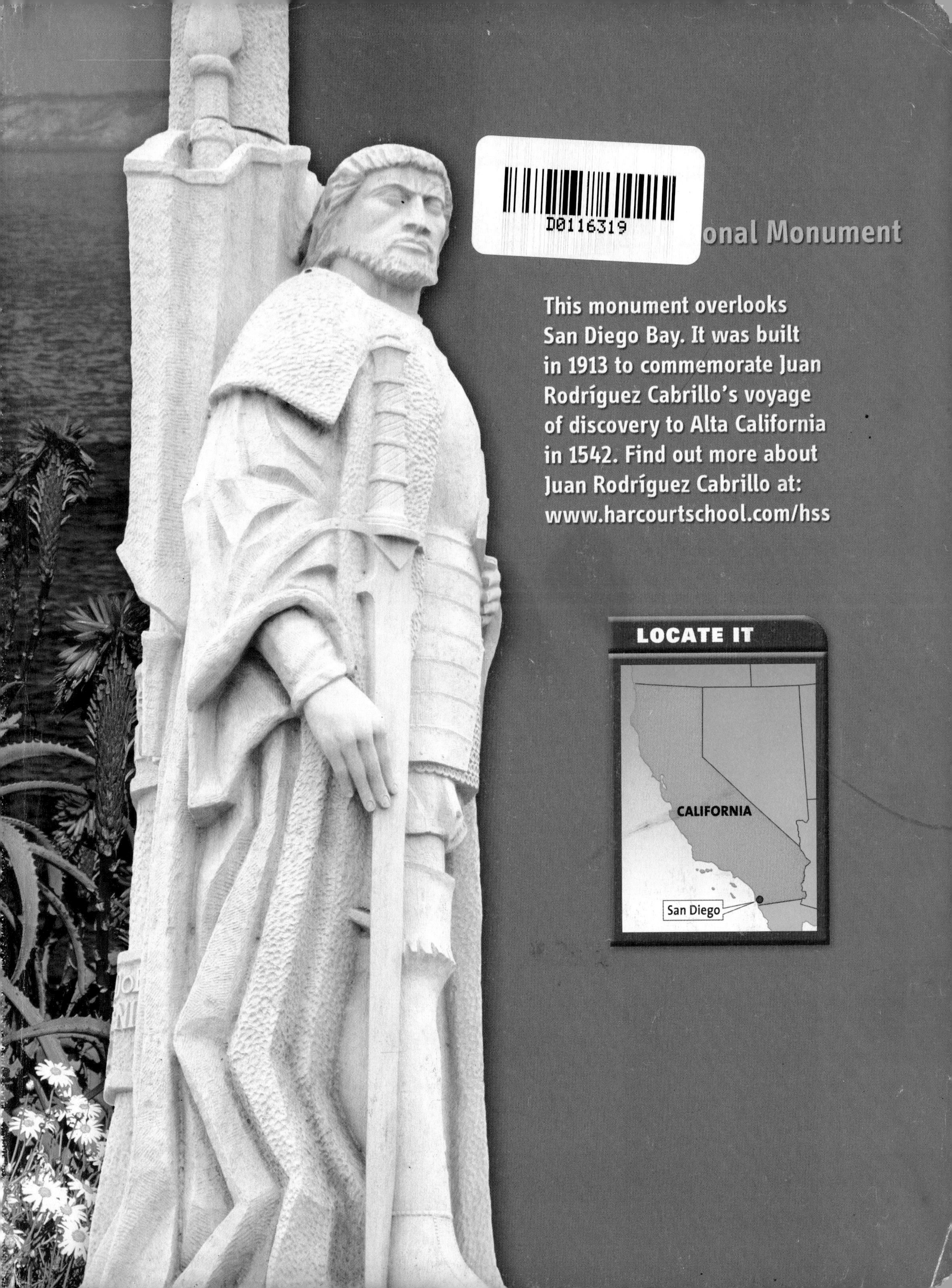

D0116319
onal Monument
This monument overlooks San Diego Bay. It was built in 1913 to commemorate Juan Rodríguez Cabrillo's voyage of discovery to Alta California in 1542. Find out more about Juan Rodríguez Cabrillo at: www.harcourtschool.com/hss
LOCATE IT
CALIFORNIA
San Diego

Reflections

California: A CHANGING STATE

Orlando Austin New York San Diego Toronto London
Visit *The Learning Site!* www.harcourtschool.com

MAPQUEST®

TIME FOR KIDS®

HARCOURT SCHOOL PUBLISHERS 

Reflections

California: A Changing State

Senior Author

Dr. Priscilla H. Porter
Professor Emeritus
School of Education
California State University, Dominguez Hills
Center for History–Social Science Education
Carson, California

Series Authors

Dr. Michael J. Berson
Associate Professor
Social Science Education
University of South Florida
Tampa, Florida

Dr. Margaret Hill
History–Social Science Coordinator
San Bernardino County Superintendent of Schools
Director, Schools of California Online Resources for Education: History–Social Science
San Bernardino, California

Dr. Tyrone C. Howard
Assistant Professor
UCLA Graduate School of Education & Information Studies
University of California at Los Angeles
Los Angeles, California

Dr. Bruce E. Larson
Associate Professor
Social Science Education/Secondary Education
Woodring College of Education
Western Washington University
Bellingham, Washington

Dr. Julio Moreno
Assistant Professor
Department of History
University of San Francisco
San Francisco, California

Series Consultants

Martha Berner
Consulting Teacher
Cajon Valley Union School District
San Diego County, California

Dr. James Charkins
Professor of Economics
California State University
Executive Director of California Council on Economic Education
San Bernardino, California

Rhoda Coleman
K–12 Reading Consultant Lecturer
California State University, Dominguez Hills
Carson, California

Dr. Robert Kumamoto
Professor
History Department
San Jose State University
San Jose, California

Carlos Lossada
Co-Director Professional Development Specialist
UCLA History–Geography Project
University of California, Los Angeles
Regional Coordinator, California Geographic Alliance
Los Angeles, California

Dr. Tanis Thorne
Director of Native Studies
Lecturer in History
Department of History
University of California, Irvine
Irvine, California

Rebecca Valbuena
Los Angeles County Teacher of the Year—2004–05
Language Development Specialist
Stanton Elementary School
Glendora Unified School District
Glendora, California

Dr. Phillip VanFossen
Associate Professor, Social Studies Education
Associate Director, Purdue Center for Economic Education
Department of Curriculum
Purdue University
West Lafayette, Indiana

Grade-Level Author

Dr. Iris H.W. Engstrand
Professor of History
University of San Diego
San Diego, California

Content Reviewers

Gordon Morris Bakken
Professor of History
California State University, Fullerton
Fullerton, California

Ramon D. Chacon
Professor of History and Ethnic Studies
Santa Clara University
Santa Clara, California

Kimberly M. Johnson
San Gabriel Band of Mission Indians
Claremont, California

Michelle Jolly
Associate Professor of History
Sonoma State University
Rohnert Park, California

Beverly R. Ortiz
Ethnographic Consultant
Walnut Creek, California

Dr. Stanley J. Underdal
Professor of History
San Jose State University
San Jose, California

Classroom Reviewers and Contributors

Paige Johnson
Teacher
Azaveda Elementary School
Fremont, California

Ruth M. Landmann, M.A.
Teacher
Rio del Mar Elementary School
Aptos, California

Maps
researched and prepared by

Readers
written and designed by

Acknowledgments appear in the back of this book.

Printed in the United States of America

ISBN 0-15-338502-2

3 4 5 6 7 8 9 10 032 15 14 13 12 11 10 09 08 07 06

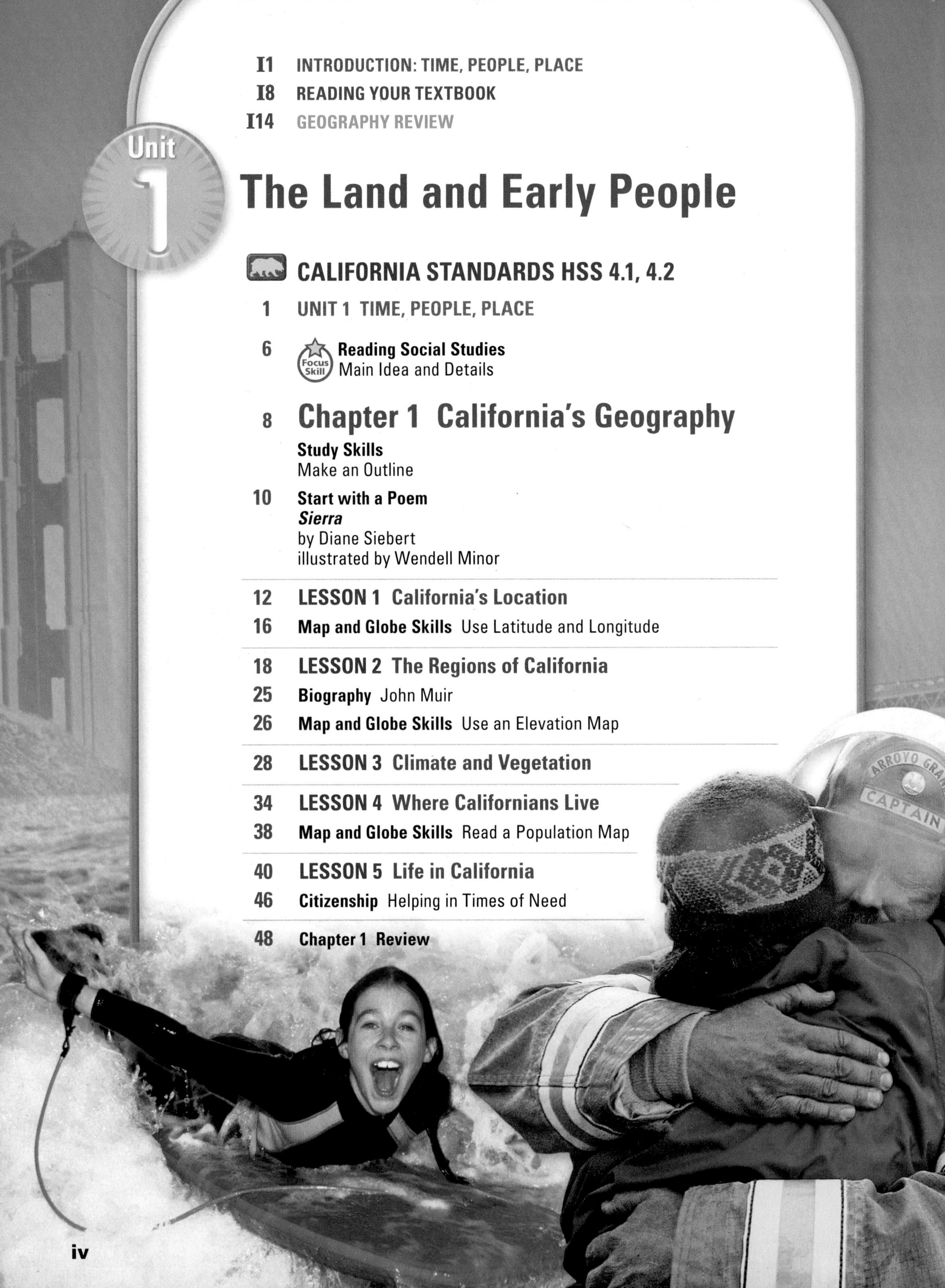

I1 INTRODUCTION: TIME, PEOPLE, PLACE
I8 READING YOUR TEXTBOOK
I14 GEOGRAPHY REVIEW

Unit 1 The Land and Early People

CALIFORNIA STANDARDS HSS 4.1, 4.2

1 UNIT 1 TIME, PEOPLE, PLACE

6 Focus Skill **Reading Social Studies** Main Idea and Details

8 **Chapter 1 California's Geography**
Study Skills Make an Outline

10 **Start with a Poem** ***Sierra*** by Diane Siebert illustrated by Wendell Minor

12 **LESSON 1 California's Location**
16 **Map and Globe Skills** Use Latitude and Longitude

18 **LESSON 2 The Regions of California**
25 **Biography** John Muir
26 **Map and Globe Skills** Use an Elevation Map

28 **LESSON 3 Climate and Vegetation**

34 **LESSON 4 Where Californians Live**
38 **Map and Globe Skills** Read a Population Map

40 **LESSON 5 Life in California**
46 **Citizenship** Helping in Times of Need

48 **Chapter 1 Review**

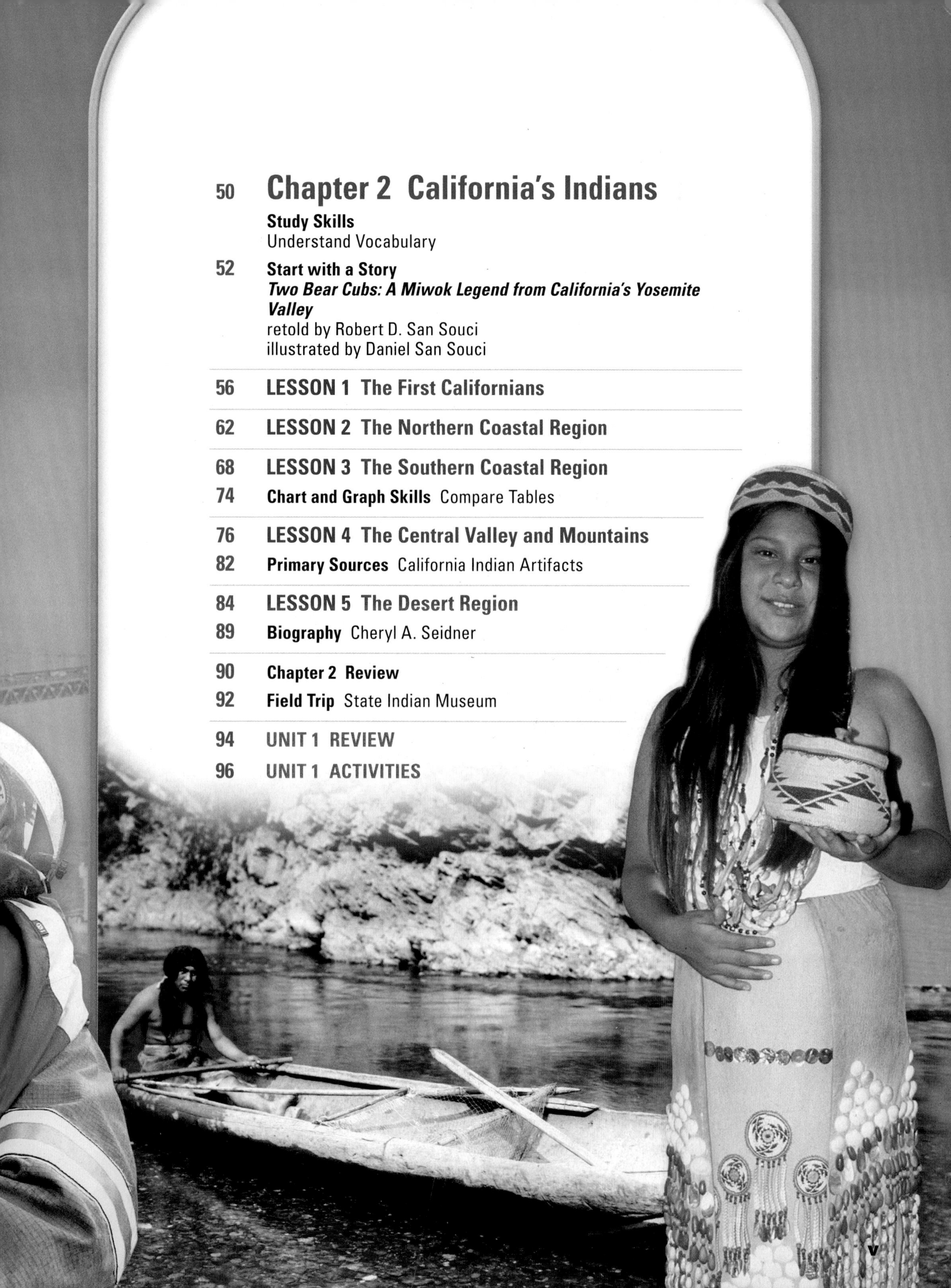

Chapter 2 California's Indians

50 **Chapter 2 California's Indians**

Study Skills
Understand Vocabulary

52 **Start with a Story**
Two Bear Cubs: A Miwok Legend from California's Yosemite Valley
retold by Robert D. San Souci
illustrated by Daniel San Souci

56 **LESSON 1 The First Californians**

62 **LESSON 2 The Northern Coastal Region**

68 **LESSON 3 The Southern Coastal Region**

74 **Chart and Graph Skills** Compare Tables

76 **LESSON 4 The Central Valley and Mountains**

82 **Primary Sources** California Indian Artifacts

84 **LESSON 5 The Desert Region**

89 **Biography** Cheryl A. Seidner

90 **Chapter 2 Review**

92 **Field Trip** State Indian Museum

94 **UNIT 1 REVIEW**

96 **UNIT 1 ACTIVITIES**

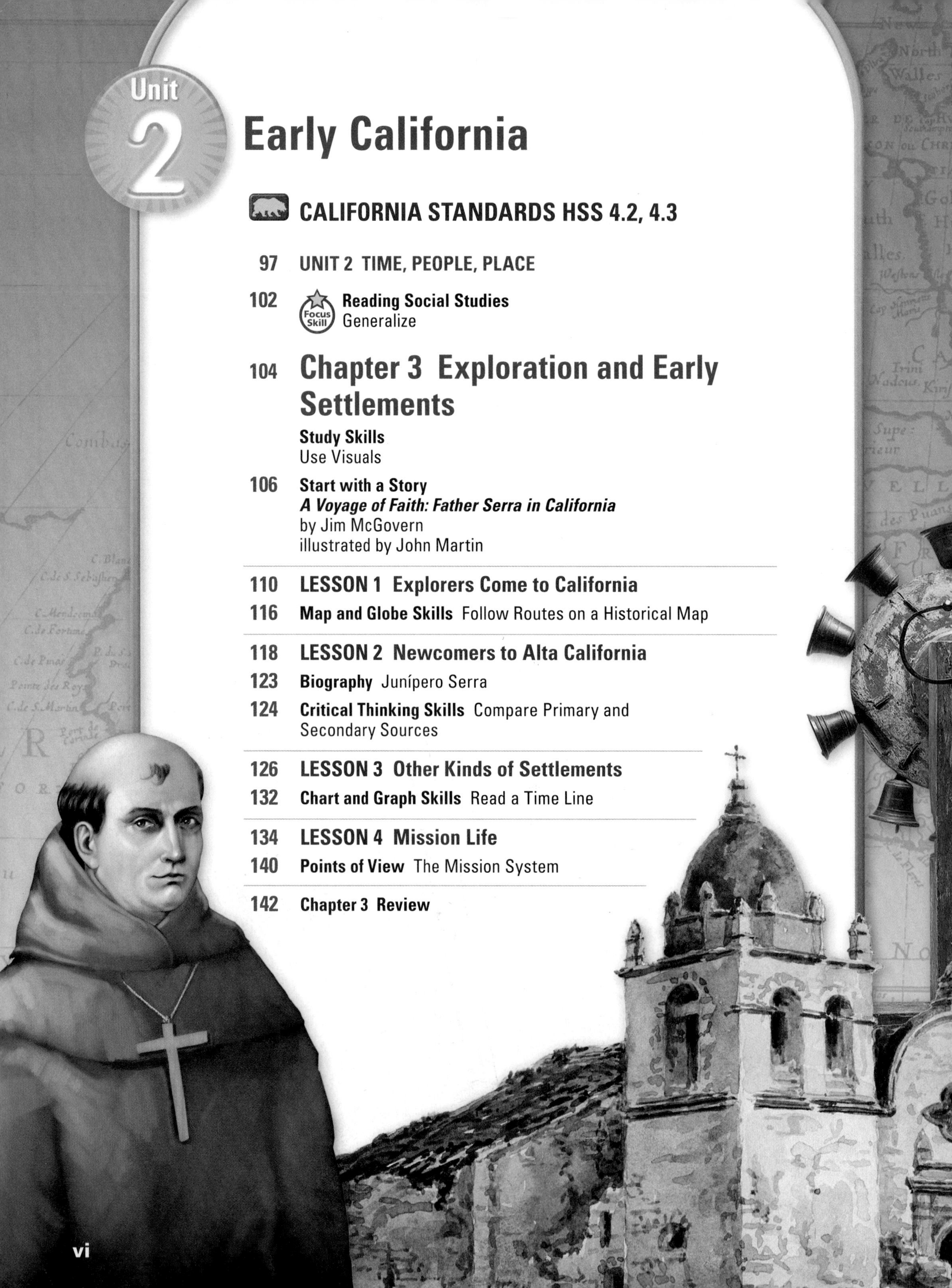

Unit 2

Early California

CALIFORNIA STANDARDS HSS 4.2, 4.3

97 UNIT 2 TIME, PEOPLE, PLACE

102 Focus Skill **Reading Social Studies**
Generalize

104 Chapter 3 Exploration and Early Settlements

Study Skills
Use Visuals

106 **Start with a Story**
A Voyage of Faith: Father Serra in California
by Jim McGovern
illustrated by John Martin

110 **LESSON 1 Explorers Come to California**

116 **Map and Globe Skills** Follow Routes on a Historical Map

118 **LESSON 2 Newcomers to Alta California**

123 **Biography** Junípero Serra

124 **Critical Thinking Skills** Compare Primary and Secondary Sources

126 **LESSON 3 Other Kinds of Settlements**

132 **Chart and Graph Skills** Read a Time Line

134 **LESSON 4 Mission Life**

140 **Points of View** The Mission System

142 **Chapter 3 Review**

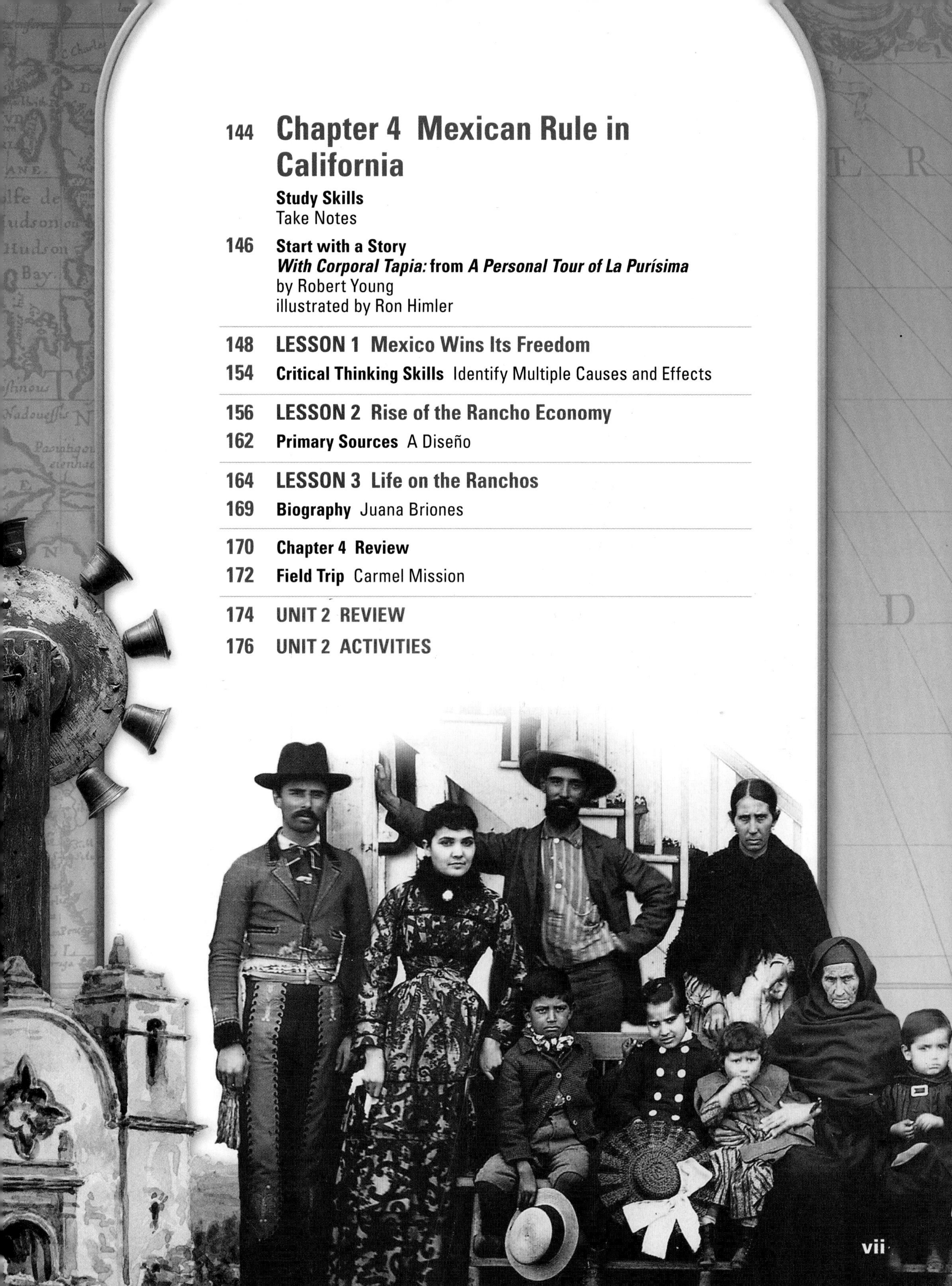

144 **Chapter 4 Mexican Rule in California**

Study Skills
Take Notes

146 **Start with a Story**
With Corporal Tapia:* from *A Personal Tour of La Purísima
by Robert Young
illustrated by Ron Himler

148 **LESSON 1 Mexico Wins Its Freedom**

154 **Critical Thinking Skills** Identify Multiple Causes and Effects

156 **LESSON 2 Rise of the Rancho Economy**

162 **Primary Sources** A Diseño

164 **LESSON 3 Life on the Ranchos**

169 **Biography** Juana Briones

170 **Chapter 4 Review**

172 **Field Trip** Carmel Mission

174 **UNIT 2 REVIEW**

176 **UNIT 2 ACTIVITIES**

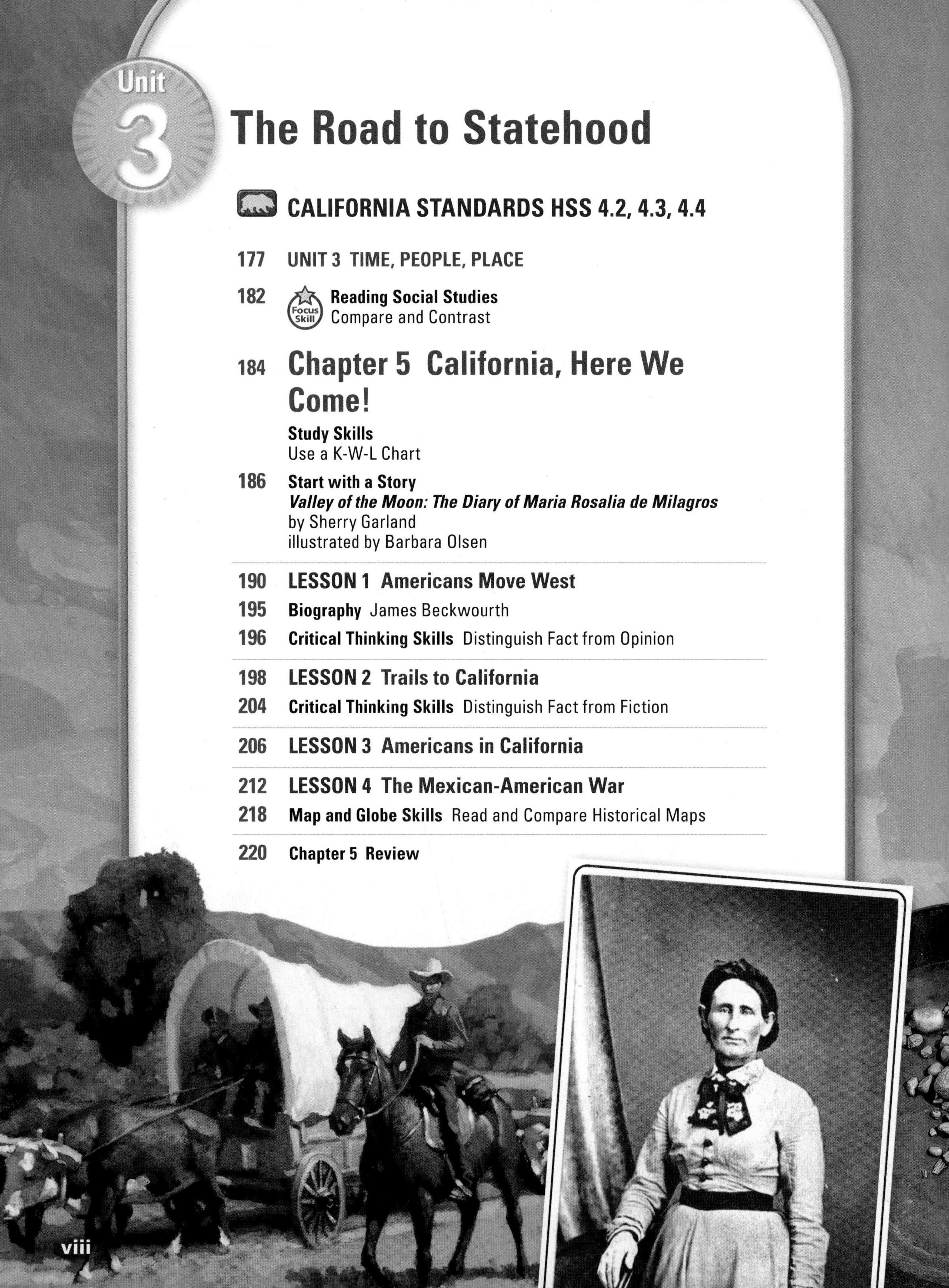

Unit 3

The Road to Statehood

CALIFORNIA STANDARDS HSS 4.2, 4.3, 4.4

177 UNIT 3 TIME, PEOPLE, PLACE

182 Focus Skill **Reading Social Studies**
Compare and Contrast

184 Chapter 5 California, Here We Come!

Study Skills
Use a K-W-L Chart

186 **Start with a Story**
Valley of the Moon: The Diary of Maria Rosalia de Milagros
by Sherry Garland
illustrated by Barbara Olsen

190 **LESSON 1 Americans Move West**
195 **Biography** James Beckwourth
196 **Critical Thinking Skills** Distinguish Fact from Opinion

198 **LESSON 2 Trails to California**
204 **Critical Thinking Skills** Distinguish Fact from Fiction

206 **LESSON 3 Americans in California**

212 **LESSON 4 The Mexican-American War**
218 **Map and Globe Skills** Read and Compare Historical Maps

220 **Chapter 5 Review**

222 **Chapter 6 Statehood for California**

Study Skills
Organize Information

224 **Start with a Biography**
Open Hands, Open Heart: The Story of Biddy Mason
by Deidre Robinson
illustrated by Colin Bootman

226 **LESSON 1 The Gold Rush**

234 **Primary Sources** The Life of a Forty-Niner

236 **LESSON 2 The Effects of the Gold Rush**

244 **Chart and Graph Skills** Read a Line Graph

246 **LESSON 3 California Becomes a State**

253 **Biography** Biddy Mason

254 **Participation Skills** Resolve Conflict

256 **Citizenship** Symbols of Pride

258 **Chapter 6 Review**

260 **Field Trip** Marshall Gold Discovery State Historic Park

262 **UNIT 3 REVIEW**

264 **UNIT 3 ACTIVITIES**

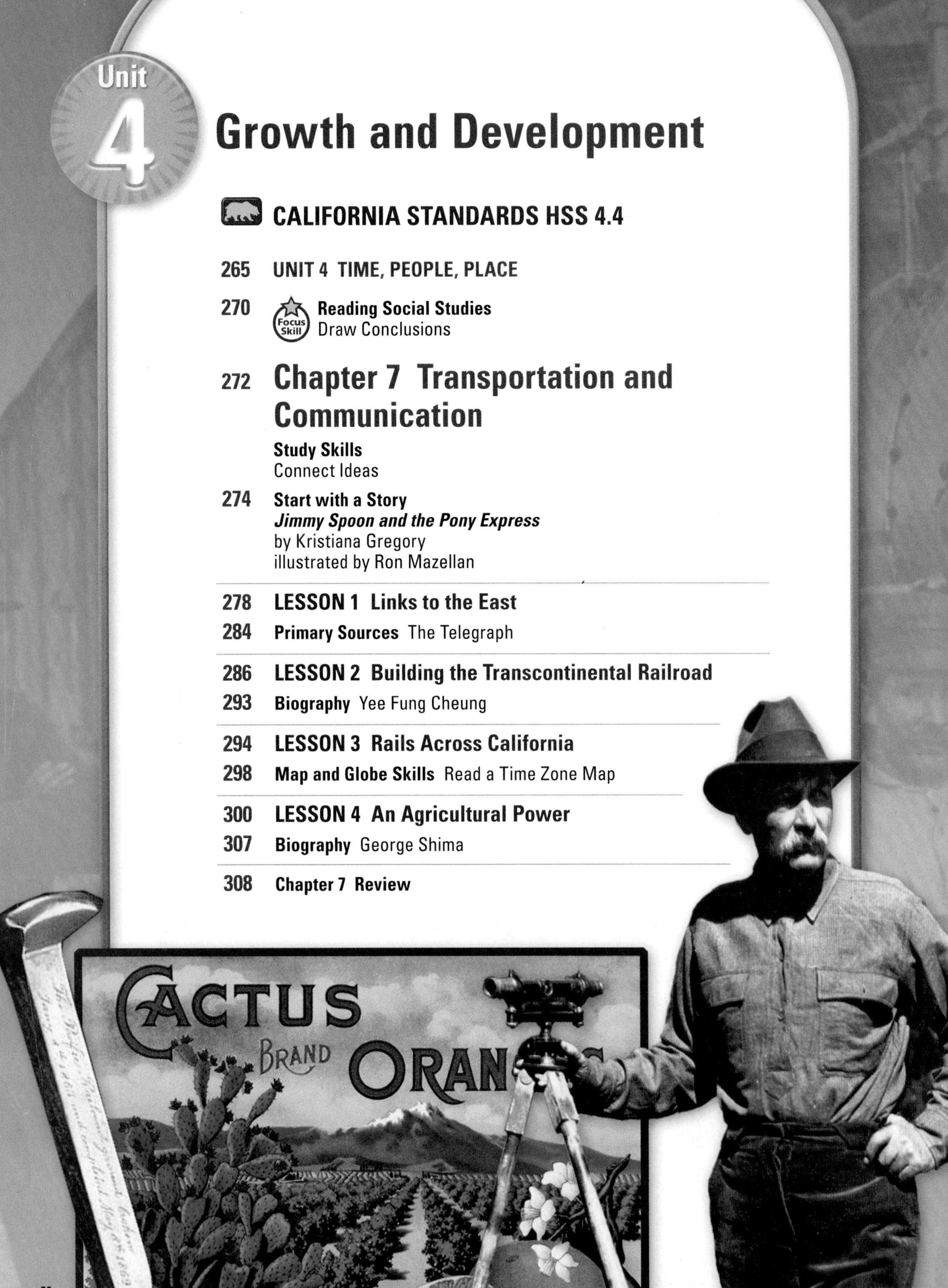

Unit 4

Growth and Development

CALIFORNIA STANDARDS HSS 4.4

265 UNIT 4 TIME, PEOPLE, PLACE

270 Focus Skill **Reading Social Studies**
Draw Conclusions

272 **Chapter 7 Transportation and Communication**

Study Skills
Connect Ideas

274 **Start with a Story**
Jimmy Spoon and the Pony Express
by Kristiana Gregory
illustrated by Ron Mazellan

278 **LESSON 1 Links to the East**

284 **Primary Sources** The Telegraph

286 **LESSON 2 Building the Transcontinental Railroad**

293 **Biography** Yee Fung Cheung

294 **LESSON 3 Rails Across California**

298 **Map and Globe Skills** Read a Time Zone Map

300 **LESSON 4 An Agricultural Power**

307 **Biography** George Shima

308 **Chapter 7 Review**

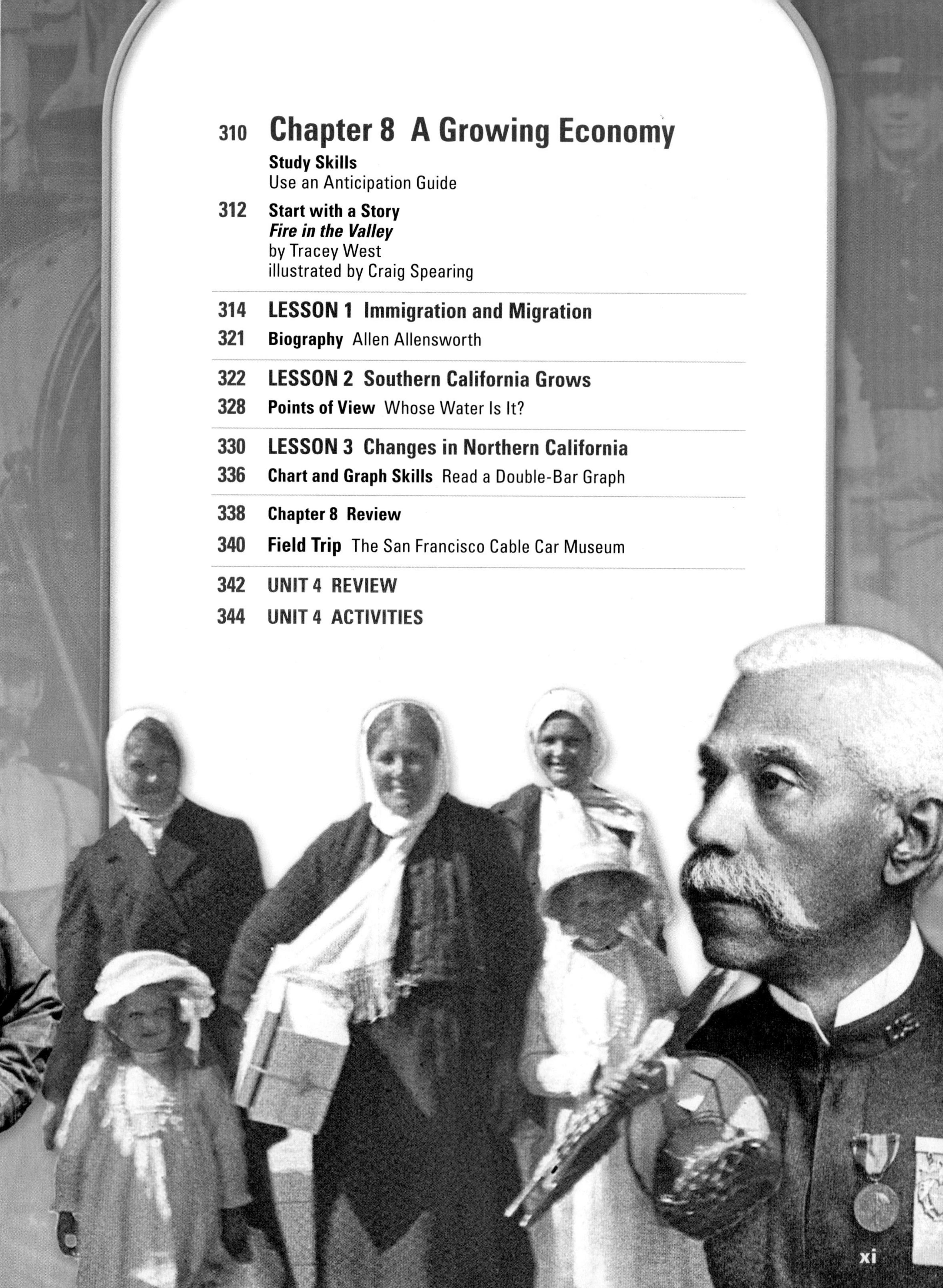

310 **Chapter 8 A Growing Economy**

Study Skills
Use an Anticipation Guide

312 **Start with a Story**
Fire in the Valley
by Tracey West
illustrated by Craig Spearing

314 **LESSON 1 Immigration and Migration**

321 **Biography** Allen Allensworth

322 **LESSON 2 Southern California Grows**

328 **Points of View** Whose Water Is It?

330 **LESSON 3 Changes in Northern California**

336 **Chart and Graph Skills** Read a Double-Bar Graph

338 **Chapter 8 Review**

340 **Field Trip** The San Francisco Cable Car Museum

342 **UNIT 4 REVIEW**

344 **UNIT 4 ACTIVITIES**

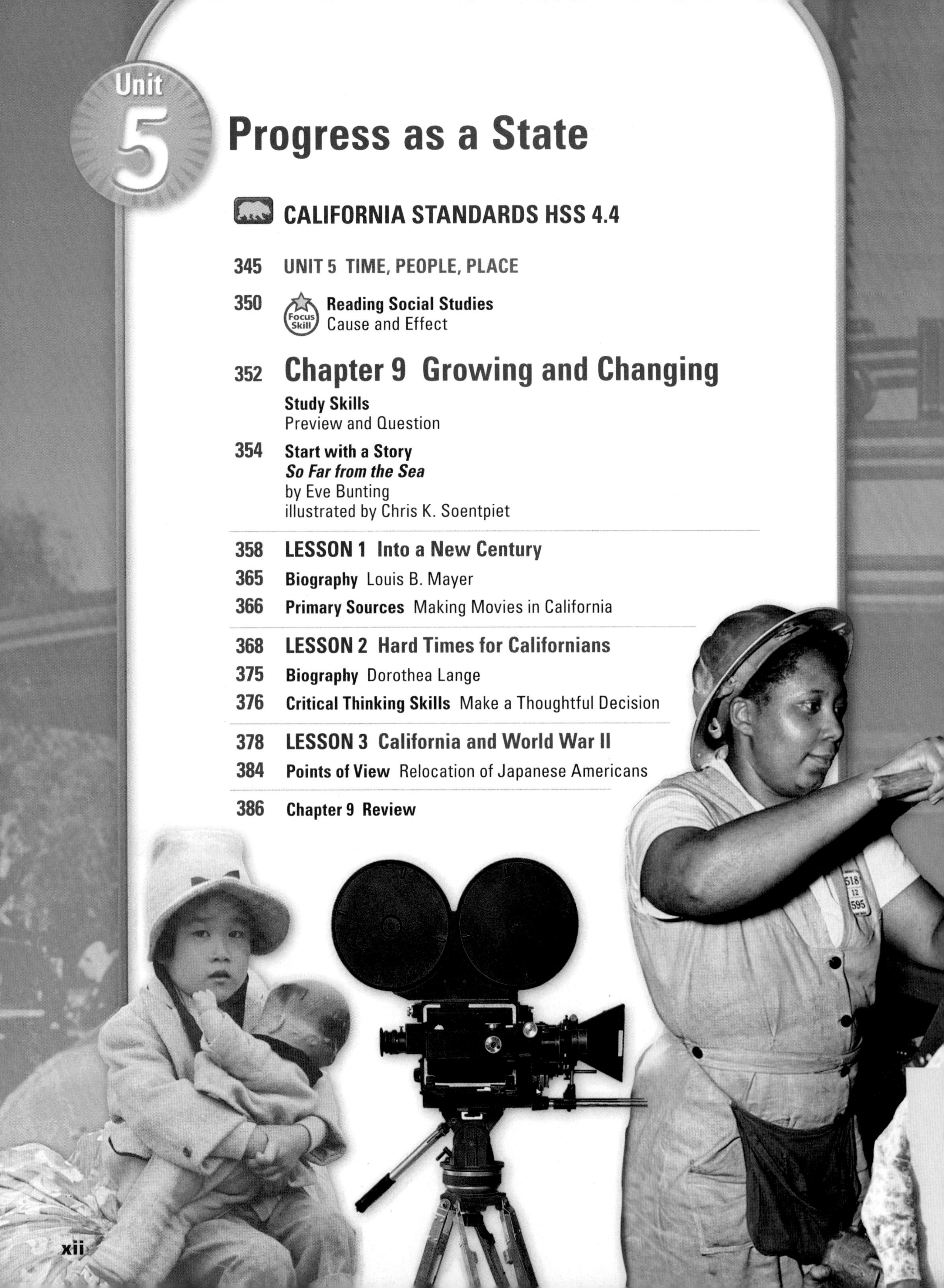

Unit 5

Progress as a State

CALIFORNIA STANDARDS HSS 4.4

345 UNIT 5 TIME, PEOPLE, PLACE

350 Focus Skill **Reading Social Studies** Cause and Effect

352 **Chapter 9 Growing and Changing**

Study Skills Preview and Question

354 **Start with a Story** ***So Far from the Sea*** by Eve Bunting illustrated by Chris K. Soentpiet

358 **LESSON 1 Into a New Century**

365 **Biography** Louis B. Mayer

366 **Primary Sources** Making Movies in California

368 **LESSON 2 Hard Times for Californians**

375 **Biography** Dorothea Lange

376 **Critical Thinking Skills** Make a Thoughtful Decision

378 **LESSON 3 California and World War II**

384 **Points of View** Relocation of Japanese Americans

386 **Chapter 9 Review**

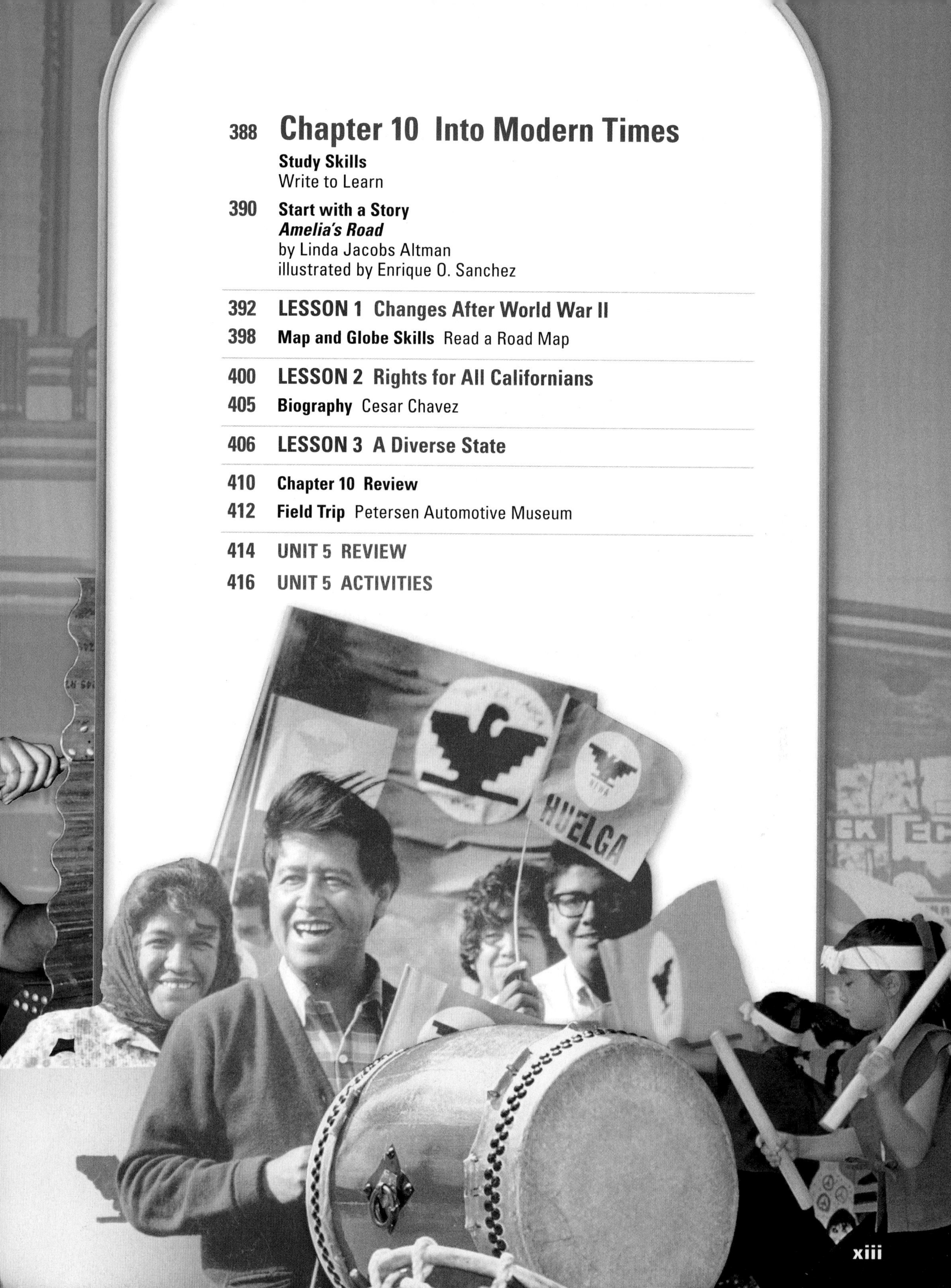

388 Chapter 10 Into Modern Times

Study Skills
Write to Learn

390 **Start with a Story**
Amelia's Road
by Linda Jacobs Altman
illustrated by Enrique O. Sanchez

392 **LESSON 1 Changes After World War II**

398 **Map and Globe Skills** Read a Road Map

400 **LESSON 2 Rights for All Californians**

405 **Biography** Cesar Chavez

406 **LESSON 3 A Diverse State**

410 **Chapter 10 Review**

412 **Field Trip** Petersen Automotive Museum

414 UNIT 5 REVIEW

416 UNIT 5 ACTIVITIES

Unit 6

California Today and Tomorrow

CALIFORNIA STANDARDS HSS 4.1, 4.4 , 4.5

417 UNIT 6 TIME, PEOPLE, PLACE

422 **Reading Social Studies** Focus Skill
Summarize

424 **Chapter 11 The Golden State**
Study Skills
Skim and Scan

426 **Start with a Story**
The Wonderful Towers of Watts
by Patricia Zelver
illustrated by Frané Lessac

430 **LESSON 1 A Modern Economy**

436 **Map and Globe Skills** Read a Land Use and Products Map

438 **LESSON 2 A State of the Arts**

443 **Biography** Walt Disney

444 **Primary Sources** Ansel Adams's Photographs

446 **LESSON 3 Education in California**

450 **LESSON 4 Overcoming Challenges**

454 **Critical Thinking Skills** Solve a Problem

456 **Chapter 11 Review**

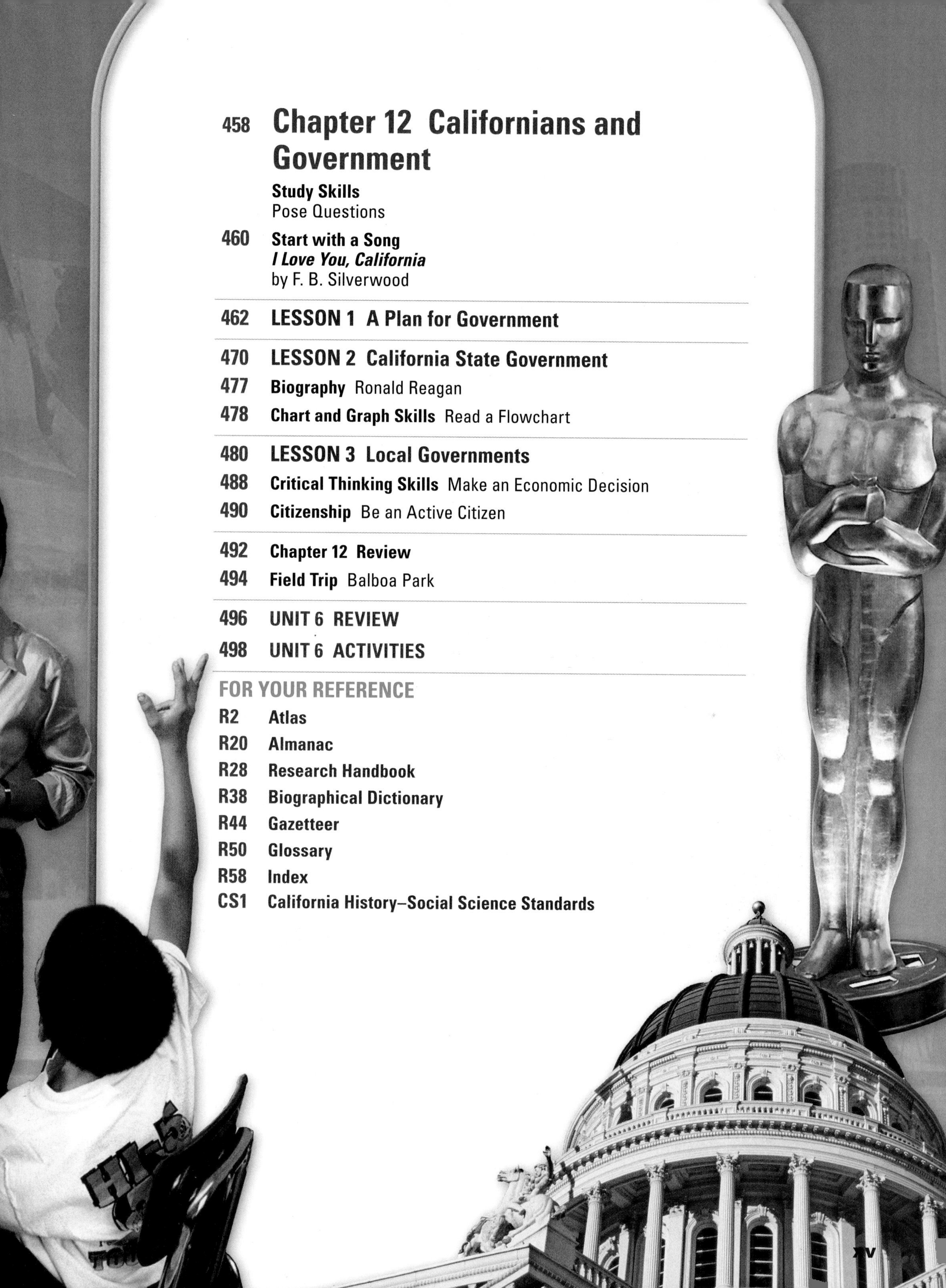

458 **Chapter 12 Californians and Government**

Study Skills
Pose Questions

460 **Start with a Song**
I Love You, California
by F. B. Silverwood

462 **LESSON 1 A Plan for Government**

470 **LESSON 2 California State Government**

477 **Biography** Ronald Reagan

478 **Chart and Graph Skills** Read a Flowchart

480 **LESSON 3 Local Governments**

488 **Critical Thinking Skills** Make an Economic Decision

490 **Citizenship** Be an Active Citizen

492 **Chapter 12 Review**

494 **Field Trip** Balboa Park

496 **UNIT 6 REVIEW**

498 **UNIT 6 ACTIVITIES**

FOR YOUR REFERENCE

R2 **Atlas**

R20 **Almanac**

R28 **Research Handbook**

R38 **Biographical Dictionary**

R44 **Gazetteer**

R50 **Glossary**

R58 **Index**

CS1 **California History–Social Science Standards**

Features

Skills

CHART AND GRAPH SKILLS

74 Compare Tables
132 Read a Time Line
244 Read a Line Graph
336 Read a Double-Bar Graph
478 Read a Flowchart

PARTICIPATION SKILLS

254 Resolve Conflict

MAP AND GLOBE SKILLS

16 Use Latitude and Longitude
26 Use an Elevation Map
38 Read a Population Map
116 Follow Routes on a Historical Map
218 Read and Compare Historical Maps
298 Read a Time Zone Map
398 Read a Road Map
436 Read a Land Use and Products Map

CRITICAL THINKING SKILLS

124 Compare Primary and Secondary Sources
154 Identify Multiple Causes and Effects
196 Distinguish Fact from Opinion
204 Distinguish Fact from Fiction
376 Make a Thoughtful Decision
454 Solve a Problem
488 Make an Economic Decision

READING SOCIAL STUDIES

6 Main Idea and Details
102 Generalize
182 Compare and Contrast
270 Draw Conclusions
350 Cause and Effect
422 Summarize

STUDY SKILLS

8 Make an Outline
50 Understand Vocabulary
104 Use Visuals
144 Take Notes
184 Use a K-W-L Chart
222 Organize Information
272 Connect Ideas
310 Use an Anticipation Guide
352 Preview and Question
388 Write to Learn
424 Skim and Scan
458 Pose Questions

Citizenship

46 Helping in Times of Need
150 Democratic Principles
248 Democratic Values
256 Symbols of Pride
359 Democratic Values
408 Democratic Institutions
464 Democratic Principles
475 Democratic Principles
490 Be an Active Citizen

Points of View

140 The Mission System
209 Californios and the United States
250 Statehood for California
328 Whose Water Is It?
384 Relocation of Japanese Americans
486 Taxes on Indian Gaming

Literature and Music

10 *Sierra* by Diane Siebert illustrated by Wendell Minor
52 *Two Bear Cubs: A Miwok Legend from California's Yosemite Valley* retold by Robert D. San Souci illustrated by Daniel San Souci
60 *How the Robin Got His Red Breast*
106 *Voyage of Faith: Father Serra in California* by Jim McGovern illustrated by John Martin
146 *With Corporal Tapia:* from *A Personal Tour of La Purísima* by Robert Young illustrated by Ron Himler
186 *Valley of the Moon: The Diary of Maria Rosalia de Milagros* by Sherry Garland illustrated by Barbara Olsen
224 *Open Hands, Open Heart: The Story of Biddy Mason* by Deidre Robinson illustrated by Colin Bootman
274 *Jimmy Spoon and the Pony Express* by Kristiana Gregory illustrated by Ron Mazellan
312 *Fire in the Valley* by Tracey West illustrated by Craig Spearing
354 *So Far from the Sea* by Eve Bunting illustrated by Chris K. Soentpiet
390 *Amelia's Road* by Linda Jacobs Altman illustrated by Enrique O. Sanchez
426 *The Wonderful Towers of Watts* by Patricia Zelver illustrated by Frané Lessac
460 *I Love You, California* by F. B. Silverwood

Primary Sources

64 A Yurok Coin Purse
82 California Indian Artifacts
162 A Diseño
234 The Life of a Forty-Niner
284 The Telegraph
292 The Transcontinental Railroad
366 Making Movies in California

402 A UFW Poster
444 Ansel Adams's Photographs
472 The Great Seal of the State of California

Biography

25 John Muir
89 Cheryl A. Seidner
123 Junípero Serra
169 Juana Briones
195 James Beckwourth
253 Biddy Mason
293 Yee Fung Cheung
307 George Shima
321 Allen Allensworth
365 Louis B. Mayer
375 Dorothea Lange
405 Cesar Chavez
443 Walt Disney
477 Ronald Reagan

Geography

14 A Western State
22 Sacramento
42 San Andreas Fault
71 Chumash Painted Cave State Historic Park
119 A Northern Passage
160 Fort Ross
305 The Imperial Valley
315 Angel Island
432 Silicon Valley

Cultural Heritage

86 California Indians Today
210 The Bear Flag
317 Chinese New Year

Children in History

80 Games for Miwok Children
138 Pablo Tac
203 Virginia Reed
318 Mamie Tape
371 Weedpatch School

A Closer Look

78 Making Acorn Flour
114 A Spanish Galleon
128 A Presidio
137 A Spanish Mission
167 A Rancho
200 A Wagon Train
241 Hydraulic Mining
290 Building the Railroad
373 The Golden Gate Bridge
471 The State Capitol

Field Trips

92 State Indian Museum
172 Carmel Mission
260 Marshall Gold Discovery State Historic Park
340 The San Francisco Cable Car Museum
412 Petersen Automotive Museum
494 Balboa Park

Charts, Graphs, and Diagrams

6 Main Idea and Details
13 California in the World
20 Major Mountains of the World
23 Plants and Animals of the Desert Region
32 The Rain Shadow
36 California's Largest Cities
75 Table A: California Indian Boats by Tribe
75 Table B: California Indian Tribes by Kind of Boat
102 Generalize
130 California's Population, 1769–1848
139 Population of California Indians
155 Causes and Effects of Mexican Rule in California
182 Compare and Contrast
229 Routes to California
237 Population of San Francisco
245 California's Population, 1850–1890
270 Draw Conclusions
283 The Original Morse Code
301 California Wheat Production, 1850–1890
316 Immigrants in California, 1900
336 Urban Population in California, 1870–1910
350 Cause and Effect
393 California's Population, 1940–1960
407 California's Foreign-Born Population, 2000
422 Summarize
431 California's Top Industries
432 High-Tech Manufacturing
433 California's Top Trading Partners, 2003
434 From Farm to Market
452 How State Tax Money Is Spent in California, 2004–2005
465 Branches of the Federal Government
466 Scope of Jurisdiction
468 Federal System of Government
478 How a Bill Becomes a Law

Maps

4 Landforms in California
14 A Western State
16 Latitude and Longitude Grid
17 California Latitude and Longitude
20 Natural Regions of California
22 Sacramento
27 Elevations in California
29 January Temperatures in California
29 July Temperatures in California
30 Precipitation in California
39 Population Density in California
42 San Andreas Fault
57 Land Routes of Early People
59 Some California Tribes

63 Some tribes of the Northern Coast
69 Some Tribes of the Southern Coast
71 Chumash Painted Cave State Historic Park
77 Some Tribes of the Central Valley and Mountains
85 Some Tribes of the Desert
95 Elevations of Southern California
100 California in New Spain, 1776
113 Early European Explorers to Alta California
117 Pacific Routes of the Spanish Galleons
119 A Northern Passage
120 Routes to Alta California, 1769–1776
127 Spanish Missions, 1769–1823
157 Mexican Settlements in California
160 Fort Ross State Historic Park
175 Anza's Expedition, 1775-1776
180 Mexican California, 1840
193 Trailblazers from the United States
202 Overland to California
215 The Mexican-American War in California
218 Map A: The United States, 1845
219 Map B: The United States, 1848
229 Routes of the Forty-Niners
232 Major Gold Mining Towns, 1849–1859
255 Free and Slave States in 1850
263 Western United States, 1845
263 Western United States, 1848
268 California in the United States, 1886
279 Sending Messages Across the Country
280 Early Mail Routes to California
289 The Transcontinental Railroad
296 Railroad Companies, Late 1880s
299 United States Time Zones
305 The Imperial Valley
315 Angel Island
326 Los Angeles Aqueduct
335 Hetch Hetchy Aqueduct
343 Pacific and Mountain Time Zones
348 California in the United States, 1985
370 The Dust Bowl
399 Road Map of California
415 Southern California
420 California in the Pacific Basin
432 Silicon Valley
437 California Land Use and Products
469 The National Park System in California
481 California Counties
487 California Tribal Lands
497 California Land Use
R2 The World: Political
R4 The World: Physical
R6 Western Hemisphere: Political
R7 Western Hemisphere: Physical
R8 United States: Overview
R10 United States: Political
R12 United States: Physical
R14 California: Political
R15 California: Physical
R16 California: Climate
R17 California: Vegetation
R18 Canada
R19 Mexico

Time Lines

Unit 1 Preview Time Line, **1**
Unit 1 People Time Line, **2**
John Muir Time Line, **25**
Chapter 2 Lesson Time Line, **56**
Cheryl A. Seidner Time Line, **89**
Chapter 2 Review Time Line, **90**
Unit 2 Preview Time Line, **97**
Unit 2 People Time Line, **98**
Chapter 3 Lesson Time Lines, **110, 118, 126, 134**
Junípero Serra Time Line, **123**
Early California History, **132**
Chapter 3 Review Time Line, **142**
Chapter 4 Lesson Time Lines, **148, 156**
Mexico and California, **151**
Juana Briones Time Line, **169**
Chapter 4 Review Time Line, **170**
Unit 3 Preview Time Line, **177**
Unit 3 People Time Line, **178**
Chapter 5 Lesson Time Lines, **190, 198, 206, 212**
James Beckwourth Time Line, **195**
The Mexican-American War, **214**
Chapter 5 Review Time Line, **220**
Chapter 6 Lesson Time Lines, **226, 236, 246**
Biddy Mason Time Line, **253**
Chapter 6 Review Time Line, **258**
Unit 4 Preview Time Line, **265**
Unit 4 People Time Line, **266**
Chapter 7 Lesson Time Lines, **278, 286, 294, 300**
The Transcontinental Railroad, **288**
Yee Fung Cheung Time Line, **293**
George Shima Time Line, **307**
Chapter 7 Review Time Line, **308**
Chapter 8 Lesson Time Lines, **314, 322, 330**
Allen Allensworth Time Line, **321**
Chapter 8 Review Time Line, **338**
Unit 5 Preview Time Line, **345**
Unit 5 People Time Line, **346**
Chapter 9 Lesson Time Lines, **358, 368, 378**
A Modern Way of Life, **362**
Louis B. Mayer Time Line, **365**
Dorothea Lange Time Line, **375**
World War II, **381**
Chapter 9 Review Time Line, **386**
Chapter 10 Lesson Time Lines, **392, 400, 406**
Advancements in Technology, **396**
Cesar Chavez Time Line, **405**
Chapter 10 Review Time Line, **410**
Unit 6 Preview Time Lines, **417**
Unit 6 People Time Line, **418**
Walt Disney Time Line, **443**
Ronald Reagan Time Line, **477**

The Story Well Told

"California's future and its promise are nothing less than the future and promise of America."*

Kevin Starr, State Librarian Emeritus of California

Have you ever wondered how California came to be and how its past continues to affect you today? This year you will find out. You will be studying the history and geography of California. You will read about what it was like to live during the **time** when important events in our state took place. You will learn about some of the **people** who took part in those events and about the **place** where each event happened. Read now the story of *California: A Changing State.*

*Kevin Starr. "California–The Dream, The Challenge". California State Library.

California:
A CHANGING STATE

The Story of California is about Time

Studying history helps you see how the present is connected to the past. It helps you understand how the past and the present are alike and different. It also helps you see how some things change over time and some things stay the same. As you learn to recognize these links, you will begin to think more like a historian. A historian is a person who studies the past.

Historians **research**, or carefully study, the time in which events happened. They look for clues in the objects and papers that people left behind. They read diaries, journal entries, letters, newspaper articles, and other writings by people who experienced the events. They look

at photographs, films, and artwork. They also listen to oral histories. These are stories told aloud by people who lived at the time. By carefully studying such **evidence**, or proof, historians are better able to piece together the historical context for the events—what the world was like at the time. The context helps them **interpret**, or explain, the past.

Historians must look closely at how events are connected to one another. They can better see such connections by studying the **chronology**, or time order, in which events happened. One way historians do this is by using time lines. A time line shows key events from the period. A time line can suggest how one event may have led to another.

The Story of California is about People

Historians study the people who lived during times in the past. Using the evidence they collect, historians try to imagine what life was like for those people. They try to explain why people did the things they did and how events affected their feelings and beliefs.

Historians also study people's points of view. A person's **point of view** is how he or she sees things. A point of view is shaped by a person's background and experiences. It can depend on whether a person is old or young, a man or a woman, or rich or poor. People with different points of view may see the same event very differently.

People from the past can often serve as role models for how to act—or how not to act—when troubling events occur. Historians identify key **character traits**, such as trustworthiness, respect, responsibility, fairness, compassion, and patriotism, that people from the past displayed. They look at how these character traits help make people into good leaders, then and now.

The Story of California is about Place

Historians must also think about the places in which events happened. Every place on Earth has features that set it apart from all other locations. Often, those features affected where events occurred. They may also have affected why the events unfolded as they did.

To better understand the features, or characteristics, of a particular place, historians often study maps. Maps show a place's location, but they can also tell historians about the land and the people who lived there. They can show the routes people followed, where they settled, and how they used the land.

Maps, like other evidence, help historians write a clearer story of the past. They are just one valuable tool historians use to better understand how time, people, and place are linked.

MAP OF HOLLYWOOD
PACIFIC OCEAN
OCEAN VIEW AVE.
PROSPECT
FOR PARTICULARS apply to H. H.
34 N. Spring St.
October 1887
ROUTE
US
66
TACOS
SPEED LIMIT 10

Reading Your Textbook

GETTING STARTED

Unit Title

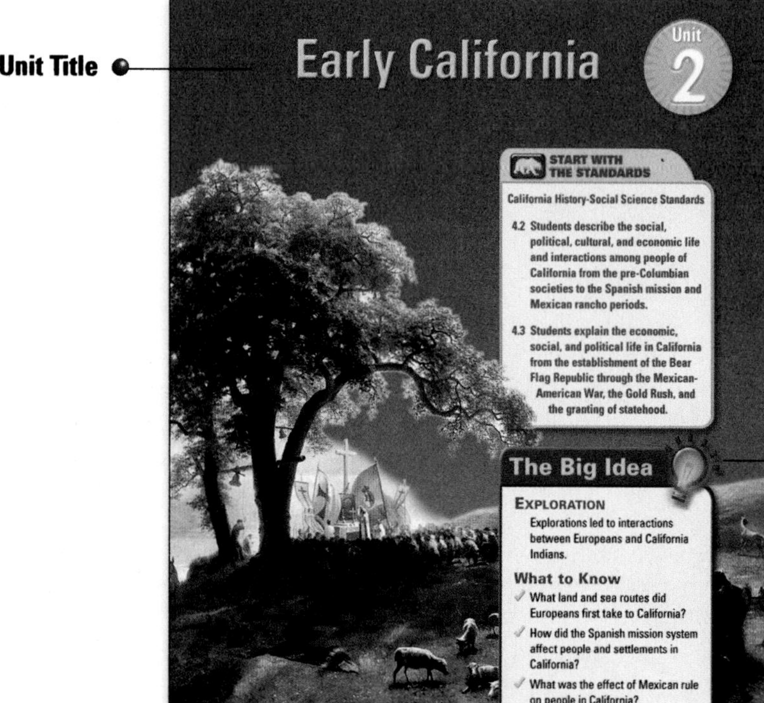

Your textbook is divided into six units.

Each unit begins with a list of the California History–Social Science Standards covered in the unit.

The BIG IDEA tells you the key idea you should understand at the end of the unit.

These questions help you focus on the Big Idea.

To show that you understand the California History–Social Science Standards and the Big Idea, your teacher may have you complete one or more of these.

LOOKING AT TIME, PEOPLE, AND PLACE

TIME pages identify important events and tell you when those events took place. You will read about these events in the unit.

PEOPLE pages introduce you to some of the men and women you will read about in the unit.

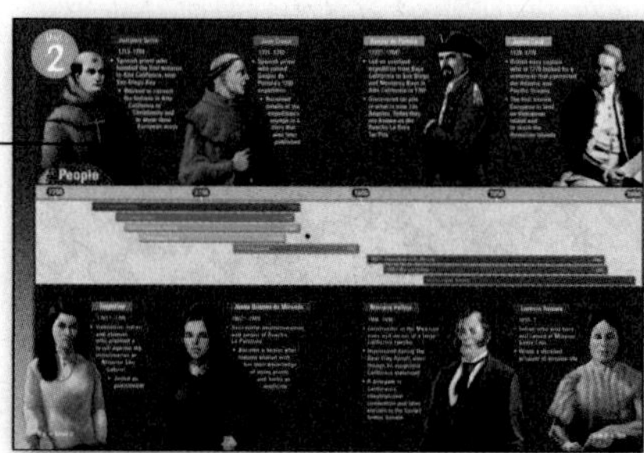

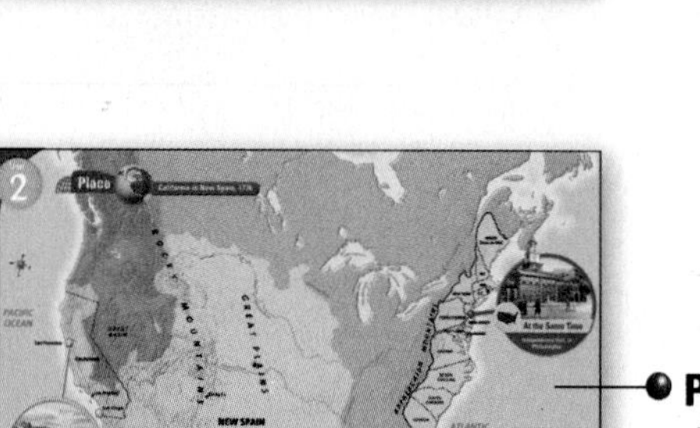

PLACE pages show where some of the events in the unit took place.

READING SOCIAL STUDIES

The Reading Social Studies Focus Skill will help you better understand the events you read about and make connections among them.

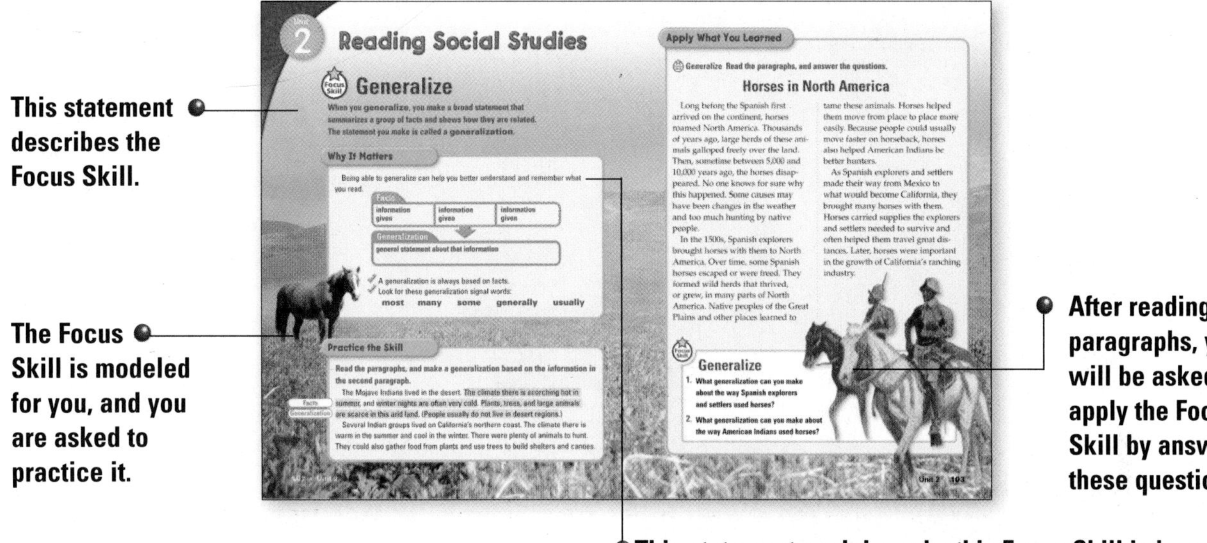

This statement describes the Focus Skill.

The Focus Skill is modeled for you, and you are asked to practice it.

After reading some paragraphs, you will be asked to apply the Focus Skill by answering these questions.

This statement explains why this Focus Skill is important.

BEGINNING A CHAPTER

Each unit is divided into chapters, and each chapter is divided into lessons.

This Study Skill provides you with a strategy that you can use to remember and organize what you read.

Chapter title and number

Each chapter has a list of the California History–Social Science Standards covered in the chapter.

Each chapter begins with a song, poem, journal, story, or other special reading selection.

READING A LESSON

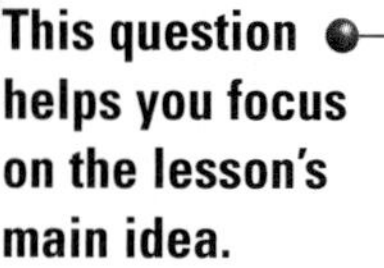

This question helps you focus on the lesson's main idea.

These statements tell you what you should be able to do at the end of the lesson.

These are the new vocabulary terms you will learn in a lesson.

Some of the people and places you will read about are listed.

Remember to apply the Reading Social Studies Focus Skill as you read the lesson.

A time line shows when some of the key events in the lesson took place.

Lesson title

You Are There puts you in the time when events in the lesson took place.

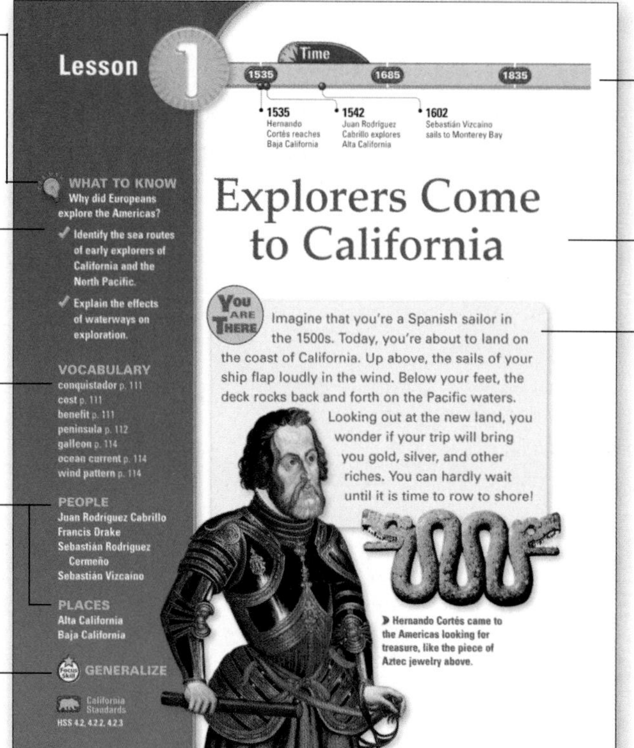

Lesson 1

Time

1535 1685 1835

1535 Hernando Cortés reaches Baja California

1542 Juan Rodríguez Cabrillo explores Alta California

1602 Sebastián Vizcaíno sails to Monterey Bay

WHAT TO KNOW
Why did Europeans explore the Americas?

✓ Identify the sea routes of early explorers of California and the North Pacific.

✓ Explain the effects of waterways on exploration.

VOCABULARY
conquistador p. 111
cost p. 111
benefit p. 111
peninsula p. 112
galleon p. 114
ocean current p. 114
wind pattern p. 114

PEOPLE
Juan Rodríguez Cabrillo
Francis Drake
Sebastián Rodríguez Cermeño
Sebastián Vizcaíno

PLACES
Alta California
Baja California

GENERALIZE

California Standards
HSS 4.2, 4.2.2, 4.2.3

110 ▪ Unit 2

Explorers Come to California

You Are There

Imagine that you're a Spanish sailor in the 1500s. Today, you're about to land on the coast of California. Up above, the sails of your ship flap loudly in the wind. Below your feet, the deck rocks back and forth on the Pacific waters. Looking out at the new land, you wonder if your trip will bring you gold, silver, and other riches. You can hardly wait until it is time to row to shore!

Hernando Cortés came to the Americas looking for treasure, like the piece of Aztec jewelry above.

Key people and places are boldfaced.

Some lessons have special features where you can read about Citizenship, Children in History, Geography, Primary Sources, and Points of View.

Vocabulary terms are highlighted in yellow.

Each short section concludes with a READING CHECK question, which helps you check whether you understand what you have read. Be sure that you can answer this question correctly before you continue reading the lesson.

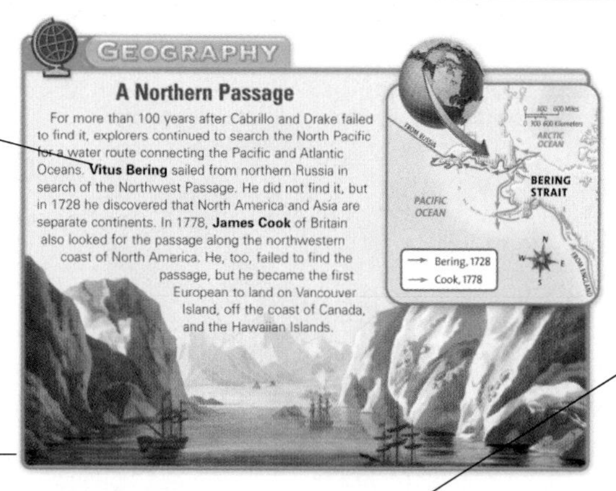

GEOGRAPHY

A Northern Passage

For more than 100 years after Cabrillo and Drake failed to find it, explorers continued to search the North Pacific for a water route connecting the Pacific and Atlantic Oceans. **Vitus Bering** sailed from northern Russia in search of the Northwest Passage. He did not find it, but in 1728 he discovered that North America and Asia are separate continents. In 1778, **James Cook** of Britain also looked for the passage along the northwestern coast of North America. He, too, failed to find the passage, but he became the first European to land on Vancouver Island, off the coast of Canada, and the Hawaiian Islands.

Settling in California

More than 150 years after Vizcaíno sailed into Monterey Bay, Spain decided to start a colony in Alta California. A **colony** is a settlement that is ruled by a faraway government. The decision to start a colony in Alta California came about in the mid-1700s. Russian explorers and fur traders had arrived in what is now Alaska. King Carlos III feared that the Russians might move south along the coast and into Alta California.

Spanish leaders hoped that a colony in Alta California would be successful. Spain had already started colonies in what would become Florida, Texas, and New Mexico by building **missions**, or religious settlements. The missions had strengthened Spain's hold on New Spain and Latin America. The king hoped to follow the same plan in Alta California.

Missions were run by missionaries. A **missionary** is a person who teaches a religion to others. In California, Catholic priests and other church workers served as missionaries. They tried to convert Indians to the Catholic religion. Missionaries also wanted to teach Indians the Spanish language and Spanish ways of life.

READING CHECK GENERALIZE
Why did Spain decide to start a colony in Alta California?

Chapter 3 ▪ 119

Each lesson, like each chapter and unit, ends with a review. Questions and activities help you check your understanding of the standards covered by the lesson.

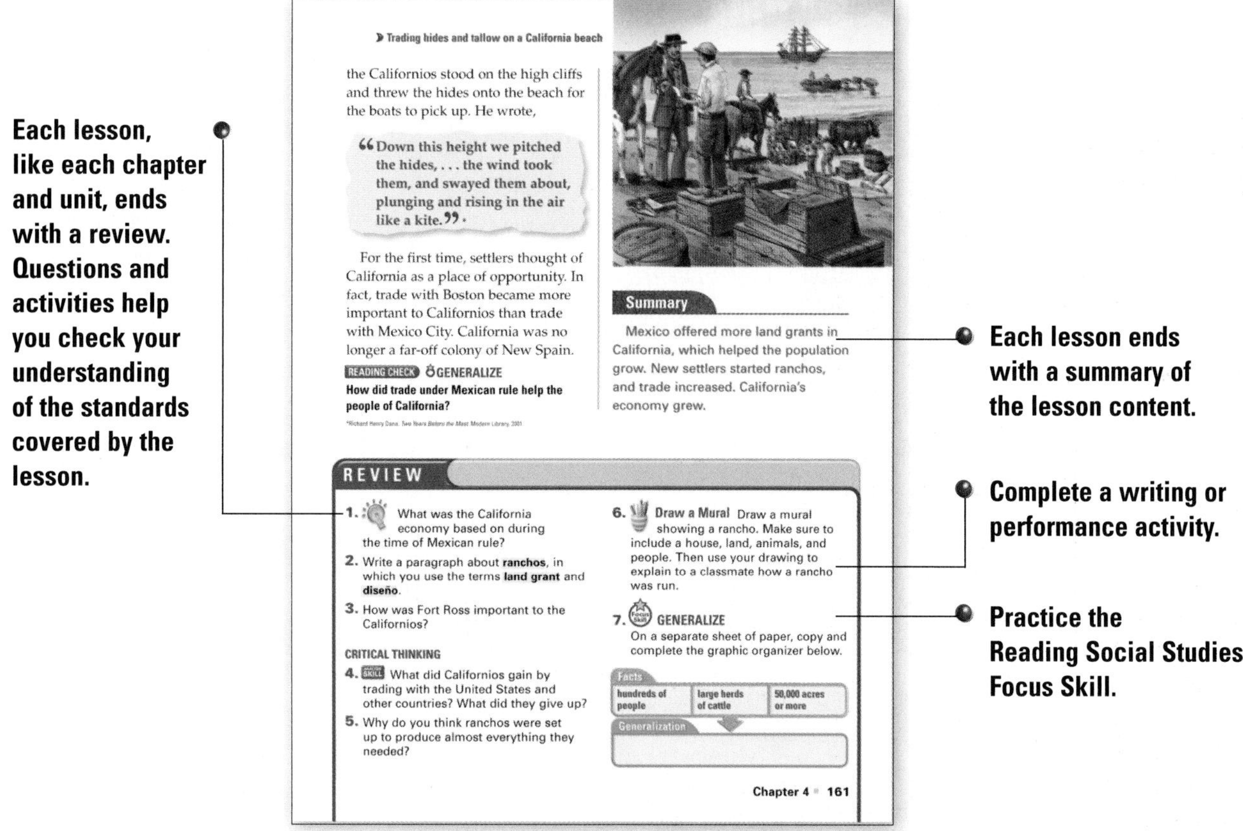

Trading hides and tallow on a California beach
the Californios stood on the high cliffs and threw the hides onto the beach for the boats to pick up. He wrote,
"Down this height we pitched the hides, . . . the wind took them, and swayed them about, plunging and rising in the air like a kite."
For the first time, settlers thought of California as a place of opportunity. In fact, trade with Boston became more important to Californios than trade with Mexico City. California was no longer a far-off colony of New Spain.
READING CHECK GENERALIZE
How did trade under Mexican rule help the people of California?
Summary
Mexico offered more land grants in California, which helped the population grow. New settlers started ranchos, and trade increased. California's economy grew.
REVIEW
1. What was the California economy based on during the time of Mexican rule?
2. Write a paragraph about ranchos, in which you use the terms land grant and diseño.
3. How was Fort Ross important to the Californios?
CRITICAL THINKING
4. What did Californios gain by trading with the United States and other countries? What did they give up?
5. Why do you think ranchos were set up to produce almost everything they needed?
6. Draw a Mural Draw a mural showing a rancho. Make sure to include a house, land, animals, and people. Then use your drawing to explain to a classmate how a rancho was run.
7. GENERALIZE
On a separate sheet of paper, copy and complete the graphic organizer below.
Facts
hundreds of people
large herds of cattle
50,000 acres or more
Generalization
Chapter 4 161

Each lesson ends with a summary of the lesson content.

Complete a writing or performance activity.

Practice the Reading Social Studies Focus Skill.

LEARNING SOCIAL STUDIES SKILLS

Your textbook has lessons that help you build your Participation Skills, Map and Globe Skills, Chart and Graph Skills, and Critical Thinking Skills.

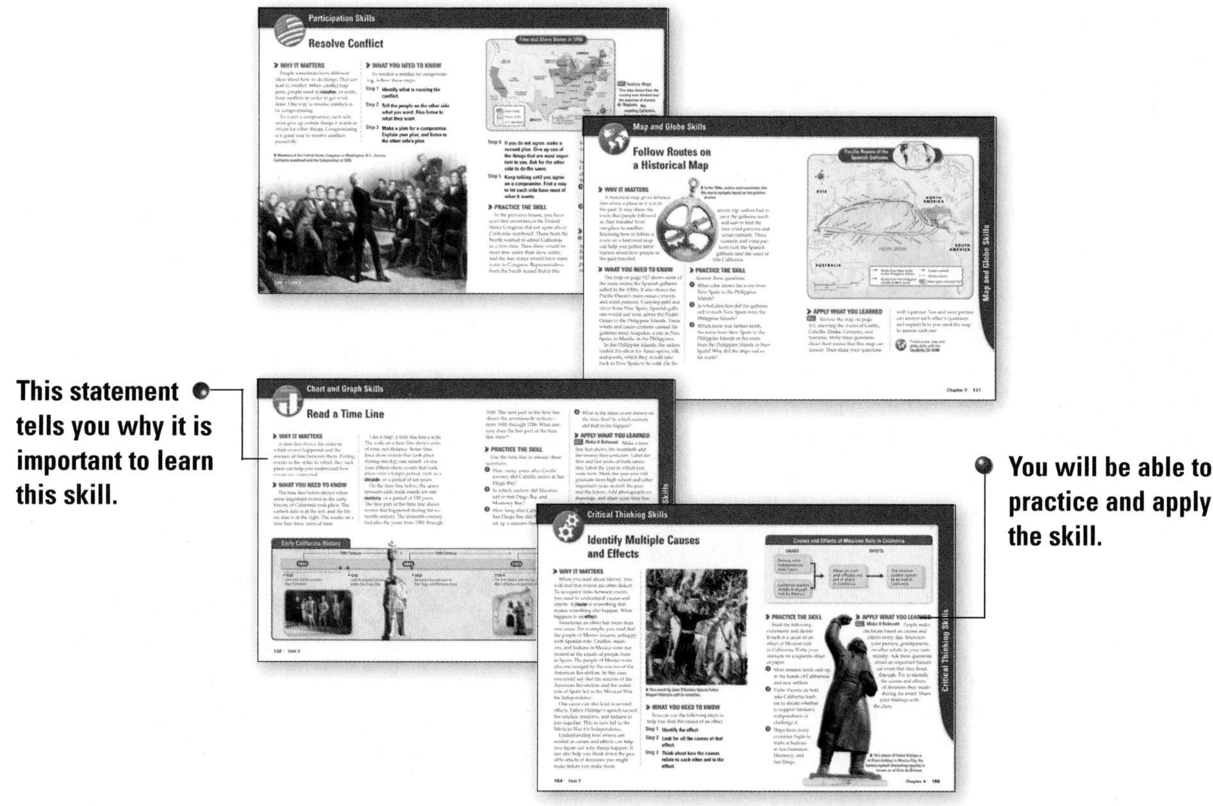

Participation Skills
Resolve Conflict
Map and Globe Skills
Follow Routes on a Historical Map
Chart and Graph Skills
Read a Time Line
Critical Thinking Skills
Identify Multiple Causes and Effects

This statement tells you why it is important to learn this skill.

You will be able to practice and apply the skill.

SPECIAL FEATURES

Biographies give in-depth background about some of the people who lived at the time.

Each biography focuses on a trait that the person showed.

Junípero Serra

Biography

Trustworthiness
Respect
Responsibility
Fairness
Caring
Patriotism

*"I trust that God will give me the strength to reach San Diego. . . . Even though I [might] die on the way, I shall not turn back."**

Miguel José Serra became a Catholic priest in Spain at the age of 24. Twelve years later, he sailed to New Spain. There he taught and worked with native peoples for many years. In 1769, he traveled to Alta California with Gaspar de Portolá. During the trip, he suffered from pain in his leg. Years earlier, he had been bitten by a snake or an insect, and his leg had never healed. Portolá urged him to return home, but Serra would not.

Today, Serra is known as the Father of the California Missions. Serra started the first California mission at San Diego in 1769. He started a total of 9 missions, which helped the new California colony grow. For many California Indians, the missions also led to the end of their traditional ways of life.

Father Junípero Serra founded the mission of San Diego de Alcalá on July 16, 1769.

Why Character Counts

In what ways did Serra help Spain increase its control of Alta California?

How did Serra show responsibility to New Spain?

Bio Brief

1713 Born — 1749 Becomes a missionary in New Spain — 1769 Sets up first mission in Alta California — 1771 Works from Mission San Carlos — 1784 Died

GO ONLINE Interactive Multimedia Biographies Visit MULTIMEDIA BIOGRAPHIES at www.harcourtschool.com/hss

123

A time line shows when the person was born and died and some key events in his or her life.

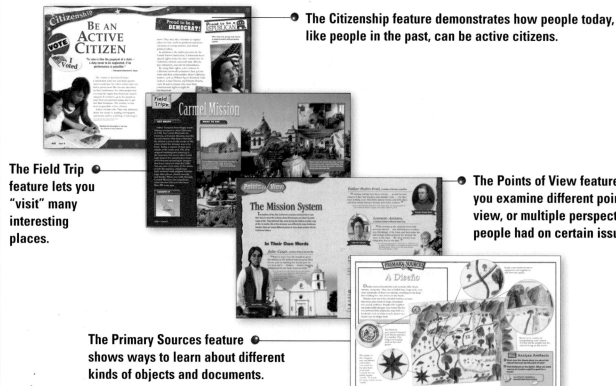

The Citizenship feature demonstrates how people today, like people in the past, can be active citizens.

The Field Trip feature lets you "visit" many interesting places.

The Points of View feature lets you examine different points of view, or multiple perspectives, people had on certain issues.

The Primary Sources feature shows ways to learn about different kinds of objects and documents.

FOR YOUR REFERENCE

At the back of your textbook, you will find different reference tools. You can use these tools to look up words or to find out information about people, places, and other topics.

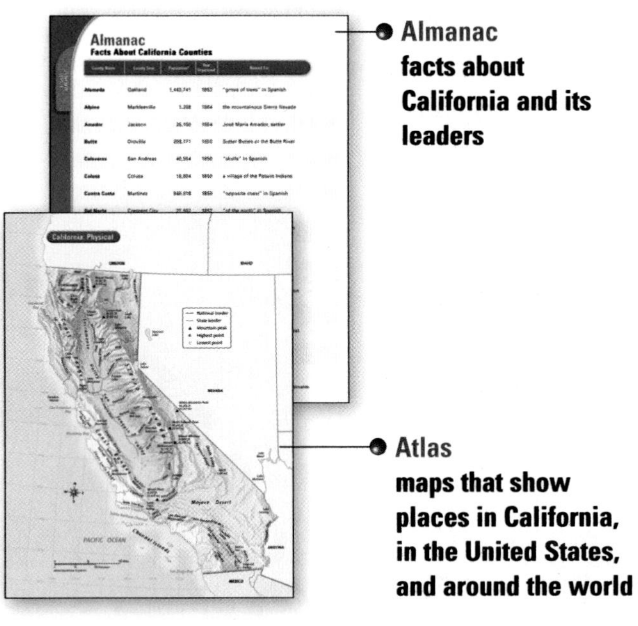

Almanac
facts about California and its leaders

Atlas
maps that show places in California, in the United States, and around the world

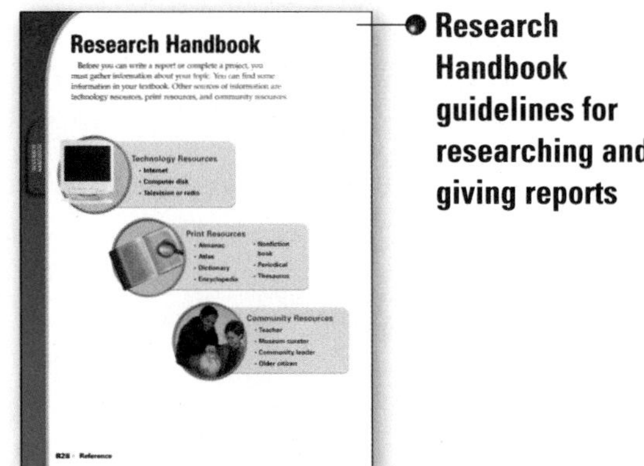

Research Handbook
guidelines for researching and giving reports

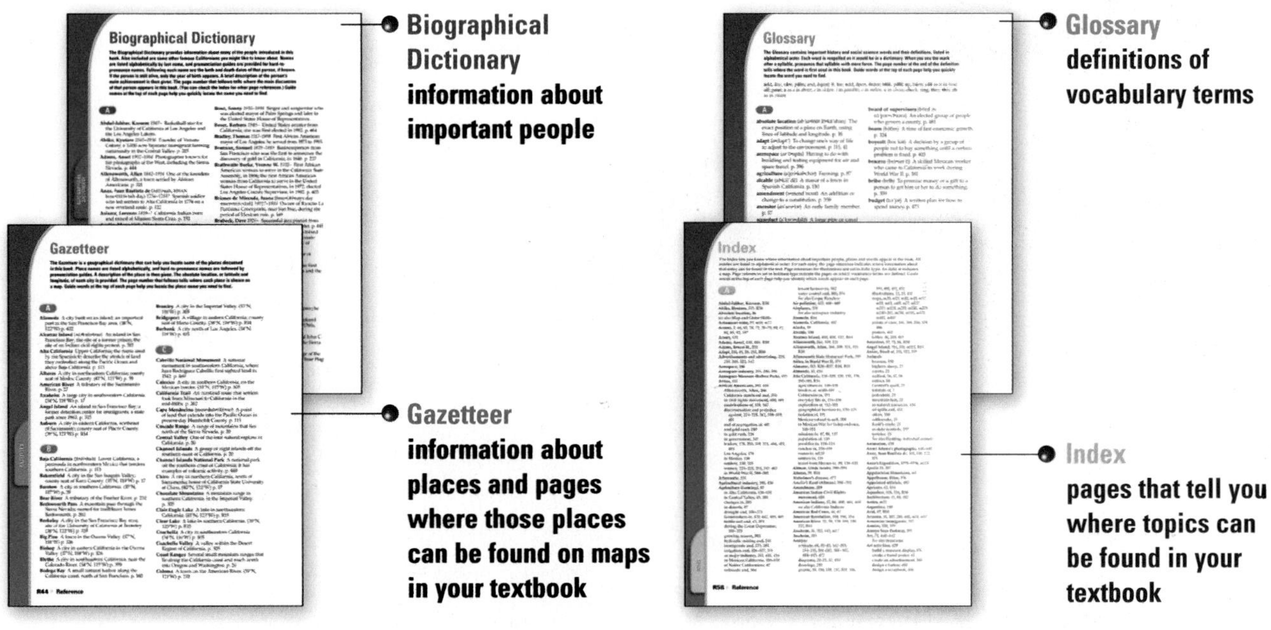

Biographical Dictionary
information about important people

Glossary
definitions of vocabulary terms

Gazetteer
information about places and pages where those places can be found on maps in your textbook

Index
pages that tell you where topics can be found in your textbook

The Five Themes of Geography

Learning about places is an important part of history and geography. Geography is the study of Earth's surface and the way people use it. When geographers study Earth and its geography, they often think about five themes, or topics. Keeping these themes in mind as you read will help you think like a geographer.

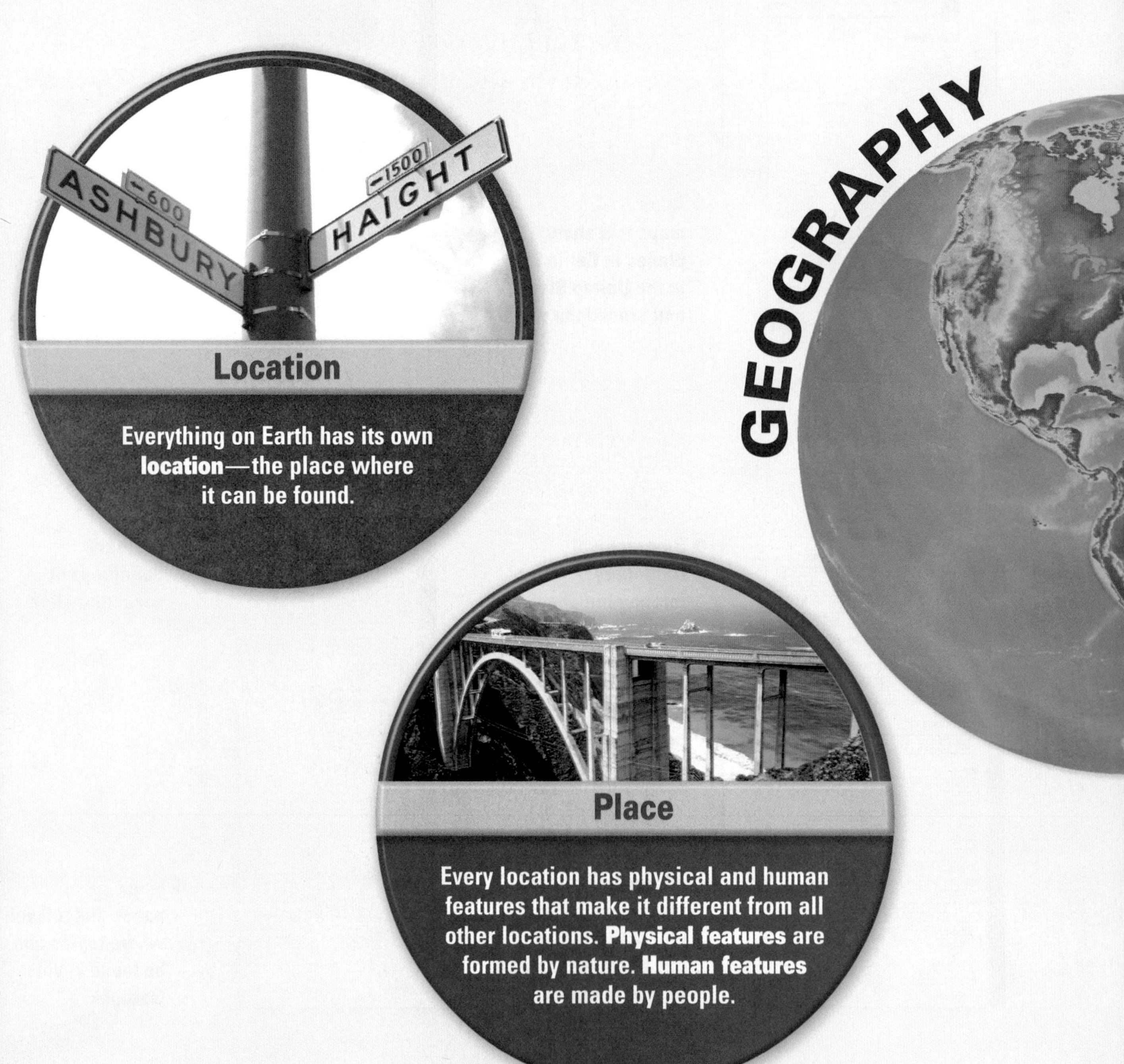

ASHBURY
600
HAIGHT
1500
GEOGRAPHY
Location
Everything on Earth has its own **location**—the place where it can be found.
Place
Every location has physical and human features that make it different from all other locations. **Physical features** are formed by nature. **Human features** are made by people.

Human-Environment Interactions

People and their surroundings interact. People's actions change the environment, but the environment also affects people. Sometimes people must change how they live to fit into their surroundings.

Movement

People, things, and ideas move every day. They move in our state, our country, and around the world.

THEMES

Regions

Areas of Earth whose main features make them different from other areas are called regions. A **region** can be described by its physical features or its human features.

Looking at Earth

A distant view from space shows Earth's round shape. You probably have a globe in your classroom. A globe is a sphere, or ball. It is a model of Earth. It shows Earth's major bodies of water and its **continents**. Continents are the largest land masses. Earth's seven continents, from the largest to the smallest, are Asia, Africa, North America, South America, Antarctica, Europe, and Australia.

Because of its shape, you can see only one half of Earth at a time when you look at a globe. Halfway between the North Pole and the South Pole on a globe is a line called the **equator**.

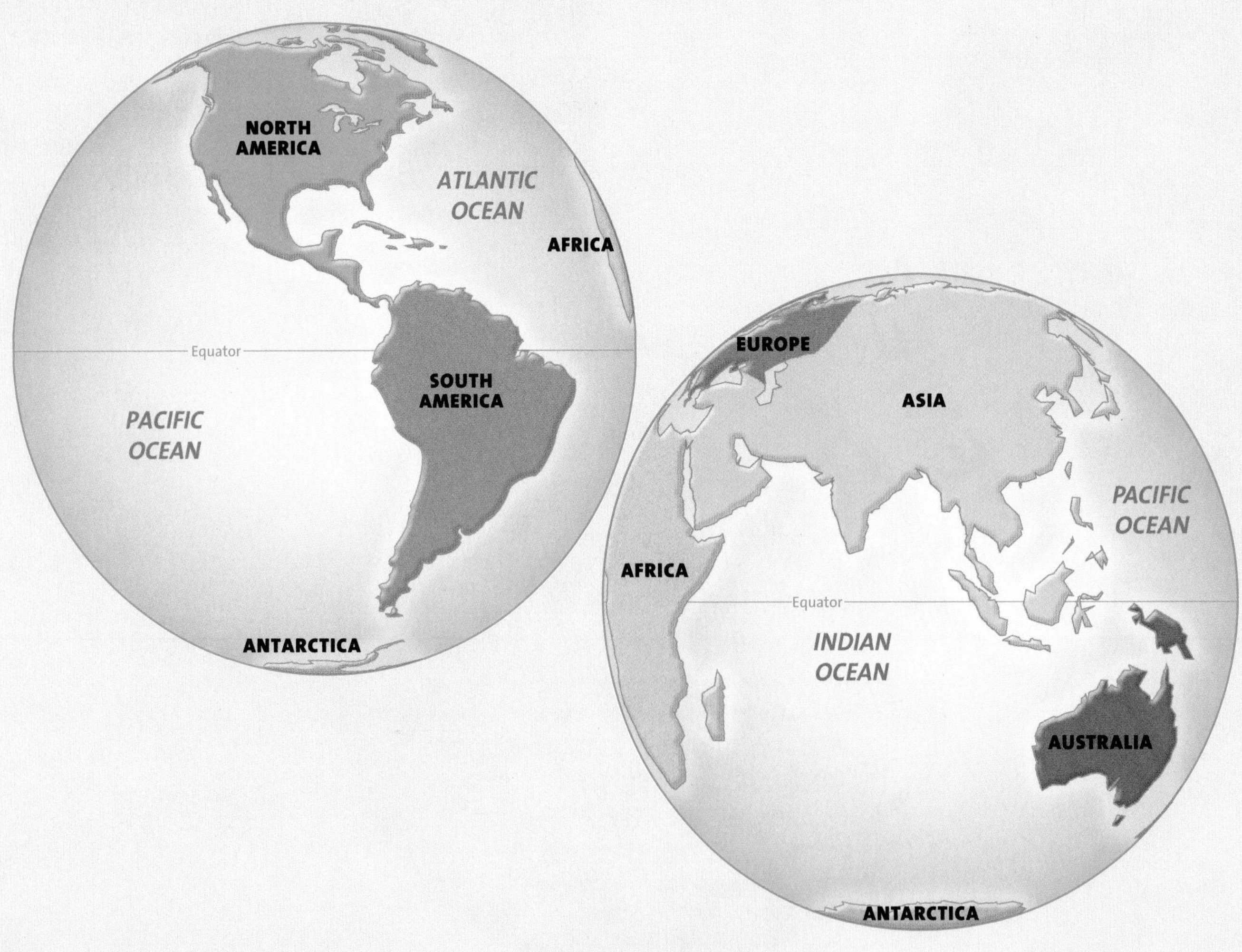

The equator divides Earth into two equal halves, or **hemispheres**. The Northern Hemisphere is north of the equator, and the Southern Hemisphere is south of it. Another line on the globe is called the **prime meridian**. It divides Earth into the Western Hemisphere and the Eastern Hemisphere.

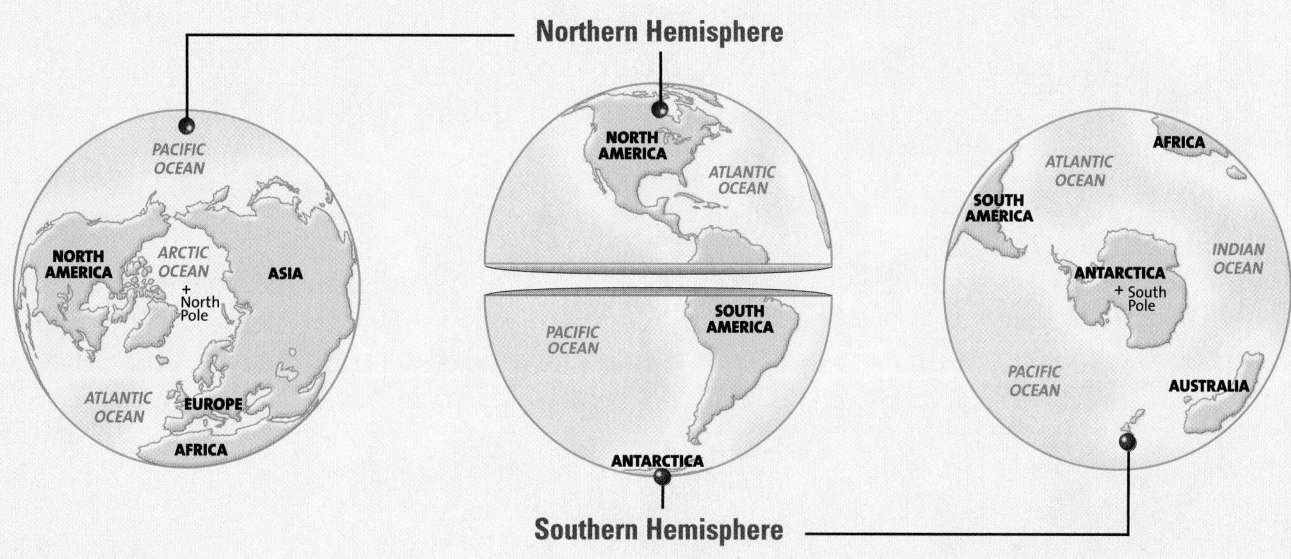

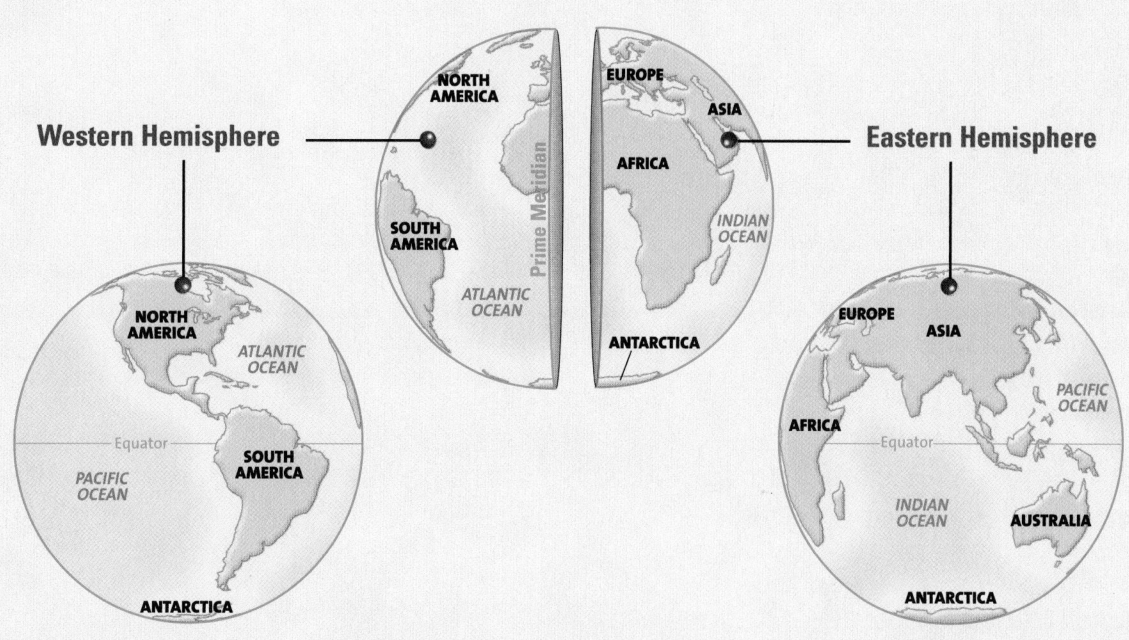

Geography Terms

1 **basin** bowl-shaped area of land surrounded by higher land

2 **bay** an inlet of the sea or some other body of water, usually smaller than a gulf

3 **bluff** high, steep face of rock or earth

4 **canyon** deep, narrow valley with steep sides

5 **cape** point of land that extends into water

6 **cataract** large waterfall

7 **channel** deepest part of a body of water

8 **cliff** high, steep face of rock or earth

9 **coast** land along a sea or ocean

10 **coastal plain** area of flat land along a sea or ocean

11 **delta** triangle-shaped area of land at the mouth of a river

12 **desert** dry land with few plants

13 **dune** hill of sand piled up by the wind

14 **fall line** area along which rivers form waterfalls or rapids as the rivers drop to lower land

15 **floodplain** flat land that is near the edges of a river and is formed by silt deposited by floods

16 **foothills** hilly area at the base of a mountain

17 **glacier** large ice mass that moves slowly down a mountain or across land

18 **gulf** part of a sea or ocean extending into the land, usually larger than a bay

19 **hill** land that rises above the land around it

20 **inlet** any area of water extending into the land from a larger body of water

21 **island** land that has water on all sides

22 **isthmus** narrow strip of land connecting two larger areas of land

23 **lagoon** body of shallow water

24 **lake** body of water with land on all sides

25 marsh lowland with moist soil and tall grasses

26 mesa flat-topped mountain with steep sides

27 mountain highest kind of land

28 mountain pass gap between mountains

29 mountain range row of mountains

30 mouth of river place where a river empties into another body of water

31 oasis area of water and fertile land in a desert

32 ocean body of salt water larger than a sea

33 peak top of a mountain

34 peninsula land that is almost completely surrounded by water

35 plain area of flat or gently rolling low land

36 plateau area of high, mostly flat land

37 reef ridge of sand, rock, or coral that lies at or near the surface of a sea or ocean

38 river large stream of water that flows across the land

39 riverbank land along a river

40 savanna area of grassland and scattered trees

41 sea body of salt water smaller than an ocean

42 sea level the level of the surface of an ocean or a sea

43 slope side of a hill or mountain

44 source of river place where a river begins

45 strait narrow channel of water connecting two larger bodies of water

46 swamp area of low, wet land with trees

47 timberline line on a mountain above which it is too cold for trees to grow

48 tributary stream or river that flows into a larger stream or river

49 valley low land between hills or mountains

50 volcano opening in the earth, often raised, through which lava, rock, ashes, and gases a forced out

51 waterfall steep drop from a high pla lower place in a stream or river

Reading Maps

Maps help you see where places are in the world. A map is a drawing that shows all or part of Earth on a flat surface. To help you read maps more easily, mapmakers add certain features to their maps. These features usually include a title, a map legend, a compass rose, a locator, and a map scale.

Mapmakers sometimes need to show certain places on a map in greater detail. Sometimes they must also show places that are located beyond the area shown on a map.

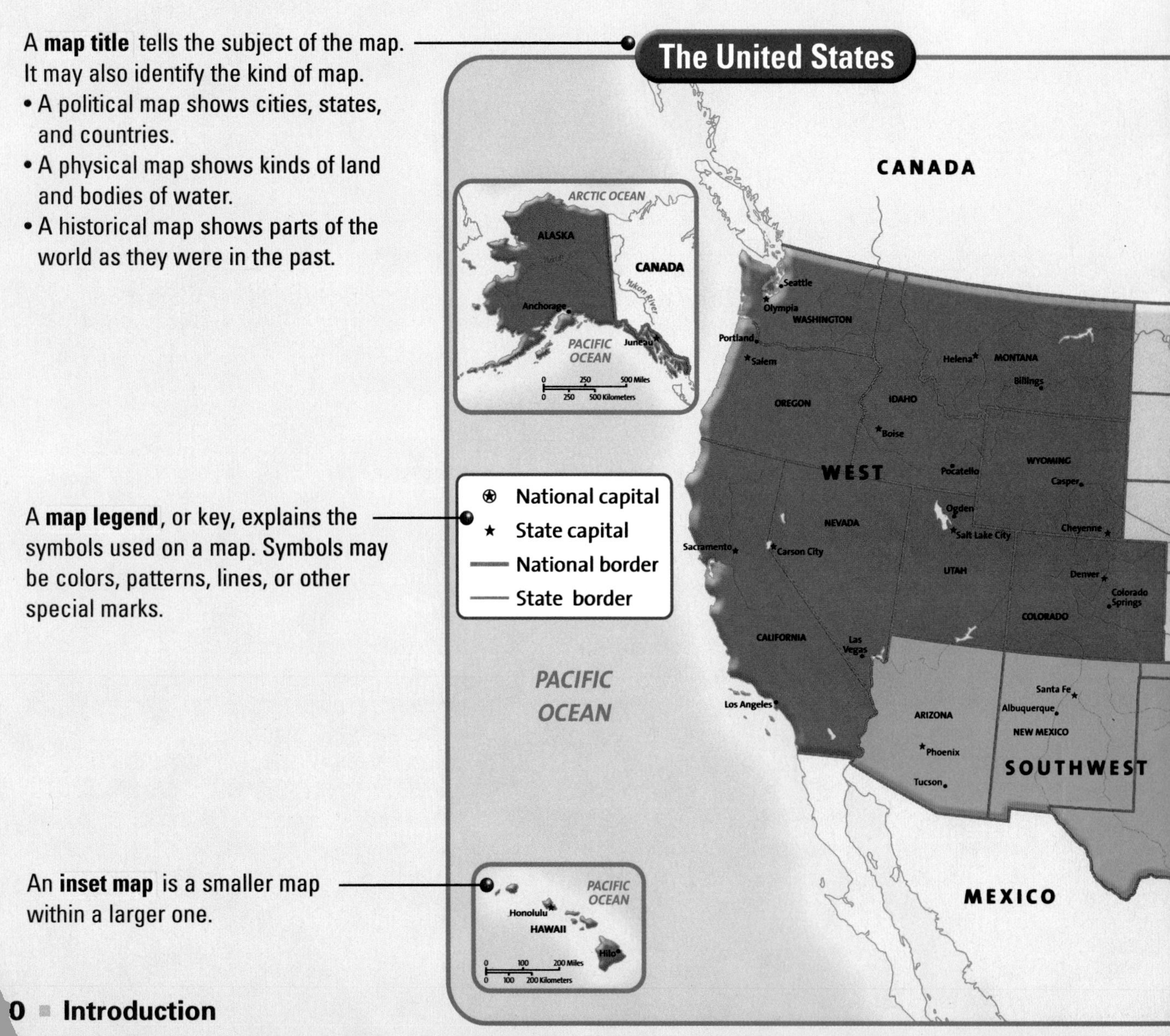

Find Alaska and Hawaii on the map of the United States on pages R8–R9. The map there shows the location of those two states in relation to the location of the rest of the country.

Now find Alaska and Hawaii on the map below. To show this much detail for these states and the rest of the country, the map would have to be much larger. Instead, Alaska and Hawaii are each shown in a separate inset map, or a small map within a larger map.

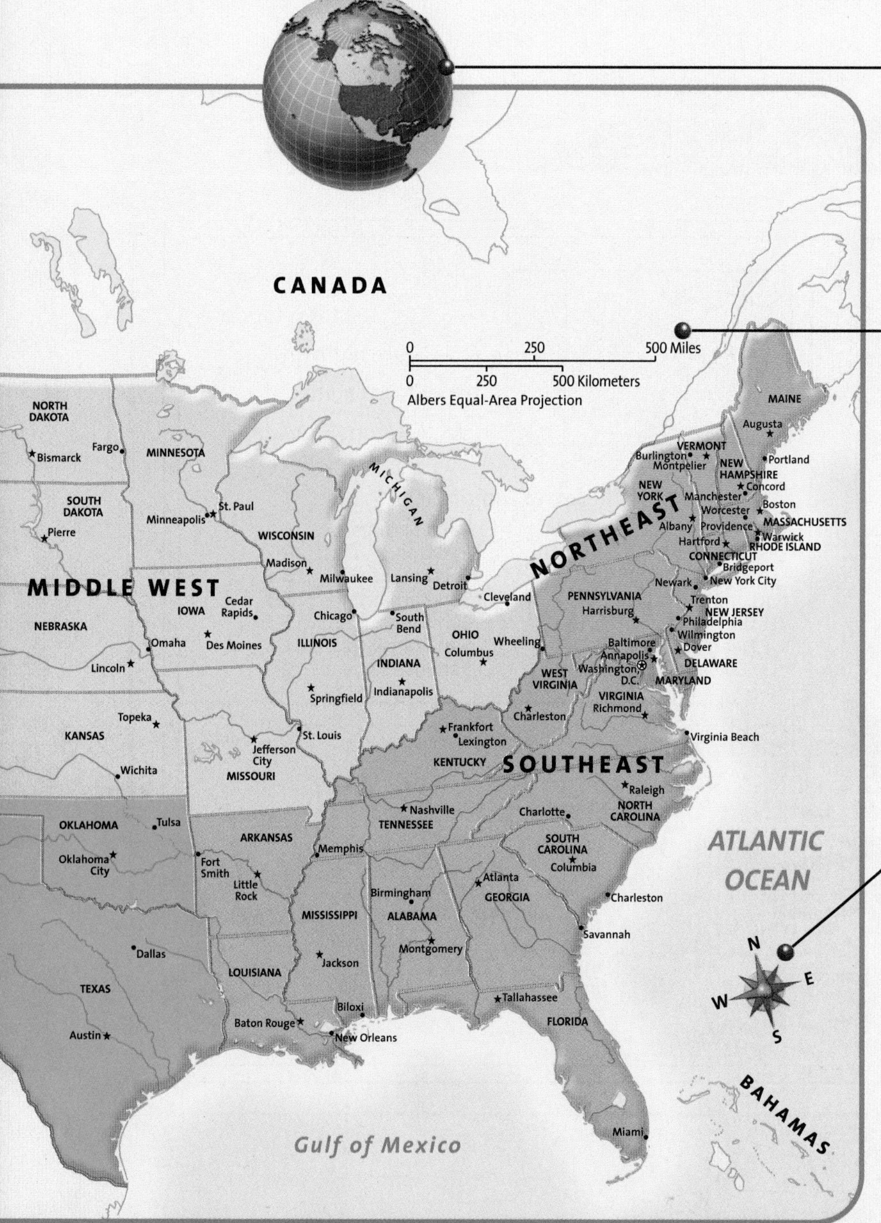

A **locator** is a small map or globe that shows where the place on the main map is located within a larger area.

A **map scale** compares a distance on the map to a distance in the real world. It helps you find the real distance between places on a map.

A **compass rose**, or direction marker, shows directions.

- The **cardinal directions** are north, south, east, and west.
- The **intermediate directions**, or directions between the cardinal directions, are northeast, northwest, southeast, and southwest.

Finding Locations

To help people find places on maps, mapmakers sometimes add lines that cross each other to form a pattern of squares called a **grid system**. Look at the map of California below. Around the grid are letters and numbers. The columns, which run up and down, have numbers. The rows, which run from left to right, have letters. Each square on the map can be identified by its letter and number. For example, the top row of squares on the map includes square A-1, square A-2, square A-3, and so on.

The Land and Early People

START WITH THE STANDARDS

California History-Social Science Standards

4.1 Students demonstrate an understanding of the physical and human geographic features that define places and regions in California.

4.2 Students describe the social, political, cultural, and economic life and interactions among people of California from the pre-Columbian societies to the Spanish mission and Mexican rancho periods.

The Big Idea

GEOGRAPHY

People in California have always interacted with their environment and been affected by it.

What to Know

- What are the major physical and human features of California, and how do they affect life in the state?
- What are some nations of California Indians, and where did they live?
- How were California Indians affected by their environment?

Show What You Know

- ★ Unit 1 Test
- Writing: A Summary
- Unit Project: A California Atlas

Unit 1

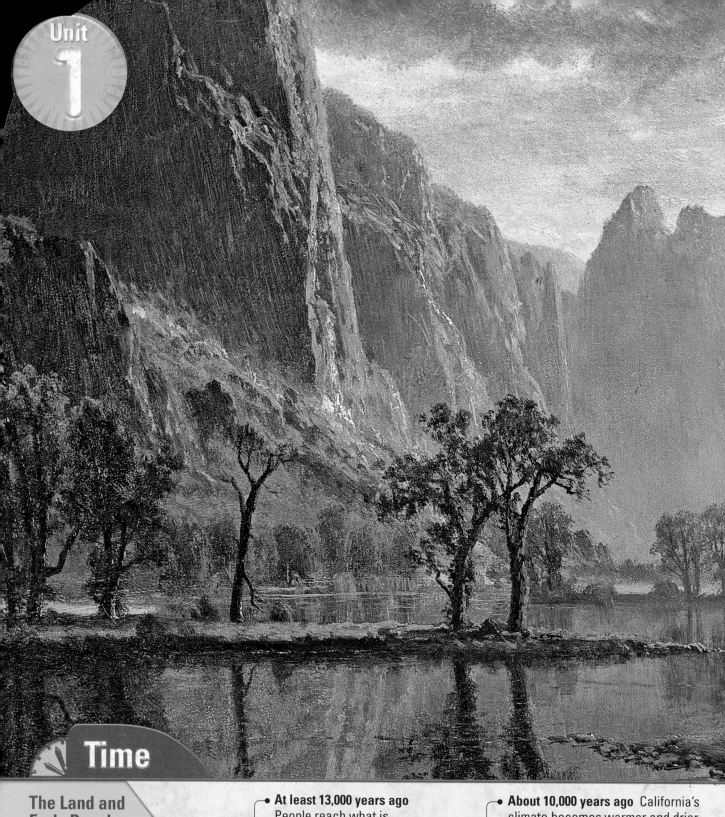

The Land and Early People

At least 13,000 years ago People reach what is now California, p. 57

About 10,000 years ago California's climate becomes warmer and drier, and many of the large animals die out, p. 58

15,000 YEARS AGO

10,000 YEARS AGO

At the Same Time

About 10,000 years ago People in different parts of the world begin to grow crops and raise animals

The Land and Early People

About 4,000 years ago
California Indians begin to form villages, p. 59

5,000 YEARS AGO

PRESENT

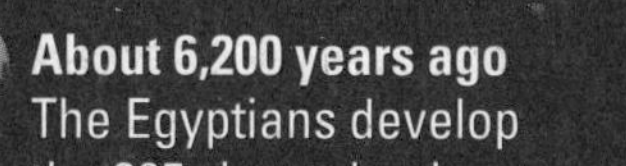

About 6,200 years ago
The Egyptians develop the 365-day calendar

About 3,600 years ago
The Shang Dynasty begins in China

About 1,600 years ago
Christianity becomes the official religion of the Roman Empire

Unit 1

People

The Gabrielino

The Yurok

- Lived along the Klamath River and the Pacific Ocean in northern California
- Wealth was important to the Yurok. Someone who owned many strings of shells was considered wealthy.

The Gabrielino

- The Gabrielino, also called the Tongva, lived in what are now Los Angeles and Orange Counties
- Believed in a spirit called *Qua-o-ar*, or "Giver of Life"
- Carved animal figures and bowls out of soapstone

The Chumash

- Lived along the Pacific Ocean in southern California, in the Cuyama and San Joaquin Valleys, and among the northern Channel Islands
- Built plank canoes, and waterproofed them with tar

The Yurok

The Chumash

The Cahuilla

- Lands included the foothills and desert areas at the base of the San Bernardino and San Jacinto Mountains
- Traveled long distances to gather acorns
- Made clay pottery

The Yokuts

- Lived in the San Joaquin Valley and in the foothills of the Sierra Nevada
- Had symbols to represent each family. The symbol was an animal that the family would praise.

The Maidu

- Lived in the Sacramento Valley and in the foothills of the Sierra Nevada
- Each Maidu village group was made up of three to five smaller villages around a main village

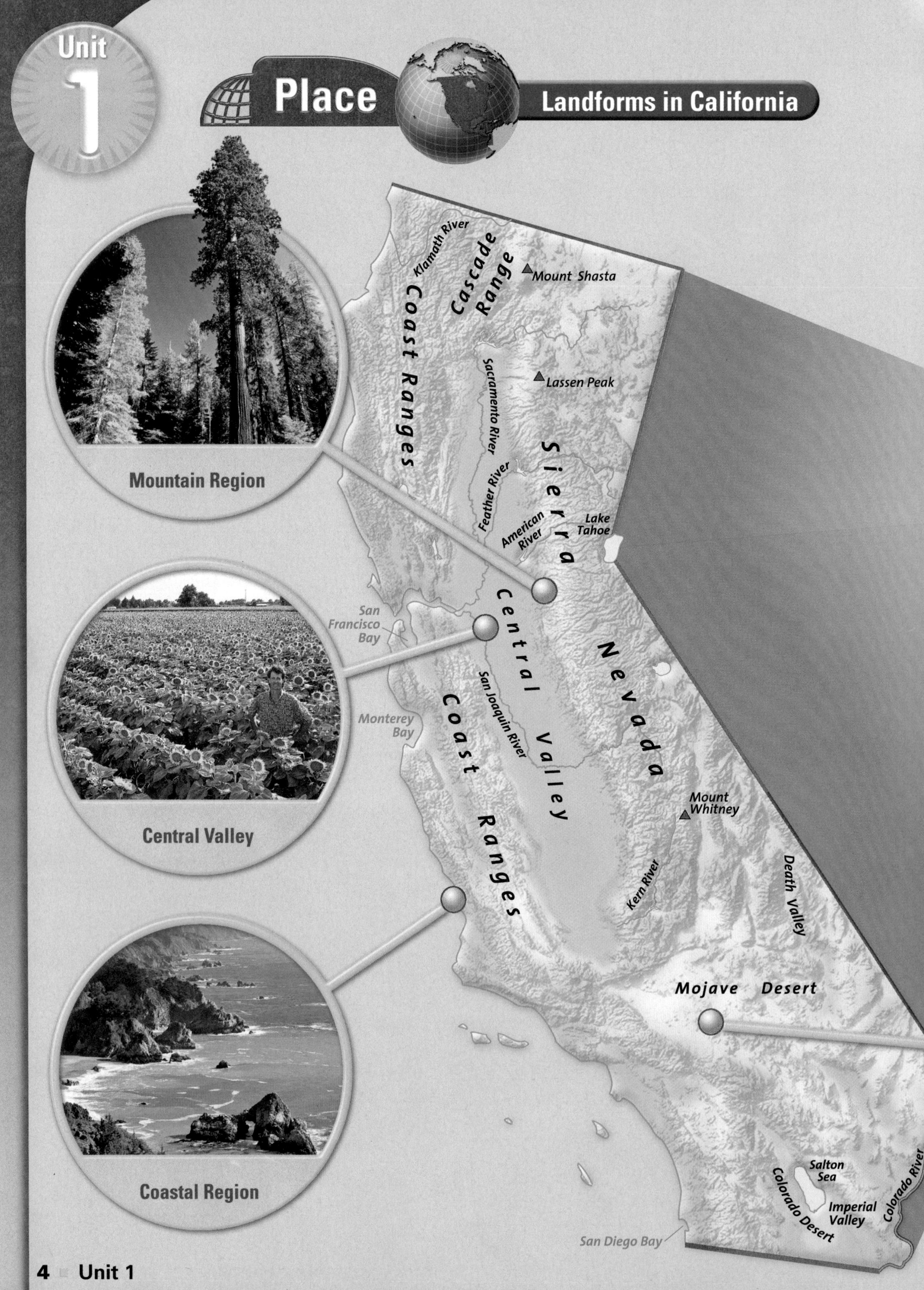

Unit 1
Place
Landforms in California
Mountain Region
Central Valley
Coastal Region
Klamath River
Cascade Range
Mount Shasta
Coast Ranges
Sacramento River
Lassen Peak
Sierra Nevada
Feather River
American River
Lake Tahoe
San Francisco Bay
Central Valley
San Joaquin River
Monterey Bay
Coast Ranges
Mount Whitney
Kern River
Death Valley
Mojave Desert
Salton Sea
Colorado Desert
Imperial Valley
Colorado River
San Diego Bay

CANADA
UNITED STATES
MEXICO
ROCKY MOUNTAINS
GREAT PLAINS
GREAT BASIN
INTERIOR PLAINS
CENTRAL PLAINS
APPALACHIAN MOUNTAINS
Missouri River
Mississippi River
Platte River
Ohio River
Colorado River
Rio Grande
ATLANTIC OCEAN
Gulf of Mexico
PACIFIC OCEAN
N
E
S
W
0 250 500 Miles
0 250 500 Kilometers
Albers Equal-Area Projection
National border
State border
Mountain peak
Desert Region

Reading Social Studies

Main Idea and Details

The main idea is the most important idea of a paragraph or passage. Details give more information about the main idea.

Why It Matters

When you identify and understand the main idea and details, you are more likely to remember what you read.

Main Idea

The most important idea

Details

facts about the main idea	facts about the main idea	facts about the main idea

- ✓ In a long article, each paragraph has a main idea and details. The whole article also has a main idea and details.
- ✓ The main idea is often the first sentence in a paragraph.

Practice the Skill

Read the paragraphs that follow. Identify the main idea and details in the second paragraph.

Main Idea
Details

Lake Tahoe is California's deepest natural lake. It is located high in the northern Sierra Nevada. At 22 miles long and 10 miles wide, Lake Tahoe is the largest mountain lake in the United States.

The Salton Sea is another of California's largest bodies of water. The Salton Sea is salty, like the ocean, but is really a large lake. It is located in the Imperial Valley and was formed when the Colorado River flooded.

Apply What You Learned

Find Main Idea and Details **Read the paragraphs, and answer the questions.**

They Call It Death Valley

In southern California is a place called Death Valley. Death Valley got its name during the California gold rush in 1849. A group of people got lost in the valley on their way to California. They were trapped there without enough supplies. Only one person died before the group was rescued. However, without water and food, the whole group was sure that they would not survive. William Lewis Manly said of what he saw, ". . . not a sign of life in nature's wide domain [territory] had been seen for a month or more."*

Thousands of years ago, the valley was full of lakes formed by melting ice. In time, the lakes dried up and became desert. The Badwater Basin is the site of a former salt-water pool that lies 282 feet below the level of the sea. It is the lowest place in Death Valley and also the lowest point in all of North America.

The name Death Valley might make you wonder whether anything at all lives there. In fact, the area is the home of many desert plants and animals. Animals that live in Death Valley include rabbits, foxes, snakes, and lizards. There are also birds, such as quails and doves. Some plants, such as cactus, grow there, too.

*William Lewis Manly. *Death Valley in '49: An Important Chapter of California Pioneer History.* Time-Life Books, 1982.

Find Main Idea and Details

1. **What is the main idea of the first paragraph?**
2. **Which sentence states the main idea of the second paragraph?**
3. **What details explain the idea that although Death Valley is a harsh environment, there is still life there?**

The desert collared lizard is one type of animal that lives in Death Valley.

Study Skills

MAKE AN OUTLINE

An outline is a good way to record main ideas and details.

- **Topics in an outline are shown by Roman numerals.**
- **Main ideas about each topic are shown by capital letters.**
- **Details about each main idea are identified by numbers.**

California's Geography

I. California's Location
  A. California in the world
    1. One of 50 states in United States
    2. On the continent of North America
    3. ____________________
  B. A Pacific Coast state
    1. ____________________
    2. ____________________

Apply As You Read

As you read this chapter, remember to pay attention to the topics, main ideas, and details. Use that information to complete an outline of the chapter.

California History-Social Science Standards, Grade 4

4.1 Students demonstrate an understanding of the physical and human geographic features that define places and regions in California.

CHAPTER

California's Geography

The Lone Cypress, Monterey Peninsula

SIERRA

by Diane Siebert
illustrated by Wendell Minor

Stretching north and south across much of California, the Sierra Nevada (see•AIR•ah neh•VAH•dah) is among California's many natural wonders. Read now to discover more about these majestic mountains.

I am the mountain,
Young, yet old.
I've stood, and watching time unfold,
Have known the age of ice and snow
And felt the glaciers come and go.
They moved with every melt and freeze;
They shattered boulders, leveled trees,
And carved, upon my granite rocks,
The terraced walls of slabs and blocks
That trace each path, each downward course,
Where through the years, with crushing force,
The glaciers sculpted deep ravines
And polished rocks to glossy sheens.

terraced formed into series of horizontal ridges

ravine a steep-sided valley

At last this era, long and cold,
Began to lose its frigid hold
When, matched against a
  warming sun,
Its final glacier, ton by ton,
Retreated, melting, making way
For what I have become today:

A place of strength and lofty height;
Of shadow shot with shafts of light;
Where meadows nestle in between
The arms of forests, cool and green;
Where, out of clefted granite walls,
Spill silver, snow-fed waterfalls.

Here stand the pines, so straight
  and tall,
Whose needles, drying and dying, fall
Upon my sides to slowly form
A natural blanket, soft and warm;

frigid very cold

retreated turned back

clefted cracked open

Their graceful, swaying branches sing
In gentle breezes, whispering
To junipers, all gnarled and low,
That here, in stubborn splendor,
  grow.

And on my western slope I hold
My great sequoias, tall and old;
They've watched three thousand
  years go by,
And, in their endless quest for sky,
This grove of giants slowly grew
With songs of green on silent blue.

Response Corner

1. Work with a partner to explain the meaning of each stanza in "Sierra." Then share your explanation with the class.
2. Why do you think the author had the mountains describe themselves?

Lesson 1

California's Location

WHAT TO KNOW
Where is California located, and what is important about its location?

- Explain where California is in relation to the North and South Poles, the equator, and the prime meridian.
- Describe California's location relative to its neighboring states, the Pacific Ocean, and other countries.

VOCABULARY
hemisphere p. 13
equator p. 13
prime meridian p. 13
relative location p. 14

PLACES
North America
Northern Hemisphere
Southern Hemisphere
North Pole
South Pole
Western Hemisphere
Eastern Hemisphere
Pacific Basin

MAIN IDEA AND DETAILS

California Standards
HSS 4.1, 4.1.1, 4.1.2, 4.1.4

YOU ARE THERE

"You have e-mail!" your computer tells you. The message is from your new pen pal in Japan. It asks you to describe where you live. What do you say? You could give your street address. You might also tell the name of your community. You could even say that you live near an important place, such as your school.

You decide to say that you live in California. Now your pen pal writes, "Where in the world is California?"

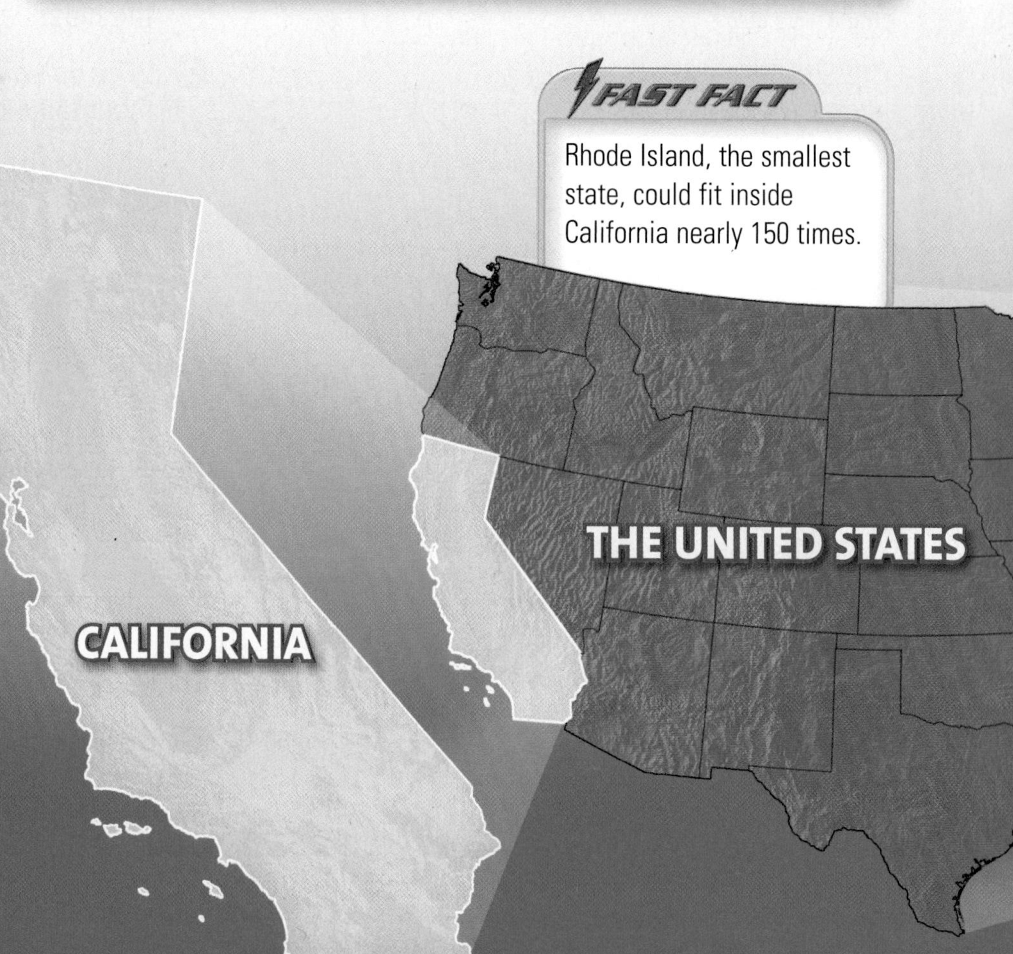

FAST FACT
Rhode Island, the smallest state, could fit inside California nearly 150 times.

California in the World

You can describe California's location to your pen pal in different ways. You could say that California is one of the 50 states that make up the United States of America. Because the United States is on the continent of North America, you could also say that California is in **North America**.

You might decide to explain in which **hemisphere**, or half of Earth, California is located. On a globe, Earth is divided into the **Northern Hemisphere** and the **Southern Hemisphere** by an imaginary line called the **equator**. The equator lies halfway between the North and South Poles. The **North Pole** is Earth's northernmost point, and the **South Pole** is its southernmost point. California is north of the equator, so it is in the Northern Hemisphere.

Another line, the **prime meridian**, divides Earth into the **Western Hemisphere** and the **Eastern Hemisphere**. The continent of North America, including California, is in the Western Hemisphere.

You can now give this answer to your pen pal—California is in the United States of America, a country in North America, in the Northern and Western Hemispheres.

READING CHECK **MAIN IDEA AND DETAILS**
Where in the world is California located?

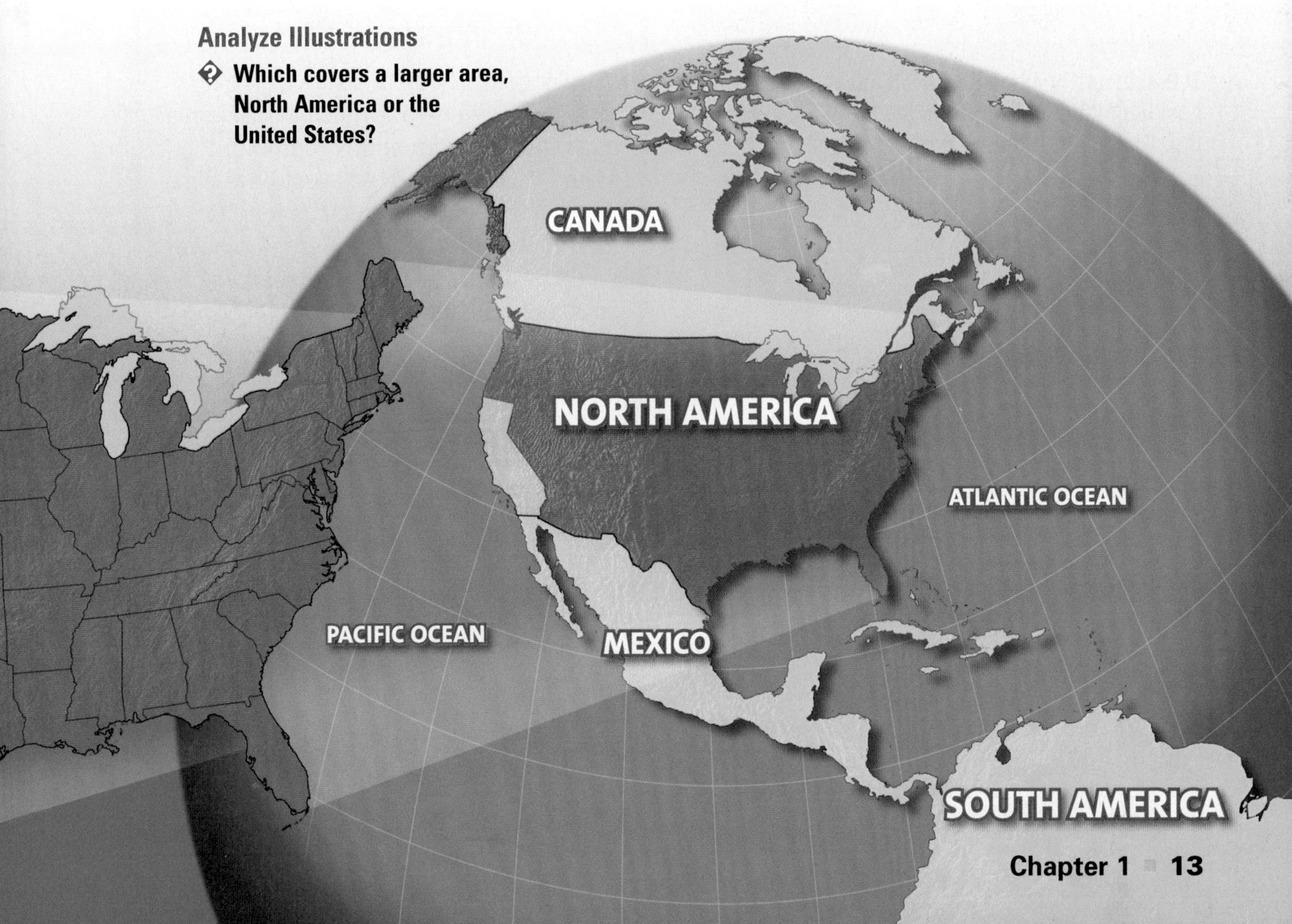

A Pacific Coast State

"Now find the country of Mexico on a map," you write your pen pal. "California is just north of it." You go on to explain that California is south of the state of Oregon and west of both Nevada and Arizona. Then you write that the Colorado River forms part of California's eastern border.

When you describe California's location in these ways, you are giving its relative location. The **relative location** of a place is where it is in relation to one or more other places on Earth.

"In the West" is another way to describe California's relative location. California is at the western edge of North America. It is one of 11 states that make up the region of the United States called the West. California is also one of five states that border the Pacific Ocean. This makes it a Pacific Coast state, too.

From the California coast, the Pacific Ocean might look big and empty to you. Actually, though, ships carrying people and goods cross the Pacific all the time. Many of these ships sail to and from other states and countries that border the Pacific Ocean. All these places are part of a larger world region

GEOGRAPHY

A Western State

California is in the West. Mountain ranges stretch across much of California and other western states. Some of the states that make up the West have similar physical features, such as forests, mountains, and deserts. They also have some of the same natural resources, such as minerals and timber.

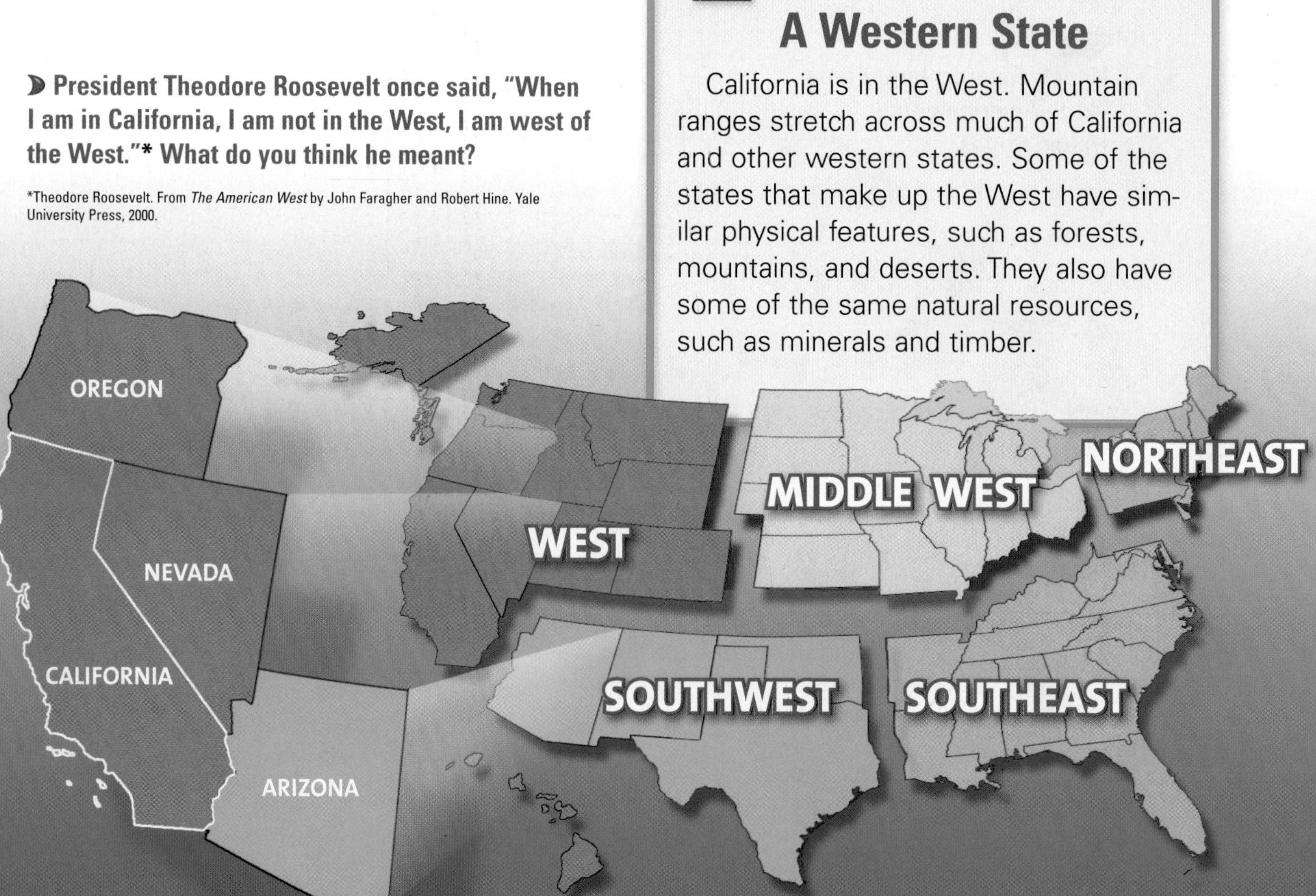

➤ **President Theodore Roosevelt once said, "When I am in California, I am not in the West, I am west of the West."* What do you think he meant?**

*Theodore Roosevelt. From *The American West* by John Faragher and Robert Hine. Yale University Press, 2000.

A cargo ship passes under the Golden Gate Bridge.

called the **Pacific Basin**. Because Japan also borders the Pacific Ocean, you could tell your pen pal that you both live in the Pacific Basin.

California's location in the western United States and on the edge of the Pacific Ocean has made it important in many ways. It is a place where people, goods, and ideas from all over the world have come together.

READING CHECK MAIN IDEA AND DETAILS
What is California's location in relation to the Pacific Ocean?

Summary

California is in the United States, in North America, and in the Northern and Western Hemispheres. Its location on the Pacific coast makes it a place where people, goods, and ideas come together from around the world.

REVIEW

1. Where is California located, and what is important about its location?
2. How are the words **equator** and **hemisphere** related?
3. What are the North Pole and the South Pole?

CRITICAL THINKING

4. ANALYSIS SKILL How has California's location in the Pacific Basin affected the state?
5. **Create a Chart** Write these terms on index cards: *the West, Earth, California, Western Hemisphere, North America, United States.* Start with *Earth* and put the cards on a chart in order from the largest region to the smallest. Use the chart to explain California's global address.
6. Focus Skill **MAIN IDEA AND DETAILS** On a separate sheet of paper, copy and complete the graphic organizer below.

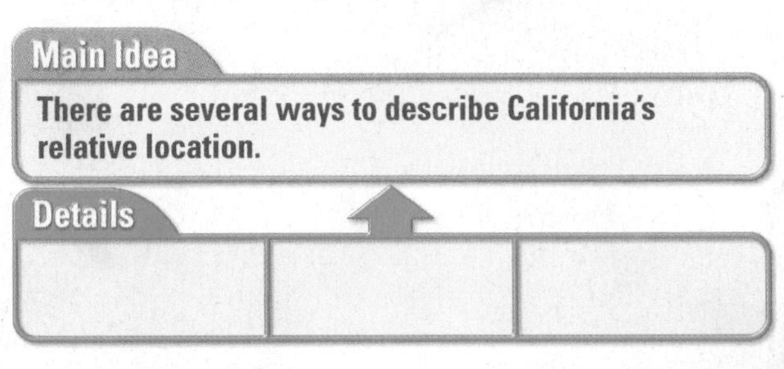

Main Idea
There are several ways to describe California's relative location.
Details

Use Latitude and Longitude

WHY IT MATTERS

To describe the exact location, or **absolute location**, of a place, you can use lines of latitude and longitude.

WHAT YOU NEED TO KNOW

Lines of latitude on a map or globe run east and west. They are measured in degrees (°) north and south from the equator. They go from 0° at the equator to 90° at each of the poles. North of the equator, lines of latitude are marked *N* for *north*. South of the equator, they are marked *S* for *south*.

Like the equator, some other lines of latitude have special names. The Tropic of Cancer and the Tropic of Capricorn mark the northern and southern boundaries of Earth's warmest region—the **tropics**. Places north of the Arctic Circle and south of the Antarctic Circle are Earth's coldest regions.

Maps and globes also have a set of lines that run north and south, from the North Pole to the South Pole. These lines are called **lines of longitude**. They are measured in degrees (°) east and west from the prime meridian. They go from 0° at the prime meridian to 180°. West of the prime meridian, lines of longitude are marked *W* for *west*. East of it, they are marked *E* for *east*.

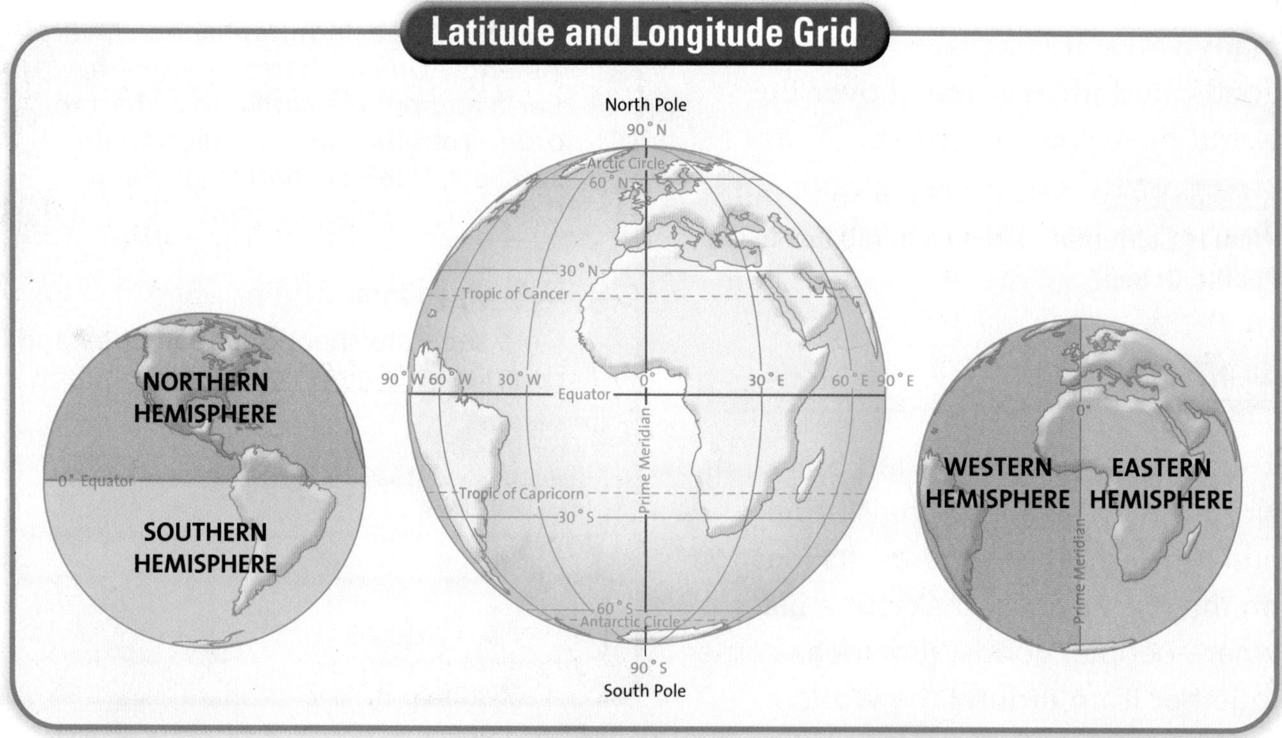

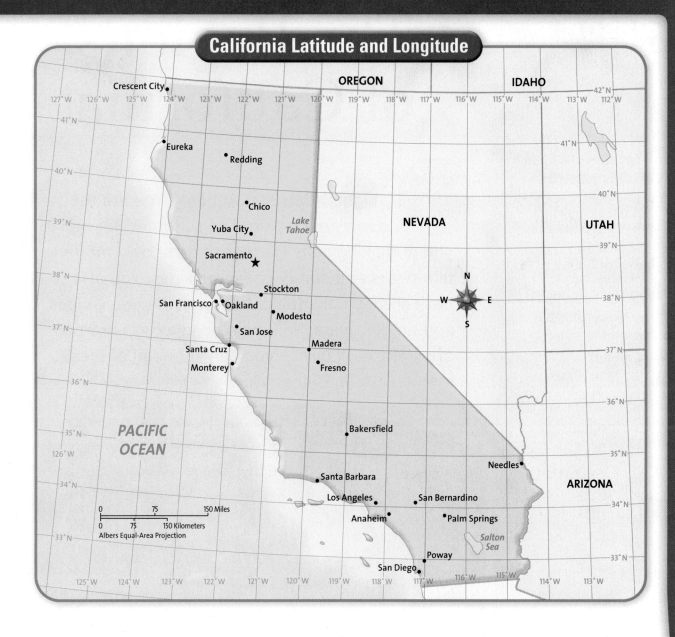

California Latitude and Longitude

OREGON
IDAHO
NEVADA
UTAH
ARIZONA
PACIFIC OCEAN
Crescent City
Eureka
Redding
Chico
Yuba City
Lake Tahoe
Sacramento
Stockton
San Francisco
Oakland
Modesto
San Jose
Santa Cruz
Monterey
Madera
Fresno
Bakersfield
Santa Barbara
Los Angeles
Anaheim
San Bernardino
Palm Springs
Salton Sea
Needles
Poway
San Diego
0 75 150 Miles
0 75 150 Kilometers
Albers Equal-Area Projection

Lines of latitude and longitude on a map or globe cross each other to form a **coordinate grid system**. You can give the absolute location of a place by first naming the line of latitude and then the line of longitude closest to it.

PRACTICE THE SKILL

Answer these questions.

1. On which line of latitude is California's northern border?
2. Which line of latitude is closest to Poway? which line of longitude?
3. What city is near 37°N, 122°W?

APPLY WHAT YOU LEARNED

ANALYSIS SKILL **Make It Relevant** Use latitude and longitude to tell your community's location.

Practice your map and globe skills with the **GeoSkills CD-ROM**.

Lesson 2 The Regions of California

WHAT TO KNOW
What are California's four natural regions like?

- ✓ **Explain how California is divided into natural regions.**
- ✓ **Identify some of the major physical features found in each natural region.**

VOCABULARY

natural region p. 19
coastal plain p. 20
harbor p. 20
tributary p. 22
delta p. 22
fertile p. 22
irrigation p. 23
sea level p. 24

PLACES

Mount Whitney
Death Valley
Coast Ranges
Sierra Nevada
Cascade Range
San Joaquin River
Sacramento River
Mojave Desert
Colorado River

MAIN IDEA AND DETAILS

California Standards
HSS 4.1, 4.1.3, 4.1.4, 4.1.5

YOU ARE THERE "Lights! Camera! Action!" You are the director of a film. The script for the movie you're making calls for scenes on snowy mountain peaks and sunny ocean beaches. You also have scenes in sunbaked deserts, in wide valleys, and on big rivers. You even need to film in front of a volcano! Luckily, you can shoot all of these scenes right in California.

California's Natural Wonders

As you travel through California making your film, you learn that there are amazing sights in every part of the state. One reason California has so many different sights is because it covers such a large area. California is a very large state. In fact, only Texas and Alaska are larger. In the eastern part of California, you see some of the highest waterfalls in North America. In the northwest, you find forests with some of the world's tallest trees. Nearby are steaming-hot springs and geysers.

In another part of California, you discover **Mount Whitney**, the highest point in the 48 connected states. Only about 100 miles away is **Death Valley**, the lowest point in the Western Hemisphere.

Because the land in California is not the same all over, geographers sometimes divide the state into four **natural regions**. Each of these regions is made up of places that share the same kinds of physical, or natural, features. They have similar landforms, bodies of water, climates, and plants. California's four natural regions are the Coastal Region, the Mountain Region, the Central Valley Region, and the Desert Region.

READING CHECK **MAIN IDEA AND DETAILS**
What is one way that geographers divide the state of California?

California has rocky coastlines, tall mountains, rich farmlands, and dry deserts. One type of flower you will find in many places in California is the golden poppy. It is the state flower of California.

The Coastal Region

California's Coastal Region stretches for more than 800 miles along the Pacific Ocean. Low mountains, called the **Coast Ranges**, follow much of the coastline.

In northern California, the mountains drop sharply into the Pacific Ocean, forming steep cliffs. Along California's southern coast, the mountains give way to a **coastal plain**. This area of low land has sandy beaches along the shoreline.

Much of California's coast is rocky, but the state has two large natural **harbors** where ships can dock safely. One of these harbors is San Francisco Bay. The other is San Diego Bay. Smaller bays also dot the coast.

Broad valleys lie between the mountains of the Coast Ranges. To the north of San Francisco are the Napa and Sonoma Valleys. To the south are the Santa Clara and Salinas Valleys. These valleys have rich soil and are important farming areas.

Two groups of islands are also part of California's Coastal Region. West of San Francisco are the Farallon (FAIR•uh•lahn) Islands. Eight other islands make up the Channel Islands, off the coast of southern California. The largest of these is Santa Catalina.

READING CHECK **COMPARE AND CONTRAST**
How is California's northern coast different from its southern coast?

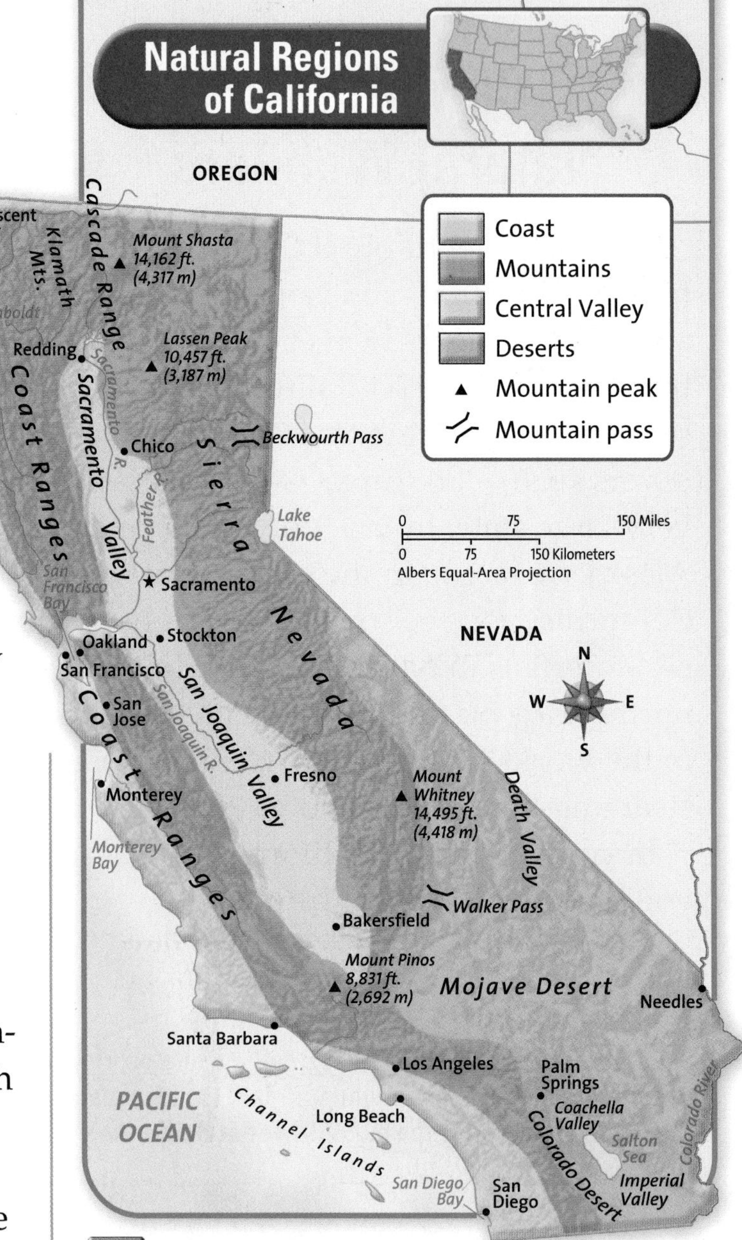

Analyze Maps

Place **What natural features surround the Central Valley Region?**

Major Mountains of the World

Analyze Diagrams

How much taller is Mount McKinley than Mount Whitney?

Mount Whitney
(California)
14,495 feet

Mont Blanc
(Europe)
15,771 feet

The Mountain Region

Mountains cover more than half of California. The state's largest mountain range is the **Sierra Nevada**. It stretches north and south across much of the eastern part of the state. Unlike the Coast Ranges, more than 100 peaks in the Sierra Nevada rise higher than 13,000 feet. Mount Whitney is the tallest, at 14,495 feet.

Between the tall peaks of the Sierra Nevada are deep valleys. One of the most famous valleys is Yosemite (yoh•SEH•muh•tee) Valley, part of Yosemite National Park. It has North America's highest waterfall, Ribbon Falls, which drops 1,612 feet.

Lake Tahoe lies high in the Sierra Nevada. It is California's deepest natural lake. In some places, Lake Tahoe is more than 1,600 feet deep.

The **Cascade Range** in northern California extends into the states of Oregon and Washington. Two of its peaks—Mount Shasta and Lassen Peak—are volcanoes.

READING CHECK **COMPARE AND CONTRAST**
How are the Sierra Nevada different from the Coast Ranges?

FAST FACT

Some mountain climbers test their skills by climbing California's *fourteeners*—mountains taller than 14,000 feet. There are 15 fourteeners in the state.

Some people enjoy rock climbing in California's Mountain Region.

Kilimanjaro
(Africa)
19,340 feet

Mount McKinley
(Alaska)
20,320 feet

Mount Everest
(Asia)
29,022 feet

The Central Valley Region

Between the Coast Ranges and the Sierra Nevada is a region of low land called the Central Valley. The **San Joaquin** (wah•KEEN) **River** flows through the southern part of the Central Valley, which is sometimes called the San Joaquin Valley. In the northern part, the Sacramento Valley is named for the **Sacramento River**.

On their journeys through the Central Valley, the San Joaquin and Sacramento Rivers are joined by a number of smaller rivers, or **tributaries** (TRIH•byuh•tair•eez).

Where the San Joaquin and Sacramento Rivers meet, a broad delta has formed. A **delta** is land that has been built up from soil carried by rivers.

California's Central Valley is one of the most productive farming regions in the world. Over time, fertile soil from the Sierra Nevada has washed down into the valley. Soil that is **fertile** is good for growing crops.

READING CHECK **MAIN IDEA AND DETAILS**
What are some of the physical features of the Central Valley?

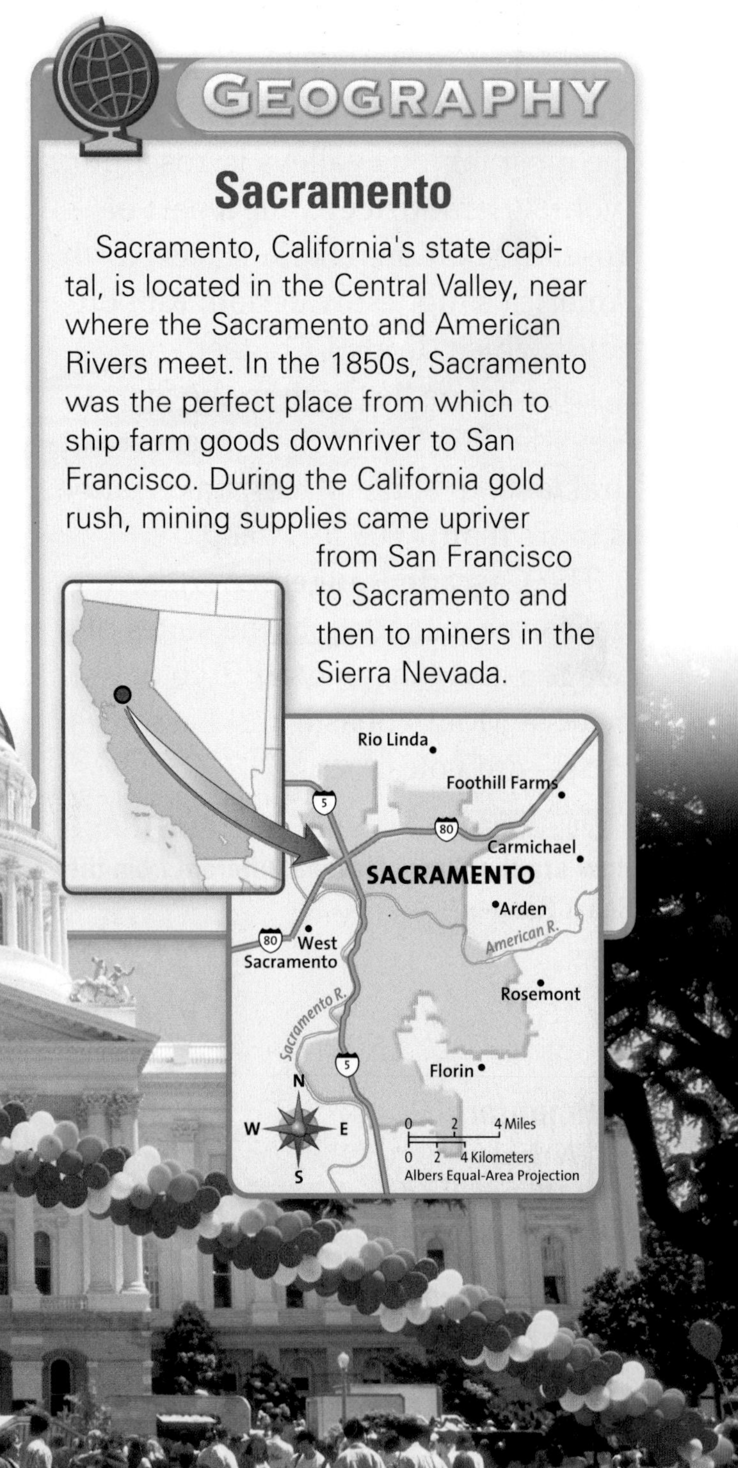

Sacramento

Sacramento, California's state capital, is located in the Central Valley, near where the Sacramento and American Rivers meet. In the 1850s, Sacramento was the perfect place from which to ship farm goods downriver to San Francisco. During the California gold rush, mining supplies came upriver from San Francisco to Sacramento and then to miners in the Sierra Nevada.

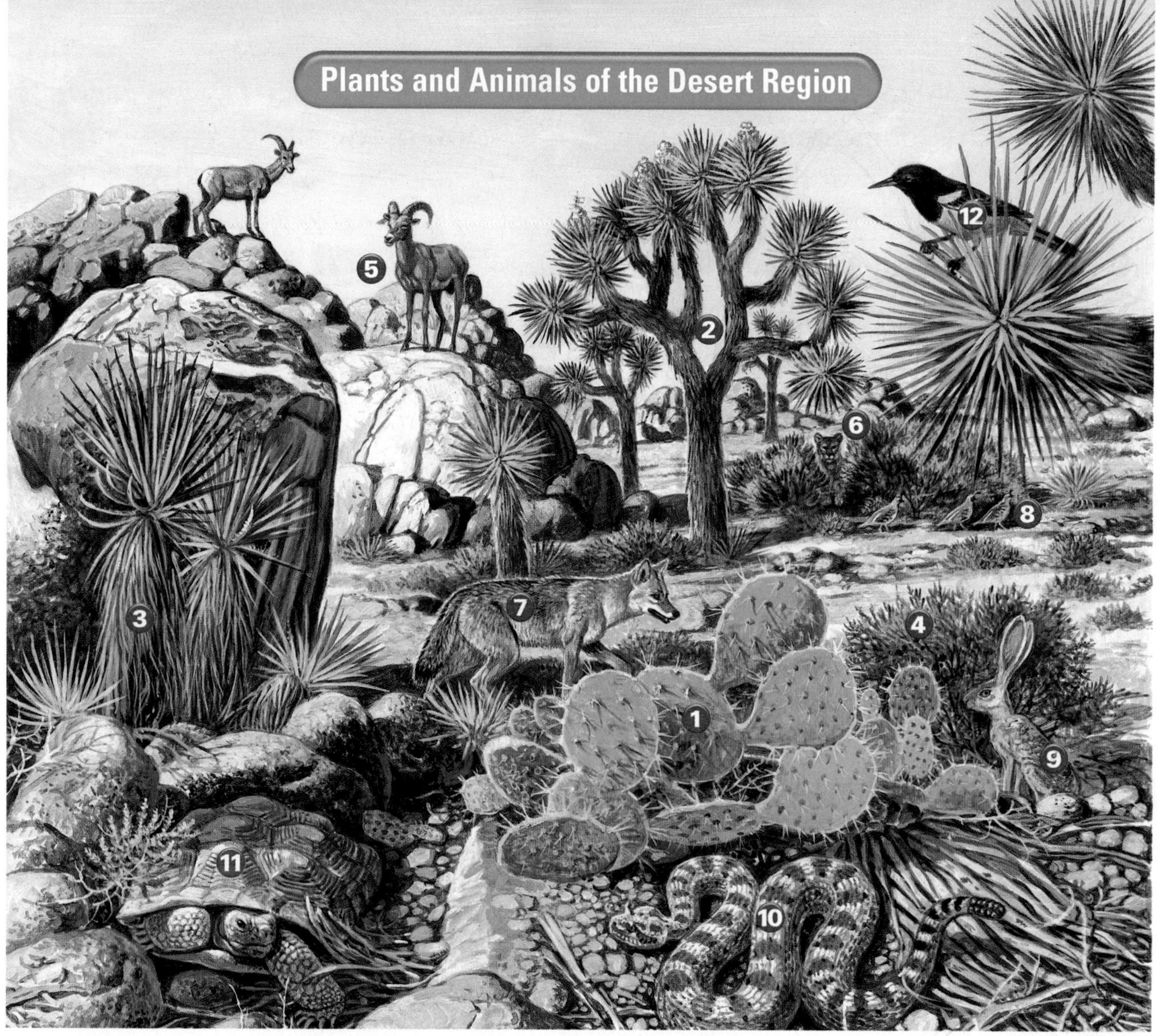

Analyze Illustrations The Desert Region has a wide variety of wildlife.

1. Prickly pear cactus
2. Joshua Tree
3. Yucca
4. Creosote bush
5. Bighorn sheep
6. Mountain lion
7. Coyote
8. Gambel's quail
9. Jackrabbit
10. Rattlesnake
11. Tortoise
12. Scott's oriole

What are some of the plants that grow in the Desert Region?

The Desert Region

Deserts stretch across most of southeastern California. The **Mojave** (moh•HAH•vee) **Desert** covers a large area between the southern Sierra Nevada and the **Colorado River**. The Colorado Desert lies farther south, near the border with Mexico.

Within California's Desert Region are several large valleys. Near the Mexican border are the Imperial and Coachella (koh•CHEL•uh) Valleys. People there have used irrigation to water their farmland. **Irrigation** is the use of canals, ditches, or pipes to carry water to dry places.

The Salton Sea—which is really a large, salty lake—lies in the Desert Region. It was formed between 1905 and 1907, when the Colorado River flooded.

Some parts of the Desert Region are too hot and dry for most people to live there. Death Valley, near the Nevada border, is one of the driest and hottest places in the United States. It is also the lowest point in the Western Hemisphere. One place in Death Valley lies 282 feet below sea level. **Sea level** refers to land that is level with the surface of the ocean.

READING CHECK **MAIN IDEA AND DETAILS**
What are some physical features of the Desert Region?

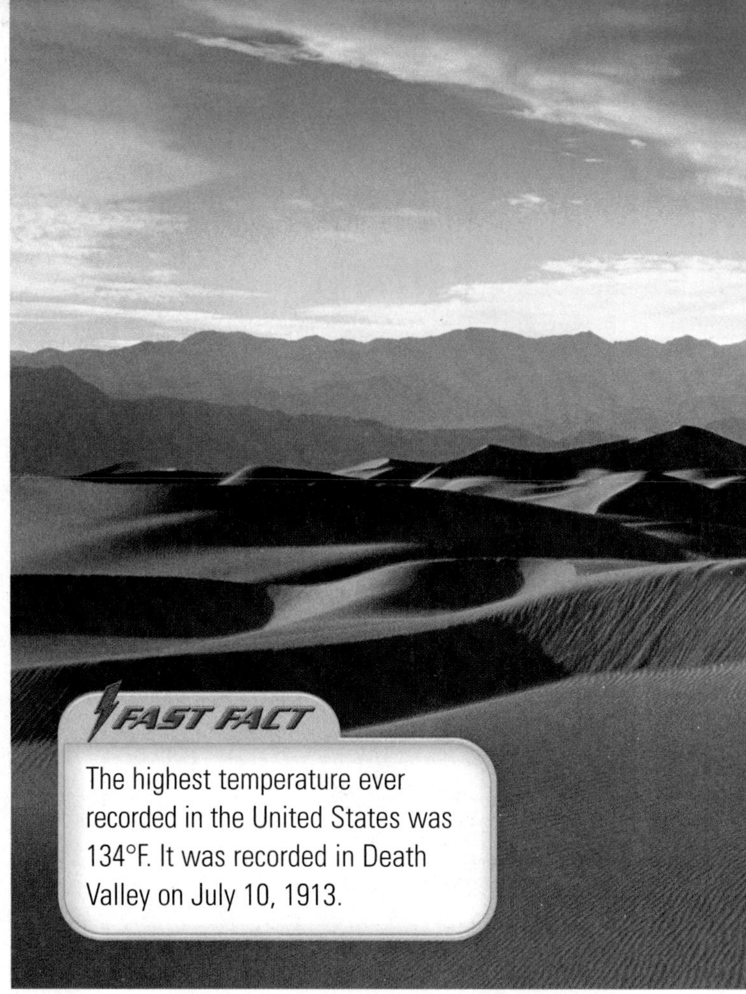

FAST FACT

The highest temperature ever recorded in the United States was 134°F. It was recorded in Death Valley on July 10, 1913.

With an area of about 5,270 square miles, Death Valley is the largest national park in the United States outside of Alaska.

Summary

California's four natural regions are the Coastal Region, the Mountain Region, the Central Valley, and the Desert Region. The Sierra Nevada, the Coast Ranges, and the Cascade Range are mountain ranges in the state.

REVIEW

1. What are California's four natural regions like?
2. Use the terms **irrigation** and **fertile** to tell about farming in California.
3. In which region are California's two largest natural harbors?
4. Which two river valleys make up the Central Valley Region?

CRITICAL THINKING

5. **Make It Relevant** Which region do you live in? What are some of the physical features near your home that are common to this region?
6. ANALYSIS SKILL How do you think irrigation affected the population of the Desert Region?
7. **Make a Map** Draw a map of the natural regions of California. Use your map to tell about the physical features in each region.
8. Focus Skill **MAIN IDEA AND DETAILS** On a separate sheet of paper, copy and complete the graphic organizer below.

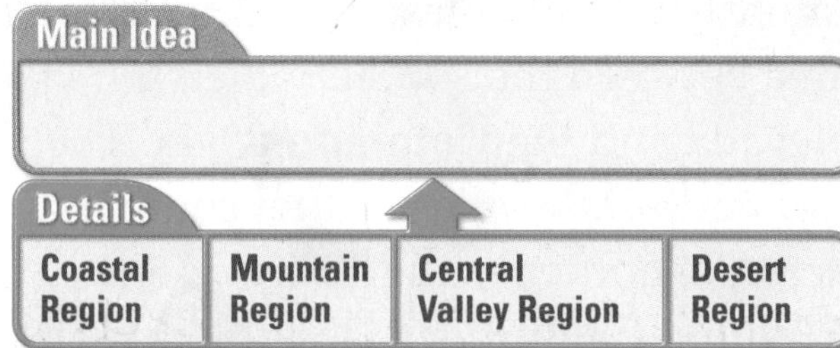

John Muir

*"The mountains are calling me and I must go . . ."**

Growing up, John Muir (MYUR) loved the outdoors and respected nature. After college, he spent months hiking in the wilderness in Canada. Later, he went to work in a factory in Indiana. One day in 1867, Muir injured his eyes at work. Muir decided he would rather spend the rest of his life looking at nature than at machines. When his eyes healed, he left his job. The next year he went to California, where he quickly fell in love with the land. "The whole State . . .," he wrote, "is one block of beauty."**

John Muir took many of the country's leaders, including President Theodore Roosevelt, on tours of Yosemite Valley.

In California, Muir became a conservationist, a person who respects nature and works to protect wild areas. He helped convince the United States government to set aside natural areas. Several of these areas, including Yosemite Valley, later became national parks.

*California Chronicles (*High Sierra*), January 2000. Quote traced to video—*John Muir: The Man, The Poet, The Legacy.*
**John Muir. *Overland Monthly*, 1872. Reprinted in *Wilderness Essays.* Peregrine Smith, Inc., 1980.

Biography

Trustworthiness
Respect
Responsibility
Fairness
Caring
Patriotism

Why Character Counts

How did John Muir's work as a conservationist show that he respected California's natural beauty?

Bio Brief

1838 Born — **1914** Died

- **1849** Muir and his family leave Scotland to settle in Wisconsin
- **1867** Injures his eyes and quits his factory job
- **1868** Settles in California

Interactive Multimedia Biographies
Visit MULTIMEDIA BIOGRAPHIES at
www.harcourtschool.com/hss

Map and Globe Skills

Use an Elevation Map

WHY IT MATTERS

In some parts of California, the tops of mountains rise more than 2 miles above sea level. In other parts, valleys lie below sea level. **Elevation** (eh•luh•VAY•shuhn), or the height of the land, is always measured from sea level. The elevation of land at sea level is zero.

WHAT YOU NEED TO KNOW

The elevation map on page 27 uses color to show elevation. Each color stands for a range of elevations. That means each color stands for an area's highest and lowest elevations and all of the elevations in between.

The map also shows **relief**, or the differences in the heights of land in an area. Relief is shown by shading. Heavy shading shows steep rises and drops in elevation. Light shading shows gentle rises and drops.

PRACTICE THE SKILL

Use the elevation map of California to answer these questions.

1. Most of the Central Valley is colored green on the map. What is the elevation of this area?
2. What is the elevation of the land around Lake Tahoe?
3. Which city has a higher elevation, Palm Springs or Fresno?

APPLY WHAT YOU LEARNED

ANALYSIS SKILL **Make It Relevant** Imagine that you are planning to travel from Sacramento to Long Beach. On a separate sheet of paper, write the name and the approximate elevation of each city. What is the highest and lowest land you might cross along the way?

Practice your map and globe skills with the **GeoSkills CD-ROM**.

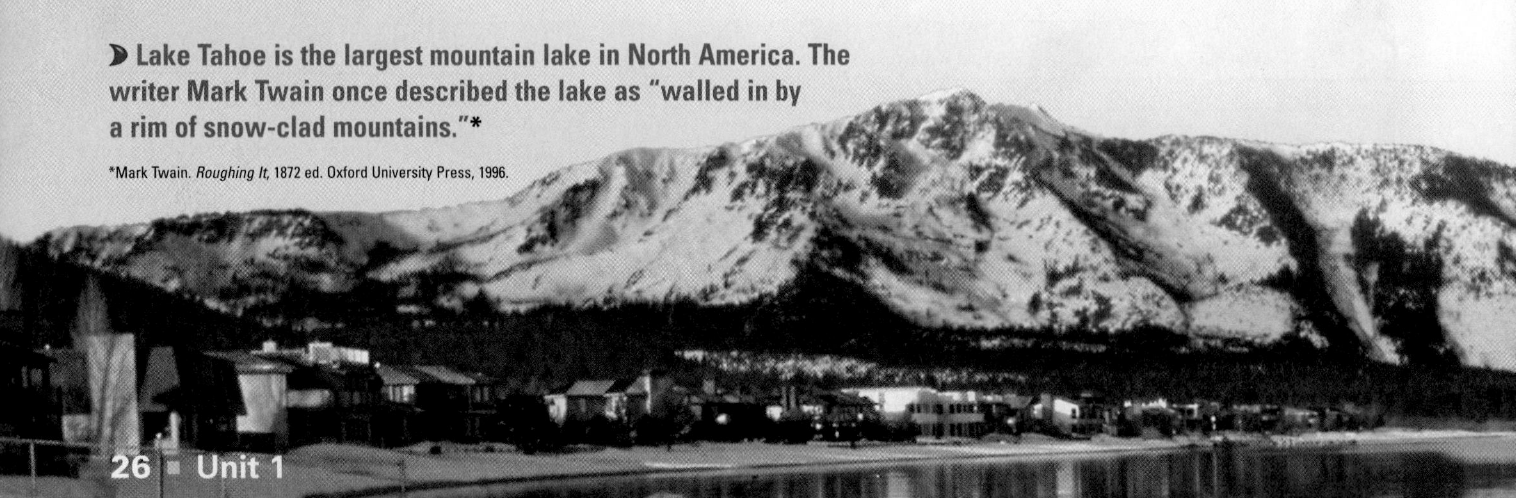

Lake Tahoe is the largest mountain lake in North America. The writer Mark Twain once described the lake as "walled in by a rim of snow-clad mountains."*

*Mark Twain. *Roughing It*, 1872 ed. Oxford University Press, 1996.

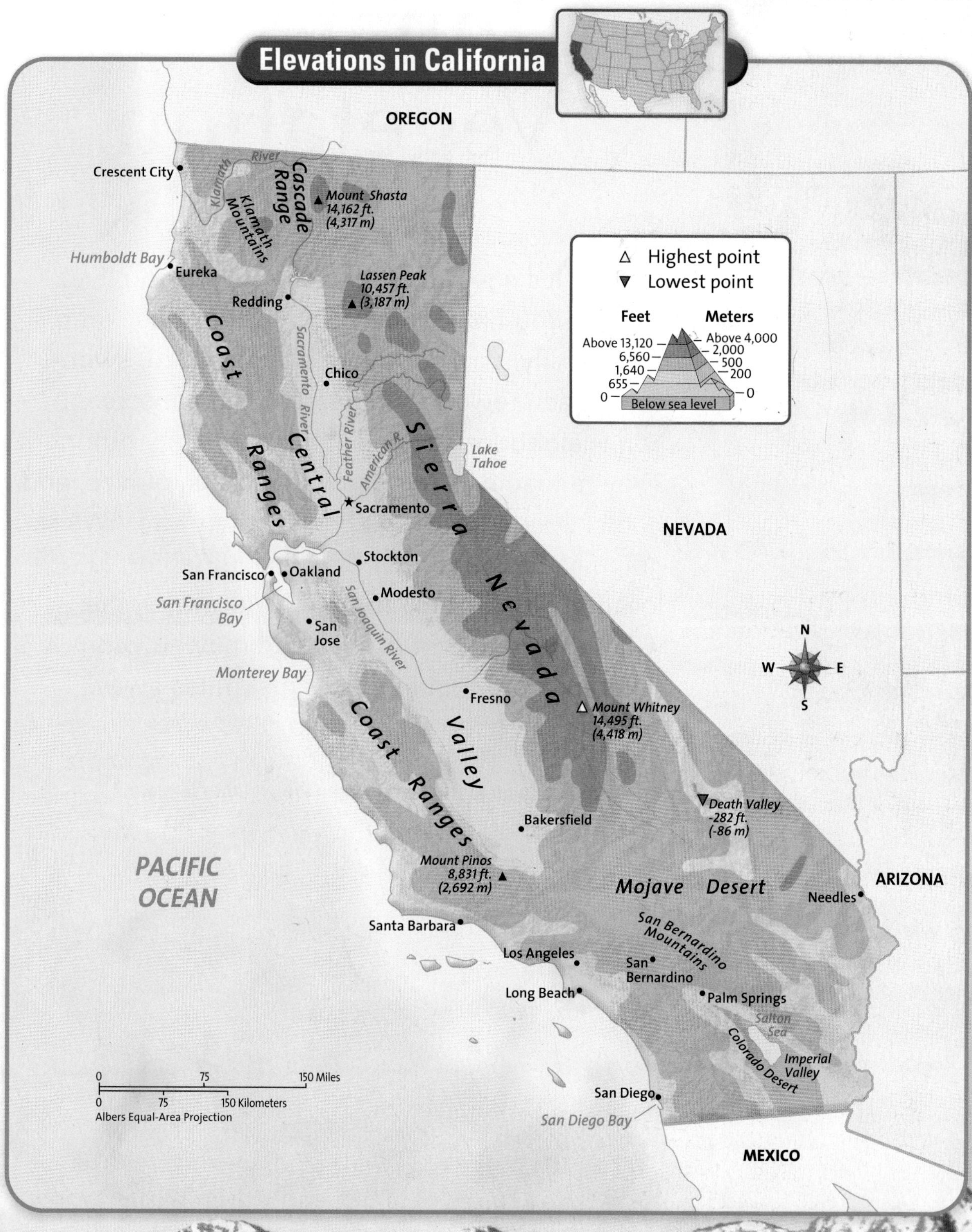

Elevations in California
OREGON
NEVADA
ARIZONA
MEXICO
PACIFIC OCEAN
Crescent City
Klamath River
Cascade Range
Klamath Mountains
Mount Shasta 14,162 ft. (4,317 m)
Humboldt Bay
Eureka
Redding
Lassen Peak 10,457 ft. (3,187 m)
Coast Ranges
Sacramento River
Chico
Feather River
American R.
Central Valley
Lake Tahoe
Sierra Nevada
Sacramento
Stockton
San Francisco
Oakland
San Francisco Bay
Modesto
San Jose
San Joaquin River
Monterey Bay
Fresno
Mount Whitney 14,495 ft. (4,418 m)
Coast Ranges
Bakersfield
Death Valley -282 ft. (-86 m)
Mount Pinos 8,831 ft. (2,692 m)
Mojave Desert
Needles
Santa Barbara
Los Angeles
San Bernardino Mountains
San Bernardino
Long Beach
Palm Springs
Salton Sea
Colorado Desert
Imperial Valley
San Diego
San Diego Bay
Highest point
Lowest point
Feet
Meters
Above 13,120
6,560
1,640
655
0
Above 4,000
2,000
500
200
0
Below sea level
N
S
E
W
0 75 150 Miles
0 75 150 Kilometers
Albers Equal-Area Projection

Map and Globe Skills

Lesson 3

Climate and Vegetation

WHAT TO KNOW

What is California's climate like, and how does it affect our state's people?

- ✓ Describe how climate affects the lives of Californians.
- ✓ Explain why places in California have different climates.

VOCABULARY

precipitation p. 29
climate p. 29
vegetation p. 30
humid p. 32
rain shadow p. 32
drought p. 32

PLACES

San Francisco
San Diego
Sequoia National Park
Feather River Valley

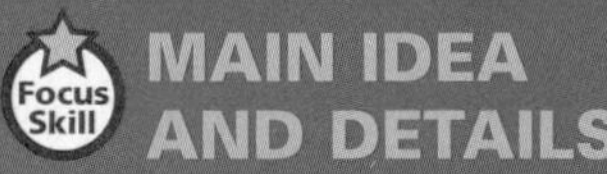

HSS 4.1, 4.1.2, 4.1.3, 4.1.5

YOU ARE THERE

It's a warm, sunny day where you live. You have plans to go to the beach with your family. You pack your boogieboard, swimsuit, beach towels, sunglasses, and sunscreen. Your neighbors have also planned a day outdoors. They're loading their car with jackets, gloves, and boots. "Have fun at the beach," they say. "We're going snowboarding!" Because of California's location, landforms, and bodies of water, the weather in one part of the state may be very different from that in places just miles away.

▶ **Do you like to go to the beach when the weather is warm?**

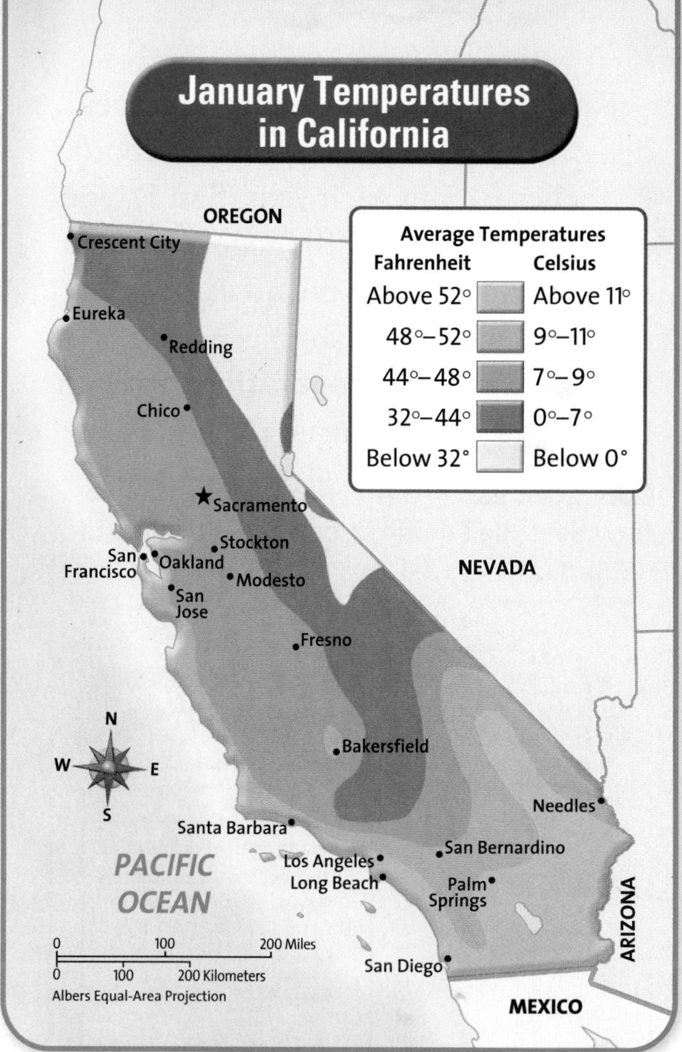

Analyze Maps

Place Which city, San Diego or Eureka, is generally warmer in January?

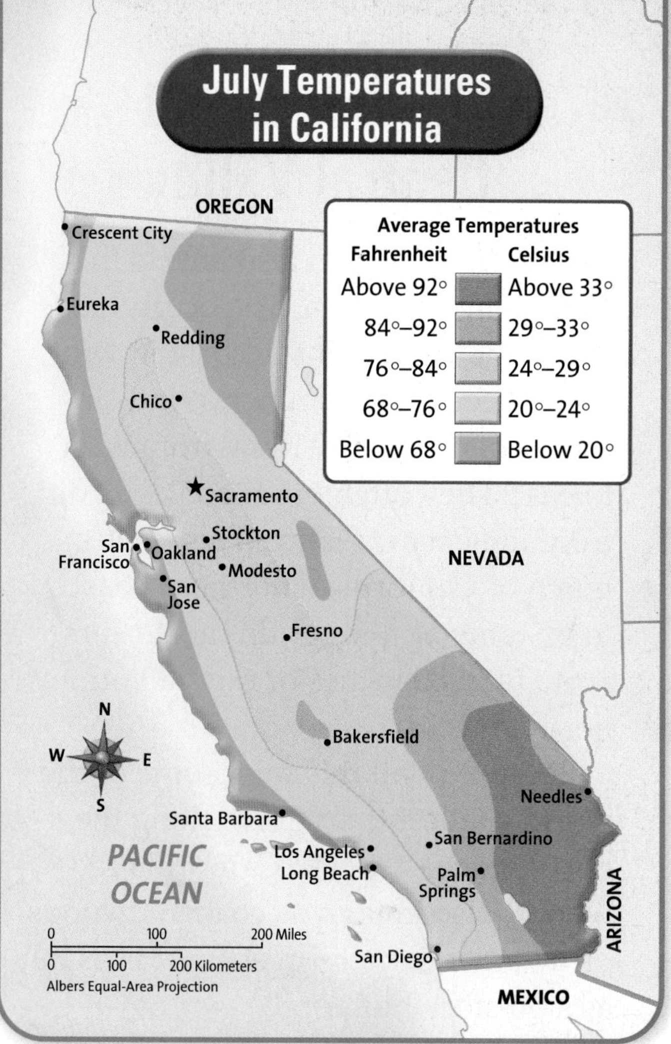

SKILL **Analyze Maps**

Place What is the average temperature in Redding in July?

Weather and Climate

How would you describe the weather where you live? You could talk about the temperature. You could also talk about the wind and precipitation (prih•sih•puh•TAY•shuhn). **Precipitation** is water that falls to Earth's surface as rain, sleet, hail, or snow. The temperature, precipitation, and wind in a place on any given day make up the weather.

The kind of weather a place has most often, year after year, is its **climate**. Because California is such a large state, different regions of the state have very different climates.

California, like the rest of the United States, is located between the equator and the North Pole. This means that temperatures in California fall between the year-round heat of most places at the equator and the year-round cold of most places near the North Pole. In general, however, temperatures are cooler in northern California than in southern California.

READING CHECK **MAIN IDEA AND DETAILS**
How does the location of a place affect its climate?

The Coast and Central Valley

The Pacific Ocean also affects the climate in California. The ocean helps warm the land near the coast in winter and cool it in summer. Winds in California generally blow from west to east. They often bring cool, wet air from the Pacific Ocean. This causes much of California's northern coast to be rainy and foggy. In most years, more than 80 inches of rain fall on the northern coast.

Because of all this rain, some of the world's tallest trees grow along the northern coast. Some California redwoods, also known as coast redwoods, grow taller than 350 feet. That is as tall as a 30-story building!

Farther south, the climate becomes drier. While **San Francisco** gets about 22 inches of rain each year, **San Diego** gets far less—about 10 inches. Parts of the Central Valley have an even drier climate. Grasses, bushes, and small trees are the main **vegetation**, or plant life, in these drier areas.

READING CHECK **MAIN IDEA AND DETAILS**
How does the Pacific Ocean affect climate in California?

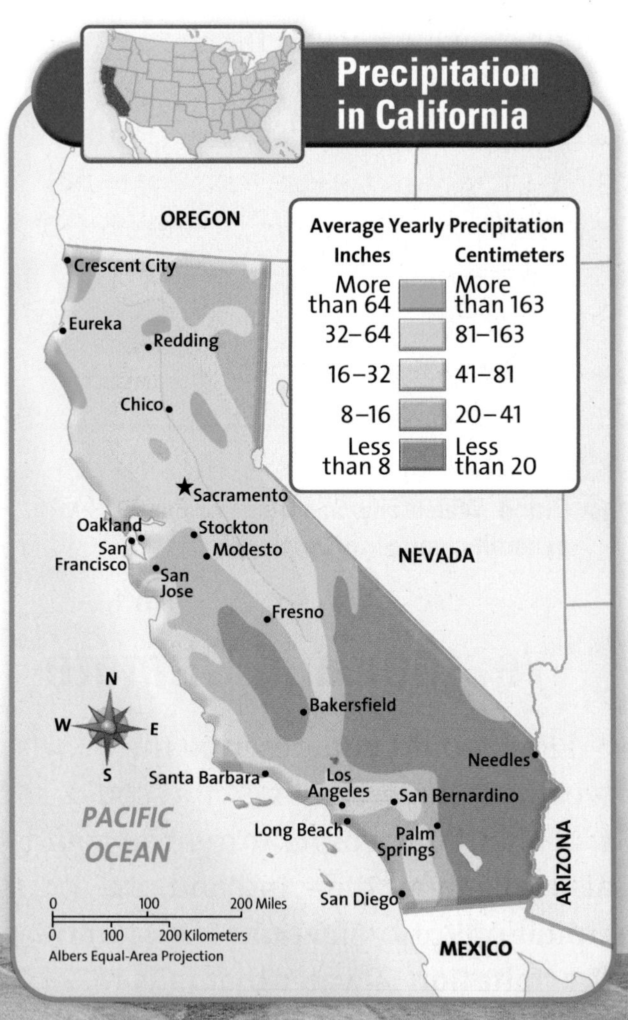

ANALYSIS SKILL Analyze Maps The Central Valley (below) and most other regions of California have a wet season during the winter months. Most of the year's precipitation falls during that time.

Place Which city, Bakersfield or Chico, gets more precipitation each year?

The Mountain Region

Mountains also affect climate in California. Temperatures usually drop about 3°F for every 1,000 feet of elevation. Because of this, on a warm day along the coast, there might be freezing temperatures and snow in the mountains.

In California, most precipitation falls on the western sides of mountains. As wet air blows in from the Pacific Ocean, it is pushed up the mountains. The air cools as it is pushed up. Clouds form, and rain or snow falls.

Large amounts of snow fall on the Sierra Nevada in most winters. John Muir once described winter there. He wrote, "Storm succeeds [follows] storm, heaping snow on snow, until thirty to fifty feet has fallen."* It is not surprising, then, to learn that *sierra nevada* means "snowy mountain range" in Spanish.

Among the trees that grow in the Sierra Nevada are the giant sequoias (sih•KWOY•uhz). They do not grow nearly as tall as the coast redwoods, but their trunks can reach more than 80 feet around. The General Sherman, a tree in **Sequoia National Park**, is Earth's largest tree at 275 feet tall and 103 feet around.

READING CHECK SUMMARIZE
How does elevation affect temperatures in California?

*John Muir. *The Mountains of California*. The Century Company, 1894.

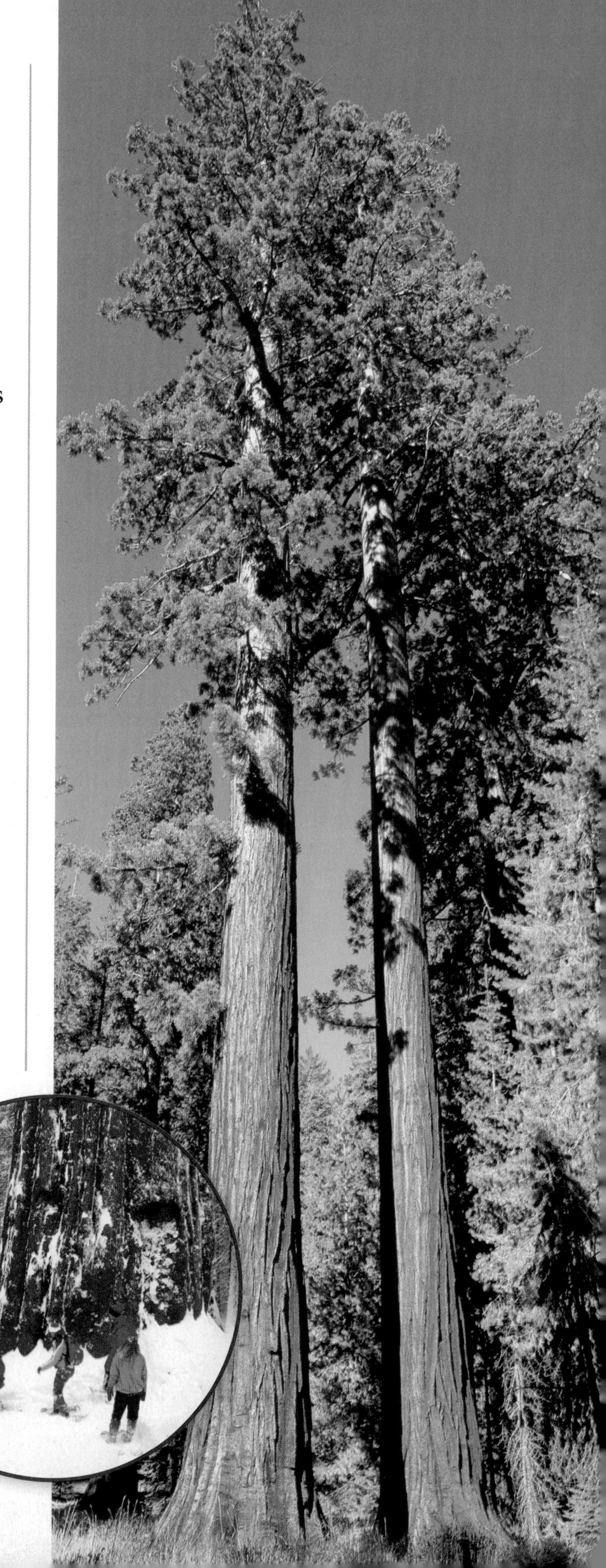

People look tiny next to giant sequoias.

Desert Climate

Mountains affect California's climate in another way, too. They act like huge walls that block **humid**, or moist, air from reaching the eastern side of the mountains. Places there lie on the drier side of the mountains, in the **rain shadow**.

In the rain shadow's driest areas, deserts form. Death Valley once went without rain for 760 days! Only plants that do not require a lot of water, such as cacti, can grow there.

READING CHECK **SUMMARIZE**
How do mountains affect precipitation?

Severe Weather

Sometimes California has dry spells that last longer than the normal dry season. A long time with little or no rain is called a **drought** (DROWT). Droughts can cause severe problems, especially for farmers. Crops can die, and soil can blow away.

Droughts can also increase the threat of forest and brush fires. In 2003, a huge brush fire burned areas of San Bernardino and San Diego Counties. Many people lost their homes.

Too much rain can also cause problems. In most years, the **Feather River Valley**—in northern California—gets less than 32 inches of rainfall. But in January 1997, the area received 25 inches of rainfall in just a few days. In the floods that followed, eight people died, and many bridges and roads were washed away.

READING CHECK **CAUSE AND EFFECT**
What can happen when a place does not get enough rain?

The Rain Shadow

Analyze Diagrams **Places in the rain shadow receive little precipitation.**
What happens after winds push clouds up the mountains?

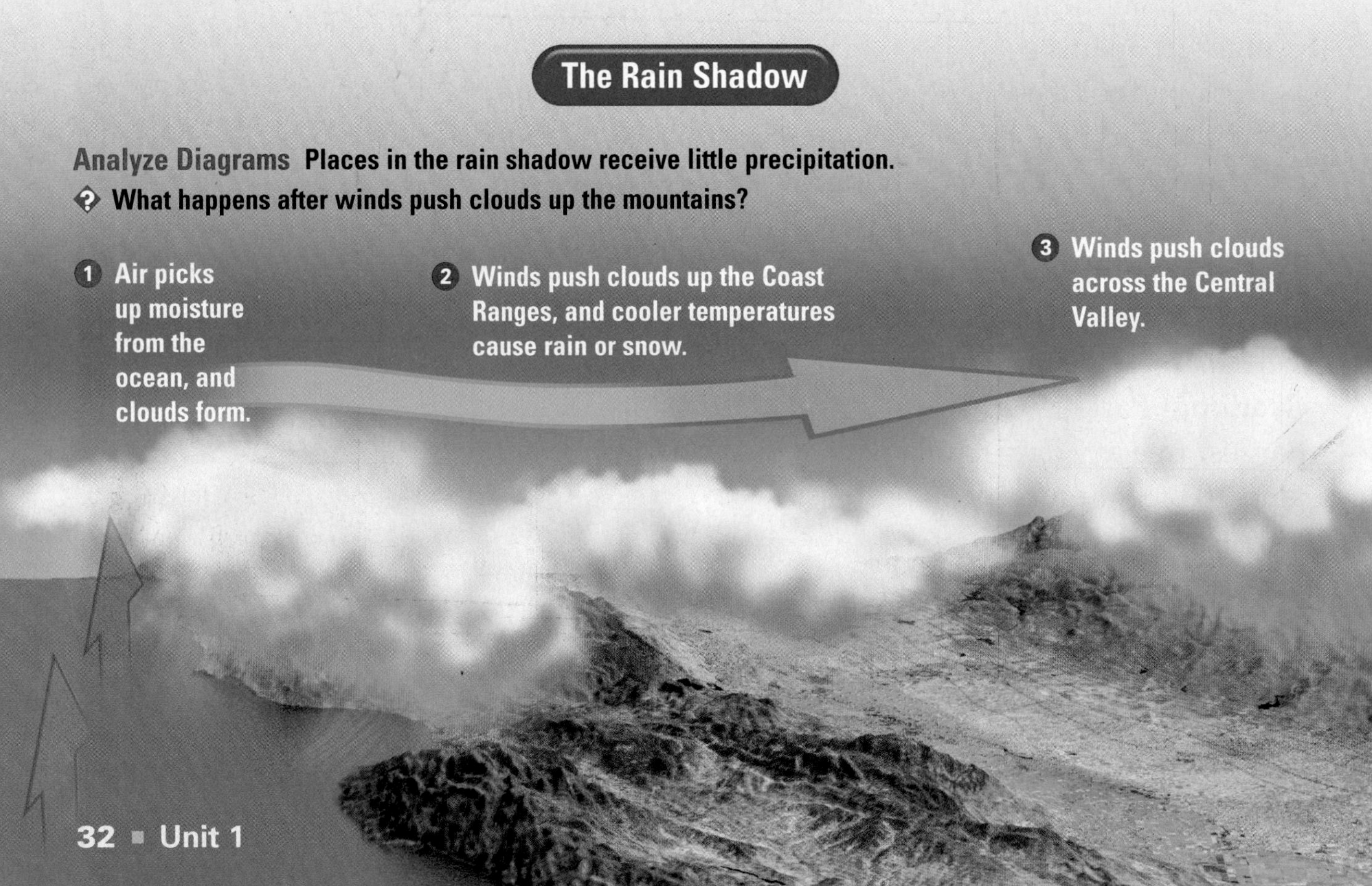
1 Air picks up moisture from the ocean, and clouds form.
2 Winds push clouds up the Coast Ranges, and cooler temperatures cause rain or snow.
3 Winds push clouds across the Central Valley.

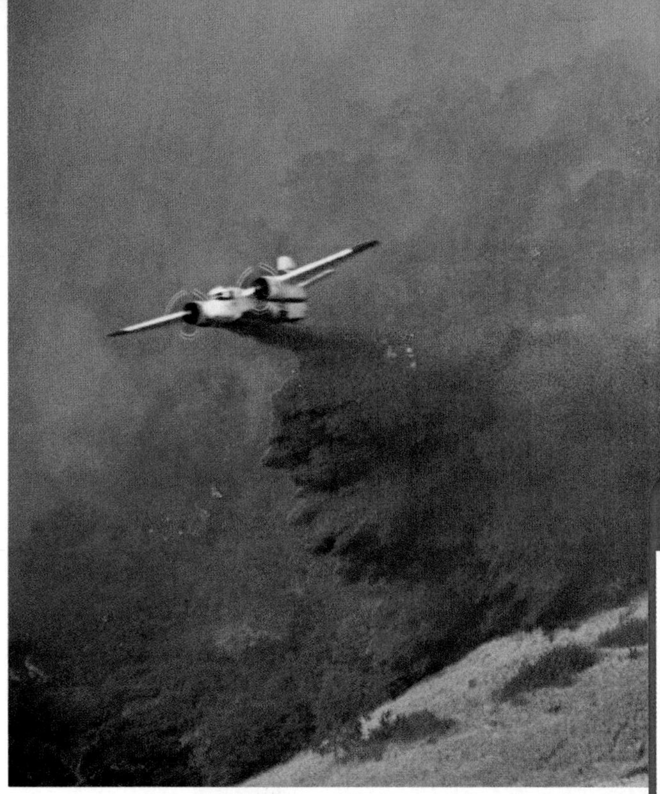

A plane sprays chemicals to put out a forest fire in southern California.

Summary

Climate in California is affected by many things. Different parts of California have different temperatures and get different amounts of precipitation, depending on their location, their closeness to the ocean, and their elevation.

4 Winds push clouds up the Sierra Nevada, and cooler temperatures cause more rain or snow.

5 Remaining clouds have little moisture.

REVIEW

1. What is California's climate like, and how does it affect our state's people?
2. How are the terms **humid** and **precipitation** related?
3. How are weather and climate different?
4. What part of the state receives the most rain? Why?

CRITICAL THINKING

5. **Make It Relevant** How does the climate where you live affect the way you live?
6. ANALYSIS SKILL How do you think climate has affected the location of cities in California?
7. **Create a Weather Chart** Over a period of one week, chart the daily high temperatures and precipitation amount in your community. Do the same for a city in another part of the state. What conclusions can you draw about the climate in the two places?
8. Focus Skill **MAIN IDEA AND DETAILS** On a separate sheet of paper, copy and complete the graphic organizer below.

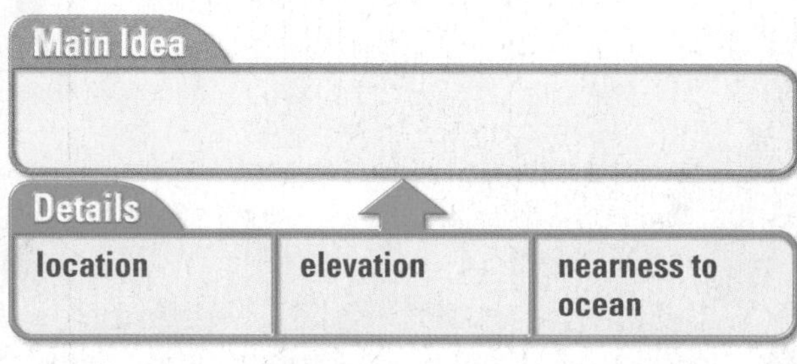

Lesson 4

Where Californians Live

WHAT TO KNOW
Why do Californians live where they do?

- ✓ Explain how landforms and bodies of water in California have affected the growth of towns.
- ✓ Analyze the locations of cities in California.

VOCABULARY
physical environment p. 35
natural resource p. 35
urban p. 36
metropolitan area p. 36
suburb p. 36
rural p. 36
modify p. 37

HSS 4.1, 4.1.3, 4.1.4, 4.1.5

YOU ARE THERE Imagine setting your eyes on California for the first time. Stretching before you are wide valleys below towering mountains. You have also heard stories of California's rugged coast and vast deserts. Where might you choose to live?

When people first came to live in what is now California, they made their homes where they found fresh water and food. Over time, they settled throughout California. People still live in every region of the state. However, more people live in certain places than in others. And they live in those places for different reasons.

Today, as in the past, San Francisco Bay is important to the people of San Francisco.

Patterns of Settlement

Today, more than 35 million people live in California—more than in any other state. However, California's population is not spread out evenly.

The **physical environment**—which includes a place's physical features, landforms, and climate—often affects where people live. In California, for example, San Francisco Bay and San Diego Bay were important parts of early transportation routes, and large cities grew up around them.

Physical features also discourage people from settling in areas. In the past, California's rugged mountains and the harsh climate of its deserts made it difficult for people to settle there. These regions still have the fewest people.

The ways in which people use natural resources can affect where they live. A **natural resource** is something found in nature, such as water, soil, and minerals, that people can use to meet their needs. People in the past often settled where the land was fertile and good for farming. This explains why so many people still live in the Central Valley today.

Some people choose to settle where they can find work. People also settle along transportation routes, such as rivers, roads, and railroads.

Culture also can affect where people live. People may live in a place because they were born there. Many people settle near their families or near others who share their ways of life.

READING CHECK **MAIN IDEA AND DETAILS**
What kinds of things affect where people live?

FAST FACT

California's population is larger than that of all the other western states combined.

Present

Both Urban and Rural

Most Californians live in **urban**, or city, areas. In fact, about 93 of every 100 Californians live in or near a city. Most larger cities are found in the Coastal and Central Valley Regions.

California's largest city is Los Angeles. About one-fourth of California's people live in the city's metropolitan (meh•truh•PAH•luh•tuhn) area. A **metropolitan area** is a large city together with nearby cities and suburbs. A **suburb** is a town or small city near a large city.

Like Los Angeles, most of the largest cities in California lie on or near the Pacific coast. San Jose, San Francisco, and Oakland are in the San Francisco Bay area. Long Beach, Riverside, and Santa Ana are near Los Angeles. San Diego, California's second-largest city, lies on San Diego Bay, near the state's southern edge.

California's other largest cities are in the Central Valley. Sacramento, the state capital, lies on the banks of the Sacramento River. To the south are Fresno and Bakersfield. All three are at the center of important farming areas.

Although California has many large cities, most of the state's land area is **rural**, or country. In rural areas, houses are farther apart and towns are smaller. There are fewer freeways and crowded streets, and the land is mostly forests, farms, or ranches.

In recent years, California's population has spread into desert areas such as San Bernardino and the Palm Springs area. This is partly because

Analyze Tables **The population of Los Angeles (below) is more than three times that of the next largest city in California.**

Which city has a larger population, San Francisco or San Diego?

California's Largest Cities

RANK	CITY	POPULATION
1	Los Angeles	3,864,000
2	San Diego	1,275,100
3	San Jose	925,000
4	San Francisco	791,000
5	Long Beach	481,000
6	Fresno	448,000
7	Sacramento	433,000
8	Oakland	412,000
9	Santa Ana	347,000
10	Anaheim	337,000

Californians are now better able to **modify**, or change, the land to meet their needs. People are now able to live in parts of the state where few people lived in the past. For example, the ability to bring water to dry regions of the state has helped these areas grow. In some places, land that was once desert is now rich farmland.

READING CHECK **GENERALIZE**
In which areas are California's largest cities found?

Summary

Physical environment, natural resources, transportation, jobs, and culture all affect where people live. Most Californians today live in cities. Even so, most of the state's land area is rural. People now live where few people lived in the past.

People have modified part of the desert near the Salton Sea and built communities.

REVIEW

1. Why do Californians live where they do?
2. Use the words **urban** and **suburb** to describe a **metropolitan area**.
3. How are California's rural areas different from its urban areas?

CRITICAL THINKING

4. ANALYSIS SKILL **Make It Relevant** How do you think the landforms and natural resources around your community have played a role in its history?
5. **Make It Relevant** Would you rather live in a metropolitan area or rural area? Explain your answer.
6. **Write a Report** Write a report describing your community. Tell whether it is an urban or rural area, and explain why you think people have chosen to settle there.
7. Focus Skill **MAIN IDEA AND DETAILS** On a separate sheet of paper, copy and complete the graphic organizer below.

Main Idea

Many things affect where Californians choose to settle and live.

Details

Map and Globe Skills

Read a Population Map

WHY IT MATTERS

Do you live in one of California's large cities? Or do you live in a rural part of the state? The population density (DEN•suh•tee) of each of these places is different. **Population density** tells how many people live in an area of a certain size. Places with a high population density are crowded. Places with a low population density have more open space.

WHAT YOU NEED TO KNOW

Population density is measured by the number of people living in an area of 1 square mile. The population map on page 39 uses colors to show the population densities in different parts of California. You can use the map legend to find out what population density each color stands for.

PRACTICE THE SKILL

Use the information on the map to answer the questions below.

1. Find Modesto on the map. What is the population density of the area in which it is located?
2. Which city has a higher population density, Alturas or Chico?
3. Which city has a lower population density, Fresno or Needles?
4. Which parts of the state generally have the lowest population densities? Why do you think this is the case?

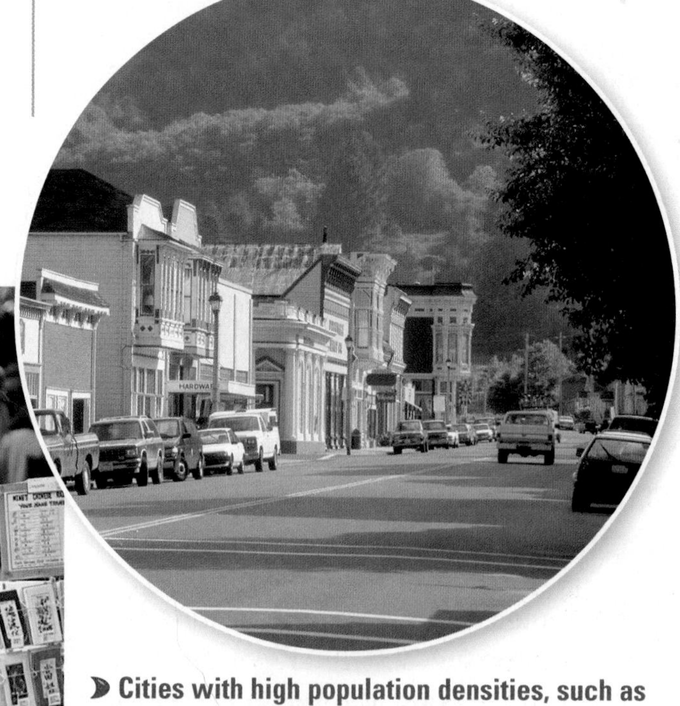

Cities with high population densities, such as San Francisco (left), are often crowded. The town of Ferndale (above) has a low population density.

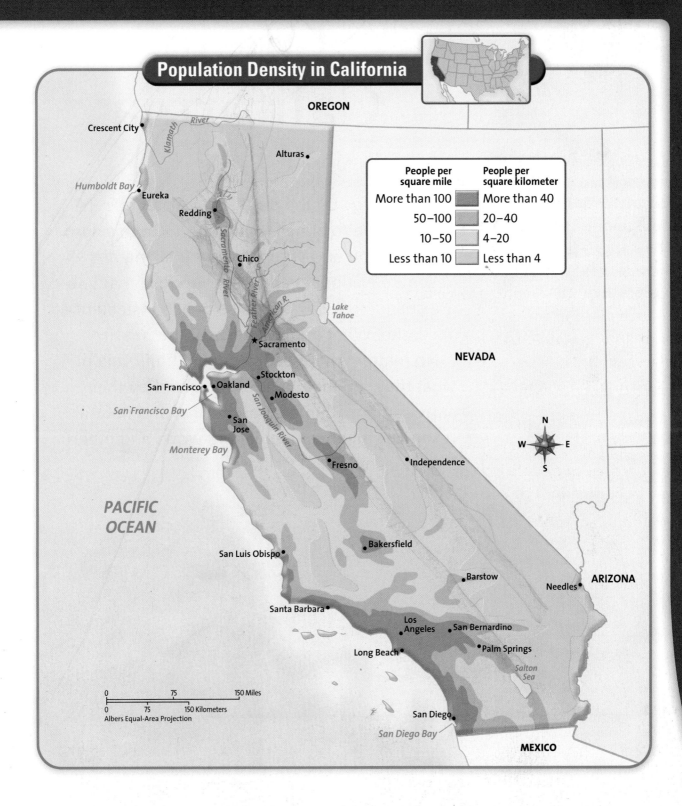

Population Density in California

People per square mile	People per square kilometer
More than 100	More than 40
50–100	20–40
10–50	4–20
Less than 10	Less than 4

OREGON
NEVADA
ARIZONA
MEXICO
PACIFIC OCEAN
Crescent City
Klamath River
Alturas
Humboldt Bay
Eureka
Redding
Sacramento River
Chico
Feather River
American R.
Lake Tahoe
Sacramento
Stockton
San Francisco
Oakland
Modesto
San Francisco Bay
San Jose
San Joaquin River
Monterey Bay
Fresno
Independence
Bakersfield
San Luis Obispo
Barstow
Needles
Santa Barbara
Los Angeles
San Bernardino
Palm Springs
Long Beach
Salton Sea
San Diego
San Diego Bay

0 75 150 Miles
0 75 150 Kilometers
Albers Equal-Area Projection

APPLY WHAT YOU LEARNED

ANALYSIS SKILL Choose five of the cities shown on the population map. List the population density of the area around each city. Then make a bar graph showing the population densities of the cities you have chosen.

Practice your map and globe skills with the **GeoSkills CD-ROM**.

Lesson 5

Life in California

WHAT TO KNOW
How do landforms, climate, and natural resources affect ways of life in California?

✓ Describe how communities and ways of life are different in the different regions of California.

VOCABULARY
adapt p. 41
service p. 41
industry p. 41
fault p. 42
growing season p. 43
scarce p. 44

MAIN IDEA AND DETAILS

California Standards
HSS 4.1, 4.1.3, 4.1.4, 4.1.5

YOU ARE THERE

"Stay on the trail," your sister shouts. "We're almost at the top." On this summer day, you and your family are hiking in Yosemite National Park. Now suppose that you are spending a day at Venice Beach instead of at Yosemite. What might you do at the beach?

No matter where people live in California or what they do, their lives are affected by their surroundings. Climate, landforms, and natural resources all affect recreation, work, and other human activities in California.

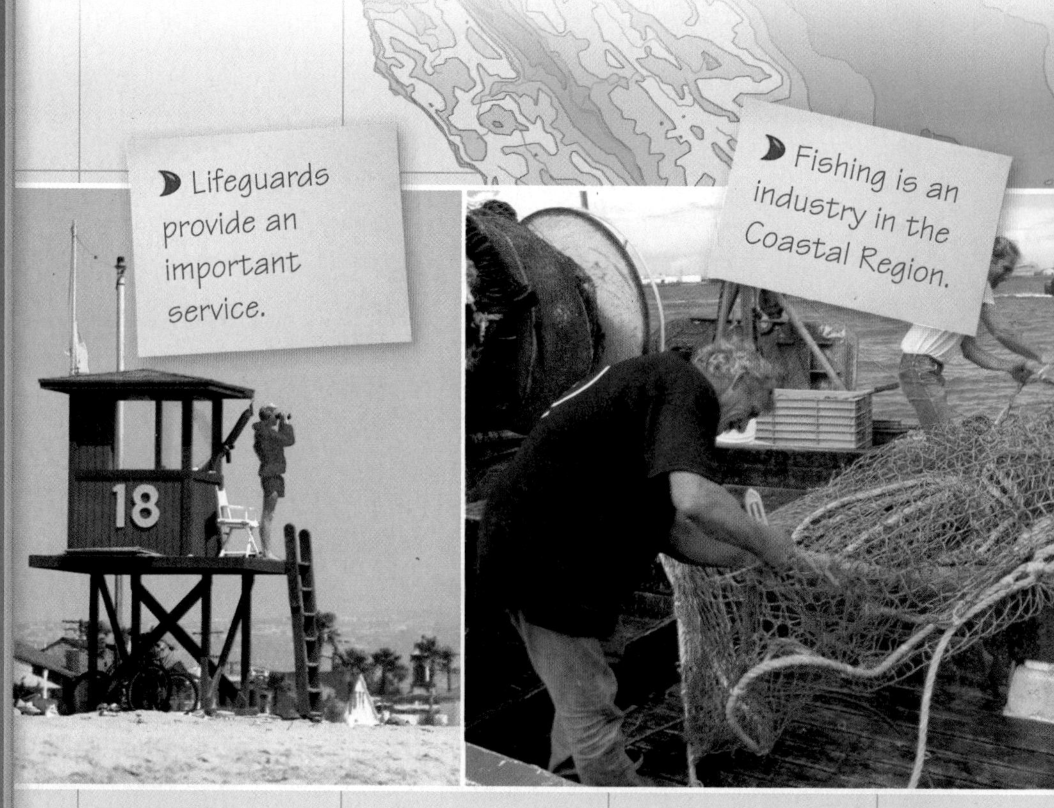

Lifeguards provide an important service.

Fishing is an industry in the Coastal Region.

Life in the Coastal Region

Many cities in the Coastal Region have large populations. Some of these cities, such as San Francisco and Oakland, are close to one another. This creates high population densities in the region.

Over time, people in the Coastal Region have **adapted**, or changed their ways of life, to adjust to the high population density. For example, many larger cities have mass-transit systems, such as buses or trains. When people use these transportation systems they help reduce traffic.

As in other parts of the state, workers in the Coastal Region have different kinds of jobs—both in manufacturing and in services. A **service** is an activity that someone does for others for pay, such as serving a meal in a restaurant.

Fishing and timber are important industries in the Coastal Region. Near Los Angeles and off the coast near Long Beach, oil production is another important industry. An **industry** is all the businesses that make one kind of product or provide one kind of service. Many people in the region also work at ports as part of the shipping industry.

The Pacific coast is important for travel and trade, as well as recreation. Surfing and swimming are just a few of the activities that people enjoy.

READING CHECK **MAIN IDEA AND DETAILS**
How does the Pacific Ocean affect life in the Coastal Region?

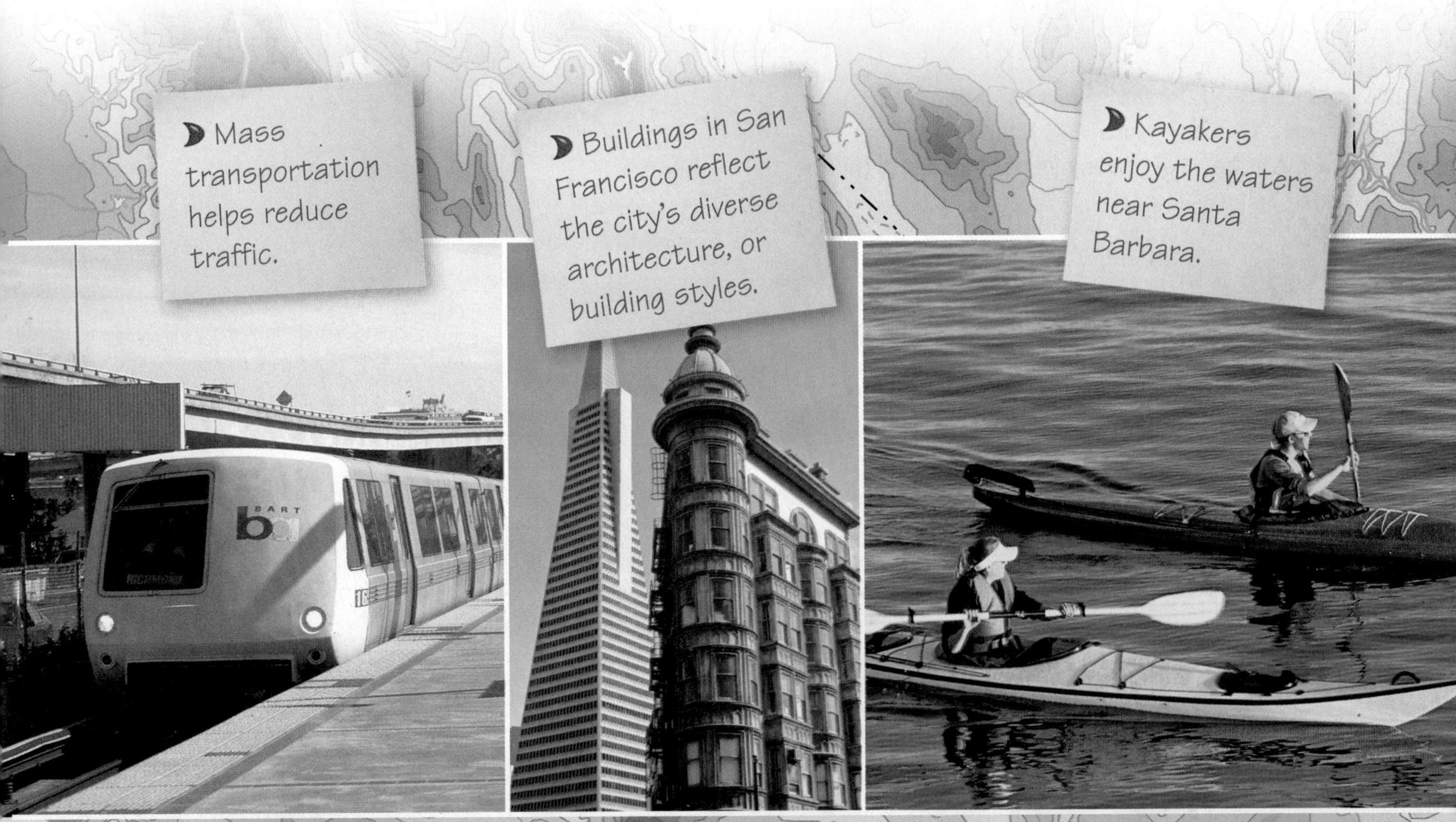

Mass transportation helps reduce traffic.

Buildings in San Francisco reflect the city's diverse architecture, or building styles.

Kayakers enjoy the waters near Santa Barbara.

Earthquakes

Suddenly the ground begins to shake. At first, it shakes only slightly. Then it moves a little faster. Dishes in the cupboard rattle. Then, just as suddenly, the shaking ends.

Throughout California, but especially in the Coastal Region, people share a danger—earthquakes. Earthquakes happen when layers of rock deep within Earth move. This movement occurs along **faults**, or cracks in Earth's surface.

Many small earthquakes shake the Coastal Region each year. Often people do not even feel them, and most buildings and roads are built to survive them. However, strong earthquakes can cause much damage. In recent years, large earthquakes have shaken San Francisco and Los Angeles.

A strong earthquake struck southern California the morning of January 17, 1994. Erik Pearson was asleep when his third-floor Los Angeles apartment came crashing down. "All I remember is the walls opening up and then dropping straight down...," he said. "The floor [had] opened up about four feet."*

READING CHECK **CAUSE AND EFFECT**
What causes earthquakes?

*Erik Pearson. From "Survivors Haunted After '94 L.A. Quake." *The Miami Herald*, January 18, 2004.

The earthquake that shook southern California on January 17, 1994, caused $40 billion in damage—making it the most expensive earthquake in United States history.

GEOGRAPHY

San Andreas Fault

More than 60 major faults lie beneath California. The longest one is the San Andreas (an•DRAY•uhs) Fault. It stretches more than 600 miles, from northern California south into Mexico.

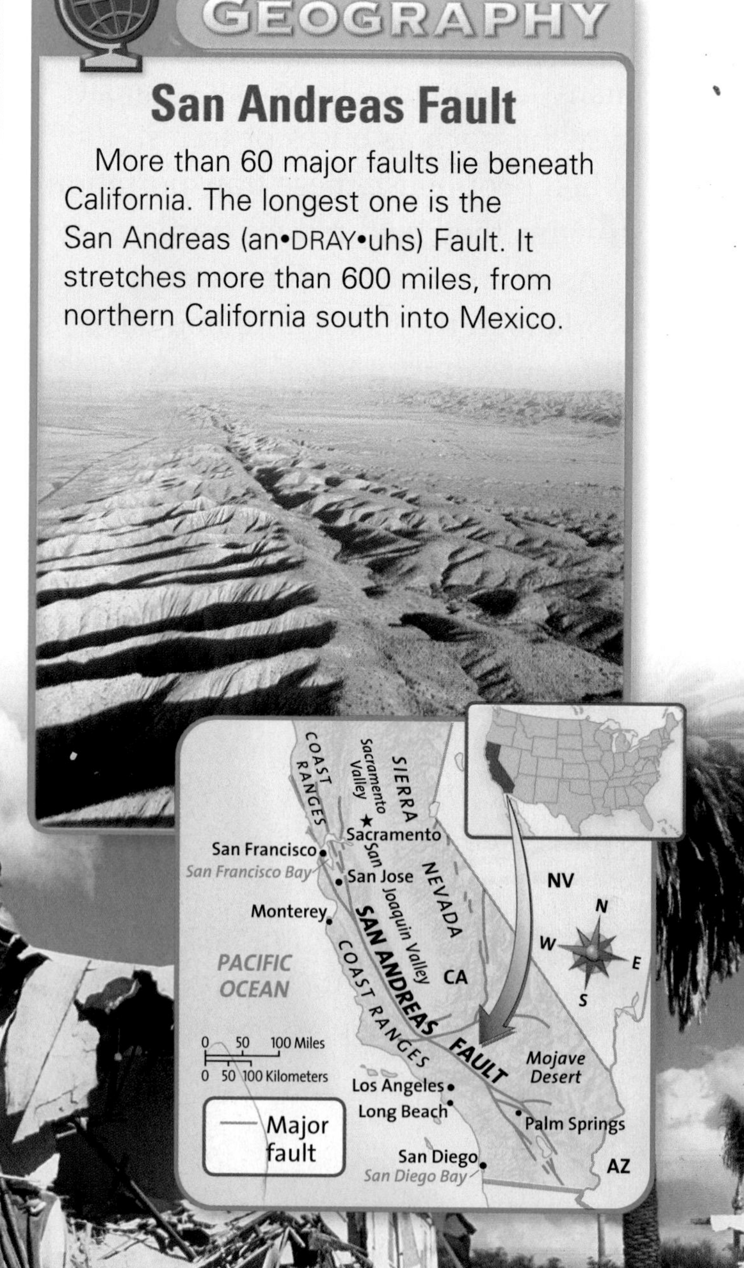

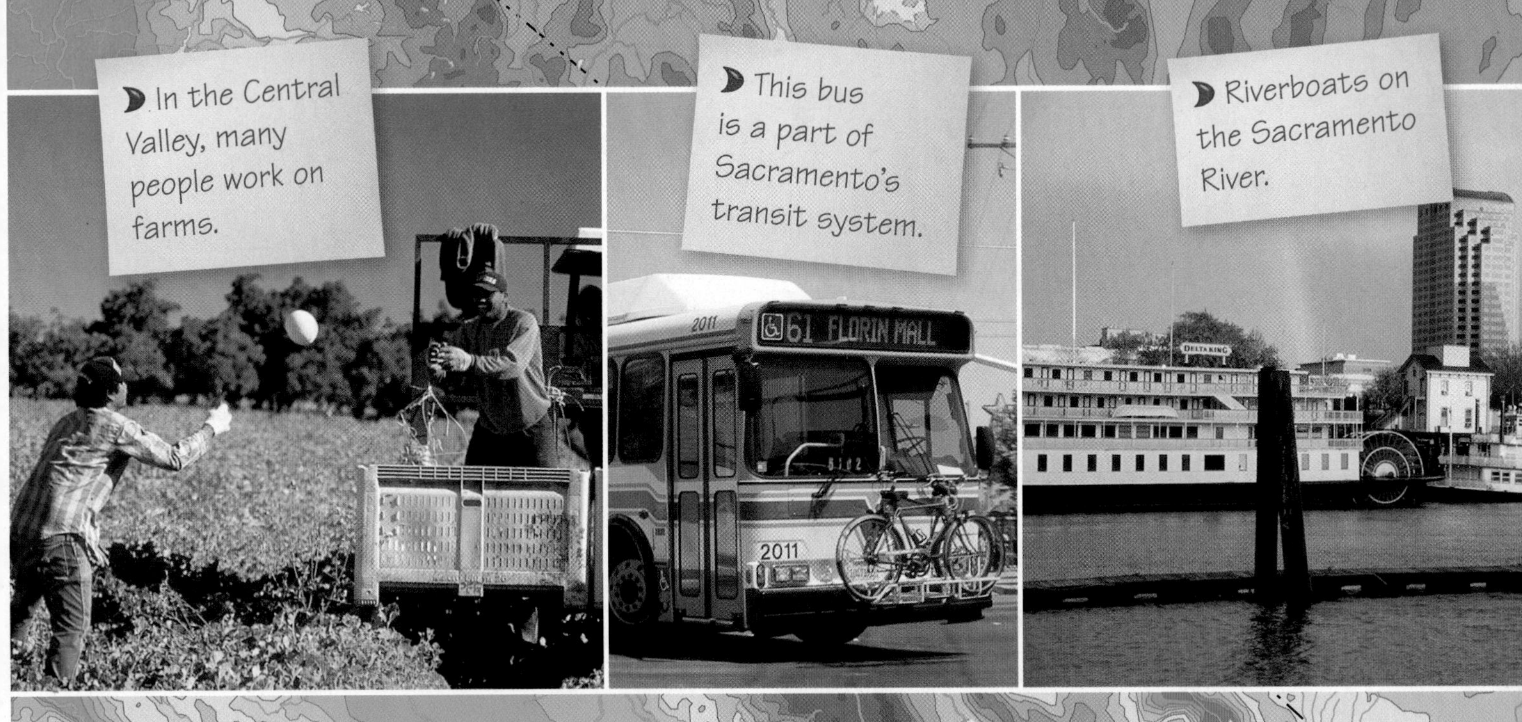

In the Central Valley, many people work on farms.

This bus is a part of Sacramento's transit system.

Riverboats on the Sacramento River.

Life in the Central Valley

Other than Sacramento and Fresno, there are few large cities in the Central Valley. Instead, flat farm fields stretch across much of the region. The Central Valley's fertile soil makes it California's most important farming area. About three-fifths of the state's farmland lies in this region.

Because the Central Valley's climate is dry, farmers there must use irrigation to water their fields. However, the Central Valley has one of the country's longest **growing seasons**. The weather is warm enough so that farmers can grow crops about ten months each year.

Central Valley farmers choose crops that grow best in the climate. For example, they grow almonds, walnuts, kiwifruits, apricots, olives, peaches, melons, and other crops that can handle the warm, dry weather. Other workers prepare these crops for market. Some farmers also raise livestock, such as cattle.

The many rivers and lakes in the Central Valley are popular places, especially in summer. In these areas, people enjoy water sports such as swimming, boating, and fishing. The climate of the Central Valley allows people to enjoy these activities almost year-round.

READING CHECK **MAIN IDEA AND DETAILS**
How do many people in the Central Valley earn their living?

The Mountain Region is a favorite place for camping.

Steep roofs allow snow to slide off of mountain homes.

Drivers in the Mountain Region sometimes face icy conditions.

Life in the Mountain and Desert Regions

Of California's four natural regions, the Mountain Region and the Desert Region have the lowest population densities. Much of the land is rural. In some places, people live many miles from schools, stores, and hospitals.

The Mountain Region is popular with visitors, however. People spend summers there fishing, hiking, rock climbing, and river rafting. In winter, they enjoy sports such as skiing and snowboarding. They may see bears, wildcats, deer, and mountain sheep.

Winter storms bring many feet of snow to the Mountain Region. Snow can weigh a lot, and it can damage buildings. Because of this, many buildings there have steep, sloping roofs. These roofs allow snow to slide off.

Trees are an important natural resource in the Mountain Region. Many people there work in the timber industry. They cut down trees to use as lumber and for making paper. In both the Mountain and the Desert Regions, minerals are an important resource. Many people work in the mining industry.

In the Desert Region, water is **scarce**, or limited, and summers are hot. People use irrigation to bring water to the cities. In some places, water is used to grow grass for golf courses in the deserts or to supply the needs of large hotels. In other places, people have used water for farmland.

Many people who live in the Desert Region do not try to change their environment. For example, many people do not grow grass in their yards. Instead, they landscape with rocks and with desert plants.

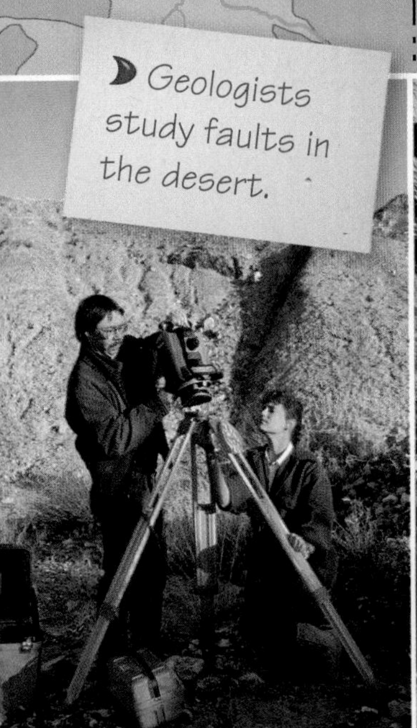

Geologists study faults in the desert.

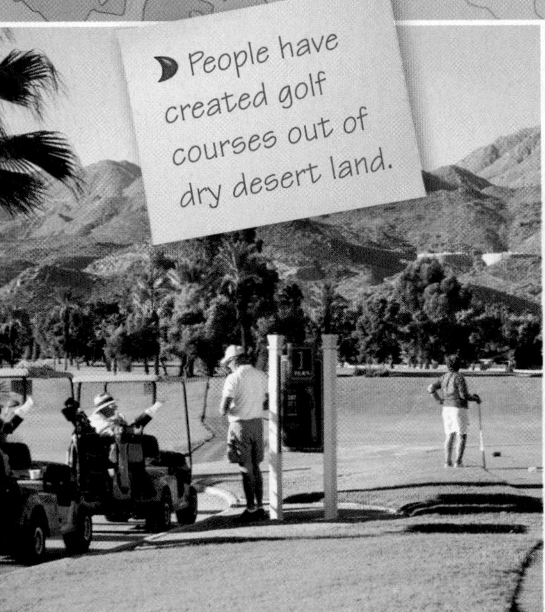

People have created golf courses out of dry desert land.

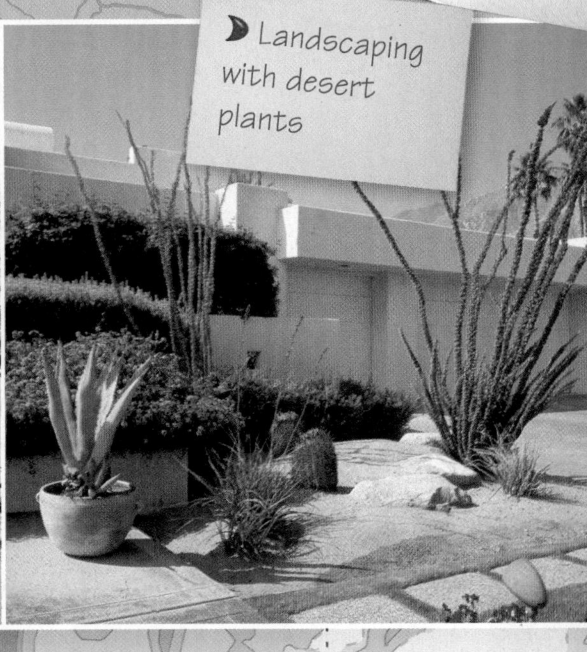

Landscaping with desert plants

Many buildings in the Desert Region reflect the region's Spanish and Mexican heritage. Some have tile roofs or brightly colored murals.

READING CHECK **MAIN IDEA AND DETAILS**
How does climate affect life in the Mountain and Desert Regions?

Summary

The Coastal, Central Valley, Mountain, and Desert Regions have different landforms, climates, and natural resources. This affects people's activities and their ways of life.

REVIEW

1. How do landforms, climate, and natural resources affect ways of life in California's different regions?
2. Use the term **growing season** to describe agriculture in your region.
3. How do landforms and natural resources affect how people use the land in different regions?
4. Which region is especially at risk for earthquakes?

CRITICAL THINKING

5. ANALYSIS SKILL What disadvantages did people in the Desert Region once face? How has that changed over time?
6. **Create a Travel Poster** Work with a group to create a travel poster showing ways of life in one of California's regions.
7. Focus Skill **MAIN IDEA AND DETAILS** On a separate sheet of paper, copy and complete the graphic organizer below.

Main Idea

Details		
outdoor activities	jobs	buildings

Citizenship

HELPING IN TIMES OF NEED

"Disaster relief of this magnitude . . . takes a committed workforce of volunteers and employees. . . . "*

— Marsha J. Evans, President and CEO of the American Red Cross

Living in California sometimes means living with natural disasters. These include earthquakes, brush and forest fires, floods, and landslides.

When major disasters occur, people need help from others to recover. In the fall of 2003, severe wildfires burned thousands of acres in southern California. Californians cared for those who were injured, served food to residents who had been evacuated, and rebuilt neighborhoods.

Firefighters often risk their lives to help people in need.

*Marsha J. Evans. From an American Red Cross press release. November 26, 2003.

After the Northridge earthquake in 1994, people rushed to help their neighbors escape from damaged buildings. They also provided food and shelter to those who had lost their homes.

Later, something interesting was noticed in neighborhoods that had Neighborhood Watch groups. People in these crime-prevention groups were familiar with their neighborhoods. They were able to tell quickly if anyone was missing. Police and city leaders decided to form disaster teams from Neighborhood Watch groups. Members were trained in first aid and were given emergency checklists to use in the future.

People can help each other through programs like Neighborhood Watch.

Think About It!

Make It Relevant Why is it important to help others in times of need?

Volunteers with the American Red Cross (below) help out during natural disasters like earthquakes (below left).

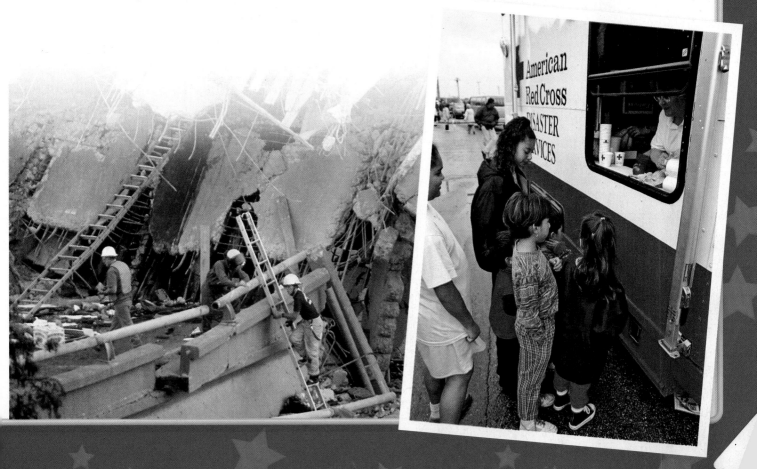

Reading Social Studies

The **main idea** is the most important idea of a passage. **Details** are facts, reasons, or examples that support the main idea.

Main Idea and Details

Complete this graphic organizer to show that you understand important ideas and details about California's natural regions. A copy of this graphic organizer appears on page 12 of the Homework and Practice Book.

California's Geography

Main Idea

California's natural regions have different physical and human features.

Details

The Coastal Region has low mountains, a rocky coastline, broad valleys, and islands.			

California Writing Prompts

Write an Information Report Write a report that describes the climate and physical features of the place where you live. Include facts and details that tell what makes your area different from other areas.

Write a Summary Think about the many different factors that affect where people choose to live. Then write a summary that tells some of the reasons why Californians live where they do.

Use Vocabulary

Identify the term that correctly matches each definition.

equator, p. 13
harbor, p. 20
drought, p. 32
suburb, p. 36
fault, p. 42

1. a crack in Earth's surface
2. an imaginary line on a globe dividing Earth into the Northern and Southern Hemispheres
3. a long period of time with little or no rain
4. a town or small city near a large city
5. a body of water where ships can dock safely

Apply Skills

ANALYSIS SKILL Use Latitude and Longitude

6. Examine the map of California on page 17. Find Crescent City, Stockton, and Madera. Then write down the lines of latitude and longitude that best describe the absolute location of each city.
7. Examine the map of California on page 17. Find San Francisco and Sacramento. Which city is closest to 39°N, 122°W?

ANALYSIS SKILL Use an Elevation Map

8. Examine the map of California on page 27. What is the elevation of the land around Chico?

Recall Facts

Answer these questions.

9. In which hemispheres is California located?
10. Where is California located in relation to the prime meridian and the equator?
11. How do the physical features and climate of the Desert Region affect the things people do there?
12. How have people in the Coastal Region adapted to the high population density?

Write the letter of the best choice.

13. Where do most Californians live?
    A in the Mountain Region
    B in the Desert Region
    C in urban areas
    D in rural areas
14. Why is the Central Valley a good area for farming?
    A The region has several mountains.
    B The region has fertile soil.
    C The region has a large population.
    D The region receives little rain.

Think Critically

15. 

How is the place where you live affected by its relative location?
16. ANALYSIS SKILL How are the coasts of northern California and southern California different? How are they alike?

Study Skills

UNDERSTAND VOCABULARY

Using a dictionary can help you learn new words that you find as you read.

- **A dictionary shows all the meanings of a word and tells where the word came from.**
- **You can use a chart to list and organize unfamiliar words that you look up in a dictionary.**

spring (spring′) *n.* **1.** A source or supply of water coming from the ground. **2.** The season between winter and summer. **3.** An elastic object or device that returns to its original shape after being crushed or changed. **4.** The act of leaping up or forward [from Middle English *springe*, wellspring].

Word	Syllables	Origin	Definition
spring	SPRING	Middle English	A source or supply of water coming from the ground

Apply As You Read

As you read, look up unfamiliar words in the dictionary. Add them to a chart like the one above. Fill in each column to help you remember the word's meaning.

California History-Social Science Standards, Grade 4

4.1 Students demonstrate an understanding of the physical and human geographic features that define places and regions in California.
4.2 Students describe the social, political, cultural, and economic life and interactions among people of California from the pre-Columbian societies to the Spanish mission and Mexican rancho periods.

CHAPTER

California's Indians

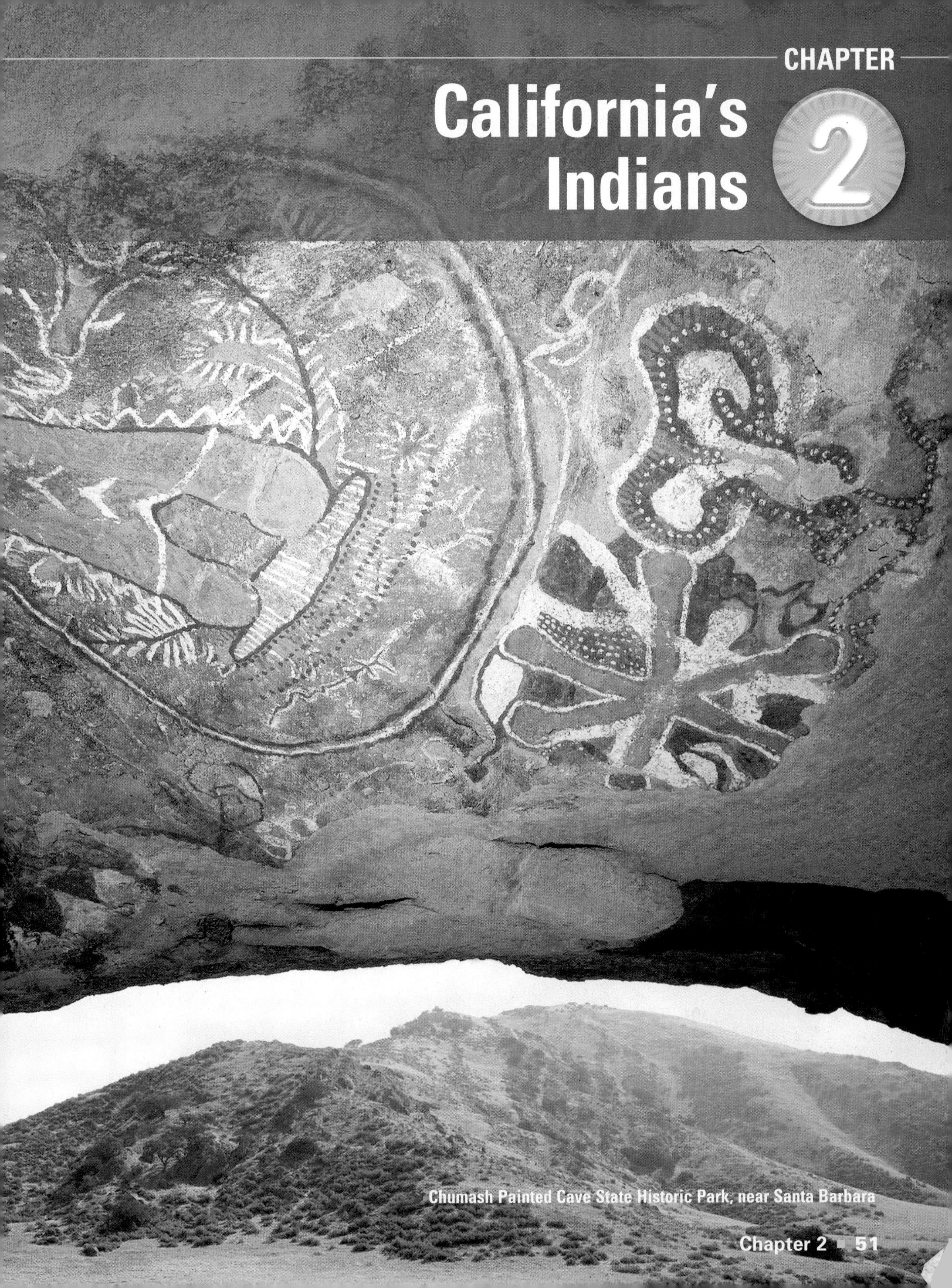

Chumash Painted Cave State Historic Park, near Santa Barbara

Start with a Story

Two Bear Cubs

A Miwok Legend from California's Yosemite Valley

retold by Robert D. San Souci
illustrated by Daniel San Souci

The Miwok (MEE•wahk) Indians who lived in Yosemite Valley called their land *Ah-wah'-nee*. They often told a story about how El Capitan, one of the valley's landforms, came to be. According to the story, two bear cubs wandered away from their mother. While the cubs slept on a rock beside the Merced River, the rock grew higher—as high as a mountain.

Red-Tailed Hawk spotted them sleeping on top of the rock. Badger, Gray Fox, Mother Deer, and Mountain Lion all tried to rescue the cubs, but none of the animals could reach them. Read now to find out how the cubs were rescued by Measuring Worm.

So Measuring Worm began to creep up the rock, curling himself into an arch, anchoring himself with his four short back legs, then stretching out his body until his six front legs could grasp another bit of stone. Curling and stretching, he inched his way up. While he climbed he chanted, *"Tú-tok! Tú-tok!"* When he curved his body, that was *"Tú,"* and when he stretched out, that was *"tok."*

As he went, he marked the safe path with a sticky thread, for Measuring Worm can make a string like a spider.

In time, he went even higher than Mountain Lion. The animals below could no longer see him, or hear his little song, *"Tú-tok! Tú-tok!"*

Up and up and up he went. Day turned to night over and over, and still he climbed. Beneath him, Mother Grizzly and the other animals kept anxious watch. Above, the cubs slept peacefully, wrapped in cloud-blankets.

Once Measuring Worm looked down and saw that the mighty river now seemed only a thin band of silver, decorated with sparkling rapids and green islands. The forests and meadows of the valley floor looked no bigger than bunches of twigs and moss. At this sight, Measuring Worm grew afraid. For a time, he could not move at all. But he found his courage again. He began to sing, *"Tú-tok! Tú-tok!"* as loudly as he could, and crept still higher up the wall.

Day after day, Measuring Worm climbed, until at last, early one morning, he reached the top of the vast stone. He softly whispered into the ears of the two cubs, "Wake up!" He was afraid that if he woke them too quickly, they might become frightened and fall off the slippery rock.

When they saw how high above the river they were, the cubs began to cry. But Measuring Worm comforted them. "Follow me," he said. "I will guide you safely down the mountain, for I have marked a safe path with my string."

To the brown cub Measuring Worm said, "Older Brother, you follow right behind me." Then, to the one with cinnamon-colored fur, he said, "Younger Brother, follow your brother and make your every step the same as his. Do this, and you will not fall."

Still the cubs were fearful. But Measuring Worm said, " Surely Mother Grizzly's children are not cowards, for she is the bravest creature in *Ah-wah'-nee.*"

Then the two little bears puffed out their chests and said, "We are brave. We will follow you."

So they began the slow climb down, both cubs doing just what Measuring Worm told them.

After a long time, sharp-eyed Gray Fox spotted them. He told Mother Grizzly, "See! Your cubs are returning." Anxiously she looked where her friend was pointing. Sure enough, there she saw her cubs making their way down the face of the mountain, as Measuring Worm guided their every step and called encouragement to them.

At last the little bears and their rescuer reached the valley floor. Then how joyfully Mother Grizzly gathered her cubs to her heart and hugged them and scolded them for not minding her and then hugged them again. Loudly she praised Measuring Worm for his courage and resourcefulness.

Then all the animals decided to call the rock that grew to be a mountain *Tu-tok-a-nu-la*, which means Measuring Worm Stone, in honor of the heroic worm who had done what no other creature could do. And so the towering landmark was known for many years, until newcomers renamed the huge granite wall, "El Capitan."

Response Corner

1. How was Measuring Worm able to rescue the bear cubs when the other animals could not?
2. Explain how people use stories, poems, and songs to explain the world around them.

Lesson 1

Time

15,000 YEARS AGO — PRESENT

- **More than 13,000 years ago** People arrive in California
- **About 4,000 years ago** Native Californians settle in villages
- **Present** More than 330,000 American Indians live in California

WHAT TO KNOW
How did the early people of California change their ways of life as their environment changed?

- ✓ Tell how people may have first come to live in California.
- ✓ Describe how early people in California lived.

VOCABULARY
glacier p. 57
ancestor p. 57
surplus p. 58
tribe p. 59
culture p. 59
artifact p. 60
legend p. 60

Focus Skill **MAIN IDEA AND DETAILS**

HSS 4.2, 4.2.1

The First Californians

YOU ARE THERE "Shhh! I see one," the hunter next to you whispers. Standing in the distance is a woolly mammoth. You're excited—and a little scared. Lately, the large animals have been harder and harder to find. A successful hunt is important to your people. This mammoth will provide meat, and its hide will provide warmth and shelter.

A Time Long Ago

In the past, Earth has had long periods of freezing cold, known as Ice Ages. During these periods, much of Earth's water was frozen in **glaciers**. So much water was trapped in these slow-moving masses of ice that the water levels of the oceans dropped. At different times, the lower water levels exposed a "bridge" of dry land between Asia and North America.

Many scientists say that people from Asia may have crossed this land bridge to reach North America. These early people most likely led a nomadic (noh•MA•dik) way of life. They moved from place to place, following herds of animals, which they hunted for food. They probably gathered wild plants for food, too.

Over thousands of years, the children of early people and their children's children spread out over North and South America. They were the **ancestors**, or early family members, of present-day American Indians.

More than 13,000 years ago, people reached what is now California. At that time, the climate was cooler and wetter than it is today. Huge animals, such as mastodons and woolly mammoths, still roamed the land. The early Indians used spears with stone points to hunt the animals. From one mammoth, a group of Indians could get meat to last for several days. They likely used the hide to make clothing and shelters.

READING CHECK **MAIN IDEA AND DETAILS**
How did early people depend on large animals?

ANALYSIS SKILL Analyze Maps **The first people to reach North America were likely nomads. A nomad is a person who keeps moving from place to place.**

Movement In which general direction did early people travel to reach what is now California from Asia?

A New Way of Life

To kill the large animals, Indians had to work in groups. They also developed tools to help them be better hunters. One of those tools was the atlatl (AHT•lah•tuhl), which allowed hunters to throw their spears faster and farther.

Over time, the climate changed, becoming warmer and drier. Many of the plants that the large animals ate could no longer grow. This may be one reason why those animals died out about 10,000 years ago.

Because people could no longer depend on the hunting of large animals, they had to adapt their way of living. They began to fish more and to hunt smaller animals, such as deer, rabbits, and birds. To hunt these animals, they developed new hunting tools. Among these were the bow and arrow.

People also gathered more nuts and berries, and they ate more plants. In time, they learned where certain plants grew best and what time of year nuts and berries became ripe. Each season, they traveled to places where they could hunt or gather food.

Sometimes the Indians gathered more food than they could use at one time. They used baskets or clay pots to store the **surplus**, or extra food.

READING CHECK **CAUSE AND EFFECT**
How did people adapt to the change in climate?

When large animals died out, early people began hunting smaller animals, such as elk, deer, and rabbits.

The California Indians

About 4,000 years ago, people began to live in villages all year. Some groups formed what are now called bands or tribes. A **tribe** is an American Indian group with its own leaders and lands. Its members work together to obtain the things they need. The members of a tribe have the same customs and speak a common language.

Over time, most tribes in California came to have their own beliefs and ways of speaking, acting, and dressing. These ways of living made up a tribe's **culture**. A tribe's culture made it different from other tribes. California had more diverse tribes than other areas north of what is now Mexico. In fact, more than 100 different languages were spoken there.

Cultures were shaped in part by the environment. Because tribes lived in different regions, they had different natural resources to use. Where forests grew, people used wood to build homes. In places with only shrubs or small trees, they mostly covered their shelters with branches or grasses. Most California tribes made tightly woven grass baskets to carry water. People who lived in the desert stored water in pots made of clay.

Even though the cultures were different, all the tribes depended on their physical environments to meet their needs. They used the land and the plants and animals around them carefully. This way, they could make sure that there would always be plenty of plants and animals in the future.

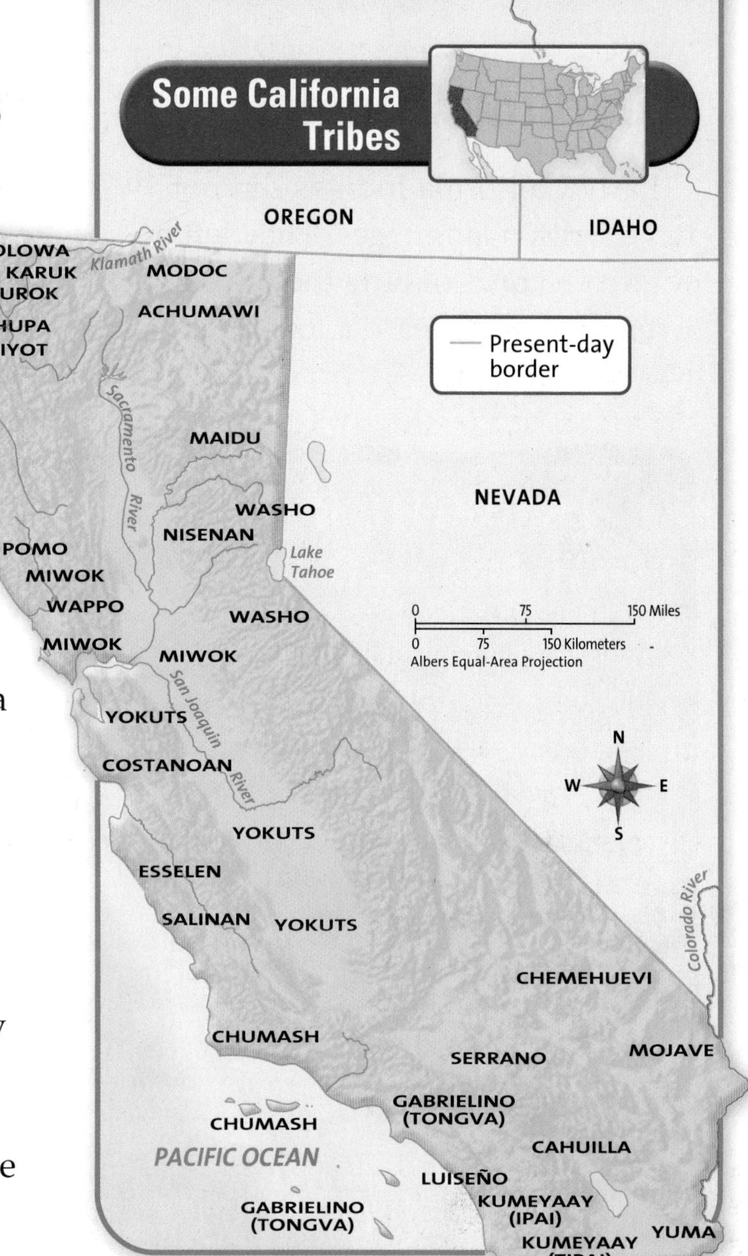

ANALYSIS SKILL Analyze Maps

Location Which tribes once lived close to where you live now?

READING CHECK MAIN IDEA AND DETAILS
How did the environment shape the ways of life of early California Indians?

Learning from the Past

Early California Indians did not have written languages. They left no written records of how they lived. Even so, we can learn a lot about their ways of life.

How the Robin Got His Red Breast

This legend was told by the Miwok Indians of the Central Valley to explain how people got fire and why the feathers on a robin's breast are red.

"A long time ago the world was dark and cold, and the people had no fire. ***Wit'-tab-bah*** the Robin learned where the fire was, and went on a far journey to get it. After he had traveled a great distance, he came to the place and stole it and carried it back to the people. Every night on the way, he lay with his breast over it to keep it from getting cold; this turned his breast red. Finally he reached home with it and gave it to the people. Then he made the Sun out of it, but before doing this he put some into the ***oo'-noo*** tree (the buckeye) so the people could get it when they needed it. From that day to this, all the people have known that when they want fire they can get it by rubbing an oo'-noo stick against a piece of dry wood; this makes the flame come out."

The Dawn of the World: Myths and Tales of the Miwok Indians of California. C. Hart Merriam. Kessinger Publishing.

Much of what we know about early California Indians comes from the artifacts (AR•tih•fakts) they left behind. An **artifact** is any object made by people in the past. Artifacts can include clothing, baskets, pots, and tools. From artifacts such as spear points, scientists can learn how people in the past hunted and where they hunted. From animal bones, they can tell what people ate.

We can also learn about early California Indians by studying the stories, songs, and teachings that they have passed down from adults to children for many, many years. Like people everywhere, California Indians wondered about the world around them. They told **legends**, or stories handed down over time, to explain how people and everything in the world came to be. Some legends

Scientists dig for American Indian artifacts in the Yosemite Valley.

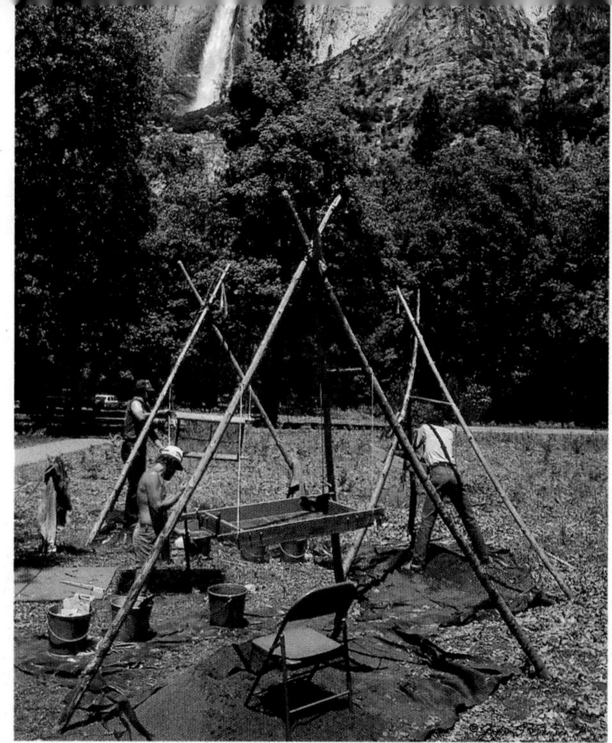

explain natural events such as storms. Others tell about a tribe's history. Some legends explain the belief that the Indians' ancestors had not come here across a land bridge. Instead, they tell that Indians have always lived in the Americas.

Children listened carefully as their elders told legends. The children had great respect for their elders, and they repeated each line until they had learned the legends for themselves. Through legends, children learned proper behavior and the knowledge they needed to survive. Later in life, they would retell the legends to their own children.

READING CHECK **MAIN IDEA AND DETAILS**
How were legends important to California Indians?

Summary

At first, people in California led a mostly nomadic life, following herds of large animals. As the climate changed, people fished more, hunted smaller animals, and ate more plants. In time, they settled in villages.

REVIEW

1. How did the early people of California change their ways of life as their environment changed?
2. Use the term **legend** to describe how California Indian tribes passed down their history.
3. How did the region in which a group of California Indians lived affect their use of resources?

CRITICAL THINKING

4. ANALYSIS SKILL From what you know about California's geography, why do you think different tribes developed different cultures?
5. **Write a Legend** Write a legend that offers an explanation for a natural event, such as a thunderstorm or an earthquake.
6. Focus Skill **MAIN IDEA AND DETAILS** On a separate sheet of paper, copy and complete the graphic organizer below.

Main Idea

California Indians adapted to a changing environment.		

Details

Lesson 2

The Northern Coastal Region

WHAT TO KNOW
How did the Indians of the northern Coastal Region of California depend on the natural resources around them?

- ✓ Describe the cultures of some tribes in the northern Coastal Region of California.
- ✓ Compare some major groups of Indians of the northern Coastal Region of California.

VOCABULARY
weir p. 64
ceremony p. 64
shaman p. 64
trade p. 67

PEOPLE
Yurok
Karuk
Hupa
Wiyot
Pomo

PLACES
Klamath River
Trinity River
Russian River
Clear Lake

MAIN IDEA AND DETAILS

California Standards
HSS 4.1, 4.1.3, 4.2, 4.2.1

YOU ARE THERE

It's a busy day in the Yurok (YOOR•ahk) village in which you live. You jump as the redwood tree your father has been cutting falls to the ground. The wood is strong and sturdy. It'll be perfect for your father's new dugout canoe.

You watch as your father starts a fire to burn the inside of the giant log. This will make the log easier to hollow out. Later, he will use tools made of stone and elk antlers to form the canoe. You know the work will take many days, but your father will soon have a new dugout canoe for fishing and for traveling to other villages.

The Land and People

The rainy northern coast of California was home to many groups of Indians, including the **Yurok**, the **Karuk** (KAHR•uhk), the **Hupa** (HOOP•uh), and the **Wiyot** (WEE•ot).

Each group developed its own culture. However, all the groups shared a similar environment, and their cultures were alike in many ways.

Trees were an important resource for all the tribes living along the northern coast. Huge redwoods and giant cedars towered above the land. Oak trees, berry bushes, and other plants also grew there. Like people today, the California Indians used the region's resources to meet their needs. They cut down trees and used the wood to build shelters and canoes.

This wet, green environment was also home to many animals. The people hunted sea lions, deer, elk, and other animals. They dug for clams and other kinds of shellfish.

The region's many rivers were also important. People traveled on and fished in the rivers. Some tribes, such as the Karuk and the Hupa, built their villages along the rivers. Others, such as the Wiyot, built some of their villages along the coast.

READING CHECK **MAIN IDEA AND DETAILS**
What natural resources did tribes in the northern Coastal Region use?

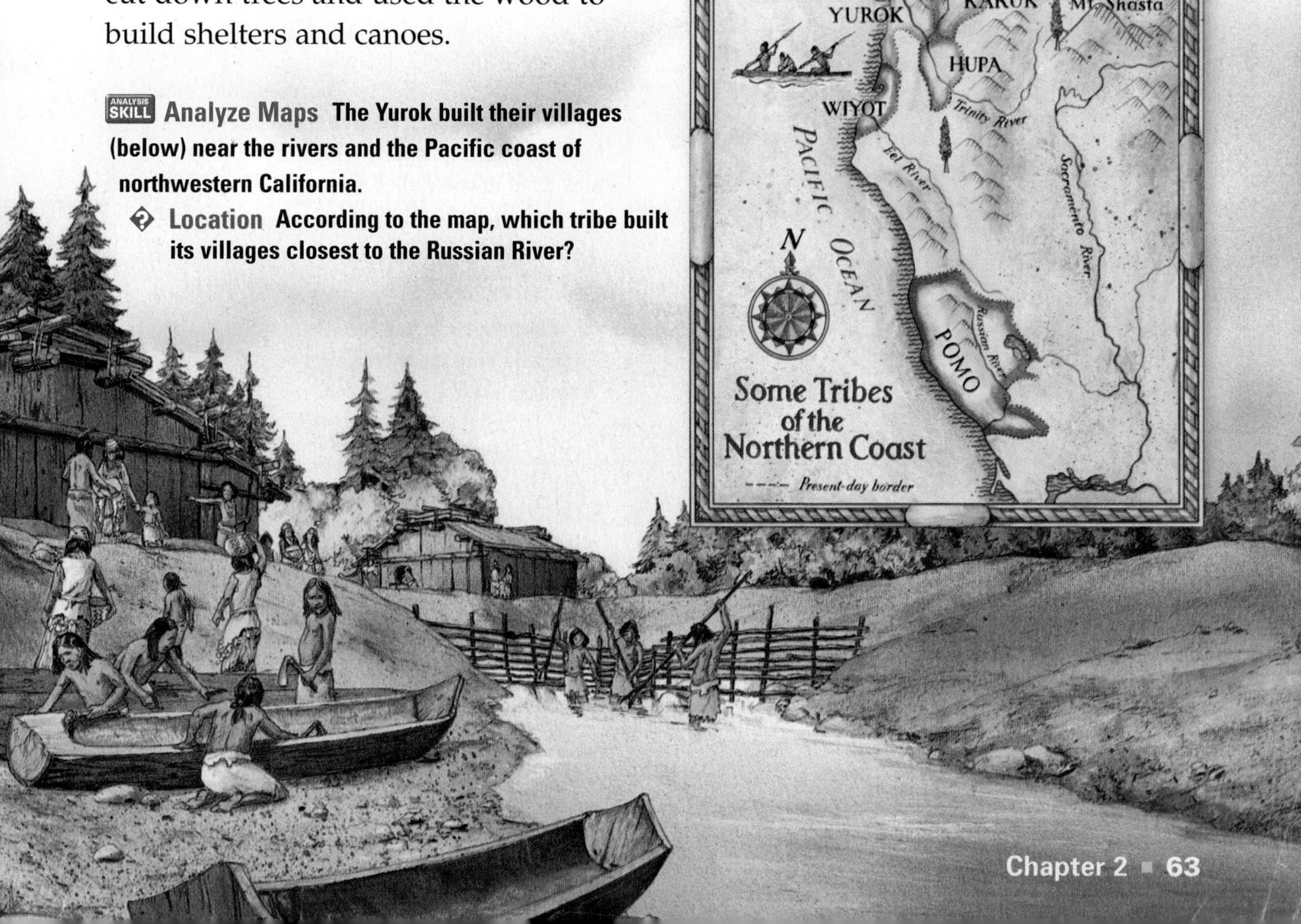

ANALYSIS SKILL **Analyze Maps** **The Yurok built their villages (below) near the rivers and the Pacific coast of northwestern California.**

Location **According to the map, which tribe built its villages closest to the Russian River?**

Yurok and Hupa

The Yurok lived along the **Klamath River** and the Pacific Ocean. In this rainy climate, they used wood from the large trees to build sturdy homes. They used tools made from elk antlers to split tree trunks into planks, or boards. They built their houses with slanted roofs so that water would run off when it rained.

The Yurok were hunters and gatherers. Men hunted animals in the forests and caught fish in the rivers. They also used dugout canoes to travel along the coast to hunt sea animals. Women gathered berries, fruits, nuts, and wild plants for food.

For the Yurok and most California Indians, acorns were an important food. However, the Yurok's most important food was salmon. To catch salmon, the Yurok stretched **weirs** (WIRZ) across the rivers. Then they captured the fish that got trapped behind these "fences."

The Yurok believed that salmon came from a being named Nepewo (nuh•PAY•oh). Each year, the Yurok honored Nepewo in the First Salmon ceremony. A **ceremony** is a celebration to honor a cultural or religious event. For the First Salmon ceremony, a **shaman**, or religious leader, had to catch and eat the first salmon of the season.

▶ The Yurok traveled up and down rivers and along the coast in dugout canoes, like the one here.

A Yurok Coin Purse

ANALYSIS SKILL **Analyze Artifacts** **The Yurok and other tribes in the Coastal Region traded by using beads made from shells. This Yurok coin purse was used to carry shell money.**

1. **The coin purse was made from an elk antler.**
2. **Shell money**

What else can you learn about the Yurok by studying the materials that the purse is made from?

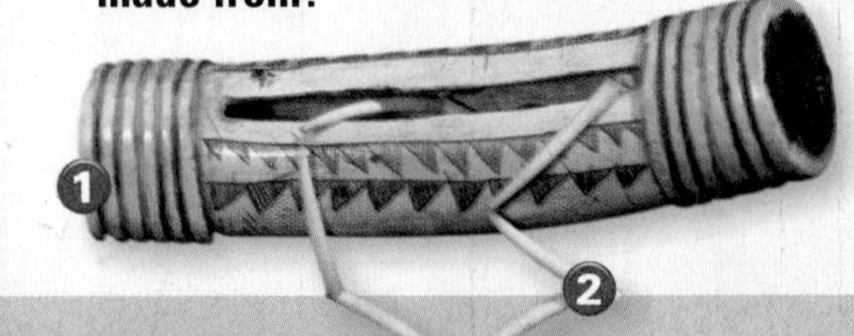

In this 1923 photograph, a Hupa man is using a weir to catch salmon.

The Hupa lived in the valleys along the **Trinity River**, upstream from the Yurok. The two groups spoke different languages, but their cultures were similar. The Hupa also built plank houses and ate salmon and acorns.

Food was usually plentiful in the northern Coastal Region, so the Hupa did not have to spend very much of their time finding food. They had time to make beautiful, useful objects. The Hupa and their neighbors made beautiful baskets from reeds and grasses. They used the baskets for storage, as dishes, and as cradles. Hupa women wore basket hats.

The Hupa also used natural materials to make clothes. Women wore deerskin skirts that were sometimes decorated with shells. They wore shell necklaces, too. Men sometimes wore headdresses with bright-red woodpecker feathers.

Like many other tribes in the region, the Hupa lived in small villages. Most villages had fewer than ten houses. Each Hupa village also had a sweat lodge. A fire burning inside a sweat lodge kept it very hot. On special occasions, the men of the village gathered there to think and pray. When they finished, they would go to the river to cool and clean themselves.

READING CHECK SUMMARIZE

Why were the Hupa able to make many beautiful objects?

Pomo

The **Pomo** lived along the coast, north of San Francisco Bay. They also built villages inland, near the **Russian River** and **Clear Lake**.

Like many other California Indians, the Pomo were hunters and gatherers. The men hunted animals and fished. Women and children gathered berries and nuts. Among the Pomo, families pruned, or trimmed, the oak and pine trees around them so that the trees would produce lots of acorns and pine nuts.

Pomo villages might have had as few as 100 people or more than 1,500 people. Along the coast, the Pomo lived in cone-shaped houses. They made these houses by piling redwood bark against poles that came together at the top. Each house was used by only one family.

The Pomo who lived farther inland used the resources around them to build a different kind of house. They used wooden poles to build a frame, which they covered with brush, plant stems, or grasses. These houses were usually large enough to hold several families at one time.

The Pomo were best known for their baskets. They wove finely crafted baskets and sometimes decorated them with feathers and shell beads.

READING CHECK COMPARE AND CONTRAST
How were Pomo houses along the coast different from those built inland?

These photographs from the early 1900s show a Pomo house (left) and a Pomo man (below) wearing a headdress and a necklace made from polished clamshells.

Wealth and Trade

Wealth was important to many of the peoples in the northern Coastal Region. They made and inherited objects they thought were beautiful and valuable. Among these objects were jewelry and strings of shells. Someone who owned many strings of shells was thought to be wealthy.

Strings of shells were often used for trade. **Trade** is the exchanging, or buying and selling, of goods. People traded shells for things they could not make or get from the resources around them.

Land was another sign of wealth. Yurok families and individual members could keep some lands for their own use. In other groups, land was shared by the whole tribe.

READING CHECK **MAIN IDEA AND DETAILS**
What did people in the northern Coastal Region use for trade?

Summary

The tribes of the northern Coastal Region developed different cultures, but they used natural resources in similar ways. Wealth was important to many of them, and they traded with other tribes.

To show their wealth, the Yurok and other tribes of the northern Coastal Region decorated their clothing with strings of shells.

REVIEW

1. How did the Indians of the northern Coastal Region of California depend on the natural resources around them?
2. Use the terms **ceremony** and **shaman** to describe how the Yurok honored Nepewo.
3. What did California Indians in the northern Coastal Region use for money, and for what did they trade?
4. What are some things that made the tribes of northern coastal California unique?

CRITICAL THINKING

5. ANALYSIS SKILL Do you think strings of shells would have been valuable to Indian groups in other regions? Explain.
6. **Make Illustrations** Use what you have read to make illustrations of the houses of northern coastal tribes. Identify the tribe that made each house and describe the materials they used. You may wish to find more information about each tribe at the library or on the internet.
7. Focus Skill **MAIN IDEA AND DETAILS**
On a separate sheet of paper, copy and complete the graphic organizer below.

Main Idea

The Yurok, the Hupa, and the Pomo lived in the northern Coastal Region of California.

Details

Lesson 3

The Southern Coastal Region

WHAT TO KNOW
How did the Indians of the southern Coastal Region of California use both land and sea resources?

- ✓ Describe how the Indians in California's southern Coastal Region traded with each other.
- ✓ Compare the religion and legends of groups in California's southern Coastal Region.

VOCABULARY
government p. 70
cooperate p. 71

PEOPLE
Chumash
Gabrielino
Luiseño
Kumeyaay

PLACES
Channel Islands
San Diego

MAIN IDEA AND DETAILS

California Standards
HSS 4.1, 4.1.3, 4.2, .4.2.1

YOU ARE THERE The leaders in your Chumash (CHOO•mash) village declare that the trading is finished. The strangers who have come to your village to trade are busy loading their canoes along the southern coast of California.

You step closer to see what the strangers have received. You see shell beads, baskets of seeds, and bows and arrows. You wonder what items your village received in exchange. You hope that the trade was a fair one.

The Land and People

Among the tribes of the southern Coastal Region of California were the **Chumash**. They lived along the Pacific Ocean, from present-day Paso Robles to Malibu. They also lived in the Cuyama Valley and in the Transverse Mountain Ranges. Some lived on the northern **Channel Islands**.

South of the Chumash lived the **Gabrielino** (gah•bree•uh•LEEN•oh), who are also known as the Tongva. Gabrielino lands stretched from Topanga south to Laguna Beach and included what is now greater Los Angeles. The Gabrielino also lived on the southern Channel Islands. The **Luiseño** (lu•ih•SA•nyoh) and the **Kumeyaay** (KOO•mee•ay), also called the Diegueño (dee•eg•EH•nyoh), lived further south. The Kumeyaay were made up of the Ipai (EE•py) and the Tipai (TEE•py). Their lands included the area around what is now **San Diego**.

The people of the southern Coastal Region used the natural resources around them to meet their needs. But the climate where they lived is warmer and drier than that farther north. There are no redwoods or giant cedars, and there are fewer rivers. The Indians in this area used different resources.

READING CHECK **MAIN IDEA AND DETAILS**
Which tribes in the Coastal Region lived farthest south?

ANALYSIS SKILL Analyze Maps **Some Chumash villages (below) had as many as 1,000 people.**

Regions **Which tribes shown on the map bordered the Chumash?**

Chumash

The Pacific Ocean was the main source of food for the Chumash. They fished its waters. They caught crabs and collected mussels and abalone in its shallow waters and dug for clams along its shore. Acorns were another major source of food. The Chumash also hunted animals and gathered plants.

Like most California Indians, the Chumash built their villages where they found fresh water. For their houses, the Chumash bent and tied willow branches into dome-shaped frames. Then they covered the frames with thick layers of tule (TOO•lee), a tall, flexible marsh plant with a spongy stem.

The Chumash were expert traders and canoe builders. They made dug-out canoes and canoes built out of tule. They also built a kind of canoe called a *tomol* (TOH•mohl). This large canoe was built with wooden planks. To make the planks, the Chumash split logs that washed up along the shore. They sewed the planks together with ropes made from plant fibers.

The Chumash had a natural resource that many other tribes did not have. On some of their lands, tar bubbled up from the ground. The Chumash used this tar to make their baskets and their plank canoes waterproof.

Like other California tribes, the Chumash had a government. A **government** is a system for deciding what is best for a group of people.

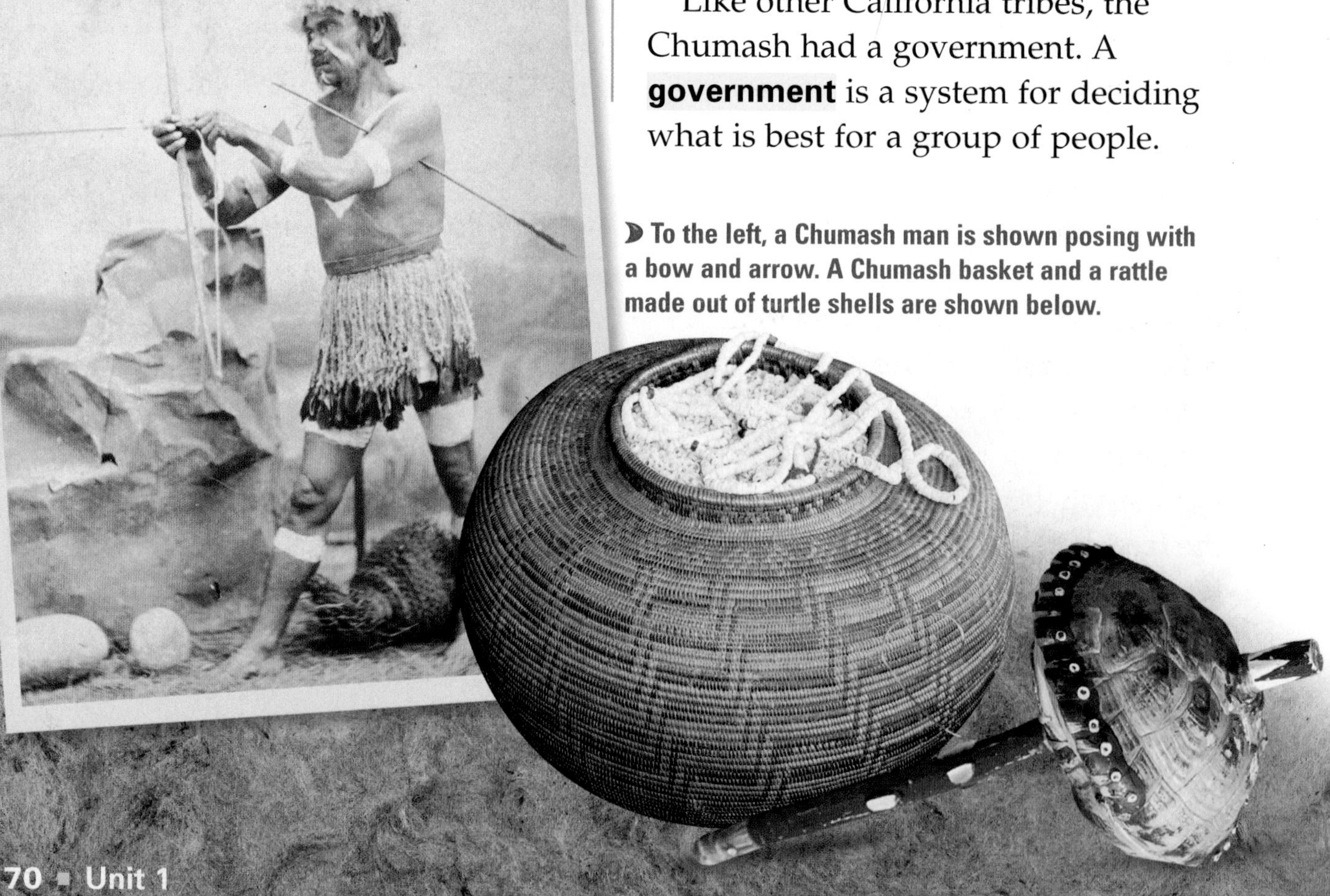

To the left, a Chumash man is shown posing with a bow and arrow. A Chumash basket and a rattle made out of turtle shells are shown below.

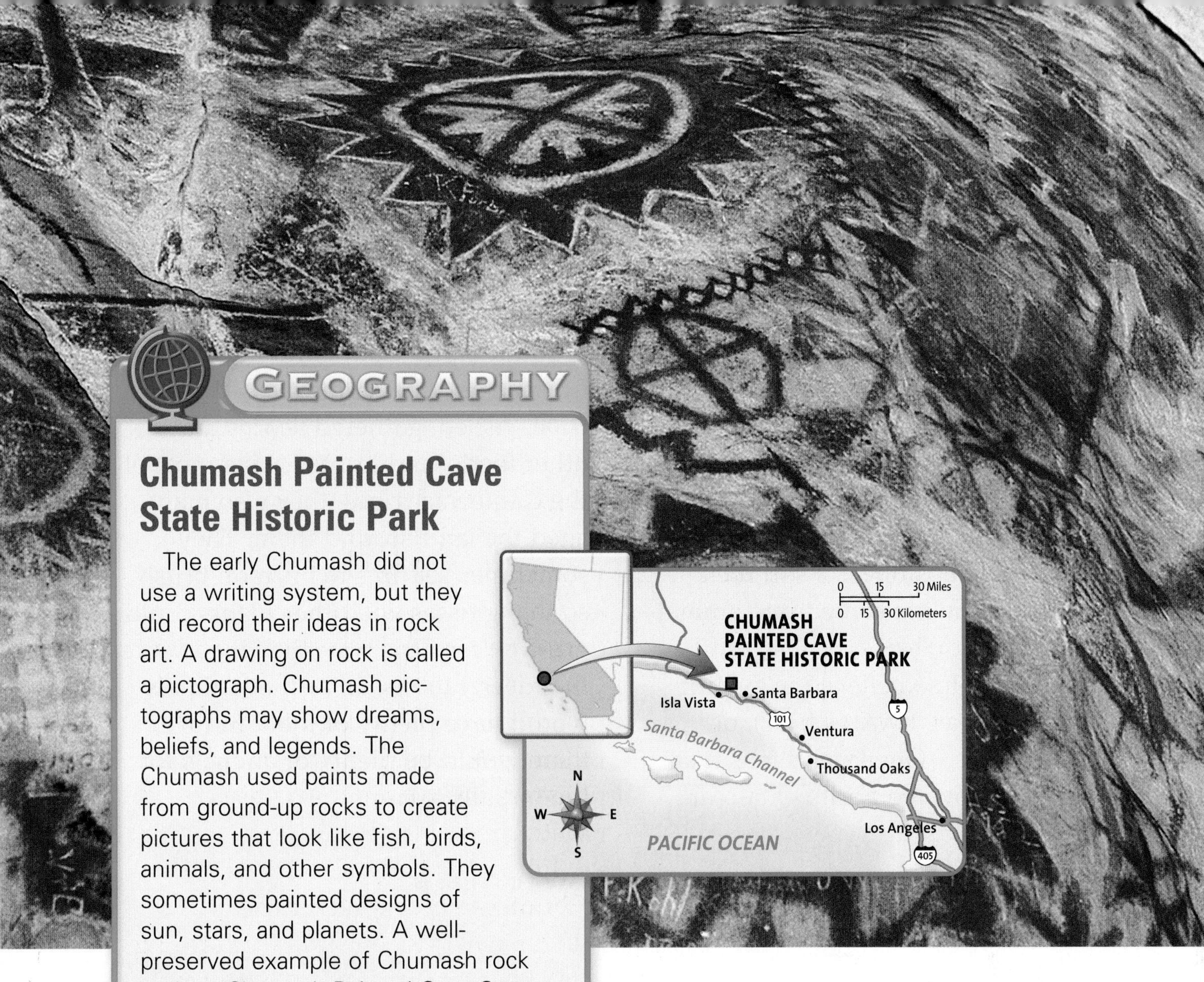

GEOGRAPHY

Chumash Painted Cave State Historic Park

The early Chumash did not use a writing system, but they did record their ideas in rock art. A drawing on rock is called a pictograph. Chumash pictographs may show dreams, beliefs, and legends. The Chumash used paints made from ground-up rocks to create pictures that look like fish, birds, animals, and other symbols. They sometimes painted designs of sun, stars, and planets. A well-preserved example of Chumash rock art is at Chumash Painted Cave State Historic Park near Santa Barbara.

It provides a way for groups to make rules and choose leaders.

Each Chumash village had a leader. When the leader died, the leader's son usually became the next leader. If the leader had no son, then a daughter, sister, or brother became leader. The village leader decided who could hunt animals or gather food in each area. He or she also met with the leaders of other villages. Those meetings helped the villages **cooperate**, or work together. A Chumash village had several houses, a place for storing food, a sweat lodge, and a public area for ceremonies.

Like many Indian groups, the Chumash used legends to explain the world. One told of how Sun carried a torch that gave light to the world. The torch was made of rolled-up bark. When Sun snapped the burning bark, the sparks that flew off became stars.

READING CHECK **MAIN IDEA AND DETAILS**
How did the Chumash make use of the tar that bubbled up on their lands?

Gabrielino, Luiseño, and Kumeyaay

The Gabrielino lived south of the Chumash, but the two tribes had similar cultures. They used many of the same resources, and they often traded with each other. Like the Chumash, the Gabrielino built plank canoes, fished, and hunted sea mammals. The tribes also lived in similar kinds of houses. They used tar, shells, and soapstone. Soapstone is a soft rock that the Gabrielino carved into animal figures and bowls.

The Gabrielino believed in a spirit called Qua-o-ar (KWAH•oh•ar), or "Giver of Life." One legend tells that water once covered Earth. Qua-o-ar ordered seven giant turtles to hold the land up out of the water. He told the turtles to be still so that things could grow on the land. But the turtles grew restless and moved, causing the Earth to shake. With this legend, the Gabrielino explained earthquakes.

South of the Gabrielino lived the Luiseño and the Kumeyaay. These tribes fished, gathered acorns and other foods, and hunted. Like most of the California tribes, they also managed the land around them. They sometimes set fires to burn off brush so that grasses and other plants could grow better. This way, they made sure that deer, rabbits, and other animals would have plenty of food. In turn, there would be plenty of animals for the Indians to hunt.

This photograph of a Kumeyaay house was taken in 1924. What materials is the house made from?

Before hunting or harvesting, the Luiseño and the Kumeyaay held ceremonies. They believed that ceremonies were a way to give thanks and to keep themselves in harmony with nature, with each other, and with their ancestors. They also believed the ceremonies would repair the harm done to Earth over the previous year and prevent sickness in the new year.

READING CHECK **COMPARE AND CONTRAST**
How is the Gabrielino turtle legend similar to the Chumash Sun legend?

California Indians today carry on the traditions of their ancestors. This dancer participates in a Gabrielino ceremony called the Harvest Dance.

Summary

The Chumash, Gabrielino, Luiseño, and Kumeyaay depended on the natural resources available to them in the dry, warm environment of the southern Coastal Region of California.

REVIEW

1. How did the Indians of the southern Coastal Region of California use both land and sea resources?
2. Use the term **cooperate** in a sentence about Chumash **government**.
3. Where were Chumash lands in relation to Gabrielino lands?
4. How did ceremonies reflect the religious beliefs of California Indians?

CRITICAL THINKING

5 ANALYSIS SKILL Why do you think people who did not live along the southern coast of California would have wanted to trade for tar, shell beads, and soapstone?

6. **Role-Play Indian Traders** Imagine that you belong to a tribe from the southern Coastal Region and that a classmate belongs to a tribe from another region. Have a conversation in which you describe to each other what resources you might trade and why.

7. Focus Skill **MAIN IDEA AND DETAILS**
On a separate sheet of paper, copy and complete the graphic organizer below.

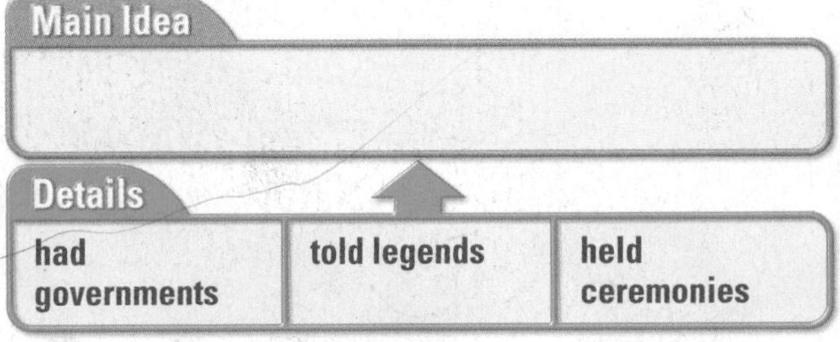

Main Idea
Details
had governments
told legends
held ceremonies

Compare Tables

WHY IT MATTERS

A table is a good way to organize information. By looking at a table, you can quickly compare numbers, facts, and other information. Tables can **classify**, or group, the same information in different ways.

WHAT YOU NEED TO KNOW

Many California Indians used boats to travel on rivers, lakes, and coastal waters. Tribes made different kinds of boats, depending on where they lived and what resources were available.

The tables on page 75 show the kinds of boats different tribes used. Both tables give the same information, but they classify it in different ways.

In Table A, the first column lists the California Indian tribes in alphabetical order. The second column lists the kinds of boats that each tribe used. Table B shows the same information about the California Indians. In this table, however, the kinds of boats are listed in alphabetical order in the first column. The second column lists the tribes that used each kind of boat.

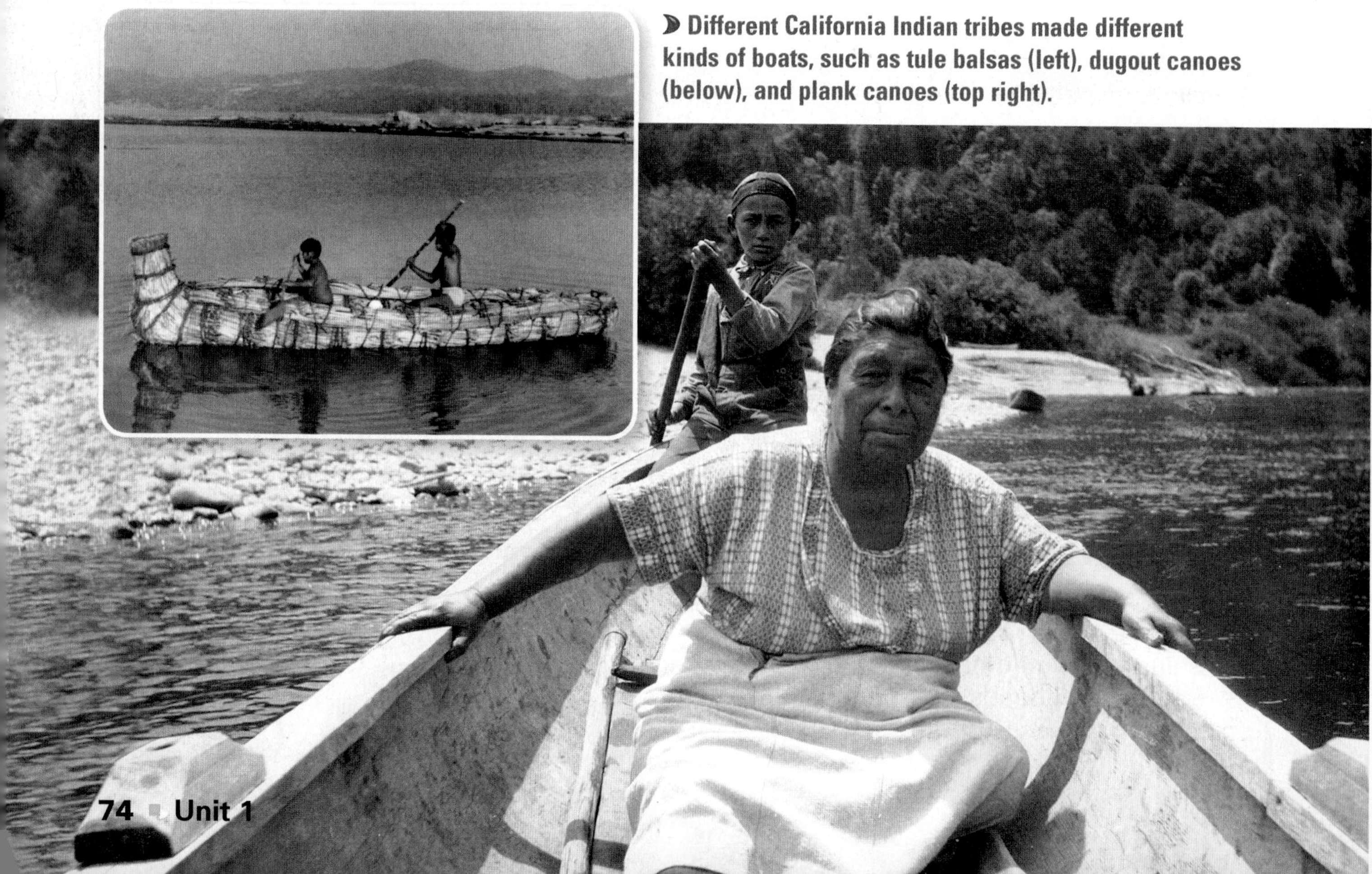

Different California Indian tribes made different kinds of boats, such as tule balsas (left), dugout canoes (below), and plank canoes (top right).

PRACTICE THE SKILL

Use the tables to answer the questions.

1. Study Table A. Which type of boat did the Miwok use? How did you find that information?
2. Study Table B. It gives the same information as Table A but in a different way. How is the information in Table B grouped?
3. Which table makes it easier to find which tribes used tule balsa? Explain.
4. Which table makes it easier to find what kind of boat a particular tribe used? Explain.

APPLY WHAT YOU LEARNED

Copy Table A onto a separate sheet of paper. Add a column labeled *Materials*. In that column, add information about the materials each tribe used to make boats. You may want to use the library or the internet to find additional information.

Table A: California Indian Boats by Tribe

TRIBE	KIND OF BOAT
Chumash	dugout canoe plank boat tule balsa
Gabrielino	dugout canoe plank boat tule balsa
Hupa	dugout canoe
Maidu	dugout canoe tule balsa
Miwok	tule balsa
Modoc	dugout canoe tule balsa
Mojave	tule balsa
Pomo	tule balsa
Yokuts	tule balsa
Yurok	dugout canoe

Table B: California Indian Tribes by Kind of Boat

KIND OF BOAT	TRIBE
dugout canoe	Chumash Gabrielino Hupa Maidu Modoc Yurok
plank boat	Chumash Gabrielino
tule balsa	Chumash Gabrielino Maidu Miwok Modoc Mojave Pomo Yokuts

Lesson 4

The Central Valley and Mountains

WHAT TO KNOW
How did the California Indians of the Central Valley and Mountain Regions depend on the natural resources around them?

- ✓ Describe how Indians of the Central Valley and Mountain Regions built their homes.
- ✓ Explain how division of labor was important to California Indians.

VOCABULARY
granary p. 78
division of labor p. 79
specialize p. 79

PEOPLE
Achumawi
Maidu
Miwok
Nisenan
Yokuts

PLACES
Sierra Nevada
Central Valley
Sacramento River
San Joaquin Valley

Focus Skill **MAIN IDEA AND DETAILS**

California Standards
HSS 4.1, 4.1.3, 4.2, 4.2.1

YOU ARE THERE

"When I was a small girl, I went on root-digging trips with my mother and helped her to collect plenty of roots to dry for winter use. These would be gathered in baskets. I also remember, as a child, living in the cedar bark house with my grandparents."*

This is how Marie Potts, a Maidu (MY•doo) woman, describes learning her people's traditional ways of life. In many ways, the way of life that Marie Potts learned is not different from the way of life of the people of the Central Valley and Mountain Regions of California of long ago.

*Marie Potts. From *The Way We Lived* by Malcolm Margolin. Co-published by Heyday Books and the California Historical Society, 1993.

The Land and People

Long before Marie Potts grew up in California, people lived on the western slopes of the **Sierra Nevada**. Even more people lived in the **Central Valley**. At one time, more than half of all California Indians may have lived in the Central Valley and Mountain Regions. Among the tribes were the **Achumawi** (ah•choo•MAH•wee), **Maidu, Miwok, Nisenan** (nee•SEE•nuhn), and **Yokuts**.

The climate of central California supported a large population. As in other regions of California, there was usually plenty of food. There were animals and fish and many plants, nuts, and berries to eat.

The tribes who lived in the Central Valley and Mountain Regions were alike in many ways. Most groups spoke related languages and used similar kinds of natural resources. At different times of the year, they traveled to different places to enjoy better weather and to gather food. In summer, for example, people traveled to higher elevations to escape hot temperatures in the Central Valley.

As in other places in California, basket making was a common activity. Tribes in the Central Valley and Mountain Regions produced many basket designs.

READING CHECK **MAIN IDEA AND DETAILS**
Why were many people able to live in the Central Valley Region?

ANALYSIS SKILL Analyze Maps **As many as 200 people sometimes lived in each Maidu village community (below).**
Regions **What river ran through Yokuts lands?**

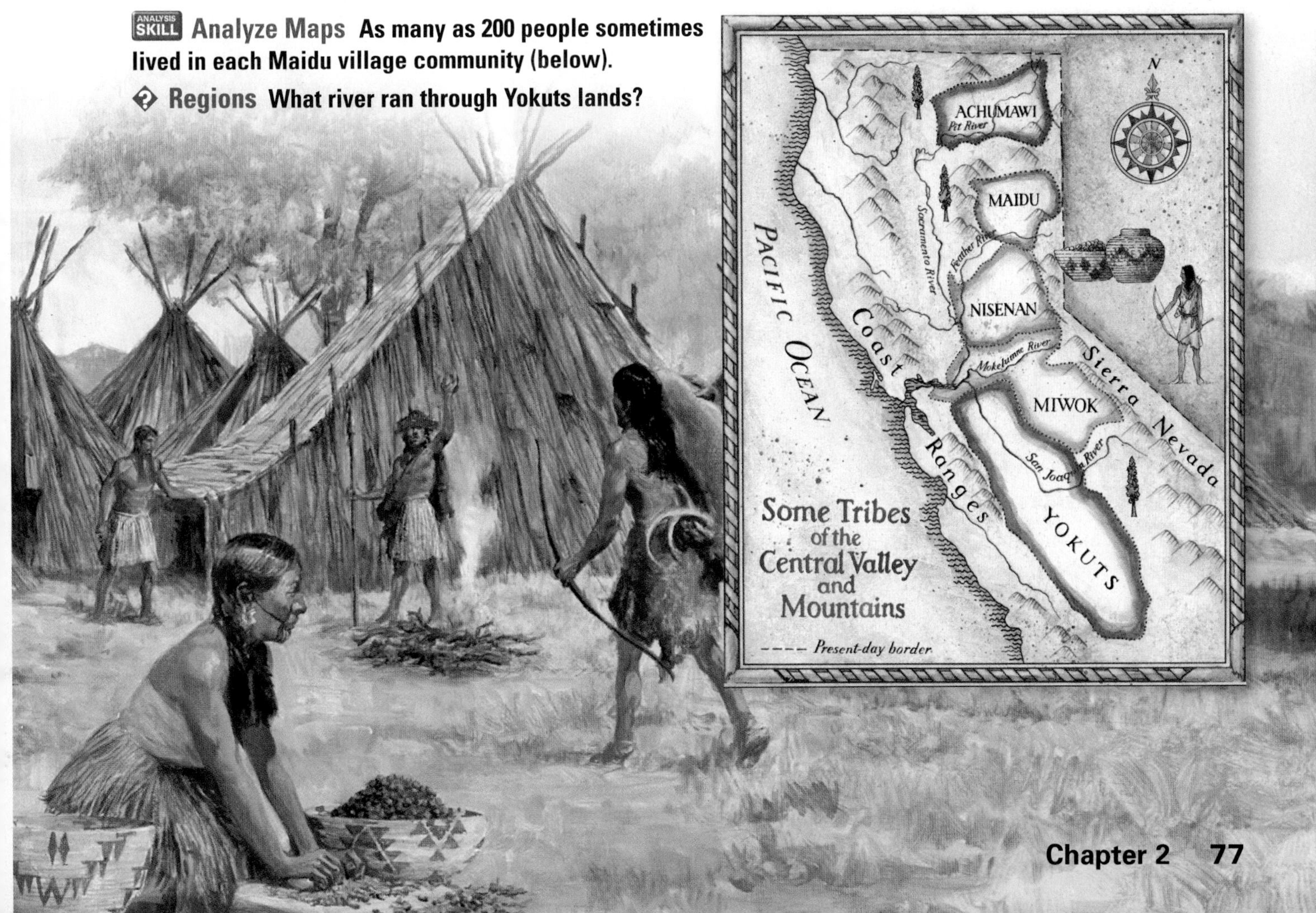

Maidu

The Maidu were one of the largest tribes in California. Most Maidu lived along the tributaries of the **Sacramento River**, including the Feather, Yuba, and American Rivers. Others lived in the foothills of the Sierra Nevada.

The Maidu lived in village groups. Each group was made up of about three to five villages around a main village. The villages in a group shared a hunting and fishing area.

Most Maidu villages had fewer than ten houses. Some houses were made of tree branches that were tied together in a cone shape and then covered with bark. Other houses were made with poles and covered with brush and dirt.

The Maidu were skilled hunters, but they had several staple, or main, foods. Among them were acorns. The Maidu sang this song when they harvested acorns. They believed it would help them have a bigger harvest.

> **"The acorns come down**
> **from heaven.**
> **I plant the short acorns in**
> **the valley.**
> **I plant the long acorns in**
> **the valley.**
> **I sprout, I, the black**
> **acorn, sprout, I sprout."***

Many villages had a special building for storing extra acorns. This building was called a **granary** (GRAY•nuh•ree).

Maidu women gathered acorns and nuts by hand, but they used a special tool, called a seed beater, to collect seeds. The women hit grasses with the

*From *The First Americans: California Indians.* C.L. Keyworth. Facts On File, 1991.

A Closer Look

Making Acorn Flour

These are the steps that California Indians followed to make acorn flour.

1. **Crush the acorns with rocks, and take off the shells.**
2. **Pound the acorns into flour.**
3. **Sift the flour through a basket to get rid of large pieces.**
4. **Spread out the flour, and rinse it many times with water to make it less bitter. To improve the taste, the Indians also added berries, nuts, or herbs.**
5. **Dry the flour in the sun.**

? Why did California Indians rinse the acorn flour with water?

seed beater, which caused the seeds to fall into a basket.

Like other California Indians, the Maidu divided work among adults in the village. Sometimes children helped. This way of having different workers do different jobs is called **division of labor**. Division of labor made it easier for the Maidu to meet their needs. The people worked together for the good of the village.

In division of labor, people specialize (SPEH•shuh•lyz). To **specialize** is to work at one kind of job and learn to do it well. Some men made arrow points or bows. Others made fishing nets or other kinds of tools. Women made baskets and prepared food.

READING CHECK **SUMMARIZE**
How was work divided among the Maidu men and women?

This woman uses a traditional seed beater to collect seeds.

3

4

5

Miwok and Yokuts

Some Miwok lived along the coast, north of San Francisco Bay. Others lived on the western slopes of the Sierra Nevada and in the **San Joaquin Valley**. Still others lived near Mount Diablo and between what are now Sacramento and Stockton.

Miwok villages varied in size. Most had a large building that was used as a place for ceremonies. These ceremonial houses were dug right into the earth. The floor was 3 or 4 feet below the ground. Above it was a wooden frame covered with brush and dirt. Each village also had a sweat lodge.

Miwok houses varied, depending on where they were. The Miwok near the coast built cone-shaped homes. They leaned branches together and covered them with grass or tule. In the mountains, they made houses by leaning wide slabs of cedar bark against each other.

Part of an old Yokuts prayer says: "My words are tied in one with the great mountains . . . with the great trees."* Trees were important to the Yokuts. Many oak trees grew where they lived, in the San Joaquin Valley and in the foothills of the Sierra Nevada. The Yokuts used wood from the oak trees to build their homes and gathered the acorns for food.

Acorns, seeds, roots, and fish were all important food for the Yokuts. The Yokuts were also excellent hunters, although animals and birds were only a small part of their diet. They built enclosures called blinds where they could trap pigeons.

Some Yokuts built rounded houses, while others built cone-shaped ones. Men made frames for the houses out of willow poles by tying the poles together at the top. Women wove tule

Children IN HISTORY

Games for Miwok Children

As with other California tribes, games were important to the Miwok. Many of the games that children play today—including tag, hide-and-seek, and racing games—were also enjoyed by Miwok children.

Some Miwok games taught important skills. In the ring-and-dart game, one player would roll a wooden ring along a course. The other player would then try to throw a 5-foot dart through the ring. Games like this helped children develop hunting skills.

Make It Relevant Think about some of the games you like to play. What skills do you learn by playing those games?

*From *Earth Always Endures: Native American Poems.* Neil Philip. Viking, 1996.

This Yokuts woman demonstrates a traditional way to use stone tools to remove the shells of acorns.

mats to cover the houses. Some of the houses were large enough for several families to live in. In summer, some Yokuts also made more open houses that were covered with brush.

Each Yokuts village had its own leaders and shamans. Many Yokuts chiefs had messengers who carried news to nearby villages. Chiefs also had criers, or spokespeople, who made announcements for them.

READING CHECK **MAIN IDEA AND DETAILS**
How were oak trees important to the Yokuts?

Summary

More California Indians lived in the Central Valley and Mountain Regions than in any other region. The tribes in these regions had similar cultures and used similar resources.

REVIEW

1. How did the California Indians of the Central Valley and Mountain Regions depend on the natural resources around them?
2. Use the term **specialize** to describe **division of labor** among California Indians.
3. Explain how the plants that grew in the Central Valley and Mountain Regions affected the kinds of homes people built there.

CRITICAL THINKING

4. ANALYSIS SKILL Some Miwok groups lived near the coast. How do you think the ways of life of the Miwok on the coast were different from those of the Miwok who lived in the mountains?
5. **Illustrate a Map** Draw an outline map of California, and color the regions in which the Miwok and Yokuts lived. Add notes and pictures that show how the Indians in each place used the resources to meet their needs.
6. Focus Skill **MAIN IDEA AND DETAILS** On a separate sheet of paper, copy and complete the graphic organizer below.

Main Idea

The Central Valley and Mountain Regions had the largest population of California Indians.

Details

PRIMARY SOURCES

California Indian Artifacts

California Indians used the natural resources around them to make items they wanted. Baskets were made in many shapes and sizes for many uses. Designs were woven into the baskets with colored grasses. In the southeast corner of the state, people made pottery out of clay and water. Utensils, such as knives and spoons, were made out of wood, animal horns, and other materials.

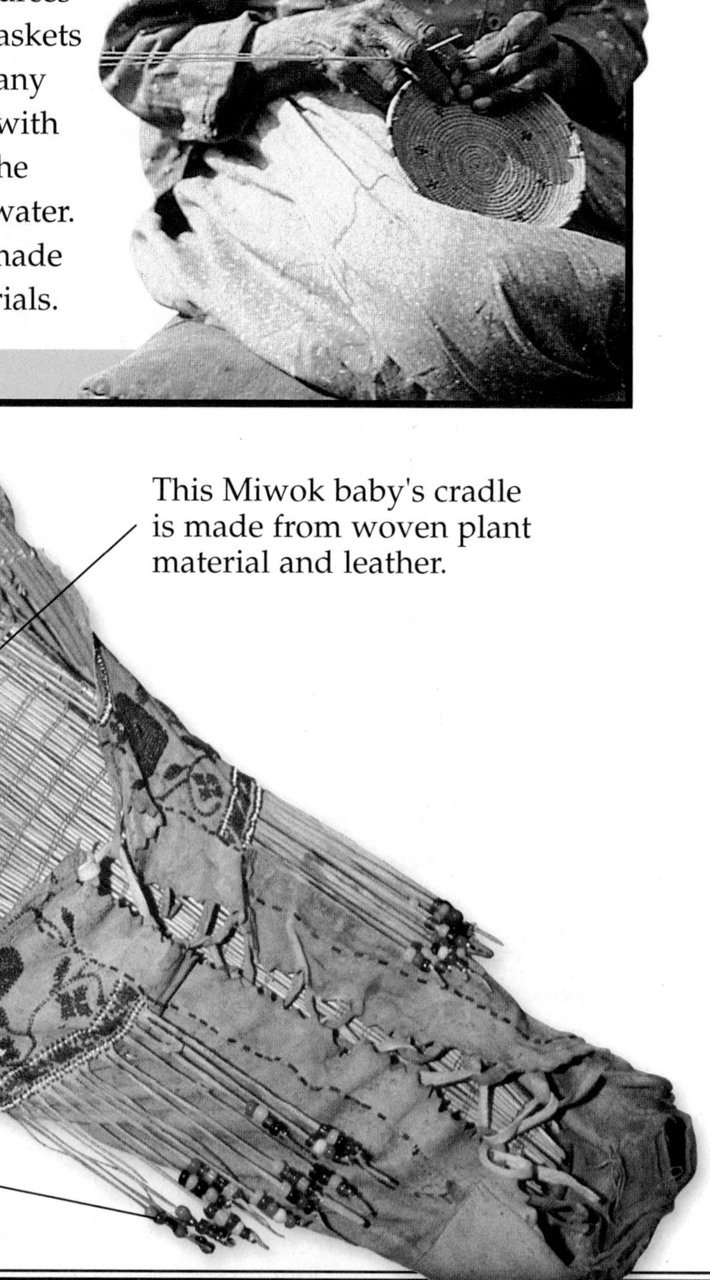

This Miwok baby's cradle is made from woven plant material and leather.

The cradle is decorated with colorful beads.

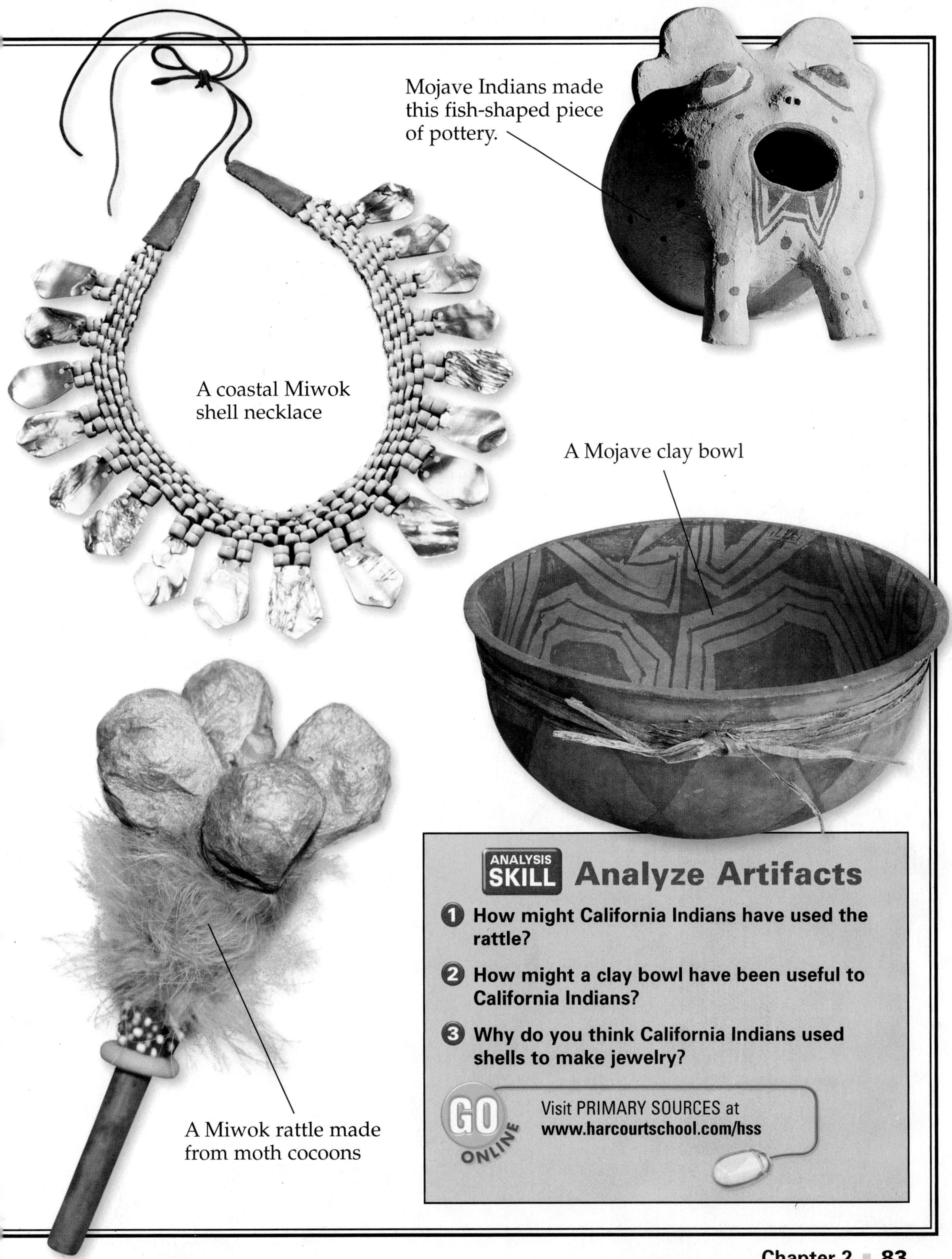

Mojave Indians made this fish-shaped piece of pottery.

A coastal Miwok shell necklace

A Mojave clay bowl

A Miwok rattle made from moth cocoons

ANALYSIS SKILL **Analyze Artifacts**

1. How might California Indians have used the rattle?
2. How might a clay bowl have been useful to California Indians?
3. Why do you think California Indians used shells to make jewelry?

GO ONLINE Visit PRIMARY SOURCES at **www.harcourtschool.com/hss**

Lesson 5

The Desert Region

WHAT TO KNOW
How did California Indians in the Desert Region adapt to or modify their dry environment?

- **Tell how the Indians of the Desert Region used the natural resources available to them.**
- **Explain how the Indians of the Desert Region developed lifeways different from those of most other California Indians.**

VOCABULARY
spring p. 85
arid p. 87
silt p. 87
agriculture p. 87

PEOPLE
Cahuilla
Serrano
Mojave

PLACES
San Bernardino Mountains
Colorado River

Focus Skill **MAIN IDEA AND DETAILS**

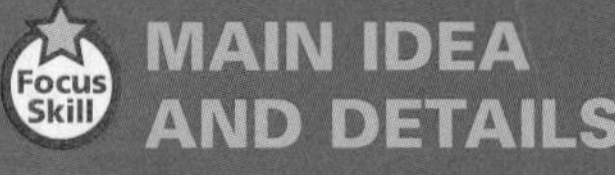
California Standards
HSS 4.1, 4.1.3, 4.2, 4.2.1

YOU ARE THERE You and your mother have been walking for several days. You think of your grandmother, who stayed behind in your village at the foot of the Santa Rosa Mountains. Though home in the desert seems far away, you know it's important to reach areas in which oak trees grow, so that you can gather enough acorns to feed your family through the winter. Adjusting the carrying net attached to your headband, you hurry to keep up with the others.

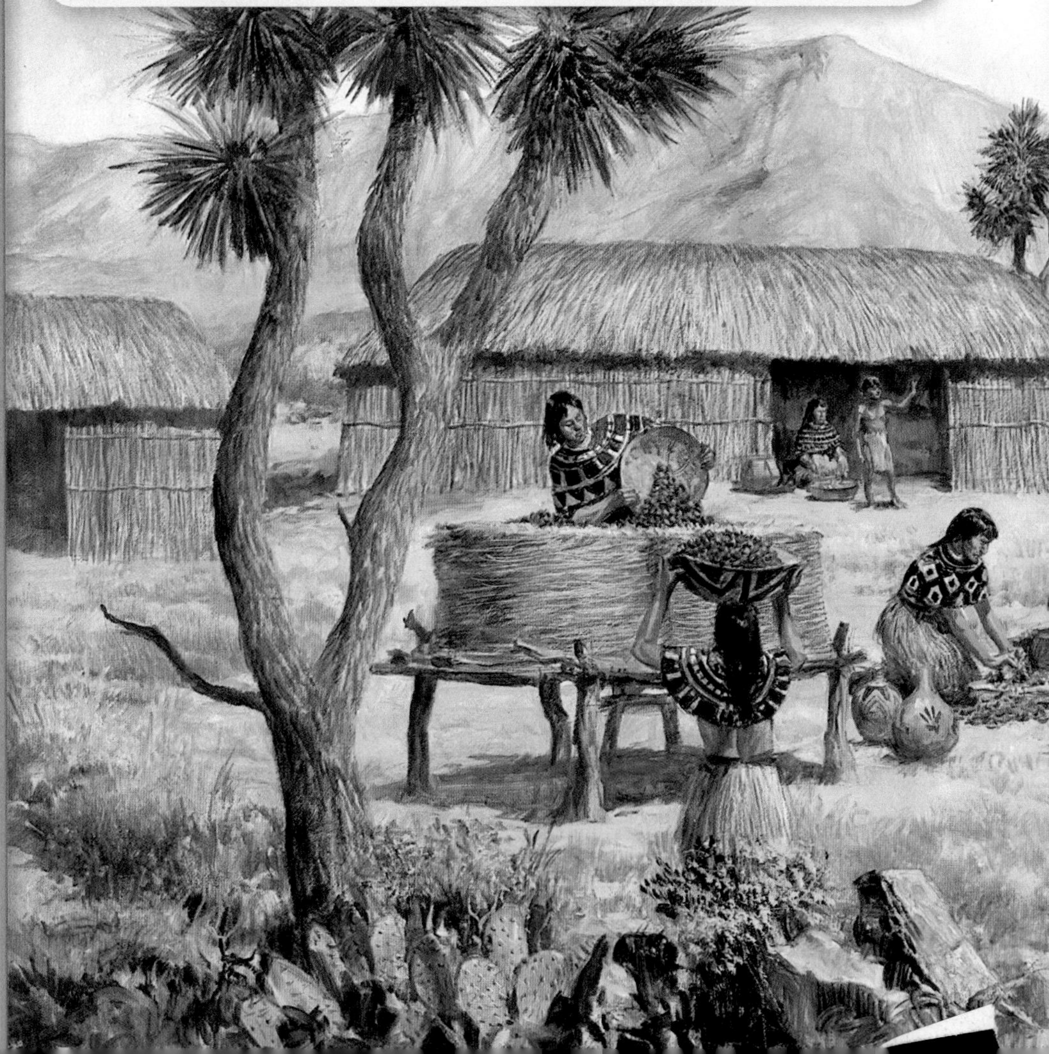

Cahuilla

Fewer people lived in the Desert Region than in other regions of California. Food was harder to find there, and people were always trying to hunt enough animals or to gather enough food to eat. They often spent part of the year in nearby mountain areas, where they gathered food and other resources. Some desert groups farmed and raised corn, beans, and squash.

Among the groups that lived in the Desert Region were the **Cahuilla** (kuh•WEE•yuh). Their lands stretched from the **San Bernardino Mountains** across the valleys of the San Jacinto and Santa Rosa Mountains. They included the foothills and desert areas at the base of the mountains.

The Cahuilla often built their villages in canyons, near streams or springs. At **springs**, water flowed through openings in the ground. In some areas, high canyon walls provided shade and protected the villages from strong winds.

Each year, during acorn gathering season, large numbers of Cahuilla Indians left their villages to gather acorns. At other times of the year, the Cahuilla gathered cactus, mesquite (muh•SKEET) beans, screwbeans, and piñon (PIN•yohn) nuts.

READING CHECK **MAIN IDEA AND DETAILS**
Why did the Cahuilla sometimes leave their villages?

ANALYSIS SKILL Analyze Maps **Cahuilla villages (below) were linked by a system of trading and hunting trails.**
Movement **In which direction did the Mojave travel to trade with groups along the Pacific coast?**

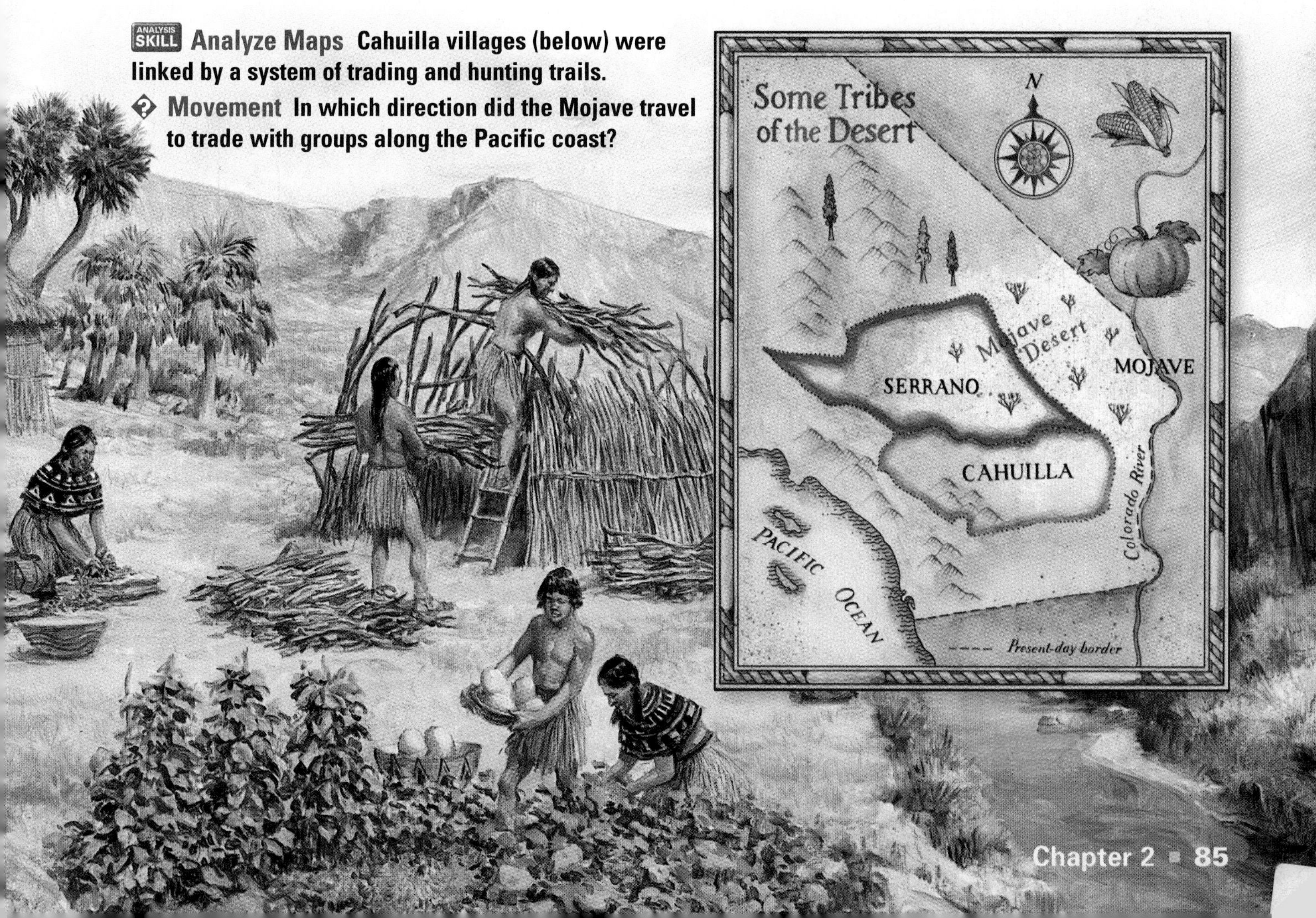

Cultural Heritage

California Indians Today

Today, more than 330,000 American Indians live in California. They belong to more than 100 different tribes. The greatest numbers live in the northwestern and central parts of the state. Most have come from tribes outside of California, however.

No matter where they live, Indian people in California are working to keep their cultures alive. They often gather to celebrate their traditional ways of life. At these gatherings, men and women wear traditional clothing and perform traditional dances.

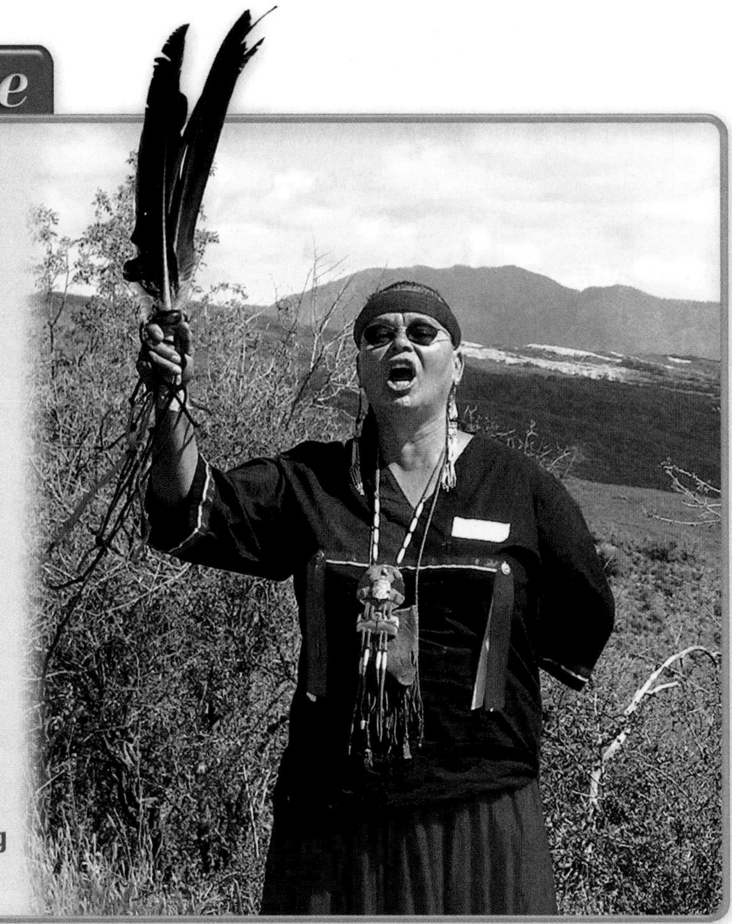

This Chumash religious leader is carrying on a tradition of his ancestors.

Cahuilla Lifeways

The Cahuilla built their houses out of brush. Some houses were dome-shaped. Others were rectangular. The Cahuilla built the largest houses for their village leaders and for special ceremonies.

Like other California Indians, the Cahuilla held ceremonies to celebrate important events. During these ceremonies, they wore special feathered headdresses, shook rattles, and performed dances and songs.

Mountains and deserts separated the Cahuilla from other Indian groups. Still, the Cahuilla traded with each other, with neighboring groups, and with groups who lived farther away. Their most important trading partners were the **Serrano**, who lived to the north, and the Gabrielino, who lived to the west.

Among the goods traded were shell beads, furs, and baskets. The Cahuilla also traded something that most other California Indians did not make—clay pots. They made these pots by coiling ropes of clay and then smoothing the sides. After the pots dried, they painted some of them. The Cahuilla used the pots for cooking as well as for storing food and water.

READING CHECK **COMPARE AND CONTRAST**
What item did the Cahuilla make that most other California Indians did not?

Mojave

The **Mojave** (moh•HAH•vee) Indians lived east of the Cahuilla Indians, in desert lands near the **Colorado River**. Not many plants or trees grow in this **arid**, or dry, land. Large animals are also scarce there. To survive in such a harsh environment, the Mojave developed ways of life very different from those of most other tribes in what is now California.

The Mojave built homes that protected them in the desert climate. In summer, they made open-sided, flat-topped shelters so that the wind could cool them. In winter, they made walls of logs and arrowweeds. They then covered the walls and roofs with mud to make them strong. Families built basket granaries on platforms to store food through the winter. They also made clay pots for storing food and water and for cooking.

The Colorado River was the most important source of water for the Mojave. It allowed them to grow some crops in the desert. Every spring, snow in the Rocky Mountains melted, causing water levels in the rivers to rise. Some years, the Colorado River overflowed and left a layer of silt along its banks. **Silt** is fine grains of soil and rock. The Mojave grew corn, beans, melons, and pumpkins in this rich soil.

The Mojave did not get all their food from **agriculture**, or farming. Women gathered seeds, cactus fruits, and mesquite beans. These foods were especially important when crops were poor due to drought. Men fished in the Colorado River and hunted small animals, such as rabbits, raccoons, and rattlesnakes.

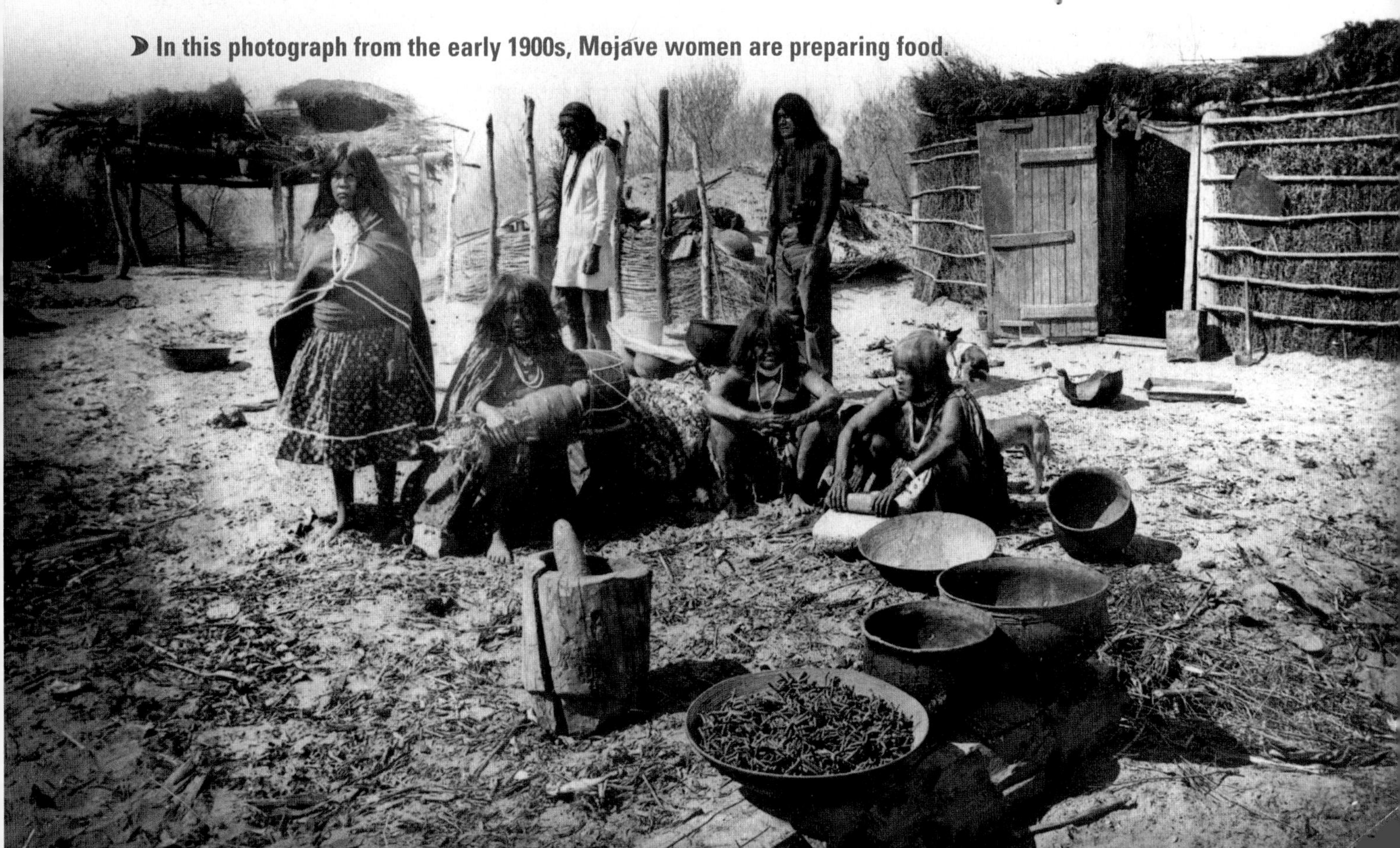

In this photograph from the early 1900s, Mojave women are preparing food.

The Mojave got most of what they needed from the lands around them. Like the Cahuilla, however, the Mojave sometimes traveled to gather food. At different times of the year, they went where they could find berries and nuts. For the Mojave, the desert made travel and trade difficult. Still, they are known to have traveled all the way to the Pacific coast to trade. Mojave traders sometimes ran most of the way.

READING CHECK SUMMARIZE
How was the Colorado River important to the Mojave?

This photograph of a Mojave woman with a clay pot was taken in 1900.

Summary

The Indians of the Desert Region adapted their ways of life to their arid environment. They hunted, farmed, and traveled long distances to gather food and to trade.

REVIEW

1. How did the California Indians in the Desert Region adapt to or modify their dry environment?
2. Use the term **silt** in describing Mojave farming.
3. How were Mojave and Cahuilla ways of life different from those of other California Indians?
4. What was one important difference between the Cahuilla and the Mojave?

CRITICAL THINKING

5. ANALYSIS SKILL How were the homes built by the Mojave well suited for the region?
6. **Draw a Mural** Make a mural showing that the Mojave and the Cahuilla had different ways of life, even though both lived in the desert.
7. Focus Skill **MAIN IDEA AND DETAILS** On a separate sheet of paper, copy and complete the graphic organizer below.

Main Idea		
Details		
traveled to gather food and to trade	made clay pots	Colorado River an important resource

Cheryl A. Seidner

*". . . My culture is in my blood. Whether I speak the language, sing the songs or weave the baskets. I know it's in me. . . ."**

Many American Indians today have worked to preserve the traditions of their culture. As tribal chairperson of the Wiyot tribe, Cheryl Seidner tries to keep alive the culture of what is left of her people. She also works to regain the land that once belonged to them.

In 1860, European settlers drove the Wiyot off their most sacred land. This land is an island, now called Indian Island, off the northern coast of California. With the loss of their land and of many tribe members, the Wiyots stopped performing traditional ceremonies, and stopped speaking their language.

By listening to old recordings, Seidner has been trying to learn the Wiyot language. She is also helping bring back her tribe's tradition of basket weaving. She encourages young girls of her tribe to learn this craft. Seidner has even helped her tribe get back more than 67 acres of the 270-acre island.

*Cheryl A. Seidner. From *Original Voices*, "Human Price of Gold Rush." http://www.originalvoices.org

Biography

Trustworthiness
Respect
Responsibility
Fairness
Caring
Patriotism

Why Character Counts

How has Cheryl Seidner taken responsibility for the future of her tribe?

Bio Brief

1950? Born — **PRESENT**

1996 Elected chairperson of the Wiyot tribe

2000 Helps her tribe buy back 1.5 acres of land on Indian Island

2004 Signs the deed to 40 additional acres of land on Indian Island

GO ONLINE Interactive Multimedia Biographies
Visit MULTIMEDIA BIOGRAPHIES at
www.harcourtschool.com/hss

Time

15,000 YEARS AGO

10,000 YEARS AGO

More than 13,000 years ago
People arrive in California

Reading Social Studies

The **main idea** is the most important idea of a passage. **Details** are facts, reasons, or examples that support the main idea.

Main Idea and Details

Complete this graphic organizer to show that you understand important ideas and details about how California Indians lived. A copy of this graphic organizer appears on page 24 of the Homework and Practice Book.

California's Indians

Main Idea

California Indians adapted to their environment and used the natural resources around them to meet their needs.

Details

used trees to build shelters and boats			

California Writing Prompts

Write a Report Make a list of the main sources of food of California Indians. Then write a brief report about the diets of different tribes and how and where they obtained their food. Use correct grammar, spelling, punctuation, and capitalization.

Write a Summary Think about games played by the Miwok. Write a paragraph that tells in your own words why games were important to them. Be sure that your paragraph has a clearly stated main idea and includes details to support that idea.

5,000 YEARS AGO

About 4,000 years ago
People in California begin to settle in villages

Present
More than 330,000 American Indians live in California

Use Vocabulary

Write the word from the box that best completes each sentence.

surplus, p. 58
artifact, p. 60
shaman, p. 64
granary, p. 78
silt, p. 87

1. The _____ led tribe members in a special ceremony.
2. Indians often stored their _____, or extra food, in baskets or clay pots.
3. Rivers that overflow often leave behind a layer of _____.
4. The villagers stored acorns in a _____.
5. An _____ is any object made by people in the past.

Use the Time Line

Use the chapter summary time line above to answer these questions.

6. When did people first come to the area that is now California?
7. When did Native Californians first settle in villages?

Apply Skills

Compare Tables

8. Examine the tables on page 75. Then write a paragraph that summarizes the information in each.

Recall Facts

Answer these questions.

9. How do artifacts help people learn about the early California Indians?
10. What natural resource did the Chumash use to waterproof their canoes?
11. How were the Mojave different from most other California Indian tribes?

Write the letter of the best choice.

12. How did the Yurok use the large trees that grew around them?
    - **A** They climbed them to look out over the forest.
    - **B** They used them to make bridges.
    - **C** They used them to build plank houses.
    - **D** They burned them to scare away wild animals.
13. Why did the Miwok build different types of homes?
    - **A** Miwok groups lived in different areas.
    - **B** They were a wealthy group.
    - **C** They moved often.
    - **D** They had to adapt to the desert climate.

Think Critically

14. ANALYSIS SKILL How did division of labor help California Indians meet their needs? Is this idea used today?
15. How were California Indians affected by the resources around them?

STATE INDIAN MUSEUM

GET READY

The State Indian Museum in Sacramento celebrates the cultures of California Indians. Exhibits and demonstrations at the museum reflect the heritage of more than 150 tribes, helping visitors experience a different way of life. Some artifacts on display include basketry, clothing, and beadwork. You can also see many historic photographs. As you learn about the ways of life of American Indians, you can try using the tools that they used. Hands-on exhibits allow you to experience what life was like for California Indians before European settlers arrived.

LOCATE IT

WHAT TO SEE

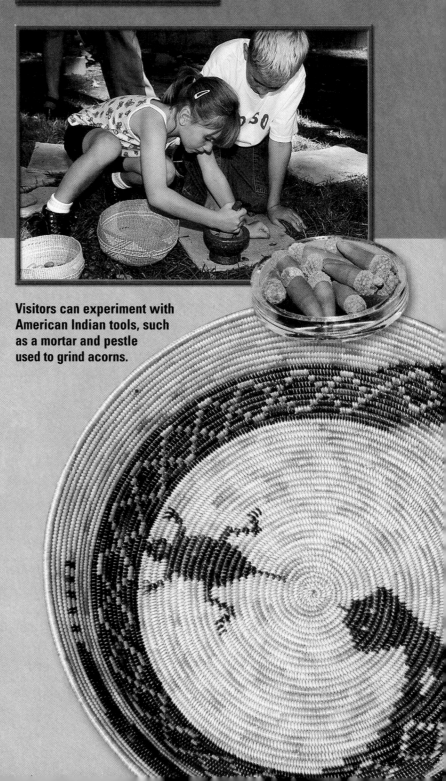

Visitors can experiment with American Indian tools, such as a mortar and pestle used to grind acorns.

Visitors to the State Indian Museum can see the different kinds of bows and arrows that American Indians used for hunting.

The museum features a display about Ishi, the last known Yahi Indian.

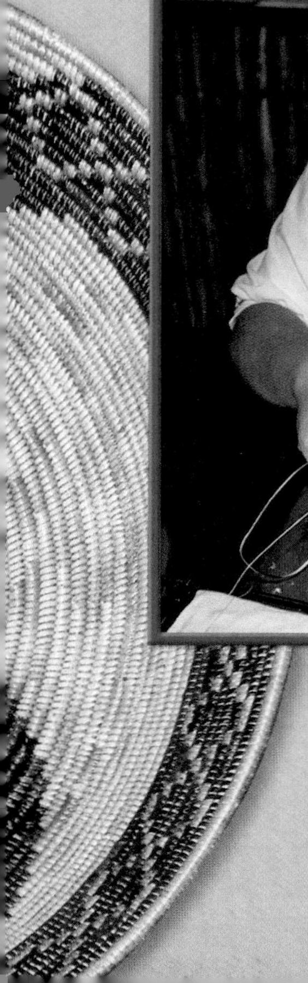

A girl learns the Pomo tradition of basket weaving. These baskets can be woven tightly enough to hold water, and many have designs and decorations.

A VIRTUAL TOUR

GO ONLINE Visit VIRTUAL TOURS at www.harcourtschool.com/hss

Review

THE BIG IDEA

Geography People in California have always interacted with their environment and been affected by it.

Summary

The Land and Early People

California is in the Northern Hemisphere, on the continent of North America. Its location on the Pacific coast makes it a place where people, goods, and ideas come together.

The state can be divided into four natural regions: the Coastal Region, the Mountain Region, the Central Valley, and the Desert Region. Thousands of years ago, groups of people came to California and explored these regions. Different groups found places to settle in each region. Living in different places, the groups developed their own cultures. However, they did share some things in common. They all used natural resources, and they all adapted to the land.

The California Indians' way of life was shaped by their surroundings, but they also changed their surroundings to meet their needs. In order to survive, the different groups also had to cooperate with each other by trading what they had for what they wanted.

Main Ideas and Vocabulary

Read the summary above. Then answer the questions that follow.

1. What is the meaning of the word hemisphere?
   A a line of latitude
   B a small ball
   C half of Earth
   D a natural region

2. How many natural regions are there in California?
   A three
   B four
   C five
   D six

3. What is the meaning of the word cooperate?
   A to fight with each other
   B to run machines
   C to build a single shelter
   D to work together

4. What was something that all California Indian groups had in common?
   A They all ate the same foods.
   B They all shared the same culture.
   C They all had to adapt to the land.
   D They all spoke the same language.

Recall Facts

Answer these questions.

5. What is California's location relative to Nevada and Arizona?
6. How do you find the absolute location of a place?
7. Why do the Desert and Mountain Regions have fewer people than other regions?
8. What makes the Central Valley such a good region for farming?
9. What are some ways we can learn about early California Indians?
10. How did the Chumash get the materials they used to build plank canoes?
11. Why did the Yurok perform the First Salmon Ceremony?
12. Why did the Mojave develop a way of life that was different from that of most other California Indians?

Write the letter of the best choice.

13. Which of these phrases describes California's relative location?
    - **A** south of the equator
    - **B** in the Eastern Hemisphere
    - **C** west of the prime meridian
    - **D** near the North Pole
14. Which of the following statements is true about the southern coast of California?
    - **A** It has mountains that drop sharply into the Pacific Ocean.
    - **B** It has flat land with sandy beaches.
    - **C** It has no natural harbors.
    - **D** It has no islands.
15. Why were acorns an important food source for many California Indians?
    - **A** They were easy to cook.
    - **B** They were plentiful in many regions.
    - **C** They could be grown in gardens.
    - **D** There were no other food sources.

Think Critically

16. ANALYSIS SKILL What places in California would you expect to have the warmest temperatures?
17. ANALYSIS SKILL How does having a dependable supply of food affect a society?

Apply Skills

Use an Elevation Map

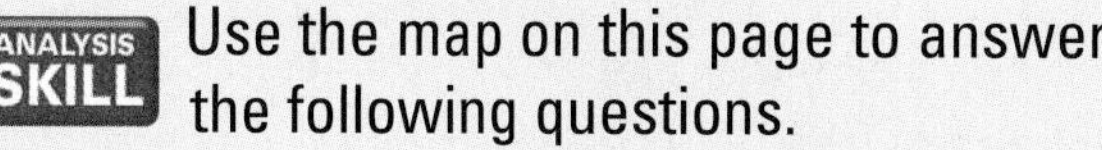

Use the map on this page to answer the following questions.

18. What is the elevation of the land around Long Beach?
19. Which city has a higher elevation, Los Angeles or San Bernardino?
20. Which city has a lower elevation, San Diego or Palm Springs?

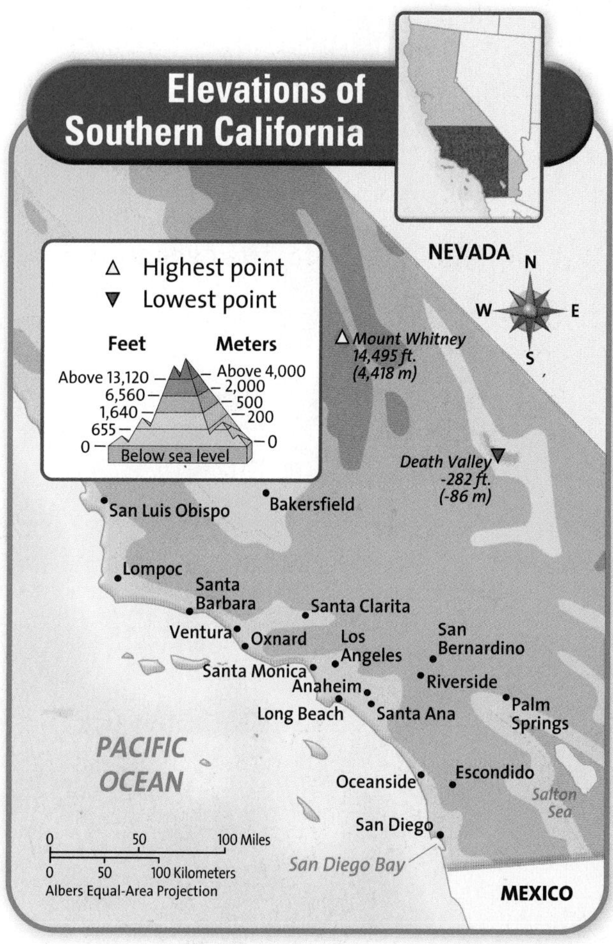

Unit 1

Activities

Read More

- *Ishi* by Sheila Sweeny.

- *Channel Islands National Park* by Renee Skelton.

- *Saving the Redwoods* by Sheila Sweeny.

Show What You Know

Unit Writing Activity

Write a Summary The natural regions of California have different physical and human features. Write a summary that explains the differences in the physical and human features among the regions. Tell how the features of each region affected both early groups living there and people living in the region today. Make sure to include significant details and to express main ideas in your summary.

Unit Project

Make a California Atlas Gather information about the geography of one of California's natural regions, and research the early groups of American Indians who lived there. Then make an atlas about the region. Illustrate it with maps and drawings. Include information about the region's people and their lives, both now and in the past.

GO ONLINE Visit ACTIVITIES at **www.harcourtschool.com/hss**

Early California

Unit 2

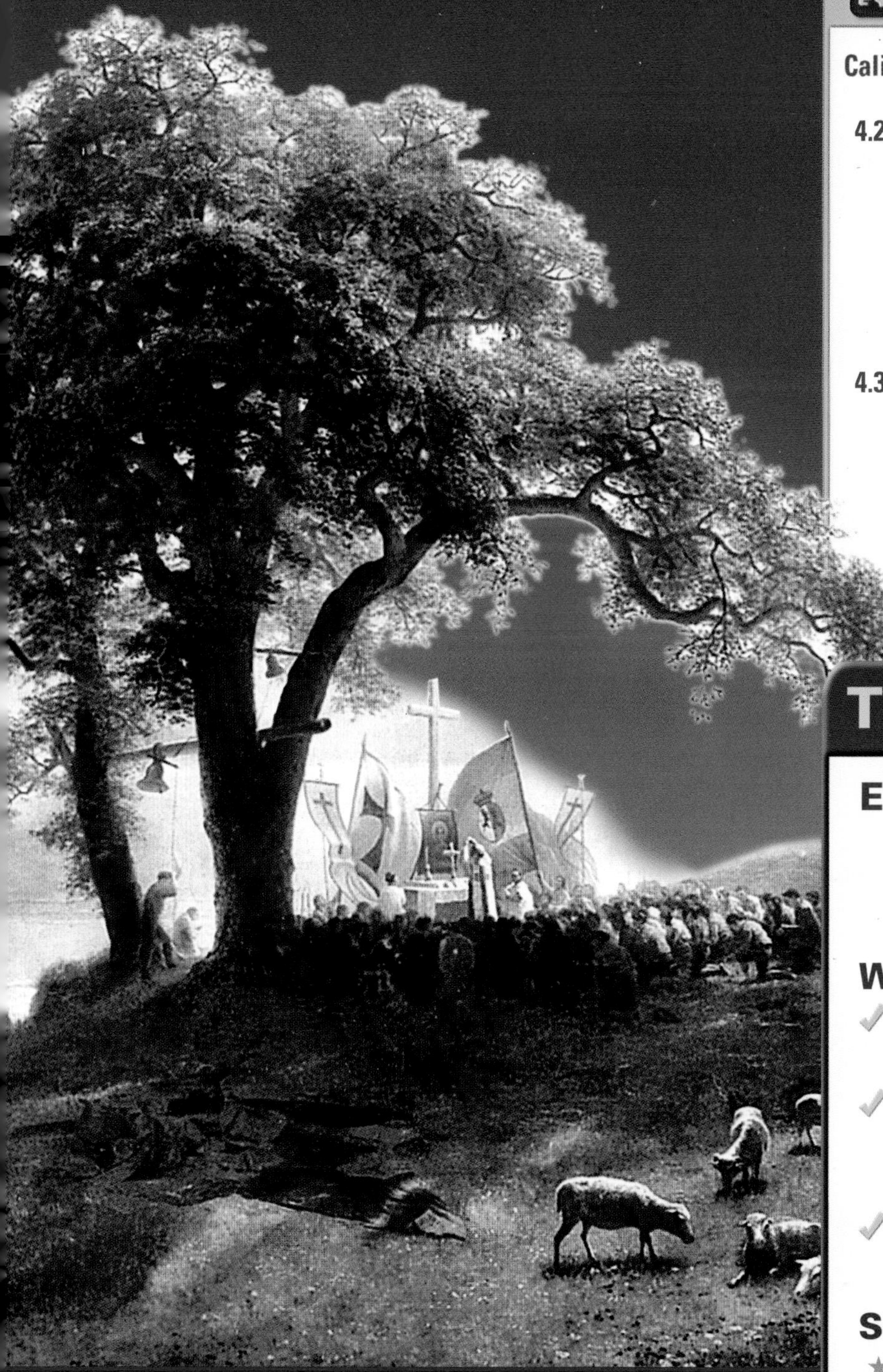

California History-Social Science Standards

4.2 Students describe the social, political, cultural, and economic life and interactions among people of California from the pre-Columbian societies to the Spanish mission and Mexican rancho periods.

4.3 Students explain the economic, social, and political life in California from the establishment of the Bear Flag Republic through the Mexican-American War, the Gold Rush, and the granting of statehood.

The Big Idea

Exploration

Explorations led to interactions between Europeans and California Indians.

What to Know

- ✓ What land and sea routes did Europeans first take to California?
- ✓ How did the Spanish mission system affect people and settlements in California?
- ✓ What was the effect of Mexican rule on people in California?

Show What You Know

- ★ Unit 2 Test
- Writing: A Narrative
- Unit Project: A California Museum Display

Unit 2

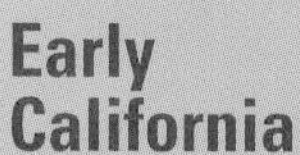

Time

Early California

1535 Hernando Cortés reaches Baja California, p. 112

1542 Juan Rodríguez Cabrillo explores Alta California and claims the area for Spain, p. 112

1535

1635

At the Same Time

1620 The Pilgrims land in what is today Massachusetts

Early California

1769 Junípero Serra establishes the first missions in Alta California at San Diego, p. 121

1821 Mexico wins independence from Spain, p. 151

1834 The end of church rule of the missions is ordered, p. 152

1735

1835

1776 The 13 English colonies declare their independence

1806 Meriwether Lewis and William Clark reach the Pacific Ocean

1825 Almost all of Spanish South America is independent

Unit 2

People

Junípero Serra

1713–1784

- Spanish priest who founded the first mission in Alta California, near San Diego Bay
  - Worked to convert the Indians in Alta California to Christianity and to show them European ways

Juan Crespí

1721–1782

- Spanish priest who joined Gaspar de Portolá's 1769 expedition
  - Recorded details of the expedition's voyage in a diary that was later published

1700 | 1750

1713 • Junípero Serra 1784

1721 • Juan Crespí 1782

1723? • Gaspar de Portolá 1784?

1728 • James Cook 1779

1761? • Toypurina

Toypurina

1761?–1799

- Gabrielino Indian and shaman who planned a revolt against the missionaries at Mission San Gabriel
  - Jailed as punishment

Juana Briones de Miranda

1802?–1889

- Successful businesswoman and owner of Rancho La Purísima Concepción
  - Became a healer after Indians shared with her their knowledge of using plants and herbs as medicine

Gaspar de Portolá

1723?–1784?

- Led an overland expedition from Baja California to San Diego and Monterey Bays in Alta California in 1769
- Discovered tar pits in what is now Los Angeles. Today they are known as the Rancho La Brea Tar Pits

James Cook

1728–1779

- British navy captain who in 1778 looked for a waterway that connected the Atlantic and Pacific Oceans
- The first known European to land on Vancouver Island and to reach the Hawaiian Islands

1800 | 1850 | 1900

1799

1802? • Juana Briones de Miranda 1889

1808 • Mariano Vallejo 1890

1819 • Lorenzo Asisara ?

Mariano Vallejo

1808–1890

- Commander in the Mexican army and owner of a large California rancho
- Imprisoned during the Bear Flag Revolt, even though he supported California statehood
- A delegate to California's constitutional convention and later elected to the United States Senate

Lorenzo Asisara

1819–?

- Indian who was born and raised at Mission Santa Cruz
- Wrote a detailed account of mission life

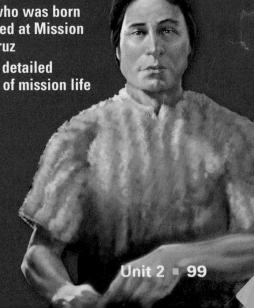

Unit 2

Place

California in New Spain, 1776

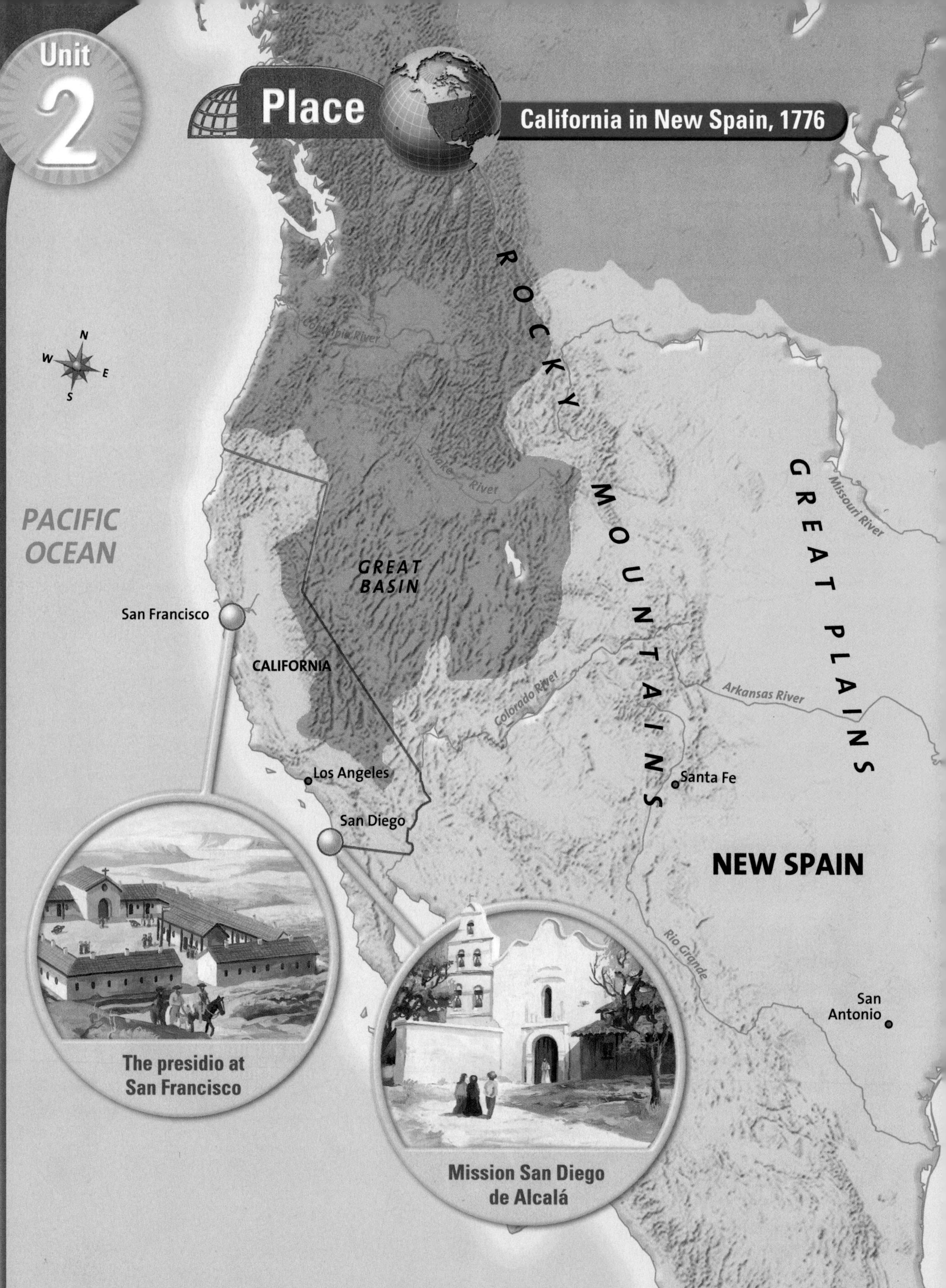

The presidio at San Francisco

Mission San Diego de Alcalá

MAINE
(PART OF MA)
NH
MA
RI
CT
NEW YORK
PENNSYLVANIA
NEW JERSEY
MARYLAND
DELAWARE
VIRGINIA
NORTH CAROLINA
SOUTH CAROLINA
GEORGIA
APPALACHIAN MOUNTAINS
Lake Superior
Lake Michigan
Lake Huron
Lake Ontario
Lake Erie
St. Lawrence River
Mississippi River
Ohio River
New Orleans
ATLANTIC OCEAN
Gulf of Mexico
At the Same Time
Independence Hall, in Philadelphia
Spanish lands
British lands
The 13 British colonies
Unclaimed lands
Present-day California border
0
250
500 Miles
0
250
500 Kilometers
Lambert Equal-Area Projection

Unit 2

Reading Social Studies

Focus Skill Generalize

When you **generalize**, you make a broad statement that summarizes a group of facts and shows how they are related. The statement you make is called a **generalization**.

Why It Matters

Being able to generalize can help you better understand and remember what you read.

Facts

information given	information given	information given

Generalization

general statement about that information

- ✓ A generalization is always based on facts.
- ✓ Look for these generalization signal words:

most **many** **some** **generally** **usually**

Practice the Skill

Read the paragraphs, and make a generalization based on the information in the second paragraph.

Facts / Generalization

The Mojave Indians lived in the desert. The climate there is scorching hot in summer, and winter nights are often very cold. Plants, trees, and large animals are scarce in this arid land. (People usually do not live in desert regions.)

Several Indian groups lived on California's northern coast. The climate there is warm in the summer and cool in the winter. There were plenty of animals to hunt. They could also gather food from plants and use trees to build shelters and canoes.

Apply What You Learned

 **Generalize Read the paragraphs, and answer the questions.**

Horses in North America

Long before the Spanish first arrived on the continent, horses roamed North America. Thousands of years ago, large herds of these animals galloped freely over the land. Then, sometime between 5,000 and 10,000 years ago, the horses disappeared. No one knows for sure why this happened. Some causes may have been changes in the weather and too much hunting by native people.

In the 1500s, Spanish explorers brought horses with them to North America. Over time, some Spanish horses escaped or were freed. They formed wild herds that thrived, or grew, in many parts of North America. Native peoples of the Great Plains and other places learned to tame these animals. Horses helped them move from place to place more easily. Because people could usually move faster on horseback, horses also helped American Indians be better hunters.

As Spanish explorers and settlers made their way from Mexico to what would become California, they brought many horses with them. Horses carried supplies the explorers and settlers needed to survive and often helped them travel great distances. Later, horses were important in the growth of California's ranching industry.

Generalize

1. **What generalization can you make about the way Spanish explorers and settlers used horses?**
2. **What generalization can you make about the way American Indians used horses?**

Study Skills

USE VISUALS

Visuals can help you better understand and remember what you read.

- **Photographs, illustrations, diagrams, charts, and maps are different kinds of visuals. Many visuals have titles, captions, or labels that help readers understand what is shown.**
- **Visuals often show information from the text, but in a different way. They may also add information.**

Checklist for Visuals	
✓	What kind of visual is shown? a photograph
	What does the visual show?
	What does the visual tell you about the topic?
	How does the visual help you understand what you are reading?

Apply As You Read

Look closely at the visuals and the text that goes with them. Answer the questions in the checklist to better understand how a visual can help as you read.

California History-Social Science Standards, Grade 4

4.2 Students describe the social, political, cultural, and economic life and interactions among people of California from the pre-Columbian societies to the Spanish mission and Mexican rancho periods.

CHAPTER

Exploration and Early Settlements

Cabrillo National Monument, San Diego

A Voyage of Faith

Father Serra in California

by Jim McGovern
illustrated by John Martin

In 1769, the Spanish government sent four expeditions to California to build settlements. Two of the expeditions traveled over land. The other two traveled by sea. One of the land expeditions was led by an army captain, Gaspar de Portolá (pawr•toh•LAH). A Catholic priest named Junípero Serra (hoo•NEE•pay•roh SAIR•rah) traveled with him. Read now about their journey to San Diego, where the Spanish expeditions were to meet and build their first settlement.

Mile after mile, day after day, week after week, the group traveled across the rugged terrain. As their food ran low, many of the men grew tired and sick. Father Serra himself suffered from a sore on one leg that grew worse each day. And yet he never gave up, calling on his faith in God to keep himself going.

Finally, as the month of June passed, the land around them grew less harsh. They found wild grapes along the route, and roses that reminded Father Serra of his native Spain. Although most of the men were sick and weak, they felt sure that they would soon reach San Diego.

As they grew closer to their goal, the men came across several large villages, home to Tipai (also called Kumeyaay) Indians. The Tipai had never seen anyone like the Spanish, who wore heavy cloth shirts, loose trousers called pantaloons, sturdy boots, and leather jackets.

terrain an area of land

native related to a person's place of birth

The Indian translators who had come with the Spanish could not understand the Tipai language. Of course, the Tipai could not speak a word of Spanish. Still, the Tipai and the Spanish were curious about one another. Together, they found ways to communicate with hand gestures.

In a letter to a fellow priest, Father Serra reported that the Indians were friendly to their strange visitors. He also described how the two groups came together to trade. The Indians, Father Serra reported, were only interested in the cloth that the Spanish carried with them. The Spanish wanted the fish and other food the Indians had. Back and forth the trading went, until both sides were satisfied.

As the expedition moved still closer to San Diego, Father Serra was pleased to find many more villages. As the Spanish and the Indians came together to visit and trade, the Indians often brought their babies and children with them. In one village a mother placed her baby in Serra's arms, which brought a smile to the priest's face. As the baby squirmed in his arms, Serra longed to baptize the baby and to make her a member of the Catholic Church. In his mind, Father Serra could already see the missions he would build. Here this baby and other Indians would come to learn the Catholic religion. Their children would go to school and new settlements would grow up around each mission. As he left the village, Serra made a sign of the cross over the Tipais, blessing them.

On the morning of July 1, the expedition finally came within sight of San Diego Bay. Looking out across the bright blue waters, sparkling in the sunshine, they could see two Spanish ships. Finally, there was to be some relief for the weary expedition! Although he was thrilled at the sight, Father Serra later wrote of the difficult voyage these ships had made. One of the ships, the *San Carlos*, had gotten lost trying to find the bay. Much of the water on board had turned out to be unfit to drink. Many of the crew had died before the ship finally found its way to San Diego.

Still, despite all of these hardships, Father Serra's faith stayed strong. And he knew that he would need that faith as he continued his work. First, he would build the mission at San Diego. And then, there would be many, many others.

expedition a trip made for a special reason, such as to explore a place or find a treasure

mission a religious settlement

Response Corner

1. Why do you think the Spanish sent priests as well as soldiers to California?
2. Work with a partner. Imagine that one of you is a Tipai Indian. One of you is a Spanish soldier. Role-play a trade, using gestures only.

Lesson 1

Time

1535 | 1685 | 1835

1535 Hernando Cortés reaches Baja California

1542 Juan Rodríguez Cabrillo explores Alta California

1602 Sebastián Vizcaíno sails to Monterey Bay

WHAT TO KNOW
Why did Europeans explore the Americas?

- ✓ Identify the sea routes of early explorers of California and the North Pacific.
- ✓ Explain the effects of waterways on exploration.

VOCABULARY
conquistador p. 111
cost p. 111
benefit p. 111
peninsula p. 112
galleon p. 114
ocean current p. 114
wind pattern p. 114

PEOPLE
Juan Rodríguez Cabrillo
Francis Drake
Sebastián Rodríguez Cermeño
Sebastián Vizcaíno

PLACES
Alta California
Baja California

GENERALIZE

California Standards
HSS 4.2, 4.2.2, 4.2.3

Explorers Come to California

YOU ARE THERE Imagine that you're a Spanish sailor in the 1500s. Today, you're about to land on the coast of California. Up above, the sails of your ship flap loudly in the wind. Below your feet, the deck rocks back and forth on the Pacific waters. Looking out at the new land, you wonder if your trip will bring you gold, silver, and other riches. You can hardly wait until it is time to row to shore!

Hernando Cortés came to the Americas looking for treasure, like the piece of Aztec jewelry above.

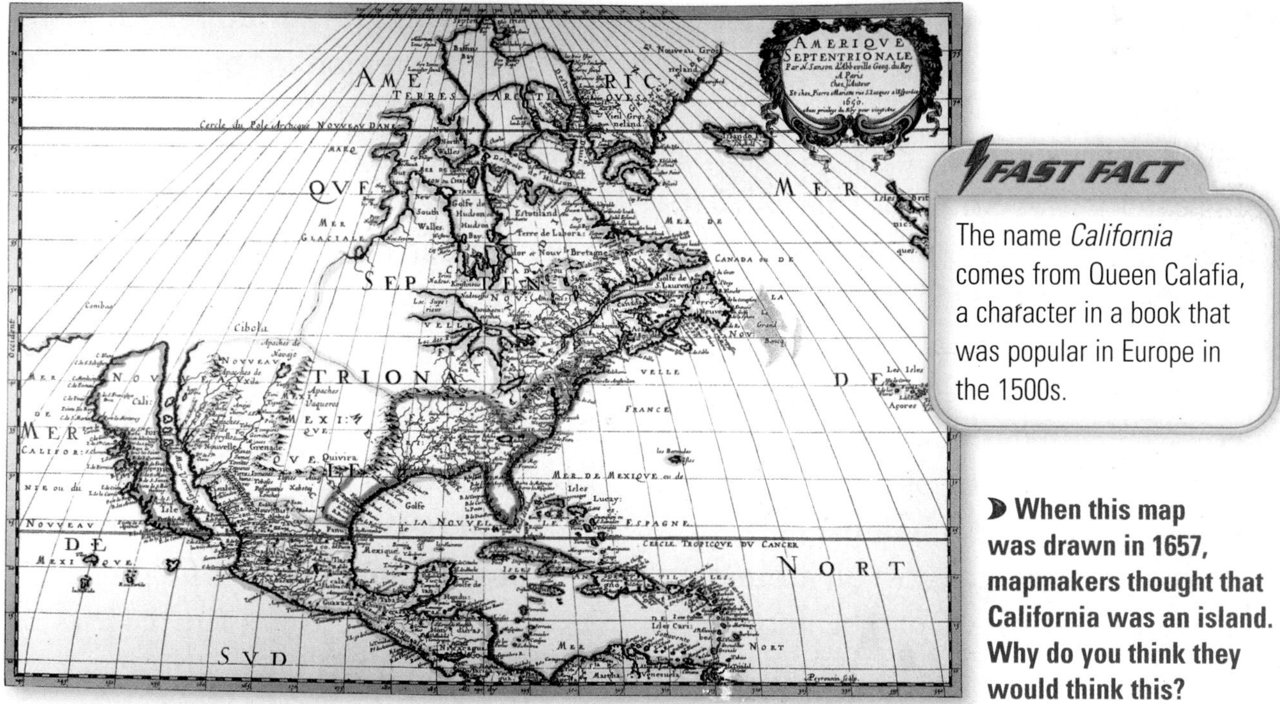

FAST FACT

The name *California* comes from Queen Calafia, a character in a book that was popular in Europe in the 1500s.

When this map was drawn in 1657, mapmakers thought that California was an island. Why do you think they would think this?

The Conquistadors

By the early 1500s, Spain had claimed large parts of the Americas. Some Spanish explorers came in search of riches. Others wanted to change the beliefs of the native peoples, or convert them, to Christianity. These explorers are known as **conquistadors** (kahn•KEES•tuh•dawrz), or conquerors. The lands they conquered became known as New Spain.

In 1521, a conquistador named Hernando Cortés (er•NAHN•doh kawr•TEZ) attacked the Aztec Indians in Mexico. Cortés and his soldiers defeated the Aztec and took their gold, silver, and jewels. Then he tore down the city of Tenochtitlán (tay•nawch•teet•LAHN). In its place, the Spanish built Mexico City as the capital of New Spain.

Explorers in the Americas also searched for a shortcut to Asia. Europeans wanted to trade for silk and spices there. At the time, however, European ships had to sail all the way around the tip of either South America or Africa to reach Asia.

Spanish explorers had heard stories about a narrow waterway called the Strait of Anián (ah•nee•AHN). It was supposed to connect the Atlantic and Pacific Oceans. Finding this strait would come with a high **cost**. It meant that Spain would have to send ships and sailors into the northern Pacific Ocean. Still, if the route were found, it would be of great **benefit**, or help, to the Spanish. It would shorten the trip to Asia, making trade with Asia easier.

READING CHECK **GENERALIZE**
Why did conquistadors travel to New Spain?

Looking for a Shortcut

TIME 1542
PLACE Alta California

In search of the Strait of Anián, Cortés sailed north from the western coast of Mexico. In 1535, he reached what he thought was an island and claimed it for Spain. Other explorers discovered later that the region was not an island. It was a peninsula (puh•NIN•suh•luh). A **peninsula** is land that has water almost all around it. The area would come to be known as **Baja California**. *Baja* (BAH•hah) means "lower" in Spanish.

Cortés never found the Strait of Anián, but other Spanish explorers continued to look for it. In June 1542, **Juan Rodríguez Cabrillo** (rohd•REE•ges kah•BREE•yoh) set out from Mexico to explore the area that Spain would later call **Alta California**. *Alta* means "high" or "upper" in Spanish. The region is "higher," or farther north, than Baja California. Cabrillo's ships carried 250 sailors and soldiers. They reached San Diego Bay in September 1542.

Cabrillo and his crew continued to sail north and met Chumash Indians. Of the meeting, Cabrillo wrote:

> **"We saw an Indian town on the land next to the sea, with large houses built much like those of New Spain. Many fine canoes each with twelve or thirteen Indians came to the ships."***

Cabrillo and his crew sailed even farther north. They found neither treasures nor a shortcut to Asia. However, Cabrillo's voyage did help the Spanish learn about the coast of Alta California.

*Juan Rodríguez Cabrillo. From *Relation of the Voyage of Juan Rodríguez Cabrillo, 1542–1543.* American Journeys Collection, Document No. AJ-001. Wisconsin Historical Society, 2003.

FAST FACT

During Cabrillo's voyage to California, he broke one of his legs. The leg became infected and, as a result, Cabrillo died.

This painting shows what Cabrillo's landing in Alta California in 1542 might have looked like.

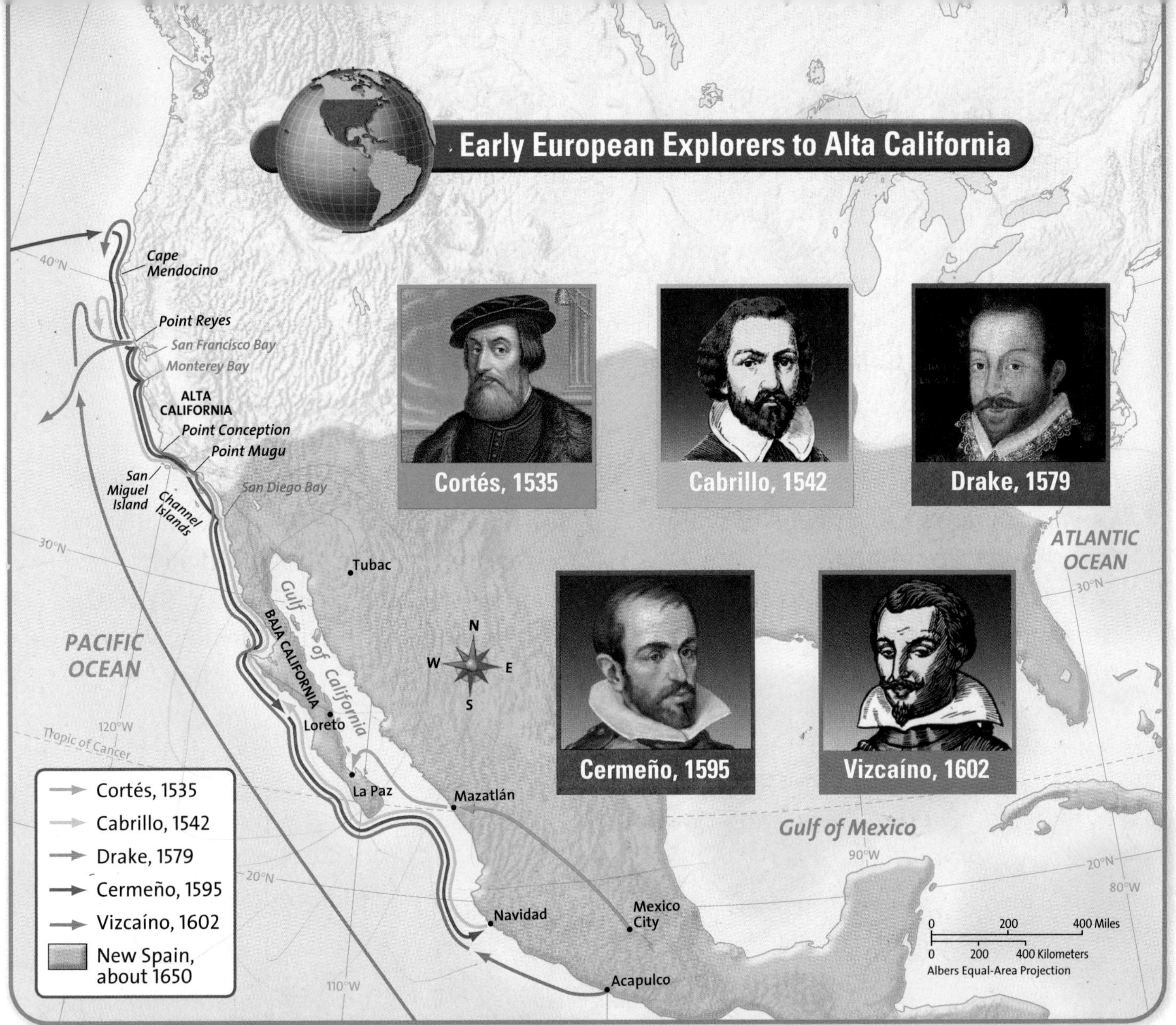

ANALYSIS SKILL Analyze Maps

Movement Which explorer sailed farthest north?

Soon other European countries joined in the search for a waterway between the Atlantic and Pacific Oceans. In December 1577, English explorer **Francis Drake** set sail for New Spain. There, he attacked Spanish ships and settlements and took their gold and other riches.

Drake crossed the Atlantic and sailed through the Strait of Magellan at the southern tip of South America. While sailing north along the Pacific coast, Drake attacked several Spanish settlements. In one raid, Drake's crew took 80 pounds of gold!

In the summer of 1579, Drake reached the California coast. He claimed the land for England and then circled the globe before returning home to England.

READING CHECK SUMMARIZE

How would a waterway connecting the Atlantic and Pacific Oceans be helpful to Europeans?

Spanish Trading Ships

Before Drake sailed along the coast of California, Spain began sending **galleons** (GA•lee•uhnz) full of gold and silver across the Pacific Ocean. These large trading ships traveled west to the Philippine Islands, in Asia. Winds and ocean currents helped move the ships quickly across the ocean—often in about three months. **Ocean currents** are streams of water that move through the ocean.

The galleons returned to New Spain, carrying spices and other treasures from Asia. On the trip back, ocean currents and **wind patterns**, or the general direction of the winds, were different. This journey took much longer—often half a year or more—and food supplies and fresh water often ran low.

In 1595, **Sebastián Rodríguez Cermeño** (sair•MAY•nyoh) sailed from the Philippines to the coast of California. He was to look for a safe harbor where sailors could stop for repairs and supplies. **Sebastián Vizcaíno** (vees•kah•EE•noh) also wanted to find a good harbor. In 1602, he traveled north from Mexico. When Vizcaíno entered Monterey Bay, he

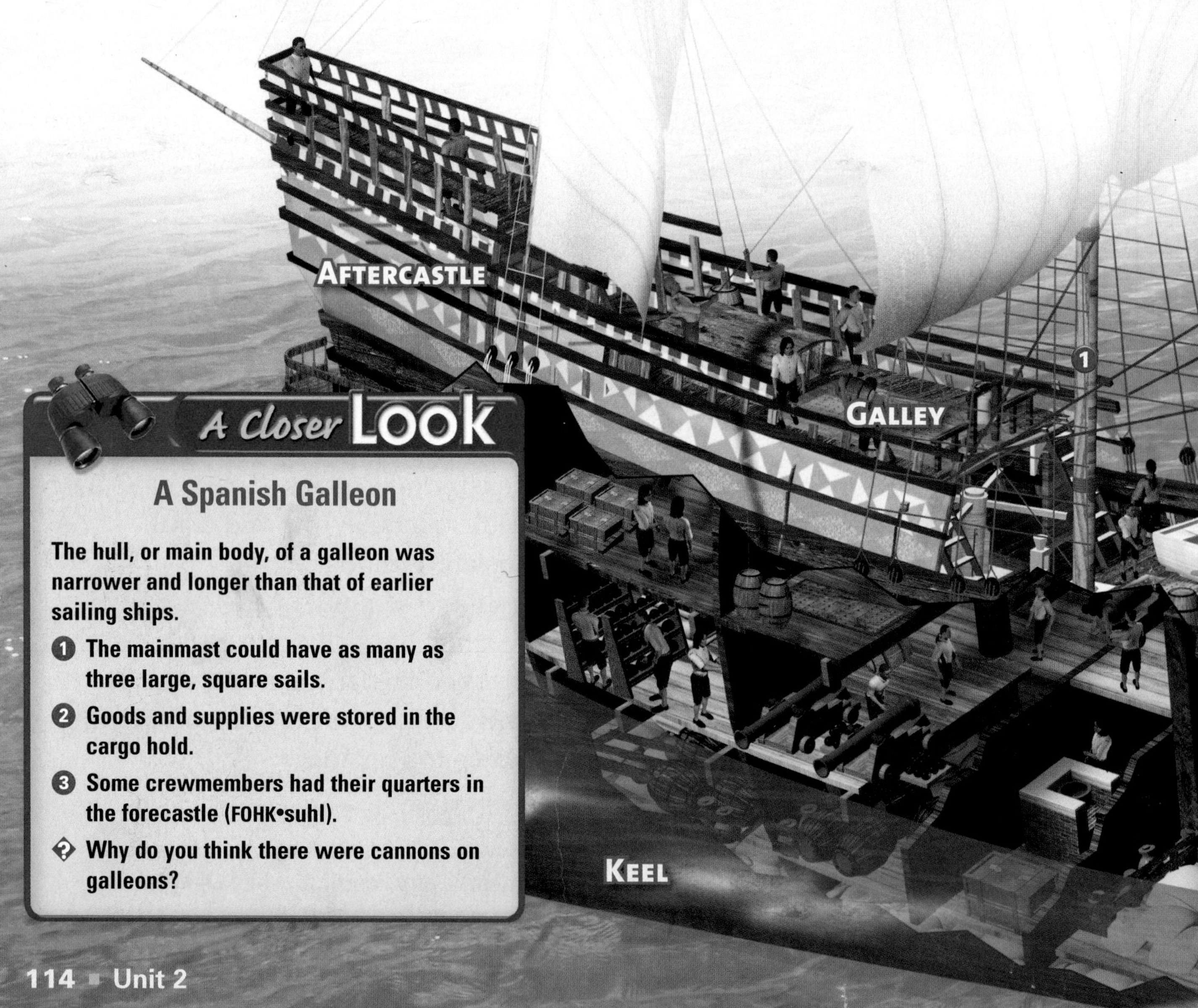

A Closer LOOK

A Spanish Galleon

The hull, or main body, of a galleon was narrower and longer than that of earlier sailing ships.

1. The mainmast could have as many as three large, square sails.
2. Goods and supplies were stored in the cargo hold.
3. Some crewmembers had their quarters in the forecastle (FOHK•suhl).

? Why do you think there were cannons on galleons?

reported that it was "the best port that could be desired," and "sheltered from all winds."* However, Spain quickly lost interest in Alta California because it did not seem to have gold or silver.

READING CHECK **CAUSE AND EFFECT**
Why did people who sailed from the Philippines want a harbor in California?

*Sebastián Vizcaíno. From *Diary of Sebastián Vizcaíno, 1602–1603.* American Journeys Collection, Document No. AJ-002. Wisconsin Historical Society, 2003.

Summary

The first Spanish explorers in the Americas hoped to find riches, and they looked for a strait connecting the Atlantic and Pacific Oceans. Later, explorers looked for safe harbors in Alta California for galleons.

FORECASTLE

3

BEAKHEAD

2

REVIEW

1. Why did Europeans explore the Americas?
2. Use the terms **galleon** and **ocean current** in a sentence about Spanish trade.
3. How did ocean currents and wind patterns affect galleons sailing across the Pacific Ocean?

CRITICAL THINKING

4. ANALYSIS SKILL How would finding the Strait of Anián have helped Spanish traders?
5. **Write a Journal Entry** Imagine that you are one of the crew of a galleon exploring the coast of California. Write a journal entry telling the reason for the trip.
6. Focus Skill **GENERALIZE**
On a separate sheet of paper, copy and complete the graphic organizer below.

Facts

Generalization

Europeans had different reasons for exploring the western coast of North America.

FAST FACT

Many sailors on galleons died from disease, pirate attacks, or starvation. Most galleons returned to Mexico from the Philippines with only a few survivors.

Map and Globe Skills

Follow Routes on a Historical Map

WHY IT MATTERS

A historical map gives information about a place as it was in the past. It may show the route that people followed as they traveled from one place to another. Knowing how to follow a route on a historical map can help you gather information about how people in the past traveled.

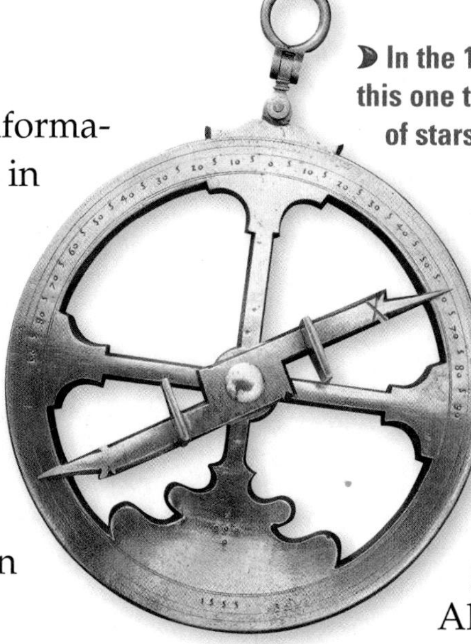

In the 1500s, sailors used astrolabes like this one to navigate based on the position of stars.

WHAT YOU NEED TO KNOW

The map on page 117 shows some of the main routes the Spanish galleons sailed in the 1500s. It also shows the Pacific Ocean's main ocean currents and wind patterns. Carrying gold and silver from New Spain, Spanish galleons would sail west across the Pacific Ocean to the Philippine Islands. Trade winds and ocean currents carried the galleons from Acapulco, a city in New Spain, to Manila, in the Philippines.

In the Philippine Islands, the sailors traded the silver for Asian spices, silk, and jewels, which they would take back to New Spain to be sold. On the return trip, sailors had to steer the galleons north and east to find the best wind patterns and ocean currents. These currents and wind patterns took the Spanish galleons near the coast of Alta California.

PRACTICE THE SKILL

Answer these questions.

1. What color shows the route from New Spain to the Philippine Islands?
2. In what direction did the galleons sail to reach New Spain from the Philippine Islands?
3. Which route was farther north, the route from New Spain to the Philippine Islands or the route from the Philippine Islands to New Spain? Why did the ships sail so far north?

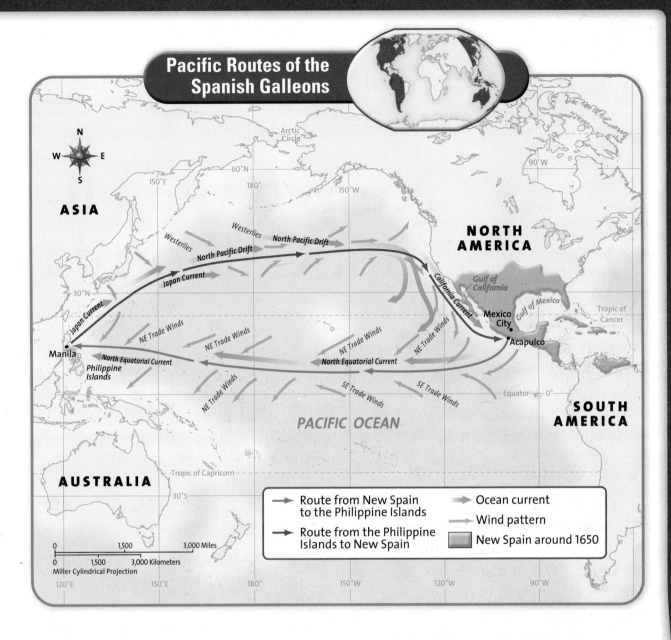

Pacific Routes of the Spanish Galleons

ASIA
NORTH AMERICA
SOUTH AMERICA
AUSTRALIA
PACIFIC OCEAN
Arctic Circle
Tropic of Cancer
Equator 0°
Tropic of Capricorn
60°N
30°N
30°S
150°E
180°
150°W
120°W
90°W
120°E
Westerlies
North Pacific Drift
Japan Current
California Current
NE Trade Winds
SE Trade Winds
North Equatorial Current
Gulf of California
Gulf of Mexico
Mexico City
Acapulco
Manila
Philippine Islands
N
S
E
W

0 | 1,500 | 3,000 Miles
0 | 1,500 | 3,000 Kilometers
Miller Cylindrical Projection

Route from New Spain to the Philippine Islands
Route from the Philippine Islands to New Spain
Ocean current
Wind pattern
New Spain around 1650

APPLY WHAT YOU LEARNED

ANALYSIS SKILL Review the map on page 113, showing the routes of Cortés, Cabrillo, Drake, Cermeño, and Vizcaíno. Write three questions about their routes that this map can answer. Then share your questions with a partner. You and your partner can answer each other's questions and explain how you used the map to answer each one.

Practice your map and globe skills with the **GeoSkills CD-ROM**.

Lesson 2

Time

1535 | 1685 | 1835

1769 Father Junípero Serra starts the first mission in Alta California

1770 Serra sets up a mission near Monterey Bay

1775–1776 Juan Bautista de Anza leads settlers overland to Alta California

WHAT TO KNOW
How did Spain begin to settle Alta California?

- ✓ Identify the land and sea routes taken to California by early settlers.
- ✓ Describe the hardships the Spanish faced in settling Alta California.

VOCABULARY
colony p. 119
mission p. 119
missionary p. 119
expedition p. 120

PEOPLE
Vitus Bering
James Cook
Gaspar de Portolá
Junípero Serra
Fernando Rivera y Moncada
Juan Crespí
Juan Bautista de Anza

PLACES
San Diego Bay
San Diego de Alcalá

GENERALIZE

California Standards
HSS 4.2, 4.2.2, 4.2.3

Newcomers to Alta California

YOU ARE THERE The year is 1765. Leaders in New Spain have sent King Carlos III of Spain a troubling report. They say that the Russians and other Europeans want to explore the coast of Alta California. So do the English, now known as the British.

Spanish explorers claimed Alta California more than 150 years before. But Spain has not yet sent settlers there. If other Europeans settle in Alta California, Spain will have no one there to defend its claim to the region.

King Carlos III of Spain

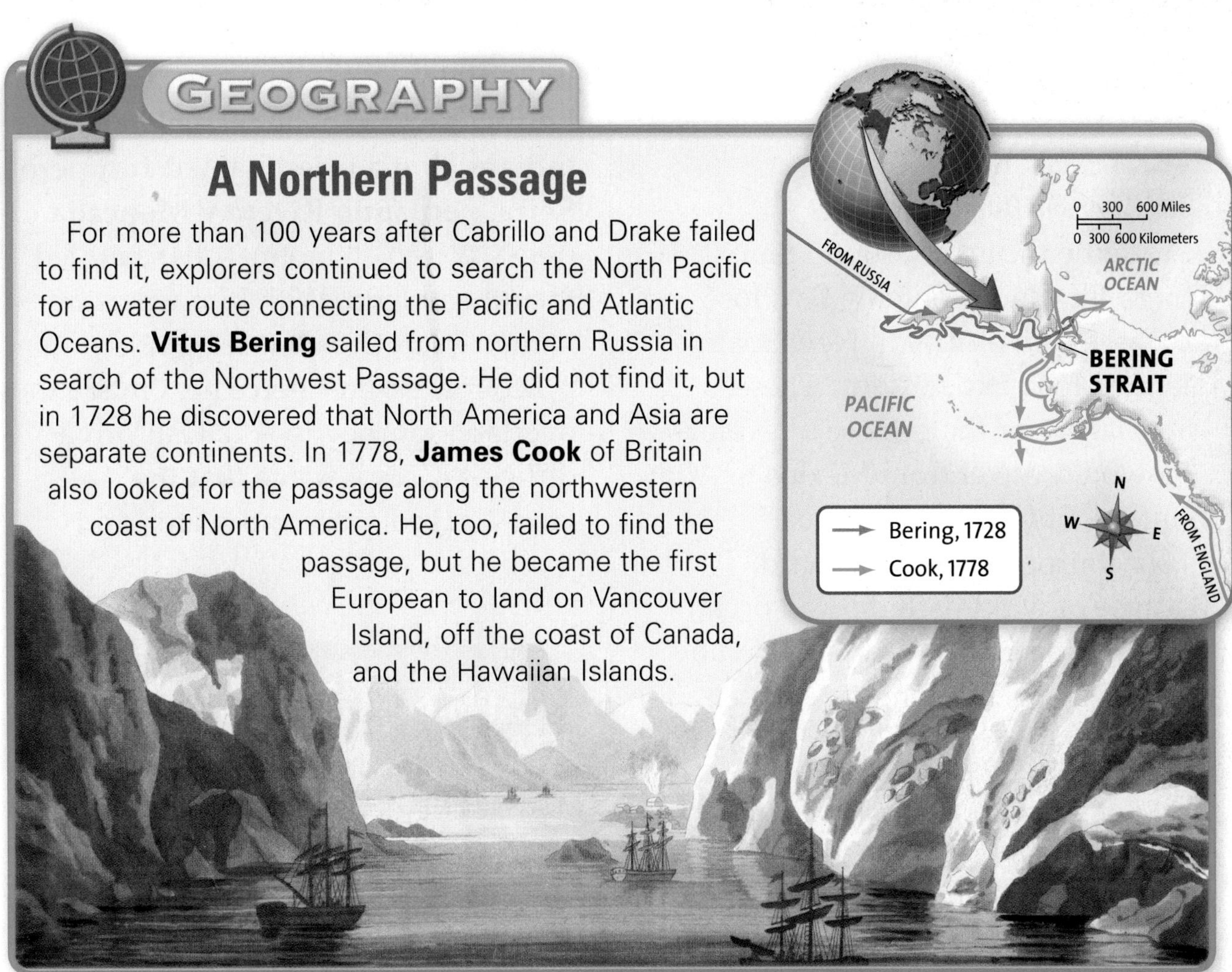

A Northern Passage

For more than 100 years after Cabrillo and Drake failed to find it, explorers continued to search the North Pacific for a water route connecting the Pacific and Atlantic Oceans. **Vitus Bering** sailed from northern Russia in search of the Northwest Passage. He did not find it, but in 1728 he discovered that North America and Asia are separate continents. In 1778, **James Cook** of Britain also looked for the passage along the northwestern coast of North America. He, too, failed to find the passage, but he became the first European to land on Vancouver Island, off the coast of Canada, and the Hawaiian Islands.

Settling in California

More than 150 years after Vizcaíno sailed into Monterey Bay, Spain decided to start a colony in Alta California. A **colony** is a settlement that is ruled by a faraway government. The decision to start a colony in Alta California came about in the mid-1700s. Russian explorers and fur traders had arrived in what is now Alaska. King Carlos III feared that the Russians might move south along the coast and into Alta California.

Spanish leaders hoped that a colony in Alta California would be successful. Spain had already started colonies in what would become Florida, Texas, and New Mexico by building **missions**, or religious settlements. The missions had strengthened Spain's hold on New Spain and Latin America. The king hoped to follow the same plan in Alta California.

Missions were run by missionaries. A **missionary** is a person who teaches a religion to others. In California, Catholic priests and other church workers served as missionaries. They tried to convert Indians to the Catholic religion. Missionaries also wanted to teach Indians the Spanish language and Spanish ways of life.

READING CHECK **GENERALIZE**
Why did Spain decide to start a colony in Alta California?

The Spanish Return

TIME July 1769

PLACE San Diego Bay

To settle the areas around **San Diego Bay** and Monterey Bay, José de Gálvez, an official in New Spain, planned four **expeditions**. These trips, taken for the pupose of exploring, would travel from Mexico to Alta California by land and by sea.

The journey by sea was hard. Because of wind patterns and ocean currents, the groups who traveled by sea had trouble staying on course.

The groups who took the land route also faced hardships. **Gaspar de Portolá** led one group overland. Portolá's group included soldiers, Indians, and a priest named **Junípero Serra. Fernando Rivera y Moncada** (ree•VAY•rah ee mohn•KAH•dah) led the other group. With him was a priest named **Juan Crespí** (kres•PEE).

Mountains and fierce heat made the overland journey to Alta California difficult. Crespí wrote that the land "lacked grass and water, and

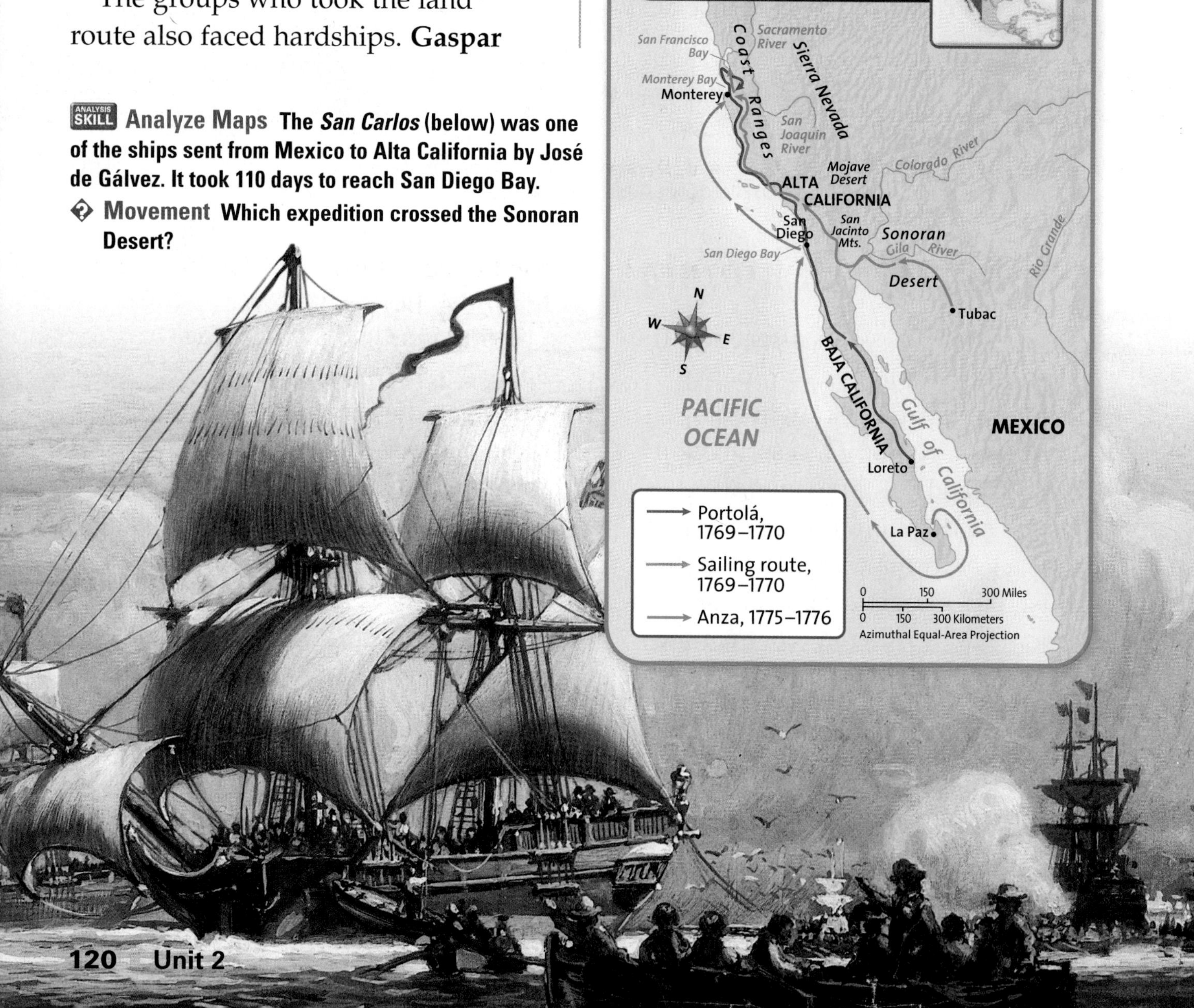

SKILL **Analyze Maps The *San Carlos* (below) was one of the ships sent from Mexico to Alta California by José de Gálvez. It took 110 days to reach San Diego Bay.**

Movement Which expedition crossed the Sonoran Desert?

Father Serra started Mission San Diego de Alcalá on July 16, 1769. The bells in the tower (inset) are rung together on the birthday of the mission.

abounded in [had a lot of] stones and thorns."*

By July 1, 1769, the groups had reached San Diego Bay. Only half of the people who had begun the trip survived, and many were sick and hungry. Soon after, Portolá and some of the crew set out on land to find Monterey Bay. Father Serra and many others stayed in San Diego.

Portolá traveled north, looking for the bay that Vizcaíno had described. Because Monterey Bay is long and gently curving, he passed by it without stopping. He went as far as San Francisco Bay before returning to San Diego in January 1770. Portolá tried a second time and finally found Monterey Bay on May 24.

While Portolá looked for Monterey Bay, Father Serra began the first mission in Alta California, called **San Diego de Alcalá** (ahl•kah•LAH). In 1770, Father Serra began Mission San Carlos Borroméo at Monterey. In 1771 the mission was moved five miles away to the Carmel Valley.

Father Serra made his headquarters at Monterey and stayed in California for 16 years. Before his death in 1784, he had started nine missions.

READING CHECK CAUSE AND EFFECT
What caused the overland journey to Alta California to be difficult?

*Father Crespí. From *the California Missions: A Pictorial History.* Edited by Dorothy Krell. Lane Publishing Company, 1979.

A New Overland Route

In 1774, Spain sent **Juan Bautista de Anza** (bow•TEES•tah day AHN•sah) to find a new land route to Alta California. He traveled across northern Mexico to reach Monterey.

The next year, Anza led a group of 240 settlers to California. The group took hundreds of cattle, mules, and horses along. Anza's route took them through the Sonoran Desert and over the San Jacinto Mountains. The group reached Monterey in March 1776.

Because of the desert and mountains, Anza's route proved to be no easier than the others. Land travel to Alta California remained very difficult. As a result, most supplies were still sent by sea.

READING CHECK **MAIN IDEA AND DETAILS**
Why was Anza sent on his expedition?

Juan Bautista de Anza

Summary

Junípero Serra founded the first missions in Alta California near San Diego Bay and Monterey Bay. Juan Bautista de Anza tried to find an easy land route from Mexico to Alta California.

REVIEW

1. How did Spain begin to settle Alta California?
2. Use the words **missionary** and **mission** to explain Spain's plan for settling Alta California.
3. Why was traveling overland to Alta California difficult?

CRITICAL THINKING

4. ANALYSIS SKILL Why do you think the missionaries wanted the California Indians to learn about Spanish ways of life?
5. ANALYSIS SKILL **Make It Relevant** Do you think that it would still be difficult to travel from Mexico to California by land today? Explain.
6. **Write a Letter** Imagine that you are Father Junípero Serra or Juan Bautista de Anza. Write a letter to King Carlos III. Tell what happened during your last expedition.
7. Focus Skill **GENERALIZE**
   On a separate sheet of paper, copy and complete the graphic organizer below.

Facts

Generalization

The expeditions sent by Gálvez faced difficult journeys.

Junípero Serra

Biography

Trustworthiness
Respect
Responsibility
Fairness
Caring
Patriotism

*"I trust that God will give me the strength to reach San Diego. . . . Even though I [might] die on the way, I shall not turn back."**

Miguel José Serra became a Catholic priest in Spain at the age of 24. Twelve years later, he sailed to New Spain. There he taught and worked with native peoples for many years. In 1769, he traveled to Alta California with Gaspar de Portolá. During the trip, he suffered from pain in his leg. Years earlier, he had been bitten by a snake or an insect, and his leg had never healed. Portolá urged him to return home, but Serra would not.

Father Junípero Serra founded the mission of San Diego de Alcalá on July 16, 1769.

Today, Serra is known as the Father of the California Missions. Serra started the first California mission at San Diego in 1769. He started a total of 9 missions, which helped the new California colony grow. For many California Indians, the missions also led to the end of their traditional ways of life.

*Junípero Serra. From *The History of San Diego: The Explorers 1492–1774* by Richard F. Pourade. Union-Tribune, 1960.

Why Character Counts

- In what ways did Serra help Spain increase its control of Alta California?
- How did Serra show responsibility to New Spain?

Bio Brief

- **1713** Born
- **1749** Becomes a missionary in New Spain
- **1769** Sets up first mission in Alta California
- **1771** Works from Mission San Carlos
- **1784** Died

GO ONLINE

Interactive Multimedia Biographies
Visit MULTIMEDIA BIOGRAPHIES at
www.harcourtschool.com/hss

Compare Primary and Secondary Sources

WHY IT MATTERS

People who study the past look for many sources of information. These sources give information about what actually happened.

WHAT YOU NEED TO KNOW

A **primary source** is a record made by people who were present as an event took place. An example might be a letter, diary, book, or interview. Drawings, paintings, or photographs can also be primary sources if they were made or used by people who saw what happened.

Another way to learn about past events is from a secondary source. A **secondary source** is a record of an event that was made by people who were not there. An encyclopedia is a secondary source. Newspaper stories and magazine articles written by people who did not take part in the event are secondary sources. So, too, are paintings and drawings by artists who did not see the event.

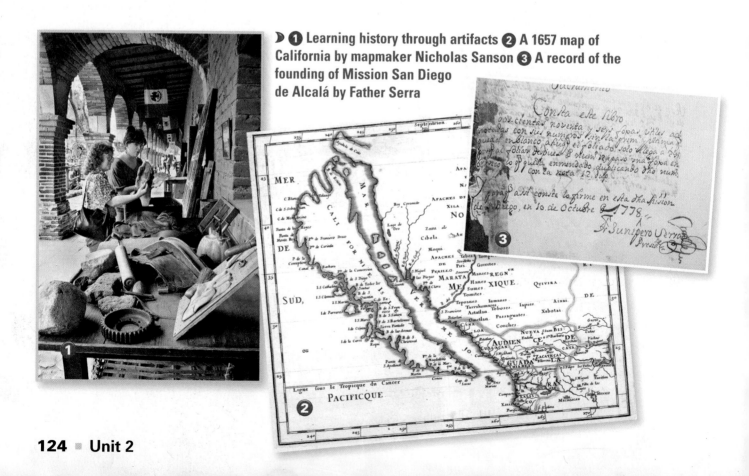

1 Learning history through artifacts **2** A 1657 map of California by mapmaker Nicholas Sanson **3** A record of the founding of Mission San Diego de Alcalá by Father Serra

Sometimes the words in a source can help you tell whether it is a primary source or a secondary source. Words such as *I*, *we*, *my*, and *our* are often found in primary sources. A date or a name on a map or drawing can help you figure out when it was created, and who created it.

PRACTICE THE SKILL

Examine the images on pages 124 and 125. Then answer the questions.

1. Which images are primary sources? Which are secondary sources?
2. Why might the map on page 124 also be considered a secondary source?
3. When is a book a primary source? When is a book a secondary source?

APPLY WHAT YOU LEARNED

ANALYSIS SKILL Your textbook is a secondary source that also has primary sources in it. Work with a partner to find primary and secondary sources in your textbook. Discuss why you think each source is either a primary source or a secondary source.

You can learn about the past from 4 historical reenactments, 5 websites, and 6 reference books.

Lesson 3

Time

1535 | 1685 | 1835

1776 The northernmost presidio is built at the mouth of San Francisco Bay

1777 The first pueblo in Alta California, San José de Guadalupe, is settled

1823 The last of 21 missions in Alta California, San Francisco Solano, is founded in Sonoma

WHAT TO KNOW
How was the Spanish mission system in California organized?

- Describe the relationships among soldiers, missionaries, and California Indians.
- Analyze the reasons for building each kind of settlement in Alta California.
- Tell how the mission system increased Spain's power and spread Christianity.

VOCABULARY
presidio p. 128
pueblo p. 130
plaza p. 130
alcalde p. 131

PLACES
El Camino Real

GENERALIZE

California Standards
HSS 4.2, 4.2.3, 4.2.4, 4.2.5

Other Kinds of Settlements

YOU ARE THERE Your boots are so dusty that it's hard to tell if they are black or brown. The dirt is from a well-traveled road called **El Camino Real** (el kah•MEE•noh ray•AHL). It is 1775, and you are a soldier. You have been ordered to go from a small fort near Mission San Carlos Borroméo to Mission San Luís Obispo.

You have been walking all day. Halfway to Mission San Luís Obispo, you come upon Mission San Antonio. The priests there give you a meal and a place to sleep. Tomorrow, you will put your boots back on and walk again.

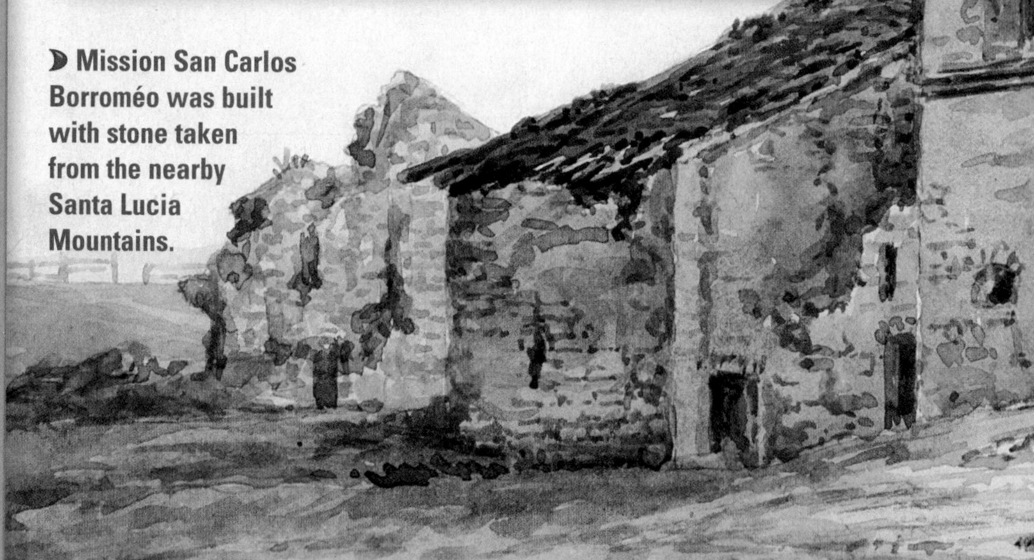

Mission San Carlos Borroméo was built with stone taken from the nearby Santa Lucia Mountains.

The Mission System

Starting in 1769, under the direction of the Franciscan priests, the Indians were forced to build a chain of missions in Alta California. These 21 missions were planned to stretch along the coast from San Diego, in the south, to Sonoma, in the north. Each mission was about a day's walk from the next on El Camino Real.

At the missions, the priests worked to create loyal Spanish subjects, or supporters of the king. To do so, the priests followed a system, or plan, that had been used in other parts of New Spain. They would move the California Indians into the missions, teach them to be Christians, and show them European ways.

Most missions were built near Indian villages or along Indian trails so they could use the Indians as labor. These locations were usually near fertile soil and fresh water. In these places, people at the missions could grow the food they needed to survive. Each mission had a church, houses for priests and Indians, workshops, farmland, and pastures for cattle and sheep.

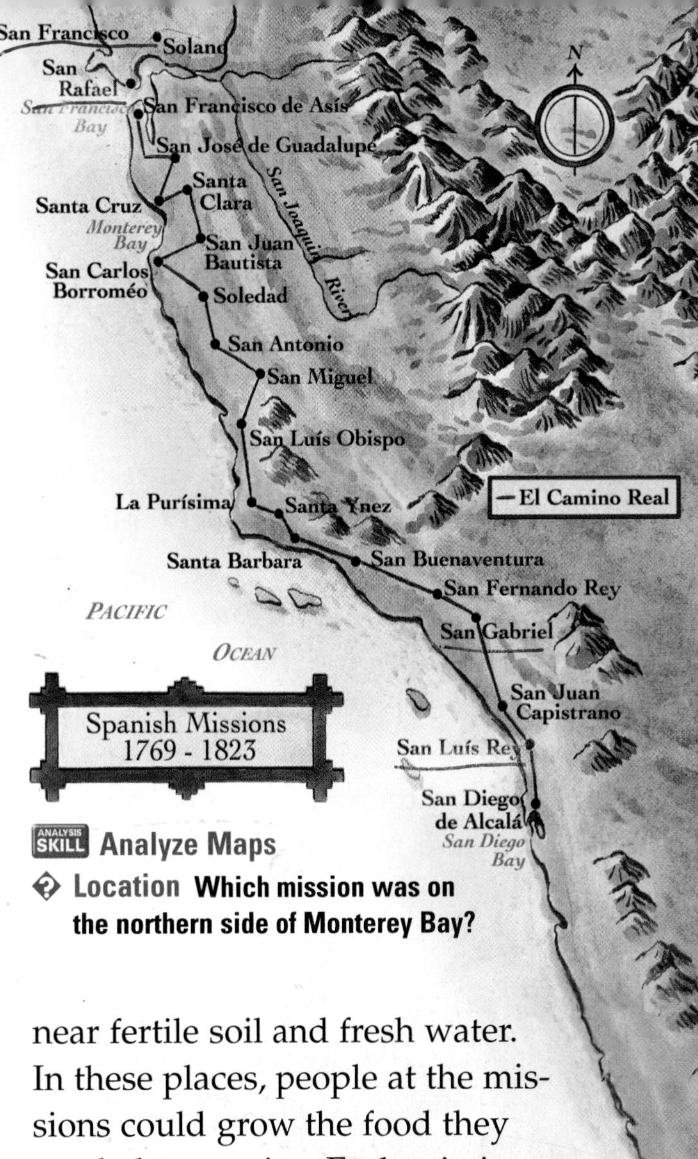

ANALYSIS SKILL Analyze Maps

Location Which mission was on the northern side of Monterey Bay?

By the late 1700s, the Franciscan priests had brought about 20,000 Indians into the missions. To attract Indians, the priests gave them glass beads and colored cloth. Often soldiers used force to bring in Indians.

READING CHECK GENERALIZE
Why were missions built near Indian villages?

Presidios for Protection

TIME Late 1700s

PLACE Alta California

The Spanish believed that the missions alone were not enough to help them hold their claim to Alta California. As in other parts of New Spain, they built forts called **presidios** (prih•SEE•dee•ohs) to protect their settlements.

In Alta California, the presidios were often built on natural harbors not far from missions. Soldiers at the presidios could defend the harbors against attacks by enemy ships. Presidios near missions could also help protect missionaries and other settlers from attacks by Indians.

The first presidio in Alta California was built near San Diego Bay in 1769. It stood near the mission, on a hill overlooking the bay. Later, three other presidios were built in Alta California, near the missions at Santa Barbara, Monterey, and San Francisco.

All the presidios were built by Indian workers and in much the same way. Each was built in the shape of a square and had an open courtyard on the inside. The buildings included a chapel, storage rooms, workshops, sleeping areas for soldiers and their families, and a house for the commander.

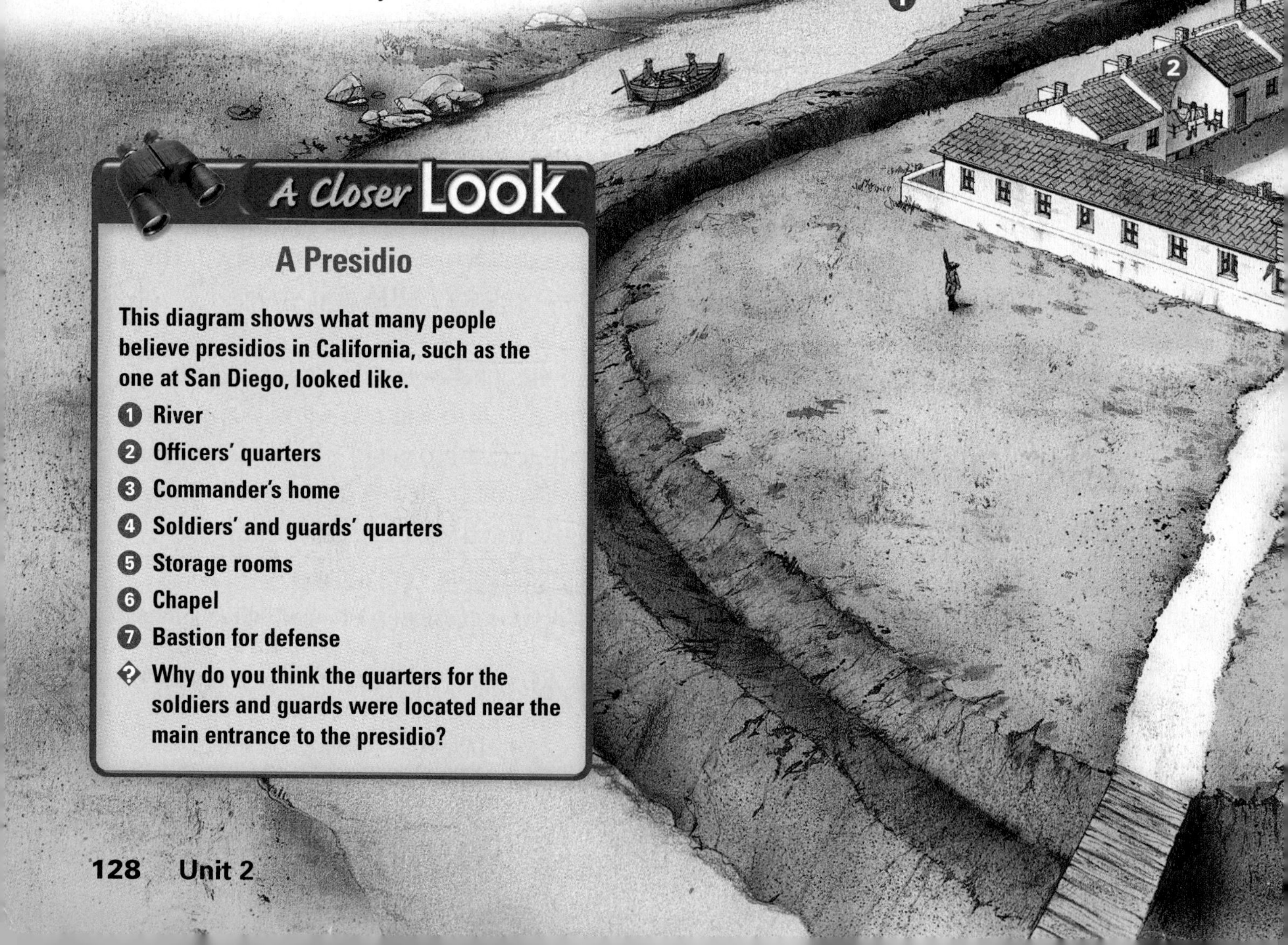

1

2

A Closer Look

A Presidio

This diagram shows what many people believe presidios in California, such as the one at San Diego, looked like.

1. **River**
2. **Officers' quarters**
3. **Commander's home**
4. **Soldiers' and guards' quarters**
5. **Storage rooms**
6. **Chapel**
7. **Bastion for defense**

? Why do you think the quarters for the soldiers and guards were located near the main entrance to the presidio?

At first, the presidios were very simple structures. The early buildings of the San Francisco presidio had dirt floors, window openings without glass, and very little furniture. When British sea captain George Vancouver toured the San Francisco presidio in 1792, he said that in cold and wet weather, the soldiers' houses "must be . . . uncomfortable dwellings."*

The soldiers at the presidios had many duties, or jobs. They hunted, worked in the fields, cared for the livestock, built and repaired structures, and delivered mail. They were often put in charge of Indian workers.

At times, the Spanish and the California Indians had conflicts. Soldiers at presidios sometimes had to stop Indians who fought against Spanish rule. The soldiers had guns and rode horses. The Indians were poorly armed and had to fight on foot.

READING CHECK **SUMMARIZE**
What kinds of duties did the soldiers have at a presidio?

*George Vancouver. From *A Voyage of Discovery to the North Pacific and Round the World, 1791-1795.* Ed. by W. Keye Lamb. The Hakluyt Society, 1984.

FAST FACT

Presidios were actually not well armed. Each presidio had only one or two cannons. Many cannons became rusty or were broken. Also, powder to shoot the cannons was often in short supply.

Pueblos for Farming

The soldiers at the presidios needed a supply of food. To meet this need, farming communities called **pueblos** (PWEH•blohz) were started. In Spanish, *pueblo* means "village."

In 1777, Felipe de Neve, the governor of Alta and Baja California, gathered soldiers and their families from the presidios in Monterey and San Francisco. Near the southern end of San Francisco Bay, they built a small settlement called San José de Guadalupe (gwah•dah•LOO•pay). It became Alta California's first pueblo.

That same year, Neve chose a spot near Mission San Gabriel for a second pueblo. In 1781, a group of 44 settlers established a pueblo that would later be known as Los Angeles. The next pueblo, Santa Cruz, was built in 1797. At the center of each pueblo was a plaza. A **plaza** is an open square where people can gather. Important buildings, such as a church, bordered the plaza.

The people in the pueblos often had Spanish, Indian, or African ancestors. In the pueblo that became Los Angeles, for example, almost half of the original settlers had Native American ancestors. Twenty-six of the first settlers had African ancestors.

While many of the people were farmers, others were store owners or craftworkers. Each pueblo also had

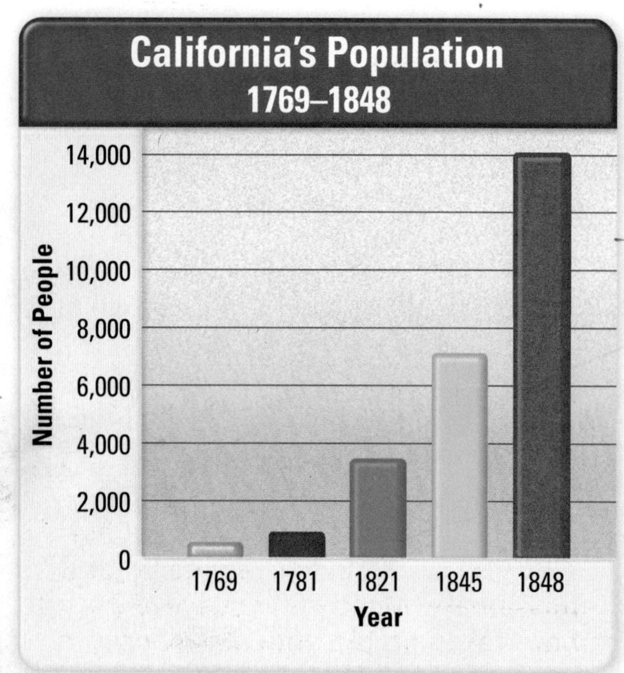

Analyze Graphs **Even with the founding of pueblos, such as the one at Monterey (below), the population of Spanish settlers in early Alta California grew at a rate of less than 100 people per year.**

During which period on this graph did the population grow most slowly?

an **alcalde** (ahl•KAHL•day), or mayor, who also served as a judge.

Spanish leaders hoped that the pueblos would attract new settlers to Alta California, but few people wanted to live there. It was a long, hard trip to reach California from most places in New Spain. There were few roads and no large towns or cities.

The Spanish wanted to encourage settlers to travel to the pueblos. Many of the new settlers were rewarded for their efforts. They were given land, farming tools, farm animals, and money. In return, they had to sell their surplus, or extra, crops to the soldiers at the presidios.

By bringing people to the pueblos, the Spanish hoped to strengthen their claim to Alta California. However, the population of Spanish settlers grew very slowly. By 1781, only 600 settlers, mostly men, lived in all of Alta California.

READING CHECK **GENERALIZE**
How did the Spanish hope to use pueblos to strengthen their claim to California?

▶ **Settlers used olive presses like this one to get oil from olives they grew.**

Summary

The Spanish established missions, presidios, and pueblos in Alta California. Presidios protected the missions. New settlers were rewarded for moving to the pueblos.

REVIEW

1. How was the Spanish mission system in Alta California organized?
2. What is the difference between a **presidio** and a **pueblo**?
3. How did the missions affect the California Indians' traditional ways of life?

CRITICAL THINKING

4. ANALYSIS SKILL Why do you think Alta California grew slowly even though there were many settlements?
5. ANALYSIS SKILL Look at the map on page 127. Describe the placement of the missions in California and explain why El Camino Real was important.
6. **Role-Play a Discussion** Imagine you are an Indian, a soldier, or a missionary. Meet with classmates who have taken on the other roles. As a group, talk about your functions at the Spanish missions.
7. Focus Skill **GENERALIZE**
On a separate sheet of paper, copy and complete the graphic organizer below.

Facts		

Generalization

Building a Spanish settlement in Alta California was a long and difficult process.

Chart and Graph Skills

Read a Time Line

WHY IT MATTERS

A time line shows the order in which events happened and the amount of time between them. Putting events in the order in which they took place can help you understand how events are connected.

WHAT YOU NEED TO KNOW

The time line below shows when some important events in the early history of California took place. The earliest date is at the left, and the latest date is at the right. The marks on a time line show units of time.

Like a map, a time line has a scale. The scale on a time line shows units of time, not distance. Some time lines show events that took place during one day, one month, or one year. Others show events that took place over a longer period, such as a **decade**, or a period of ten years.

On the time line below, the space between each mark stands for one **century**, or a period of 100 years. The first part of the time line shows events that happened during the sixteenth century. The sixteenth century includes the years from 1501 through

Early California History
16th Century
17th Century
1501
1601
1535
Hernando Cortés reaches Baja California
1542
Juan Rodríguez Cabrillo enters San Diego Bay
1602
Sebastián Vizcaíno sails to San Diego and Monterey Bays

1600. The next part of the time line shows the seventeenth century—from 1601 through 1700. What century does the last part of the time line show?

PRACTICE THE SKILL

Use the time line to answer these questions.

1. How many years after Cortés' journey did Cabrillo arrive at San Diego Bay?
2. In which century did Vizcaíno sail to San Diego Bay and Monterey Bay?
3. How long after Cabrillo entered San Diego Bay did Father Serra set up a mission there?
4. What is the latest event shown on the time line? In which century did that event happen?

APPLY WHAT YOU LEARNED

ANALYSIS SKILL **Make It Relevant** Make a time line that shows the twentieth and the twenty-first centuries. Label the first and last years of both centuries. Label the year in which you were born. Mark the year you will graduate from high school and other important years in both the past and the future. Add photographs or drawings, and share your time line with classmates.

Chart and Graph Skills

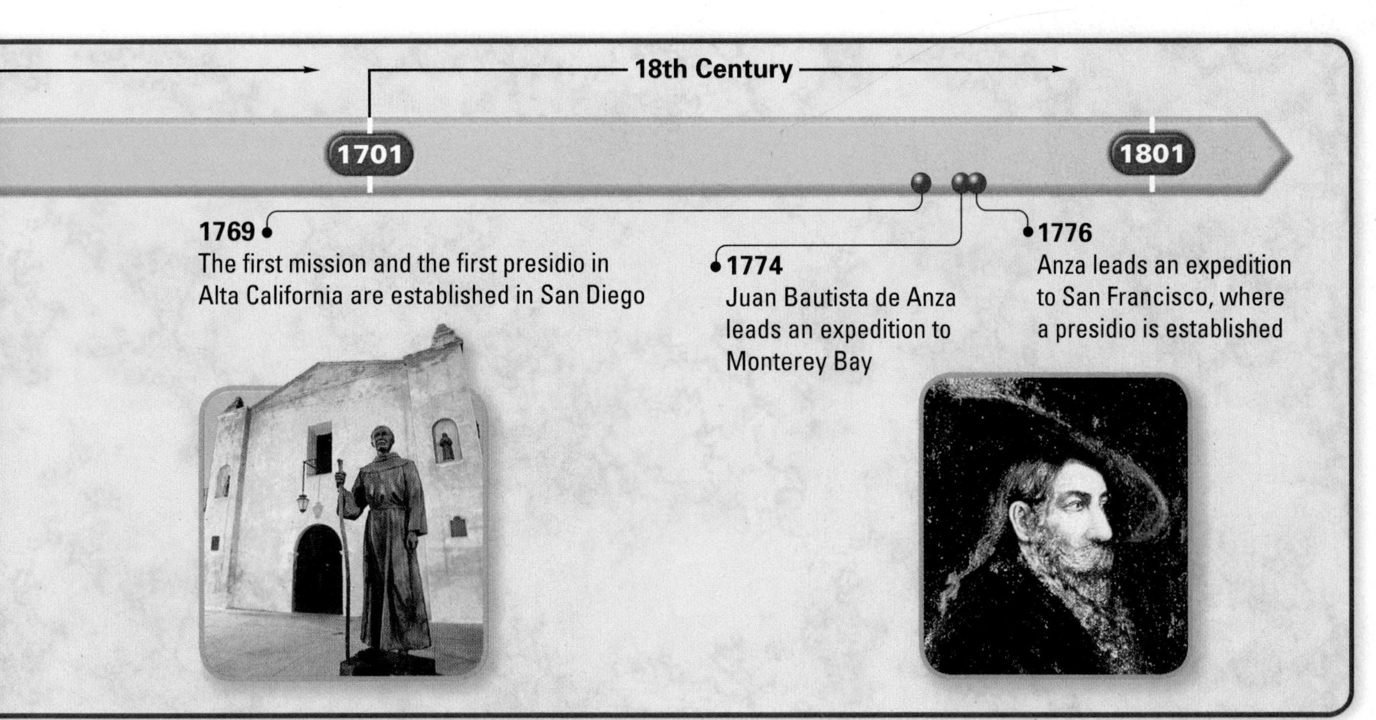
18th Century
1701
1801
1769
The first mission and the first presidio in Alta California are established in San Diego
1774
Juan Bautista de Anza leads an expedition to Monterey Bay
1776
Anza leads an expedition to San Francisco, where a presidio is established

Lesson 4

1771 Mission San Gabriel is founded

1785 Indians plan an uprising at Mission San Gabriel

1824 Indians along the central coast reject mission life

WHAT TO KNOW
How did the mission system affect the ways of life of California Indians?

- Describe the daily lives of people living at missions in Alta California.
- Identify reasons why some Indians resisted the mission system.

VOCABULARY
economy p. 135
neophyte p. 135
revolt p. 136
custom p. 138

PEOPLE
Nicolas José
Toypurina

PLACES
Mission Santa Barbara
Mission San Gabriel

GENERALIZE

California Standards
HSS 4.2, 4.2.4, 4.2.5, 4.2.6

Mission Life

YOU ARE THERE Bells at **Mission Santa Barbara** are ringing. You and the other California Indians who live there start each day when the bells call you to the church for prayer. Until you break for your midday meal, you study with the mission priests. They are teaching you new words, new ideas, and new ways to live. Other Indians at the mission build homes or work in the fields.

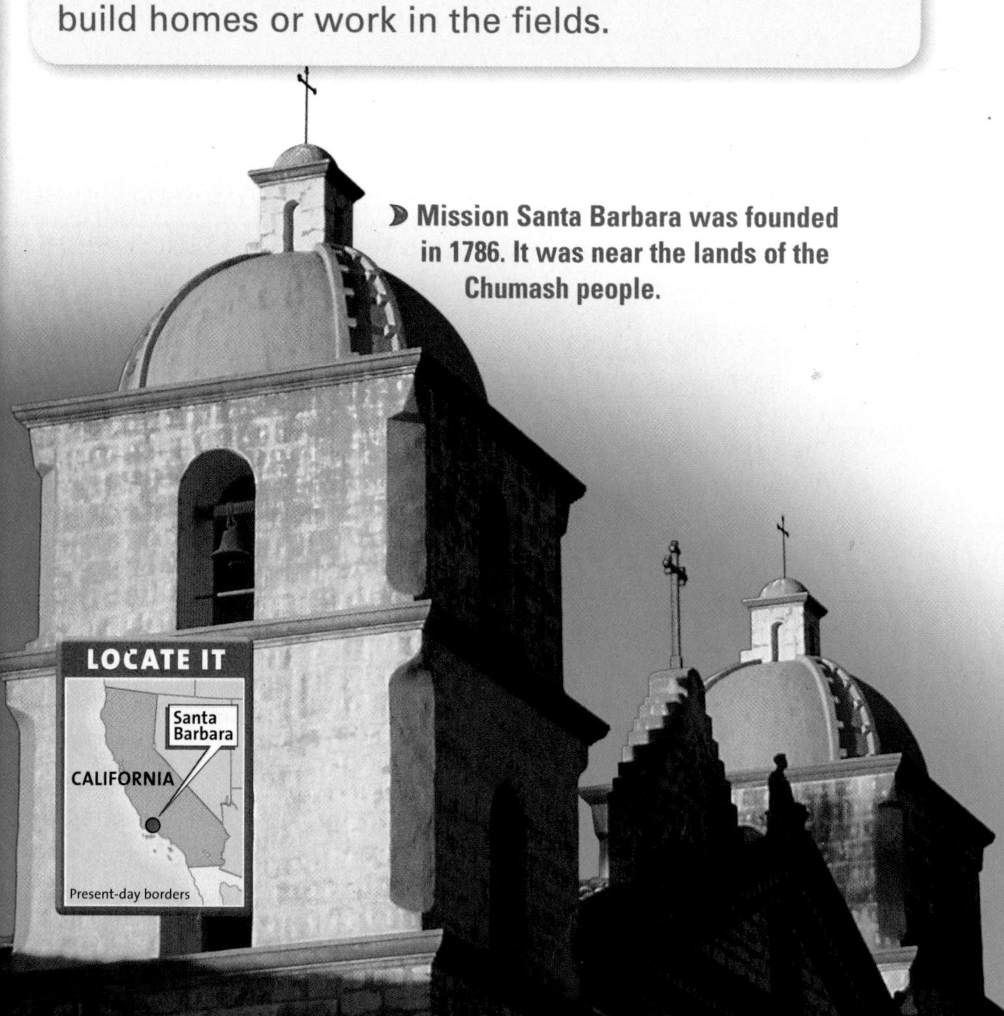

Mission Santa Barbara was founded in 1786. It was near the lands of the Chumash people.

Soldiers, priests, and Indians gathered together for prayer.

Changes Begin

Population in the California colony grew slowly at first. The missionaries worked hard to survive. In time, they brought more California Indians into the mission system. Indians provided the workers that the missions needed. Some Indians came to the missions on their own. Others were forced to the missions by soldiers.

At the missions, priests taught the Indian families about Christianity and Spanish ways of life. They taught them new skills, such as how to take care of horses, cattle, sheep, goats, and chickens. The Indians learned about carpentry and metalworking as well.

For the Indians, life at the missions was unlike their traditional ways of life. Before the arrival of the Spanish, most California Indians were hunters and gatherers. The Franciscan priests taught the Indians to farm. They grew food for the mission. This slowly changed the economy of California to one based on farming. An **economy** is the way people in a place or region use resources to meet their needs.

The cultural ways of life of the Indians changed as well. When they moved to a mission, Indians became **neophytes** (NEE•uh•fyts), or people new to the Catholic faith. They were not allowed to practice their traditional beliefs. Those who did could be punished, although many did so anyway.

READING CHECK GENERALIZE

How did the Spanish change the economy of California from one based on hunting and gathering?

Mission bells called people to prayer, work, and meals. The altar at Mission San Francisco Solano is shown to the left.

Work and Prayer

Mission life for the Indians consisted mostly of work and prayer. In fact, each day started with prayer. At sunrise, the mission bells rang to call neophytes to church.

Bells also rang when it was mealtime or time to begin and end work. There were many jobs at a mission. The Indians plowed and planted fields, dug ditches, and harvested crops. They also raised horses, cattle, sheep, goats, and chickens.

Indian men built adobe houses. Indian women wove cloth and made soap. They cooked the meals and did the cleaning. Children went to church and school. They also weeded the gardens.

READING CHECK MAIN IDEA AND DETAILS
What did mission life for the California Indians mostly consist of?

Some Indians Resist

Many Indians were unhappy with mission life and tried to resist, or act against, the missionaries. Some ran away. Others **revolted**, or fought, against the missionaries.

As part of a revolt in the 1770s, Indians burned the missions at San Diego and San Luis Obispo. Then, in 1785, a neophyte named **Nicolas José** and a Gabrielino woman named **Toypurina** (toy•poo•REE•nuh) planned a revolt at **Mission San Gabriel**. The plan was discovered, and José and Toypurina were jailed.

Some Indians were able to escape from the missions, but many were forced to return. The mission workers worried that Indians who left would give up Christianity.

READING CHECK DRAW CONCLUSIONS
Why did some Indians resist mission life?

A Closer LOOK

A Spanish Mission

At the center of a typical Spanish mission in Alta California was a courtyard. In the courtyard workers did such chores as weave cloth, make candles, and grind corn. Also, missionaries gave the Indians lessons about Christianity there.

1. Church
2. Priests' quarters
3. Workshops
4. Kitchen
5. Storerooms
6. Well
7. Indian huts
8. Irrigation ditch
9. River

? How was water brought from the river to the fields?

Children IN HISTORY

Pablo Tac

Pablo Tac, a Luiseño Indian, was born at Mission San Luis Rey in 1822. Tac was considered an excellent student by the priests at his mission. At the age of ten, he was sent to Italy to receive special schooling.

While in Europe, Tac wrote a diary about his life at the mission. The diary told about how the Indians' ways of life had changed after the Spanish arrived.

Tac dreamed of becoming a missionary himself. However, he became ill with smallpox in 1841. Pablo Tac died before he reached the age of 20.

Make It Relevant Do you think Tac's diary would be important to people today? Explain.

Indian Ways of Life End

By the late 1700s, about 20,000 Indians lived at the missions in Alta California. At the missions, they were expected to give up their old religious beliefs and customs. A **custom** is a usual way of doing things. Mission Indians were not allowed to wear their traditional clothing. They also could not hold the celebrations that were important to them.

One of the most serious threats to the mission Indians was disease. Without knowing it, some Europeans brought diseases such as smallpox, measles, and influenza. The Indians had no protection against these diseases, and their bodies could not fight them off. The diseases spread quickly and sometimes killed whole villages. After the deaths of many Indians at Mission Santa Clara, one priest wrote:

> **"Sickness is always with us, and I fear it is the end of the Indian race. What can we do?"***

*Father Jose Viader. From *Digger: The Tragic Fate of the California Indians from the Missions to the Gold Rush* by Jerry Stanley. Random House, 1997.

The missionaries had believed they were bringing a better way of life to the Indians of Alta California. Instead, their diseases had brought death to many Indians. After the first 75 years of life at the missions, only about one-third of California Indians remained.

READING CHECK **DRAW CONCLUSIONS**
How were California Indian ways of life affected by Spanish settlements?

Summary

The mission system caused changes in the lives of many California Indians. Some Indians learned new skills from the priests. At the same time, these mission Indians had to give up their traditional ways of life. Some ran away, and others tried to revolt. Many died of diseases.

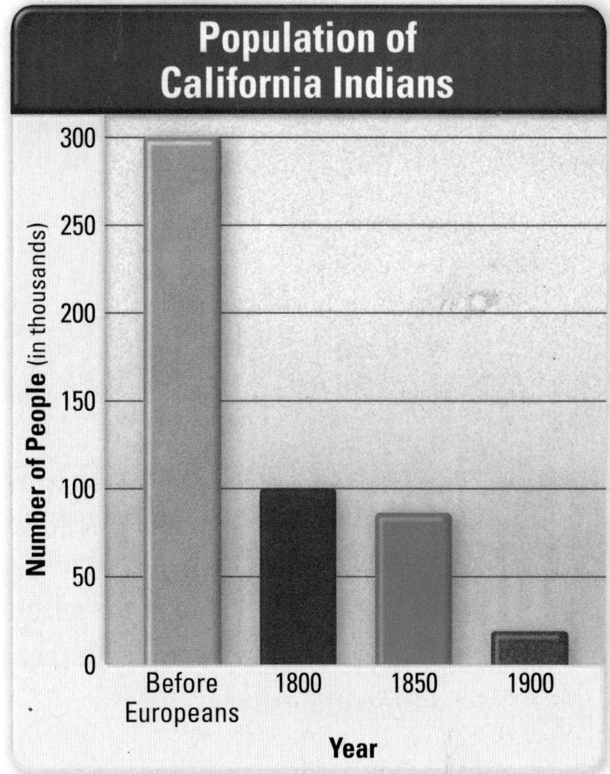

Analyze Graphs **At one point, more Indians lived in California than in any other area north of what is now Mexico.**

About how many Indians were living in California before the first Europeans arrived?

REVIEW

1. How did the mission system affect the ways of life of California Indians?
2. Use the word **neophyte** to describe a mission Indian.
3. How did the Indians who worked at the missions contribute to the success of the missions?

CRITICAL THINKING

4. ANALYSIS SKILL How do you think the drop in population of California Indians affected their traditional ways of life?
5. **Make It Relevant** How might your life have been different if you were forced to live at a California mission?
6. **Write a Letter** Suppose that the king of Spain has asked you to visit one of the missions in Alta California and to report to him what life there is like. Write a letter to him. Describe the daily lives of the priests and the neophytes who live there.
7. Focus Skill **GENERALIZE**
On a separate sheet of paper, copy and complete the graphic organizer below.

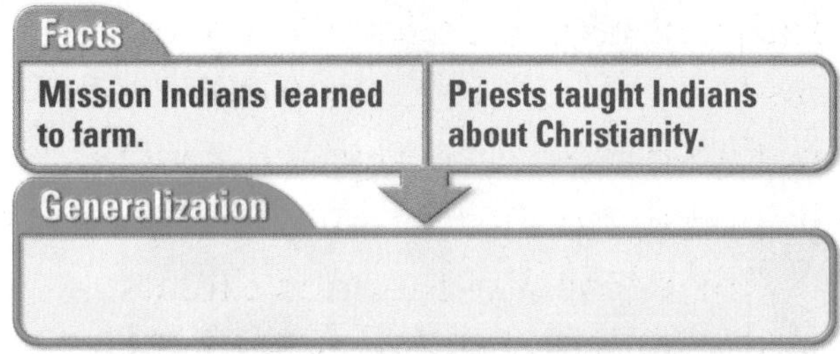

Facts
Mission Indians learned to farm.
Priests taught Indians about Christianity.
Generalization

The Mission System

The leaders of the Alta California missions believed that it was their duty to teach the Indians about Christianity and about Spanish ways of life. They believed they were giving the Indians a better way of life. In reality, life at the missions was difficult for many California Indians. Here are some different points of view about mission life for California Indians.

In Their Own Words

Julio Cesar, a mission Indian at San Luis Rey

"When I was a boy, the treatment given the Indians at the mission was not good. They did not pay us anything but merely gave us our food and a . . . blanket . . . besides flogging [whipping] for any fault, however slight."

—from *Recollections of My Youth at San Luis Rey Mission,* 1878 by Julio Cesar. Reprinted in *Native American Perspectives on the Hispanic Colonization of Alta California* by Edward D. Castillo. Garland, 1991.

JULIO CESAR

Father Pedro Font, a member of the Anza expedition

FATHER PEDRO FONT

“I surmise [think] that these Indians . . . would become experts if they had teachers and suitable tools . . . , for they have nothing more than flints [sharp rocks], and with them and their steady industry [work] they make artifacts.”

—from the diary of Father Pedro Font, 1776. Reprinted in *The Anza Expedition of 1775–1776* by Frederick J. Teggart. University of California, 1913.

LORENZO ASISARA

Lorenzo Asisara, a California Indian at Mission Santa Cruz

“The Indians at the missions were very severely treated . . . any disobedience or infraction [breaking] of the rules, and then came the lash [whip] without mercy, the women the same as the men. . . . We were always trembling with fear of the lash.”

—from the autobiography of Lorenzo Asisara, 1890. Reprinted in *Impact of Colonization on the Native California Societies* by Robert Heizer. The Journal of San Diego History, Volume 24, Number 1, 1978.

Father Fermín Francisco de Lasuén, head of the mission system in Alta California from 1785 to 1803

“Here are [Indians] whom we are teaching to be men, people of vicious and ferocious habits who know no law but force. . . . Such is the character of the men we are required to correct.”

—from a report in defense of the mission system, 1800. Reprinted in *Indian Labor at the California Missions Slavery or Salvation?* by Robert Archibald. The Journal of San Diego History, Volume 24, Number 2, 1978.

FATHER FERMÍN FRANCISCO DE LASUÉN

It's Your Turn

ANALYSIS SKILL **Analyze Points of View** How are the points of view of Father Lasuén and Father Font alike? How are they different from those of Julio Cesar and Lorenzo Asisara?

Make It Relevant Why might people have different points of view about the same subject?

1535 | 1600

1535
Hernando Cortés sails to Baja California and claims it for Spain

1542
Juan Cabrillo enters San Diego Bay

Reading Social Studies

When you **generalize**, you make a broad statement about the facts and details you have read.

Generalize

Complete this graphic organizer to make a generalization about European exploration and settlement of California. A copy of this graphic organizer appears on page 35 of the Homework and Practice Book.

Exploration and Early Settlements

Facts

The Spanish explorer Cabrillo reaches San Diego Bay.			

Generalization

Over time, the Europeans explored California, and the Spanish established missions to settle California.

California Writing Prompts

Write a Narrative Write a description of a European explorer or priest that came to California in which that person tells about himself. Do not mention the name of the explorer or priest. Read your description to the class and see if they can guess who you are describing.

Write a Report Write two or three paragraphs describing the effects of the missions on the lives of California Indians. Be sure to include information and facts from the textbook in your paragraphs to support your opinion.

1665 | 1730 | 1795

1602
Sebastián Vizcaíno sails to Monterey Bay

1769
Father Junípero Serra founds the first mission in Alta California

Use Vocabulary

Identify the term that correctly matches each definition.

galleon, p. 114
mission, p. 119
presidio, p. 128
alcalde, p. 131
neophyte, p. 135

1. a fort
2. a religious settlement
3. a person new to the Catholic faith
4. the mayor of a pueblo
5. a ship used in the 16th and 17th centuries mostly by Spanish traders

Use the Time Line

ANALYSIS SKILL **Use the summary time line above to answer the questions.**

6. Which Spanish explorer sailed to Baja California in 1535?
7. In what century was the first mission founded in California? What was the year?

Apply Skills

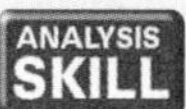

Compare Primary and Secondary Sources

8. Look at the map on page 111. Is this map a primary or secondary source? Explain your answer.

Recall Facts

Answer these questions.

9. What were some of the reasons that European explorers came to the Americas?
10. Why did Spain send explorers to what is now California?
11. Why were some California Indians unhappy with mission life?

Write the letter of the best choice.

12. Who led the first overland expedition to San Diego?
    A Cortés
    B Portolá
    C Cabrillo
    D Vizcaíno
13. How many Spanish missions were built in Alta California?
    A 5
    B 9
    C 21
    D 33

Think Critically

14. ANALYSIS SKILL What were the benefits and the costs of the Spanish exploration of California?
15. ANALYSIS SKILL How did the arrival of Spanish missionaries in Alta California change the lives of many Native Americans?

Study Skills

TAKE NOTES

Taking notes can help you remember important ideas.

- **Write only important facts and ideas. Use your own words. You do not have to write in complete sentences.**
- **One way to organize notes is in a chart. Write down the main ideas in one column and facts in another.**

Mexican Rule in California	
Main Ideas	Facts
Lesson 1: Mexico Wins Its Freedom • Mexico won independence from Spain • ______	• Father Hidalgo asked Mexicans to fight for freedom • ______
Lesson 2: Rise of the Rancho Economy • ______ • ______	• ______ • ______

Apply As You Read

As you read this chapter, use a two-column chart to take notes about each lesson.

California History-Social Science Standards, Grade 4

4.2 Students describe the social, political, cultural, and economic life and interactions among people of California from the pre-Columbian societies to the Spanish mission and Mexican rancho periods.
4.3 Students explain the economic, social, and political life in California from the establishment of the Bear Flag Republic through the Mexican-American War, the Gold Rush, and the granting of statehood.

CHAPTER

Mexican Rule in California

This painting shows workers on a ranch in Mexican California.

With Corporal Tapia

from *A Personal Tour of La Purísima*
by Robert Young
illustrated by Ron Himler

By 1804, settlers in New Spain were fighting for independence from Spain. During this time, the missionaries and soldiers at the missions and presidios in New Spain had to make do with few supplies and little support from the government. Read now about the problems one soldier at La Purísima Mission faced.

Corporal Tapia looked down at his red wool vest. The holes in it seemed to get bigger every month. He smoothed the vest then reached for his uniform jacket, which had faded from its original dark blue color. The red piping along the edges of the jacket was dull and frayed.

Tapia had hoped that he and the five soldiers under his command would be getting new uniforms. He had even spoken with Father Payeras about it this morning. But, once again, the padre told him there would be no uniforms coming from Mexico City. There would be no new supplies or wages either.

The reason was simple, as Tapia knew. The colony of New Spain was fighting for its independence from Spain. The government of New Spain was spending most of its money on the war. As a result, the missions would suffer.

piping a narrow trim

frayed worn down to loose threads

Corporal Tapia buttoned the shiny brass buttons on the front of his jacket. He adjusted his black head scarf, then straightened his shoulders, puffed out his chest, and lowered his chin. Despite the tattered uniform and the lack of supplies, Tapia was proud to be a soldier and a Californian.

tattered torn

The soldiers under his command, though, were another story. Some of them had been picked off the streets of Mexico City. Others were criminals who had been sent to Alta California as punishment. These men were in a strange land far from home. They knew little about the Chumash and cared even less. The soldiers were tired of not being paid and of not being fed properly.

Response Corner

1. Suppose New Spain had been able to pay and provide supplies to the soldiers at the missions and presidios. What do you think might have happened?
2. Why do you think Corporal Tapia stayed at La Purísima despite hardships?

Lesson 1

Time

1535 | 1685 | 1835

1810 The Mexican War for Independence begins

1821 Mexico wins its independence

1834 The end of church rule of the missions is ordered

WHAT TO KNOW
How did Mexican independence affect life in Alta California?

- ✓ **Describe the effects on Alta California of the Mexican War for Independence.**
- ✓ **Explain how the Mexican War for Independence affected borders in North America.**

VOCABULARY
independence p. 149
criollo p. 149
mestizo p. 149
Californio p. 151
secularization p. 152

PEOPLE
Miguel Hidalgo y Costilla
Pablo Vicente de Solá
José Figueroa
Lorenzo Asisara

PLACES
Dolores, Mexico
Monterey

GENERALIZE

California Standards
HSS 4.2, 4.2.7, 4.2.8

Mexico Wins Its Freedom

YOU ARE THERE

"Clang! Clang! Clang!" Church bells are ringing all over the city of **Dolores**, in central Mexico. It's the morning of September 16, 1810, and you are standing near the city square. Excited people pass you, hurrying toward the church. Wanting to find out what's happening, you follow the crowd. A woman tells you that the priest has just called for Mexicans to fight for freedom from Spanish rule. Life as you know it is about to change.

The Road to War

TIME September 16, 1810
PLACE Dolores, Mexico

September 16, 1810, marked an important day in Mexico's history. On that morning, Father **Miguel Hidalgo y Costilla** (mee•GAYL ee•DAHL•goh ee kohs•TEE•yah) called on people to join against Spanish rule. His speech came to be called *el Grito de Dolores*, or "the Cry of Dolores."

Hidalgo asked Mexicans to fight for freedom, crying "Death to bad government!"* He and many other colonists did not like the Spanish government. They wanted **independence**, or freedom, from Spanish rule.

Just as the 13 British colonies had become the United States of America, many people in Mexico wanted to have their own country. Many of these people were **criollos** (kree•OHL•yohz), or people born of Spanish parents in Mexico. Because criollos were not born in Spain, they were not allowed to hold the best jobs in the government or the church. They were angry that they were not treated as the equals of people born in Spain. Indians and **mestizos** (meh•STEE•zohz), or people of both European and Indian heritage, were treated even less fairly.

READING CHECK **GENERALIZE**
Why did criollos, Indians, and mestizos want independence from Spain?

*Father Miguel Hidalgo y Costilla, in a speech at Dolores, Mexico, September 16, 1810. From *Mexico: A History* by Robert Ryal Miller. University of Oklahoma Press, 1985.

This illustration shows what it might have looked like when Father Hidalgo gave his famous speech in Dolores, Mexico, in 1810.

CITIZENSHIP

Democratic Principles

The right to take part in one's own government is an important freedom.

Mexico's people were not the only ones in the Americas to want independence from colonial leaders. By the late 1700s, the ideas that had led to the American Revolution had become well known. Among these was the idea that people have the right to take part in their government. Between 1776 and 1825, the people of Colombia, Chile, Paraguay, Venezuela, and Argentina gained independence from Spain. Using the United States as a model, they wrote new plans of governments that declared that all people are equal.

This mural by Juan O'Gorman honors the leaders of the Mexican War for Independence.

Mexico Gains Independence

For 11 years, the colonists in Mexico fought against Spain. Thousands of people died during the war. Spain was too busy fighting in Mexico to pay much attention to far-off California. However, the war had an effect on life in California. For years, the soldiers in the presidios and other settlers received few supplies from Spain.

Only one battle took place in Alta California during the Mexican War for Independence. In 1818, sailors from a Spanish colony in South America burned the capital at **Monterey**. The commander of the ship said he was fighting for Mexican independence, but he was little more than a pirate.

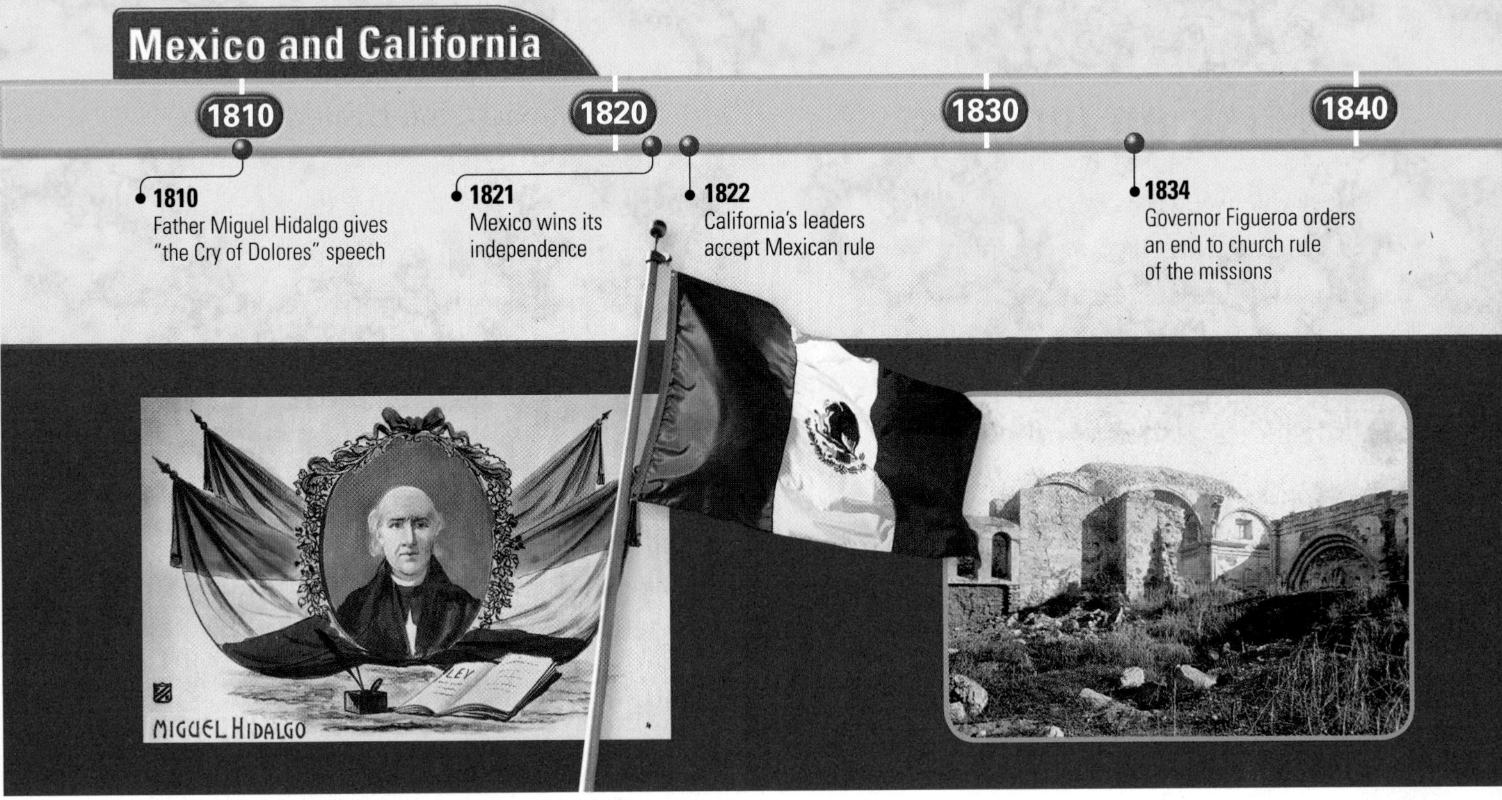
Mexico and California
1810
1820
1830
1840
1810
Father Miguel Hidalgo gives "the Cry of Dolores" speech
1821
Mexico wins its independence
1822
California's leaders accept Mexican rule
1834
Governor Figueroa orders an end to church rule of the missions
LEY
MIGUEL HIDALGO

ANALYSIS SKILL Analyze Time Lines

How long after Father Hidalgo's speech did Mexico win independence?

In 1821, Mexico finally won its independence. A large part of the land that was once New Spain, including Alta California, was now under the control of the new country of Mexico.

In 1822, people in Alta California heard the news of Mexico's independence. The Spanish governor of Alta California, **Pablo Vicente de Solá**, did not know what to do. He asked the leaders of the presidios, missions, and pueblos to decide whether they supported or opposed being ruled by Mexico. After meeting in Monterey in April 1822, the leaders decided to accept Mexican rule. Most **Californios**, as the Spanish-speaking people of Alta California called themselves, welcomed Mexican rule.

After independence was won, Mexico's new leaders wanted to get rid of everything from the old Spanish government. Mexican leaders and new laws were quickly put in place in Alta California.

Under Spanish law, the colonies in New Spain had not been allowed to trade with other countries. The new government of Mexico quickly changed that. Before long, ships from many countries, including the United States, Russia, and Britain, began to sail into the harbors at San Francisco, Monterey, and San Diego. The trade that took place helped California's economy grow.

READING CHECK GENERALIZE

How did new laws change life in California?

Problems for the Mission Indians

The new Mexican government also wanted to end the mission system in Alta California. The missions had become very powerful, and they reminded people of Spanish rule. The missions also controlled much of California's best land.

In 1834, Governor **José Figueroa** ordered the **secularization** (seh•kyuh•luh•ruh•ZAY•shuhn), or the end of church rule, of the missions. Under his plan, all the missions would become pueblos within 15 years, and each mission's church would become the pueblo's church. Half of the mission's land was to be given to the Indians who had worked at the mission, and the rest would be managed by the local government. Some of this land would become available to settlers from Mexico, the United States, and other countries.

Mexican leaders hoped that this plan would help the Indians and add to California's population. As it turned out, however, the Indians got very little mission land. Most mission lands eventually ended up in the hands of Californios and new settlers.

The Indians who kept their lands often lacked the tools and animals they needed for farming. **Lorenzo Asisara**, an Indian living at Mission Santa Cruz, said that Indians got only "old mares that were no longer productive"* instead of healthy horses.

After the missions closed, some Indians tried to return to their old villages. But their lands had changed greatly during Spanish settlement.

*Lorenzo Asisara. California Historical Society, 2000. californiahistory.net.

By 1880, Mission San Juan Capistrano lay in ruins.

Much of the land had been taken over by others. Many Indians, like Asisara, had been born and raised in missions. They had learned Spanish ways of life and agriculture from the Franciscan priests, and they could not return to being hunters and gatherers. In the end, many Indians had no choice but to work for the Californios and the new settlers.

READING CHECK **MAIN IDEA AND DETAILS**
How did life change for mission Indians under Mexican rule?

Summary

The Mexican War for Independence began in 1810. After Mexico won its independence from Spain, California became a part of Mexico. The new Mexican government brought important changes to California.

This 1881 painting shows the ruins of Mission San Carlos.

REVIEW

1. How did Mexican independence affect life in Alta California?
2. Write a sentence about Father Hidalgo, using the term **independence**.
3. What was the location of the only battle fought in Alta California during the Mexican War for Independence?

CRITICAL THINKING

4. ANALYSIS SKILL Why do you think the new Mexican government wanted to trade with other countries?
5. ANALYSIS SKILL Why did the Mexican government close the missions, and how did this affect California Indians?
6. **Write Headlines** Write three headlines for a newspaper in the 1830s. Each should tell about a change the new Mexican government is bringing to California.
7. Focus Skill **GENERALIZE**
On a separate sheet of paper, copy and complete the graphic organizer below.

Facts

Generalization

Life for Californios changed under Mexican rule.

Identify Multiple Causes and Effects

WHY IT MATTERS

When you read about history, you will find that events are often linked. To recognize links between events, you need to understand causes and effects. A **cause** is something that makes something else happen. What happens is an **effect**.

Sometimes an effect has more than one cause. For example, you read that the people of Mexico became unhappy with Spanish rule. Criollos, mestizos, and Indians in Mexico were not treated as the equals of people born in Spain. The people of Mexico were also encouraged by the success of the American Revolution. In this case, you could say that the success of the American Revolution and the unfair rule of Spain led to the Mexican War for Independence.

One cause can also lead to several effects. Father Hidalgo's speech caused the criollos, mestizos, and Indians to join together. This in turn led to the Mexican War for Independence.

Understanding how events are related as causes and effects can help you figure out why things happen. It can also help you think about the possible effects of decisions you might make before you make them.

This mural by Juan O'Gorman depicts Father Miguel Hidalgo's call to revolution.

WHAT YOU NEED TO KNOW

You can use the following steps to help you find the causes of an effect.

Step 1 **Identify the effect.**

Step 2 **Look for all the causes of that effect.**

Step 3 **Think about how the causes relate to each other and to the effect.**

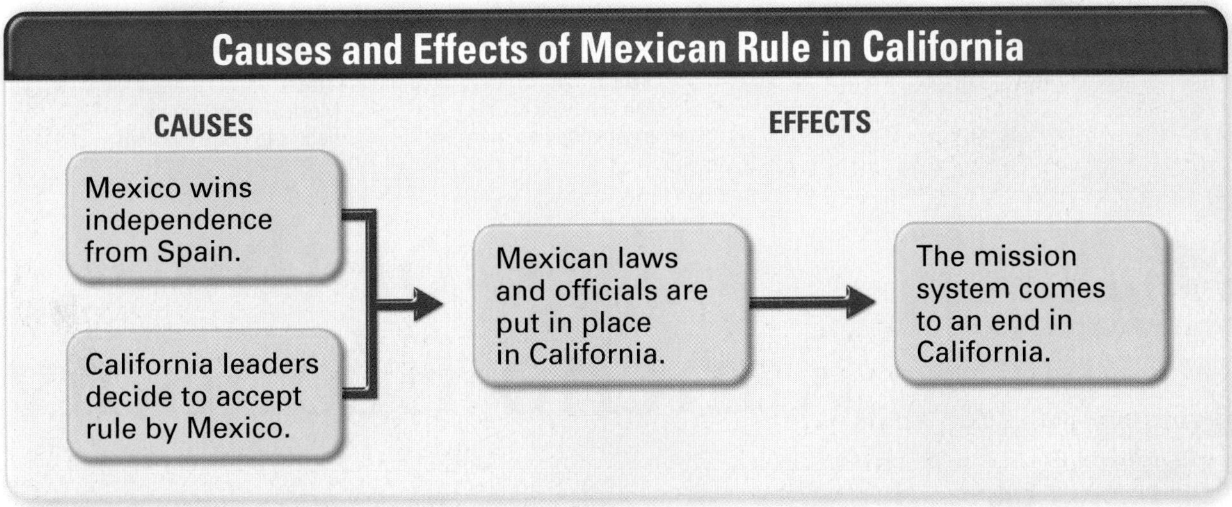

Causes and Effects of Mexican Rule in California

CAUSES		EFFECTS
Mexico wins independence from Spain.	Mexican laws and officials are put in place in California.	The mission system comes to an end in California.
California leaders decide to accept rule by Mexico.		

PRACTICE THE SKILL

Read the following statements and decide if each is a cause or an effect of Mexican rule in California. Write your answers on a separate sheet of paper.

1. Most mission lands end up in the hands of Californios and new settlers.
2. Pablo Vicente de Solá asks California leaders to decide whether to support Mexico's independence or challenge it.
3. Ships from many countries begin to trade at harbors in San Francisco, Monterey, and San Diego.

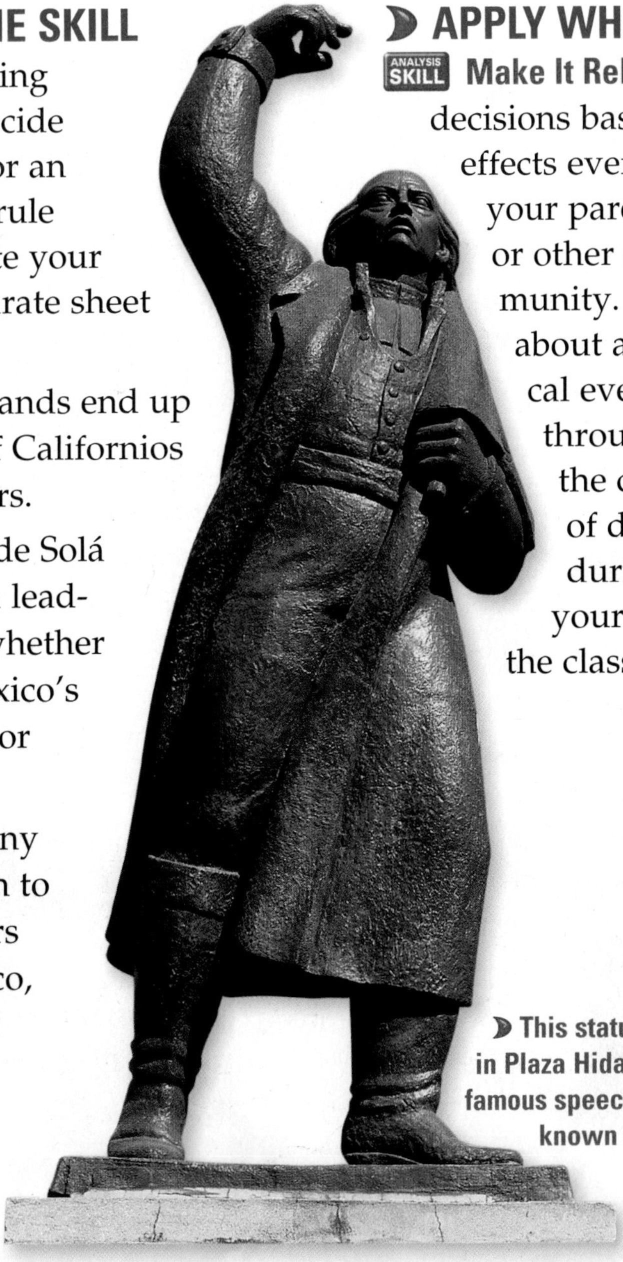

APPLY WHAT YOU LEARNED

ANALYSIS SKILL **Make It Relevant** People make decisions based on causes and effects every day. Interview your parents, grandparents, or other adults in your community. Ask them questions about an important historical event that they lived through. Try to identify the causes and effects of decisions they made during the event. Share your findings with the class.

This statue of Father Hidalgo is in Plaza Hidalgo in Mexico City. His famous speech demanding equality is known as *el Grito de Dolores*.

Lesson 2

Time

1535 1685 1835

1821 Mexico wins its independence

1834 Mexican government begins to close missions

WHAT TO KNOW
What was the California economy based on during the time of Mexican rule?

- ✓ Explain how offers of land grants changed California.
- ✓ Describe how new Mexican trading rules and the rise of ranchos helped California's economy.

VOCABULARY
land grant p. 157
diseño p. 157
rancho p. 158
hacienda p. 159
barter p. 160
tallow p. 160

PEOPLE
Pío Pico
Mariano Vallejo
Richard Henry Dana

PLACES
Monterey
Rancho Petaluma
Fort Ross

GENERALIZE

California Standards
HSS 4.2, 4.2.5, 4.2.8, 4.3, 4.3.1, 4.3.2

Rise of the Rancho Economy

YOU ARE THERE

The year is 1835. You are a sailor on board a trading ship from Boston. As your ship sails into Monterey Bay, you look at the land in front of you. Through the fog, you notice cattle grazing on hills. Then you see the town.

Compared to the big cities of the United States, **Monterey** looks quite small. Even so, it's where your captain plans to land to trade the ship's cargo of furniture, clothes, and other items. You've heard that the Californios will trade fine cattle hides for these goods.

FAST FACT

By 1830, there were about 500,000 cattle and many thousands of horses in California.

Land Grants

To attract people to California, the Mexican government began offering more **land grants**, or gifts of land, to settlers. A person seeking a land grant had to send a letter to the government, explaining why he or she wanted the land. The person had to promise to bring cattle or other animals to live on the land. The letter also had to include a **diseño** (dih•SAYN•yoh), or "design." This hand-drawn map showed the boundaries of the land grant.

Under Spanish rule, land grants in California had been very difficult to get. Most went to people who were already wealthy or had friends or family members in government. Now, the Mexican government said that all people who would accept the Catholic religion and become Mexican citizens could own land. As a result, getting a land grant became much easier. People from other countries, especially the United States, began to move to California.

Most land grants went to white men. However, women and Indian men could also receive them. Unlike women in the United States at that time, married women in Mexico could own land.

READING CHECK GENERALIZE
Why did California's population increase under Mexican rule?

ANALYSIS SKILL Analyze Maps

Location Where in California were most land grants located?

New Land Owners

Most people who received land grants wasted no time in starting **ranchos**, or cattle ranches. A rancho was made up of the owner's house, fields for crops, and pastures for cattle and horses. Because there were few people in California and so much land, some of the ranchos were very large. Some covered 50,000 acres or more—an area larger than the present-day city of San Francisco.

Ranchos needed a lot of land to produce enough grass for the cattle to eat. The animals roamed freely on the rancho land, eating most of the wild grasses in one place and then moving to another place.

At first, the number of ranchos in California grew slowly. As the Mexican government began closing the missions, more land grants were given. The government also gave new rancho owners cattle from the missions. Between 1834 and 1846, more than 700 new ranchos were started. Ranchos soon became the center of California life and an important part of California's economy.

Living on a large rancho was almost like living in a small town. Hundreds of people might live on a large rancho. These people included the rancher, his or her family, and the rancho workers. Many workers were Indians who had worked at missions before the missions closed.

Among the many rancho owners in California was **Pío Pico** (PEE•oh

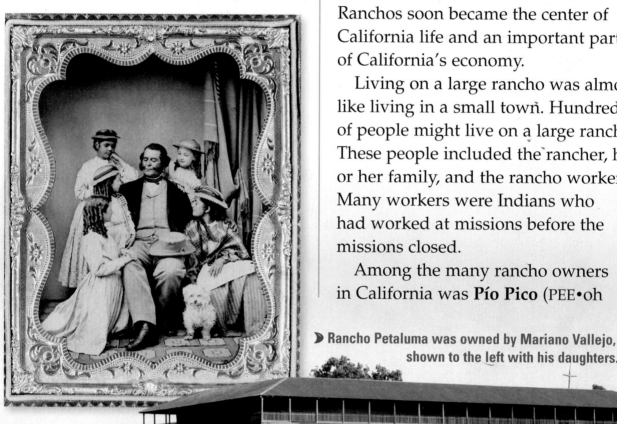

Rancho Petaluma was owned by Mariano Vallejo, shown to the left with his daughters.

LOCATE IT

CALIFORNIA

Petaluma

Present-day borders

This illustration shows rancho owner Andrés Pico, the brother of Pío Pico, at his hacienda near Los Angeles.

PEE•koh), whose father had traveled north from Mexico to California in 1801. Pico was born in Los Angeles, and his family was among the area's first settlers. Pico grew up to be a rancher and the last governor of Mexican California.

Mariano Vallejo (vuh•LAY•hoh), a wealthy rancher in northern California, owned several ranchos. One was in Petaluma, north of San Francisco. **Rancho Petaluma** was like many other large California ranchos. It had a **hacienda** (hah•see•EN•dah), or main house, built around an open courtyard. A veranda, or porch, ran along the inside of the courtyard walls.

In all, Vallejo's ranchos totaled about 175,000 acres of land. On this land, Vallejo kept about 25,000 cows as well as thousands of sheep and horses. He had fields planted with corn, wheat, barley, peas, beans, and other crops. The rancho also had space and equipment for workers to make items such as blankets, nails, and horseshoes. Not all rancho owners were wealthy, however. On poorer ranchos, families often lived in small houses that had dirt floors. Doors and windows were covered with cowhides.

Not all people in California lived on ranchos at this time. Some people continued to live in pueblos. In pueblos, there were skilled workers such as blacksmiths and saddlemakers, and there were often stores and inns.

READING CHECK **GENERALIZE**

Why did many of the ranchos cover large areas of land?

Growing Trade

Mexican laws allowing Californios to trade with other countries also helped the economy in California grow. Trading ships from the United States, Britain, and all over the world began to arrive at California ports.

In 1834, a young sailor named **Richard Henry Dana** traveled to California on a trading ship from Boston. Later, in his book *Two Years Before the Mast*, he wrote: "We had . . . teas, coffee, sugar, spices, raisins, molasses, hardware, . . . clothing of all kinds, boots and shoes. . . ."*

When Californios saw a ship sail into the harbor, they got ready to barter. To **barter** is to trade one kind of item for another. Traders on the ships wanted cowhides. They also wanted **tallow**. People used this animal fat to make soap and candles. In return for the hides and tallow, the traders offered goods that the Californios could not make or grow themselves.

*Richard Henry Dana. *Two Years Before the Mast*. Modern Library, 2001.

Many places along the California coast did not have good harbors. To trade at these places, ships had to remain at sea and send small boats to trade for hides. Dana described how

Fort Ross

In 1812, Russian fur traders built a fort along the Pacific coast, north of Bodega (boh•DAY•guh) Bay. The Spanish called the fort *Fuerte de los Rusos*, which means "Fort of the Russians." It later became known as **Fort Ross**.

The Russians became trading partners with the Californios—something Spanish law did not allow. The Californios traded their cattle and crops for goods made in Russia, such as plows and axes. In 1824, Russia agreed to stop building settlements south of Alaska. In 1841, the Russians left the fort, and a settler named John Sutter bought the buildings.

Trading hides and tallow on a California beach

the Californios stood on the high cliffs and threw the hides onto the beach for the boats to pick up. He wrote,

> "Down this height we pitched the hides, . . . the wind took them, and swayed them about, plunging and rising in the air like a kite."*

For the first time, settlers thought of California as a place of opportunity. In fact, trade with Boston became more important to Californios than trade with Mexico City. California was no longer a far-off colony of New Spain.

READING CHECK **GENERALIZE**
How did trade under Mexican rule help the people of California?

*Richard Henry Dana. *Two Years Before the Mast.* Modern Library, 2001.

Summary

Mexico offered more land grants in California, which helped the population grow. New settlers started ranchos, and trade increased. California's economy grew.

REVIEW

1. What was the California economy based on during the time of Mexican rule?
2. Write a paragraph about **ranchos**, in which you use the terms **land grant** and **diseño**.
3. How was Fort Ross important to the Californios?

CRITICAL THINKING

4. ANALYSIS SKILL What did Californios gain by trading with the United States and other countries? What did they give up?
5. Why do you think ranchos were set up to produce almost everything they needed?
6. **Draw a Mural** Draw a mural showing a rancho. Make sure to include a house, land, animals, and people. Then use your drawing to explain to a classmate how a rancho was run.
7. Focus Skill **GENERALIZE**
On a separate sheet of paper, copy and complete the graphic organizer below.

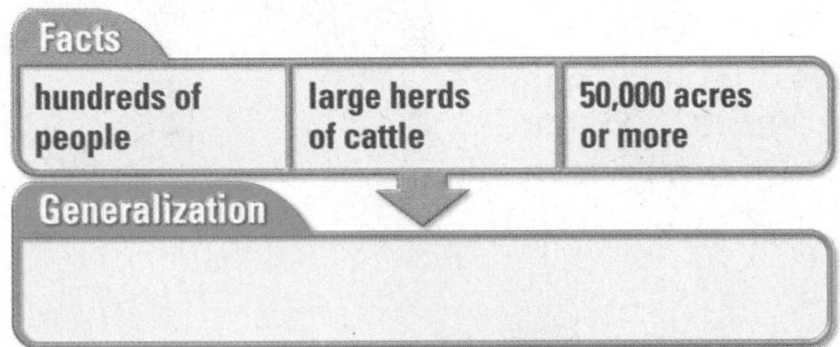

Facts
hundreds of people
large herds of cattle
50,000 acres or more
Generalization

PRIMARY SOURCES

A Diseño

Diseños showed landmarks such as roads, hills, rivers, streams, and ponds. They also included trees, large rocks, and other landmarks. If there was already a building on the land, that building was also shown on the diseño.

Diseños were much less detailed and less accurate than most other kinds of maps. Sometimes this caused problems. People with neighboring lands might disagree over where the line was between their properties, especially if a landmark, such as a tree or rock, shown on a diseño was no longer there.

The Mexican government stamped each diseño and gave it a number. This helped in keeping track of the land grants.

The points on this compass rose are labeled with letters that stand for the directions in Spanish. *S* stands for *sur*, which means "south." *N* stands for *norte*, which means "north."

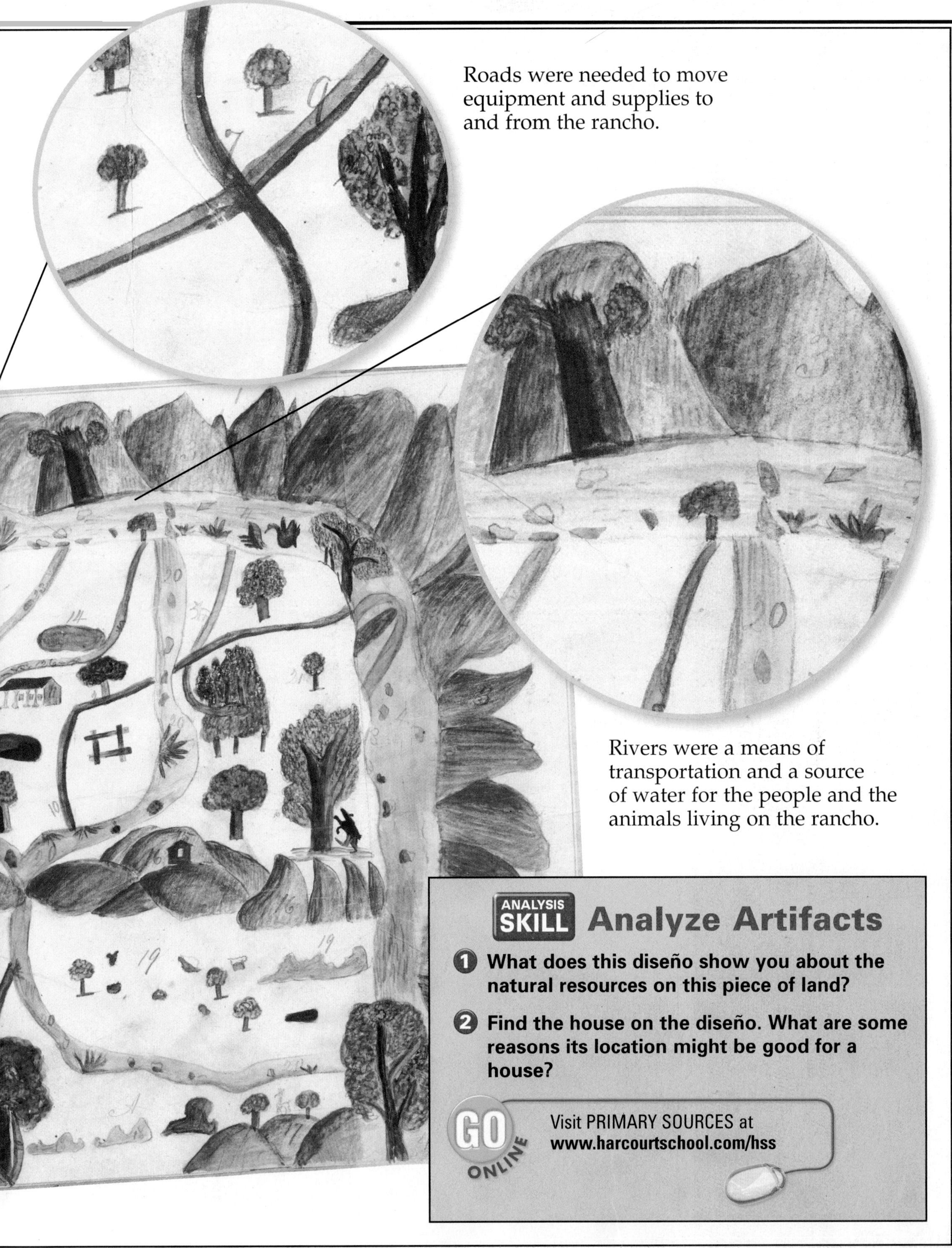

Roads were needed to move equipment and supplies to and from the rancho.

Rivers were a means of transportation and a source of water for the people and the animals living on the rancho.

ANALYSIS SKILL **Analyze Artifacts**

1. **What does this diseño show you about the natural resources on this piece of land?**
2. **Find the house on the diseño. What are some reasons its location might be good for a house?**

GO ONLINE Visit PRIMARY SOURCES at **www.harcourtschool.com/hss**

Lesson 3

Life on the Ranchos

WHAT TO KNOW
How did ranchos become the center of life in California during the period of Mexican rule?

- ✓ Explain the roles of people who lived and worked on ranchos.
- ✓ Describe the social life of people who lived and worked on ranchos.

VOCABULARY
vaquero p. 165
labor p. 166
fiesta p. 167

PEOPLE
William Davis
Juana Briones de Miranda

GENERALIZE

California Standards
HSS 4.2, 4.2.5, 4.2.8

YOU ARE THERE It is barely three o'clock in the morning, but it's already time to start the day's work on the rancho. You know that your horse will be working hard today, so you feed and water it first. Then you swing up into the saddle to round up the other horses your group will need for the day.

It's still dark outside when you return to the main house to eat breakfast. After a hearty meal, you strap a rope and a water canteen to your saddle. Now you're ready to ride many miles to look for the rancho's cattle.

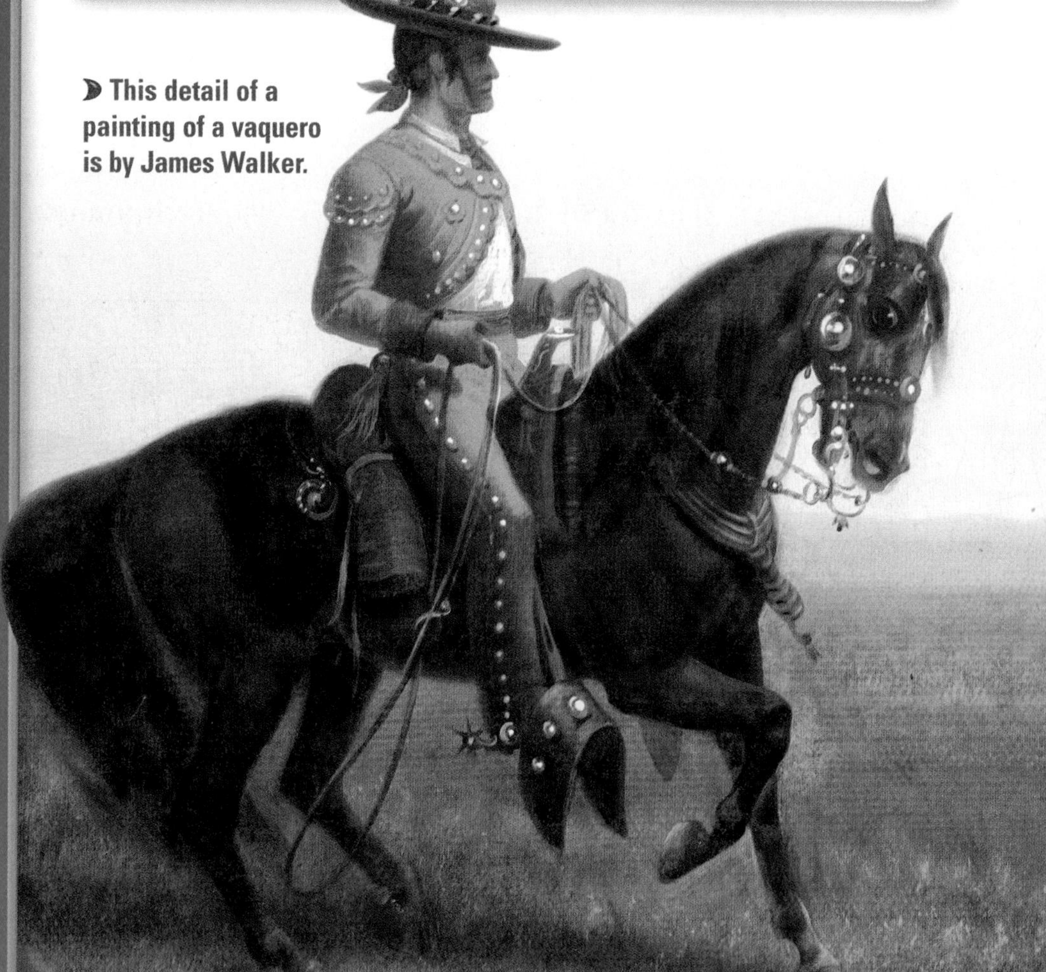
This detail of a painting of a vaquero is by James Walker.

Vaqueros were skilled workers and riders. These vaqueros are using lassos to capture a cow.

Vaqueros

Some of the most important work on a rancho was done by **vaqueros** (vah•KEH•rohz), or cowhands. The main job of the vaquero was to round up the rancho's cattle. The cattle were not fenced in, so they wandered around the countryside.

Vaqueros needed to be skillful riders. Working with ranch animals also meant that a vaquero had to be able to use a reata (ray•AH•tuh), or lasso. **William Davis**, who visited California twice before starting work there in 1838, described the reata as "a slender woven cord about 80 feet in length, and made of very strong leather or strips of hide untanned."* A good vaquero could catch any animal by throwing the reata and looping it around the animal's neck.

Since there were no fences between ranchos, cattle from different ranchos sometimes got mixed together. The vaqueros could separate the cattle by looking at their brands. A brand is a mark burned into a cow's hide to show which rancho owned it. Each rancho had its own brand.

At least once a year, the vaqueros rounded up all the rancho's cattle. A large herd of cattle could be one mile across. The vaqueros counted and sorted the cattle and branded the calves, or young cattle.

READING CHECK GENERALIZE
What was a vaquero's main job?

*William H. Davis. *Sixty-Years in California.* A.J. Leary, 1889.

Women and Indian Workers

Women on the ranchos had many jobs. Some women ran their own ranchos and even worked with the cattle. Edward Vischer was washing his clothes one day when two women from a rancho rode up. He recalled, "The wife and daughter came out to assist in getting in the cattle. Well mounted, they managed their horses superbly, and just as I was up to my elbows in soapsuds, along they came, with a herd of several hundred cattle."*

Women did much more on ranchos than chores, however. Some, such as **Juana Briones de Miranda**, owned their own ranchos. In 1844 she bought a rancho of more than 4,000 acres near San Jose.

Indians, too, did much of the **labor**, or work, on the ranchos. They worked as vaqueros, cooks, farmers, and much more. Most Indian workers were not paid with money. Instead, the ranchers gave them food, some clothes, and a place to live. Some lived in small villages, called *rancherias*, that were built on the rancho.

After the missions closed, many Indians had no place to go. Often, their lands had been taken over by others. Some had been away from their old ways of life too long to return to them.

READING CHECK **SUMMARIZE**
What did many of the mission Indians do after the missions were closed?

*Edward Vischer. From "Hispano-Mexican Childrearing Practices in Pre-American Santa Barbara" by Gloria Miranda. *Southern California Quarterly* 65, no. 4, 1983.

Social Life

Imagine this scene: A woman is sitting on a fine horse. She is wearing high leather boots, a loose shirt tucked into a long, full skirt, and a short jacket. With a quick move, she sets her horse into a fast gallop. She is taking part in a horse-riding contest. As she races by on her horse, she skillfully leans down and scoops up a coin from the ground. The watching crowd cheers.

While there was always work to be done on a rancho, people also took time to get together for celebrations and to enjoy life. Vaqueros often enjoyed showing off their courage and their riding skills in horse races and at bullfights.

Californios were well known for their **fiestas** (fee•ES•tuhz), or parties. To attend a fiesta, people often traveled long distances to visit one another and stayed for many days. Rancho owners treated their guests well. There was always a lot of food, and people played guitars, sang, and danced.

Not all celebrations took place on the ranchos. Weddings and baptisms sometimes took place in churches in or near the pueblos. Like celebrations on ranchos, wedding parties could last a week.

Even without guests, ranchos were often lively places. Many Californio families were very large. It was not unusual for the main house to be filled with brothers and sisters, cousins, aunts and uncles, and grandparents.

A Closer LOOK

A Rancho

Nearly every day on a rancho was filled with work.

1. **The cattle had to be brought in from all parts of the rancho to be counted and sorted.**
2. **In the summer and fall, some of the cattle were killed. After removing the meat, the vaqueros scraped and cleaned the hides. Once the hides were dried in the tannery, they could be used to make leather.**
3. **The oven was built outside the rancho house.**

? What other jobs are people doing in this diagram?

School was not always part of the day for a child on a rancho. There were no public schools, and most people living on ranchos had little chance to learn to read or write.

The children of some wealthy rancho owners, however, learned from traveling teachers. Such teachers went from rancho to rancho, spending a few weeks in each home.

READING CHECK **DRAW CONCLUSIONS**
Why did people living on ranchos have little chance to learn to read or write?

Summary

Most people in Mexican California lived on ranchos. People on ranchos worked hard, but they also enjoyed fiestas and other celebrations. Many Indians lived and worked on the ranchos because they had few other choices.

The Lugo family owned a large rancho near what is now Los Angeles.

REVIEW

1. How did ranchos become the center of life in California during the period of Mexican rule?
2. Use the terms **vaquero** and **labor** in a sentence about rancho life.
3. How did rancho owners identify their cattle?

CRITICAL THINKING

4. ANALYSIS SKILL Why do you think the games and contests held at fiestas tested courage and riding skills?
5. **Write a Letter** Imagine that you are visiting a California rancho in the 1800s. Write a letter to a friend who lives in a city. Describe what life is like at the rancho.
6. Focus Skill **GENERALIZE** On a separate sheet of paper, copy and complete the graphic organizer below.

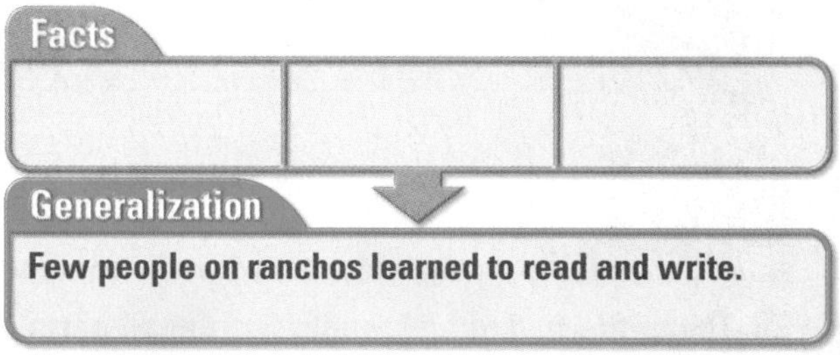

Facts

Generalization

Few people on ranchos learned to read and write.

Juana Briones

Biography

Trustworthiness
Respect
Responsibility
Fairness
Caring
Patriotism

*"She . . . extended the love, nurturing, and care [that] she gave to her immediate family to the larger community of people. . . ."**

In 1836, Juana Briones decided to change her life. Because her husband had been treating her badly for a long time, she took her eight children and moved from the family's home to the town of Yerba Buena (YAIR•bah BWAY•nah), a settlement that would later become part of the city of San Francisco.

Juana Briones built this home at Rancho La Purísima Concepción.

Worried that her husband or the government would take her Yerba Buena home, Juana Briones began to save money. She grew crops and sold fruits and vegetables. With her money, she bought Rancho La Purísima Concepción in 1844.

At the rancho, she continued to make money. While managing the rancho work, she also adopted six children. At Yerba Buena, Juana Briones gave medical help to the sick.

In 1997, the city of San Francisco dedicated a plaque in her honor in the neighborhood known as North Beach, near her Yerba Buena home.

*Albert Camarillo, from the speech "The Legacy of Juana Briones," dedicating California Registered Historical Landmark number 1024, in 1997.

Why Character Counts

Which of Juana Briones's actions do you think best shows that she was a caring person?

Bio Brief

1802 Born

1889 Died

1820 Marries Apolinario Miranda

1836 Moves with her children to Yerba Buena

1844 Buys a 4,400-acre ranch, La Purísima Concepción

GO ONLINE
Interactive Multimedia Biographies
Visit MULTIMEDIA BIOGRAPHIES at www.harcourtschool.com/hss

Time

1805

1815

1810
The Mexican War for Independence begins

Reading Social Studies

When you **generalize**, you make a broad statement about the facts and details you have read.

Generalize

Complete this graphic organizer to make a generalization about the settlement of Mexican California from the early 1800s to 1850. A copy of this graphic organizer appears on page 46 of the Homework and Practice Book.

Mexican Rule in California

Facts

Mexico won its independence from Spain.			

Generalization

The economy of California grew stronger and its population increased under Mexican rule.

California Writing Prompts

Write a Narrative Imagine you are a Californio living in Alta California. Write a story in which you ask the Mexican government for a land grant. Include a description of the land you want, and explain what you will do if the land is granted to you.

Write a Report Write a short report describing the lives of either California Indians or women on ranchos. Visit your library and use your textbook and the Internet to gather information, facts, and details for your report.

1825

1835

1812
Fort Ross is founded

1821
Mexico wins its independence

1834
The Mexican government begins to close missions

Use Vocabulary

Write a definition for each word. Then use each word in a sentence that explains its meaning.

1. **independence,** p. 149
2. **land grant,** p. 157
3. **rancho,** p. 158
4. **barter,** p. 160
5. **tallow,** p. 160
6. **vaquero,** p. 165
7. **labor,** p. 166

Use the Time Line

Use the summary time line above to answer the questions.

8. In what year did Mexico gain independence from Spain?
9. How long did it take the Mexican government to begin closing missions after Mexico won its independence?

Apply Skills

Identify Multiple Causes and Effects

10. What are some reasons why ranchos became the center of life in California after Mexico gained independence from Spain?

Recall Facts

Answer these questions.

11. What changes did Mexico's independence from Spain bring to Alta California?
12. How did life for California Indians change after the missions were closed?
13. How did California's economy develop under Mexican rule?

Write the letter of the best choice.

14. Which of the following received most of the land grants in California?
    A Californio women
    B Californio men
    C California Indians
    D settlers from the United States
15. What was a popular trading item in California in the 1830s?
    A jewelry
    B corn
    C tallow
    D soap

Think Critically

16. ANALYSIS SKILL In what ways would your life be different if you lived on a rancho during the 1800s?
17. ANALYSIS SKILL If you were living in Alta California in the 1830s, would you want to live on a rancho or in a pueblo? Why?

Carmel Mission

GET READY

Father Junípero Serra began establishing missions in Alta California in 1769. San Carlos Borroméo de Carmelo, or Carmel Mission, was the second mission that Serra founded. He placed a cross in the center of the place where the mission was to be built. Today, a replica of that cross stands at the same spot. The only original building left standing is the museum, but many other buildings around the mission have been reconstructed according to designs that have survived from the 1780s. You can also visit some of the rooms inside the mission, which have been restored with original furnishings, altar pieces, church records, and books. When you walk through Carmel Mission, you experience what mission life was like more than 200 years ago.

LOCATE IT

WHAT TO SEE

Carmel Mission began to fall into ruins after it was abandoned in the 1830s. By the time reconstruction began in 1931, little remained of the original building.

When Serra founded Carmel Mission, he placed a cross where the mission would be.

Rooms inside the mission have been restored. Some even have the original furnishings. You can see the bedrooms, the kitchen, and other living areas when you visit.

A VIRTUAL TOUR

GO ONLINE Visit VIRTUAL TOURS at www.harcourtschool.com/hss

Unit 2

Review

 **THE BIG IDEA**

Exploration Explorations led to interactions between Europeans and California Indians.

Summary

Early California

In 1769, the Spanish began to build presidios and missions along the coast of Alta California. As they had done in other parts of New Spain, the Spanish wanted to start a colony of loyal subjects to protect their claim to the area. The settlements the Spanish built changed the lives of many California Indians.

Missionaries tried to teach Spanish ways to local Indians and convert them to the Catholic religion. While some Indians were willing to change, others were not. Many California Indians resisted the Spanish.

In 1821, the people of Mexico defeated the Spanish in the Mexican War for Independence. After the war, California became part of Mexico. Life in California changed under Mexican rule. New laws closed the missions and supported the growth of ranchos. These changes had far-reaching effects on people in California.

Main Ideas and Vocabulary

Read the summary above. Then answer the questions that follow.

1. What is the meaning of the word missionaries?
A Spanish explorers
B governors of California
C people who own large cattle ranches
D people who teach their religion to others

2. Why did the Spanish want to start a colony in Alta California?
A to fight against the Indians
B to open more ranchos
C to keep missionaries busy
D to defend their claim to the area

3. What is a rancho?
A a small town
B a large cattle ranch
C a brick made out of mud and grass
D a ship used by European traders

4. Who controlled Alta California immediately after the Mexican War for Independence?
A Mexico
B Russia
C the United States
D Spain

Recall Facts

Answer these questions.

5. Looking for the Strait of Anián was very costly. Why did Spain continue to send explorers to search for it?
6. Why did Spain want to find a good harbor in Alta California?
7. Why did Spain establish missions and presidios in California?
8. Why was it hard to get to Alta California from the rest of New Spain?
9. What were some of the duties of soldiers in Alta California?
10. How did the missions affect California's economy?
11. How did some California Indians at the missions resist the Spanish?
12. Who worked with the cattle and horses on ranchos?
13. How did the growth of ranchos affect California's economy?

Write the letter of the best choice.

14. Where was the first mission built in California?
    A San Diego de Alcalá
    B Monterey
    C San Francisco de Asís
    D Santa Barbara
15. What was El Camino Real?
    A a road
    B a rancho
    C a pueblo
    D a Spanish galleon
16. What happened to the missions in California after the Mexican government took control?
    A They were torn down.
    B They became larger.
    C They were changed into presidios.
    D They were no longer ruled by the church.

Think Critically

17. ANALYSIS SKILL Why do you think most missions in California were built near Indian villages?
18. ANALYSIS SKILL Why do you think some ranchos were extremely large?

Apply Skills

Follow Routes on a Historical Map

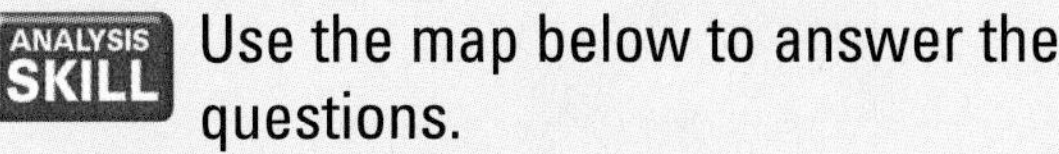

Use the map below to answer the questions.

19. What city did Anza start from?
20. Which river did Anza follow as he approched Yuma?
21. Which mission did Anza reach first? San Luís Obispo or San Gabriel?

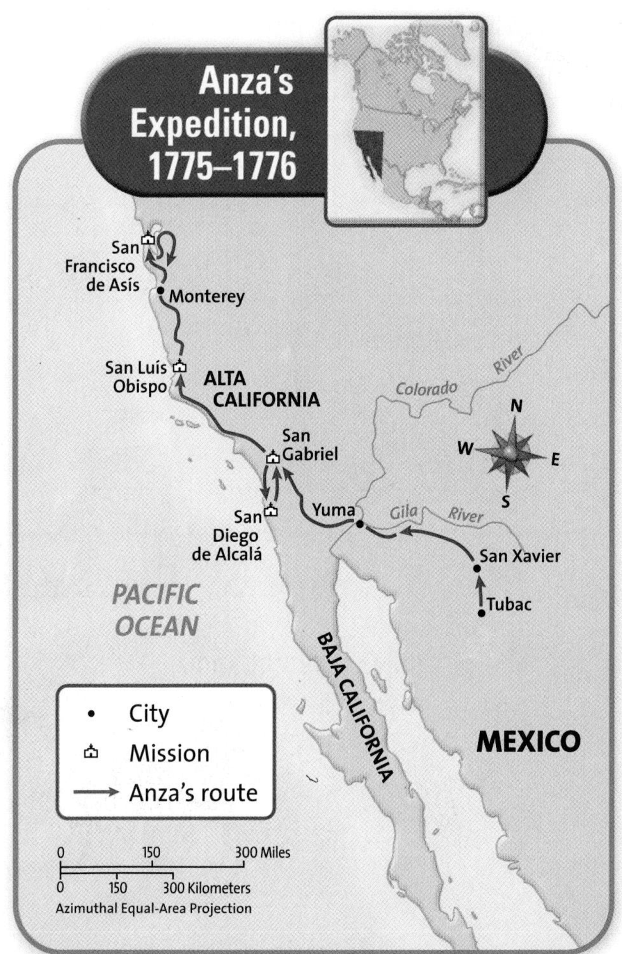

Unit 2

Activities

Read More

- *California Cowhands* by Richie Chevat.

- *Mission Santa Barbara* by Ellen Appelbaum.

- *Exploring California's Coast* by Nan Friedman.

Show What You Know

Unit Writing Activity

Write a Narrative Imagine that you are part of a Spanish expedition to California. Write a letter to a friend in Spain telling a story about your travels. Tell where you are going, and describe the land and California Indians you meet. Include sensory details such as sights and sounds to illustrate time and place.

Unit Project

Build a Museum Display Build a museum exhibit about early California. Choose people, places, and events to include in your display, and write brief reports about them. Create artifacts, drawings, maps, and journal entries to go with your reports.

GO ONLINE Visit ACTIVITIES at **www.harcourtschool.com/hss**

The Road to Statehood

Unit 3

START WITH THE STANDARDS

California History-Social Science Standards

4.2 Students describe the social, political, cultural, and economic life and interactions among people of California from the pre-Columbian societies to the Spanish mission and Mexican rancho periods.

4.3 Students explain the economic, social, and political life in California from the establishment of the Bear Flag Republic through the Mexican-American War, the Gold Rush, and the granting of statehood.

4.4 Students explain how California became an agricultural and industrial power, tracing the transformation of the California economy and its political and cultural development since the 1850s.

The Big Idea

Growth and Change

New opportunities and discoveries attracted many people to California.

What to Know

- Why did people travel to California, and what routes did they take?
- How did the discovery of gold change life in California?
- What events led to statehood?

Show What You Know

- ★ **Unit 3 Test**
- **Writing: An Information Report**
- **Unit Project: A Fact Book**

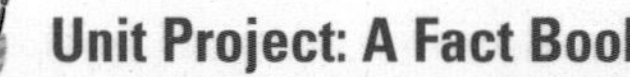

Time

The Road to Statehood

1834 Joseph Reddeford Walker finds a pass through the Sierra Nevada, p. 194

1825 | 1830 | 1835 | 1840

At the Same Time

1830 Peter Cooper designs and builds the *Tom Thumb,* the first locomotive made in the United States

1836 Texans and Mexican troops fight at the Alamo

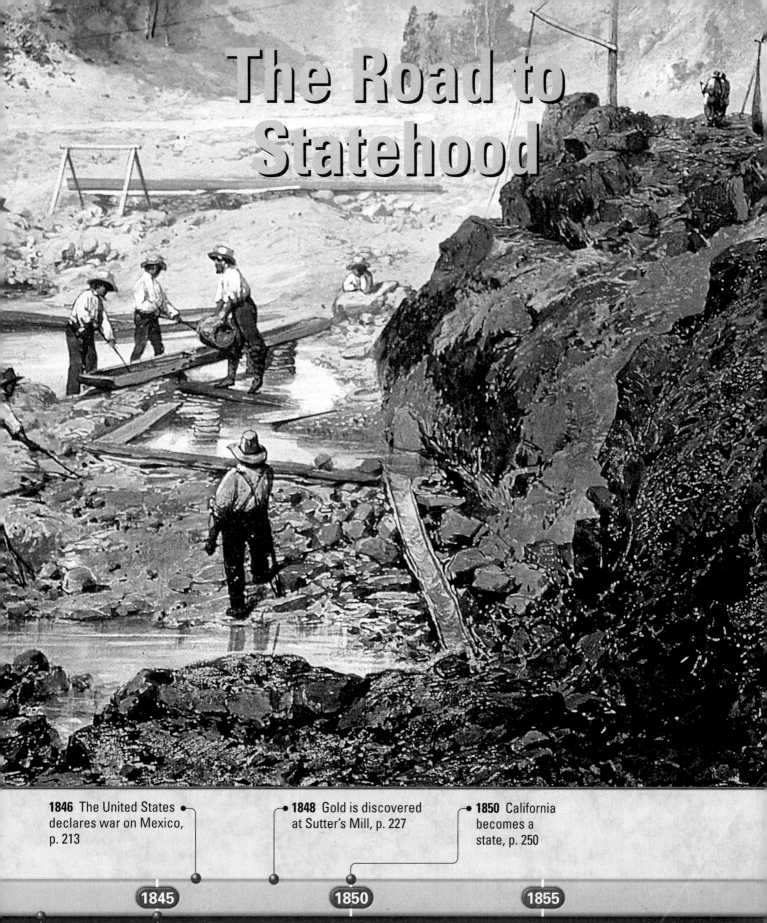

The Road to Statehood

1846 The United States declares war on Mexico, p. 213

1848 Gold is discovered at Sutter's Mill, p. 227

1850 California becomes a state, p. 250

1845

1850

1855

1842 The border between the United States and Canada is established by the Webster-Ashburton Treaty

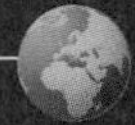

1845 Irish Potato Famine begins

Unit 3

People

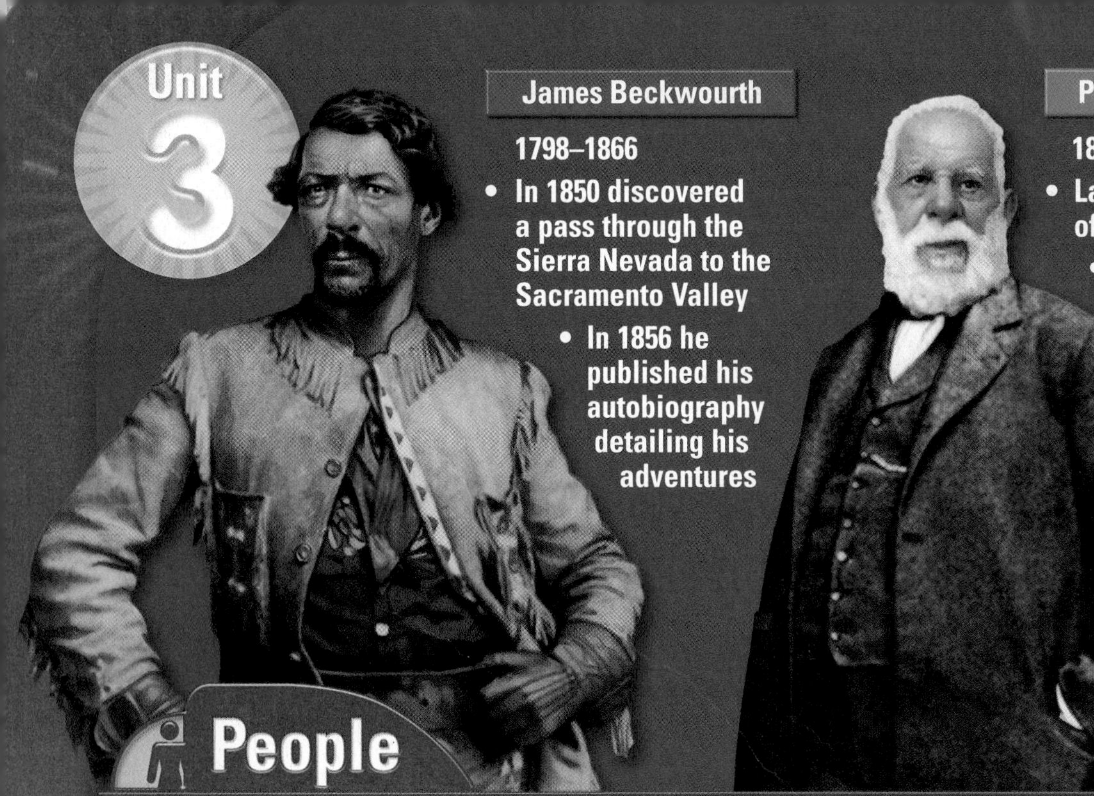

James Beckwourth

1798–1866

- In 1850 discovered a pass through the Sierra Nevada to the Sacramento Valley
- In 1856 he published his autobiography detailing his adventures

Pío Pico

1801–1894

- Last Mexican governor of Alta California
- Later became a Los Angeles city councilman
- Owner of the 8,893-acre"El Ranchito"

1790
1820

- 1798 • James Beckwourth
- 1801 • Pío Pico
- 1802 • Bernarda Ruíz
- 1803 • John Sutter
- 1813 • John C. Frémont
- 1818 • Bridget "Biddy" Mason
- 1819 • John Bidwell
- 1819 • Louise Clappe

John C. Frémont

1813–1890

- Became known as the Great Pathfinder after two expeditions on the western frontier in the early 1840s
- Served as one of the first senators from California
- Was a U.S Presidential candidate in 1856

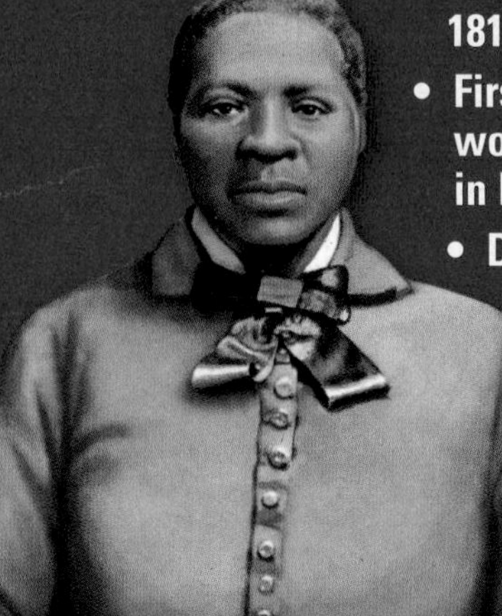

Bridget "Biddy" Mason

1818–1891

- First African American woman to own property in Los Angeles
- Donated money to many charities and churches, including the First African Methodist Episcopal Church, which she co-founded

Bernarda Ruíz

1802–1880

- Helped convince John C. Frémont not to punish the Californios for fighting the Americans in the Mexican-American War

John Sutter

1803–1880

- Built Sutter's Fort, which marked the end of the Oregon Trail for many pioneers
- Gold was discovered on his land along the American River in 1848

1850 1880 1910

1866

1894

1880

1880

1890

1891

1900

1906

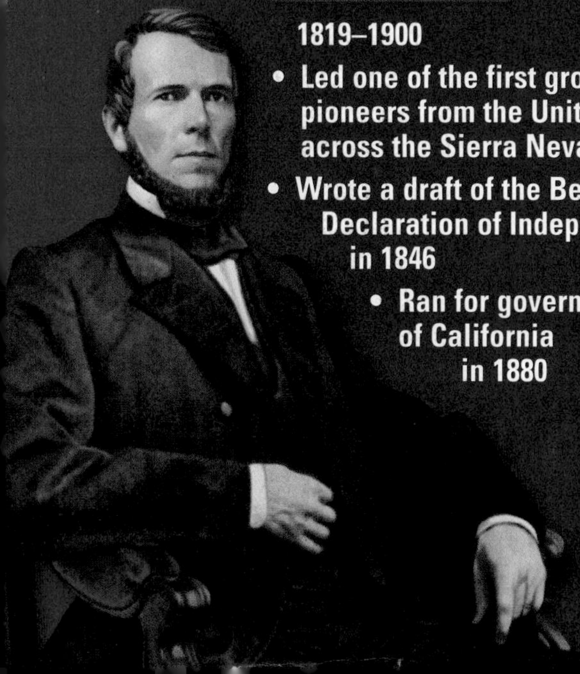

John Bidwell

1819–1900

- Led one of the first groups of pioneers from the United States across the Sierra Nevada
- Wrote a draft of the Bear Flag Declaration of Independence in 1846
- Ran for governor of California in 1880

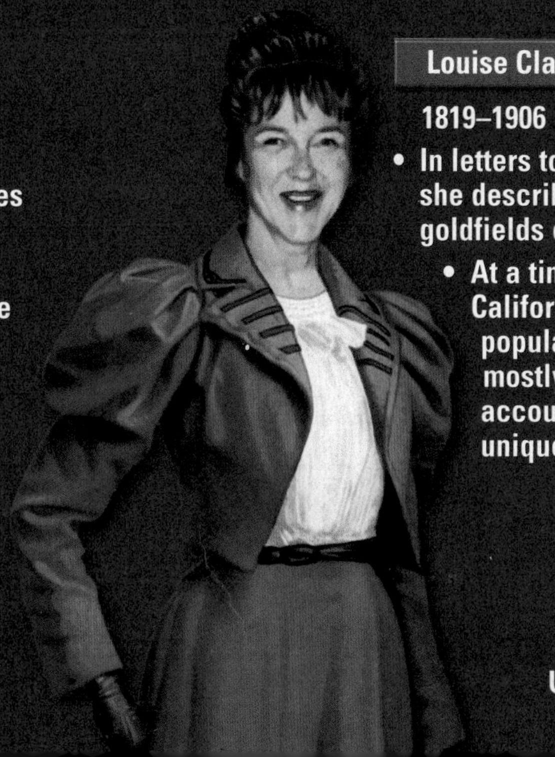

Louise Clappe

1819–1906

- In letters to her sister, she described life in the goldfields of California
- At a time when California's population was mostly male, her accounts provided a unique point of view

Unit 3

Place

Mexican California, 1840

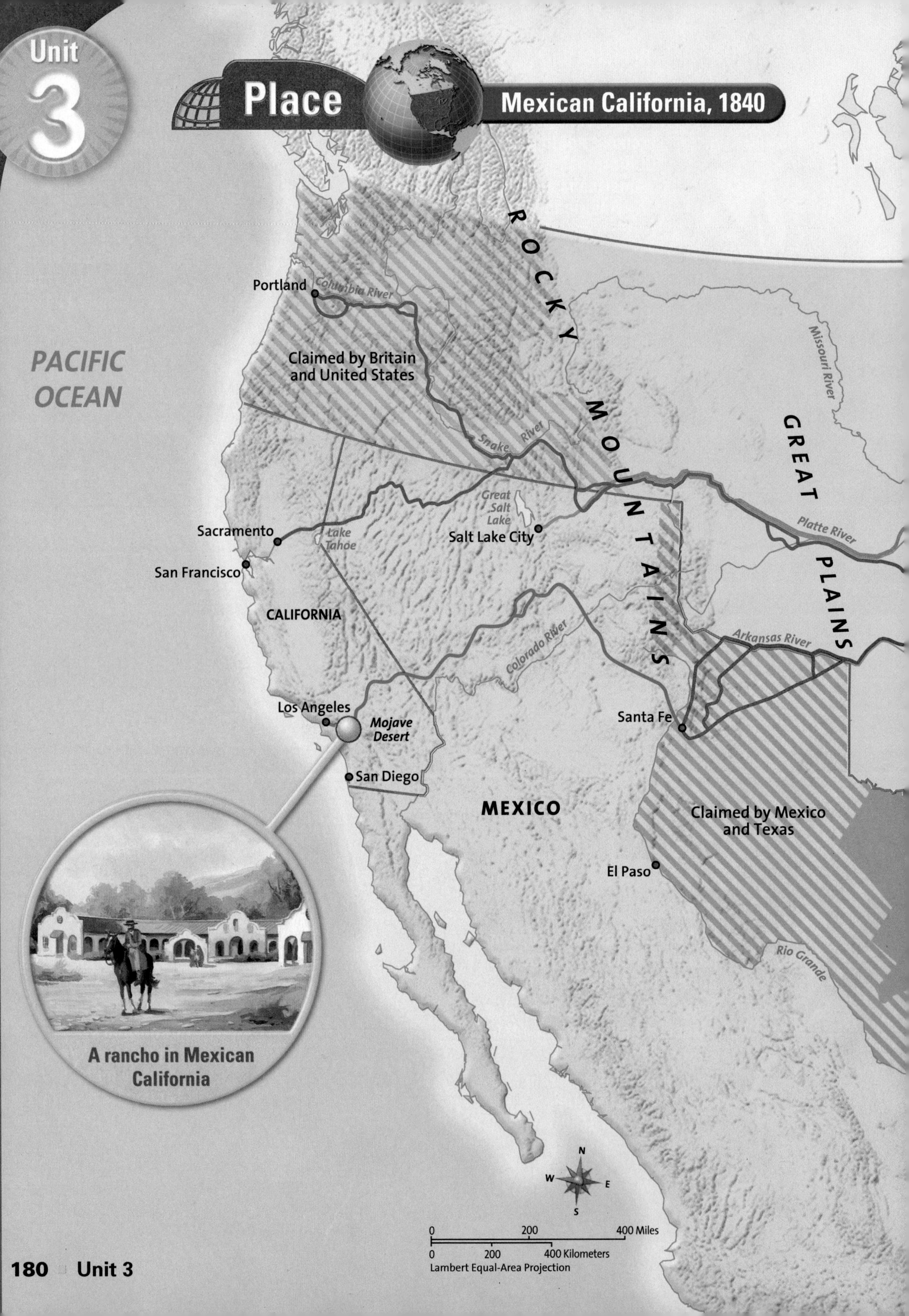

PACIFIC OCEAN

ROCKY MOUNTAINS

GREAT PLAINS

Portland

Columbia River

Claimed by Britain and United States

Missouri River

Snake River

Great Salt Lake

Salt Lake City

Platte River

Sacramento

Lake Tahoe

San Francisco

CALIFORNIA

Colorado River

Arkansas River

Los Angeles

Mojave Desert

Santa Fe

San Diego

MEXICO

Claimed by Mexico and Texas

El Paso

Rio Grande

A rancho in Mexican California

N E S W

0 200 400 Miles
0 200 400 Kilometers
Lambert Equal-Area Projection

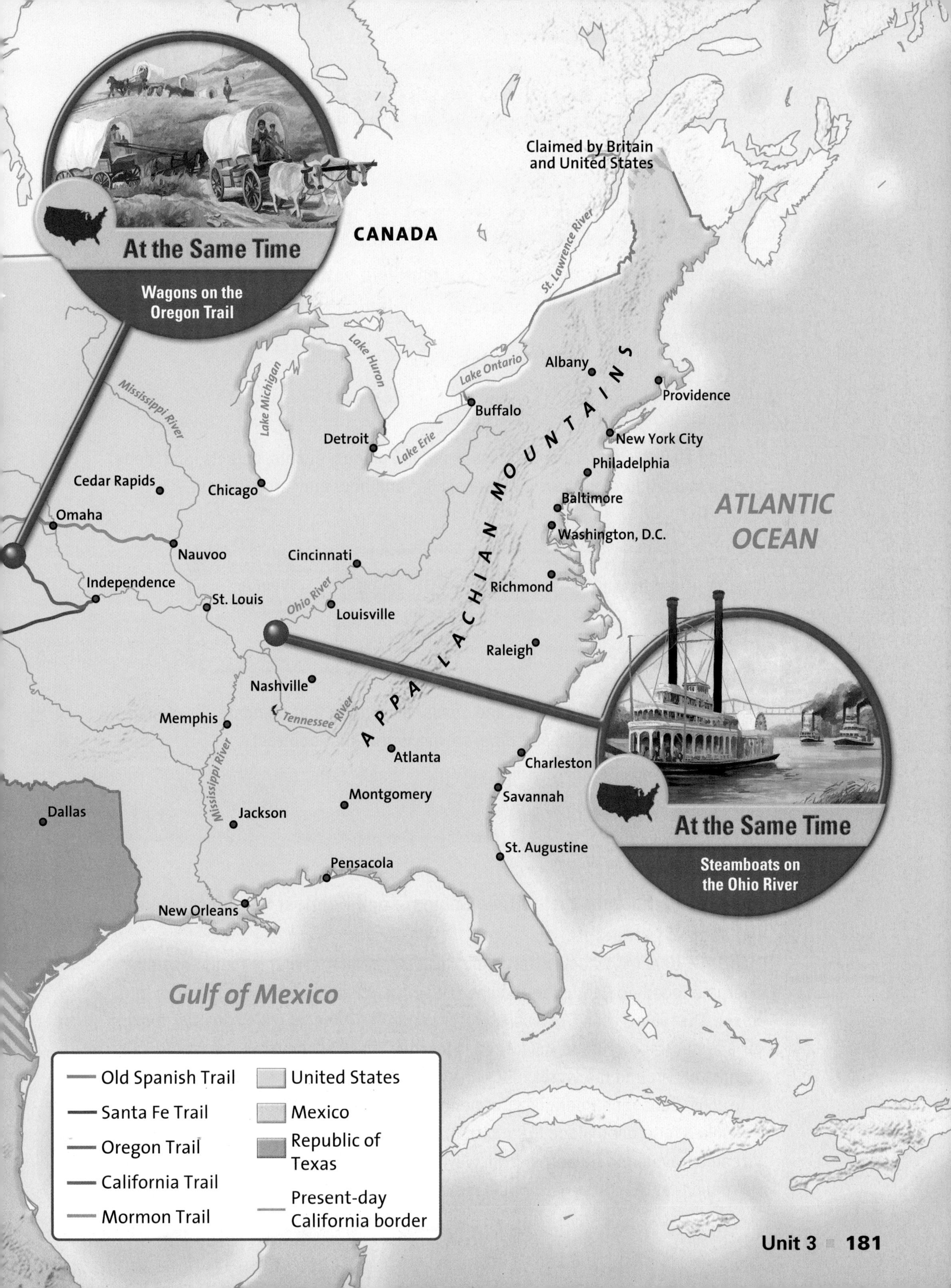

At the Same Time
Wagons on the Oregon Trail
CANADA
Claimed by Britain and United States
St. Lawrence River
Lake Ontario
Lake Huron
Lake Michigan
Lake Erie
Mississippi River
APPALACHIAN MOUNTAINS
Albany
Providence
Buffalo
New York City
Detroit
Philadelphia
Cedar Rapids
Chicago
Baltimore
ATLANTIC OCEAN
Omaha
Washington, D.C.
Nauvoo
Cincinnati
Richmond
Independence
St. Louis
Ohio River
Louisville
Raleigh
Nashville
Memphis
Tennessee River
Atlanta
Charleston
Mississippi River
Montgomery
Savannah
Dallas
Jackson
At the Same Time
St. Augustine
Steamboats on the Ohio River
Pensacola
New Orleans
Gulf of Mexico
Old Spanish Trail
Santa Fe Trail
Oregon Trail
California Trail
Mormon Trail
United States
Mexico
Republic of Texas
Present-day California border

Reading Social Studies

Focus Skill Compare and Contrast

When you compare, you think about how two or more things are alike, or similar. When you contrast, you think about how they are different.

Why It Matters

Being able to compare and contrast people, places, events, objects, and ideas can help you figure out how they are similar and how they are different.

Topic 1	Similar	Topic 2
What is different	What is similar	What is different

- *Like, alike, both, also, same,* and *similar* are words that compare.
- *But, instead, however,* and *different* are words that contrast.

Practice the Skill

Read the paragraphs that follow. Compare and contrast the information in the second paragraph.

Similar
Different

In 1519, Spanish explorer Hernando Cortés set sail for what is today Mexico. There he found and conquered the wealthy Aztec Empire, claiming the area for Spain. That same year, Spanish explorer Ferdinand Magellan also set sail, looking for a faster trade route to Asia. On this journey, his crew became the first to sail completely around the world.

In 1595, Sebastián Rodríguez Cermeño sailed from the Philippines to California. He looked for a good place for a port, but he did not find one. In 1602, Sebastián Vizcaíno traveled to California from New Spain. He also wanted to find a good port. He found that Monterey Bay would make a good port.

Apply What You Learned

 **Compare and Contrast Read the paragraphs, and answer the questions.**

Ships Bound for California

In the mid-1800s, many people in the eastern United States were eager to get to California. The easiest route was by sea around South America. Different kinds of ships traveled those waters. Many people wanted to arrive in California as quickly as possible. Those who had enough money could travel on clipper ships.

Clipper ships were the fastest ships of their time. Unlike other ships that took as long as six to eight months to travel to California, clipper ships took only about three to four months. What gave clipper ships such speed? They had long, narrow hulls, flat bottoms, and three masts with up to five sails on each.

In 1851, the clipper ship *Flying Cloud* sailed from New York to San Francisco in just 89 days! Just a few years earlier, the steamship *California* had made the same journey in 145 days. Because the *California* was powered by steam, it had to carry tons of coal. The *Flying Cloud* was much lighter, since it was powered by wind.

The clipper ships were the fastest boats for only a short time. By the late 1800s, steamships had been greatly improved. New engines gave them more power and speed. They no longer needed to carry as much coal. By the 1900s, clipper ships had almost disappeared.

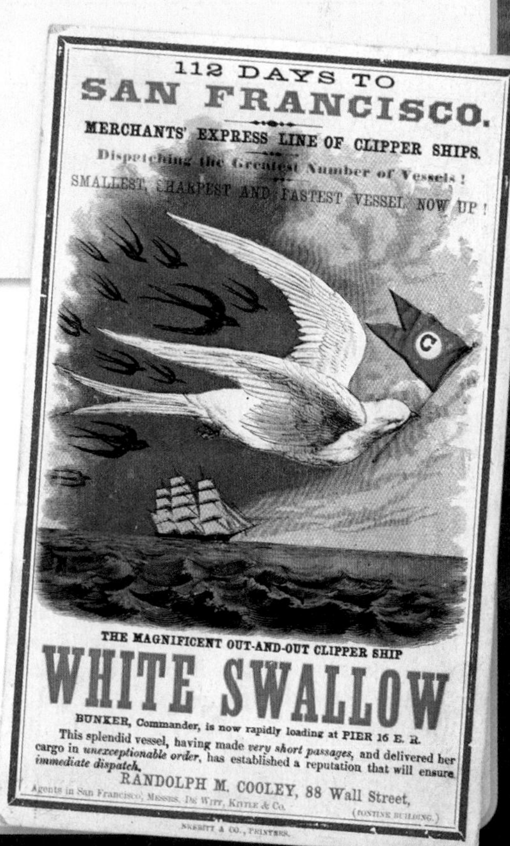

Compare and Contrast

1. **How did the way clipper ships were powered differ from the way steamships were powered?**
2. **How were the clipper ship *Flying Cloud* and the steamship *California* similar? different?**
3. **How would you describe the popularity of clipper ships in the mid-1800s compared to their popularity in the 1900s?**

Study Skills

USE A K-W-L CHART

A K-W-L chart can help you focus on what you already know about a topic and what you want to learn about it.

- **Use the K column to list what you know about a topic.**
- **Use the W column to list what you want to know about the topic.**
- **Use the L column to list what you have learned about the topic after reading.**

California, Here We Come!		
What I Know	What I Want to Know	What I Learned
Many people came to California in the 1800s.	Was it difficult to get to California? Why?	

Apply As You Read

Complete your own K-W-L chart as you read this chapter.

California History-Social Science Standards, Grade 4

4.2 Students describe the social, political, cultural, and economic life and interactions among people of California from the pre-Columbian societies to the Spanish mission and Mexican rancho periods.
4.3 Students explain the economic, social, and political life in California from the establishment of the Bear Flag Republic through the Mexican-American War, the Gold Rush, and the granting of statehood.

CHAPTER

California, Here We Come!

Traveling overland to California from the United States in the 1840s

Start with a Story

Valley of the Moon

The Diary of Maria Rosalia de Milagros

by Sherry Garland • illustrated by Barbara Olsen

In her diary, 12-year-old Maria Rosalia de Milagros (mah•REE•ah ro•sah•LEE•ah deh mee•LAH•grohs) describes life as a servant on the Medina family's *rancho* near Sonoma in 1845. She writes about her friendship with Señor Johnston, an American trader. At this time, more and more Americans were traveling overland to settle in California. As you read, notice the hardships that many of these pioneers, including Señor Johnston's family, faced on the journey to California.

Sunday October 19

Horrible, horrible news! After the meal, a messenger pounded at the door. Señor Johnston's brother, wife, and their two youngest children were killed in an awful accident while crossing the Sierras. Their oxen slipped near a cliff, and while trying to upright the wagon, the parents and children plunged to their deaths. Only Nelly and an older brother survived.

Poor Johnston was inconsolable. He wept openly, then said he must go immediately to Sutter's Fort to get his nephew and niece. He asked Señor Medina if I could accompany him, thinking it might be a comfort to his niece to have a companion her own age in this sad time and because I am an orphan, too. Señor Medina quickly consented and is sending along supplies, extra horses, and an Indian guide to show Johnston the quickest route to Sutter's Fort.

I must close for now; the horses are packed and ready.

inconsolable not able to be comforted

consented agreed

October 21

We have been pushing the horses hard for over two days. We awake before dawn and travel even after dark. We are passing through the most beautiful country—pleasant hills and valleys lush with autumn wildflowers, pine trees, live oaks, and *manzanita* shrubs. Occasionally we pass shepherds bringing their herds down from the mountains for winter grazing. The air is crisp and reminds me that light snows are already falling on top of the distant Sierras. I can only imagine the misery of the American settlers who have the misfortune of not getting across before winter sets in.

We changed horses at a small, bleak *rancho* and set out again. I have never been so far from home. It is frightening, yet exciting. I only wish we did not travel at such a pace. My bottom is so saddle sore, I may never walk again.

manzanita (mahn•zah•NEE•tah) a type of evergreen shrub

October 22

Señor Johnston is resting a moment. We are on a hillock and I can see Sutter's Fort below beside a slough that runs to the Sacramento River. The fort is a large rectangular building with a tall, armed bastion at each end . . .

From the top of each bastion roof flies a flag. The adobe walls are several feet thick and contain few windows. Johann Sutter hails from a far-off country called Switzerland, so he named his settlement New Helvetia, the Latin word for Switzerland. Everyone else calls it Sutter's Fort or simply Sacramento, after the nearest river.

Near the fort is a corral for livestock, and in the distance fields of grain are being harvested. I can clearly see the Indian laborers loading big *carretas* pulled by oxen. Fur, cattle hides, tallow, and handicrafts are being loaded onto barges at the slough. The barges will carry the goods down the river all the way to San Francisco Bay to waiting merchant ships. The ships, many of them American, will haul the goods around the tip of South America to the United States.

hillock a small hill

slough (SLOO) a muddy river inlet

bastion (BAS•chuhn) a heavily guarded place

corral a pen for holding livestock

It is almost dark, and I hear bells from the fort signaling the laborers to stop work and return to their quarters. I see smoke rising from chimneys and I can smell bread baking. Johnston is ready to ride again, so I must close for now.

Later that night

It is dark now, and I am in a room set aside for arriving emigrants. Nelly Johnston is sound asleep. She had not slept well for a week because of grief and has finally cried herself out. She is a very quiet girl, thin from nearly starving on the long trip from Missouri. Her wavy hair is the color of an oak leaf turning bronze, and she has a few freckles on her nose.

Nelly does not speak a word of Spanish, but through Johnston and with the little English I know, she communicated her feelings. She is still in shock because she traveled so far, so long, through such hardships, only to lose her parents on the final leg of the journey. Not to hostile Indians when they crossed the Great Plains, or to thirst, or to disease or hunger, or to vicious animals, but to a stupid mishap, to the slipping of an ox's hoof.

emigrant a person who has moved away from a place

hostile unfriendly

Response Corner

1. Why was the overland journey to California so difficult?
2. Why do you think hardships did not stop pioneers from coming to California?

Lesson 1

Time

1825 | 1840 | 1855

1826 Jedediah Strong Smith goes to California

1827 Smith crosses the Sierra Nevada

1834 Joseph Walker finds Walker Pass

WHAT TO KNOW
Why did trappers from the United States head west to California?

- ✓ Explain why trappers and others traveled to California.
- ✓ Describe the routes that many trappers took to get to California.

VOCABULARY
demand p. 191
supply p. 191
frontier p. 191
trailblazer p. 192
pass p. 194

PEOPLE
Jedediah Strong Smith
James Ohio Pattie
Sylvester Pattie
Ewing Young
Joseph Reddeford Walker
James Beckwourth

PLACES
Mission San Gabriel
Sierra Nevada

Focus Skill **COMPARE AND CONTRAST**

California Standards
HSS 4.2, 4.2.8, 4.3, 4.3.2

Americans Move West

YOU ARE THERE Up ahead, you catch sight of a beaver sliding into a stream. The year is 1830, and many of the animals in your area have already been trapped. Other trappers have told you about large numbers of beavers and otters in the unmapped lands beyond the Rocky Mountains. You know that to continue trapping animals and trading furs, you'll soon need to move west. But that land is part of Mexico.

Trappers Head West

For nearly 25 years, California remained a part of Mexico. It also remained a hard place to reach. Sun-baked deserts and steep mountains separated it from other parts of Mexico and from the United States.

For years, the only way for people from the United States to get to California was by ship. In the 1820s, however, trappers began to open up new overland routes through the West. They discovered these routes while looking for new places to trap beavers and other animals.

At that time, beaver furs were used to make hats and other kinds of clothing. There was a high **demand**, or desire, for those products in the United States and in Europe. People were willing to pay a lot of money for them.

By the 1820s, so many beavers had been caught and killed that the supply of beaver fur in the United States was nearly used up. **Supply** is the amount of a good or service that is offered for sale. Because the demand was high and the supply was low, the prices that people were willing to pay for furs went up.

Trappers from the United States began to travel farther and farther into what they called the frontier, looking for fur-bearing animals. The **frontier** was land beyond the settled parts of the United States. At the time, the borders of the United States reached as far west as the Rocky Mountains. However, few people lived in these far western lands.

READING CHECK **COMPARE AND CONTRAST**
Earlier settlers in California came for land. Why did trappers come to California?

These trappers search a western river for fur-bearing animals.

FAST FACT

Trappers in the West would meet every year at a gathering called the Rendezvous (RAHN•dih•voo) to sell their furs and buy needed supplies.

Jedediah Strong Smith

TIME 1826

PLACE Alta California

As trappers from the United States moved west, they opened up new paths. One of these trailblazers was **Jedediah Strong Smith**. A **trailblazer** is someone who makes a new path for others to follow.

Smith was a young man in his twenties and was eager to explore California. In August 1826, Smith led 17 men on a trapping expedition that left from the Great Salt Lake area, in what is now Utah. They headed southwest and eventually reached the Colorado River. Then they made their way across the Mojave Desert.

Indian guides helped the trappers, but travel was extremely difficult. There was little shelter from the sun and little water. As Smith wrote, "I travelled . . . over a country of complete barrens . . . from morning until night without water."*

In November, the men went through the San Bernardino Mountains and became the first people from the United States to travel by land to California. They arrived at **Mission San Gabriel**. Father José Bernardo Sánchez gave them food and a place to stay. Next, the trappers went south to San Diego, where they met José María Echeandía (eh•chay•ahn•DEE•ah), the Mexican governor of California.

Smith asked Echeandía for permission to explore California. Echeandía felt that Smith might be an American spy, so he ordered him to leave California.

*Jedediah Strong Smith. From *The Ashley-Smith Explorations and the Discovery of a Central Route to the Pacific, 1822–1829* by Harrison Clifford Dale. Arthur H. Clark Company, 1941.

This painting shows Jedediah Smith and fellow trailblazer James Clyman.

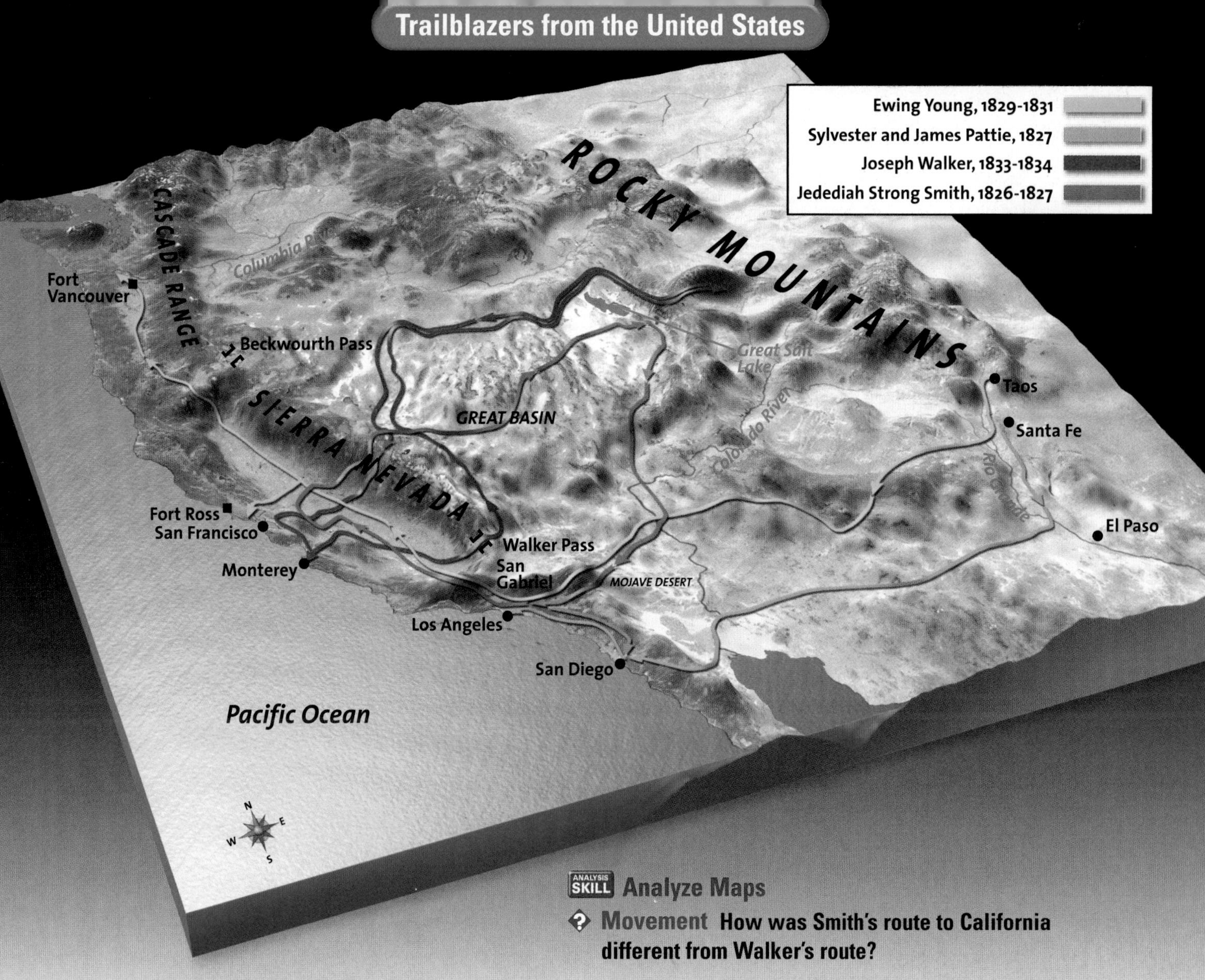

Analyze Maps

Movement **How was Smith's route to California different from Walker's route?**

Smith agreed to leave California. But before he did, he spent several months trapping in the San Joaquin Valley. Smith and his men survived freezing temperatures and rough lands as they crossed the **Sierra Nevada** and continued on to what is now Utah. They were the first people from the United States to cross those mountains.

READING CHECK **COMPARE AND CONTRAST**
How did Smith's route into California differ from his route out of California?

More Trailblazers

After Smith's expedition, other people set out to find new land routes into California. **James Ohio Pattie** and his father, **Sylvester Pattie**, began an expedition in 1827. These trappers were no more welcome in California than Smith had been. They were put in jail for entering California without permission. James Pattie was later freed, but his father died in jail.

Walker Pass became the main route for many settlers traveling to California.

Trailblazers opened new paths to California for other people from the United States to follow. **Ewing Young's** travels during the 1830s helped develop the Old Spanish Trail from Santa Fe, New Mexico, to southern California. **Joseph Reddeford Walker** was the first American to cross the Sierra Nevada from the east. He found a **pass**, or opening between mountains, that was later named for him. In 1850, **James Beckwourth** found a new pass through the northern Sierra Nevada. Today, this pass is called Beckwourth Pass.

READING CHECK **DRAW CONCLUSIONS**
What risk did explorers and trappers from the United States face by going to California?

Summary

The demand for furs led trappers from the United States to blaze new trails to California. Settlers coming to California would later use the new trails.

REVIEW

1. Why did trappers from the United States head west to California?
2. How did **trailblazers** help other explorers and settlers?
3. What land routes did people from the United States use to get to California?

CRITICAL THINKING

4. SKILL Think about how Father Sánchez and Governor Echeandía first reacted to the arrival of people from the United States. Which reaction do you think was more appropriate? Why?
5. Group the trailblazers, based on the routes they followed. Explain how you chose each group.
6. **Give a Speech** Imagine that you are Jedediah Strong Smith. You are asking Governor Echeandía to allow you to explore California. Write a speech to try to persuade him to let you do so.
7. Focus Skill **COMPARE AND CONTRAST** On a separate sheet of paper, copy and complete the graphic organizer below.

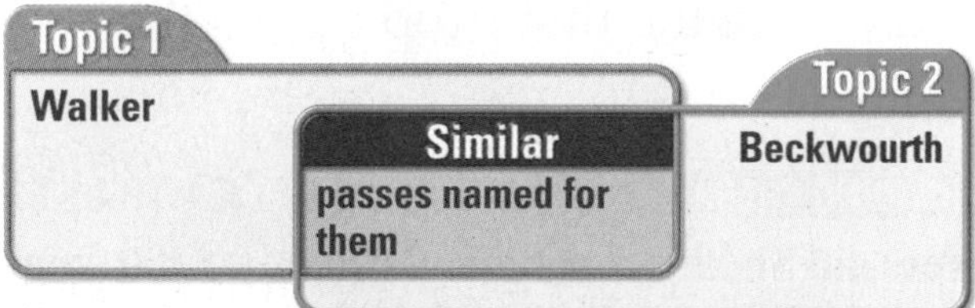

James Beckwourth

Biography

Trustworthiness
Respect
Responsibility
Fairness
Caring
Patriotism

*"[A]ll busied themselves in searching for gold; but my errand was of a different character: I had come to discover what I suspected to be a pass."**

In about 1828, James P. Beckwourth was on a trapping expedition in the Rocky Mountains when he was taken prisoner by Crow Indians. They thought he was the son of a Crow chief. They adopted Beckwourth to live with them, and he followed their ways of life. He became known as one of their best warriors. Beckwourth later said that he was chosen as chief of the Crow Indians.

Beckwourth first came to California in 1844 to trap animals. While traveling to California through the Sierra Nevada, he found a mountain pass. For several years, the new trail was used by settlers on their way to California. The trail is still known today as Beckwourth Pass.

Beckwourth Trading Post, near Beckwourth Pass in California

*James Beckwourth. From *The Life and Adventures of James P. Beckwourth* by T.D. Bonner. Ayer Company Publishers, 1969

Why Character Counts

The Crow Indians prided themselves on their skills in battle. How do you think Beckwourth was able to gain the respect of the Crow people and become a leader?

1798 Born

1824 Joins the Ashley-Henry trapping expedition up the Missouri River

1828 Is captured and later adopted by the Crow Indians

1850 Discovers a new pass through the Sierra Nevada

1866 Died

Interactive Multimedia Biographies
Visit MULTIMEDIA BIOGRAPHIES at
www.harcourtschool.com/hss

Critical Thinking Skills

Distinguish Fact from Opinion

WHY IT MATTERS

A statement that can be checked and proved to be true is a **fact**. A statement that tells what a person thinks or believes is an **opinion**. Knowing whether a statement is a fact or an opinion can help you better understand what you hear or read.

WHAT YOU NEED TO KNOW

Some of the statements that you may read about early Americans in California are *facts*. Here is an example: *In 1850, Beckwourth found a new pass through the northern Sierra Nevada.* You could check whether the statement is true by looking in an encyclopedia or other reference book about California.

Facts often give dates, numbers, or other information. To tell whether a statement is a fact, you can ask yourself questions like these:

- Do I know this idea to be true from my experience?
- Can the idea be proved true by testing?
- Is the idea from a source that I can trust?

This 1906 painting shows Jedediah Strong Smith and his fellow trailblazers crossing the Mojave Desert.

Other statements that you may read are opinions. For example, when settler John Marsh wrote to friends in Missouri about California, he said, *This is beyond all comparison the finest country and the finest climate.** This statement is an opinion because there is no way to prove that California is the finest country or has the finest climate.

Words such as *I think, I believe,* and *in my opinion* tell you that you are reading or hearing an opinion. Words such as *best, worst,* and *greatest* are often part of an opinion.

PRACTICE THE SKILL

Identify each statement that follows as a fact or an opinion.

1. In 1834, Joseph Reddeford Walker became the first American to cross the Sierra Nevada from the east.
2. The Old Spanish Trail was the best route into California.
3. Governor Echeandía should have let Smith explore California.
4. In the 1820s, the demand for beaver fur was high, but the supply of it was low.

*John Marsh. From *Eye-Witness to Wagon Trains West* by James Hewitt. Charles Scribner's Sons, 1973.

The author Washington Irving once described Joseph Reddeford Walker as "strong built, . . . brave in spirit, though mild in manners."*

*Washington Irving. From *The Adventures of Captain Bonneville*, Twayne Publishers, 1977.

APPLY WHAT YOU LEARNED

Reread Lesson 1, "Americans Move West." What are your opinions about the information presented? Write four statements about the information in the lesson—two that state facts and two that are your own opinions. Trade your paper with a classmate, and challenge each other to identify which statements are facts and which are opinions.

Critical Thinking Skills

Lesson 2

Time

1825	1840	1855

1829 Abel Stearns settles in the Los Angeles area

1841 The Bartleson-Bidwell expedition travels to John Marsh's California ranch

1846 The Donner party sets out for California

WHAT TO KNOW
Why did more and more settlers begin to travel to California from the United States?

- ✓ Compare the routes used by people traveling to California.
- ✓ Identify the location of Sutter's Fort, and describe its importance to early settlers.

VOCABULARY
immigrant p. 199
pioneer p. 200
wagon train p. 200

PEOPLE
John Augustus Sutter
John Marsh
John Bidwell
John C. Frémont
George Donner
Jacob Donner

PLACES
Sutter's Fort

COMPARE AND CONTRAST

California Standards
HSS 4.3, 4.3.1, 4.3.2

Trails to California

YOU ARE THERE Your parents are busy reading the book a neighbor has given them. It describes California's fertile lands and mild climate and the wonderful opportunities that await people who are willing to make the journey west. They've read the book many times, and they've now come to a decision. Your family will join a group of settlers heading to California in the spring.

LOCATE IT

Early Settlers

In the 1820s and 1830s, people began looking at California as a place where they could get plenty of land. Some people continued to move north from Mexico to settle in California. Others came as immigrants (IH•mih•gruhnts). An **immigrant** is someone who comes from one country to live in another.

Abel Stearns was born in Massachusetts, moved to Mexico in 1826, and became a Mexican citizen. He went to Los Angeles in 1829 and started a rancho, eventually becoming the largest landowner in southern California.

Another immigrant to California was **John Augustus Sutter**. He traveled from Switzerland to North America and arrived in California in 1839. Sutter became a Mexican citizen and was given a large land grant in the Sacramento Valley. There he built a settlement called New Helvetia (hel•VEE•shuh). It included a wheat farm, a cattle ranch, and a fort. **Sutter's Fort** stood near a pass leading through the Sierra Nevada. This is where Sacramento is located today.

Most people in the 1820s and 1830s traveled to California by ship, but over time, settlers had begun to travel to California from the United States by land. For many, Sutter's Fort was the end of the long journey west. There they could get food, supplies, or even jobs.

READING CHECK **COMPARE AND CONTRAST**
How were the reasons for settlers coming to California different from those of trappers?

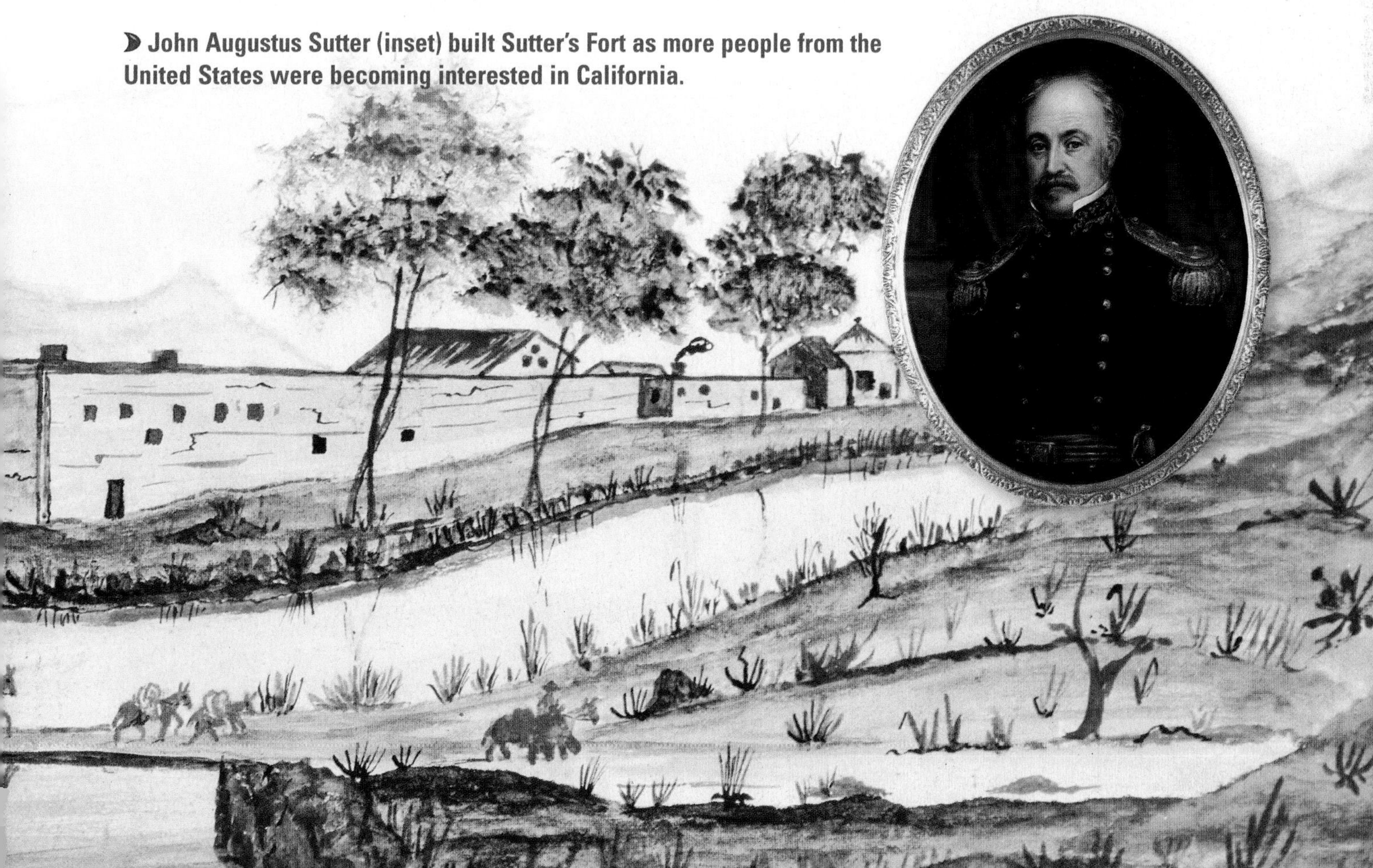

John Augustus Sutter (inset) built Sutter's Fort as more people from the United States were becoming interested in California.

More Trails West

One of the settlers from the United States was **John Marsh**, who came to Los Angeles in 1836. A year later, he bought a rancho in the Central Valley.

In 1840, Marsh wrote to friends in Missouri, praising California. He told them that "this is beyond all comparison the finest country and the finest climate."* His words inspired other pioneers from the United States to make the long, difficult journey over land. A **pioneer** is one of the first people to settle in a new land.

In May 1841, a group of 69 men, women, and children set out for California from Missouri. The group chose John Bartleson as their leader. **John Bidwell** took over later. The Bartleson-Bidwell expedition was one of the first groups to make the overland trip to California. They traveled in a **wagon train**, or a group of wagons, each pulled by horses or oxen.

The group set out on the Oregon Trail, the main route from Missouri to Oregon—the lands north of California. Their plan was to follow the trail for a while and then turn southwest and cross the Great Basin to California.

The maps the group had were not very good. When the time came to

*John Marsh. From *Eye-Witness to Wagon Trains West* by James Hewitt. Charles Scribner's Sons, 1973.

A Closer Look

A Wagon Train

The wagons used by pioneers were called prairie schooners, because their white covers looked like sails.

1. **Wagons were pulled by oxen or horses.**
2. **Settlers packed as many houshold items in their wagons as they could. They would need these things to begin their lives on the frontier.**
3. **A cloth cover protected passengers and cargo from rain and snow. The covers were coated with oil to make them waterproof.**
4. **Wagon train guides kept the wagons together and on the correct trail.**

? Why do you think wagon trains traveling across the frontier would need guides?

John Frémont and his wife, Jessie, became famous after they published a book about exploring California.

leave the trail, about half of the people decided to go to Oregon. The other half of the group turned southwest toward California.

It was nearly winter when the party came to the Sierra Nevada. The settlers knew they had to cross the mountains before the snow fell. Luckily, the first snowfall came late that year, and the group reached John Marsh's rancho in the Central Valley in November. The trail they followed was later called the California Trail. It became the main overland route to California.

Later pioneers were helped by the work of mapmakers and explorers, such as **John C. Frémont**. Frémont first came west in 1842 as the leader of a U.S. Army expedition to explore and map the Oregon Trail. During a second trip in 1844, he explored the San Joaquin Valley. Later, with the help of Joseph Walker, he went farther south and eventually reached the Old Spanish Trail.

After these expeditions, Frémont wrote a book about California with the help of his wife, Jessie. The book became very popular. As news of his travels spread, Frémont became a national hero.

READING CHECK **SUMMARIZE**
Why did John Frémont travel to the West?

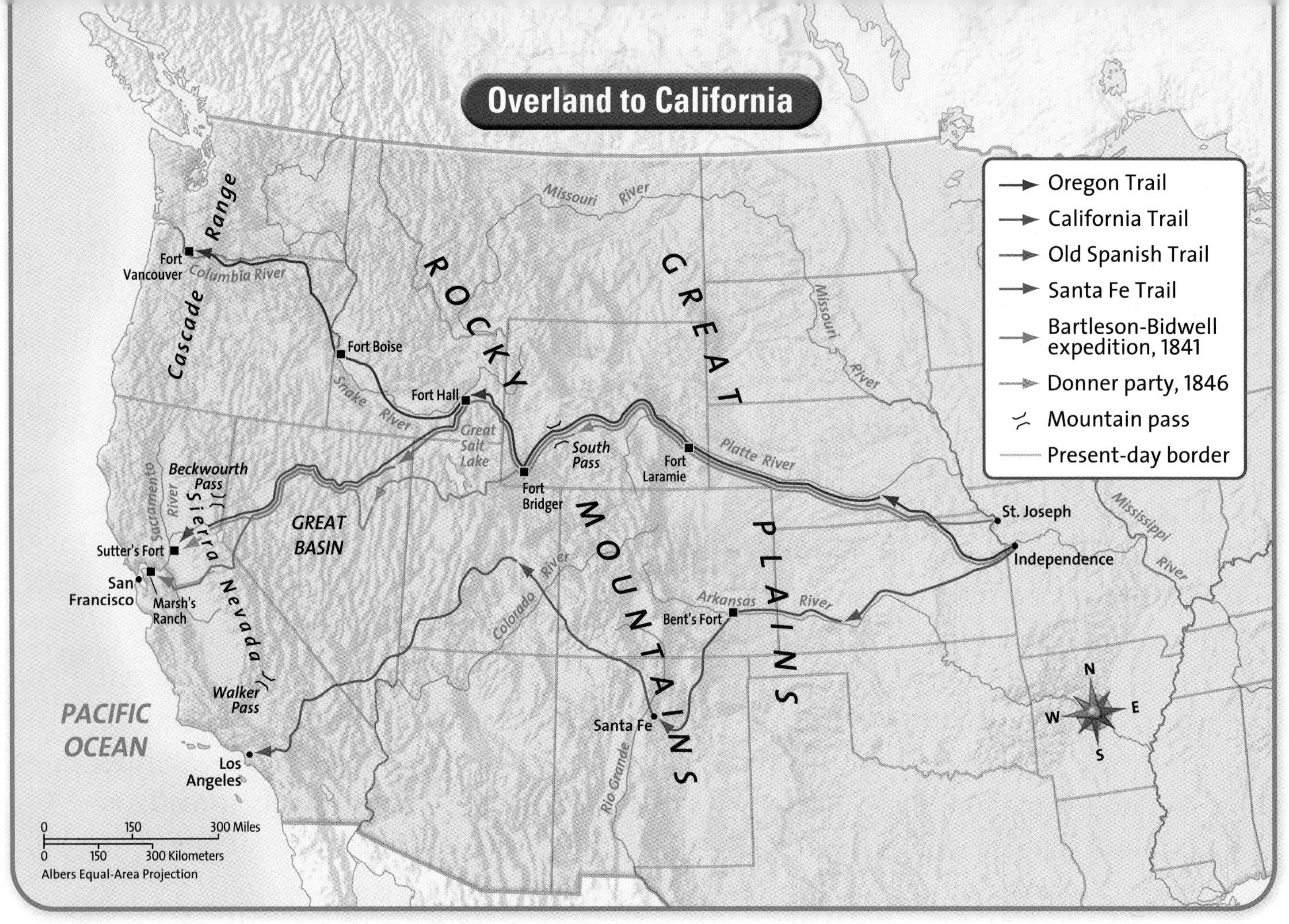

ANALYSIS SKILL Analyze Maps If pioneers traveled 15 miles a day, a journey in a wagon train from Missouri to California could take about five months.

Movement Which trail ended at Sutter's Fort?

The Donner Party

Because of the favorable stories being told about California, more and more people gathered to travel west in wagon trains. One such group was the Donner party, led by brothers **George** and **Jacob Donner**. The Donner party, which would eventually total 87 men, women, and children, left Missouri for California in April 1846.

In 1845, Lansford W. Hastings had published *The Emigrants' Guide to Oregon and California*. In his book, Hastings also told of a new route south of the Great Salt Lake. It was supposed to be a shortcut. However, Hastings had never traveled the route. It turned out to be much more difficult than the well-traveled California Trail.

Unfortunately, the Donner party decided to follow Hastings's new route. The route led the group over ground so rough that it took nearly a month longer to go that way. It was winter when the Donner party reached the Sierra Nevada.

As the weary travelers struggled across the mountains, they were caught in a heavy snowfall. The group set up shelters around what is now Donner Lake. Some of the strongest members hiked out into the deep snow to look for help. In February, after three months of snowstorms, help finally arrived. Almost half of the party had died from the freezing temperatures and lack of food. The survivors eventually made their way to Sutter's Fort.

READING CHECK **CAUSE AND EFFECT**
Why did the Donner party get stuck in the Sierra Nevada?

Summary

Beginning in the 1840s, greater numbers of settlers from the United States traveled to California by ship and by wagon train. The trip was often long, difficult, and dangerous.

Children IN HISTORY

Virginia Reed

Virginia Reed was the daughter of James Reed, a leader of the Donner party. Virginia was 12 years old when her family set out for California from Missouri. When they reached the Sierra Nevada, heavy snows trapped them there. Virginia recalled that the snowstorms "often lasted ten days at a time." Virginia later wrote that the "children were crying with hunger, and the mothers were crying because they had so little to give their children." *

Make It Relevant
Do you think the Sierra Nevada are easier to cross today? Explain.

*Virginia Reed Murphy. *Across the Plains in the Donner Party.* Linnet Books, 1996.

REVIEW

1. Why did more and more settlers begin to travel to California from the United States?
2. How was John Marsh a **pioneer**?
3. What route did the Donner party take to reach California?

CRITICAL THINKING

4. SKILL How did Marsh, Frémont, and Hastings influence people's ideas about California in the 1840s?
5. **Make It Relevant** Identify some reasons that people move to California today. Are these reasons similar to those of the early settlers?
6. **Write a Guidebook** Write a guidebook for immigrants coming to California. Be sure to include information about your route and the supplies that immigrants will need.
7. **COMPARE AND CONTRAST** On a separate sheet of paper, copy and complete the graphic organizer below.

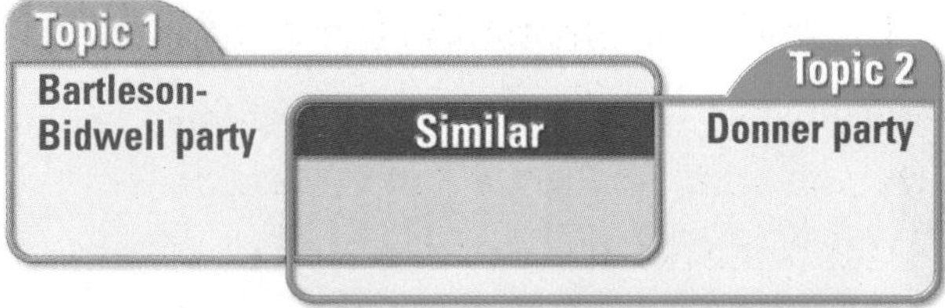

Distinguish Fact from Fiction

WHY IT MATTERS

When you are reading about history, it is important to know whether what you are reading is true or made up. In other words, you need to be able to tell facts from **fiction**, or made-up writing.

WHAT YOU NEED TO KNOW

One way to check facts is to find the same information in a trusted reference source. For example, you could use a dictionary or an encyclopedia, or a nonfiction book such as a textbook.

Other sources of facts are letters, diaries, and other documentary sources. **Documentary sources** are often produced at the time an event takes place, often by a person who actually experiences the event. However, documentary sources must be studied carefully. They can contain opinions or statements by the writer that may not be true.

Sometimes fiction writers base their stories on real people and events. But the writers add made-up details, such as words that the people did not say.

PATTY REED'S DOLL

"Those who headed for California had two choices—to go on with the Oregon people . . . and then turn south, or to take the new Hastings Cutoff that was described in Mr. Hastings' book. . . .

"This Hastings seems to know what he is talking about," Mr. Reed said. "I understand that he has guided several parties across safely."

"But not by that route, Mr. Reed," Mrs. Donner said. "George says that mountain man, Mr. Clyman, . . . advised us not to take it. . . ."

Patty and I and the little Donner girls were sitting [nearby], listening. Mrs. Donner didn't seem convinced. . . . Patty's mother said she was sure that the men knew best, and it was very important to get across the mountains as soon as possible. Remembering Grandma's story about the folks who were caught in the snow, . . . crossing the Cumberland Mountains back in Kentucky, my wooden head was inclined to agree with her."

From *Patty Reed's Doll: The Story of the Donner Party* by Rachel Kelly Laurgaard. Tomato Enterprises, 1989.

This doll was owned by Patty Reed.

PRACTICE THE SKILL

The two passages on these pages are both about the Donner party expedition to California in 1846. The passage on page 204 is from the book *Patty Reed's Doll*. Patty Reed was a member of the Donner party. The speaker is a doll belonging to Patty Reed. The passage on this page is from the diary of Eliza P. Donner Houghton, another member of the Donner party. Read the passages, and answer these questions.

1. How are the passages similar? How are they different?
2. Which passage is a documentary source? Which passage is fiction? How are you able to tell?

APPLY WHAT YOU LEARNED

ANALYSIS SKILL Compare the two passages. List any statements that are similar. See if you can find information in a trusted nonfiction source to prove that they are facts.

THE DIARY OF ELIZA P. DONNER HOUGHTON

"On the nineteenth of July we reached the Little Sandy River and there found four distinct companies [groups of settlers]. . . . There my father and others deliberated over [talked about] a new route to California.

They were led to do so by "An Open Letter,". . . The letter was written by Lansford W. Hastings, author of "Travel Among the Rocky Mountains, Through Oregon and California." It . . . urged those on the way to California to concentrate their numbers and strength, and to take the new and better route which he had explored . . . by way of the south end of Salt Lake. It emphasized . . . that this new route was nearly two hundred miles shorter than the old one. . . .

The proposition seemed so feasible [sensible] that after . . . discussion, a party was formed to take the new route.

After parting from us, Mr. Thornton made the following note in his journal: "The Californians were much elated and in fine spirits, with the prospect of better and nearer road to the country of their destination. Mrs. George Donner, however, was an exception. She was gloomy, sad, and dispirited in view of the fact that her husband and others could think of leaving the old road, and confide [trust] in the statement of a man of whom they knew nothing . . ."

From *The Expedition of the Donner Party and Its Tragic Fate* by Eliza P. Donner Houghton. University of Nebraska Press, 1997.

Eliza Donner was a young girl when her family and a group of other settlers left Missouri for California. As an adult in 1911, she wrote a book about the ill-fated trip.

Critical Thinking Skills

Lesson 3

1825 · 1840 · 1855

1845 James K. Polk becomes President

1846 The Bear Flag Revolt occurs on June 14

1846 The United States flag is raised over Monterey

Americans in California

WHAT TO KNOW
What was the Bear Flag Republic?

- Explain the meaning of *manifest destiny* and how it relates to California.
- Tell why the Bear Flag Revolt took place and who was involved in it.

VOCABULARY
manifest destiny p. 207
squatter p. 209
rebel p. 210
republic p. 210

PEOPLE
James K. Polk
José Castro
Mariano Vallejo

PLACES
Monterey
Sonoma

COMPARE AND CONTRAST

California Standards
HSS 4.2, 4.2.7, 4.2.8, 4.3, 4.3.2

YOU ARE THERE Today you have visitors. They bring bad news—that the tensions between American settlers and Mexican leaders are getting worse. In fact, a number of Americans are planning an uprising. You have worked hard on your farm since you arrived several years ago. But you don't own the farm, since you're not a Mexican citizen. You must decide whether you should join in the revolt.

By 1847, about half of San Francisco's 450 residents were American-born.

In this painting, the symbol of manifest destiny, the woman in white, leads settlers west.

American Interest in California Grows

By 1845, there were almost 700 people from the United States living in California. Settlers could own land, but only if they became Mexican citizens.

In the United States, a new idea was gaining popularity. Many people felt that the United States should expand to reach from the Atlantic Ocean to the Pacific Ocean. This idea became known as **manifest destiny**.

Manifest destiny became a popular idea for many reasons. The population of the United States had swelled from about 5 million in 1800 to more than 23 million in the 1840s.

Many Americans wanted California to be part of the United States so that citizens would have more places to live and work. Because trade was rapidly growing in the area, some Americans wanted the United States to have control of ports along the Pacific coast. One person who placed a high value on California was President **James K. Polk**. Soon after he took office in 1845, President Polk offered Mexico $40 million for what is now California, Arizona, and New Mexico.

READING CHECK **COMPARE AND CONTRAST**
How did the population of the United States change between the years 1800 and 1840?

Mexican Control Weakens

Mexico refused to sell California to the United States. Yet, it had little control over the region. The Mexican government in California was weak. In the 20 years after Mexico won its independence, California had more than a dozen governors.

The economy of Mexican California was also weak. The church no longer had control of the missions, and much of the mission property had been sold or given away as land grants. Rancho owners were able to buy more land at low prices.

Because they owned much of the land, the rancho owners gained power. Most of these landowners were Californios, but they had different opinions about Mexican rule. Some agreed that Mexico should rule California. Others supported the United States.

The government in Mexico City did not have the money to pay soldiers in California. With few Mexicans willing to move to the distant region, there was little hope of keeping order there. To add to Mexico's troubles, more and more Americans continued to move westward. The Mexican government was unable to stop the settlers.

John C. Frémont and United States soldiers enter Monterey in 1846.

Points of View

Californios were deeply divided over what to do about American settlers in California.

Pío Pico, governor of Mexican California

"Shall we remain supine [lying down], while these daring strangers [American settlers] are overrunning our fertile plains . . . until we have become strangers in our own land?"*

From *The Los Angeles Almanac.* www.losangelesalmanac.com

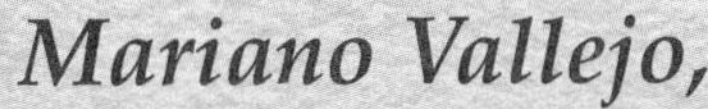

Mariano Vallejo, government official and rancho owner in Sonoma

"[A]ll our minds were prepared to give a brotherly embrace [hug] to the sons of the Great Republic [the United States], whose . . . spirit had filled us with admiration."*

From *Historical and Personal Memoirs Relating to Alta California,* translated by Earl R. Hewitt, 1875

It's Your Turn

ANALYSIS SKILL Analyze Points of View

1. How do you think Pico would have reacted to news of Frémont's actions in northern California?
2. Do you think Vallejo agreed with the idea of manifest destiny? Why or why not?

During his first expedition to the West, John C. Frémont noticed that California was not well defended. He returned to **Monterey** in 1846 with about 60 soldiers. Frémont hoped to take control of California. General **José Castro**, California's Mexican military leader, ordered Frémont to leave.

As Frémont and his men headed north to Oregon, they spread a rumor that Castro was going to make all American settlers leave California. Although some American settlers had become Mexican citizens and owned their land, many others were squatters. A **squatter** is someone who lives in a place without permission. Squatters did not have the same rights and protections as Mexican citizens.

The squatters worried that Castro would attack. In northern California, a group of American settlers decided to try to gain control of California. They hoped that the United States would support their efforts.

READING CHECK CAUSE AND EFFECT
Why was the Mexican government unable to stop Americans from settling in California?

Cultural Heritage

The Bear Flag

The Osos designed a flag to represent their new republic. On a piece of cloth, they painted a lone star, a grizzly bear, and the words *California Republic.* A single red stripe was sewn across the bottom. Explaining their choice of symbols, one of the Bear Flaggers said, "A bear stands his ground always, and as long as the stars shine, we stand for the cause."* In 1911, the bear flag became California's official state flag. These same images are still found on the flag of California today.

*From *California: A History, Fourth Edition* by Andrew Rolle. Harlan Davidson, Inc. 1987

The original bear flag (top) and the California state flag as it looks today (below)

The Bear Flag Revolt

TIME June 1846

PLACE Sonoma

On June 14, 1846, a group of about 30 settlers marched into the town of **Sonoma** at dawn. They called themselves the Osos. *Oso* is the Spanish word meaning "bear." This group wanted to take control of California away from Mexico.

The rebels went to the house of **Mariano Vallejo**, the most important Mexican official in Sonoma. A **rebel** is someone who fights against the government. The rebels made Vallejo agree to give up control of Sonoma. Because Vallejo shared the idea that California would be better off separated from Mexico, he did not oppose the rebels. Even so, they arrested him and took him to Sutter's Fort.

The rebels declared California to be a free republic. A **republic** is a form of government in which people elect their leaders. The rebels then raised a handmade flag over Sonoma's main plaza to announce the California Republic, later called the Bear Flag Republic.

General Castro quickly tried to end the rebellion. However, the 50 soldiers he sent to take back Sonoma failed. They lost the Battle of Olompali (oh•LOM•pah•lee) on June 24.

John C. Frémont returned to California and soon aided the rebels, known now as the Bear Flaggers. During this time, the United States was already at war with Mexico. The people in California did not know this. They found out only after American warships landed at Monterey. The arrival of American troops quickly brought an end to the California Republic.

READING CHECK **SUMMARIZE**

What were the main events of the Bear Flag Revolt?

Summary

Mexico struggled to keep American settlers out of California. American settlers rebelled and created the Bear Flag Republic. The republic ended when the United States took control of the region.

The Bear Flaggers celebrate their victory.

REVIEW

1. What was the Bear Flag Republic?
2. Use the term **manifest destiny** to explain the westward movement of American settlers.
3. What was one sign that the Mexican government of California was weakening?

CRITICAL THINKING

4. ANALYSIS SKILL How do you think people in the United States responded to news of the Bear Flag Revolt? Why?
5. **Write a Script** Work with a classmate to write a dialogue that might have taken place between Mariano Vallejo and a Bear Flagger. Then perform your dialogue for the rest of the class.
6. Focus Skill **COMPARE AND CONTRAST** On a separate sheet of paper, copy and complete the graphic organizer below.

Lesson 4

1825	1840	1855

1836 Texas declares itself an independent republic

1846 The United States declares war on Mexico

1848 The Treaty of Guadalupe Hidalgo is signed

WHAT TO KNOW
What effects did the Mexican-American War have on California?

- ✓ Analyze the reason for the Mexican-American War.
- ✓ Explain how the Mexican-American War affected the people living in California.

VOCABULARY
right p. 213
treaty p. 216

PEOPLE
John D. Sloat
Robert F. Stockton
Archibald Gillespie
Stephen Watts Kearny
Andrés Pico
Bernarda Ruíz

PLACES
Monterey
Domínguez Rancho

COMPARE AND CONTRAST

California Standards
HSS 4.3, 4.3.1, 4.3.4, 4.3.5

The Mexican-American War

YOU ARE THERE It is July 1846. Each morning, the United States flag is raised over Los Angeles. For days now, American soldiers have marched around your town. They have been telling people that California is now part of the United States. You wonder how the lives of you and your family will change.

War Comes to California

The Mexican-American War was partly the result of a disagreement about Texas. Texas had won independence from Mexico in 1836. However, Mexican leaders still considered Texas to be part of Mexico. The Mexican government became angry when United States leaders invited Texas to become a state.

Mexican leaders also disagreed about the border between Texas and Mexico. When United States soldiers crossed the border that Mexico had set, Mexican troops attacked them. In turn, the United States declared war on Mexico on May 13, 1846.

Many Americans saw the war as a chance to take control of California, which was still part of Mexico. President Polk ordered **John D. Sloat**, a commander in the United States Navy, to sail to **Monterey**, the capital of Mexican California.

Sloat reached Monterey on July 2 and took over the city without firing a shot. On July 7, 1846, Sloat raised the United States flag at Monterey. He declared that California was now a part of the United States. He told Californians that they would now have the same rights as other United States citizens. A **right** is a freedom that belongs to a person.

READING CHECK **COMPARE AND CONTRAST**
How did the views of Mexican and American leaders differ about Texas?

United States soldiers raise the United States flag over Monterey on July 7, 1846.

The Fight for California

After Sloat's capture of Monterey, the United States flag was raised at San Francisco and Sonoma on July 9 and at Sutter's Fort on July 11. When Sloat gave up his command, he named Commodore **Robert F. Stockton** as the new leader.

Stockton made the Bear Flaggers a part of the United States Army. He named John C. Frémont and **Archibald Gillespie**, a United States Marine, leaders of the Bear Flaggers. Stockton sent the group out to take control of other California cities. Most American settlers and Californios did not resist the American forces.

Frémont and Gillespie captured Los Angeles on August 12. Soon after, Stockton declared, "California is entirely free from Mexican dominion [rule]."* However, this victory did not last long.

Stockton left Gillespie in charge of Los Angeles. Gillespie made strict rules about when and where people could travel. These rules made the people angry. When some Californios rebelled against the soldiers, Gillespie and his soldiers marched to San Pedro. There, they met up with soldiers sent south by Stockton. The two groups marched back to Los Angeles and fought the Californios at **Domínguez** (doh•MEEN•gehs) **Rancho**. The Californios won again.

About this time, General **Stephen Watts Kearny** was heading west from New Mexico with 300 soldiers. On the way, Kearny met the famous scout Kit

*Robert F. Stockton. From a letter to the people of California, August 17, 1846. Reprinted in "What I Saw in California" by Edwin Bryant. Ross and Haines, 1967.

ANALYSIS SKILL Analyze Time Lines

How long after the Treaty of Cahuenga was signed was the Treaty of Guadalupe Hidalgo signed?

The Mexican-American War
1846
1847
1848
1849
May 1846
President Polk asks Congress to declare war on Mexico
January 1847
The signing of the Treaty of Cahuenga ends the fighting in California
September 1847
General Winfield Scott and the United States Army capture Mexico City
February 1848
The Mexicans and the Americans sign the Treaty of Guadalupe Hidalgo, ending the Mexican-American War

SKILL Analyze Maps

Place Which battles were fought near Los Angeles?

Carson. Carson had not heard about the fighting, and told Kearny that California was safely under United States control.

Because of Carson's report, Kearny sent 200 of his soldiers back to New Mexico. Carson led Kearny and the remaining soldiers to California. As soon as they reached California, however, they were attacked by a group of Californios. The Californios retreated—but it was a trick. They circled back, surprised the American soldiers, and won the Battle of San Pasqual (pahs•KWAHL).

READING CHECK CAUSE AND EFFECT
Why did Kearny send most of his soldiers back to New Mexico?

Conflicts End

TIME 1847
PLACE Cahuenga Pass

The victory at San Pasqual was the last one for the Californios. General Kearny and Commodore Stockton launched another attack, and took control of Los Angeles on January 10, 1847.

Mexican governor Pío Pico and his brother, General **Andrés Pico**, organized the surrender of California. They asked to meet with John Frémont. Before the meeting took place, a woman named **Bernarda Ruíz** (bair•NAR•dah roo•EES) asked to talk with Frémont.

Ruíz advised Frémont to offer easy peace terms to the Californios. Frémont took her advice and decided not to punish the Californios. She told Frémont that he should

> "... win the Mexican Californians over to your side, rather than make enemies of them by inflicting [enforcing on them] harsh peace terms."*

The Treaty of Cahuenga ended the fighting in California. A **treaty** is a written agreement between groups or nations. Another treaty, the Treaty of Guadalupe Hidalgo, officially ended the Mexican-American War. Mexico agreed to give up lands that included all of present-day California, Utah, and Nevada and parts of New Mexico, Arizona, Colorado, and Wyoming. In return, the United States agreed to pay Mexico $15 million.

As a result of the Treaty of Guadalupe Hidalgo, the United States had achieved its dream of manifest destiny. The

*Bernarda Ruíz. From *Old Spanish Santa Barbara: From Cabrillo to Frémont* by Walker A. Tompkins. McNally and Leftin, 1967.

Andrés Pico (left) and Bernarda Ruíz (right)

On January 13, 1847, Mexican and United States leaders signed the Treaty of Cahuenga, which ended the fighting in California.

treaty also pleased many Californios. It made them citizens of the United States and allowed them to keep land they had owned before the war.

READING CHECK **CAUSE AND EFFECT**
What was the result of the Treaty of Guadalupe Hidalgo?

Summary

The Mexican-American War began in May 1846. As a result of the Treaty of Guadalupe Hidalgo, which ended the war, California became part of the United States.

REVIEW

1. What effects did the Mexican-American War have on California?
2. Use the term **treaty** to describe the agreement that ended the Mexican-American War.
3. Why did Bernarda Ruíz want to talk with John Frémont?

CRITICAL THINKING

4. ANALYSIS SKILL Do you think the people of Los Angeles were right in deciding to rebel? Why or why not?
5. What do you think some Californios believed were the benefits of becoming part of the United States?
6. **Write a Journal Entry** Imagine you are Bernarda Ruíz, Andrés Pico, or Stephen Kearny. Write a journal entry describing what you have seen happen in California and what you would like to see happen next. Include facts from the lesson in your entry.
7. Focus Skill **COMPARE AND CONTRAST** On a separate sheet of paper, copy and complete the graphic organizer below.

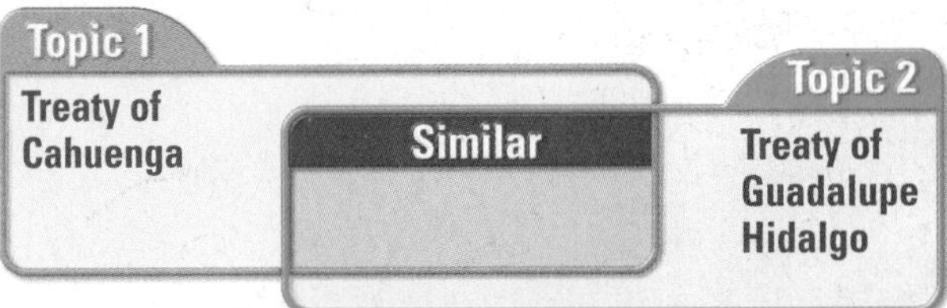

Read and Compare Historical Maps

WHY IT MATTERS

Historical maps can give you information about places as they were in the past. These maps may show the political boundaries of a place during a certain time. A **political boundary** is the imaginary line marking the limits of a nation. By comparing maps of the same area from different times, you can see how political boundaries change.

WHAT YOU NEED TO KNOW

The map below shows the United States in 1845, before the Mexican-American War. At this time, California and areas of the Southwest were part of Mexico. The map on page 219 shows the same area in 1848, after the United States won the war against Mexico. At this time, California and some areas of the Southwest became part of the United States.

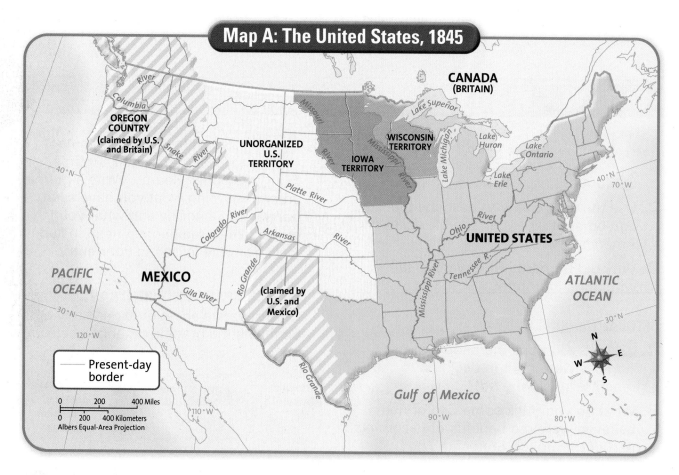

Map A: The United States, 1845

CANADA (BRITAIN)
OREGON COUNTRY (claimed by U.S. and Britain)
UNORGANIZED U.S. TERRITORY
IOWA TERRITORY
WISCONSIN TERRITORY
UNITED STATES
MEXICO
(claimed by U.S. and Mexico)
PACIFIC OCEAN
ATLANTIC OCEAN
Gulf of Mexico
Present-day border
0 200 400 Miles
0 200 400 Kilometers
Albers Equal-Area Projection

Mapmakers often use different colors to show different regions. Sometimes they also use a pattern of diagonal stripes, called **hatch lines**. Hatch lines are often used in historical maps to show lands that were claimed by two or more countries.

PRACTICE THE SKILL

Use the historical maps of the United States and nearby lands to answer these questions.

1. What color is used on both maps to show lands that belonged to the United States?
2. How did Mexico change between 1845 and 1848?
3. What do the hatch lines stand for on the map of the United States in 1845?
4. How did California change between 1845 and 1848?

APPLY WHAT YOU LEARNED

ANALYSIS SKILL Write three or four sentences about these historical maps. In your sentences, leave blanks where dates belong. Then trade papers with a partner. Have your partner fill in the correct date in each sentence.

Practice your map and globe skills with the **GeoSkills CD-ROM**.

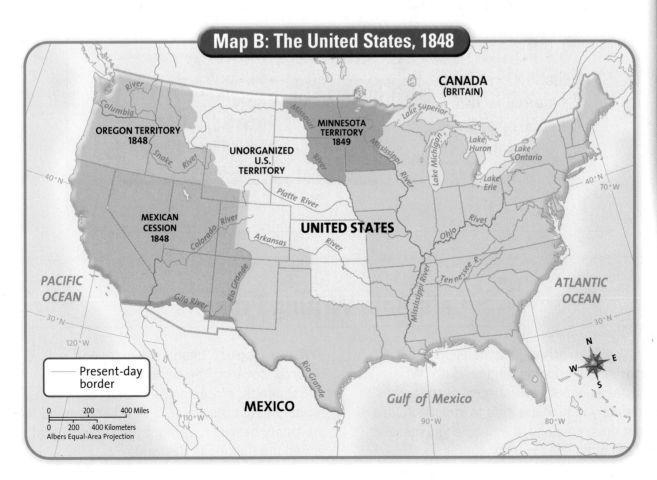

Map B: The United States, 1848

CANADA (BRITAIN)
OREGON TERRITORY 1848
MINNESOTA TERRITORY 1849
UNORGANIZED U.S. TERRITORY
MEXICAN CESSION 1848
UNITED STATES
MEXICO
PACIFIC OCEAN
ATLANTIC OCEAN
Gulf of Mexico
Columbia River
Snake River
Missouri River
Mississippi River
Platte River
Arkansas River
Colorado River
Gila River
Rio Grande
Ohio River
Tennessee R.
Lake Superior
Lake Michigan
Lake Huron
Lake Ontario
Lake Erie
40°N
30°N
120°W
110°W
90°W
80°W
70°W
N
E
S
W
Present-day border
0 200 400 Miles
0 200 400 Kilometers
Albers Equal-Area Projection

Time

1825 — 1835

1826
Jedediah Strong Smith goes to California

Reading Social Studies

To **compare** is to think about how two or more things are alike. To **contrast** is to think about how two or more things are different.

Compare and Contrast

Complete this Venn diagram to show that you understand how the journeys of Jedediah Strong Smith and of Sylvester and James Pattie were alike and how they were different. A copy of this graphic organizer appears on page 58 of the Homework and Practice Book.

California, Here We Come!

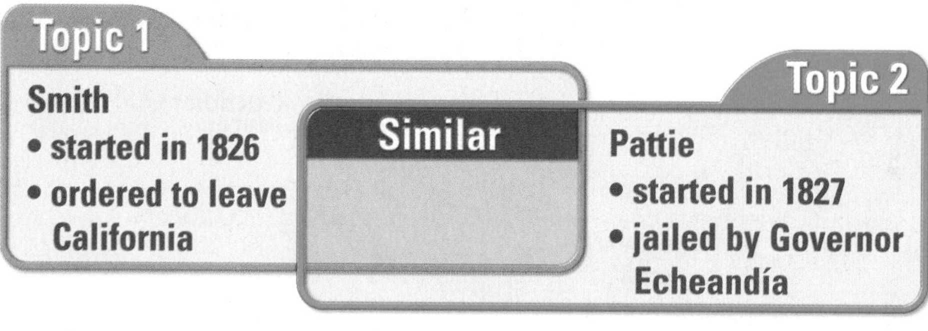

California Writing Prompts

Write a Narrative Imagine you are a trailblazer to California during the 1820s. Write a narrative about your journey, describing the route you take. Be sure to include details about the landscape, the people you meet, and the difficulties you encounter.

Write a Report Imagine you are a reporter covering the signing of the Treaty of Cahuenga. Write an article that tells your readers about the event. Give a background to the treaty by summarizing the key events that ended the fighting in California.

1845

1855

1841
The Bartleson-Bidwell expedition arrives in California from Missouri

1846
California settlers begin the Bear Flag Revolt

1848
The Mexican-American War ends

Use Vocabulary

Write a term from the list to complete each sentence.

demand, p. 191
trailblazer, p. 192
wagon train, p. 200
treaty, p. 216

1. The war ended after both sides signed a ______.
2. Many early settlers traveled to California by ______.
3. In the late 1700s, there was great ______ for beaver and otter pelts.
4. A ______ makes new paths for others to follow.

Use the Time Line

Use the summary time line above to answer the questions.

5. In which decade did Jedediah Smith go to California?
6. When did the Bear Flag Revolt begin?

Apply Skills

Distinguish Fact from Opinion Identify each statement as a fact or an opinion.

7. The Californios were the very best horse riders in the world.
8. General Kearny and his troops lost the Battle of San Pasqual.

Recall Facts

Answer these questions.

9. Why was it difficult for the Mexican government to control California?
10. Why did some people think it was a good idea for California to join the United States?
11. What events started the Mexican-American War?

Write the letter of the best choice.

12. Who led the first group of Americans across the Sierra Nevada?
    - **A** John C. Frémont
    - **B** Bernarda Ruíz
    - **C** Jedediah Strong Smith
    - **D** Jacob Donner
13. Which of the following was the capital of Mexican California?
    - **A** Fort Ross
    - **B** Los Angeles
    - **C** Monterey
    - **D** Santa Barbara

Think Critically

14. ANALYSIS SKILL What were some benefits of moving to California during the early 1800s? What were the costs?
15. ANALYSIS SKILL How does the way people move to new places today differ from the way people moved to California in the 1800s?

Study Skills

ORGANIZE INFORMATION

A graphic organizer can help you make sense of the facts you read.

- **Tables, charts, and webs are graphic organizers that can show main ideas and important details.**
- **A graphic organizer can help you classify and categorize information. It can also help you understand the relationship between the subject of the chapter and each lesson.**

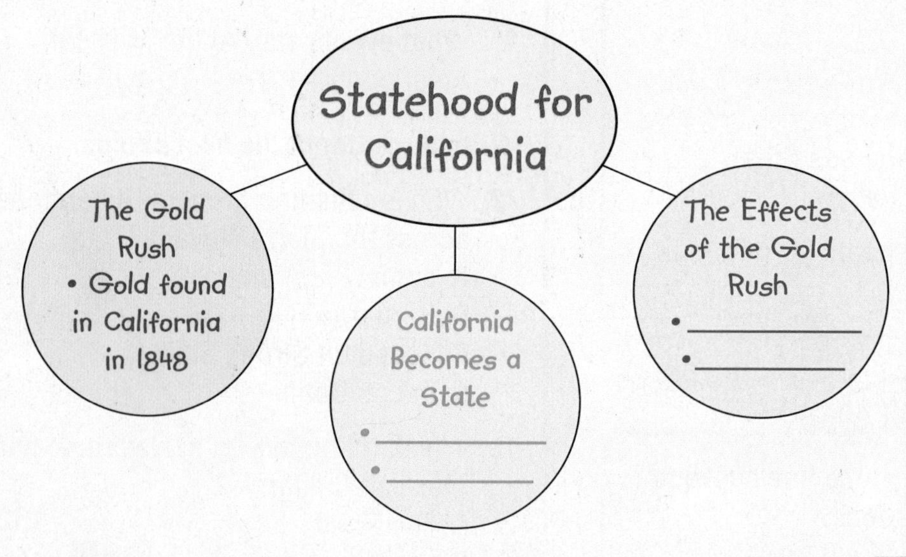

Apply As You Read

As you read this chapter, fill in each circle of a web like the one above with facts from each lesson.

California History-Social Science Standards, Grade 4

4.3 Students explain the economic, social, and political life in California from the establishment of the Bear Flag Republic through the Mexican-American War, the Gold Rush, and the granting of statehood.
4.4 Students explain how California became an agricultural and industrial power, tracing the transformation of the California economy and its political and cultural development since the 1850s.

CHAPTER

Statehood for California

Delegates to the Monterey Convention met in this room in Colton Hall to discuss statehood for California.

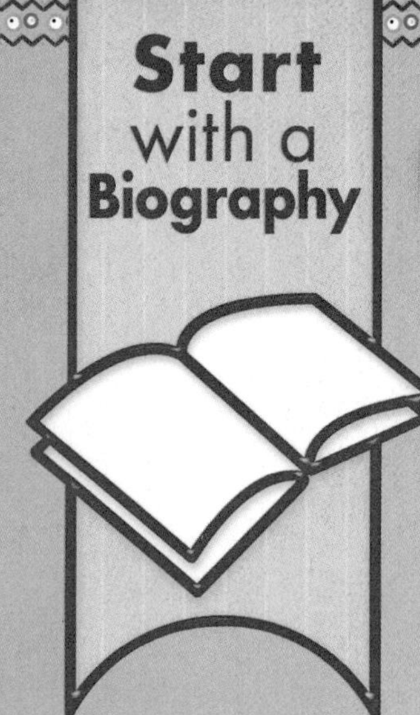

Open Hands, Open Heart

THE STORY OF BIDDY MASON

by Deidre Robinson
illustrated by Colin Bootman

California joined the United States in 1850. Even though it joined as a free state, some slave owners still brought slaves with them to California. Bridget "Biddy" Mason was an enslaved African American woman who was brought to California in 1852 by her owner, Robert Smith. When Smith decided to move from California to the slave state of Texas, Biddy Mason went to court to fight for the right to stay in California and be free. Read now to find out what happened to Biddy Mason.

Biddy and her group appeared before Judge Benjamin Hayes in Santa Monica, California. On the first day of the trial, Smith told the judge that these fourteen people were not his slaves but his hired help. Instead of paying them wages, he provided them with food and shelter. He considered them a part of his family. They were moving to Texas with him willingly.

Biddy was unable to testify against Smith in the courtroom because of the Civil Practice Act of 1850, which stated that black people could not testify against white people in a court of law. Judge Hayes had to question Biddy and the other slaves in the chamber of his courtroom. Biddy told the judge and his two witnesses, "I have always done what I have been told to do; I always feared this trip to Texas, since I first heard of it. Mr. Smith told me I would be just as free in Texas as here." The other slaves stated, also, they did not know Texas was a slave state.

Judge Hayes was from the East coast and was opposed to slavery. He was certain that no slave would willingly move from a free state to a state which allowed slavery. He felt Smith took advantage of his slaves because they did not know how to read, write, or know their rights under the law.

After listening to the testimony of Biddy and her group, Judge Hayes returned to the courtroom and told Smith he could not understand why Smith wanted to support an additional fourteen people. According to the court records, Smith owned only one suit and had five hundred dollars. He could barely afford to feed and support his wife and six children. Judge Hayes accused Smith of planning to sell his slaves once he got to Texas.

On January 21, 1856, Robert Smith failed to appear in court. Judge Hayes granted freedom to Biddy, her daughters, and the rest of Smith's slaves. He declared, "All men should be left to their own pursuit of freedom and happiness." Judge Hayes also said for the "petitioners to become settled and go to work for themselves—in peace and without fear."

Response Corner

1. How did Biddy Mason's need for freedom improve her own life and the lives of other people?
2. Write a paragraph describing how you think Biddy Mason felt when she was granted her freedom.

Lesson 1

Time

1825 | 1840 | 1855

1848
Gold is discovered near Sutter's Mill on January 24

1849
Forty-niners begin arriving in California

WHAT TO KNOW
How did the discovery of gold change California?

- **Explain how the discovery of gold affected California's population and settlements.**
- **Describe the routes that gold seekers used to reach California.**

VOCABULARY
gold rush p. 227
forty-niner p. 228
isthmus p. 228
claim p. 230

PEOPLE
John Sutter
James Marshall
Sam Brannan
Lu Ng
Louise Clappe

PLACES
American River
Coloma
Sutter's Mill
Isthmus of Panama

COMPARE AND CONTRAST

California Standards
HSS 4.3, 4.3.2, 4.3.3, 4.3.4

The Gold Rush

YOU ARE THERE You are standing by the river when you see a shining rock in the gravel. Your heart beats faster as you scoop it up. The year is 1848, and until a few days ago, you were working to build a sawmill on the **American River** in northern California. Then somebody found a shining yellow rock in the river. Now everybody is looking for yellow rocks. If the nuggets you find are gold, you'll be rich!

AUTOGRAPH OF
Jas. W. Marshall
THE DISCOVERER OF GOLD IN CALIFORNIA
January 19th, 1848.

This photograph of James Marshall was taken in the 1870s, many years after gold was discovered at Sutter's Mill. Marshall handed out autograph cards (below).

Gold!

TIME **January 24, 1848**

PLACE **Coloma, California**

John Sutter had decided to build a sawmill at **Coloma** (kuh•LOH•muh), on the banks of the American River. He hired a carpenter named **James Marshall** and several other workers to build the sawmill. On January 24, while digging at the site, the workers found a small nugget, or lump, of something that looked like gold. Marshall quickly reported the discovery to Sutter, who had the nugget tested. It was indeed gold!

No one is sure who found the first gold nugget, but Marshall said that he did. By the time Sutter and Marshall arrived back at the sawmill, the workers had found more gold. Soon, the workers stopped working and spent all their time looking for gold. They had caught "gold fever."

Gold is a valuable natural resource.

In time, word of the discovery at **Sutter's Mill** leaked out, and a gold rush started. A **gold rush** is a huge movement of people going to a place to look for gold. **Sam Brannan** traveled from San Francisco to Coloma to see if the stories were true. When he returned to the city, he held up a bottle filled with gold dust and ran through the streets yelling, "Gold! Gold! Gold from the American River!"*

READING CHECK **COMPARE AND CONTRAST**
How did the daily lives of Sutter's workers change after they learned about the gold?

*Sam Brannan. From *The World Rushed In: The California Gold Rush Experience* by J. S. Holliday. Simon & Schuster, 1981.

When word of the discovery of gold leaked out, almost all of the 800 residents of San Francisco left to go to Coloma, near Sutter's Mill (below).

Bound for California

Gold fever spread further when President James K. Polk announced the discovery. In a short time, about 90,000 fortune seekers traveled to California. They were called **forty-niners** because many of them arrived in 1849. Most of the forty-niners were men, but some were women. Most women came with their husbands, fathers, or brothers.

As many as 1,000 African Americans also joined the gold rush. Some were free. Others were brought as enslaved workers from the South—the states in the southern part of the United States—to mine gold. Sometimes an owner would agree to give a slave freedom if that slave mined $2,000 worth of gold. Many slaves earned enough money to buy their freedom and the freedom of their family members as well.

There were three main routes to California from the United States. The fastest of these took travelers across the **Isthmus** (IS•muhs) **of Panama**. An **isthmus** is a narrow piece of land that connects two larger land areas. The Isthmus of Panama connects North America and South America. Forty-niners traveled across the isthmus by riverboat, on mules, and by foot. In the hot climate, many people caught diseases and died. Those who made it to the Pacific coast waited there to catch ships to California.

The second route was by ship around the tip of South America. This route was the longest and could take from three to eight months.

The third route to California was all by land. Overland travelers had to cross deserts and mountain ranges. Other challenges they faced included accidents, illness, and lack of food and water.

Some forty-niners sped to California on clipper ships, the fastest ships of the time. Traveling on a clipper ship was very expensive, but people paid the price, believing that they would find a fortune in gold in California.

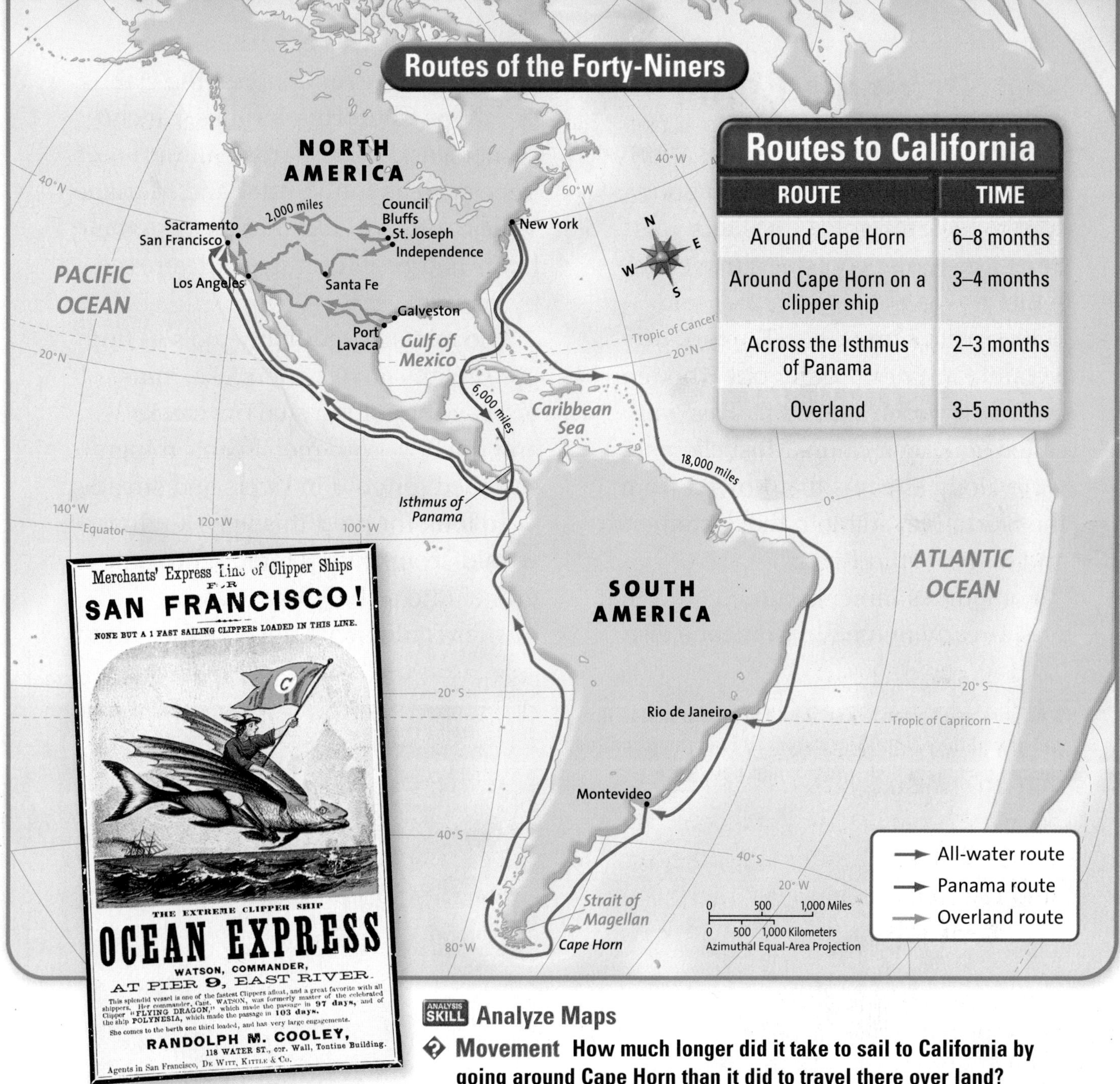

Routes to California

ROUTE	TIME
Around Cape Horn	6–8 months
Around Cape Horn on a clipper ship	3–4 months
Across the Isthmus of Panama	2–3 months
Overland	3–5 months

ANALYSIS SKILL Analyze Maps

Movement How much longer did it take to sail to California by going around Cape Horn than it did to travel there over land?

Most forty-niners came from the United States, but many came from Mexico, South America, Europe, Australia, and Asia. By 1852, thousands of Chinese had also joined the gold rush. In fact, about one of every four gold seekers was Chinese. To them, California was *Gum Sam*, or "Gold Mountain."

While most forty-niners headed to California to get rich quickly and then return home, others came to escape wars and other hardships in their homelands. **Lu Ng** (LOO ING) traveled to California from China. He explained his decision this way: "Crops had failed and floods had ruined our fields. . . . What else could I do?"*

READING CHECK COMPARE AND CONTRAST
What is one thing that is true for all three routes from the United States to California?

*Lu Ng. From *The Gold Rush of 1849: Staking a Claim to California* by Arthur Blake. Millbrook, 1995.

Staking a Claim

Upon arriving in California, a forty-niner's first task was to find a good spot to look for gold. Once this was done, the miner could set up a claim. A **claim** was the area a miner said belonged to him or her. To mark off a claim, a miner usually put wooden stakes, or posts, around it. This was called staking a claim. Most claims were along streams that flowed from the Sierra Nevada into the Sacramento and San Joaquin Rivers.

Sometimes miners claimed land that was already owned by someone else. Some miners even ignored the claims of others. California Indians, rancho owners, and other early California settlers, such as John Sutter and Mariano Vallejo, often found that parts of their lands had been dug up or destroyed by miners.

The miners used many tools to find gold. With shovels and picks, miners dug for gold in shallow creeks and ditches. With metal pans, miners searched for gold in rivers and streams.

To look for gold this way, a miner would scoop river water, sand, and gravel into a shallow pan. Next, he or she would swirl the water around.

Miners used pans to separate the gold from the dirt and gravel they dug. They also used long ramps called sluices through which water could flow (inset).

FAST FACT

Most gold seekers were under 30 years of age. More than nine out of ten were men.

It was not uncommon for miners to work long days, often up to their knees in water and mud.

This made the heavy bits, including the gold, sink to the bottom. Then, the miner carefully spilled out the water and dirt.

Sometimes two miners worked together to use a tool that was called a cradle because it was rocked like a baby's cradle. The cradle had two trays, one above the other. The miners filled the top tray with sand, soil, and gravel. Then one miner poured water over the dirt, and the other miner rocked the cradle. Any large pieces of gravel were trapped in the top tray, and the water and the rest of the dirt flowed through openings into the bottom one. The water washed the dirt out through an opening in the bottom tray, leaving the heavier gold behind.

Looking for gold was hard work. Miners often worked six days a week. Many got up before dawn, and they stopped only when it became too dark to see. A miner named Prentice Mulford wrote that mining ". . . combines, within itself, the various arts of canal-digging, ditching, laying stone walls, ploughing [plowing]. . . ."*

READING CHECK SUMMARIZE

What were some methods of searching for gold?

*Prentice Mulford. From *Days of Gold: The California Gold Rush and the American Nation* by Malcolm J. Rohrbough. University of California Press, 1997.

Major Gold Mining Towns, 1849–1859

Mining town
Other city or town
Gold-mining area
Present-day border

0 20 40 Miles
0 20 40 Kilometers
Albers Equal-Area Projection

The Mining Camps

The forty-niners set up camps wherever they thought they could find gold. Life in these camps was very hard. Tents and shacks offered little protection from rain, wind, and cold weather. The dirt streets in the camps were usually filled with trash. Food was often scarce, and there was little medicine.

When they stopped working for the day, the miners in the camps found ways of entertaining themselves. They might play cards, read books if they

ANALYSIS SKILL Analyze Maps If enough gold was found in an area over time, the mining camps, like the one below, in that area might become permanent towns.

Human-Environment Interactions On which river did miners set up Chinese Camp?

could find them, play music and sing songs, or just sit and talk.

Sunday was most often a day of rest from mining. Preachers who traveled from one camp to another held religious services. Miners also spent the day cleaning or mending clothes and doing other chores.

Many forty-niners were lured to California by tall tales of gold nuggets just waiting to be picked up. In fact, however, few people got rich from mining gold. In letters to her sister, **Louise Clappe**—who had moved with her husband from New England to the mining camps—wrote about the truth of the gold rush. "A man may work in a claim for many months," she wrote, "and be poorer in the end; or he may 'take out' thousands in a few hours. It is a mere matter of chance."* These letters were later published, and are among the first true accounts of the gold rush.

READING CHECK **COMPARE AND CONTRAST How were Louise Clappe's accounts of the gold rush different from earlier reports?**

*Louise Clappe. From a letter to her sister, April 10, 1852. *The Shirley Letters: From the California Mines, 1851–1852.* Heyday Books, 1998.

Louise Clappe's letters were published under the pen name "Dame Shirley."

Summary

Gold was discovered in California in 1848. Within a year, thousands of people arrived in California. Gold mining was hard work, and few people got rich from mining gold.

REVIEW

1. How did the discovery of gold change California?
2. Describe the three routes forty-niners could take to California. Use the term **isthmus**.
3. How did conditions in other countries affect immigration to California during the gold rush?

CRITICAL THINKING

4. Why were people willing to make the difficult trip to California?
5. ANALYSIS SKILL What do you learn from the quotation on this page by Louise Clappe? Is it a primary source or a secondary source? Explain.
6. **Write a Diary Entry** Imagine that you live in a mining camp in 1850. Write a diary entry to describe a day in your life. Be sure to include a description of the camp and the kinds of activities you do.
7. Focus Skill **COMPARE AND CONTRAST** On a separate sheet of paper, copy and complete the graphic organizer below.

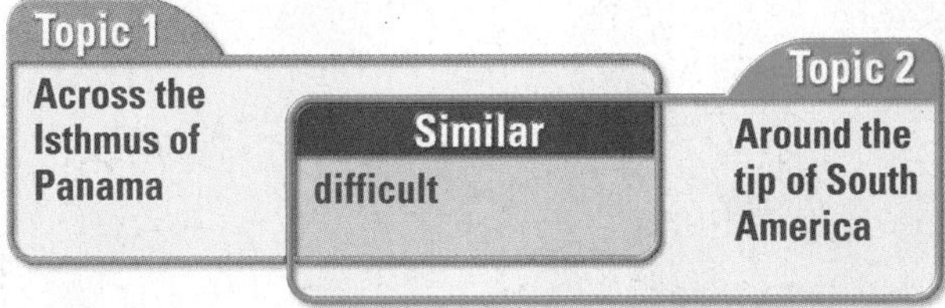

PRIMARY SOURCES

The Life of a Forty-Niner

At the time of the gold rush, much of California was wilderness. Forty-niners often lived in simple mining camps located many miles away from the nearest town. They needed sturdy tools to help them do their work. In time, forty-niners developed new tools that made searching for gold easier.

Miners used metal pans like this one to find gold in rivers and streams.

Miners needed clothes that would be long-lasting. In 1873 Levi Strauss and a partner designed pants that had metal rivets on the pockets to make them strong. Jeans such as these are still popular today.

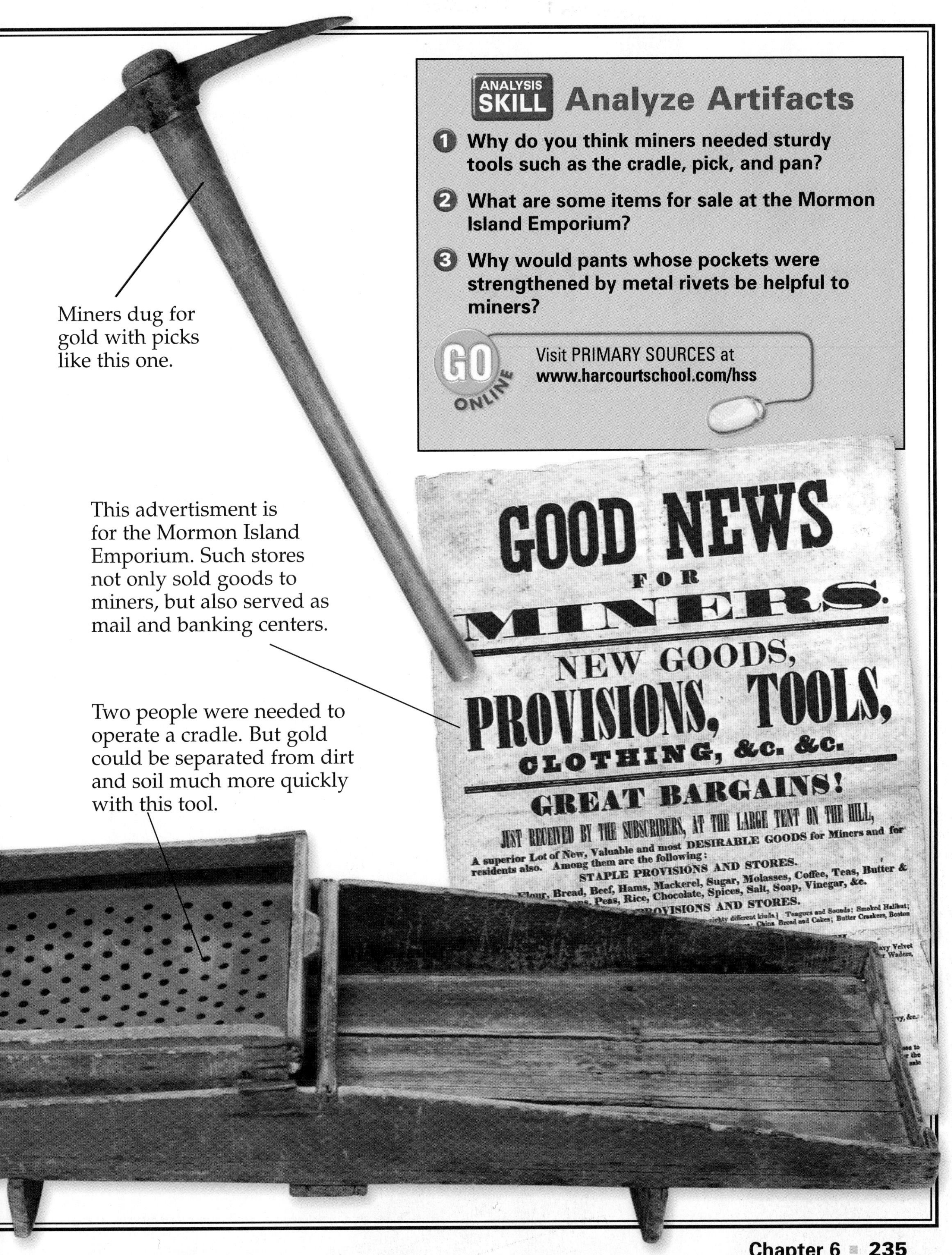
GOOD NEWS
FOR
MINERS.
NEW GOODS,
PROVISIONS, TOOLS,
CLOTHING, &c. &c.
GREAT BARGAINS!
JUST RECEIVED BY THE SUBSCRIBERS, AT THE LARGE TENT ON THE HILL,
A superior Lot of New, Valuable and most DESIRABLE GOODS for Miners and for residents also. Among them are the following:
STAPLE PROVISIONS AND STORES.
Flour, Bread, Beef, Hams, Mackerel, Sugar, Molasses, Coffee, Teas, Butter &
Peas, Rice, Chocolate, Spices, Salt, Soap, Vinegar, &c.
PROVISIONS AND STORES.
Tongues and Sounds; Smoked Halibut;
China Bread and Cakes; Butter Crackers, Boston

ANALYSIS SKILL Analyze Artifacts

1. Why do you think miners needed sturdy tools such as the cradle, pick, and pan?
2. What are some items for sale at the Mormon Island Emporium?
3. Why would pants whose pockets were strengthened by metal rivets be helpful to miners?

GO ONLINE Visit PRIMARY SOURCES at **www.harcourtschool.com/hss**

Miners dug for gold with picks like this one.

This advertisment is for the Mormon Island Emporium. Such stores not only sold goods to miners, but also served as mail and banking centers.

Two people were needed to operate a cradle. But gold could be separated from dirt and soil much more quickly with this tool.

Lesson 2

Time

1825 1840 1855

1851 The Committee of Vigilance is formed in San Francisco

1855 Mifflin Gibbs publishes the *Mirror of the Times*

WHAT TO KNOW
How did the gold rush affect California?

- Analyze the effects of the gold rush on California's economy, people, settlements, and politics.
- Explain how the gold rush changed California's physical environment.

VOCABULARY
consumer p. 238
entrepreneur p. 238
inflation p. 239
discrimination p. 242
vigilante p. 242

PEOPLE
Levi Strauss
Mary Jane Megquier
Mifflin Gibbs

PLACES
San Francisco
Stockton
Marysville

COMPARE AND CONTRAST

HSS 4.3, 4.3.2, 4.3.3, 4.3.4, 4.4, 4.4.2

The Effects of the Gold Rush

YOU ARE THERE The sounds of saws and hammers can be heard day and night. Builders can't keep up with the growing population. The year is 1849, and **San Francisco** keeps growing bigger and bigger. Every day, more people arrive at the harbor. Most leave quickly for the gold fields, but some stay to start businesses.

Settlements Grow and Change

The discovery of gold in California set off one of the largest movements of people in history. In just a few years, San Francisco changed from a town of about 800 people to a city of 35,000. Ships entered and left San Francisco by the thousands.

Ferries and riverboats made regular trips up and down the Sacramento and San Joaquin Rivers. Sacramento grew quickly, and so did **Stockton** and **Marysville**. They became trading and supply centers for the mining camps in the foothills of the Sierra Nevada. Other towns that had been mining camps just months earlier now had banks, food stores, and doctors' offices. As a miner named Charles Peters described, ". . . [mining towns] were not laid out and built according to any definite plan . . . they just growed [grew]."*

Population of San Francisco

YEAR	NUMBER OF PEOPLE
1848	🧍
1849	🧍🧍🧍🧍🧍🧍🧍🧍🧍🧍🧍🧍🧍🧍🧍 🧍🧍🧍🧍🧍🧍🧍🧍🧍🧍
	🧍 = 1,000 people

Analyze Graphs **At times in 1849, the population of San Francisco doubled every ten days.**

What was the city's population in 1849?

Many miners gave up on the dream of finding gold but decided to stay in California anyway. Some became merchants and shopkeepers. Others claimed farmland in the Central Valley, where they began to grow food for the miners and others.

READING CHECK **COMPARE AND CONTRAST**
How was San Francisco different after the gold rush?

*Charles Peters. *The Autobiography of Charles Peters.* La Grave, 1915.

Ships that brought the forty-niners to California were often abandoned once they reached San Francisco. At one time, five hundred ships were left in the harbor.

FAST FACT

During the gold rush, buildings were needed so badly in San Francisco that some abandoned ships in the harbor were made into hotels, stores, and warehouses.

The New Economy

Not only did the gold rush bring thousands of people to California, but it also transformed, or changed, California's economy. The gold rush made some people in California rich. While many workers mined gold, others started businesses. They provided goods and services to the miners and other consumers. A **consumer** is a person who buys a good or service.

Most newcomers arrived in California with only what they could carry. These people needed places to live, food to eat, clothes to wear, and much more. This created demand for workers of many kinds. Carpenters built homes and buildings, and merchants sold supplies. Towns also needed police officers, bankers, grocers, blacksmiths, and other workers.

Levi Strauss

Many entrepreneurs became wealthy selling goods and services to miners. An **entrepreneur** (ahn•truh•pruh•NER) is a person who sets up a new business.

One of the most successful entrepreneurs was **Levi Strauss**. He developed a product that miners liked and needed—blue jeans. Strauss and Jacob Davis, a tailor, designed the jeans to be tough and to last a long time. The jeans were made from denim, a rugged material, and had

Some businesspeople who offered services to the gold miners, such as tinsmiths (left) and bankers (below) made more money from their businesses than miners made searching for gold.

Some store owners "mined the miners." That is, they often charged very high prices for scarce goods. How does this cartoon illustrate this?

metal rivets at the corners of their pockets to make them strong.

Entrepreneurs, such as Strauss, often had better chances of becoming rich than did people searching for gold. Because so many people had come to California in such a short time, many goods that people consumed became scarce, or hard to find. Almost everything had to be imported, or brought to California from somewhere else. In time, imported goods also included costly items, such as fine furniture and clothing. Wealthy miners and business owners were willing to pay for these products.

In addition to a shortage of goods, there was a shortage of labor, or workers. Most people wanted to look for gold rather than work at other jobs.

The shortages of goods and labor caused **inflation**, or a sharp increase in prices. In fact, some miners found that it was cheaper to have their laundry sent to China and back than to have it cleaned in San Francisco! Clothing, food, haircuts, and pots and pans often cost ten times more in California.

READING CHECK **COMPARE AND CONTRAST**
How did the economy of California change during the gold rush?

Mifflin Gibbs (above) and this Chinese worker (left) represent the diversity of California's population in the late 1800s.

New Opportunities

Despite the high cost of living, people saw California as a place of freedom and opportunity. The gold rush economy in California meant that some people had opportunities that were not available to them in other places. Many women opened hotels, restaurants, and laundries. They worked long days, buying and cooking food, changing beds, washing sheets, cleaning, and sewing. **Mary Jane Megquier**, who had come to California from Maine with her husband, wrote,

> "Women's help is so very scarce . . . that a woman that can work will make more money than a man."*

In California, women could earn their own money. In many other places at the time, women were not allowed to own property or start their own businesses.

Many free African Americans came to California as entrepreneurs. **Mifflin Gibbs** opened a shoe store in San Francisco during the gold rush. He later helped start the *Mirror of the Times*, the first newspaper in California that was owned by African Americans. Like other free African Americans in California, Gibbs used some of the money he earned to help buy the freedom of enslaved African Americans in the South.

READING CHECK GENERALIZE
Why did some women and free African Americans come to California during the gold rush?

Damage to the Land

At the beginning of the gold rush, there were no strong laws in California

*Mary Jane Megquier. From *Apron Full of Gold: The Letters of Mary Jane Megquier from San Francisco, 1849-1856* by Polly Welts Kaufman. University of New Mexico Press, 1994.

to protect the land from the effects of mining. As a result, the miners generally did what they wanted. As gold became harder to find, miners often tore up land or built dams to change the flow of rivers. This killed fish and kept the water from reaching farms and towns downstream.

Perhaps the most harmful mining method was hydraulic (hy•DRAW•lik) mining. Hydraulic mining used waterpower to reach gold deeper in the ground. This method uncovered large amounts of gold, but it also caused big problems for the environment. It sent tons of dirt into the rivers that fed into San Francisco Bay. The mud stopped ships from traveling up some rivers. It also caused the waterways to flood after heavy rainfalls, damaging nearby farmlands.

In 1884, lawmakers in California put a stop to hydraulic mining. Yet some of the damage done by this and other mining methods is still visible today.

READING CHECK MAIN IDEA AND DETAILS
What did hydraulic mining do to the land?

Hydraulic Mining

Miners used water power to reach the gold that was deeper in the ground.

1 **Water was pumped through hoses from rivers and lakes at higher elevations.**

2 **The hoses were attached to big nozzles called water cannons, which in turn were aimed at hillsides. The spray turned solid earth into a mixture of mud, sand, and rocks.**

3 **The muddy mixture was carried into a series of sluices (SLOO•siz), troughs through which water flows. Grooves in the bottom of a sluice held gold and other heavier metals as lighter materials were washed away.**

Why do you think the miners pumped water from higher elevations?

A Changing Population

People of nearly every race, religion, and background came to California during the gold rush. Immigrants from around the world brought different customs, languages, and cultures. Most people learned to get along with people of other groups, but sometimes there were conflicts.

Chinese and Mexican immigrants, California Indians, African Americans, Californios and other groups faced discrimination (dis•krih•muh•NAY•shuhn). **Discrimination** is the unfair treatment of people because of their religion, their race, or their birthplace. Some miners felt that only people from the United States had the right to search for California gold. Some people even threatened to harm immigrant miners or worked to pass laws that limited their rights.

California Indians were hurt by the gold rush in other ways as well. Many were forced off their lands when miners found gold there. Miners also cut down forests and destroyed rivers and streams. These were the places where Indians hunted, fished, and gathered their food. These actions often led to violent conflicts between miners and California Indians.

In the early days of the gold rush, violence and crime were common. Because there were few government officials, some people decided to become vigilantes (vih•juh•LAN•teez) to enforce the laws. A **vigilante** is a person who takes the law into his or

After a gang set fire to downtown San Francisco, Sam Brannan led the formation of the Committee of Vigilance. Why do you think the group chose an eye to be a symbol on its seal (left)?

her own hands. Because they did not follow the rules of law, in some cases, vigilantes punished people who had done nothing wrong.

READING CHECK **DRAW CONCLUSIONS**
How did the search for gold lead to conflicts between different groups in California?

Summary

The gold rush changed almost everything about California. The population grew rapidly and became more diverse. Entrepreneurs sold new kinds of goods and services. The gold rush also harmed the land and led to more crime. Some people suffered discrimination.

To show their dislike of Chinese immigrants, some miners in California during the gold rush would cut off the long, braided hair—called queues—worn by Chinese men at that time.

REVIEW

1. How did the gold rush affect California?
2. Use the terms **entrepreneur** and **inflation** to explain how the gold rush changed the economy of California.
3. How did the products that consumers in California wanted change during the gold rush?

CRITICAL THINKING

4. **ANALYSIS SKILL** Do you think the effects of the gold rush were mostly positive or mostly negative? Explain.
5. **ANALYSIS SKILL** **Make It Relevant** Why do people come to California today? How are these reasons for coming like those of the forty-niners? How are they different?
6. **Role-Play Forty-niners** Imagine that you are planning to go to California during the gold rush. Decide whether to become a miner or an entrepreneur. Think about the benefits and costs of each choice. Then plan the items you will need to take with you.
7. **Focus Skill** **COMPARE AND CONTRAST** On a separate sheet of paper, copy and complete the graphic organizer below.

Topic 1	Similar	Topic 2
Miners cannot afford to pay high prices of some goods and services.		Entrepreneurs become wealthy selling goods and services to miners.

Read a Line Graph

WHY IT MATTERS

The gold rush affected California in many ways, but perhaps the greatest change it caused was in population. In 1848, only about 14,000 non-Indian people lived in California. After gold was discovered, the population of California grew very quickly and then continued to grow. It went from around 100,000 in 1850 to just over 1,200,000 in 1890.

In order to see how a population changes over time, it can be helpful to show the numbers on a line graph. A **line graph** is a graph that shows changes over time.

WHAT YOU NEED TO KNOW

The line graph on page 245 shows how California's population grew rapidly in the 40-year period from 1850 to 1890. The left-hand side of the graph shows the number of people living in California. The bottom of the graph shows the years. Each point on the graph shows the population for a certain year. The line connecting the points shows how the population changed over a period of time. The steeper the line, the greater the change is. To figure out the population in California for a given year, follow these steps.

Stockton, on the San Joaquin River, experienced rapid growth during the gold rush.

Step 1 **Find a year, such as 1850, at the bottom of the graph.**

Step 2 **Move your finger straight up from that date until you reach the purple line.**

Step 3 **Move your finger left to the number of people. That is the population for that year. If your finger doesn't end up exactly at a marked number, you may need to estimate, or make a close guess.**

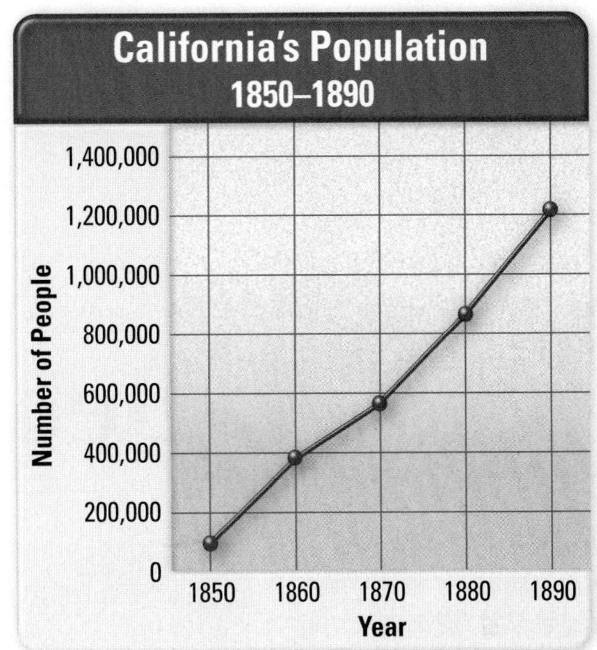

PRACTICE THE SKILL

Use the line graph on this page to answer these questions.

1. About how many people lived in California in 1860? in 1880?
2. About how many more people lived in California in 1880 than in 1860?
3. Did California's population grow more between 1860 and 1870 or between 1880 and 1890? How do you know this?

APPLY WHAT YOU LEARNED

Create a line graph that shows the changes in the population of the United States during the same period. Use these figures.

23,000,000 in 1850
31,000,000 in 1860
38,000,000 in 1870
49,000,000 in 1880
62,000,000 in 1890

Chart and Graph Skills

Lesson 3

Time

1825 | 1840 | 1855

1849
Delegates at Monterey write the California Constitution

1850
California becomes a state on September 9

California Becomes a State

WHAT TO KNOW
How did California become a state?

- ✓ Identify the challenges faced by California leaders after statehood.
- ✓ Tell how California's new government differed from those during the Spanish and Mexican periods.

VOCABULARY
convention p. 247
delegate p. 247
constitution p. 249
legislature p. 249
ratify p. 249
Congress p. 250
compromise p. 250

PEOPLE
General Bennet Riley
Mariano Guadalupe Vallejo
Peter H. Burnett

PLACES
Monterey

COMPARE AND CONTRAST

HSS 4.3, 4.3.3, 4.3.5, 4.4, 4.4.2

YOU ARE THERE San Francisco was just a small, quiet town when you arrived eight months ago. Now, in 1849, it's the largest city in the West. You were part of the gold rush that created this population boom in California. You and others are now beginning to talk about California's becoming a state. California leaders have called a meeting in **Monterey** to discuss statehood. You are excited and also nervous about California's future.

The Monterey Convention

In 1847, the United States took control of California. Since that time, California had been ruled by United States military officials. Under military rule, Californians had no rights except those given them by the military governor.

At first, people had not complained much about military rule. Then the gold rush brought tens of thousands of newcomers from the United States to California. They wanted the same rights in California as they had in the United States. So did many of the people who had already been living in California.

At this time, the United States Congress was busy dealing with rising conflicts over slavery and other issues between the Northern states and the Southern states. Its members were not able to pass laws that would create a new government for California.

General Bennet Riley, the new military governor of California, decided to call for a **convention.** At this important meeting, to be held in Monterey, decisions would be made about California's future. Delegates were elected to attend the convention. A **delegate** is a person chosen to speak and act for the people who elected him or her.

READING CHECK **COMPARE AND CONTRAST**
How did the feelings of Californians about military rule change with the gold rush?

The delegates who met at Monterey represented people from all parts of California. The delegates came from different backgrounds but worked together to make decisions for all Californians.

FAST FACT

The 48 delegates to the Monterey Convention met in Colton Hall, the only building in California at the time large enough to hold such a gathering.

A Constitution for California

TIME 1849

PLACE Colton Hall, Monterey

Californians elected 48 delegates to attend the convention. They included both new immigrants and members of old Californio families, such as **Mariano Guadalupe Vallejo**. Vallejo had lived in California since the time of Spanish rule. He was one of eight Californios elected to the convention.

The delegates quickly decided that California should become a state. Next, they had to decide what land would become the state of California. The Treaty of Guadalupe Hidalgo had set California's southern border with Mexico. The Pacific Ocean formed the state's western boundary. The northern border was the Oregon Territory. It was the eastern boundary that the delegates had to set.

The decision about the eastern border was one of the most important that the delegates had to make. Should California include all of the land that the United States had gained from Mexico? The delegates decided against this. They thought that the area would be too large to govern. They decided that the eastern boundary of California should be marked by the Sierra Nevada and the Colorado River.

Another decision the delegates faced was whether California would be a slave state or a free state. In slave states, people were allowed to own

CITIZENSHIP

Democratic Values

Being able to own your own property is a right that people value.

In California's constitution of 1849, only white men over the age of 21 were allowed to vote. This was true in the rest of the United States as well. Unlike most other state constitutions, however, the California constitution did give women the right to own property. This was a tradition in California from the time of Mexican rule. The delegates at the Monterey Convention included this right as Article XI, Section 14 of the constitution of 1849. Today, all citizens in the United States have the right to own property.

California's constitution granted Nancy Kelsey (right) and other women in California many rights that women in other parts of the United States did not have.

The members of the first graduating class of the first high school in San Francisco, shown here in 1859, were among the first people to benefit from California's public school system.

slaves. In free states, they were not. All of the delegates voted that California should be a free state.

The delegates also made decisions about education in the new state. They called for the creation of a state public school system.

These decisions and others were written into a **constitution**, or plan of government, for the new state. In just six weeks, the delegates wrote the constitution of 1849. It gave Californians new rights and freedoms.

For the first time, California citizens would have a voice in their own government. They could now vote for their leaders, such as a governor and members of the state legislature. A **legislature** (LEH•juhs•lay•cher) is a group of officials elected to make laws.

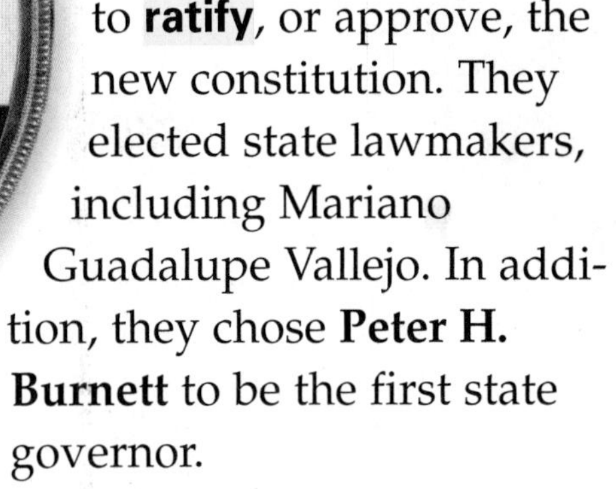

Peter H. Burnett

In November 1849, the people of California voted to **ratify**, or approve, the new constitution. They elected state lawmakers, including Mariano Guadalupe Vallejo. In addition, they chose **Peter H. Burnett** to be the first state governor.

READING CHECK **COMPARE AND CONTRAST**
How was California's new government different from its governments of the past?

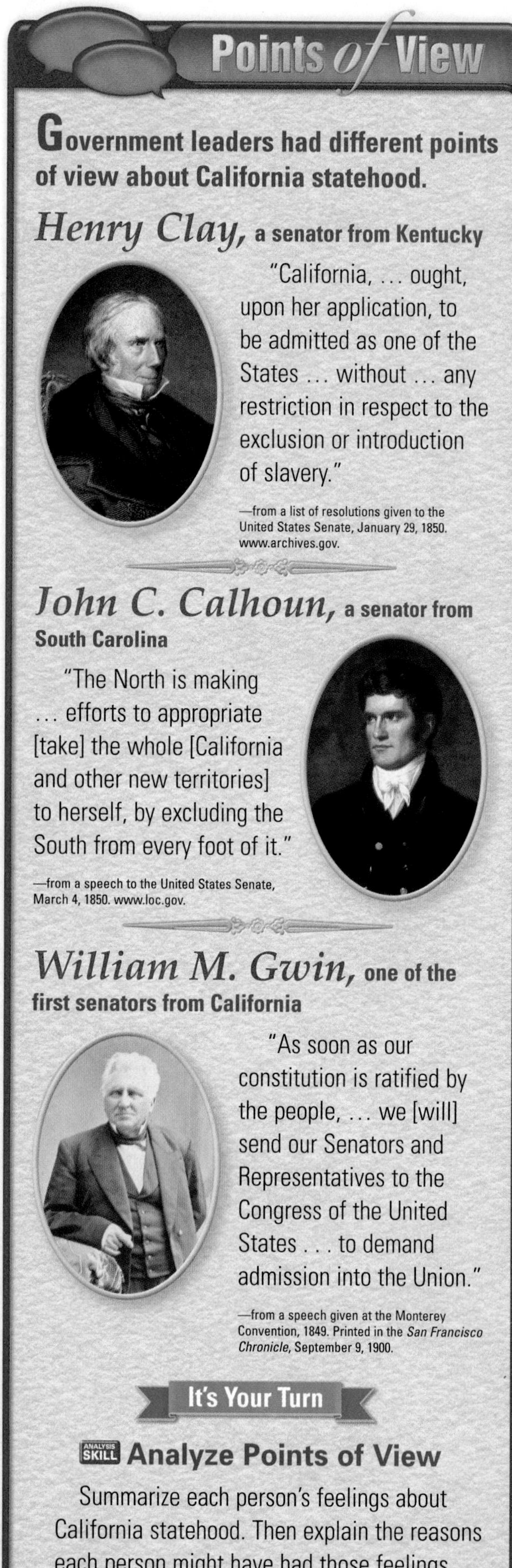

Points of View

Government leaders had different points of view about California statehood.

Henry Clay, **a senator from Kentucky**

"California, ... ought, upon her application, to be admitted as one of the States ... without ... any restriction in respect to the exclusion or introduction of slavery."

—from a list of resolutions given to the United States Senate, January 29, 1850. www.archives.gov.

John C. Calhoun, **a senator from South Carolina**

"The North is making ... efforts to appropriate [take] the whole [California and other new territories] to herself, by excluding the South from every foot of it."

—from a speech to the United States Senate, March 4, 1850. www.loc.gov.

William M. Gwin, **one of the first senators from California**

"As soon as our constitution is ratified by the people, ... we [will] send our Senators and Representatives to the Congress of the United States . . . to demand admission into the Union."

—from a speech given at the Monterey Convention, 1849. Printed in the *San Francisco Chronicle,* September 9, 1900.

It's Your Turn

ANALYSIS SKILL Analyze Points of View

Summarize each person's feelings about California statehood. Then explain the reasons each person might have had those feelings.

The Thirty-first State

After the elections in 1849, California's two senators went to Washington, D.C. There, they asked Congress to allow California to join the United States. **Congress** is the part of the United States government that makes laws.

California's request set off a huge debate. At that time, the United States had the same number of free states as slave states. Most free states were in the North, and most slave states were in the South. Southerners did not want to break this balance by letting California join as a free state.

Finally, members of Congress worked out a **compromise**. People on each side of the argument agreed to give up something. Under the Compromise of 1850, California joined the Union as a free state. In exchange, Congress passed a law—the Fugitive (FYOO•juh•tiv) Slave Act—that said anyone who was caught helping an escaped slave would be punished.

California officially became a state on September 9, 1850. The new state government faced some early challenges. First, it had to choose a location for the state capital. The capital was moved from Monterey to San Jose. Then, it was moved to Vallejo, and later to Benicia. Finally, in 1854, the capital of California was moved to Sacramento.

Another big challenge had to do with taxes. A large part of the population in California were people, such as miners, who did not own land. As a result, the state was not able to collect enough property taxes to pay its bills. Also, banks in other parts of the United States did not want to lend money to banks in California.

READING CHECK **CAUSE AND EFFECT**
Why was California having trouble paying its bills?

The End of the Ranchos

The state government also faced troubles over land ownership. Many people who stayed in California after the gold rush lived on unmarked lands that were parts of ranchos. This led to arguments over who owned the land. To settle these disputes, the United States Congress passed the Land Act of 1851. This law said that the rancheros, or rancho owners, had to prove that the land belonged to them.

Sacramento became California's capital in 1854, but the capitol building was not completed until 1874.

This was hard for some of the rancheros to do. Most of them did not speak English, and few government officials spoke Spanish. It was also difficult for some rancheros to prove that they had received their land grants legally. Most had received their grants when California was ruled by Mexico. In addition, hand-drawn diseños were often not correct.

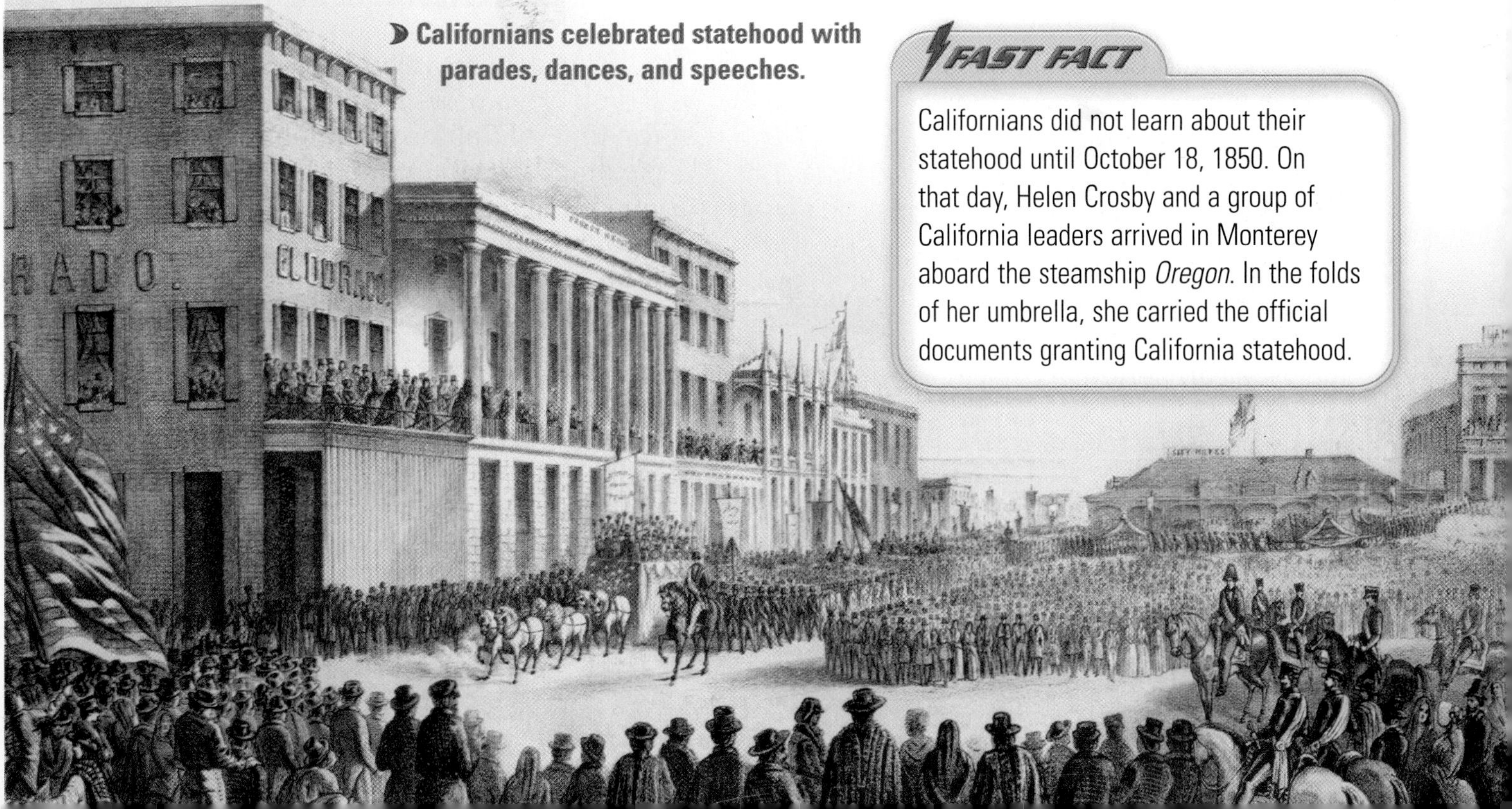

Californians celebrated statehood with parades, dances, and speeches.

FAST FACT

Californians did not learn about their statehood until October 18, 1850. On that day, Helen Crosby and a group of California leaders arrived in Monterey aboard the steamship *Oregon*. In the folds of her umbrella, she carried the official documents granting California statehood.

Many rancheros had to hire lawyers and had to sell their lands to pay their bills. In the end, most large ranchos were broken up.

The fight over land ownership affected the state's population as well. Because of the long legal arguments, many people who might have settled in California decided not to.

READING CHECK GENERALIZE
Why were there arguments over land ownership in California?

Among the state of California's early leaders were (left to right) Pablo de la Guerra, Salvador Vallejo, and Andrés Pico.

Summary

In 1848, California leaders gathered to decide California statehood and to write a state constitution. The Compromise of 1850 allowed California to become a state. The new state faced a lack of tax revenue and fights over land ownership.

REVIEW

1. How did California become a state?
2. Use the words **delegate** and **ratify** to describe the creation of the Constitution of 1849.
3. How did the California state government differ from the government during the Spanish and Mexican periods?

CRITICAL THINKING

4. ANALYSIS SKILL How might the United States be different today if Congress had not been able to compromise in order to let California become a state?
5. **Write a News Report** Imagine that you are a newspaper reporter at the time of California statehood. Write an article about the Monterey Convention, the Compromise of 1850, or another important event related to California statehood.
6. Focus Skill **COMPARE AND CONTRAST** On a separate sheet of paper, copy and complete the graphic organizer below.

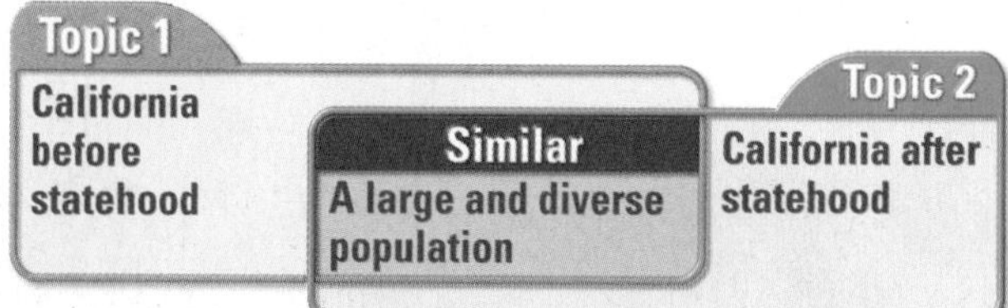

Biddy Mason

Biography

Trustworthiness
Respect
Responsibility
Fairness
Caching

*"If you hold your hand closed, nothing good can come in. The open hand is blessed, for it gives in abundance, even as it receives."**

In 1818, Bridget "Biddy" Mason was born into slavery on the Georgia plantation of Robert Smith. In 1851, Smith moved his household to San Bernardino, in southern California. When Smith wanted to move to Texas—a slave state—Mason fought to stay in California and be free. In 1856, the courts granted freedom to Mason.

For the first time in her life, Mason was allowed to work for herself. She got a job as a nurse. With the money she earned, Mason bought land in what became downtown Los Angeles. She eventually made a fortune by buying, selling, and renting land.

Biddy Mason used her money to help others. She paid the bills of her church and bought food and clothes for those in need. She also helped set up the first school for African American children in Los Angeles.

The 1866 deed that gave Biddy Mason ownership of property in Los Angeles

Why Character Counts

How did Biddy Mason show that she cared about people in her community?

*Mason family saying as recalled by Gladys Owens Smith, great-granddaughter of Biddy Mason, in 1989. *Let It Shine: Stories of Black Women Freedom Fighters* by Andrea Davis Pinkney. Harcourt, 2000.

Bio Brief

1818 Born — 1891 Died

- **1818** Born into slavery in Georgia
- **1851** Robert Smith brings his slaves, including Mason, to California
- **1856** Mason and her daughters win their freedom
- **1872** Helps found the first black church in Los Angeles

Interactive Multimedia Biographies
Visit MULTIMEDIA BIOGRAPHIES at www.harcourtschool.com/hss

Resolve Conflict

WHY IT MATTERS

People sometimes have different ideas about how to do things. That can lead to conflict. When conflict happens, people need to **resolve**, or settle, their conflicts in order to get work done. One way to resolve conflicts is by compromising.

To reach a compromise, each side must give up certain things it wants in return for other things. Compromising is a good way to resolve conflicts peacefully.

WHAT YOU NEED TO KNOW

To resolve a conflict by compromising, follow these steps.

Step 1 **Identify what is causing the conflict.**

Step 2 **Tell the people on the other side what you want. Also listen to what they want.**

Step 3 **Make a plan for a compromise. Explain your plan, and listen to the other side's plan.**

Members of the United States Congress in Washington, D.C., discuss California statehood and the Compromise of 1850.

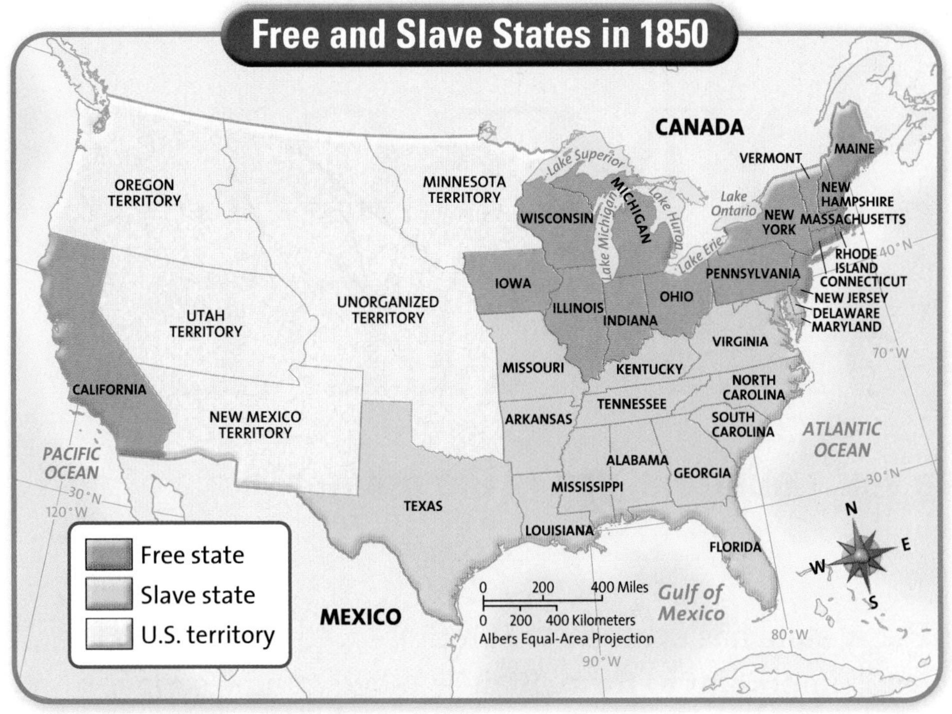

ANALYSIS SKILL Analyze Maps
This map shows how the country was divided over the question of slavery.

Regions **Not counting California, how many free states were there in 1850? How many slave states?**

Step 4 **If you do not agree, make a second plan. Give up one of the things that are most important to you. Ask for the other side to do the same.**

Step 5 **Keep talking until you agree on a compromise. Find a way to let each side have most of what it wants.**

PRACTICE THE SKILL

In the previous lesson, you have read that members of the United States Congress did not agree about California statehood. Those from the North wanted to admit California as a free state. Then there would be more free states than slave states, and the free states would have more votes in Congress. Representatives from the South feared that if this happened, the free states would try to end slavery in all the other states.

To resolve the conflict, representatives in Congress worked out the Compromise of 1850. Recall facts about that compromise. Then answer these questions.

1. What did the North get in the compromise? What did the North give up?
2. What did the South get in the compromise? What did the South give up?

APPLY WHAT YOU LEARNED

MAKE IT RELEVANT Think about a disagreement you have had recently. Review the steps for resolving conflicts by compromising. Then write a paragraph listing compromises that could have been made.

Participation Skills

Citizenship

SYMBOLS OF PRIDE

"I love you, California, you're the greatest state of all."

—from the California state song

Every state has symbols that represent its citizens and what is important to them. State symbols can be songs, flags, mottoes, animals, plants, or other objects. California has many symbols, including a state flower, a state bird, a state dance, and even a state fife-and-drum band.

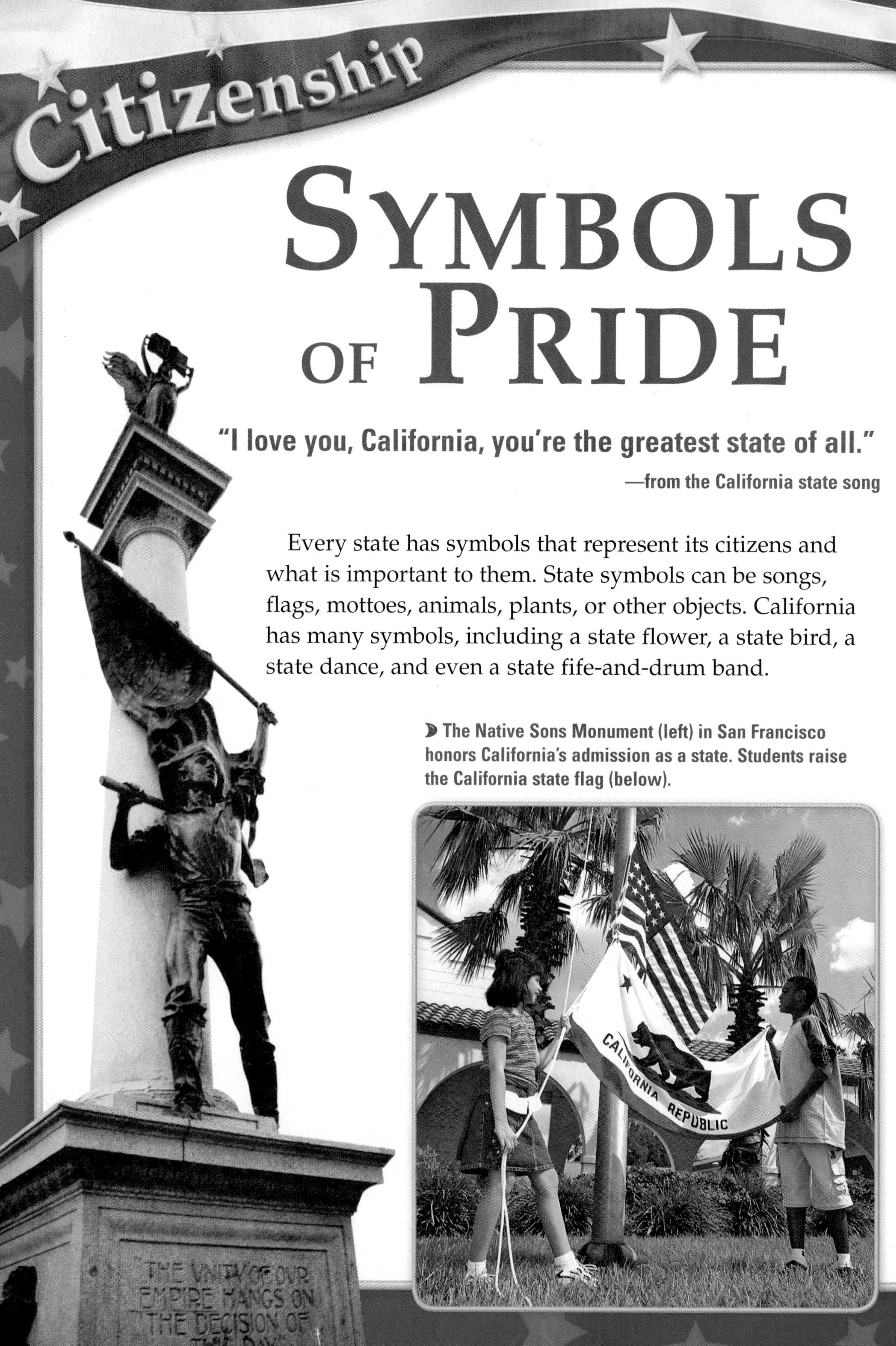
THE VNITY OF OVR
EMPIRE HANGS ON
THE DECISION OF
THIS DAY
CALIFORNIA REPUBLIC

The Native Sons Monument (left) in San Francisco honors California's admission as a state. Students raise the California state flag (below).

A stained glass representation of California's state seal (middle) can be seen at the capitol. The California Indian Seal (left) and the Spanish-Mexican Seal (right) are also state symbols and represent things Californians are proud of.

Even before California became a state in 1850, people began to adopt symbols to represent California. Some state symbols, such as the state seal, are used when conducting official state business. Others, such as the state flag, represent important events in the state's history. Still others, such as the state song and state tree, represent the pride that Californians have for their state and its natural beauty.

The state flower is the California Poppy.

Make It Relevant Why is it important to have state symbols?

The grizzly bear is the state animal. Why do you think it was chosen as a state symbol?

1835

1848
James Marshall discovers gold in California

Reading Social Studies

To **compare** is to think about how two or more things are alike. To **contrast** is to think about how two or more things are different.

Compare and Contrast

Complete the Venn diagram below to show how two of the methods forty-niners used to search for gold were alike and how they were different. A copy of this graphic organizer appears on page 70 of the Homework and Practice Book.

Statehood for California

Topic 1

Panning
- **single person**
- **river water, sand, and gravel scooped into pan**
- **water swirled around pan**

Similar

Topic 2

Cradle
- **at least two people**
- **two trays; top tray filled with sand, soil, and gravel**
- **water poured over material in top tray as cradle is rocked**

California Writing Prompts

Write a Narrative Imagine you are a forty-niner who has been working a claim for several months. Think about your experiences in California. Then write a postcard to the people back home about your life.

Write a Summary Write a report summarizing the effects of the gold rush on California. Be sure to include details about how settlements, the economy, and the environment in California changed.

1845 1850 1855

1849
Delegates meet in Monterey to write the California Constitution

1850
California becomes the thirty-first state of the United States

Use Vocabulary

Write the term that correctly matches each definition.

- **isthmus,** p. 228
- **inflation,** p. 239
- **discrimination,** p. 242
- **legislature,** p. 249
- **ratify,** p. 249

1. to approve
2. a sharp increase in prices
3. a group of people elected to make laws
4. a narrow piece of land that connects two larger land areas
5. unfair treatment of people because of their religion, race, or birthplace

Use the Time Line

Use the summary time line above to answer the questions.

6. When did James Marshall discover gold?
7. When was California admitted as the thirty-first state of the United States?

Apply Skills

Read a Line Graph

8. Look at the line graph on page 245. In which decade did California have the smallest population increase? In which decade did California have the greatest population increase?

Recall Facts

Answer these questions.

9. Where was gold first discovered in California?
10. What happened to the price of goods in California during the gold rush? Why?
11. What did members of Congress decide in the Compromise of 1850?

Write the letter of the best choice.

12. Which features were chosen to mark California's eastern border?
   A the Sierra Nevada and Colorado River
   B the Rocky Mountains and the Mojave Desert
   C the Cascade Range and the Sacramento River
   D the Pacific Ocean
13. What happened to most large ranchos after California became a state?
   A They grew bigger.
   B They were broken up.
   C They became national parks.
   D They were given to Indian tribes.

Think Critically

14. Why was hydraulic mining in the mid-1800s started? How did this method of mining affect the environment?
15. ANALYSIS SKILL How did the gold rush contribute to the diversity of California's population?

Marshall Gold Discovery

• State Historic Park •

GET READY

Gold was first discovered in California in 1848 near Coloma by James Marshall and a group of workers building a sawmill. When word of this discovery got out, people flooded into California, starting the gold rush. Today, people can visit the Marshall Gold Discovery State Historic Park to see the site of the famous event. There are 16 historic buildings and a working replica of the sawmill Marshall was building at the time of the discovery. Visitors to the park can also explore a museum that contains exhibits about the gold rush. You can even try your luck at panning for gold in the American River. Through demonstrations, exhibits, and reenactments at the park, you will see how the discovery of gold forever changed the state of California.

WHAT TO SEE

Visitors of all ages try panning for gold. Like miners of the gold rush, some present-day miners find gold and others do not.

LOCATE IT

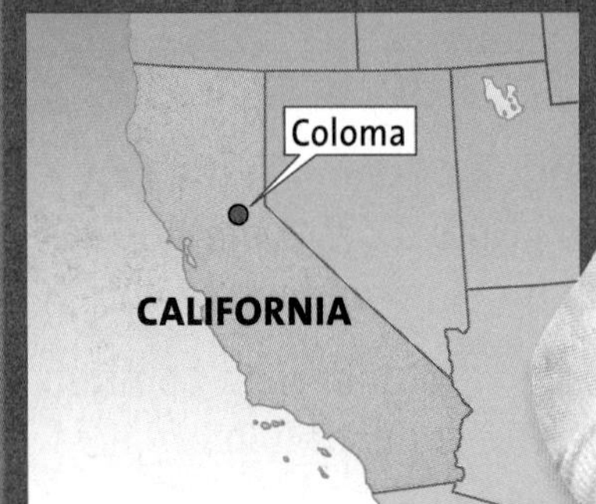

This historic building was used as Coloma's schoolhouse.

The park features many historic buildings as well as replicas to show how Coloma appeared in the mid-1800s.

A park ranger shows students the full-size working replica of Sutter's mill, the sawmill Marshall was building at the time of the gold discovery.

There are many volunteers at the park who participate in reenactments. This volunteer teaches a young visitor to play tic-tac-toe on an old slate board.

This blacksmith displays his skills during a demonstration at the park.

A VIRTUAL TOUR

Visit VIRTUAL TOURS at www.harcourtschool.com/hss

Review

THE BIG IDEA

Growth and Change New opportunities and discoveries attracted many people to California.

Summary

The Road to Statehood

Starting in the early 1800s, settlers followed paths opened by trailblazers to California. By 1845, about 700 people from the United States lived in California. Many Americans believed in manifest destiny, the idea that the United States should reach from the Atlantic Ocean to the Pacific Ocean.

The United States gained control of California in 1847, and the region was placed under military rule. In 1848, gold was discovered in California. The gold rush began as people from all over the world moved to California. People in California wanted military rule to end.

In 1849, delegates were chosen to meet at the Monterey Convention. They wrote a state constitution which was ratified, or approved, by voters later that year. Voters also elected lawmakers and the first state governor. After much debate, the United States Congress voted in 1850 to make California the thirty-first state.

Main Ideas and Vocabulary

Read the summary above. Then answer the questions that follow.

1. What event brought newcomers from around the world to California?
- **A** the discovery of gold
- **B** the Bear Flag Revolt
- **C** a convention in Monterey
- **D** the Mexican-American War

2. What are delegates?
- **A** people who fight against the government
- **B** elected officials who represent others
- **C** settlers in new lands
- **D** gold miners

3. What does ratify mean?
- **A** resist
- **B** deny
- **C** vote
- **D** approve

4. When was the state constitution of California ratified?
- **A** 1847
- **B** 1848
- **C** 1849
- **D** 1850

Recall Facts

Answer these questions.

5. How did trailblazers help open California to settlers from the East?
6. What was manifest destiny?
7. How was California's government under the United States different from its government during Mexican and Spanish rule?

Write the letter of the best choice.

8. Which group became stranded in the Sierra Nevada during an overland journey to California?
   A the Donner party
   B the Bartleson-Bidwell expedition
   C Jedediah Smith and his men
   D General Stephen Kearny and his soldiers
9. When and where was gold first discovered by a settler in California?
   A 1847 at Marysville
   B 1848 at Coloma
   C 1849 at Monterey
   D 1850 at Stockton
10. What did forty-niners hope to do in California?
   A explore the mountains
   B find gold
   C rebuild missions
   D fight against the Mexican government

Think Critically

11. ANALYSIS SKILL Why was California a good place for entrepreneurs during the gold rush?
12. ANALYSIS SKILL At the time of the Bear Flag Revolt, why might some Californios have wanted independence? Why might others have been against it?

Apply Skills

Read and Compare Historical Maps

Look at the historical maps below to answer these questions.

13. How did California change between 1845 and 1848?
14. By 1848 what had happened to land that was claimed by the United States and Mexico in 1845?

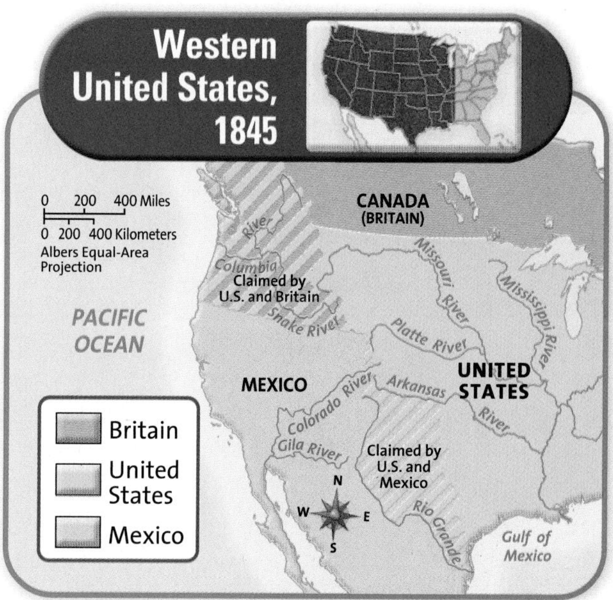

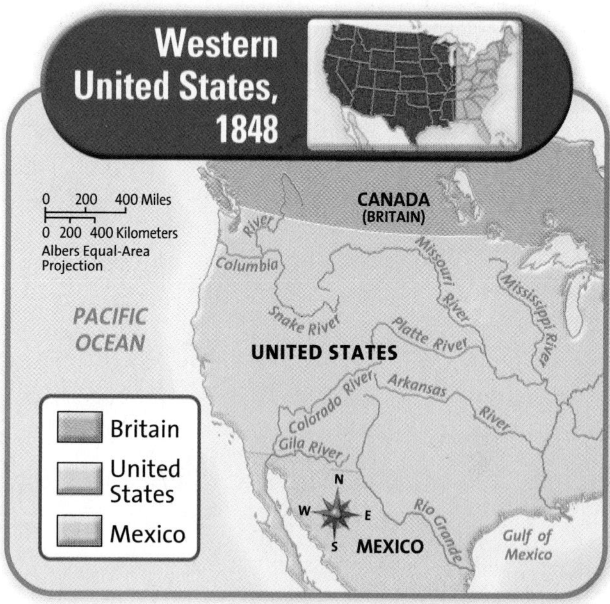

Unit 3

Activities

Read More

- *The Story of Levi Strauss* by Sandy Damashek.

- *Going for the Gold* by Sandra Widener.

- *Blazing Trails to California* by Renee Skelton.

Show What You Know

Unit Writing Activity

Write an Information Report Write an information report about an event in California that took place between 1820 and 1850. Possible topics include trailblazers, the Bear Flag Revolt, the Mexican-American War, and statehood. Be sure to include facts and details about the event you choose.

Unit Project

Publish a California Fact Book Compile a fact book about California in the years leading up to statehood. Make a list of important topics and events from the unit, and write informative entries about each one. Illustrate your entries with maps and drawings.

Visit ACTIVITIES at
www.harcourtschool.com/hss

Growth and Development

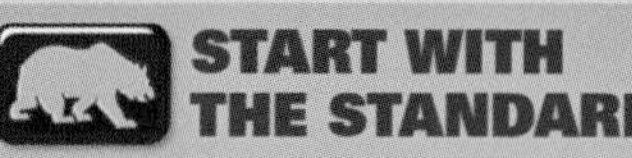

California History-Social Science Standards

4.4 Students explain how California became an agricultural and industrial power, tracing the transformation of the California economy and its political and cultural development since the 1850s.

Innovations

The years after statehood were a time of great change for California and the United States.

What to Know

- How did transportation and communication in California change?
- How did the California economy change?
- How did the movement of people to California affect the state?
- How were water and land resources modified to support California's growing population?

Show What You Know

- **Unit 4 Test**
- **Writing: A Narrative**
- **Unit Project: A California Newspaper**

Unit 4

Time

Growth and Development

1858 Mail is delivered by stagecoach from the East Coast to San Francisco, p. 280

1869 The first transcontinental railroad is completed, p. 291

1882 Congress passes the Chinese Exclusion Act, p. 318

1855

1870

1885

At the Same Time

1861 The American Civil War begins

1869 The Suez Canal, in Egypt, is completed

Growth and Development

1899 Workers begin digging San Pedro Bay, p. 323

1906 A major earthquake strikes San Francisco, p. 331

1909 California approves $18 million for a state highway system, p. 333

1900

1915

1885 The Statue of Liberty is given to the United States as a gift from France

1903 Orville and Wilbur Wright make the first successful powered flights

1914 The Panama Canal is completed

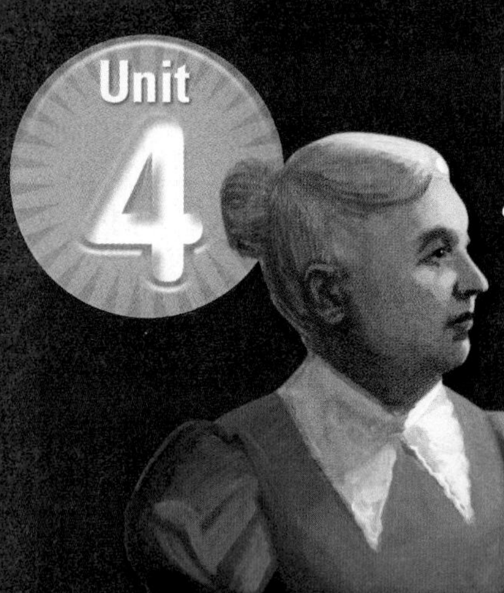

People

Eliza Tibbets

1825–1898

- With her husband, she introduced seedless navel oranges to California
- Because of the work of the Tibbets, California had become the nation's main producer of citrus fruits by 1900.

Yee Fung Cheung

1825?–1907

- Came to California from China during the gold rush, hoping to strike it rich
- Opened herbal medicine stores in Sacramento and Fiddletown in California and Virginia City in Nevada

1805 | 1825 | 1845 | 1865

- 1825 • Eliza Tibbets
- 1825? • Yee Fung Cheung
- 1826 • Theodore Judah — 1863
- 1837? • Chief Kientepoos — 1873
- 1838 • John Muir
- 1842 • Allen Allensworth
- 1855 • William Mulholland
- 1865? •

John Muir

1838–1914

- Served as a guide in the Yosemite Valley for much of his life
- Helped create a national park around Yosemite Valley and started the Sierra Club to help preserve the Sierra Nevada

Allen Allensworth

1842–1914

- In 1906 he became the highest-ranking African American officer in the U.S. Army
- Founded the town of Allensworth, in the San Joaquin Valley, where he wanted African Americans to live free from discrimination

Theodore Judah

1826–1863

- Planned the route for the first transcontinental railroad
- Faced criticism for his idea of a transcontinental railroad at first but eventually convinced Congress to support it

Chief Kientepoos

1837?–1873

- A Modoc Indian chief also known as Captain Jack
- His tribe was forced to move to a reservation with the Klamath Indians
- Led the Modocs in the Modoc War (1872–1873)

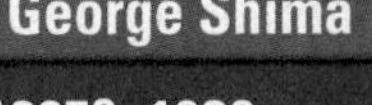

William Mulholland

1855–1935

- Engineer of the Los Angeles Aqueduct, which drained water from the Owens River and brought it to Los Angeles
- Suffered much criticism for his work on the Los Angeles Aqueduct and the St. Francis Dam

George Shima

1865?–1926

- Immigrant from Japan who reclaimed more than 100,000 acres of land in the Sacramento Delta
- In 1913 he was producing most of the potatoes in California, earning him the nickname the "Potato King"

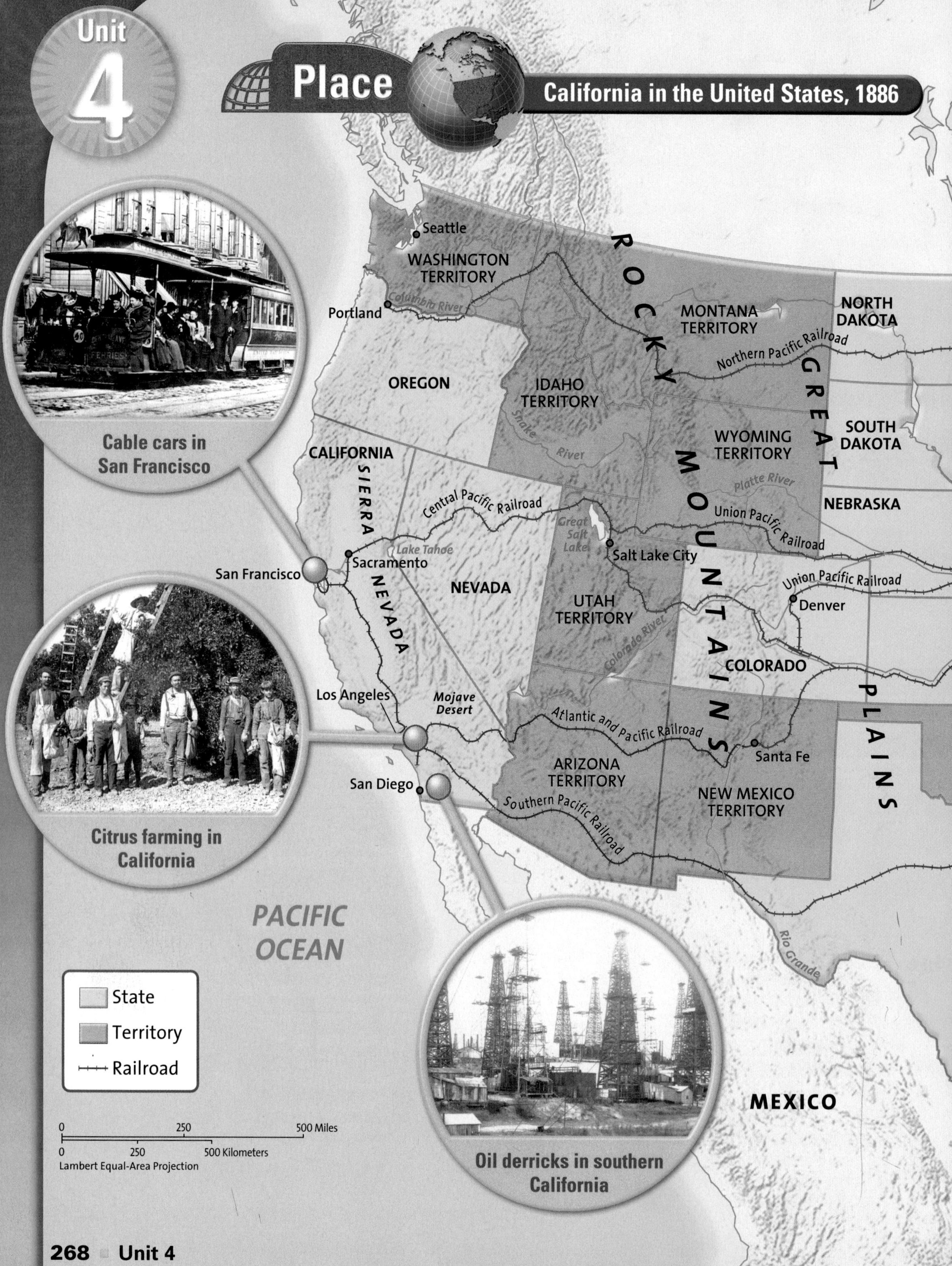

Cable cars in San Francisco

Citrus farming in California

Oil derricks in southern California

CANADA
MAINE
VERMONT
NEW HAMPSHIRE
Boston
MASSACHUSETTS
RHODE ISLAND
CONNECTICUT
NEW YORK
New York City
PENNSYLVANIA
NEW JERSEY
Philadelphia
DELAWARE
MARYLAND
ATLANTIC OCEAN
Washington, D.C.
Richmond
VIRGINIA
NORTH CAROLINA
SOUTH CAROLINA
Charleston
GEORGIA
Jacksonville
FLORIDA
ALABAMA
Birmingham
MISSISSIPPI
LOUISIANA
New Orleans
TEXAS
Dallas
Houston
Southern Pacific Railroad
Gulf of Mexico
INDIAN TERRITORY
ARKANSAS
Arkansas River
MISSOURI
Kansas City
St. Louis
KANSAS
Missouri River
TENNESSEE
KENTUCKY
Ohio River
INDIANA
Cincinnati
OHIO
Pittsburgh
Cleveland
ILLINOIS
Chicago
IOWA
Omaha
MICHIGAN
Detroit
WISCONSIN
MINNESOTA
St. Paul
Mississippi River
Lake Superior
Lake Michigan
Lake Huron
Lake Ontario
Lake Erie
APPALACHIAN MOUNTAINS
N
S
E
W
At the Same Time
Statue of Liberty, in New York Harbor

Reading Social Studies

Focus Skill Draw Conclusions

A **conclusion** is a general statement about an idea or event. It is reached by using what you learn by reading combined with what you already know.

Why It Matters

Being able to draw a conclusion can help you better understand what you read.

Evidence
What you learn

Knowledge
What you already know

Conclusion
A general statement about an idea or event

- ✓ Think about what you know about a subject. Keep in mind the new facts you learn.
- ✓ Look for clues, and try to figure out what they mean.
- ✓ Combine new facts with the facts you already know to draw a conclusion.

Practice the Skill

Read the paragraphs. Draw a conclusion for the second paragraph.

When John Sutter arrived in the Sacramento Valley in 1839, he built a fort, a wheat farm, and a cattle ranch. The location of Sutter's Fort, where the Sacramento and American Rivers join, later became the city of Sacramento. (Rivers supply transportation routes and water for people, crops, and animals. Sutter's Fort was at a good location near natural resources.)

Evidence | Knowledge | Conclusion

Sutter's Fort stood at the end of several trails crossing the Sierra Nevada. People who crossed these mountains could get food and supplies at the fort. Sutter also hired those who needed jobs to work on his land.

Apply What You Learned

Draw Conclusions Read the paragraphs, and answer the questions.

Sacramento's Place in History

Sacramento officially became a city in 1850. It became the state's capital in 1854. By that time, many people had come to the area looking for gold. There was regular steamboat service between Sacramento and the port of San Francisco. Wagon routes were well worn between Sacramento and the gold fields.

During this period, many businesses opened in the city. These businesses provided goods and services to the miners. On surrounding lands, people started farms to grow grains and fruit to feed the growing population. The area's soil, which had been made rich by flooding, proved to be very fertile. By 1860, the Sacramento Valley was one of the leading farming regions in the state.

The first passenger railroad in the West was based in Sacramento. The city was also the first in California to receive regular mail delivery. Later, Sacramento would mark the western end of the railroad crossing the nation from east to west.

In 1870, the Central Pacific Railroad built a railroad car cooled by ice. Several years later, refrigerated cars were used to ship fruit to the East Coast. This new way of keeping shipped goods cool and fresh helped Sacramento become a leading farming region in the United States.

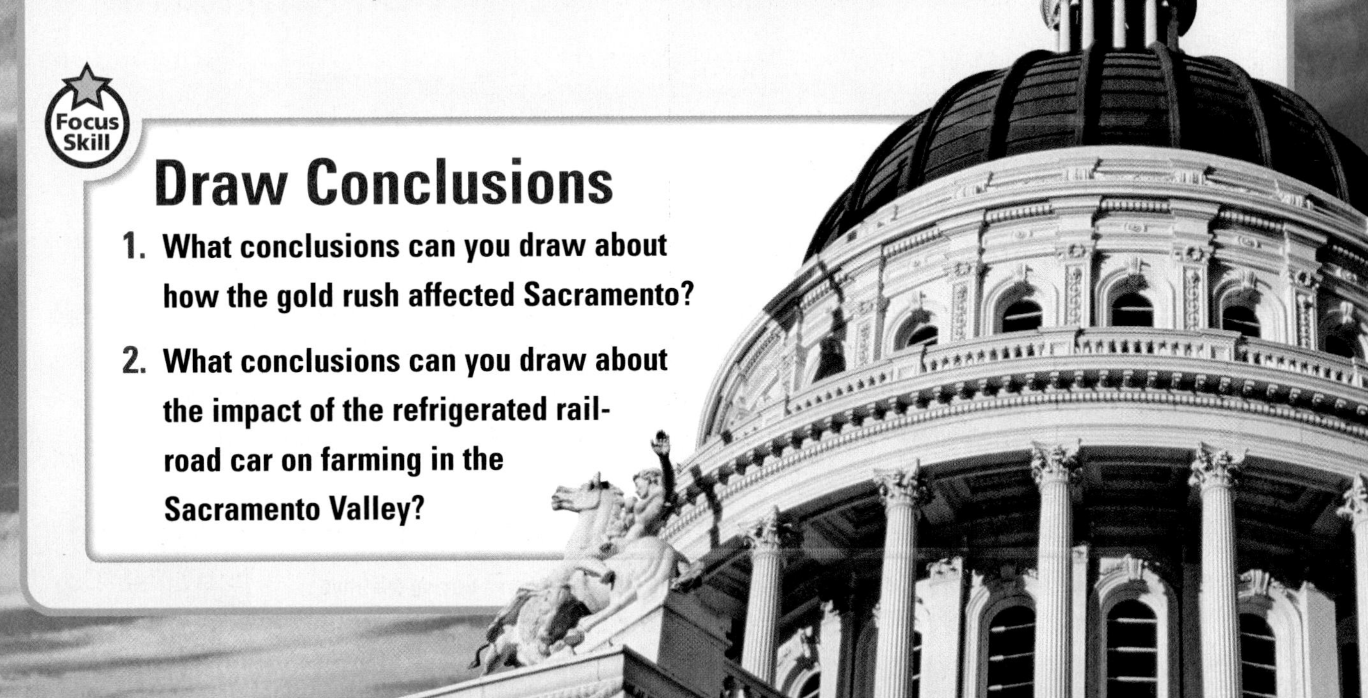

Focus Skill

Draw Conclusions

1. **What conclusions can you draw about how the gold rush affected Sacramento?**
2. **What conclusions can you draw about the impact of the refrigerated railroad car on farming in the Sacramento Valley?**

Study Skills

CONNECT IDEAS

You can use a web organizer to show how different ideas and information are related.

- **List important themes in the ovals in the web's center.**
- **Add ovals showing main ideas that support each theme.**
- **Add bubbles for the details that support each main idea.**

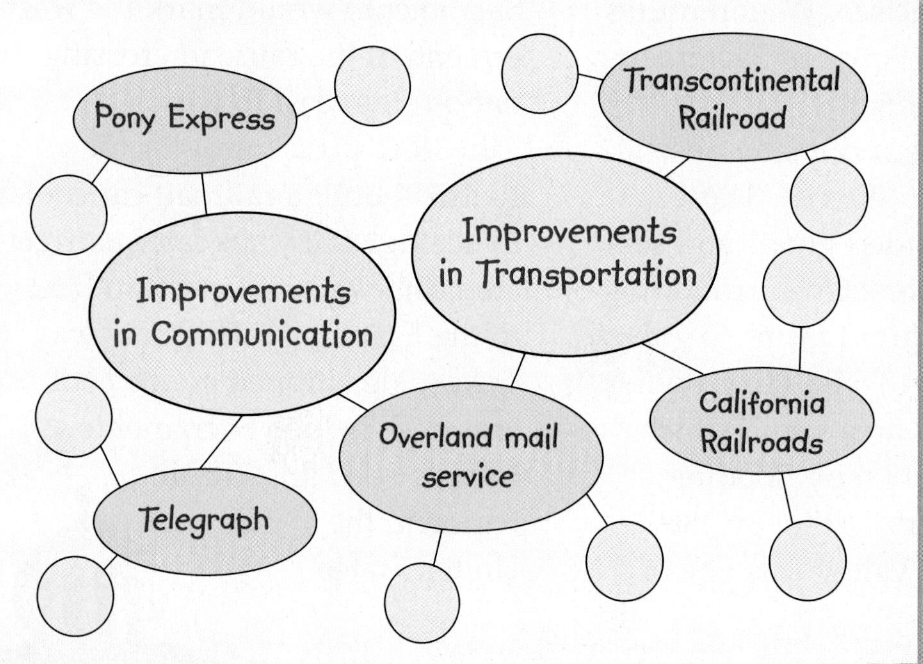

Apply As You Read

Copy and complete the web above as you read this chapter. Fill in each bubble by adding facts and details.

California History-Social Science Standards, Grade 4

4.4 Students explain how California became an agricultural and industrial power, tracing the transformation of the California economy and its political and cultural development since the 1850s.

CHAPTER

Transportation and Communication

Stagecoaches once carried mail and passengers to and from California.

Jimmy Spoon and the Pony Express

by Kristiana Gregory

illustrated by Ron Mazellan

In 1860, the company of Russell, Majors, and Waddell started the Pony Express. The Pony Express promised to deliver mail between St. Joseph, Missouri, and Sacramento, California, in 10 days. Only the fastest horses and best riders were chosen for the Pony Express. One of these riders was Jimmy Spoon. Read now about his first ride for the Pony Express.

Jimmy woke suddenly. Embers in the fireplaces were the only light in the small cabin. He lay in his bunk, listening. In the very far distance, a rider was approaching.

It was two o'clock in the morning, April 6, 1860. Three days earlier, a boy in Missouri and a boy in California began galloping full speed toward each other. Every fifteen miles a fresh horse would be waiting, and every

embers glowing coals from a fire

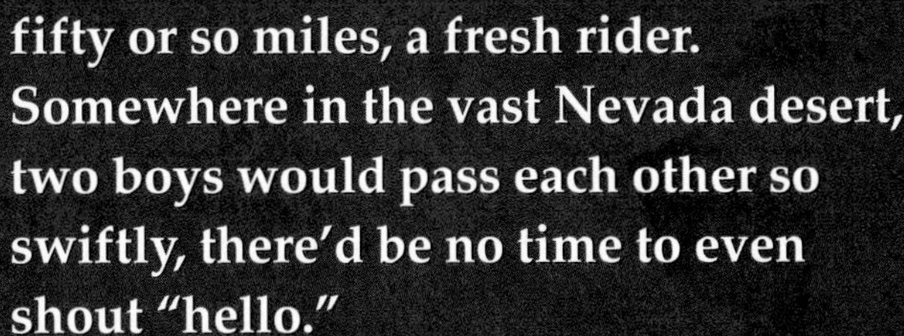

fifty or so miles, a fresh rider. Somewhere in the vast Nevada desert, two boys would pass each other so swiftly, there'd be no time to even shout "hello."

This thought made Jimmy bolt upright and hurriedly pull on his pants. *Could this be the rider he was to relieve? So soon?*

Blankets were thrown back and bare feet struggled into cold, stiff boots: A rider was coming! Mr. Tagg and Will rushed outside to ready a horse, and Pen tried to boost Jimmy's courage.

"You're the best there is, Jim. No Pie-oot will catch *you*, guaranteed."

Milo poured steaming coffee into a tin cup and handed it to Jimmy with a chunk of bread.

"Mornin', son," he said, bending close. His breath stunk from an infected tooth, but Jimmy didn't mind. Despite Milo's unwashed body and unpleasant odors, he was as kind as an old grandfather. "We're countin' on you, Jim. Soon's you reach Roberts Crik Station, ride the next relay back. Mr. Tagg'll keep the coffee on, just like always."

"Thanks, Milo. I'll try my best." Jimmy drank the scalding liquid, but tucked the bread inside his shirt. He was too nervous to eat. He lifted his coat off a peg in the wall and stepped out into the cold night.

Pie-oot Paiute Indian

scalding burning

Silhouetted against the starry horizon was a small, moving shape. It rose and fell, again and again. The faint rumbling Jimmy had heard earlier was now clearly the sound of hoofbeats. A knot clenched in his stomach, a mixture of fear and excitement. He prayed Washakie would understand he had a job to do.

Jimmy was grateful for the full moon rising in the east because it illuminated the trail like a silver ribbon. *Had Mr. Majors planned it this way, so the first riders would be guided by moonlight?*

silhouetted outlined

illuminated lit

Before he could think further, the rider, a boy named Charlie Cliff, was in front of the cabin, leaping off his foaming horse. Charlie lifted the *mochila*, which was a wafer-thin square of leather with four pockets, off the saddle, and tossed it to Mr. Tagg yelling, "Trail's clear!" This meant there were no Indians chasing him.

Jimmy's horse was rearing with impatience as Mr. Tagg slipped the *mochila* over the horn of its saddle. Nick held the halter while Jimmy swung up. Before his right boot could fit into the stirrup, the horse bolted forward and he was on his way, galloping westward across the cold night desert.

Through the thundering of hooves a wisp of a voice reached him. "Godspeed, Jimmy!" called Milo.

Jimmy's horse sped on. Moonlight behind them made it appear they were chasing their shadow. After an hour his sides ached and he was thirsty. Jimmy was relieved when ahead there appeared the dark shape of a hut. Men were leading a horse from a corral. Maybe the two minutes allowed for changing mounts would be enough for Jimmy to catch his breath.

After jumping down, he transferred the *mochila* to the fresh animal. An eager boy about nine years old pressed a cup of water into his hand.

"What's it like, Mister?" the boy asked.

Jimmy took a drink. "Trail's clear, " he responded in his deepest voice. He mounted, then, smiling down at the youngster, slapped the reins against the horse's flank.

"Yee-up!" he yelled. No one saw Jimmy's grin, or knew that his heart soared with happiness. A small boy had called him "Mister" and had pulled a souvenir strand from his pony's tail.

Yes, sir, this was his kind of job.

flank side

Response Corner

1. Why do you think the riders were given so little time to change horses?
2. Many young men wanted to be Pony Express riders even though the job was very dangerous. Why do you think they wanted to be riders?

Lesson 1

Time

1855 · 1885 · 1915

1857 Congress passes the Overland Mail Act

1860 Pony Express service begins

1861 Telegraph lines connect California to the East

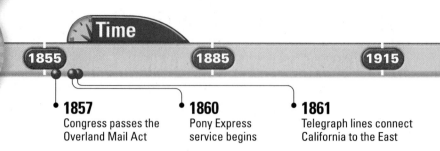

WHAT TO KNOW
What changes improved communication between California and the rest of the United States?

- ✓ Describe how the Overland Mail Service, the Pony Express, and the telegraph linked California to the rest of the United States.
- ✓ Identify the lasting influence of the new links to California.

VOCABULARY
communication p. 279
stagecoach p. 280
telegraph p. 282

PEOPLE
John Butterfield
Samuel F. B. Morse
Stephen J. Field

PLACES
Tipton, Missouri
St. Joseph, Missouri

DRAW CONCLUSIONS

California Standards
HSS 4.4, 4.4.1

Links to the East

YOU ARE THERE It is late November, 1860. You're having dinner in your family's Sacramento home. "Well," your father says, "the mail should arrive tomorrow. Maybe we'll find out who was elected President." You, too, are eager to hear news from faraway Washington, D.C. Mail from the East is now delivered in less than two weeks. You have heard people say that soon they'll be getting news from the East in less than five minutes!

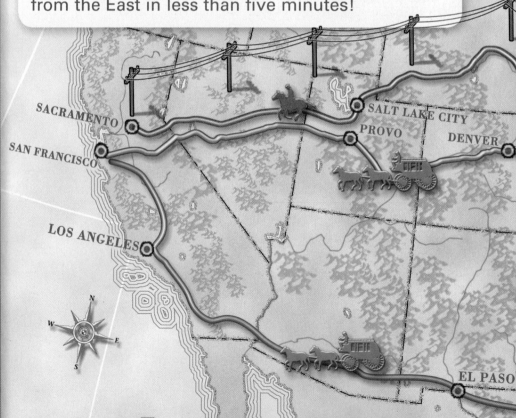

California and the East

In the 1850s, it was difficult for Californians to keep up with events that were happening in the East. Unlike today, there were no telephones and no e-mail. There was not even regular mail service to California. Most mail from the eastern states was taken by ship to the Isthmus of Panama, carried across the land there, and then put on another ship for the rest of the journey to California. It could take months for news from one side of the country to reach the other side.

Many Californians wanted to keep in touch with friends and family in the East. Now that California was part of the United States, its citizens also wanted news about the national government. People living in California wanted better forms of communication to connect them to the rest of the country. **Communication** is the sending and receiving of information. One way to get better communication was to improve the mail service.

READING CHECK **DRAW CONCLUSIONS**
How might faster mail service improve life for Californians?

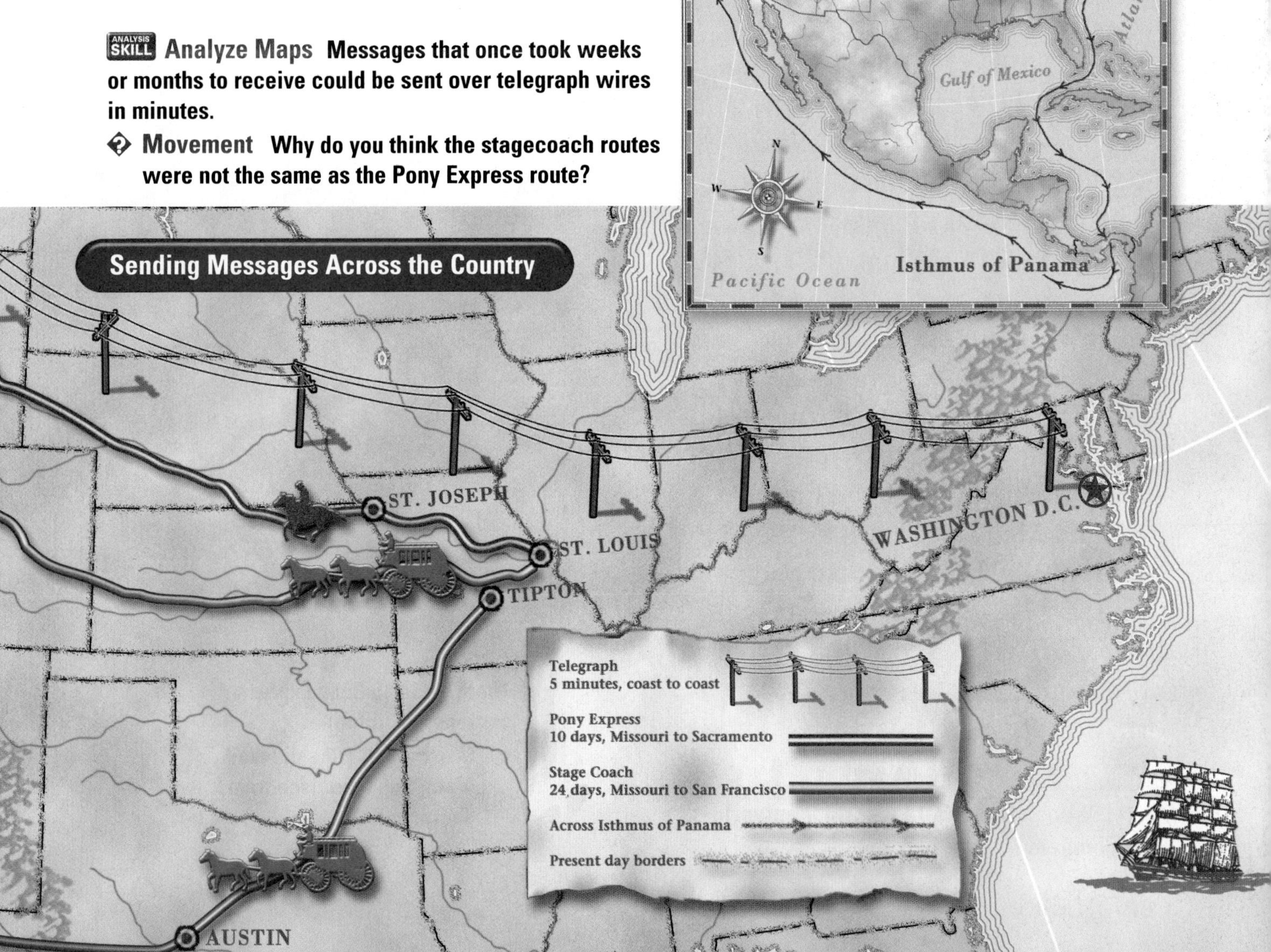

ANALYSIS SKILL **Analyze Maps** **Messages that once took weeks or months to receive could be sent over telegraph wires in minutes.**

Movement **Why do you think the stagecoach routes were not the same as the Pony Express route?**

Overland Mail Service

TIME 1857

PLACE Washington, D.C.

In 1857, the United States Congress passed the Overland Mail Act. This law helped pay for mail service between the Mississippi River and San Francisco. At that time, railroads had not yet reached California.

The Overland Mail Act called for mail to be carried by **stagecoach**—an enclosed wagon pulled by a team of horses. The plan was for coaches to set out for California twice each week.

To carry out this plan, **John Butterfield** started a stagecoach line called the Overland Mail Company. Butterfield's company built new stagecoaches. It also created 200 way stations, or stopping places, where stagecoach drivers could change horses, make repairs, and eat.

Stagecoaches could carry people as well as mail, but the trip was not very pleasant. The roads were rough and dusty. The weather was blazing hot in summer and icy cold in winter.

On October 10, 1858, the first Overland Mail stagecoach arrived in San Francisco, bringing mail and news from the East. Crowds cheered as it drove by. The stagecoach had traveled more than 2,800 miles from **Tipton, Missouri,** in only 24 days.

READING CHECK **CAUSE AND EFFECT**
What led John Butterfield to form the Overland Mail Company?

ANALYSIS SKILL **Analyze Maps**
There were 15 Pony Express stations in California.

Movement **How did mail reach San Francisco from Sacramento?**

The Pony Express

TIME **April 13, 1860**
PLACE **Sacramento**

On April 3, 1860, Johnny Fry jumped on a horse in **St. Joseph, Missouri**, carrying a bag of mail. He headed west. A few hours later, in Sacramento, Billy Hamilton headed east with another bag of mail. They were the first Pony Express riders. The Pony Express hoped to carry mail between Missouri and California in 10 days—less than half the time it took by stagecoach. The journey was made in 9 days and 23 hours!

The Pony Express worked much like a relay race. Each rider traveled about 75 miles before handing over the mail to the next rider. The riders changed horses every 10 to 12 miles.

They traveled day and night through desert heat, mountain snow, and driving rain. As one rider, George Stiers, said, "Our orders were not to stop for anything . . . I carried a snack and a canteen of water, and what eating or drinking I did was done on the hoss [horse] a-running."*

The Pony Express lasted for fewer than 18 months. It ended on October 24, 1861. But in that short time, its riders carried almost 35,000 letters.

READING CHECK **SUMMARIZE**
How was the Pony Express able to get mail to California even faster than by earlier services?

The motto of the Pony Express riders was "The mail must go through."

Utah Territory

Teams of horses pulled stagecoaches at up to 10 miles an hour.

*George S. Stiers. From an interview with Sheldon Gauthier. 1937.

The Telegraph

TIME October 24, 1861

PLACE Sacramento

The Pony Express was put out of business by an even faster form of communication—the telegraph. The **telegraph** used electricity to send messages over wires. With the telegraph, messages could be sent across the country in just minutes! For the first time, news could travel faster than people could.

Telegraph operators sent messages in Morse code, which was created by the inventor of the telegraph, **Samuel F. B. Morse**. Morse code uses groups of "dots" and "dashes," or short and long signals, to stand for the letters of the alphabet. A telegraph operator spelled words by tapping on a switch. An operator on the other end heard the signals and changed them back into letters and words.

Telegraph lines spread throughout the eastern United States in the 1840s and 1850s. By 1860, lines connected San Francisco and Los Angeles.

In 1861, the Western Union Telegraph Company finished the first telegraph line that connected California with the East. On October 24,

Samuel F. B. Morse shows how the telegraph works (left). Once telegraph lines had been strung across the country (below), the Pony Express was no longer needed.

Stephen J. Field, a judge in California, sent a message to President Lincoln in Washington, D.C. It read, "The Pacific to the Atlantic sends greetings." Field later said this about the telegraph:

> **"The people of California . . . believe it will be the means of strengthening the attachment which binds both the East and West to the Union [the United States]. . . ."***

It no longer took Californians weeks to hear about events in the East. California's ties to the rest of the United States were growing stronger.

READING CHECK **DRAW CONCLUSIONS**
What lasting effect did Field hope the telegraph would have on the East and the West?

*Stephen J. Field. From an article in *The Sacramento Dispatch*. October 29, 1861.

The Original Morse Code

a •▬	h ••••	o • •	v •••▬
b ▬•••	i ••	p •••••	w •▬▬
c •• •	j ▬•▬•	q ••▬•	x •▬••
d ▬••	k ▬•▬	r • ••	y •• ••
e •	l ▬	s •••	z ••• •
f •▬•	m ▬▬	t ▬	
g ▬▬•	n ▬•	u ••▬	

Analyze Tables
How would you write your name in Morse code?

Summary

Faster ways of communication, such as the Overland Mail Company, the Pony Express, and the telegraph, helped Californians stay in touch with the rest of the United States.

REVIEW

1. What changes improved communication between California and the rest of the United States?
2. Use the terms **stagecoach** and **telegraph** to tell how **communication** changed in the 1850s and 1860s.
3. Why did the Pony Express operate for only 18 months?

CRITICAL THINKING

4. **ANALYSIS SKILL** **Make It Relevant** What are some forms of communication today? What influence might early forms of communication have had on communication today?
5. **Conduct an Interview** Write a few questions you would want to ask a driver for the Overland Mail Company, a Pony Express rider, or a telegraph operator. Have a classmate write answers that the person might give.
6. **Focus Skill** **DRAW CONCLUSIONS**
On a separate sheet of paper, copy and complete the graphic organizer below.

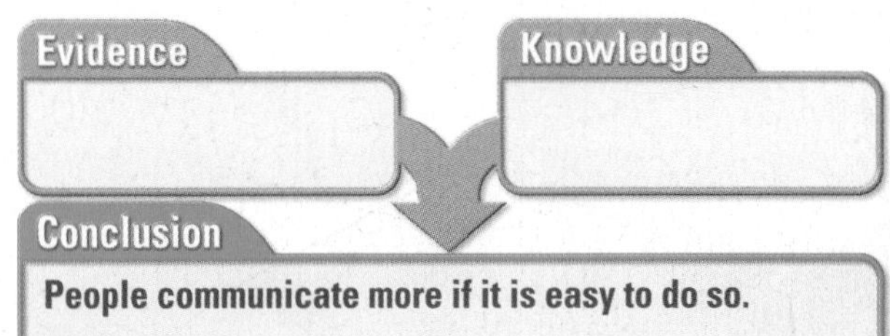
Evidence
Knowledge
Conclusion
People communicate more if it is easy to do so.

PRIMARY SOURCES

The Telegraph

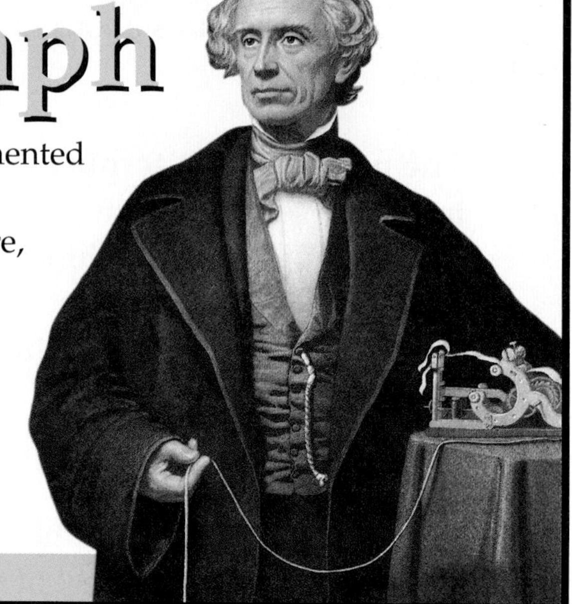

During the 1830s, Samuel F. B. Morse experimented with sending messages by electricity, along iron wires. The first telegraph line ran from Baltimore, Maryland, to Washington, D.C. By the 1860s, telegraph offices existed in every major city in the United States. Today, there are many ways of sending messages quickly over long distances, but Morse code is still used in many parts of the world.

1. To send a message by telegraph, this knob was pressed down for a short time to send a "dot" and for a longer time to send a "dash."
2. When the knob was pressed down, a signal was sent through the electrical circuit.

3. This metal strip acted as a spring to reopen the circuit.

Morse drew this diagram to show how his first telegraph worked.

FIG. 1.
FIG. 2.
MORSE FIRST TELEGRAPH INSTRUMENT
Fig. 1. A, cylinder from which paper was unrolled. B, cylinder on which paper received its records. C, cylinder on which paper was afterward wound. D, clockwork. E, weight for clockwork. F, wooden pendulum pivoted at f. g, pencil carrying a weight. h, electro-magnetic armature. I, voltaic cell.
Fig. 2. MORSE PORT-RULE. L, L, cylinders united by a linen belt. M, rule or composing stick. N, standard. O, O, lever suspended from N, which, when depressed, plunged into J and K, two cups of mercury, completing an electrical circuit.

The first telegraph message was sent by Morse, in Washington, D.C., to his assistant, in Baltimore, Maryland, on May 24, 1844. It read, "What hath God wrought?"

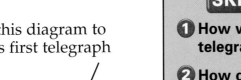

ANALYSIS SKILL Analyze Artifacts

1. **How were messages sent through the telegraph?**
2. **How do the quotes express approval and excitement about the telegraph?**
3. **How do you think the telegraph in the 1860s was like e-mail today?**

GO ONLINE Visit PRIMARY SOURCES at **www.harcourtschool.com/hss**

"The telegraph has become one of the essential means of commercial transactions."

—*St. Louis Republican*, 1847

At first, people were fearful of the telegraph. But, in time, people began to express approval and excitement about it.

"The demands for the telegraph have been constantly increasing; they have been spread over every civilized country in the world, and have become, by usage, absolutely necessary for the well-being of society."

—*The New York Times*, April 3, 1872

Lesson 2

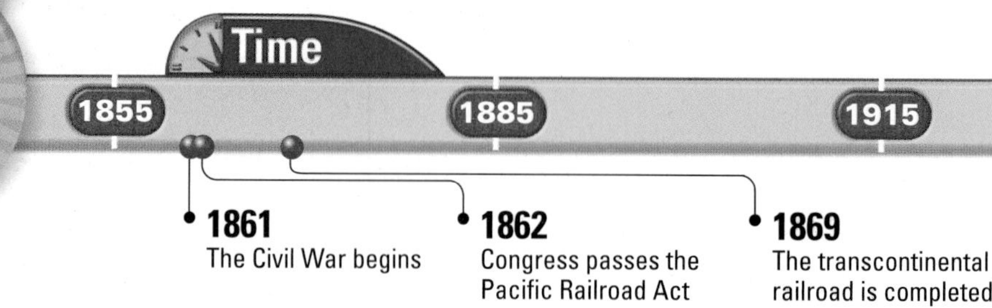
Time
1855
1885
1915
1861 The Civil War begins
1862 Congress passes the Pacific Railroad Act
1869 The transcontinental railroad is completed

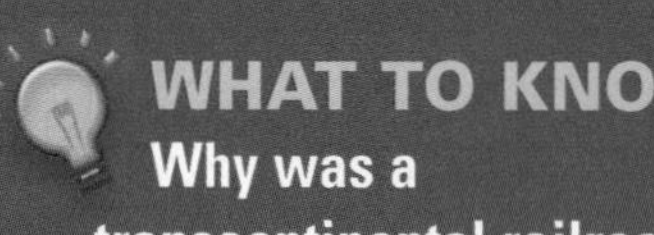

WHAT TO KNOW
Why was a transcontinental railroad needed, and how was it built?

- ✓ Describe how the transcontinental railroad was built.
- ✓ Describe the contribution of Chinese workers and other immigrant groups to the building of the transcontinental railroad.

VOCABULARY
transcontinental railroad p. 287
invest p. 288

PEOPLE
Theodore Judah
Leland Stanford
Collis P. Huntington
Mark Hopkins
Charles Crocker

PLACES
Promontory, Utah

Focus Skill **DRAW CONCLUSIONS**

California Standards
HSS 4.4, 4.4.1, 4.4.3

Building the Transcontinental Railroad

YOU ARE THERE It's been six long years of backbreaking work, but the day you've been waiting for has finally come. Workers at **Promontory, Utah**, are about to join two sets of railroad tracks. One set stretches east from Sacramento, and the other stretches west from Council Bluffs, Iowa. As the last spike is pounded into the ground, the crowd cheers wildly.

Hoping for a Railroad

With improvements in communication in place, people soon began to look at improving transportation between the East and the West. They believed that a **transcontinental railroad**, one that crossed the continent from the Atlantic to the Pacific, might help pull the country together.

Many people supported the idea of a transcontinental railroad. In addition to improving travel, many thought a transcontinental railroad would increase trade. Goods from California and goods brought to California from Asia could be carried by train to the East Coast.

A young man named **Theodore Judah** took a special interest in the idea of a transcontinental railroad. Judah was an engineer, someone who plans and builds railroads and other structures. He knew that the hardest part of building a railroad to California would be crossing the Sierra Nevada. He traveled there 23 times before finding a possible route. In 1857, he gave his opinion of such a railroad. He wrote,

> **"It is the most magnificent project ever conceived [thought of]."***

READING CHECK **DRAW CONCLUSIONS**
How could a railroad help bring the country together?

*Theodore Judah. *A Practical Plan for Building the Pacific Railroad.* H. Polkinhorn. 1857.

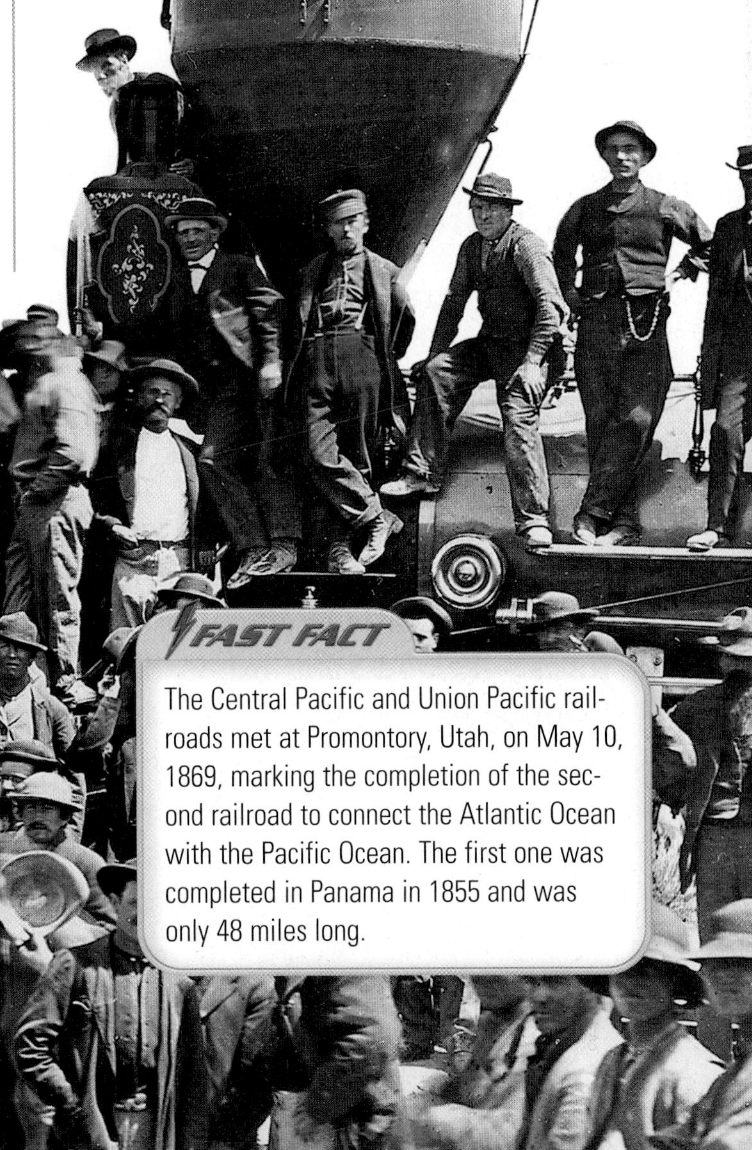

FAST FACT

The Central Pacific and Union Pacific railroads met at Promontory, Utah, on May 10, 1869, marking the completion of the second railroad to connect the Atlantic Ocean with the Pacific Ocean. The first one was completed in Panama in 1855 and was only 48 miles long.

The Transcontinental Railroad
1860
1865
1870
June 28, 1861
Judah and the Big Four form the Central Pacific Railroad Company
October 27, 1863
The Central Pacific Railroad lays track eastward from Sacramento
July 1865
The Union Pacific Railroad lays track eastward from Council Bluffs, Iowa
May 10, 1869
The "Last Spike" is driven at a ceremony at Promontory, Utah
Southern Pacific Bulletin
AUGUST, 1920
4
THE BIG FOUR

ANALYSIS SKILL Analyze Time Lines

How many years did it take the Central Pacific Railroad to lay track?

Building the Railroad

Building a transcontinental railroad would cost millions of dollars. Judah began to look for people willing to invest in the railroad. To **invest** is to buy something, such as a share or part of a company, in the hope that it will be worth more in the future. Judah found four men who wanted to invest—**Leland Stanford**, **Collis P. Huntington**, **Mark Hopkins**, and **Charles Crocker**. They became known as the Big Four.

In 1861, Judah and the Big Four formed the Central Pacific Railroad Company. That year, a civil war broke out in the United States. A civil war is a war between groups of people in the same country. Despite the war, Judah went to Washington, D.C., to discuss the railroad with members of Congress.

In 1862, Congress passed the Pacific Railroad Act. The United States would provide money and land for the Central Pacific Railroad Company to build a railroad east from Sacramento. Another railroad company, the Union Pacific, would lay tracks west from Council Bluffs, Iowa. The two railroad lines would meet in between.

The first tracks were laid in 1863. Right away, the railroads faced a serious problem. Because many people were fighting in the Civil War, there were few workers to build the railroad. However, when the Civil War ended in 1865, many former soldiers went to work for the Union Pacific. The Union Pacific also hired many immigrant workers from Ireland. At the same time, the Central Pacific hired many Chinese workers.

The Chinese workers proved to be so good that the Central Pacific began to bring over workers from China. In one year alone, more than 12,000 Chinese immigrants worked on the tracks. By the end of the project, about three-fourths of the Central Pacific workers were Chinese. For all of the hard work that they did, the Chinese workers made very little money. Their pay was between $25 and $35 per month. Irish workers also made little money, but the Chinese were paid less than the Irish and other workers.

READING CHECK **CAUSE AND EFFECT**
How did the Civil War affect the building of the transcontinental railroad?

ANALYSIS SKILL **Analyze Maps**
The Central Pacific Railroad laid 690 miles of track. The Union Pacific Railroad laid 1,086 miles of track.

Human-Environment Interactions **Why do you think the Union Pacific Railroad laid more total miles of track than the Central Pacific Railroad?**

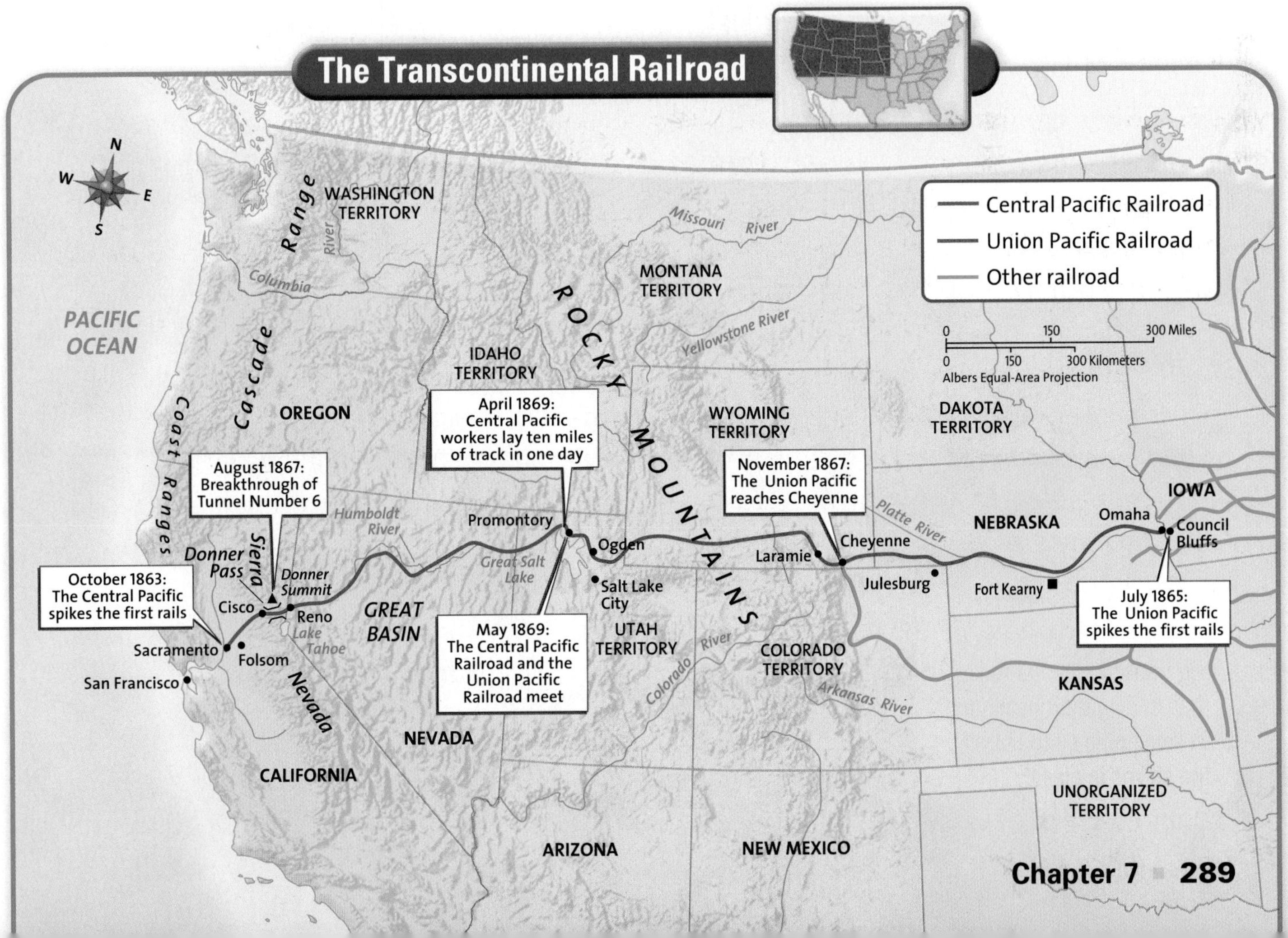

A Closer LOOK

Building the Railroad

Workers on the Central Pacific Railroad cut 15 tunnels through the solid rock of the Sierra Nevada.

1. **At times, workers were lowered down the sides of mountains to set the explosives.**
2. **Workers removed all the broken rock from the work area.**
3. **It took a crew of workers to lay the rails. Each crew member performed a different task in the process. The tampers packed down the gravel and rocks that were used to hold the ties in place. The ironmen laid the rails on the ties.**

? Why do you think workers were organized into crews?

FAST FACT

One newspaper reporter estimated that workers on the transcontinental railroad swung their hammers 21 million times to put all the spikes in place.

Completing the Railroad

TIME May 10, 1869
PLACE Promontory, Utah

Work on the railroad was difficult. The Chinese workers did some of the most dangerous jobs. Sometimes they had to set off explosives. Many workers were injured or even killed.

In some parts of the Sierra Nevada, workers moved forward only a few inches a day. To speed up work, the United States government agreed to give each company thousands of acres of land and to lend money to each railroad company based on the amount of track that the company laid.

The two companies began to work as though they were in a contest. First, workers for the Union Pacific laid 6 miles of track in a day. Then, workers for the Central Pacific laid 7 miles of track in a day. In this contest, a team of Chinese and Irish workers for the Central Pacific laid 10 miles of track in 12 hours!

Within six years, the railroad was completed. On May 10, 1869, the two lines of track met at Promontory, Utah. The final spike linking the two lines was made of solid gold. It was also engraved with a message:

> **"May God continue the unity of our Country as this Railroad unites the two great Oceans of the world."***

When the transcontinental railroad was finished, traveling from coast to coast took about one week. For $100, wealthy passengers could ride in comfort in fancy train cars. For $40–or about $536 in today's money–others rode on hard benches.

*Central Pacific Railroad Photographic History Museum. http://cprr.org

The Transcontinental Railroad

ANALYSIS SKILL Analyze Drawings

This cartoon celebrates the completion of the first transcontinental railroad.

1 People cheering

2 A train from New York and a train from San Francisco

What does it mean that the trains are greeting each other with a handshake?

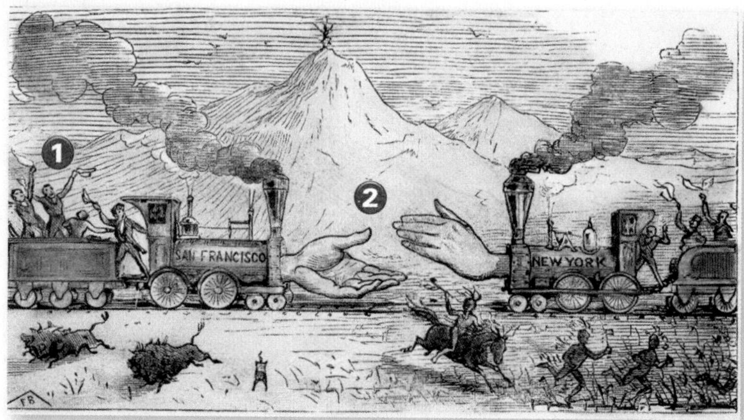

The railroad also made it easier to move goods between California and the rest of the country. As a result, those goods cost less than ever before.

READING CHECK DRAW CONCLUSIONS
What do you think the message on the final spike means?

Summary

Congress decided that a transcontinental railroad was needed. Many Chinese and Irish immigrants worked to complete the railroad. In 1869, the Central Pacific and Union Pacific met.

REVIEW

1. Why was a transcontinental railroad needed, and how was it built?
2. Use the term **invest** to write a sentence about the Big Four.
3. How did immigrant workers contribute to the construction of the transcontinental railroad?

CRITICAL THINKING

4. ANALYSIS SKILL Do you think it would have been possible to build the transcontinental railroad without the help of immigrant workers? Why or why not?
5. How do you think Theodore Judah was able to convince others to invest?
6. **Write a Speech** Write a speech about the importance of the transcontinental railroad and about the contributions of the workers who built it.
7. Focus Skill **DRAW CONCLUSIONS** On a separate sheet of paper, copy and complete the graphic organizer below.

Evidence	Knowledge
The Big Four invested money in the railroad.	

Conclusion

Trustworthiness
Respect
Responsibility
Fairness
Caring
Patriotism

Yee Fung Cheung

*"It was only a dose of his smile they needed."**

In 1850, Yee Fung Cheung (YEE FUHNG JEH•uhng) came to California from China. He was a skilled herbalist (ER•buh•list), or a person who uses herbs to treat illnesses. He came to California during the gold rush, hoping to strike it rich. Instead, in 1851, he gave up gold mining and opened an herb shop.

Inside Yee Fung Cheung's herb shop in Fiddletown

Yee Fung Cheung's shop was in Fiddletown, in the heart of the Sierra Nevada gold country. As his business grew, he opened shops in Sacramento and in Virginia City, Nevada.

His best-known customer was Jane Stanford, the wife of Leland Stanford, who had become governor of California. In 1862, she was suffering from a lung illness that her own doctors were unable to cure. Yee Fung Cheung made an herbal remedy that helped save her life.

*From the article "Chinese Transformed Gold Mountain" by Stephen Magagnini. *The Sacramento Bee*, January 18, 1998.

Why Character Counts

How do you know that Yee Fung Cheung was a trusted herbalist?

Bio Brief

1825? Born

1850 Arrives in California from China

1851 Opens an herb shop in Fiddletown

1904 Retires from his practice and returns to China

1907 Died

GO ONLINE **Interactive Multimedia Biographies** Visit MULTIMEDIA BIOGRAPHIES at www.harcourtschool.com/hss

Lesson 3

Time

1855 · 1885 · 1915

- **1862** The Pacific Railroad Act is passed
- **1869** The transcontinental railroad is completed
- **1876** The Southern Pacific Railroad reaches Los Angeles

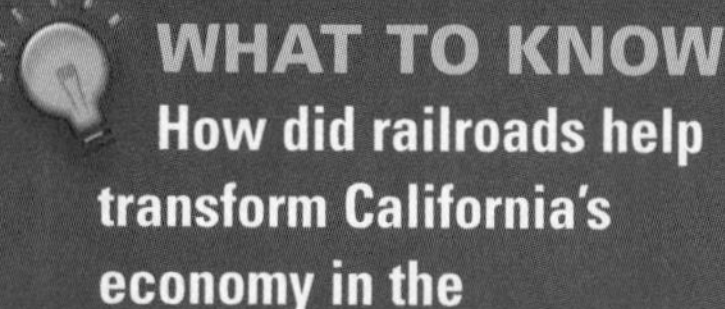

WHAT TO KNOW
How did railroads help transform California's economy in the late 1800s?

- ✓ Describe how railroads in California affected cities and businesses.
- ✓ Identify the lasting influence of the transcontinental railroad on life in California.

VOCABULARY
competition p. 296

PLACES
Stockton
Los Angeles

DRAW CONCLUSIONS

California Standards
HSS 4.4, 4.4.1, 4.4.4

Rails Across California

YOU ARE THERE

It's 1870, and you live in New York City. Your uncle owns a business in San Francisco. Last year, a new railroad connected California to the East Coast, and now you hope to travel by rail to visit your uncle. But a one-way ticket to San Francisco costs about $100. That's more than your family earns in a month! Still, this is the quickest route to California.

➤ This train stopped in Nevada on its way to Sacramento.

This detail from a painting by William Hahn shows the train station in Sacramento in 1874.

Effects of the Railroad

When the transcontinental railroad was completed, Californians were thrilled. People in Sacramento hoped that the railroad would help the city grow. In San Francisco, business owners were eager to send goods from Asia by rail to the East coast.

The railroad did lead to growth. However, it also caused problems for some businesses. It brought new products into the state that sometimes cost less than goods made and sold in California. Many businesses in the state suffered and closed.

In addition, the state faced hard economic times during the early 1870s. As a result, Sacramento did not grow as much as people had expected. In 1869, the opening of the Suez Canal, halfway around the world in Egypt, provided a new way to ship Asian goods to the East Coast. Business owners in San Francisco did not make the money they thought they would by sending Asian goods east. The economy of other California cities suffered, too.

READING CHECK **DRAW CONCLUSIONS**
Why might people have thought that the railroad would help Sacramento grow?

More Railroads

Before the transcontinental railroad was finished, the Big Four had begun building other railroads in California. One of these was the Southern Pacific Railroad. Part of this railroad ran through the Central Valley from **Stockton** to **Los Angeles.** Towns along the railroad's route—such as Bakersfield, Modesto, Fresno, and Merced—grew quickly.

In return for building tracks, the Southern Pacific Railroad had gained more than 11 million acres of land. This was a result of the Pacific Railroad Act of 1862. The act granted large areas of land surrounding railroad tracks to the railroad company that laid the tracks.

The Big Four gained more and more land with every new railroad track that they laid in California. As they grew wealthier, they bought or started other railroads, including the Western Pacific and the California Southern. The railroads owned by the Big Four stretched in so many directions that they were nicknamed "the Octopus."

For almost 20 years, the Big Four's railroads had little competition in California. In business, **competition** is a contest among companies to get the most customers or to sell the most products. Because the railroads owned

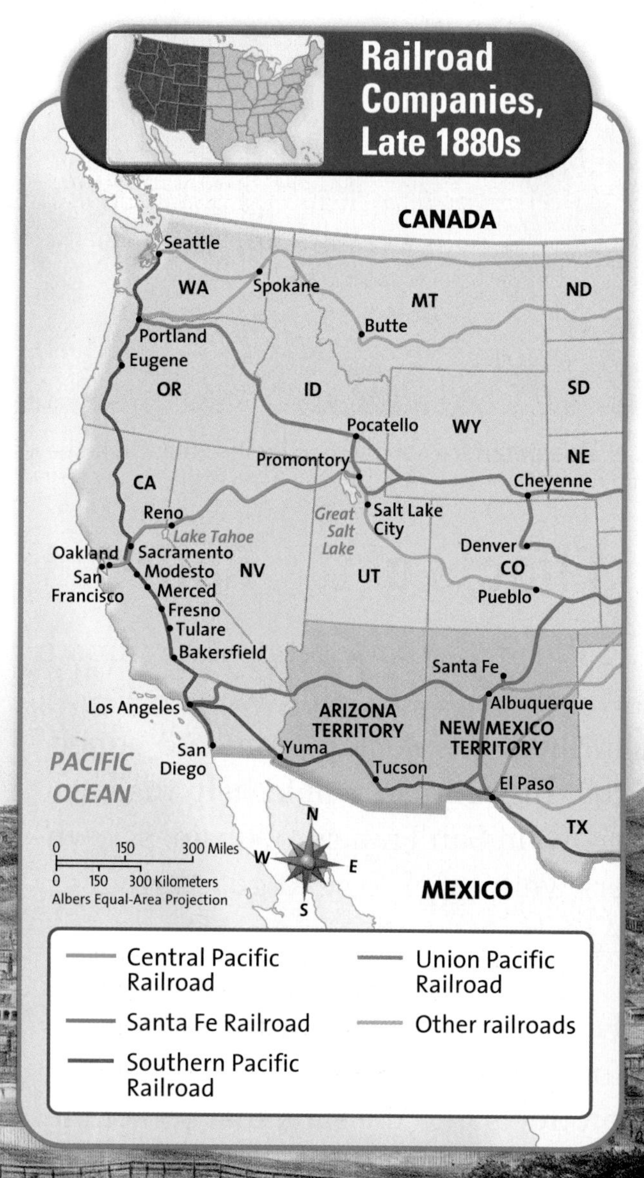

ANALYSIS SKILL Analyze Maps

Movement According to the map, which railroad line linked San Francisco (below) to Sacramento?

by the Big Four had little competition, they could charge high prices for train tickets. At one time, a round-trip ticket from the East to California cost more than $200. This is equal to about $3,578 in today's money.

READING CHECK **DRAW CONCLUSIONS**
Why were the Big Four's railroads nicknamed "the Octopus"?

Summary

Railroads across the United States allowed California businesses to ship products to the East Coast. However, the railroads also brought less-expensive goods into the state. This hurt some California businesses. Railroad owners also faced little competition and charged high prices.

An 1882 cartoon shows the railroad companies as a monster octopus.

REVIEW

1. How did railroads help transform California's economy in the late 1800s?
2. Use the term **competition** to describe railroads in California in the late 1800s.
3. Why did new goods brought by rail into California hurt some California businesses?

CRITICAL THINKING

4. What might have happened to the price of train tickets if there had been more competition between railroad companies in California in the late 1800s?
5. ANALYSIS SKILL **Make It Relevant** Would being located near a railroad line be important for a city today? Why or why not?
6. **Draw a Cartoon** Look at the editorial cartoon on this page. Notice how the artist used pictures to represent ideas. Choose another important idea from the lesson, and draw your own editorial cartoon.
7. Focus Skill **DRAW CONCLUSIONS**
On a separate sheet of paper, copy and complete the graphic organizer below.

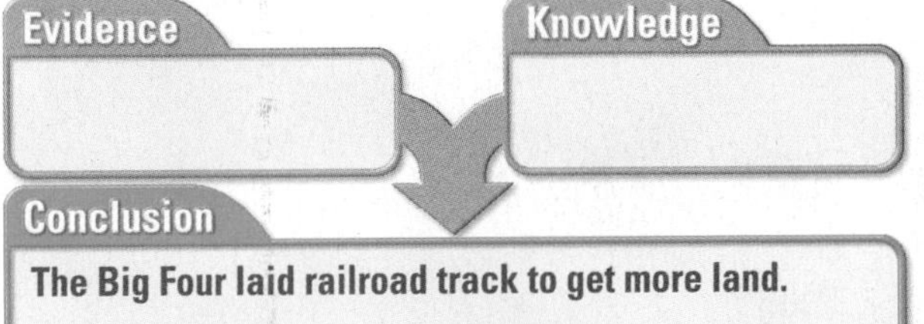

Map and Globe Skills

Read a Time Zone Map

WHY IT MATTERS

The transcontinental railroad, and similar railroads all over the world, changed how people thought about time. Towns that trains passed through had many different local times. As a result, train operators had trouble setting clear schedules.

People from all over the world realized that they needed a standard time system that everyone could use. They decided to divide the Earth into 24 time zones, one for each hour of the day. A **time zone** is a region in which all people use the same time. To figure out the time anywhere in the world, you can use a time zone map like the one on page 299.

WHAT YOU NEED TO KNOW

The United States has six standard time zones. To read a time zone map, first find the clock that goes with each time zone. All places in a standard time zone use the same time. On the map on page 299, the clock for the Pacific time zone reads 7 A.M. The clock for the mountain time zone, east of the Pacific time zone, reads 8 A.M.—one hour later. To the west, the clock for the Alaska time zone reads 6 A.M.—one hour earlier. To find the time to the east of the Pacific time zone, add the correct number of hours to the Pacific time. To find the time to the west, subtract the correct number of hours.

Did you know that when you start school each morning, it is nighttime in other parts of the world?

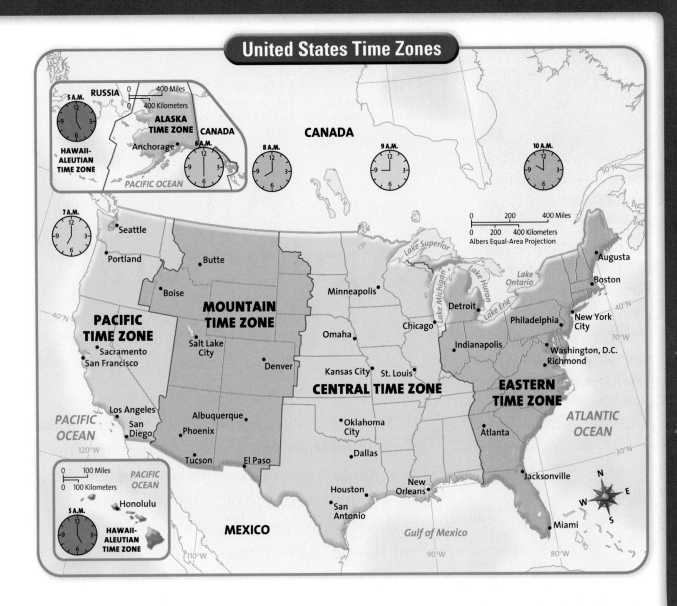

United States Time Zones

PRACTICE THE SKILL

Use the information on the time zone map to answer these questions.

1. Is the time in Sacramento earlier than, later than, or the same as the time in Salt Lake City?
2. If it is 4:00 P.M. in Omaha, what time is it in El Paso? What time is it in Detroit?
3. How many hours is the eastern time zone ahead of the Pacific time zone?

APPLY WHAT YOU LEARNED

ANALYSIS SKILL **Make It Relevant** What time is it in your time zone? Now figure out the time for each of these cities.

Denver, Colorado
New York City, New York
Honolulu, Hawaii
Portland, Oregon
Kansas City, Missouri
Anchorage, Alaska

Practice your map and globe skills with the **GeoSkills CD-ROM.**

Lesson 4

1870 California produces 20 million bushels of wheat

1873 The first navel orange trees are planted in California

1880 Fighting at Mussel Slough takes place

WHAT TO KNOW
How was California able to become an agricultural power?

- Identify the reasons for disagreements between farmers and the railroads.
- Compare farming in California before and after the development of irrigation systems.

VOCABULARY
commercial farm p. 301
export p. 301
tenant farmer p. 302
canal p. 305
levee p. 305

PEOPLE
Eliza and Luther Calvin Tibbets
Luther Burbank
George Shima

PLACES
Mussel Slough
Riverside

DRAW CONCLUSIONS

California Standards
HSS 4.4, 4.4.2, 4.4.3, 4.4.6, 4.4.7

An Agricultural Power

YOU ARE THERE You're making your way slowly through the 1878 International Exhibition in Paris. There, you see goods from all over the world. Soon the judges will announce the gold medal winner for wheat. What country will the winner be from? France? Russia? At last, the gold medal is awarded to a farmer from California! John Bidwell, a Central Valley farmer, has grown the finest wheat in the world.

John Bidwell

Wheat for the World

By 1878, John Bidwell had been farming in the Central Valley for almost 40 years. He had come to California in 1841 with the first wagon train that crossed the Sierra Nevada.

Bidwell saw the Central Valley as an ideal farming area, but others did not. He later said, "People generally look on it as the garden of the world or the most desolate [empty] place on creation [Earth]."*

Bidwell was one of the few people who were farming in the Central Valley in the early days of the California gold rush. Suddenly, there was a greater demand for farm products than California's farmers could supply. People began to pay very high prices for food, and some of the farmers became wealthy.

To meet the demand for food, new farms were started in the Central Valley during the 1850s. People began to grow crops in other valleys, too. Instead of growing crops mainly to feed themselves, many farmers grew crops only to sell. Their farms were the state's first **commercial farms**.

California's fertile valleys and long growing season were perfect for wheat. By 1873, California had become the number one wheat-producing state in the country. Because of the railroads, California was able to supply wheat to eastern cities. It was also exporting wheat to France, Italy, and other faraway places. To **export** goods is to sell them to people in another country.

READING CHECK **DRAW CONCLUSIONS**
How did the gold rush affect agriculture in California?

*John Bidwell. From *Addresses, Reminiscences, etc., of General John Bidwell*, compiled by C. C. Royce. 1907.

Analyze Graphs **By 1890, California grew more wheat than any other state except Minnesota.**

During which decade did the production of wheat in California grow the most?

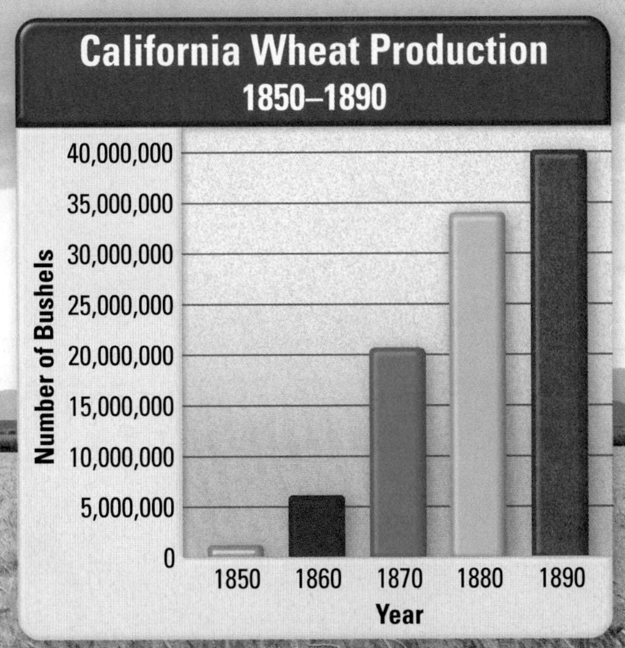

Conflicts with the Railroads

At this time, the railroad companies owned about one-eighth of the land in California. Many farmers did not want the railroads to control this much land. They also felt that the railroads charged too much to transport crops.

Disagreements between farmers and the railroad companies led to conflicts. One conflict happened at **Mussel Slough** (MUH•suhl SLOO), a part of the San Joaquin Valley. The Southern Pacific Railroad Company offered land to settlers for as little as $2.50 an acre. The company invited settlers to begin farming before the sales were final.

Thinking that they owned the land, the farmers built irrigation systems, plowed the land, and planted crops. Then the railroad company decided to raise the price of land. It set prices at $17 to $40 an acre.

Most farmers refused to pay the higher prices. Some also refused to leave the land. On May 11, 1880, fighting broke out when people from the railroad tried to force the farmers to leave. Seven people died, and the railroad took over the land.

Farmers in other parts of the state also faced hard times. They could not afford to pay the high prices the railroads charged to ship goods. Many had to sell their land. Some then stayed and paid rent on the land with money earned from the sale of their crops. These people were known as **tenant farmers**.

READING CHECK **DRAW CONCLUSIONS**
Why do you think the railroad company changed the price of land?

Disagreements between farmers and the railroad companies led to bloodshed at Mussel Slough.

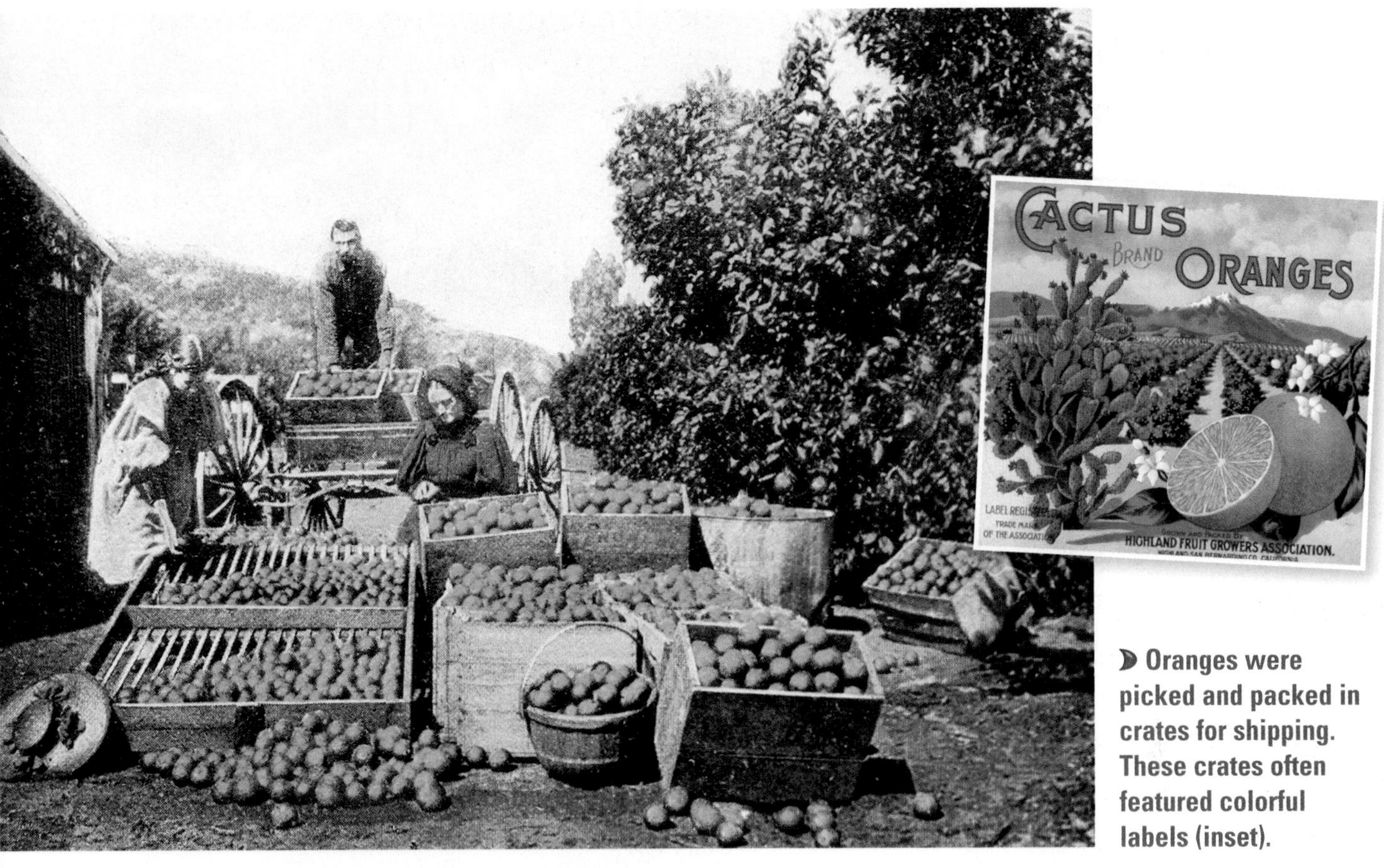

Oranges were picked and packed in crates for shipping. These crates often featured colorful labels (inset).

Citrus Is King

Oranges had been grown near the coast since the time of the missions, but those oranges were sour and full of seeds. In 1870, a group of orange farmers moved to what would soon be called **Riverside**. They discovered that the hilly land and the warm climate in that area produced better fruit than coastal areas.

In 1873, two members of the group, **Eliza and Luther Calvin Tibbets**, received a pair of orange trees that had come from Brazil. They planted the trees and discovered that the fruit was very juicy and did not have seeds. The oranges, which came to be called Washington navels, ripened in the winter. The group in Riverside also began growing a sweet type of orange from Spain called the Valencia. Valencia oranges ripened in the summer. Riverside farmers could now produce oranges year-round.

Eliza Tibbets

Orange groves soon stretched across southern California. Lemons, grapefruit, and other citrus fruits were planted there, too. By the 1890s, California had become the nation's main producer of citrus fruits.

READING CHECK **SUMMARIZE**
How did the citrus industry in California develop?

New Methods, New Markets

In the late 1800s, Californians looked for ways to create new markets for their crops and to improve farming methods. A walnut farmer named Harriet Russell Strong developed new ways to store water to irrigate dry areas. By mixing seeds from different plants, scientist **Luther Burbank** worked to create new and better kinds of plants for farmers to grow.

New ways of shipping food also helped California's farmers. Railroads started to use ice to refrigerate, or chill, some cars. These refrigerated cars could move crops to markets in the East. In the past, most fruits and vegetables spoiled on the long journey.

Even with these improvements, the costs of shipping and selling California's crops were high. Still, growers believed that they could make more money if more people in the East would buy California's crops.

To increase the demand, California growers spread the word about the importance of eating foods such as oranges. Special fruit trains were decorated with banners that said "Oranges for Health—California for Wealth."*

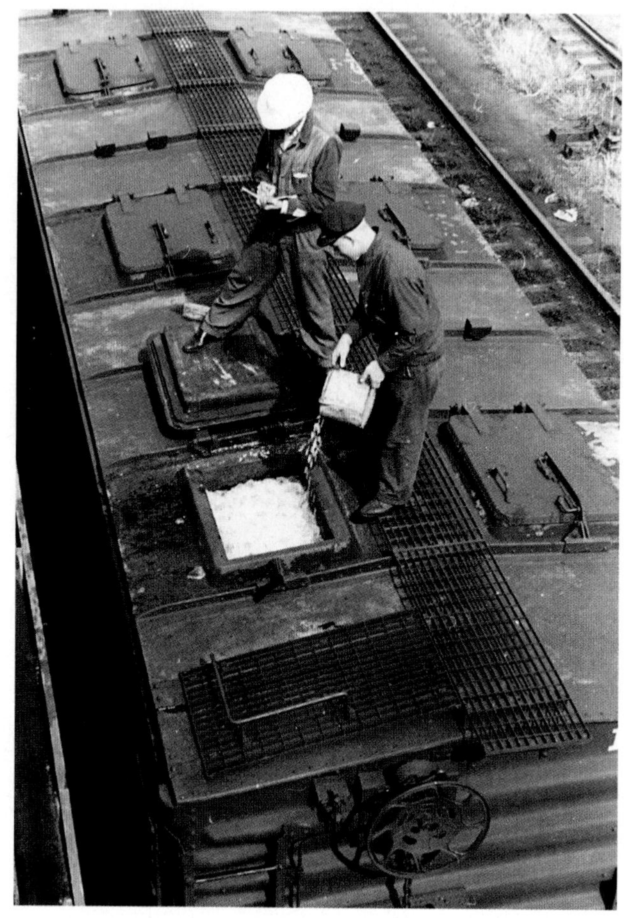

In refrigerated railroad cars, ice was poured into tanks through roof hatches.

READING CHECK **COMPARE AND CONTRAST**
How did California's agricultural industry change after the invention of the refrigerated railroad car?

*California Historical Society. californiahistory.net

The Imperial Valley in 1913 (below) and today (inset)

Water Everywhere

California's geography provides rich soil and plenty of sunshine. However, it does not always provide enough rain in the growing season. The first farms in California usually included land beside creeks or rivers.

For a long time, California's laws said that only farmers who owned land on a river had the right to use the river's water for irrigation. Then, in 1887, the Wright Act was passed. This new law allowed a group of farmers in an area to form an irrigation district. Farmers in the district had the right to take water from rivers and build canals to move it to their farms. A **canal** is a waterway dug across land. Great networks of canals were built. This opened up thousands of acres of farmland.

Some places, though, suffered from having too much water. Areas near the Sacramento River, for example, often flooded. Starting in the 1850s, landowners there built levees (LEH•veez) to protect farmland from flooding. A **levee** is a high wall made of earth.

GEOGRAPHY

The Imperial Valley

The Imperial Valley is located in the hot, dry Colorado Desert. In the late 1800s, the Colorado Desert seemed like a very unlikely place to grow crops. In 1900, however, George Chaffey led the work of building a canal from the Colorado River to turn desert land into farmland. Chaffey renamed the newly irrigated area the Imperial Valley to attract settlers.

Farmers began growing tomatoes, grapes, lettuce, and melons there. Today, many crops are farmed in the Imperial Valley. The area is sometimes called the Winter Garden of the World because farmers there can grow crops year-round.

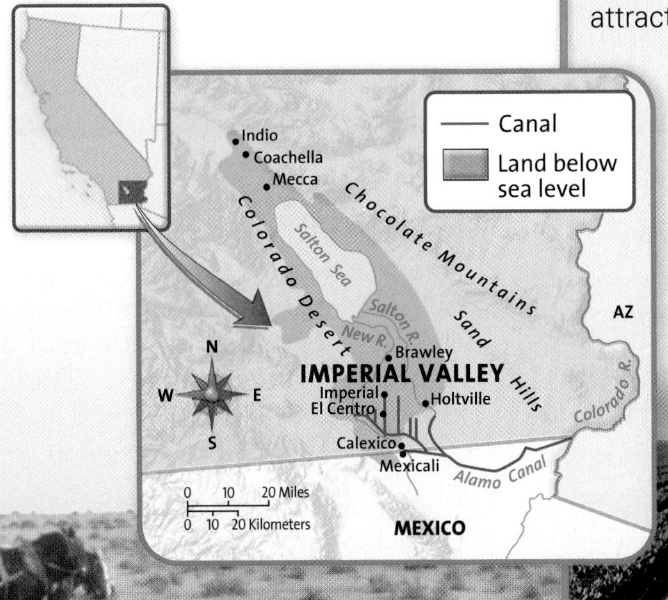

Many Chinese workers who had worked on the transcontinental railroad also helped build levees. A Japanese farmer named **George Shima** continued this work. Shima and his workers reclaimed, or took back, many acres of flooded land in the San Joaquin River delta. He used this land to grow potatoes and became a very successful farmer.

READING CHECK **DRAW CONCLUSIONS**
Why are levees important to California farmers?

Summary

In fewer than 50 years, California changed from an area with few farms into an agricultural leader. Conflicts over the use of water and land were overcome. As a result, agriculture and the economy of the state grew.

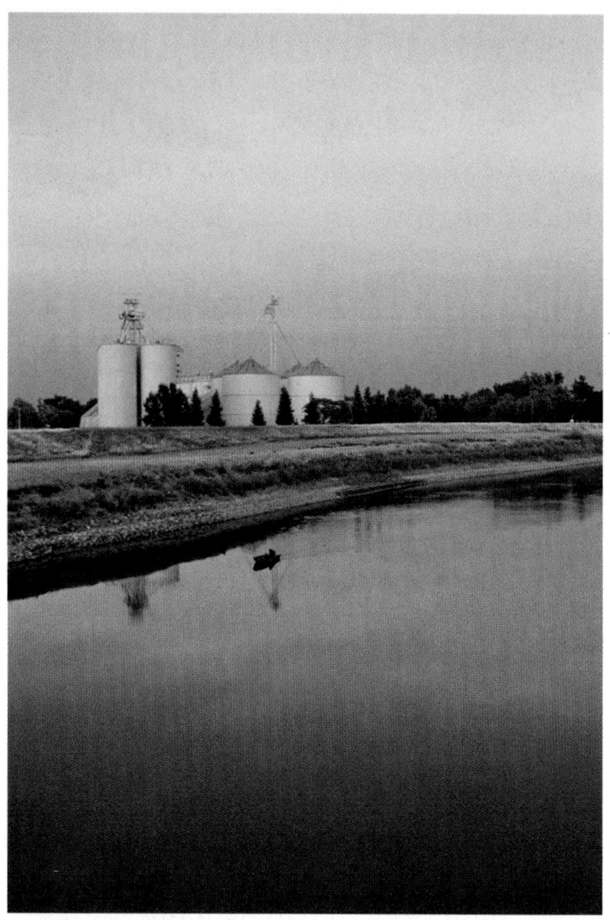

Levees are still built today to hold back floodwaters along the Sacramento River.

REVIEW

1. How was California able to become an agricultural power?
2. Tell how **levees** and **canals** helped make more land in California available for farming.
3. What was one reason orange trees in Riverside produced better fruit than trees in coastal areas?

CRITICAL THINKING

4. ANALYSIS SKILL What were some of the causes of the problems at Mussel Slough?
5. Do you think it was a good idea to ship crops east, given the high costs? Explain.
6. **Make an Advertisement** Imagine that you are a farmer who is selling wheat or oranges. Create a billboard or newspaper advertisement to persuade people to buy your crops. Share your advertisement with your classmates.
7. Focus Skill **DRAW CONCLUSIONS** On a separate sheet of paper, copy and complete the graphic organizer below.

Evidence
Knowledge
People use advertisements to sell products.
Conclusion

George Shima

Biography

Trustworthiness
Respect
Responsibility
Fairness
Caring
Patriotism

*"To shed the light of truth"**

George Shima was born in Japan in 1865. He moved to the United States in 1888, not knowing that he would one day be known as the "potato king" of California.

Shima first grew potatoes on land that he rented in San Joaquin County. The first years were not good because of bad weather, but Shima worked hard. He hired hundreds of Japanese American immigrants to work for him. When he retired in 1917, he controlled 25,000 acres of land and grew most of the potatoes in California.

George Shima never became a citizen of the United States. However, he was a respected member of his community and was considered to be a trustworthy businessperson. People there said that even though Shima never made an agreement in writing, he always kept his word. In 1926, the emperor of Japan made him a member of the Order of the Rising Sun. On that same day, Shima died at age 61.

*From the mission and goals of the Order of the Rising Sun.

Why Character Counts

How did George Shima show that he was trustworthy?

George Shima plowing his lands near Stockton

Bio Brief

1865 Born

1926 Died

1888 Leaves Japan

1891 Plants his first potato crop

1900 Brings his Japanese bride to the United States

1908 Is elected president of the Japanese Association of America

GO ONLINE **Interactive Multimedia Biographies**
Visit MULTIMEDIA BIOGRAPHIES at www.harcourtschool.com/hss

Time

1855

1865

1860
Pony Express service begins

Reading Social Studies

A **conclusion** is a decision or an idea reached by using what you read and what you already know about a subject.

Focus Skill Draw Conclusions

Complete this graphic organizer to show your understanding of the importance of the growing links between California and the rest of the United States in the late 1800s. A copy of this graphic organizer appears on page 82 of the Homework and Practice Book.

Transportation and Communication

Evidence

A telegraph line linking California to the East Coast was finished in 1861.

Knowledge

Improved communication makes it easier to exchange ideas.

Conclusion

California Writing Prompts

Write a Summary Imagine your job is to hire new riders for the Pony Express. Write an ad that summarizes the tasks involved as well as the skills and personal qualities a successful rider needs.

Write a Report Imagine that you are a news reporter covering the conflict at Mussel Slough between farmers and the railroad. Write an article about what happened, explaining the reasons behind the conflict.

1875 1885 1895

1869
The transcontinental railroad is completed

1880
Fighting at Mussel Slough takes place

Use Vocabulary

Identify the term that correctly matches each definition.

telegraph, p. 282
competition, p. 296
export, p. 301
canal, p. 305

1. a contest
2. a device that uses electricity to send messages over wires
3. a waterway dug across land
4. to send goods to another country in order to sell them to people there

Use the Time Line

ANALYSIS SKILL **Use the summary time line above to answer the question.**

5. How many years after the transcontinental railroad was completed did fighting at Mussel Slough take place?

Apply Skills

Read a Time Zone Map Use the time zone map on page 299 to answer these questions.

6. In which time zone is San Francisco?
7. If it is noon in Philadelphia, Pennsylvania, what time is it in Seattle, Washington?
8. Is Central time one hour earlier or one hour later than Mountain time?

Recall Facts

Answer these questions.

9. How did the Western Union Telegraph Company affect Pony Express service?
10. What role did Theodore Judah play in the building of the transcontinental railroad?
11. Who were the Big Four? How did they contribute to the growth of California?

Write the letter of the best choice.

12. Who was John Bidwell?
    A a successful farmer
    B a famous engineer
    C an Irish railroad worker
    D a Pony Express rider
13. What new crop did people start growing in Riverside, California, in 1873?
    A wheat
    B barley
    C navel oranges
    D asparagus

Think Critically

14. ANALYSIS SKILL What effects did the transcontinental railroad have on California's economy?
15. ANALYSIS SKILL How have transportation and communication in California changed since the late 1800s? In what ways are they still the same?

Study Skills

USE AN ANTICIPATION GUIDE

An anticipation guide can help you anticipate, or predict, what you will learn as you read.

- **Look at the lesson titles and section titles for clues.**
- **Preview the Reading Check questions. Use what you know about the subject of each section to predict the answers.**
- **Read to find out whether your predictions were correct.**

Building New Lives		
Reading Check	Prediction	Correct?
Why do you think many immigrants formed their own communities?	Immigrants in California wanted to live near people from their home countries.	✓
Contributions of Newcomers		
Reading Check	Prediction	Correct?

Apply As You Read

Use the Reading Check questions to make an anticipation guide for each lesson. Then predict an answer to each question. After reading, check to see if your predictions were correct.

California History-Social Science Standards, Grade 4

4.4 Students explain how California became an agricultural and industrial power, tracing the transformation of the California economy and its political and cultural development since the 1850s.

CHAPTER

A Growing Economy

Citrus growing became a major industry in California in the early 1900s.

Start with a Story

Fire in the Valley

by Tracey West

illustrated by Craig Spearing

Providing enough water for its growing population was a challenge and a source of conflict for California in the early 1900s. In this story, eleven-year-old Sarah Jefferson and her family are excited. They have heard about plans to bring more water to their town in the Owens Valley. Read now to learn how their happiness suddenly turns to disappointment.

Sarah had heard talk of the Reclamation Service project for the last year. She knew it was a special plan the federal government had to irrigate all of Owens Valley. There was plenty of water in the Owens River, but not all the valley residents had the money or the means to bring the water to their farms. The Reclamation Service project would make sure the farmers who worked the valley had all the water they needed.

"Do you really think it will happen soon?" Sarah asked excitedly. If the railroad came, Independence would become almost as exciting as Los Angeles. All kinds of people would come to the valley to live and open shops and other businesses.

"Things look pretty good," Uncle Will said. He nodded in the direction of the Richardson cattle ranch. "I heard Joe Richardson sold some of his land to Fred Eaton last week. Everyone knows that Eaton represents the Reclamation Service project. If he's got Richardson's land, something must be brewing."

Sarah felt like singing. "That would be wonderful, wouldn't it, Ma?"

Her mother allowed herself a small smile. "Yes, it would. We've all worked hard." . . .

The town was usually quiet, but Sarah saw today that a crowd had gathered in front of the post office. A scowling farmer galloped past the wagon. As the wagon drew closer, Sarah heard an angry buzz rising from the crowd.

irrigate to water land, usually crops

scowling making an angry face

"What's going on here?" Uncle Will asked, getting down off Rusty.

James Aguilar, a farmer from outside of town, was holding up a newspaper. "This just came in from Los Angeles."

Sarah started to jump out of the wagon, but her mother held her back. It was easy enough to read the paper's headline, which was written in large letters: "TITANIC PROJECT TO GIVE CITY A RIVER." The paper was dated July 29, 1905, just a few days before.

"What does this mean?" Uncle Will asked, grabbing the paper.

"The Los Angeles water company is planning to build an aqueduct from here to the city," James said. "They are stealing our water!"

titanic huge

aqueduct large pipe or canal that carries water

Response Corner

1. Why would a water project in the Owens Valley bring the railroad to the area?
2. Why do you think the people of Independence were upset about the aqueduct to Los Angeles?

Lesson 1

Time

1855 | 1885 | 1915

1873
The last battle in California between Indians and the United States Army takes place

1882
Congress passes a law to stop most new Chinese immigration

1900
California celebrates its fiftieth year as a state

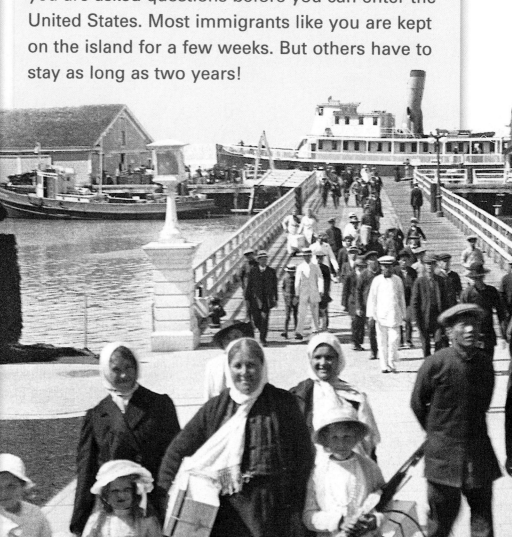

WHAT TO KNOW
How did immigration and migration affect California?

- ✓ Describe the makeup of migrants and immigrants to California in the late 1800s and early 1900s.
- ✓ Examine conflicts and accords, or agreements, among different groups in California.

VOCABULARY
immigration p. 315
migration p. 315
prejudice p. 318
reservation p. 319

PEOPLE
Kyutaro Abiko
Colonel Allen Allensworth
Chief Kientepoos

PLACES
Angel Island
Yamato Colony
Solvang
Allensworth

DRAW CONCLUSIONS

California Standards
HSS 4.4, 4.4.3, 4.4.4

Immigration and Migration

YOU ARE THERE

After a long journey across the Pacific Ocean, you step onto **Angel Island**. Here, you are asked questions before you can enter the United States. Most immigrants like you are kept on the island for a few weeks. But others have to stay as long as two years!

Building New Lives

In the late 1800s and early 1900s, **immigration** to the United States increased greatly. Millions of people arrived at ports on both the Atlantic and Pacific coasts. Some of these immigrants were escaping unfair treatment. Others wanted freedom to practice their own religions. Still others wanted the chance to own land.

A large number of immigrants arrived in California. Most came from countries in Europe, Asia, Central America, and South America. Many of the immigrants wanted to live among people from their home countries. In 1904, **Kyutaro Abiko** (KYOO•tah•roh AH•bee•koh) started the **Yamato** (yah•MAH•toh) **Colony**, a Japanese farming community in the Central Valley. In 1910, immigrants from Denmark built a community called **Solvang** in the Santa Ynez Valley.

Immigrants were not the only newcomers to California. There was also a **migration**, or movement, of people within the United States to California. Farmers from the Middle West hoped to find a better life in California and to enjoy its mild climate. Many African Americans, freed from slavery after the Civil War, hoped to make better lives there, too.

READING CHECK **DRAW CONCLUSIONS**
Why do you think many immigrants formed their own communities?

For these immigrants arriving at Angel Island in 1910, California was a land of hope and opportunity.

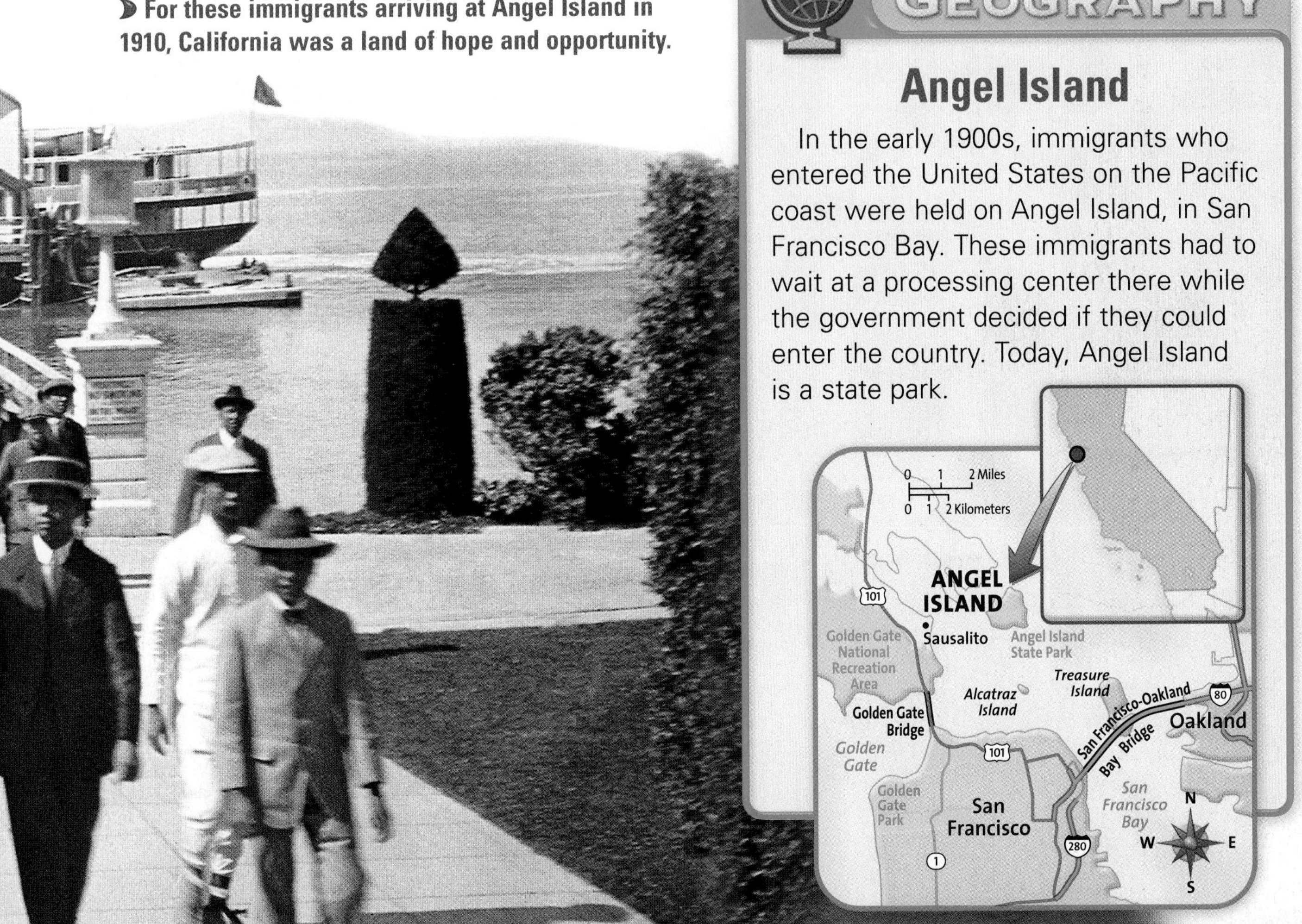

GEOGRAPHY

Angel Island

In the early 1900s, immigrants who entered the United States on the Pacific coast were held on Angel Island, in San Francisco Bay. These immigrants had to wait at a processing center there while the government decided if they could enter the country. Today, Angel Island is a state park.

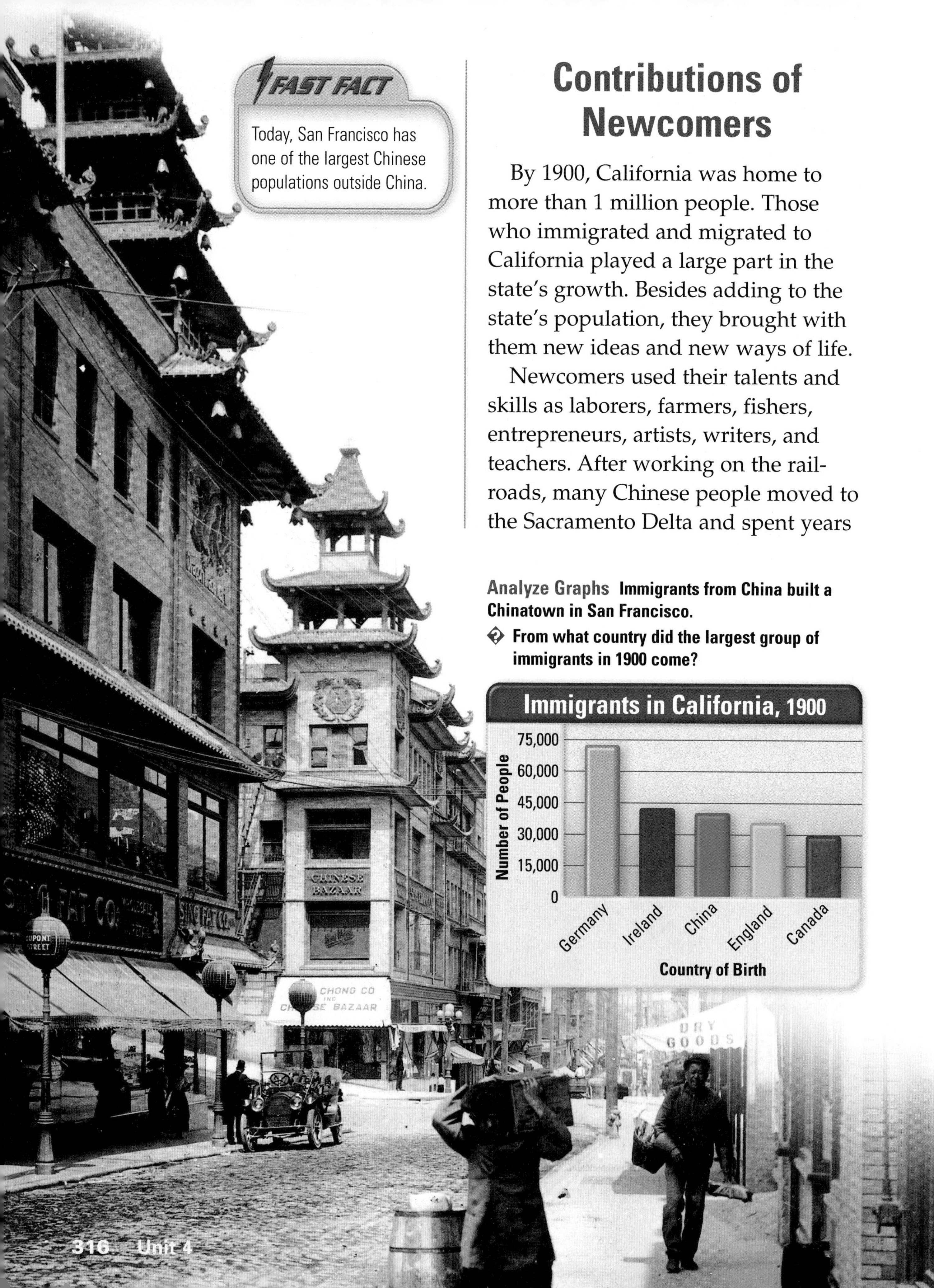

FAST FACT

Today, San Francisco has one of the largest Chinese populations outside China.

Contributions of Newcomers

By 1900, California was home to more than 1 million people. Those who immigrated and migrated to California played a large part in the state's growth. Besides adding to the state's population, they brought with them new ideas and new ways of life.

Newcomers used their talents and skills as laborers, farmers, fishers, entrepreneurs, artists, writers, and teachers. After working on the rail-roads, many Chinese people moved to the Sacramento Delta and spent years

Analyze Graphs **Immigrants from China built a Chinatown in San Francisco.**

From what country did the largest group of immigrants in 1900 come?

building the levees there that turned marshland into farmland.

Many immigrants from Japan became successful farmers in California. They grew fruits such as grapes and strawberries. Some brought rice seeds from Japan and showed that rice could be grown successfully in California.

Many people from Armenia, in western Asia, settled in the Central Valley. The geography and climate of this area reminded them of their home country. Armenian farmers grew crops from their homeland, such as figs, grapes, melons, and pistachio nuts.

Immigrants from Europe also helped make California's agricultural industry grow. At first, many Italian immigrants came to look for gold. In time, Italian miners became farmers. They, too, grew crops from their home country, such as grapes and olives.

In 1857, German immigrants built a settlement in the Santa Ana Valley. They named their community Anaheim—*Ana* after the valley and *heim*, the German word for "home." At Anaheim, they started one of the first large vineyards in California. French and Italian immigrants planted more vineyards in the Napa, Sonoma, San Joaquin, and Sacramento Valleys.

Many artists also came to California from Europe. Charles Christian Nahl of Germany became famous for his paintings of life in California's mining camps. Scottish artist William Keith made paintings of California's missions and of the Yosemite Valley.

Cultural Heritage

Chinese New Year

Each winter during the Chinese New Year, the Chinese community in San Francisco shares its heritage with the rest of the city. During the 15-day celebration, Chinese Americans greet others with "Gung Hay Fat Choy!" or "Happy New Year." A huge parade through the city's Chinatown includes colorful floats and costumes.

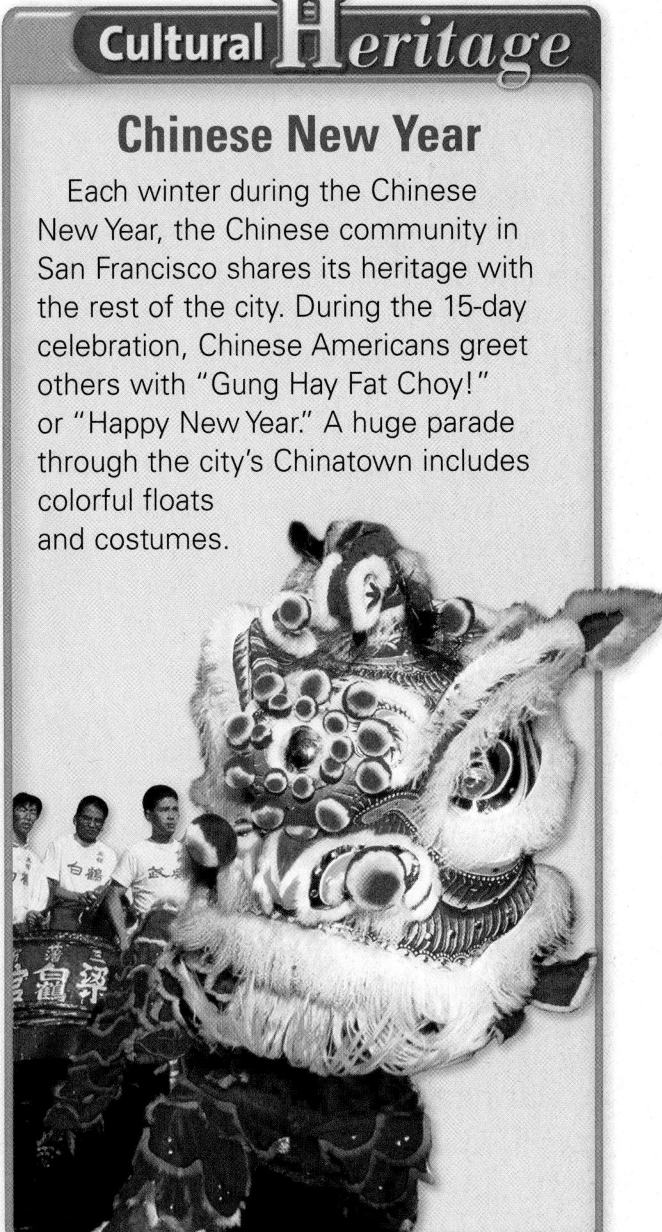

People who migrated to California also made contributions. Kate Douglas Wiggin started the first free kindergarten in San Francisco in 1878. Mary Austin, a writer, moved to California from Illinois in 1888. Her writings celebrate the beauty of California's Owens Valley.

READING CHECK GENERALIZE
How were immigrants able to grow crops in California that grew in their homeland?

Children IN HISTORY

Mamie Tape

In 1885, a Chinese girl named Mamie Tape tried to attend a public school in San Francisco. When the school refused to accept Mamie as a student, Mamie's mother, Mary, decided to fight for her child's rights. In a letter, Mary Tape asked, "Is it a disgrace [to be born] Chinese?"* Under pressure, the school board did set up a separate school that Chinese children could attend. Years later, such schools were found to be unconstitutional, and the law was changed.

Make It Relevant Why is it important for public schools today to be open to all students? Explain.

*Mary Tape. From a letter to the San Francisco school board. April 8, 1885.

Mamie Tape (center) and her family in 1884.

Facing Discrimination

During the 1870s, the United States met hard economic times. Many workers lost their jobs. In California, many people blamed the problems on immigrants. Earlier, immigrants had been needed to build the transcontinental railroad. Now many Californians felt that the immigrants were taking away their jobs.

Chinese immigrants, especially, faced discrimination. Discrimination against the Chinese and other immigrant groups grew out of prejudice (PREH•juh•duhs). **Prejudice** is the unfair feeling of hate or dislike for members of a certain group, race, or religion. Chinese immigrants were not allowed to hold certain jobs. They were also not allowed to live outside their own communities. Even so, many Chinese homes and businesses were attacked.

In 1882, Congress passed a law called the Chinese Exclusion Act. It stopped new Chinese immigrants from entering the United States unless they had family members living there. For the first time, people from a certain country were not allowed to enter the United States.

African Americans also faced prejudice and discrimination in California. Many had difficulty getting good jobs. In some places, African American children were not allowed to attend certain public schools.

In 1908, a group of African Americans decided that the best way to solve the problem of discrimination was to build their own town. The group was led by **Colonel Allen Allensworth**, a former slave. The group built its town in the San Joaquin Valley and named it **Allensworth**.

The town had its own government, school, library, post office, and church. African Americans opened stores and other businesses, but most people were farmers. When the town's well began to dry up in 1920, farmers could not get enough water. As a result, people began to leave Allensworth.

READING CHECK **DRAW CONCLUSIONS**
Why did Congress pass the Chinese Exclusion Act in 1882?

More Problems for California Indians

The large numbers of people who immigrated and migrated to California led to more problems for California Indians. As had happened during the gold rush, settlers often moved onto Indian lands, and many Indians were killed in conflicts.

The United States government tried to move Indians onto **reservations**, or lands set aside for them. However, much of the reservation land was poor, and Indians often could not find or grow enough food there to survive.

Many Indian groups fought to keep their lands. In 1864, the Modoc Indians were sent to live on a reservation in Oregon. Twice, they returned to their land in northern California.

Today, Allensworth is a state historic park. This picture of Colonel Allensworth, with a drawing of the town on it, hangs near one of the park's abandoned houses.

The United States Army was then sent to force them back onto the reservation. The Modoc, led by **Chief Kientepoos** (kih•en•TEH•pooz), fought for more than three years. In 1873, the Modoc were defeated. It was the last time Indians and the Army fought in California.

READING CHECK **CAUSE AND EFFECT**
How did immigration and migration affect California Indians?

Summary

Large numbers of people came to live and work in California in the late 1800s and early 1900s. They brought cultural and economic changes to the state, but some groups faced discrimination. California's growing population also created problems for California Indians.

Chief Kientepoos was also called Captain Jack.

REVIEW

1. How did immigration and migration affect California?
2. How are **immigration** and **migration** different?
3. Why did some immigrant groups face discrimination in California?

CRITICAL THINKING

4. Why do you think the Chinese immigrants were especially discriminated against?
5. SKILL **Make It Relevant** Do you see evidence of immigrant cultures in your community today? Explain.
6. **Write an Article** Choose an important event that you read about in this lesson. Then write a newspaper article about it. Be sure to answer these questions—who?, what?, when?, and where?—in your article.
7. Focus Skill **DRAW CONCLUSIONS**
On a separate sheet of paper, copy and complete the graphic organizer below.

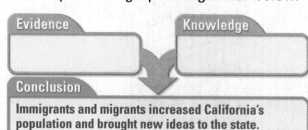

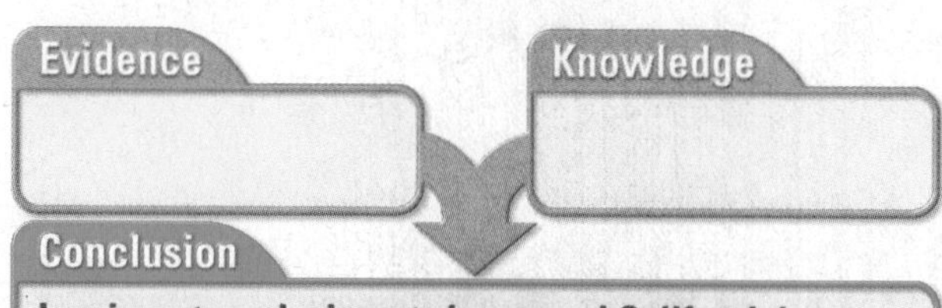
Evidence
Knowledge
Conclusion
Immigrants and migrants increased California's population and brought new ideas to the state.

Allen Allensworth

Biography

Trustworthiness
Respect
Responsibility
Fairness
Caring
Patriotism

*"We intend . . . to encourage our people to develop the best there is in them. . . ."**

Colonel Allen Allensworth was born a slave in Kentucky in 1842. After escaping slavery, he joined the United States Army and fought in the Civil War. When he retired, he had earned the highest rank of any African American in the United States military up to that time.

Allensworth encouraged other African Americans to achieve their dreams. He believed that a place that supported "intellectual and industrial freedom" would help them do that. In 1908, Allensworth and three others built a town for African Americans in the San Joaquin Valley. Named in honor of Allen Allensworth, this place was to be free from prejudice and discrimination. Allensworth led the town until his death in 1914.

Each year at the Allensworth Old Time Jubilee, descendants of Allensworth's first settlers honor the life of Allen Allensworth.

*Colonel Allen Allensworth. From a letter to Booker T. Washington, *The Booker T. Washington Papers*, Vol. 13, University of Illinois Press, 1972-1989.

Why Character Counts

How did Allen Allensworth show that he cared about the fair treatment of African Americans?

Bio Brief

1842 Born

1914 Died

1863 Joins the United States Army during the Civil War

1886 Appointed chaplain of the African American Army regiments

1908 Starts a town for African Americans

Interactive Multimedia Biographies
Visit MULTIMEDIA BIOGRAPHIES at
www.harcourtschool.com/hss

Lesson 2

1855 · 1885 · 1915

1887 The Santa Fe Railroad reaches Los Angeles

1892 Edward Doheny discovers oil in Los Angeles

1913 The Los Angeles Aqueduct opens

WHAT TO KNOW
What caused towns and cities in southern California to grow during the late 1800s and early 1900s?

- ✓ Trace the evolution of southern California's water system.
- ✓ Identify the network of dams, aqueducts, and reservoirs that supplied water to southern California.

VOCABULARY
petroleum p. 324
boom p. 324
derrick p. 324
reservoir p. 325
aqueduct p. 325
hydroelectric power p. 325

PEOPLE
Edward Doheny
William Mulholland

PLACES
San Pedro Bay
Owens Valley

DRAW CONCLUSIONS

California Standards
HSS 4.4, 4.4.4, 4.4.6, 4.4.7

Southern California Grows

YOU ARE THERE You stand beside the tracks as the train puffs slowly into the Los Angeles train station and comes to a stop. As people pour out of the railroad cars, you look for a familiar face—your grandmother's. Now that Los Angeles is linked to the East by two railroad lines, she has decided to come for a visit. Judging by the size of the crowd, it looks as if many other people have decided to come to southern California, too.

Growth to the South

In 1887, the Santa Fe Railroad reached Los Angeles. It began to compete with the Southern Pacific Railroad. Both railroads wanted to get more customers. As a result, the railroads lowered their rates for goods to be shipped and for passengers to travel. The cost of a ticket from Kansas City, Missouri, to Los Angeles fell from $125 to just $1! Low fares on railroads lured thousands of people from the East to southern California.

To get even more people to travel, the railroads wrote advertisements praising southern California's warm climate. Los Angeles, they claimed, had "a climate that makes the sick well and the strong more vigorous [energetic]."* The advertisements worked. Many people came to Los Angeles, San Diego, Long Beach, Anaheim, San Bernardino, and Santa Barbara because they believed the climate would help make them healthier.

Soon Los Angeles needed a harbor to help get supplies to its new residents. In 1899, workers began digging one in **San Pedro Bay**. The harbor was completed in 1914, and Los Angeles quickly became one of the busiest ports on the Pacific coast.

READING CHECK **DRAW CONCLUSIONS**
How did railroads affect southern California in the late 1800s?

*Advertising slogan from the late 1800s. *The Golden Book of California* by Irwin Shapiro. Golden Press, 1961

The population of Los Angeles grew from about 11,000 in 1880 to more than 300,000 in 1910. With so many newcomers, the price of land in Los Angeles doubled and doubled again.

Oil!

Discoveries of **petroleum** (puh•TROH•lee•uhm), or oil, in southern California brought more changes to the area in the late 1800s. The first important oil discoveries were made near the town of Ventura in the 1860s and 1870s. Then, in 1892, **Edward Doheny** (duh•HEE•nee) discovered large amounts of oil in Los Angeles.

The discovery started an oil **boom**, a time of fast economic growth. People began drilling for oil in all parts of Los Angeles, and within five years, about 2,300 wells had been drilled. Some people even tore out the palm trees in their yards to set up tall derricks to drill for oil. A **derrick** is a tower built over an oil well to hold drilling machines. In 1895, Los Angeles produced more than 700,000 barrels of oil.

Up until then, demand for petroleum had not been strong. Then, in the 1890s, railroad companies found that oil was a cheaper fuel for locomotives than coal. Oil also burned more cleanly. The railroads switched to oil, creating more demand for the fuel.

Later, as automobiles became popular, the demand for oil grew even more. The demand for gasoline set off a second California oil boom. Huge oil deposits had been discovered west of Bakersfield. The oil industry became a major part of California's economy.

READING CHECK SUMMARIZE
What happened to the economy in Los Angeles when oil was discovered in the area?

"Forests" of oil derricks towered above the land in some parts of Los Angeles in the early 1900s.

A crowd watches the first rush of water from the Owens River come down the Los Angeles Aqueduct, which was planned by William Mulholland.

Water for Los Angeles

TIME **1913**

PLACE **Los Angeles**

In the early 1900s, agriculture, oil, and other new industries were bringing thousands of people to the Los Angeles area. Water from the Los Angeles River and from **reservoirs** (REH•zuh•vwahrz), or human-made lakes, could no longer supply people with all the water they needed.

One man had an idea to solve the problem. **William Mulholland** (muhl•HAH•luhnd) wanted the city to get water from the Owens River—more than 200 miles away. Mulholland planned to build an aqueduct (A•kwuh•dukt) to carry the water. An **aqueduct** is a large pipe or canal that carries water from one place to another.

Work on this aqueduct began in 1908. Workers blasted tunnels through the Sierra Nevada and cleared paths across the Mojave Desert. New reservoirs were built near Los Angeles to store the water.

In 1913, the Los Angeles Aqueduct finally opened. It brought millions of gallons of water each day to the Los Angeles area. In addition, the fast-moving water was used to make **hydroelectric power**, or electricity produced by using waterpower.

READING CHECK **DRAW CONCLUSIONS**
Why do you think it took so long to build the aqueduct?

Conflicts over Water

The Los Angeles Aqueduct hurt people living in the **Owens Valley**. So much water was taken away that farmers and ranchers in the valley did not have enough for their own crops and animals.

The people of the Owens Valley were very angry, but there was little they could do. To get the water it needed, Los Angeles had secretly bought most of the land on both sides of the Owens River. Owning the land meant that the city also controlled the water.

Some people in the Owens Valley were so angry that they tried to stop the flow of water into the aqueduct. One group went so far as to use dynamite to blast holes in the aqueduct. But the damage was repaired, and water continued to flow out of the valley.

Even today, Owens Valley faces problems because of the aqueduct. Owens Lake, formed by the Owens

ANALYSIS SKILL **Analyze Maps In 1913, the Los Angeles Aqueduct was 233 miles long. By 1940, its length had grown to 338 miles.**

Human-Environment Interactions

Which two reservoirs are between the cities of Mojave and Los Angeles?

River, was dry. Dust clouds formed over the dry lake bed. These clouds created health problems for people in the area. In 2001, engineers set up pipelines to bring water back to parts of the lake to reduce the dust. Now, areas of the lower Owens River will have enough water for farming and ranching.

READING CHECK **CAUSE AND EFFECT**
How did the Los Angeles Aqueduct affect people in the Owens Valley?

Summary

The population of southern California grew quickly. New railroads, as well as the discovery of oil in the region, led to rapid growth. A port and an aqueduct were built for Los Angeles. As the population grew, conflicts over water arose.

In 1928, the St. Francis Dam, one of the dams built near Los Angeles, broke. About 12 billion gallons of water rushed through the Santa Clara Valley, killing nearly 450 people.

REVIEW

1. What caused towns and cities in southern California to grow during the late 1800s and early 1900s?
2. Explain the difference between an **aqueduct** and a **reservoir**.
3. How was Los Angeles able to get the rights to water in the Owens Valley?

CRITICAL THINKING

4. ANALYSIS SKILL How did the location of Los Angeles lead to its rapid growth? Did its location have any disadvantages?
5. What do you think would have happened to Los Angeles if the Los Angeles Aqueduct had not been built?
6. **Hold a Debate** With classmates, learn more about the building of the Los Angeles Aqueduct. Then choose a point of view for or against the water project. Find another group with the opposite point of view, and hold a debate.
7. Focus Skill **DRAW CONCLUSIONS** On a separate sheet of paper, copy and complete the graphic organizer below.

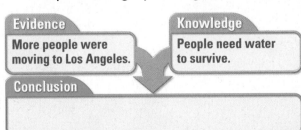

Evidence	Knowledge
More people were moving to Los Angeles.	People need water to survive.

Conclusion

Whose Water Is It?

Since the early 1900s, there has been much conflict over who should use the water from the Owens River. Officials in Los Angeles felt that the river was an ideal water source for the city's growing population. They planned to build an aqueduct to bring the water to Los Angeles. Many people in the Owens Valley, however, were worried about the damage this water project might cause. Here are three points of view on the issue of water rights in the Owens Valley.

Building the Los Angeles Aqueduct, 1908

In Their Own Words

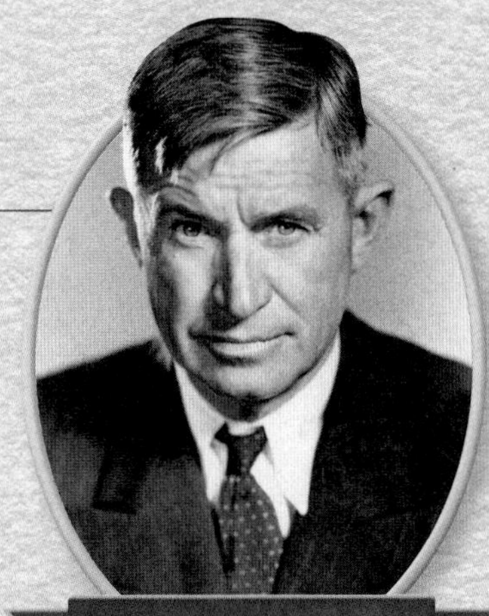
WILL ROGERS

Will Rogers, a famous humorist

“Ten years ago this was a wonderful valley. . . . But Los Angeles had to have more water . . . to drink more toasts to its growth. . . . So, now this is a valley of desolation.”

— From *The Story of Inyo* by W. A. Chalfant, 1959.

WILFRED AND MARK WATTERSON

Owens Valley residents, led by Wilfred and Mark Watterson

“The Los Angeles water officials are forcing the Valley folk to sell their lands. Our people do not want to dispose of [get rid of] their homes; they want to be left alone.”

— From *The Water Trail* by Don Kinsey. The Department of Water and Power. City of Los Angeles, 1928.

Theodore Roosevelt, twenty-sixth President of the United States

“[Water from the Owens Valley] is a hundred or a thousand fold [times] more important to the state and more valuable to the people as a whole if used by the city than if used by the people of the Owens Valley.”

— From a letter written on June 25, 1906, agreeing with the building of the Los Angeles Aqueduct. City of Los Angeles, Department of Water and Power.

It's Your Turn

ANALYSIS SKILL **Analyze Points of View** Explain why residents of the Owens Valley and the people favoring the Los Angeles Aqueduct had differing points of view.

Make It Relevant California's demand for water continues to grow. How do you think California's water resources should be shared today?

Lesson 3

Time		
1855	1885	1915

1906 An earthquake and fire destroy much of San Francisco

1909 California spends $18 million to build a state highway system

1914 Construction begins on the Hetch Hetchy Aqueduct

WHAT TO KNOW
What caused towns and cities in northern California to grow during the early 1900s?

- ✓ Trace the evolution of northern California's water system.
- ✓ Identify the network of dams, aqueducts, and reservoirs that supplied water to northern California.

VOCABULARY
naturalist p. 335

PEOPLE
Amadeo Pietro Giannini
John Muir

PLACES
San Francisco
Florin
Hetch Hetchy Valley

DRAW CONCLUSIONS

California Standards
HSS 4.4, 4.4.4, 4.4.7

Changes in Northern California

YOU ARE THERE You are asleep in your home in **San Francisco**. It's just after 5:00 A.M. on Wednesday, April 18, 1906. Suddenly a deep rumbling wakes you up. At first, it's soft and low, but it soon grows louder and louder. Your room shakes violently. As you stumble out of bed, things crash to the floor all around you. The floor is shaking so hard that you can barely stay on your feet. It's an earthquake!

➤ Before the earthquake in 1906, San Francisco was a busy, growing city. After the earthquake, much of the city lay in ruins.

After

A Great Earthquake

TIME **April 18, 1906**

PLACE **San Francisco**

Most people were asleep early in the morning on April 18, 1906, when an earthquake shook San Francisco. One citizen, Ernest H. Adams, later wrote:

> **"I was thrown out of bed and in a twinkling of an eye the side of our house was dashed to the ground. . . . I fell and crawled down the stairs amid flying glass and timber and plaster."***

Out in the streets, sidewalks cracked and broke into pieces. Glass windows crashed to the ground. Lamps swung wildly. The violent shaking lasted less than a minute, but it was long enough to destroy many buildings.

*Ernest H. Adams. From a letter to his employers, Reed and Barton of Taunton, Massachusetts. April 23, 1906.

To make matters worse, a huge fire broke out just after the earthquake. Leaking gas from broken pipes fed the flames. Most firefighters who rushed to put them out discovered that there was no water. The earthquake had broken many of the city's water pipes.

READING CHECK **DRAW CONCLUSIONS**
How do you think the 1906 earthquake affected the growth of San Francisco?

Soon after the earthquake, workers began to rebuild San Francisco's damaged buildings.

San Francisco Rebuilds

The earthquake and fire left San Francisco in ruins. Most of the city's buildings were destroyed, including the city hall, churches, and banks. Damage to the city totaled almost $500 million. After looking over the earthquake damage, United States Secretary of Labor Victor H. Metcalf reported:

> "It is almost impossible to describe the ruin wrought [caused] by the earthquake. . . . The people, however, are confident and hopeful for the future and have not in any sense lost courage."*

San Francisco was an important port city, and San Franciscans were determined to rebuild. An Italian American banker, **Amadeo Pietro Giannini** (ah•mah•DAY•oh PYEH•troh jee•uh•NEE•nee), was one of the first to help. Even before the fires were put out, Giannini began to give out loans of money. His loans helped

*Victor H. Metcalf. From a Letter to President Theodore Roosevelt, April 26, 1906.

San Franciscans were determined to rebuild their city to be bigger and better than it had been before the earthquake.

Japanese farm workers pick strawberries near Sacramento in 1910.

people rebuild their homes and businesses.

Money, food, and supplies poured in from all over the country. In fewer than ten years, a new city rose from the ruins. By 1915, San Francisco was said to be bigger and better than it had been before the earthquake.

READING CHECK **DRAW CONCLUSIONS**
Why do you think people were willing to rebuild such a damaged city?

Growth Throughout Northern California

San Francisco was not the only city in northern California that grew. Many people from San Francisco moved across the bay to Oakland. The population of Oakland more than doubled between 1900 and 1910. San Jose also grew.

The population in northern California also became more diverse. Fewer than 30 Japanese Americans lived in Sacramento. That soon changed as many Japanese immigrants began traveling to Sacramento to work on fruit farms.

A Japanese American community named **Florin** grew in Sacramento County. Florin became known as the Strawberry Capital of California. Farmers there grew enough strawberries to fill 120 railroad cars at a time!

Improvements also changed cities in northern California. In 1909, the California government spent $18 million to build a state highway system. A network of paved highways soon made it easier for people to travel from city to city.

READING CHECK **SUMMARIZE**
Why did many Japanese immigrants move to Sacramento County?

San Francisco Gets More Water

TIME 1914

PLACE San Francisco

San Francisco soon faced a shortage of water because of its growing population. City leaders asked the United States government if a dam might be built on the Tuolumne (too•AH•luh•mee) River. This dam would create a large reservoir for San Francisco. An aqueduct would carry the water from the reservoir to the city.

The plan would solve San Francisco's water problems, but it would also create new problems. The water behind the dam would flood the **Hetch Hetchy Valley**, a part of Yosemite National Park. The plan set off angry arguments. People in favor of the dam felt it was the only way to get the needed water. **John Muir**, a

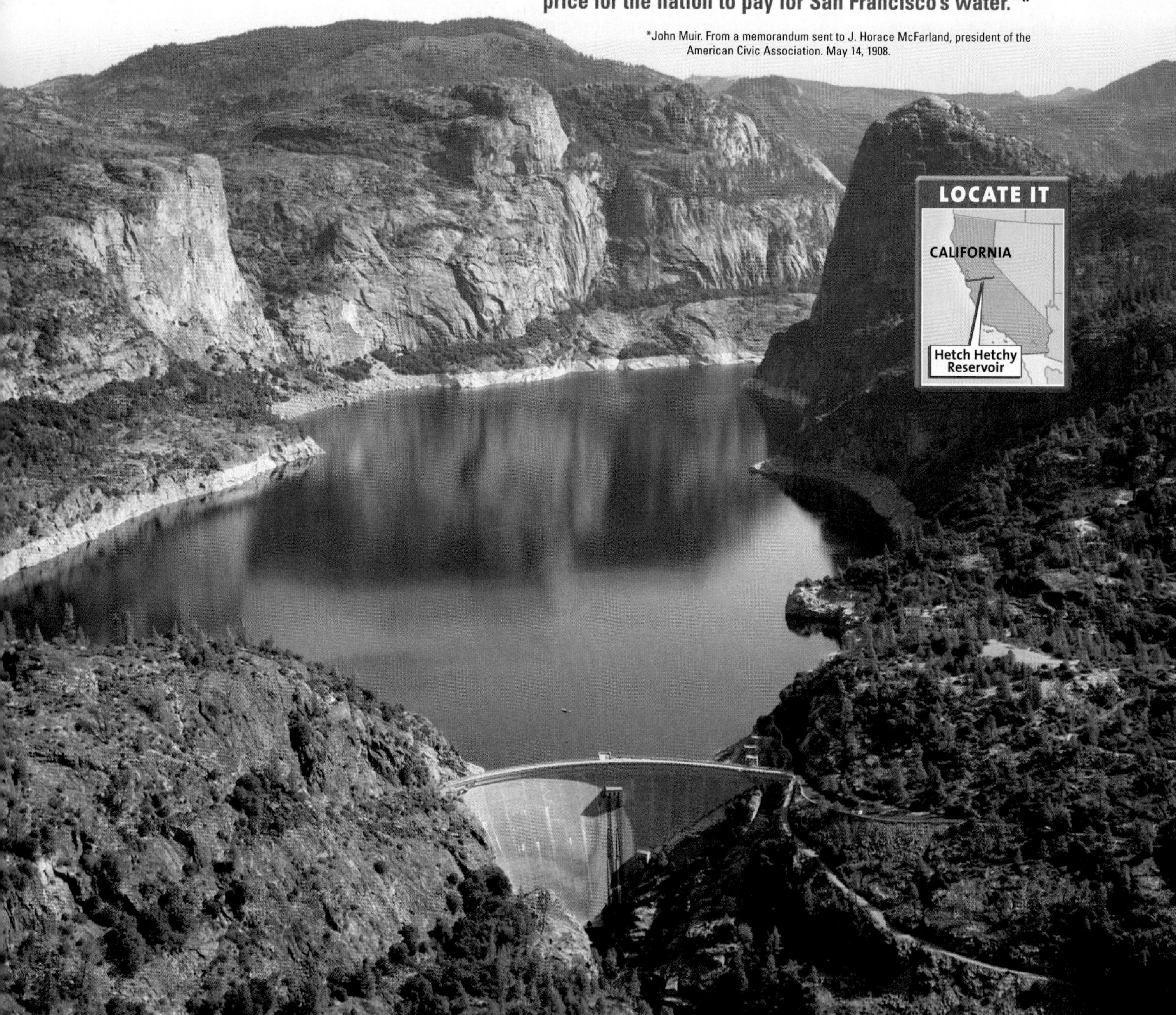

John Muir thought flooding the Hetch Hetchy Valley was a "tremendous price for the nation to pay for San Francisco's water."*

*John Muir. From a memorandum sent to J. Horace McFarland, president of the American Civic Association. May 14, 1908.

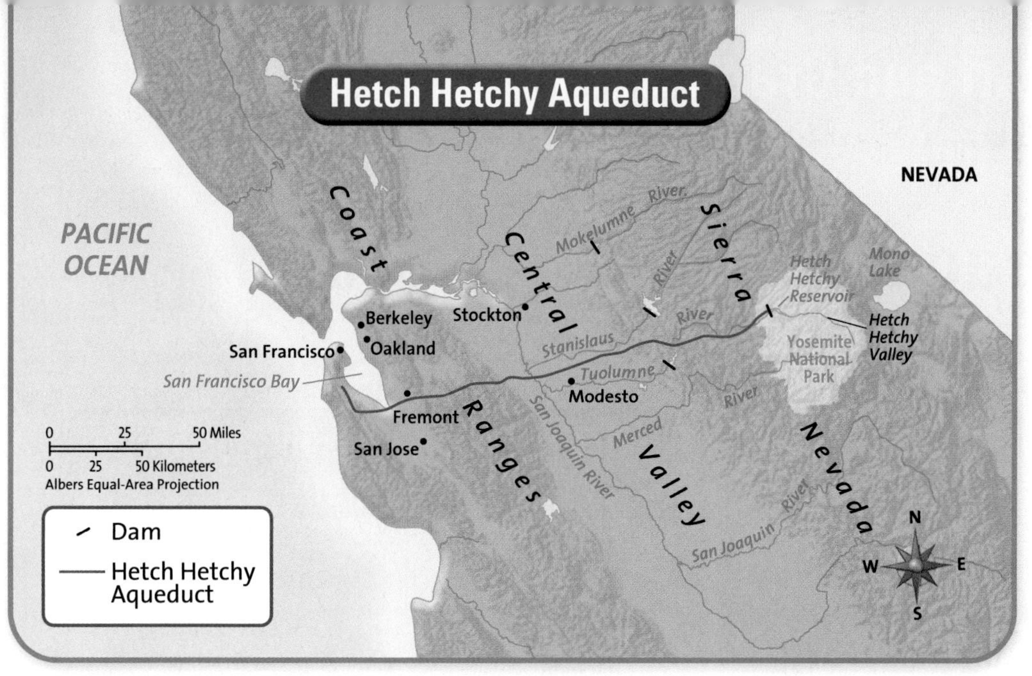

ANALYSIS SKILL Analyze Maps
Today, San Francisco gets more than three-fourths of its water from the Hetch Hetchy Reservoir.

Human-Environment Interactions
Which rivers on this map does the Hetch Hetchy Aqueduct cross?

well-known naturalist, led the fight against the project. A **naturalist** is a person who studies nature and works to protect it. Muir and his supporters did not want even part of a national park to be flooded.

Despite protests, San Francisco began building the dam and the Hetch Hetchy Aqueduct in 1914. However, Californians kept speaking against the plan for years.

READING CHECK SUMMARIZE
How did northern California meet its growing need for water in the early 1900s?

Summary

In 1906, an earthquake and fire destroyed much of San Francisco. However, the city was quickly rebuilt and kept growing. Other areas of northern California also grew quickly. The Hetch Hetchy Reservoir was built to help meet northern California's growing need for water.

REVIEW

1. What caused towns and cities in northern California to grow during the early 1900s?
2. Use the term **naturalist** to describe the conflict over the Hetch Hetchy Valley.
3. Who founded the town of Florin? Why did they come to Sacramento County?

CRITICAL THINKING

4. ANALYSIS SKILL Why do you think people had such different opinions on building a dam on the Tuolumne River?
5. **Write an Editorial** Write a newspaper editorial in favor of or against flooding the Hetch Hetchy Valley.
6. Focus Skill **DRAW CONCLUSIONS** On a separate sheet of paper, copy and complete the graphic organizer below.

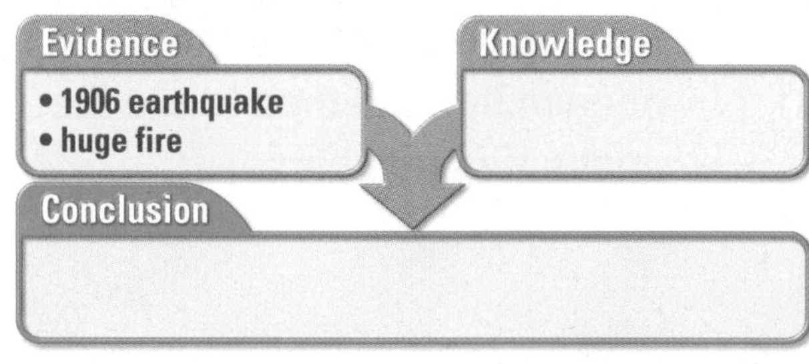

Chart and Graph Skills

Read a Double-Bar Graph

WHY IT MATTERS

As you have read, California's population grew quickly during the late 1800s and early 1900s. Suppose that you want to compare how the population of two cities in California changed during this time. Graphs make it easy to compare numbers. A **double-bar graph** makes it easy to compare two sets of numbers.

WHAT YOU NEED TO KNOW

The double-bar graph on this page shows changes in the populations of San Francisco and Los Angeles from 1870 to 1910.

Step 1 **Read the title, labels, and information in the key. The numbers of people are listed along the left-hand side of the graph. The years are listed along the bottom. Each purple bar shows the population of San Francisco during a certain year. The green bars show the population of Los Angeles.**

Step 2 **Read the double-bar graph by running your finger up to the top of each bar and then left to the population numbers.**

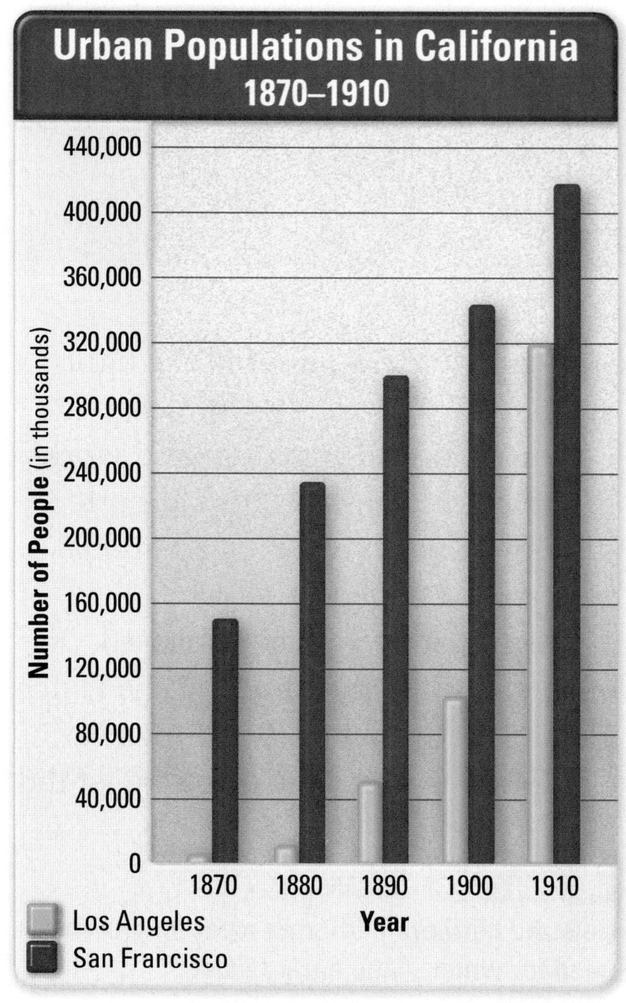

Step 3 **To compare the numbers for a certain year, look at the height of each bar. A taller bar stands for a larger population. The difference between the heights of the two bars shows the difference between the two populations.**

PRACTICE THE SKILL

Use the double-bar graph on page 336 to answer these questions.

1. Compare the populations of San Francisco and Los Angeles in 1890. Which city had a larger population? About how many more people lived in that city?
2. What was the population of San Francisco in 1900? in 1910? What were the populations in Los Angeles for those years? Which city grew more between 1900 and 1910?
3. Which city grew more between 1870 and 1910?

APPLY WHAT YOU LEARNED

Create a double-bar graph that shows the growth of Sacramento and San Diego between 1870 and 1910. Use the population numbers shown in the table below. Then write a paragraph comparing the population growth of the two cities during that time period.

Year	Sacramento	San Diego
1870	16,283	2,300
1880	21,420	2,637
1890	26,386	16,159
1900	29,282	17,700
1910	44,696	39,578

As San Francisco's population grew in the late 1800s and early 1900s, new neighborhoods were built there. Many of the homes in these neighborhoods reflect the architecture of the time.

Time

1875

1885

1882
Congress passes the Chinese Exclusion Act

1892
Oil is discovered in Los Angeles

Reading Social Studies

A **conclusion** is a decision or an idea reached by using what you read and what you already know about a subject.

Focus Skill Draw Conclusions

Complete this graphic organizer to show you understand how California's population grew and changed in the late 1800s and early 1900s. A copy of this graphic organizer appears on page 92 of the Homework and Practice Book.

A Growing Economy

Evidence
California was seen by many immigrants as a land of opportunity.

Knowledge
People from different cultures can learn from each other's ways of life and traditions.

Conclusion

California Writing Prompts

Write a Narrative Imagine you are listening to a speech given by William Mulholland. Describe what he might have said to convince city officials to support the plan for bringing more water to Los Angeles.

Write a Summary Review the contributions made by newcomers to California. Summarize how immigrants and settlers helped California grow during the late 1800s and early 1900s.

1895 1905 1915

1906
A great earthquake and fire destroy much of San Francisco

1913
The Los Angeles Aqueduct is completed

Use Vocabulary

Identify the term that correctly matches each definition.

migration, p. 315

reservations, p. 319

derricks, p. 324

aqueduct, p. 325

1. A new _____ in southern California brought more water to Los Angeles.
2. Freed slaves formed part of a large _____ to California in the late 1800s.
3. After oil was discovered in Los Angeles, some people built _____ in their yards.
4. The United States government moved many American Indians onto _____ .

Use the Time Line

Use the summary time line above to answer the question.

5. In what year did Congress pass the Chinese Exclusion Act?

Apply Skills

Read a Double-Bar Graph

6. Look at the graph on page 336.In which decade did the difference between the populations of San Francisco and Los Angeles drop below 100,000?

Recall Facts

Answer these questions.

7. In what way did Allen Allensworth try to solve the problem of discrimination?
8. What effect did the discovery of oil have on Los Angeles?
9. Why did certain parts of California need more water?

Write the letter of the best choice.

10. Which of these towns was started by Danish Americans?
    A Solvang
    B Yamato Colony
    C Florin
    D Anaheim
11. Where did the Los Angeles Aqueduct get most of its water from?
    A the Owens River
    B the Tuolumne River
    C the Hetch Hetchy Reservoir
    D the Salton Sea

Think Critically

12. ANALYSIS SKILL How are the water supply issues of the early 1900s like those of today? How are they different?
13. ANALYSIS SKILL In what ways have migrants and immigrants contributed to the unique character of California?

The San Francisco CABLE CAR Museum

GET READY

San Francisco's steep hills once presented a problem for city residents. In the 1870s, Andrew Hallidie invented a system of underground wire cables to pull cars up and down San Francisco's steep hills. The San Francisco Cable Car Museum traces the history of the cable car. On a visit to the museum, you can tour the sheave (SHEEV) room. This room houses the underground system that moves the cables and keeps the cars traveling throughout the city. You can also see photographs, models, and exhibits that show how cable cars have changed over time. As you walk through the museum, you will see how the cable car has helped shape San Francisco and become an important part of the city.

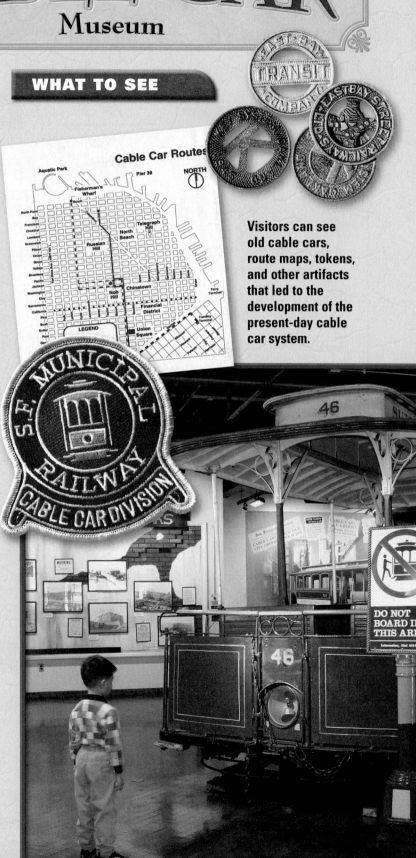

LOCATE IT

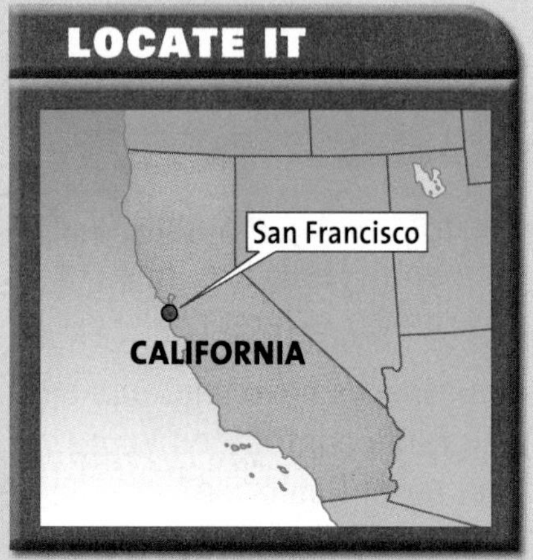

WHAT TO SEE

Visitors can see old cable cars, route maps, tokens, and other artifacts that led to the development of the present-day cable car system.

There have been many different kinds of cable cars since the original design in 1873. This is one of San Francisco's cable cars from 1890.

The conductor is responsible for collecting fares and for controlling the brakes that slow the car on steep hills.

With the help of a turntable, cable cars can turn around at the end of a line.

You can take a cable car to travel to the museum. Both the Powell-Hyde and Powell-Mason cars stop at the museum.

From the observation gallery, visitors can watch the electric motors as they keep each cable moving at nine and one-half miles per hour.

A VIRTUAL TOUR

Visit VIRTUAL TOURS at **www.harcourtschool.com/hss**

Review

THE BIG IDEA

Innovations The years after statehood were a time of great change for California and the United States.

Summary

A Growing State

In the late 1800s and early 1900s, California developed rapidly. The stagecoach, the Pony Express, and the telegraph led to faster communication between California and the East Coast. Then, in 1869, the transcontinental railroad provided a transportation link for people and goods, such as crops from California's growing farm industry.

In the late 1800s, tens of thousands of migrants and immigrants came to California. Many faced prejudice. Some were not allowed to hold certain jobs. Those who found work were often paid very little. Some, like the Chinese, were forced to live in separate communities.

In 1906, San Francisco was destroyed by an earthquake and then rebuilt. A few years later, the discovery of oil in southern California caused an oil boom. As the state's population continued to grow, large cities built water projects to bring more water and electricity to residents.

Main Ideas and Vocabulary

Read the summary above. Then answer the questions that follow.

1. What does prejudice mean?
   - **A** acceptance and fair treatment
   - **B** people from the same country or culture
   - **C** a contest among people or groups
   - **D** unfair feelings of dislike for members of a certain group, race, or religion
2. How did the transcontinental railroad affect California?
   - **A** linked California to the rest of the country
   - **B** reduced travel to the East
   - **C** brought water and electricity to California
   - **D** helped farmers grow better crops
3. What is a boom?
   - **A** a celebration
   - **B** a time of destruction
   - **C** a time of fast economic growth
   - **D** a time of slow population growth
4. How did large cities, such as Los Angeles and San Francisco, deal with water problems in the early 1900s?
   - **A** They dug more wells.
   - **B** They built dams, reservoirs, and canals.
   - **C** They brought water in on railcars.
   - **D** They asked citizens to use less water.

The Pacific Railroad ground broken Jany. 8th 1863 and completed May 8th 1869

Recall Facts

Answer these questions.

5. How did communication across the United States become faster and easier during the mid-1800s?
6. What geographical barrier did the Central Pacific Railroad have to cross when building the transcontinental railroad?
7. What dangers did workers on the transcontinental railroad face?
8. Why did Congress pass the Chinese Exclusion Act in 1882?
9. What made it possible for railroads to carry fresh fruits and vegetables from California to the East?
10. Why were some people against building the Hetch Hetchy Aqueduct?

Write the letter of the best choice.

11. Which of these people was one of the Big Four?
    A Leland Stanford
    B William Mulholland
    C Eliza Tibbets
    D John Muir
12. Where did tracks laid by the Central Pacific and Union Pacific railroad companies meet?
    A Promontory, Utah
    B Omaha, Nebraska
    C Los Angeles, California
    D St. Joseph, Missouri
13. Commercial farms
    A are located only in the Imperial Valley.
    B grow wheat only.
    C grow citrus fruit only.
    D grow crops only to sell.
14. What major natural disaster hit northern California in 1906?
    A a flood
    B a hurricane
    C an earthquake
    D a tornado

Think Critically

15. ANALYSIS SKILL Think about immigrants' contributions to the transcontinental railroad, the sacrifices they made, and the discrimination many faced. Based on this, what questions do you have about the experiences of these immigrants?
16. ANALYSIS SKILL Do you think the benefits of California's water projects make up for the costs? Explain.

Apply Skills

Use a Time Zone Map

Look at the time zone map below to answer these questions.

17. Which two states use both Pacific time and Mountain time?
18. If it is 9:30 A.M. in Sacramento, California, what time is it in Cheyenne, Wyoming? in Portland, Oregon?

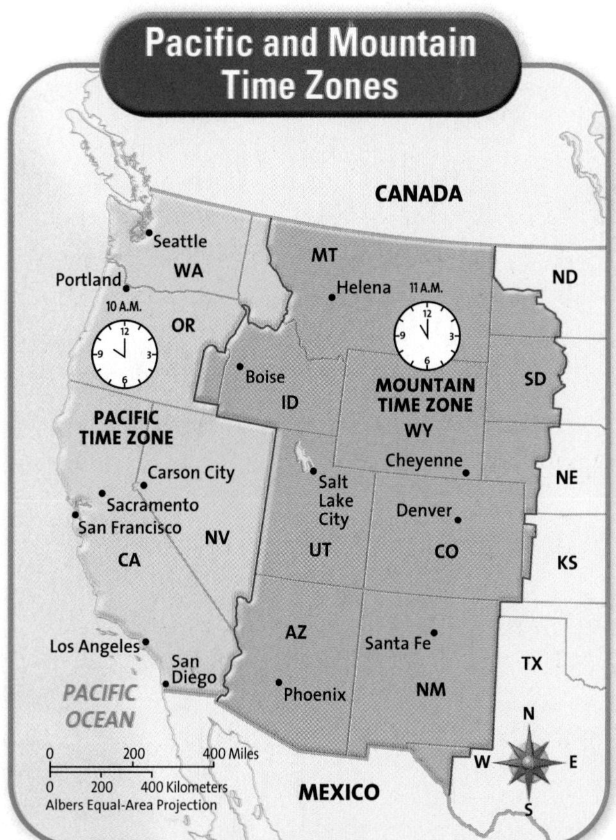

Activities

Read More

- *The Pony Express* by Renee Skelton.

- *The Golden Spike* by Renee Skelton.

- *Coming to California: Chinese Immigrants* by Susan Kim.

Show What You Know

Unit Writing Activity

Write a Narrative Imagine that you are writing a story for a California newspaper. Pick a person from the unit to interview and compose a list of questions for the person to answer. Based on information from the unit, write answers to the questions the person might have given. Use your interview to help you write about the person you chose.

Unit Project

Publish a California Newspaper Put together a newspaper that tells about some of the important events that took place in California in the years after statehood. Choose people and events to feature in articles, editorials, and cartoons. Illustrate your newspaper with drawings, and also feature advertisements of the time.

GO ONLINE Visit ACTIVITIES at **www.harcourtschool.com/hss**

Progress as a State

California History-Social Science Standards

4.4 Students explain how California became an agricultural and industrial power, tracing the transformation of the California economy and its political and cultural development since the 1850s.

The Big Idea

GROWTH AND CHANGE

Human and natural events changed California, the United States, and the world during the twentieth century.

What to Know

- ✓ How did world wars and economic depression affect Californians?
- ✓ How did agriculture and industry change in California?
- ✓ How did California's water system grow?

Show What You Know

- ★ **Unit 5 Test**
- **Writing: A Summary**
- **Unit Project: A California Scrapbook**

Unit 5

Time

Progress as a State

1911 Women in California gain the right to vote in state elections, p. 359

1937 The Golden Gate Bridge is completed, p. 373

1942 Japanese Americans are moved to relocation camps during World War II, p. 382

1905 — 1925 — 1945

At the Same Time

1914 World War I begins

1929 The stock market crashes and the Great Depression begins

Progress as a State

1962 Dolores Huerta and Cesar Chavez form the National Farm Workers Association, p. 402

1981 The first space shuttle lands at Edwards Air Force Base, p. 396

1965

1985

1939 World War II begins

1963 President John F. Kennedy is assassinated

1975 The Vietnam War ends

Unit 5

People

James Doolittle

1896–1993

- One of 13 soldiers from California to win the Congressional Medal of Honor during World War II
- First pilot to fly across the United States in fewer than 24 hours

Dalip Singh Saund

1899–1973

- Helped form the India Association of America and became its first president
- Elected judge in Imperial County but was denied the office because he had not been a citizen for a full year
- First Indian American and the first Asian American elected to Congress

1885 | 1915

- 1896 • James Doolittle
- 1899 • Dalip Singh Saund
- 1902 • John Steinbeck
- 1919 • Jackie Robinson
- 1923 • David M. Gonzales
- 1930 • Dolores Huerta
- 1932 •

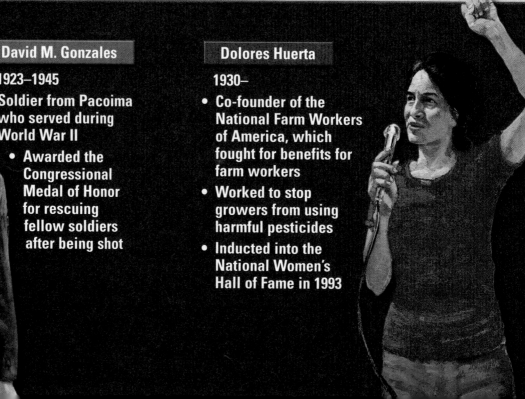

David M. Gonzales

1923–1945

- Soldier from Pacoima who served during World War II
- Awarded the Congressional Medal of Honor for rescuing fellow soldiers after being shot

Dolores Huerta

1930–

- Co-founder of the National Farm Workers of America, which fought for benefits for farm workers
- Worked to stop growers from using harmful pesticides
- Inducted into the National Women's Hall of Fame in 1993

John Steinbeck

1902–1968

- California native who wrote books about the Great Depression
  - Won the Pulitzer Prize in 1939 for *The Grapes of Wrath*
  - Awarded the Nobel Prize for Literature in 1962

Jackie Robinson

1919–1972

- UCLA athlete who in 1947 became the first African American to play major league baseball
  - Inducted into the National Baseball Hall of Fame in 1962

1945 | 1975 | PRESENT

1993

1973

1968

1972

1945

Yvonne Brathwaite Burke

1951 • Sally Ride

Yvonne Brathwaite Burke

1932–

- First African American woman in the California state assembly
- First African American woman from California elected to Congress
  - Currently serves as Los Angeles County Supervisor

Sally Ride

1951–

- First American woman in space
- Went into space twice, first in 1983 and again in 1984
- Currently on the faculty at the University of California

Unit 5

Place

California in the United States, 1985

Trinity Dam
Shasta Dam
Shasta Lake
Pit River
Sacramento River
Tehama-Colusa Canal (1971)
Feather River
Oroville Dam
American River
Lake Tahoe
Sacramento
Folsom Dam
Contra Costa Canal (1940)
Mokelumne River
Berkeley
Mokelumne Aqueduct (1929)
San Francisco
Oakland
Hetch Hetchy Aqueduct (1934)
Mono Lake
San Jose
South Bay Aqueduct (1962)
Delta-Mendota Canal (1951)
Owens River
California Aqueduct (1968–1973)
San Joaquin River
Monterey
Friant-Kern Canal (1949)
Fresno
Salinas River
Kern River
Bakersfield
Los Angeles Aqueduct (1913)
Santa Ynez River
Santa Barbara
Santa Clara R.
Los Angeles
Long Beach
Colorado River Aqueduct (1941)
Lake Havasu
Parker Dam
Palm Springs
Second San Diego Aqueduct (1960)
First San Diego Aqueduct (1947)
Coachella Canal (1949)
Colorado River
Salton Sea
San Diego
All-American Canal (1941)
Imperial Dam

A BART train in the San Francisco Bay area

Cesar Chavez leads farmworkers

CANADA
UNITED STATES
MEXICO
PACIFIC OCEAN
ATLANTIC OCEAN
Gulf of Mexico
Columbia River
Snake River
Rio Grande
WA
OR
ID
MT
ND
SD
WY
NE
NV
UT
CO
CA
AZ
NM
KS
OK
TX
MN
IA
MO
AR
LA
WI
IL
MI
IN
OH
KY
TN
MS
AL
GA
FL
SC
NC
VA
WV
PA
NY
VT
NH
ME
MA
RI
CT
NJ
DE
MD
Olympia
Salem
Boise
Helena
Bismarck
Pierre
Sacramento
Carson City
Salt Lake City
Cheyenne
Denver
Lincoln
Topeka
Santa Fe
Phoenix
Oklahoma City
Austin
St. Paul
Des Moines
Madison
Lansing
Springfield
St. Louis
Jefferson City
Little Rock
Jackson
Baton Rouge
Indianapolis
Columbus
Frankfort
Nashville
Montgomery
Atlanta
Tallahassee
Columbia
Raleigh
Richmond
Charleston
Washington, D.C.
Annapolis
Dover
Trenton
Harrisburg
Albany
Montpelier
Concord
Augusta
Boston
Providence
Hartford
At the Same Time
Kennedy Space Center, in Florida
Interstate highways
Toll roads
Other roads
Aqueduct
Canal
Dam
0 250 500 Miles
0 250 500 Kilometers
Albers Equal-Area Projection
N
S
E
W

Reading Social Studies

Focus Skill Cause and Effect

A cause is an action or event that makes something else happen. An effect is what happens as the result of that action or event.

Why It Matters

Understanding cause and effect can help you see why events and actions happen.

Cause		Effect
An event or action	→	What happens

✓ Look for these cause-and-effect signal words and phrases:

because   since   so   as a result

✓ Sometimes the effect may be stated before the cause.

Practice the Skill

Read the second paragraph, and find a cause and an effect.

Cause — In 1887, the Santa Fe Railroad and the Southern Pacific Railroad lowered their rates for goods to be shipped and for passengers to travel. The cost of a ticket from Kansas City, Missouri, to Los Angeles fell from $125 to just $1! As a result, Effect — thousands of people traveled to southern California on the railroads.

In the late 1800s, oil was discovered in southern California. In 1890, the railroad companies switched to oil as a lower-cost fuel for their trains. This and the increasing popularity of automobiles created a greater demand for oil. Soon the oil industry became a large part of California's economy.

Apply What You Learned

 **Find Cause and Effect** **Read the paragraphs, and answer the questions.**

California's Air and Space Flight Industry

Because of its mild climate, California attracted new industries during the early 1900s. Farmers, filmmakers, and airplane builders moved into the state.

When the United States entered World War II, many scientists and engineers came to California. They drew plans for new airplanes, including fighter jets. As a result, business owners built factories in southern California to make these new planes. The government also set up military training bases in the Mojave Desert to test how well the new planes flew. There, good weather and clear skies made it possible to fly nearly every day of the year.

After the war, many scientists stayed in California. They kept looking for ways to make better airplanes. They also worked on missiles, rockets, and spacecraft. By the 1950s, southern California was at the heart of the air and space flight industry.

In the 1960s, the air and space flight industry helped form the United States space program, NASA. NASA engineers directed several rockets to the moon from their lab in Pasadena. They also helped American astronauts land on the moon in 1969. Today, the air and space flight industry remains an important part of California's economy.

Cause and Effect

1. **What caused airplane manufacturers and pilots to come to southern California in the early 1900s?**
2. **What effect did World War II have on the airplane industry in southern California?**
3. **What caused the government to choose the Mojave Desert as a place to test new airplanes?**

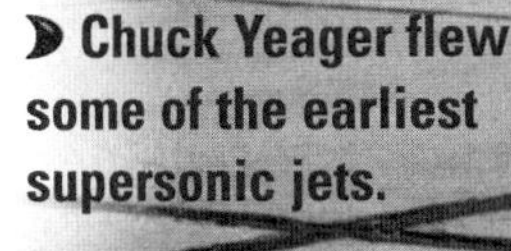

Chuck Yeager flew some of the earliest supersonic jets.

Study Skills

PREVIEW AND QUESTION

Identifying main ideas and asking questions about them can help you find important information.

- **To preview a passage, read the title. Look at the pictures, and read their captions. Try to get an idea of the main topic, and think of questions you have.**
- **Read to find the answers to your questions. Then recite, or say, the answers aloud. Finally, review what you have read.**

Growing and Changing				
Preview	Questions	Read	Recite	Review
Lesson 1 Big events and ideas shaped California in the early 1900s.	What did people try to change about government, and why?	✓	✓	✓
Lesson 2				

Apply As You Read

In a chart, identify the topic you will be reading about. Then write down questions about it. Read, recite, and review to be sure that you understand the information.

California History-Social Science Standards, Grade 4

4.4 Students explain how California became an agricultural and industrial power, tracing the transformation of the California economy and its political and cultural development since the 1850s.

CHAPTER

Growing and Changing

In the early 1900s, Hollywood became the center of the movie industry.

So far from the Sea

by Eve Bunting
illustrated by Chris K. Soentpiet

In this story, set in 1972, Laura Iwasaki (ee•wah•SAH•kee) and her family are visiting her grandfather's grave at the site of Manzanar (MAN•zuh•nar) War Relocation Camp in a desolate part of eastern California. As a boy during World War II, Laura's father and his family had been sent to live there. Read to learn about Laura's visit.

"Let's keep going, pal," Dad says, and Thomas limps on. I see he is holding Mom's hand. Thomas doesn't like to hold anyone's hand. He must feel the scariness of this awful place, too.

"Why did they put you and Grandmother and the aunts and uncles here, anyway?" he asks.

Dad pulls his head far back in his hood, like a snail going into its shell. "Because Japan attacked the United States," he says. "It was a terrible thing. Suddenly we were at war. And we were Japanese, living in California. The government thought we might do something to help Japan. So they kept us in these camps."

Dad has explained this a hundred times, but Thomas forgets because he is so little.

"It wasn't fair," I say. "It was the meanest thing in the whole world. You were Americans. Like I am. Like Thomas."

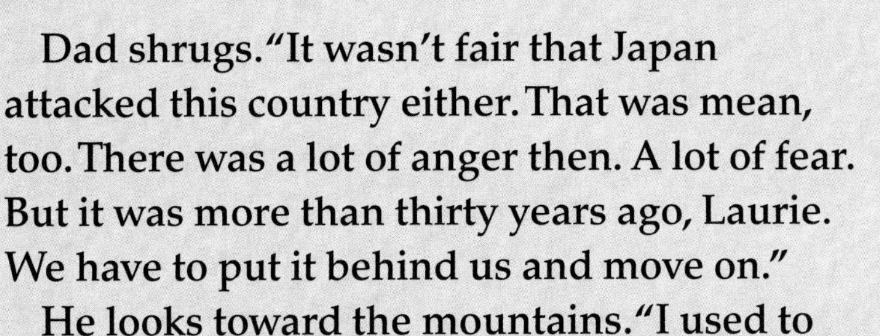

Dad shrugs. "It wasn't fair that Japan attacked this country either. That was mean, too. There was a lot of anger then. A lot of fear. But it was more than thirty years ago, Laurie. We have to put it behind us and move on."

He looks toward the mountains. "I used to watch those. They'd change with every season. In summer, at sunset, they were pink and a shadow like a giant eagle would fall across them. I'd wish I could climb on its back and fly away . . . far, far, away."

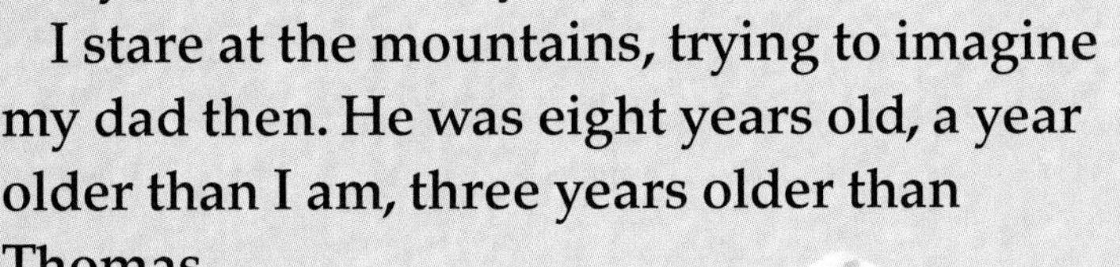

I stare at the mountains, trying to imagine my dad then. He was eight years old, a year older than I am, three years older than Thomas. . . .

"Look! Look! There's the monument," Thomas says, running ahead.

The monument is tall and thin and white. An obelisk, Dad calls it. It looks so weird standing out here in the middle of nothingness. On it, in black Japanese script, are the words MEMORIAL TO THE DEAD. It marks the cemetery that lies behind a wire fence.

We go in through an opening.

People have left offerings at the monument, held down by pieces of wood or stones. There are origami birds, their wings trapped under little rocks. A broken cup holds crumbs of a rice cake. There are bits of colored glass, some coins. A bare cherry tree branch is stuck inside one of the cracks in the base.

I turn my head and see my grandfather's grave among the others circled round with stones. He died in this camp. The doctors said it was from pneumonia, but my father says Grandfather began dying the day the soldiers came for them, to put them in buses and bring them here.

Grandfather was a tuna fisherman. He had his own boat, *Arigato*, which means "thank you" in Japanese. He was always thankful for his good life. My father never found out afterward what happened to the boat or to Grandmother and Grandfather's house. He said the government took those things and Grandfather's dignity along with them when they brought him here, so far from the sea.

Dad told me that while Grandfather was in the camp he went out every morning to check the sky and the clouds and smell the weather. "A good day for fishing," he'd say.

obelisk a pointed pillar

origami the Japanese art of folding paper

pneumonia a lung disease

Instead of a headstone, Grandfather has rocks piled one on top of the other like a small tower. His name, Shiro Iwasaki, and the date, 1943, are painted on the top stone.

Dad lifts away a tumbleweed that has blown inside the circle of rocks around the grave. Mom lays the flowers where the tumbleweed was, and Dad weighs their stems down with a heavy rock. We stand, looking at the purple and yellow and scarlet silk flowers against the brown dirt. Wind moves the petals.

Response Corner

1. Describe the fears and concerns that led the United States government to move Japanese Americans to relocation camps.
2. What do you think Laura's father meant when he told her that Grandfather began dying the day the soldiers brought him to the relocation camp?

Lesson 1

Time

1905 1945 1985

1911 California women gain the right to vote in state elections

1917 The United States enters World War I

1927 The first full-length movie with sound is released

Into a New Century

WHAT TO KNOW
What political, economic, and cultural developments occurred in California in the early 1900s?

- ✓ Explore the new industries that developed in California in the early 1900s.
- ✓ Trace California's political development in the early 1900s.

VOCABULARY
bribe p. 359
reform p. 359
amendment p. 359
suffrage p. 359
consumer goods p. 362
aviation p. 363

PEOPLE
Hiram Johnson
Caroline Severance
Louis B. Mayer

PLACES
Panama Canal
Hollywood

Focus Skill **CAUSE AND EFFECT**

California Standards
HSS 4.4, 4.4.6, 4.4.9

YOU ARE THERE The people around you are quiet, but the governor's voice booms with confidence. You are in Sacramento in 1910, listening to a speech by **Hiram Johnson**, the new governor of California. He promises to make the government more honest. He says that all Californians will have an equal say in how the state is run. You feel that a better time is coming for California.

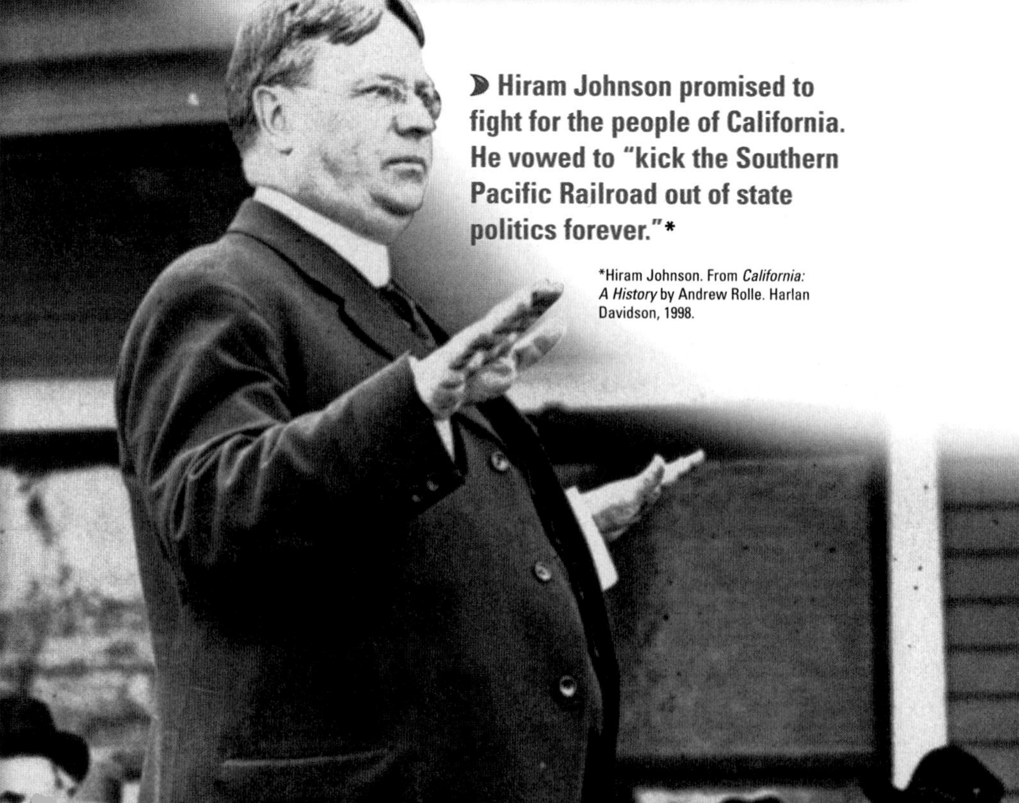

Hiram Johnson promised to fight for the people of California. He vowed to "kick the Southern Pacific Railroad out of state politics forever."*

*Hiram Johnson. From *California: A History* by Andrew Rolle. Harlan Davidson, 1998.

CITIZENSHIP

Democratic Values

Voting is a right that had to be won by many Americans.

The United States Constitution has been amended many times to approve suffrage for citizens. Amendment 15 made it unlawful for states to keep citizens from voting because they are not white, and Amendment 19 granted women the right to vote. In 1971, the 26th Amendment lowered the voting age from 21 to 18. Other laws have been written over the years to help citizens exercise the right to vote in fair elections. For example, the Voting Rights Act of 1965 was passed so that no state could tax or test citizens before allowing them to vote.

Leaders of the California Equal Suffrage Association march in Oakland in 1908.

Reforming the Government

In the early 1900s, the economy of California boomed. Yet some of the businesses that strengthened the economy also caused problems. Oil companies and other big businesses were very powerful. The government let them charge very high prices, and this gave them unfair advantages.

To get these advantages, business leaders often bribed government officials. To **bribe** is to promise or give a person money or a gift to get him or her to do something.

Some Californians wanted to **reform** the state government, or change it for the better. Electing Hiram Johnson as governor was their first step. Under Governor Johnson, Californians voted to accept 22 **amendments**, or changes, to the state constitution. The amendments gave the people more control over the state government.

In 1911, another important change happened. Women in California gained **suffrage**, or the right to vote, in state elections. **Caroline Severance** (SEH•vuh•ruhns) was the first woman to register, or sign up, to vote. She had been a leader in the suffrage movement, helping California become the sixth state to allow women to vote. Women would not win the right to vote in national elections until 1920.

READING CHECK **CAUSE AND EFFECT**
How were women in California affected by reforms in the state government?

The Panama Canal

For a long time, many people had dreamed of having a canal across the Isthmus of Panama to connect the Atlantic Ocean and the Pacific Ocean. In the late 1800s, France had tried, but failed, to build such a canal.

In 1903, the newly formed country of Panama gave the United States the right to build a 51-mile-long canal. Work began on the project in 1904, but construction of the canal was very difficult. Workers had to move tons of rock and dirt, clear thick rain forests, and battle diseases. It was not until 1914 that the **Panama Canal** opened.

Just as the transcontinental railroad had done earlier, the Panama Canal helped increase trade between California and the rest of the world. Ships no longer had to sail around South America to get from the Pacific Ocean to the Atlantic Ocean.

Californians especially were excited about the Panama Canal. The canal shortened the route between California and the East coast of the United States by more than 7,000 miles, and shortened the time to travel between the coasts to about a month. Also, many people in Los Angeles were happy that the canal would bring more ships to their city's new harbor.

READING CHECK **GENERALIZE**
How did the Panama Canal help the United States maintain its trade link with the Pacific Basin?

The battleship U.S.S. *Ohio* moves through the Panama Canal in 1915. To travel between the Pacific and Atlantic Oceans, ships passed through locks, such as Gatun Lock (inset).

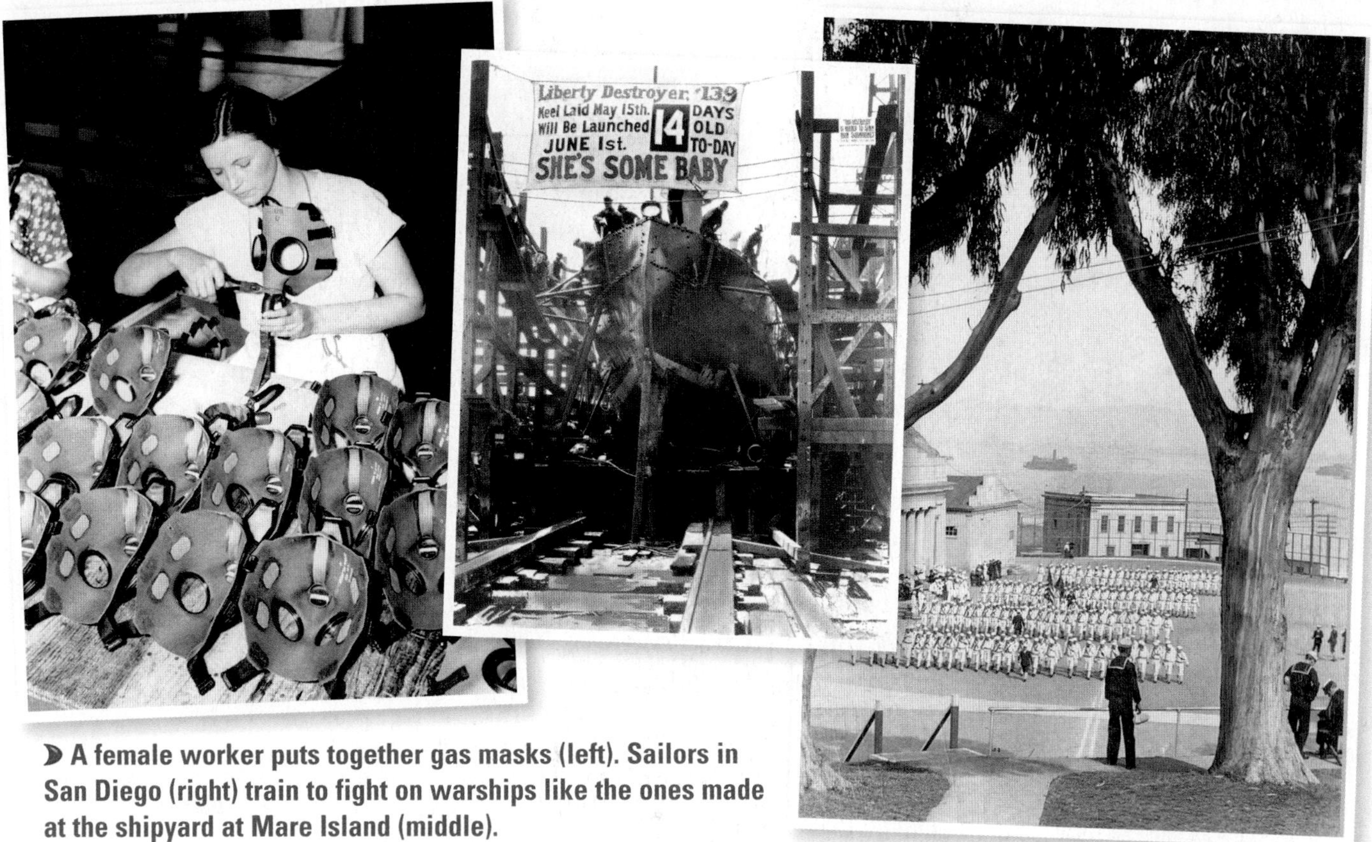

A female worker puts together gas masks (left). Sailors in San Diego (right) train to fight on warships like the ones made at the shipyard at Mare Island (middle).

A World War

The opening of the Panama Canal changed the shipping routes of the world. Soon, though, the world's attention was focused on something else—war in Europe. This war, which later became known as World War I, had begun in 1914. The United States did not enter the war until 1917, after Germany began attacking United States ships.

A famous song called Americans into battle with these words:

> **"Hear them calling,**
> **you and me,**
> **Every son of liberty,**
> **Hurry right away,**
> **No delay, go today . . ."***

Californians were among the many Americans who answered the call to service. Soldiers left their families to fight on the battlefields of Europe.

Californians who did not go overseas worked hard at home on farms and in factories. California supplied food, cotton for uniforms, oil for fuel, and ships. Some women joined the workforce, taking jobs left behind by men who had gone to fight.

As the demand for goods grew during the war, more workers were needed. Thousands of people moved to California to fill jobs. By the time the war ended in 1918, California's economy was stronger than ever.

READING CHECK **CAUSE AND EFFECT**
What effect did World War I have on the economy of California?

*From "Over There," a song written by George M. Cohan. 1917. www.loc.gov.

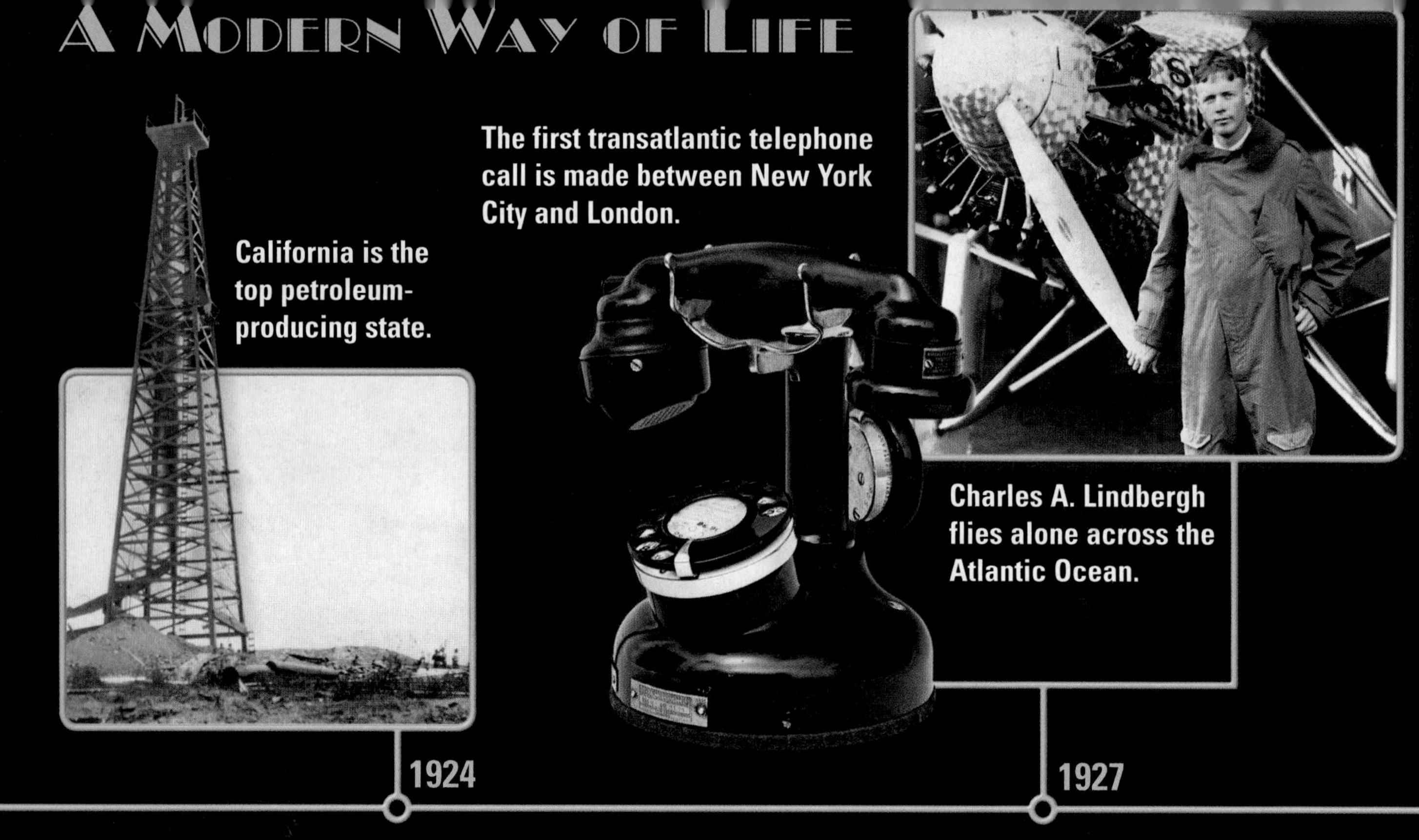

A MODERN WAY OF LIFE
California is the top petroleum-producing state.
The first transatlantic telephone call is made between New York City and London.
Charles A. Lindbergh flies alone across the Atlantic Ocean.
1924
1927

Changing Times

The years after World War I brought many changes in the ways people in California lived. New consumer goods changed ways of life at home. **Consumer goods** are products made for people to use. People in California and the rest of the United States began using new products such as vacuum cleaners, washing machines, and radios.

Another change in the way people lived was the growing popularity of the automobile. The first gasoline-powered automobiles were seen on California roads in the early 1900s. As cars became more affordable, it seemed as if everyone wanted one. By 1920, there were about 600,000 cars in California.

Californians were among the leading automobile consumers. By 1925 in Los Angeles, there was one car for every three people! The automobile changed the way people lived in California. People drove to work, to stores, and almost everywhere. They took long car trips with their families. Soon the government built a state highway system.

As more Americans bought and drove cars, the demand for oil grew, too. In the early 1900s, Californians were discovering huge deposits of oil in the southern part of the state. The oil industry in California became the biggest in the nation during the 1920s.

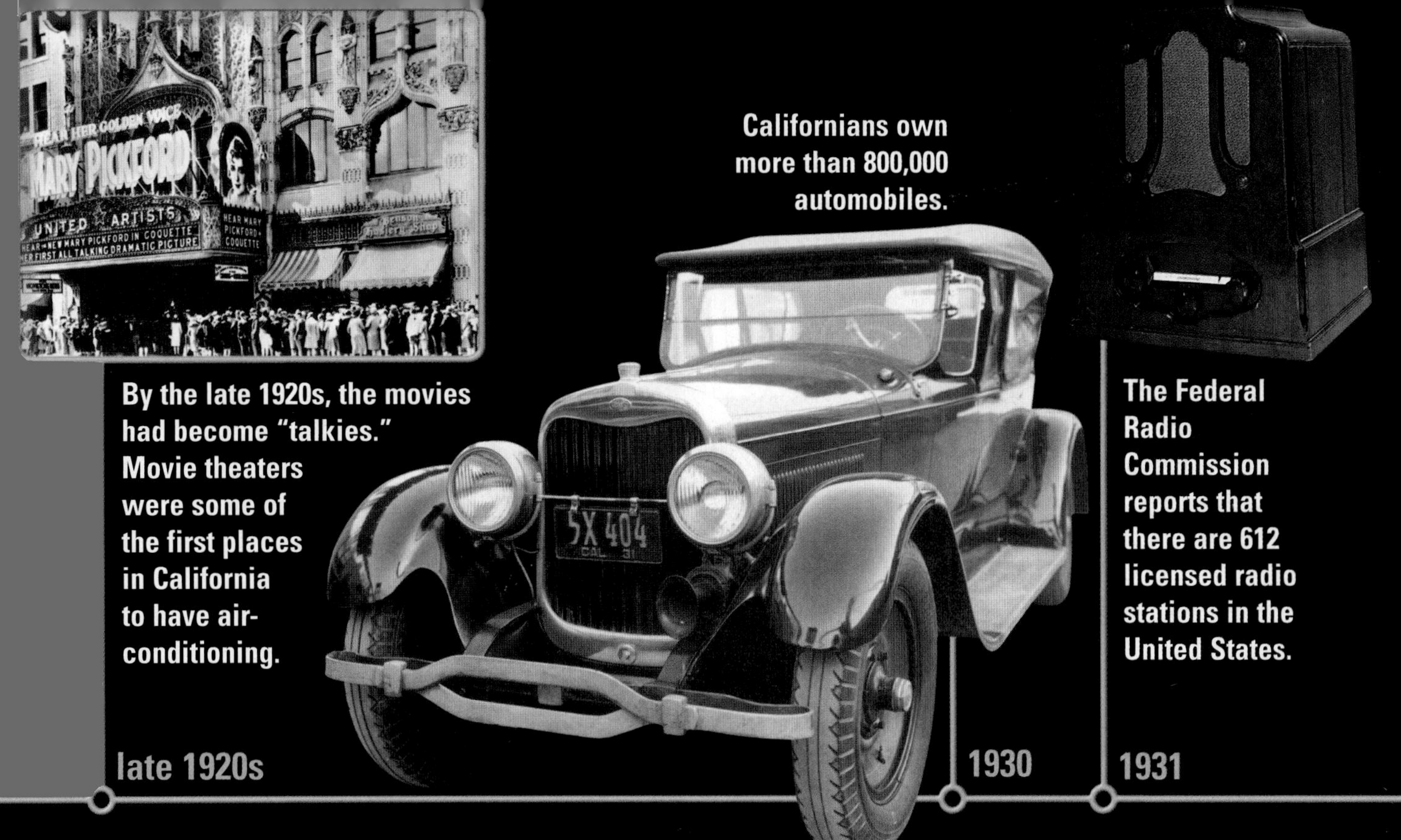

By the late 1920s, the movies had become "talkies." Movie theaters were some of the first places in California to have air-conditioning.

late 1920s

Californians own more than 800,000 automobiles.

1930

The Federal Radio Commission reports that there are 612 licensed radio stations in the United States.

1931

Another new industry also began to shape life in southern California in the early 1900s—the aviation (ay•vee•AY•shuhn) industry. **Aviation** is the making and flying of airplanes.

Because of its mild climate, southern California is a good place for making and testing airplanes. Pilots could test-fly planes during most of the year. In 1909, Glenn Martin built California's first airplane factory in Santa Ana. By the 1920s, four more top aircraft builders had factories near Los Angeles. By 1943, more than 280,000 people in southern California held jobs in the aviation industry.

READING CHECK GENERALIZE
How did southern California's climate lead to the development of the aviation industry there?

Movies Are a Hit

Moviemaking soon brought even more changes to southern California. In the early 1900s, movie cameras did not take good pictures indoors. Pictures taken outside looked better, and in California, people could film outside year-round. Southern California also had nearly every kind of landscape needed for the movies—mountains, valleys, deserts, and beaches.

The movie business grew quickly in the early 1900s. Many theater owners decided to replace live actors with films, which were less expensive. The first films were pictures with no sound, however.

One successful moviemaker was **Louis B. Mayer**. Starting with just one movie theater in 1907, he later headed a major film studio called Metro-Goldwyn-Mayer, or MGM.

In 1927, pictures with sound, also called talkies, made movies even more popular. Filmmaking soon became the state's top industry. Today, **Hollywood**, California, is the movie capital of the world.

READING CHECK **DRAW CONCLUSIONS**
Why would moviemakers like to film in a place that had many kinds of landscapes?

This director shouts instructions to his crew, filming in southern California in 1920.

Summary

In the early 1900s, Californians reformed their state government. The Panama Canal opened in 1914. During World War I, demand for goods boosted the economy. After the war, new industries grew in southern California.

REVIEW

1. What political, economic, and cultural developments occurred in California in the early 1900s?
2. How are the terms **reform** and **amendment** related?
3. How did geography affect the development of new industries in California?

CRITICAL THINKING

4. **SKILL** **Make It Relevant** What technological changes from the early 1900s are still a part of people's lives today?
5. **Write a Script** Work with a group to write a script about an event in California in the early 1900s. Read the script aloud for your classmates.
6. **CAUSE AND EFFECT** On a separate sheet of paper, copy and complete the graphic organizer below.

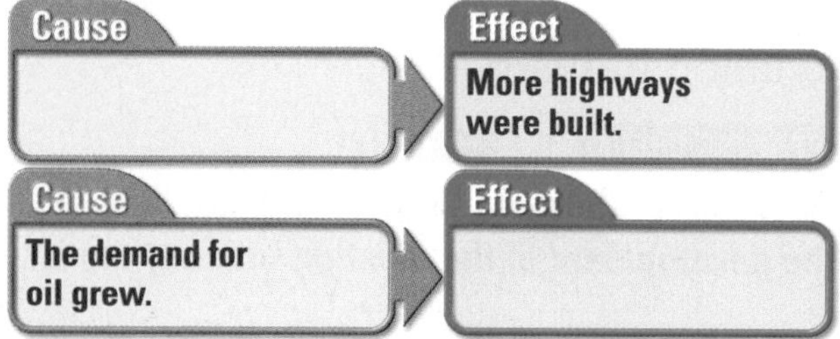
Cause
Effect
More highways were built.
Cause
The demand for oil grew.
Effect

Louis B. Mayer

Biography

Trustworthiness
Respect
Responsibility
Fairness
Caring
Patriotism

*"I will make only pictures that I won't be ashamed to have my children see."**

Louis B. Mayer was born in Russia in 1885. At the age of three, he moved with his parents to Canada. In 1904, Mayer moved to Massachusetts. It was there that he first entered the movie business.

Louis B. Mayer (right) with *Gone With the Wind* star Clark Gable (left)

In 1907, Mayer bought a small theater and began showing movies. Within a few years, he owned the largest chain of movie theaters in New England.

Mayer moved to California and started Louis B. Mayer Pictures in 1917. This moviemaking company later became part of Metro-Goldwyn-Mayer (MGM). At MGM, Mayer made some of the best-known films of the time, including *Ben-Hur* and *Grand Hotel*. Films such as these offered Americans a chance to escape into a world of adventure, music, and laughter. Going to the movies became a favorite pastime.

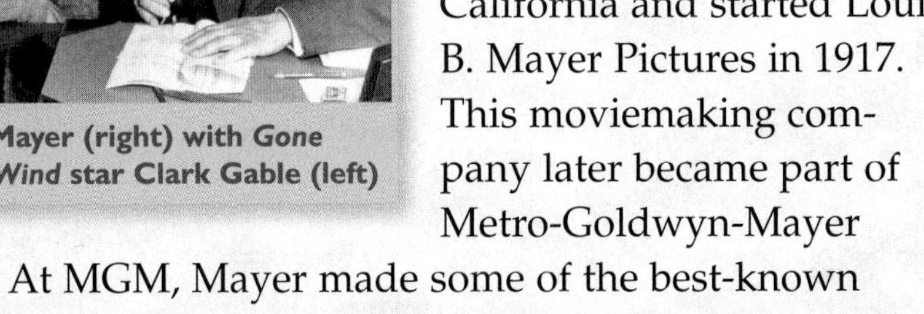

*Louis B. Mayer. From *Hollywood Rajah: The Life and Times of Louis B. Mayer* by Bosley Crowther. Holt, Rinehart, and Winston. 1960.

Why Character Counts

How does the quote show that Mayer was a responsible moviemaker?

Bio Brief

1885 Born

1907 Buys a small theater in Haverhill, Massachusetts

1917 Starts Louis B. Mayer Pictures in Hollywood, California

1924 Louis B. Mayer Pictures joins with Metro Pictures and Goldwyn Pictures to form MGM

1957 Died

GO ONLINE **Interactive Multimedia Biographies**
Visit MULTIMEDIA BIOGRAPHIES at www.harcourtschool.com/hss

PRIMARY SOURCES

Making Movies in California

At first, most films in the United States were made in New York City or New Jersey. During the early 1900s, however, some filmmakers discovered a much better place to make movies—southern California. The area's varied landscape and dry, warm climate let film directors make movies year-round.

Movie directors used megaphones to amplify their voices, or make them louder.

A poster advertising the movie *Swing Time*, which was released in 1936

Clapper boards like this one are used to identify a movie scene so that sound can later be added to it during editing.

ANALYSIS SKILL **Analyze Artifacts**

1. **Why do you think a director might need a megaphone?**
2. **How is the early movie camera similar to video cameras today? How is it different?**
3. **Who were the stars of *Swing Time*?**

GO ONLINE Visit PRIMARY SOURCES at **www.harcourtschool.com/hss**

An early movie camera

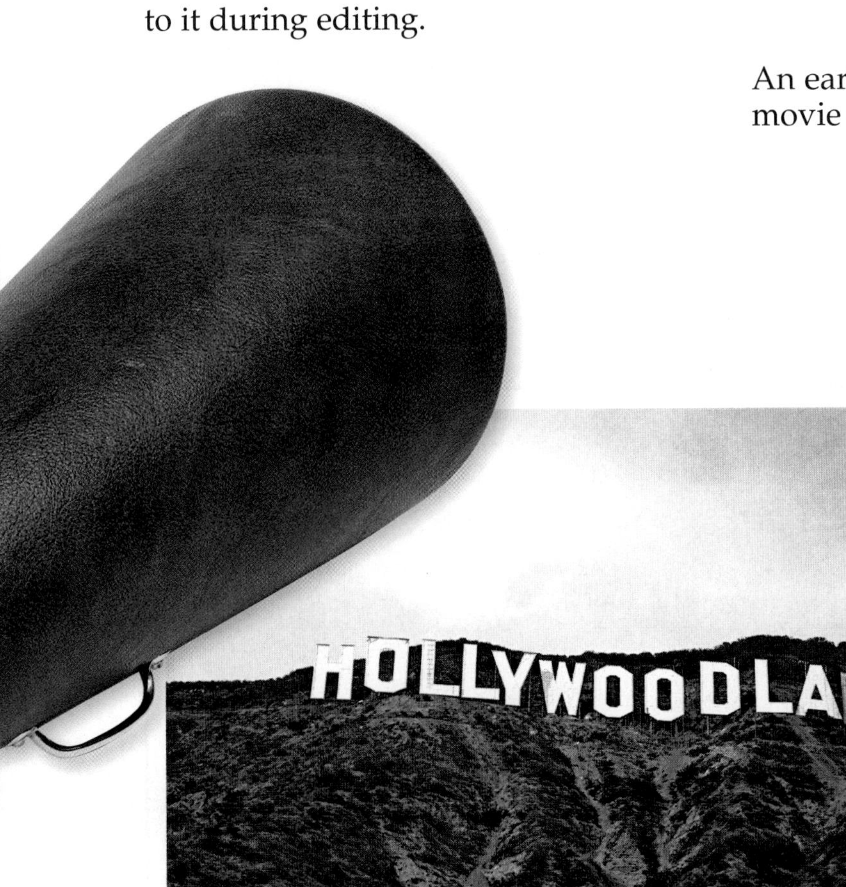

This famous symbol for Hollywood would later be shortened. In 1923, the sign was a real-estate advertisement.

Lesson 2

Time

1905 | 1945 | 1985

1929 The Great Depression begins

1932 Franklin D. Roosevelt is elected President

1933 Work begins on the Golden Gate Bridge

WHAT TO KNOW

How did the Great Depression and the Dust Bowl affect Californians?

- **Explore events that led up to the Great Depression.**
- **Describe the Dust Bowl.**
- **Tell how government programs helped Californians during the Great Depression.**

VOCABULARY

stock p. 369
depression p. 369
unemployment p. 369
migrant worker p. 371

PEOPLE

John Steinbeck
Joseph B. Strauss
Franklin D. Roosevelt
Dorothea Lange

PLACES

Dust Bowl
Golden Gate

CAUSE AND EFFECT

California Standards
HSS 4.4, 4.4.5, 4.4.9

Hard Times for Californians

YOU ARE THERE

On this cool morning in Los Angeles in 1930, you've counted at least 150 people waiting in line at the soup kitchen, where you are volunteering. The line stretches around the corner. Looking at your stack of sandwiches, you wonder whether there will be enough food for all the people who have lost their jobs and their homes since the stock market crashed last year.

The Great Depression

In California and across the United States, the 1920s brought good times for most people. Cities and businesses grew, and stocks went up in value. A **stock** is a share of ownership in a company.

To buy as many stocks as possible, many people borrowed from banks. Then, in October 1929, stock prices began to fall. Thousands of people across the country rushed to sell their stocks before the value fell even more. On October 29, stock prices fell so low that the drop was called a crash. Almost everyone who owned stocks lost money.

The stock market crash of 1929 led to an economic **depression** (dih•PREH•shuhn), a time when there are few jobs and people have little money. The depression that began in 1929 was so bad that it is known as the Great Depression.

Meanwhile, banks had been lending people too much money. As a result, many banks ran out of money and had to close. When the banks closed, people lost their savings. Because people had less money, they bought fewer goods. This caused many businesses to fail. Workers in those businesses then lost their jobs. For most of the 1930s, **unemployment**, or the number of workers without jobs, was high. In 1934, one out of every five workers in California was unemployed.

READING CHECK **CAUSE AND EFFECT**
What were some effects of the Great Depression?

Unemployed people are given a meal at the Los Angeles Plaza Church during the Great Depression. What other kinds of help would people have needed?

FAST FACT

At the start of the Great Depression, 1 million Americans were unemployed. By 1932, that number had grown to 12 million.

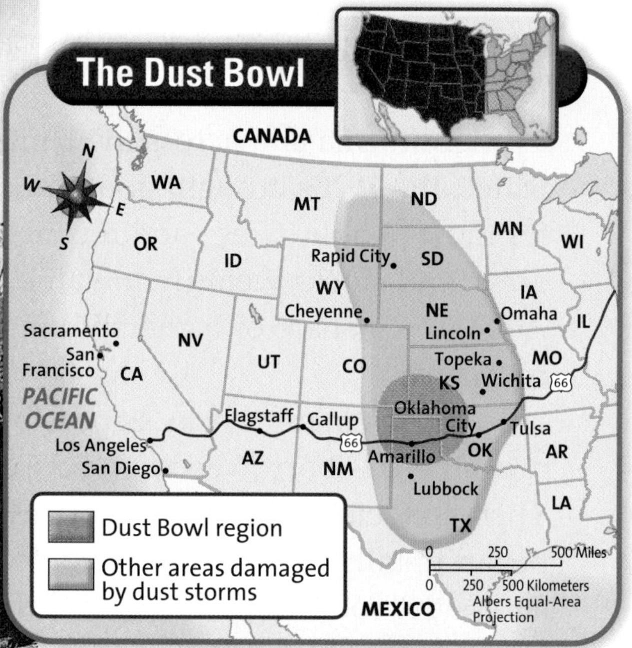

The Dust Bowl

CANADA
WA
MT
ND
MN
WI
OR
ID
Rapid City
SD
WY
Cheyenne
NE
IA
Omaha
IL
Sacramento
San Francisco
CA
NV
UT
CO
Lincoln
Topeka
MO
KS
Wichita
PACIFIC OCEAN
Flagstaff
Gallup
Oklahoma City
Tulsa
Los Angeles
San Diego
AZ
NM
Amarillo
OK
AR
Lubbock
LA
TX
MEXICO
0 250 500 Miles
0 250 500 Kilometers
Albers Equal-Area Projection

Dust Bowl region
Other areas damaged by dust storms

ANALYSIS SKILL Analyze Maps **About 350,000 people, including the family to the left, went to California to escape the Dust Bowl.**

Regions Parts of which states were in the Dust Bowl region?

The Dust Bowl

Farmers also suffered from the effects of the Great Depression, but soon things got even worse. In the early 1930s, a drought began in many of the farming states in the center of the country. The areas that suffered the worst drought were parts of Oklahoma, Texas, Kansas, Colorado, and New Mexico. The soil became so dry in some places that it turned to dust. Strong winds caused huge dust storms that blew away the dry soil in some areas. These areas became known as the **Dust Bowl**.

One of the worst dust storms happened in April 1935. The dust in the air turned the sky black, and the storm dumped so much dust on farms that crops were buried. Dust invaded the houses, blowing through every crack around windows and doors.

Many of the people who lived in the Dust Bowl wanted to leave. Many people in the Dust Bowl lost their homes and farms, and California

A camp for migrant workers in California

seemed like a good place to move to. Movies showed that the state had fertile fields and warm, sunny beaches. People said plenty of work could be found there.

During the middle and late 1930s, more than 100,000 people came to California each year. For many newcomers, life in California did not turn out as they had expected. Some Californians did not welcome them. California workers were afraid that the newcomers would take their jobs. Because some of the newcomers had come from Oklahoma, they were called Okies. Some Californians asked leaders to pass laws to keep Okies out of the state.

Most of the newcomers had been farmers. They hoped to find work in farming areas such as the Central Valley, but there were few steady jobs to be found. Many men, women, and children became **migrant workers** who moved from place to place, harvesting crops.

Migrant workers were paid very poorly. For working 16 hours a day, 7 days a week, they were paid about $4. Because they did not earn enough money to pay rent, some people set up tent camps. Others slept in cars and trucks or in shacks made from whatever they could find. They had little food and no running water in the camps. The dirty conditions in the camps made many people ill.

John Steinbeck wrote about these terrible conditions in his book *The Grapes of Wrath*, published in 1939. The book told of the unfair ways that migrant workers were treated in the San Joaquin Valley.

READING CHECK **CAUSE AND EFFECT**
What caused many farmers to move to California in the 1930s?

Children IN HISTORY

Weedpatch School

Look at your school. Could you and your friends have built it yourselves? That's what the children of Weedpatch Camp, near Bakersfield, did in 1940. The United States government had set up Weedpatch Camp for migrant families, but there was no school. With donated materials, the local superintendent of schools and the children of the camp built a school. Weedpatch School had classrooms, labs, a working farm, and a swimming pool.

Make It Relevant **What are some ways students can contribute to your school?**

The children of Weedpatch Camp made their classroom desks and chairs out of scrap lumber and orange crates.

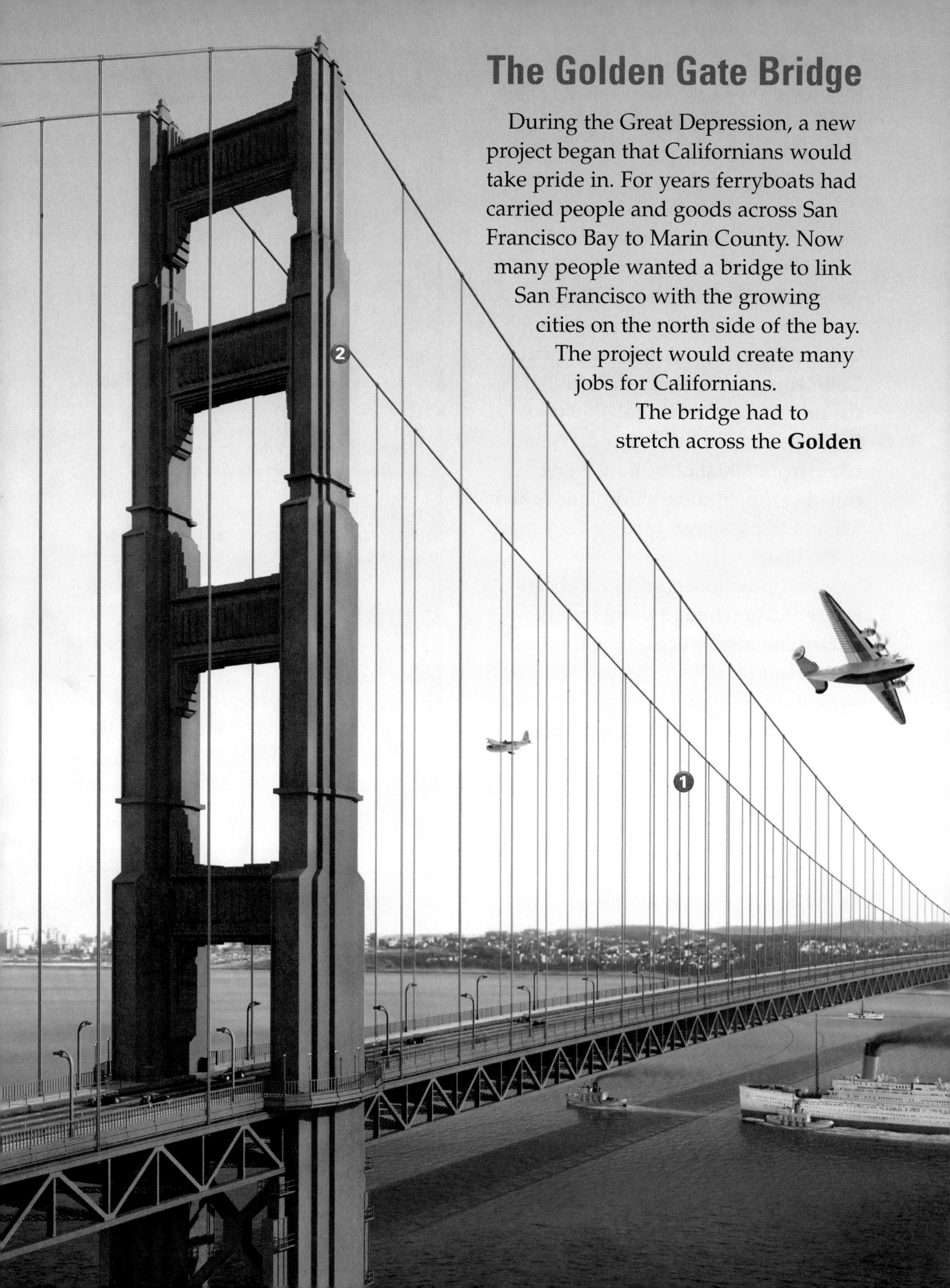

The Golden Gate Bridge

During the Great Depression, a new project began that Californians would take pride in. For years ferryboats had carried people and goods across San Francisco Bay to Marin County. Now many people wanted a bridge to link San Francisco with the growing cities on the north side of the bay. The project would create many jobs for Californians.

The bridge had to stretch across the **Golden**

Gate, a narrow body of water that connects San Francisco Bay to the Pacific Ocean. It took chief engineer **Joseph B. Strauss** and his crew of workers four years to complete the project.

Building the bridge was dangerous work. Hundreds of feet above the water, workers struggled with wind, rain, and fog. In fact, crews hung a safety net under the bridge, which saved the lives of 19 workers when they fell.

On May 27, 1937, a huge parade celebrated the completion of the Golden Gate Bridge. Almost two miles long, it was the longest bridge in the world at the time. A huge crowd of people walked across the bridge that day. The next day, it opened for automobiles. Since 1937, about 2 billion cars and other vehicles have crossed the Golden Gate Bridge.

READING CHECK **DRAW CONCLUSIONS**
How did the Golden Gate Bridge help Californians during the Great Depression?

Help for Californians

In addition to projects like the Golden Gate Bridge, United States government projects also helped workers in California. In his first speech as President, **Franklin D. Roosevelt** told Americans in 1933,

> **"The only thing we have to fear is fear itself. . . . Our greatest primary task is to put people to work."***

President Roosevelt had promised a "new deal" for Americans. The New Deal became the name for the programs that the government set up to help end the Great Depression. These programs gave people jobs building post offices, schools, and roads. One program hired people to plant trees and do other projects to help the environment.

Another program paid authors to write books and artists to paint murals

*Franklin D. Roosevelt. Inaugural Address. March 4, 1933. www.archives.gov

A Closer LOOK

The Golden Gate Bridge

Like all suspension bridges, the Golden Gate Bridge suspends—or hangs—a roadway from huge cables. These cables pass over high towers and are anchored on land at each end.

1. **If stretched out, the cables could wrap around Earth three times!**
2. **The 746-foot-high towers support most of the weight of the roadway.**
3. **The length of the bridge is 8,981 feet. The longest single span is 4,200 feet.**

Any bridge spanning the Golden Gate would have to withstand strong tides and winds. Why do you think a suspension bridge was the best kind of bridge to build across the Golden Gate?

on walls. **Dorothea Lange** took photographs of families escaping the Dust Bowl. Lange's photographs helped the government decide to help the farmworkers.

Under the New Deal, many people went to work on new water projects. One of these in California was the Central Valley Project, or CVP. This water project controlled floods on the Sacramento River and moved water to the San Joaquin Valley.

READING CHECK **SUMMARIZE**
Tell how New Deal programs helped California during the Great Depression.

The Friant-Kern Canal was part of the Cental Valley Project.

Summary

During the 1930s, the Great Depression made life difficult for people in California and the rest of the United States. Many people left the Dust Bowl and came to look for work in California. Government programs helped put people to work.

REVIEW

1. How did the Great Depression and the Dust Bowl affect Californians?
2. Use the term **unemployment** to describe the effects of a **depression**.
3. How did President Roosevelt think the New Deal programs would end the Great Depression?

CRITICAL THINKING

4. ANALYSIS SKILL What was the relationship between banks closing during the Great Depression and people losing their jobs?
5. **Write a Newspaper Article** Imagine that you are a Central Valley newspaper reporter. You have just met a migrant worker. Write an article about that person's journey and hopes for a new life.
6. Focus Skill **CAUSE AND EFFECT** On a separate sheet of paper, copy and complete the graphic organizer below.

Cause	Effect
Banks lent too much money.	
	People lost their savings.

Dorothea Lange

Biography

Trustworthiness
Respect
Responsibility
Fairness
Caring
Patriotism

*"She. . . seemed to know that my pictures might help her, and so she helped me."**

As a child, Dorothea Lange enjoyed watching people. This interest in people led to a successful career as a photographer.

When Lange was 19 years old, Arnold Genthe, a famous photographer, gave Lange her first camera. Soon after that, Lange started working for photographers in New York City. Then she moved to San Francisco and opened a photography studio.

Migrant Mother **is one of Dorothea Lange's most famous photographs.**

In 1935, the United States government hired Lange to photograph victims of the Dust Bowl and the Great Depression. Her photographs appeared in newspapers and magazines and showed Americans the suffering of the poor. Soon the government started programs to help migrant workers and other people in need.

*Dorothea Lange. Quoted in *Popular Photography*. February 1960.

Why Character Counts

How did Dorothea Lange show that she cared about the victims of the Dust Bowl?

Bio Brief

1895 Born

1919 Opens a photography studio

1935 Begins photographing rural Americans for the government

1940s Photographs Japanese American families in relocation camps

1965 Died

Interactive Multimedia Biographies
Visit MULTIMEDIA BIOGRAPHIES at www.harcourtschool.com/hss

GO ONLINE

Critical Thinking Skills

Make a Thoughtful Decision

WHY IT MATTERS

Every day, people make decisions, or choices. Some decisions are more important than others and require more thought. For example, you might not spend much time deciding what to eat for breakfast. However, you might spend a lot of time deciding what career you would like to have when you grow up. Difficult decisions take more thought because the choices may have lasting consequences. A **consequence** (KAHN•suh•kwens) is what happens because of an action. Many decisions made by people in history have consequences in your life today.

WHAT YOU NEED TO KNOW

Making wise decisions can help you reach your goals. To make a thoughtful decision, follow these steps.

Step 1 Make a list of choices to help you reach your goal.

Step 2 Gather the information you will need to make a good decision.

Step 3 Think about possible consequences of each choice. Decide which choice will have the best consequences.

Step 4 Put your decision into action.

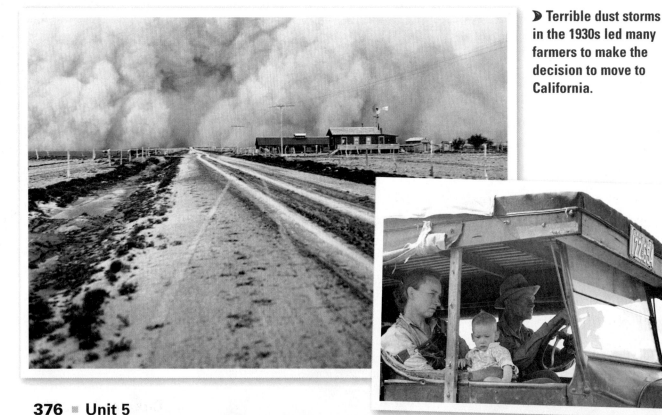

Terrible dust storms in the 1930s led many farmers to make the decision to move to California.

For many people, having to live in migrant camps was one consequence of moving to California.

PRACTICE THE SKILL

You have read that during the Great Depression, a terrible drought struck certain farming states. It created the Dust Bowl, where huge dust storms destroyed farms. Recall what many Dust Bowl farmers decided to do. Think about the challenges they faced as a result. Then answer these questions.

1. What problems did people living in the Dust Bowl area face?
2. Why did many of them decide to move to California? What other choices might they have had?
3. What were the advantages and disadvantages of moving to California? Do you think the advantages were greater than the disadvantages? Why or why not?

APPLY WHAT YOU LEARNED

Make It Relevant Recall an important decision you made recently at school. Think about how you made that decision. Identify your goals, the information you gathered, the choices available to you, and the consequences of each choice. Looking back, do you think that you made a wise decision? You may wish to share your thoughts with a classmate.

Lesson 3

Time

1905 | 1945 | 1985

1941 The United States enters World War II

1942 Japanese Americans are sent to relocation camps

1945 World War II ends

WHAT TO KNOW
What effects did World War II have on California and its people?

- Explain how California changed as a result of World War II.
- Discover where and why new industries started in California during World War II.

VOCABULARY
munitions p. 380
shortage p. 380
bracero p. 381
recycle p. 381
relocation camp p. 382

PEOPLE
Henry J. Kaiser
David Gonzales
James Doolittle

PLACES
Pearl Harbor
Fort Ord
Richmond
Tule Lake
Manzanar

CAUSE AND EFFECT

California Standards
HSS 4.4, 4.4.4, 4.4.5, 4.4.6

California and World War II

YOU ARE THERE It is an early December morning in 1941 on the island of Oahu (oh•AH•hoo), in Hawaii. As you gaze across the calm waters of **Pearl Harbor**, you hear the sound of airplanes coming. A line of planes zooms low overhead. You see the red circles on the wings and realize they are Japanese planes. Pearl Harbor is under attack!

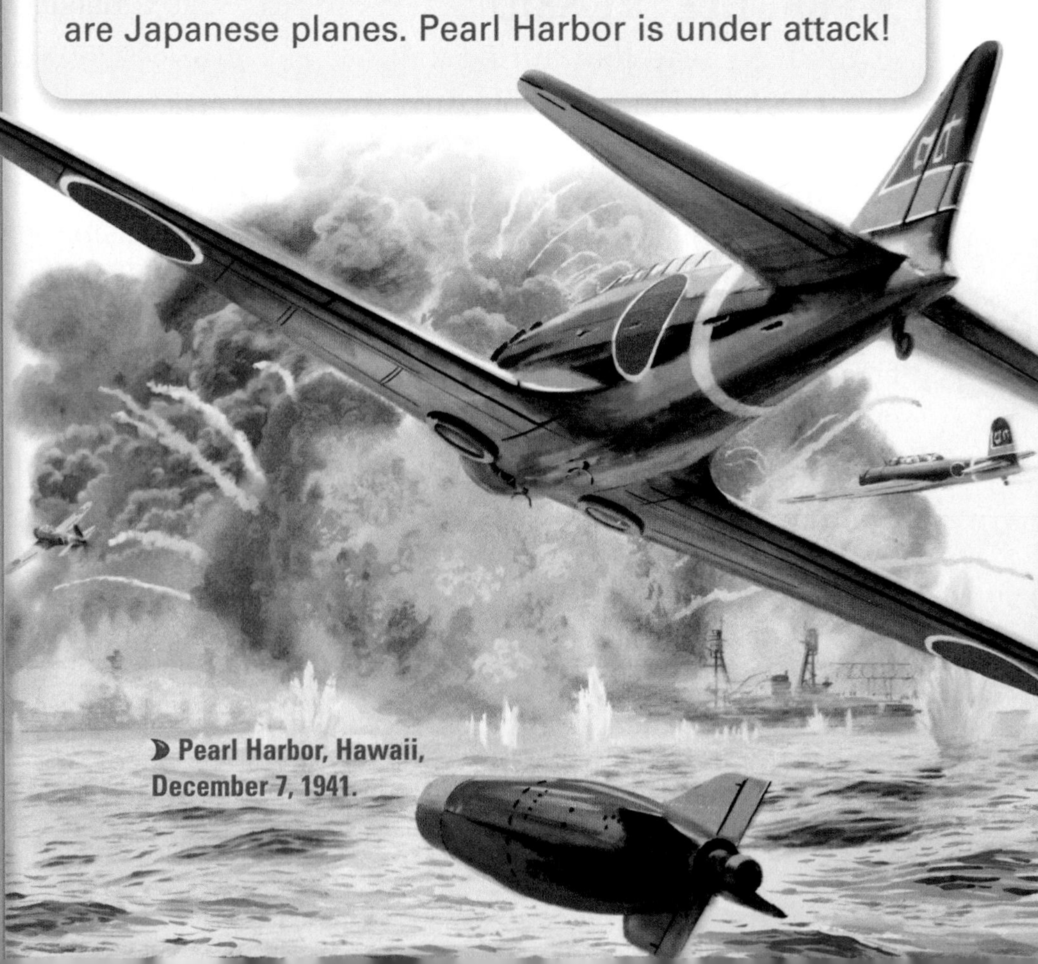
Pearl Harbor, Hawaii, December 7, 1941.

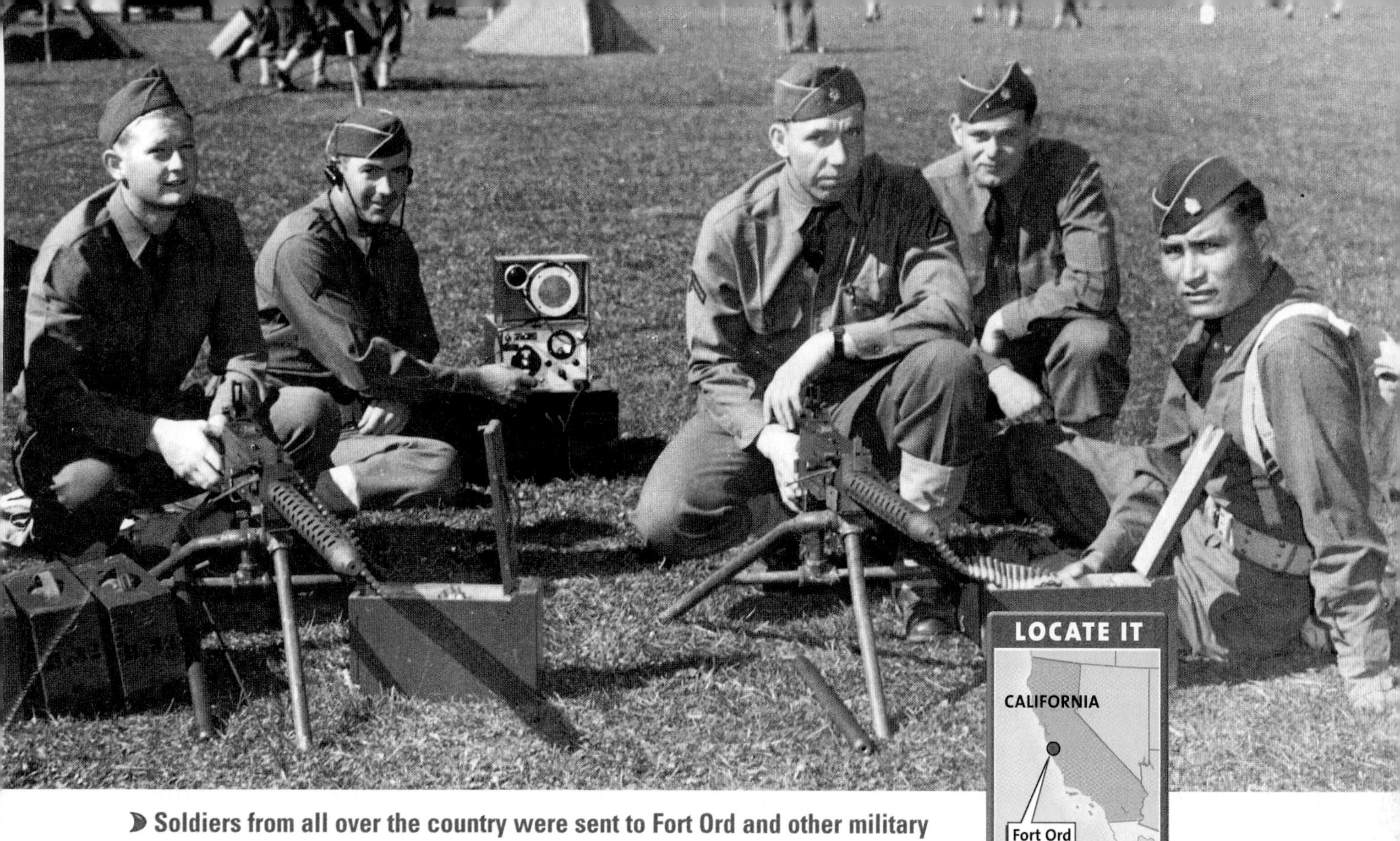

Soldiers from all over the country were sent to Fort Ord and other military bases in California for training.

World War II and Californians

Since 1939, many countries had been fighting in World War II. On one side were the Allies, made up of Britain, France, and later the Soviet Union. On the other side were the Axis Powers, made up of Germany, Italy, and Japan.

Until the Japanese attack on Pearl Harbor in 1941, the United States had stayed out of the war. During that surprise attack, Japanese bombs killed about 2,400 Americans and damaged or destroyed 21 ships and 347 aircraft. The next day, the United States declared war on Japan and entered World War II.

About 750,000 men and women from California joined the armed forces during World War II. Thousands went to fight in the South Pacific. Many others fought in North Africa and Europe.

Many soldiers were trained at military bases in California. Before the war, there had been only a few military bases in California. By the end of the war, there were dozens. **Fort Ord**, near Monterey, was one of the largest military training centers in the United States.

READING CHECK **CAUSE AND EFFECT**
What was one effect of World War II on California?

California provided troops to fight the war.

The War Effort at Home

While California soldiers, sailors, and pilots were away fighting the war, Californians at home were doing their part for the war effort. The United States needed ships and planes, and it needed factories to make **munitions** (myu•NIH•shuhnz), or military supplies and weapons. It also needed fuel for planes, ships, and tanks. Food was needed, too.

California helped meet all these needs. Oil companies went into full production. Aviation companies in southern California made old factories larger, and built new ones in Burbank, Santa Monica, Long Beach, and San Diego.

Shipbuilding, too, became a huge industry in California. One out of every four ships built during the war was made in California. Many of these were built in **Richmond** at a factory owned by **Henry J. Kaiser**. Kaiser had helped build the Shasta Dam, but during the war, he turned his attention to building ships.

There was a **shortage**, or lack, of enough local workers to build all the ships needed for the war. So Kaiser sent word across the country that workers were needed, and people came west by the thousands. Many of the newcomers who came to work in California were African Americans from the South. During the war, more than 300,000 African Americans came

▶ In aircraft factories, shipyards, and steel mills, women did much of the work of men who had left to fight the war.

World War II
1939
1941
1943
1945
1939
Germany invades Poland, marking the start of World War II
1941
The United States enters World War II
1944
The D-day invasion in France is a turning point in the war for the Allies
1945
Japan surrenders, and World War II ends
BOMBERS RAID MANILA
U. S. DECLARES WAR ON JAPAN

ANALYSIS SKILL Analyze Time Lines

For how many years was the United States involved in World War II?

to work in California shipyards and other industries.

Thousands of people went to work in the aviation industry. To meet the need for warplanes, aviation companies hired more than 200,000 new workers. As in other industries, a large number of the workers in the aviation factories were women. During the war, many women went to work outside the home for the first time. They worked in factories, steel mills, shipyards, and offices. They also ran family businesses and farms.

In 1942, the United States worked with Mexico to create the Bracero (brah•SER•oh) Program. This program brought **braceros**, or skilled Mexican workers, to California. These workers did much of the farm labor in California during the war and for years after.

Children helped in the war effort, too. They collected metal, rubber, paper, and other items that could be **recycled**, or used again, by the military.

With all the new workers coming to California to help in the war effort, the population grew quickly. During the war years, California's population grew by more than 2 million. Some cities, such as Los Angeles, became crowded because not enough new housing was built. Since building materials were needed for the war, those items were not available to people at home.

READING CHECK CAUSE AND EFFECT
How did World War II affect California's population?

Japanese Americans and the War

At the time of the attack on Pearl Harbor, about 125,000 people with Japanese ancestors lived in the United States. Most Japanese Americans lived in California. Many of them had been born in this country and were United States citizens. The attack on Pearl Harbor made them want to defend the United States. In fact, the Japanese American men of the 442nd Regimental Combat Team won more medals for bravery than any other group in the military.

However, many people in the United States feared that Japanese Americans would be loyal to Japan. In February 1942, the United States government ordered about 110,000 Japanese Americans to move to relocation camps. Each **relocation camp** was like a prison.

There were two camps in California. One camp was at **Tule Lake**, and one was at **Manzanar**, in the Owens Valley. The camps had been built quickly, and there was no heating or air-conditioning. Families shared laundry and bathing areas. Fences and barbed wire surrounded the camps.

Despite the conditions in the camps, Japanese Americans did their best to create homes there. They made furniture out of scraps of wood and metal. They started schools and sports teams.

READING CHECK GENERALIZE
Why were Japanese Americans in the United States sent to relocation camps?

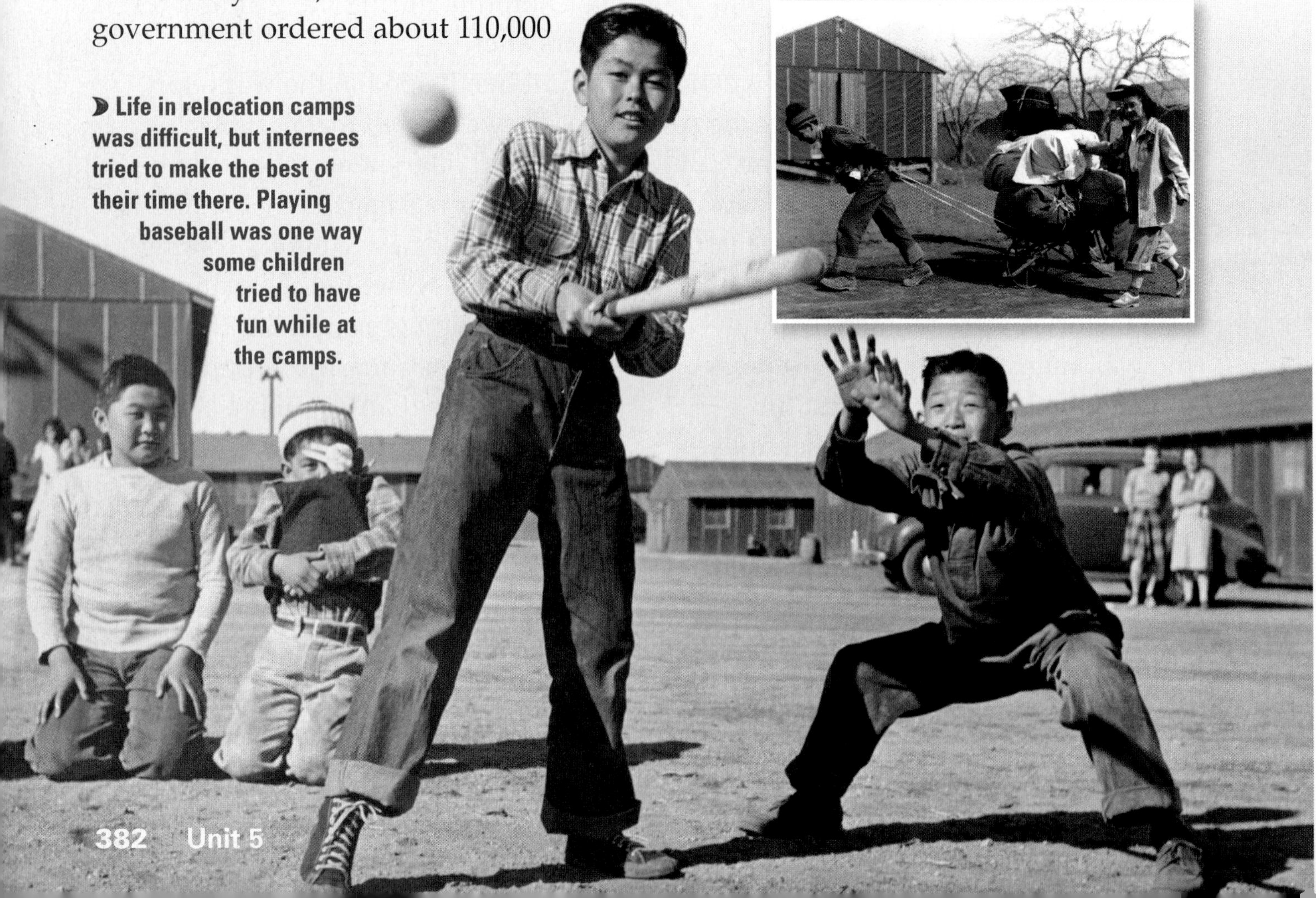

Life in relocation camps was difficult, but internees tried to make the best of their time there. Playing baseball was one way some children tried to have fun while at the camps.

The War Ends

By the end of the war in 1945, millions of people had been killed. Of about 400,000 Americans who died, more than 17,000 were from California. **David Gonzales** and **James Doolittle** were among the 13 soldiers from California who won the Congressional Medal of Honor, the highest military award in the United States.

For Japanese Americans, life after the war continued to be difficult. After being sent away to relocation camps, many Japanese Americans had no homes and no jobs. In 1990, the internees who were still alive received an apology from the United States government.

READING CHECK **DRAW CONCLUSIONS**
Why did life for Japanese Americans continue to be difficult after the war ended?

A soldier hugs his mother upon returning home to Los Angeles from the war.

Summary

Many Californians fought in World War II. Goods produced in California helped the war effort. During the war, California's Japanese Americans were held in relocation camps.

REVIEW

1. What effects did World War II have on California and its people?
2. Use the term **recycle** to explain how children helped support the war effort in World War II.
3. How did World War II affect workers in California?
4. What mistake from the past did the United States government apologize for in 1990?

CRITICAL THINKING

5. ANALYSIS SKILL Why do you think California was a good place for military bases during World War II?
6. **Create an Advertisement** During World War II, government advertisements encouraged people at home to help the war effort. Create an advertisement that encourages people to do an important job for the war.
7. Focus Skill **CAUSE AND EFFECT** On a separate sheet of paper, copy and complete the graphic organizer below.

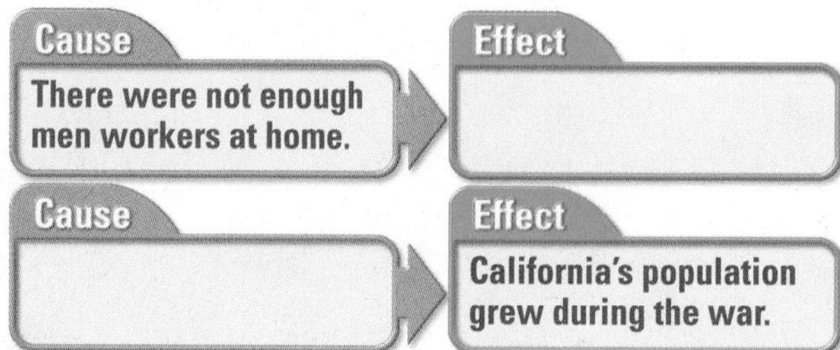

Cause
There were not enough men workers at home.
Effect
Cause
Effect
California's population grew during the war.

Relocation of Japanese Americans

People in the United States were divided over the treatment of Japanese Americans during World War II. Many people viewed the relocation camps as a necessary guarantee for safety against enemy attacks. Other people felt that the relocation was unfair treatment of fellow United States citizens. Here are some points of view about the relocation of Japanese Americans during World War II.

In Their Own Words

Central Japanese Association

"We want to live here [in the United States] in peace and harmony. Our people are 100% loyal to America."

—from a statement by the Central Japanese Association, 1941. *Encyclopedia of Japanese American History: An A-to-Z Reference from 1868 to the Present* by Brian Niiya. Facts on File, 2000.

Norman Mineta, Secretary of Transportation and former relocation camp detainee

NORMAN MINETA

“These camps were all barbed wire, guarded towers, searchlights. They were concentration camps [terrible prisons]. There's no question about it.”

—from *USA Today*, vol. 112, no. 2468, May 1984

JOHN RANKIN

John Rankin, former member of Congress

“I'm for catching every Japanese in America, Alaska, and Hawaii, now and putting them in concentration camps . . .”

—from the *Congressional Record*, December 15, 1941

San Francisco News

“Real danger would exist for all Japanese if they remained in the [war] area . . . the most [kind] way to insure against it is to move the Japanese out of harm's way . . .”

—from an editorial in the *San Francisco News*, March 6, 1942

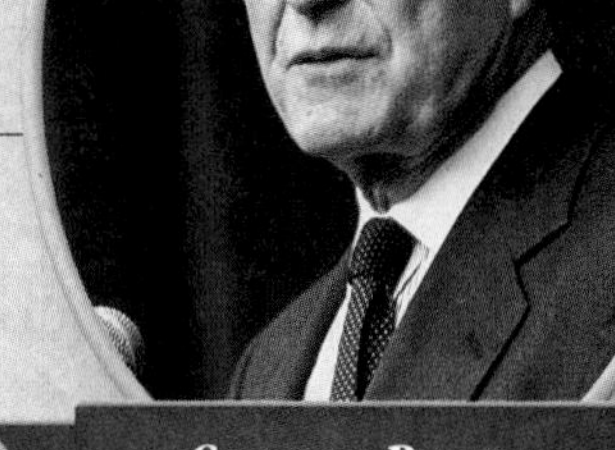
GEORGE BUSH

George Bush, former President of the United States

“We can never fully right the wrongs of the past. But we can . . . recognize that serious injustices were done to Japanese Americans during World War II.”

—from a letter of apology to Japanese Americans, 1990

It's Your Turn

ANALYSIS SKILL Analyze Points of View Discuss why you think each person or group held the view he or she did about the relocation of Japanese Americans.

Make It Relevant How do you think you might feel, as a citizen of the United States, if you were forced to live in a relocation camp?

1905

1915

1911
Women in California gain the right to vote in state elections

Reading Social Studies

A **cause** is an action or event that makes something happen. An **effect** is what happens as a result of an action or event.

Focus Skill Cause and Effect

Complete the graphic organizer below to show that you understand the causes and effects of change and growth in California from the early 1900s through World War II. A copy of this graphic organizer appears on page 103 of the Homework and Practice Book.

Growing and Changing

Cause	Effect
The stock market crashes on October 29, 1929.	
The United States enters World War II in 1941.	

California Writing Prompts

Write a Narrative Suppose you moved from the Middle West to California in the 1930s to work in a New Deal program. Write a letter to a relative telling about your new job and your life in California.

Write a Summary Imagine you are writing a script for a documentary film about California during World War II. In your script write a summary of the things Californians did to help with the war effort.

1925 1935 1945

1929 The Great Depression begins

1941 The United States enters World War II

1942 Japanese Americans are sent to relocation camps

Use Vocabulary

Write one or two sentences explaining how each pair of terms is related.

1. reform (p. 359), amendment (p. 359)
2. depression (p. 369), unemployment (p. 369)
3. migrant worker (p. 371), bracero (p. 381)
4. shortage (p. 380), recycle (p. 381)

Use the Time Line

ANALYSIS SKILL **Use the summary time line above to answer these questions.**

5. In what year did women gain the right to vote in California?
6. How many years after the beginning of the Great Depression did the United States enter World War II?

Apply Skills

Make a Thoughtful Decision

7. Some Californians asked leaders to pass laws to keep "Okies" out of the state. Imagine you are one of the leaders. What would you consider before making this decision?
8. Imagine you have been invited to come to California to work in an industry related to the war effort. What decision would you make? How and Why?

Recall Facts

Answer these questions.

9. Did the opening of the Panama Canal help or hurt California's economy?
10. What was life like in California during the Great Depression?
11. How were most Dust Bowl families treated when they arrived in California?

Write the letter of the best choice.

12. What helped attract filmmakers to southern California?
    A a reformed government
    B less expensive automobiles
    C the Golden Gate Bridge
    D a mild climate
13. What event caused the United States to enter World War II?
    A the Great Depression
    B the discovery of oil in California
    C the Japanese attack on Pearl Harbor
    D the stock market crash

Think Critically

14. ANALYSIS SKILL Why did Californians feel it was important to reform the government in the early 1900s?
15. ANALYSIS SKILL How might the point of view of many Japanese Americans about their treatment during World War II be different from the point of view held by many other Americans?

Study Skills

WRITE TO LEARN

Writing about what you read can help you understand and remember information.

- **Many students write about their reading in learning logs. The writing in a learning log can be both creative and personal.**
- **Writing about the text leads you to think about it.**
- **Writing your reactions to the text makes it more meaningful to you.**

Changes After World War II	
What I Learned	My Response
California's population grew when African Americans, braceros from Mexico, and soldiers returning from WWII decided to live in the state.	This probably made California's population more diverse.

Apply As You Read

As you read the chapter, pay attention to new and important information. Keep track of the information by completing a learning log for each lesson.

California History-Social Science Standards, Grade 4

4.4 Students explain how California became an agricultural and industrial power, tracing the transformation of the California economy and its political and cultural development since the 1850s.

CHAPTER 10

Into Modern Times

Freeways are a part of modern life in California.

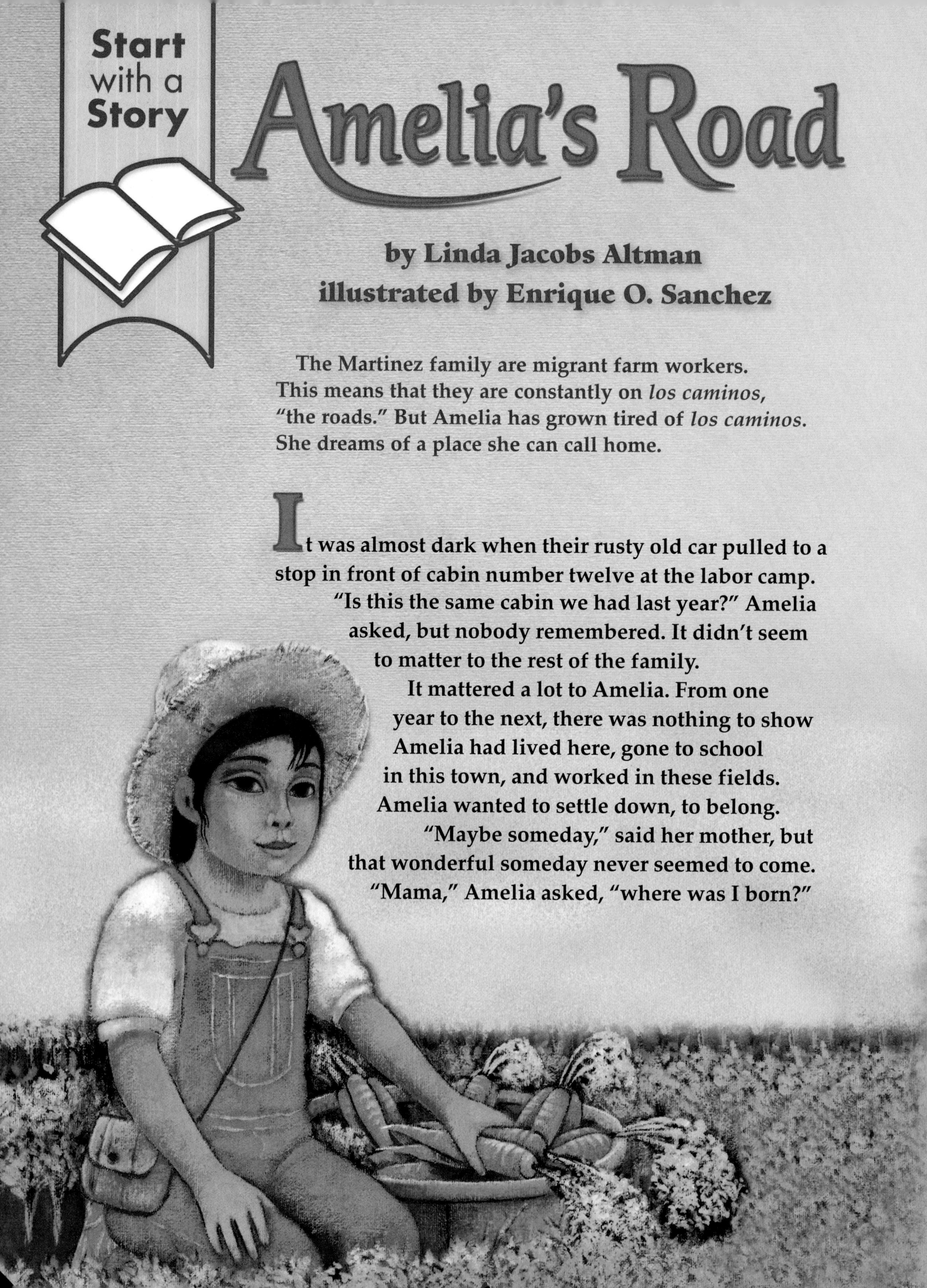

Start with a Story

Amelia's Road

by Linda Jacobs Altman
illustrated by Enrique O. Sanchez

The Martinez family are migrant farm workers. This means that they are constantly on *los caminos,* "the roads." But Amelia has grown tired of *los caminos.* She dreams of a place she can call home.

It was almost dark when their rusty old car pulled to a stop in front of cabin number twelve at the labor camp.

"Is this the same cabin we had last year?" Amelia asked, but nobody remembered. It didn't seem to matter to the rest of the family.

It mattered a lot to Amelia. From one year to the next, there was nothing to show Amelia had lived here, gone to school in this town, and worked in these fields. Amelia wanted to settle down, to belong.

"Maybe someday," said her mother, but that wonderful someday never seemed to come.

"Mama," Amelia asked, "where was I born?"

Mrs. Martinez paused for a moment and smiled. "Where? Let me see. Must have been in Yuba City. Because I remember we were picking peaches at the time."

"That's right. Peaches," said Mr. Martinez, "which means you were born in June."

Amelia sighed. Other fathers remembered days and dates. Hers remembered crops. Mr. Martinez marked all the important occasions of life by the never-ending rhythms of harvest.

The next day, everybody got up at dawn. From five to almost eight in the morning, Amelia and her family picked apples. Even though she still felt sleepy, Amelia had to be extra careful so she wouldn't bruise the fruit.

By the time she had finished her morning's work, Amelia's hand stung and her shoulders ached. She grabbed an apple and hurried off to school. . . .

This year, the teacher . . . welcomed all the new children to her classroom and gave them name tags to wear. She wore a tag herself. It said MRS. RAMOS.

Later, Mrs. Ramos asked the class to draw their dearest wishes. "Share with us something that's really special to you."

Amelia knew exactly what that would be. She drew a pretty white house with a great big tree in the front yard. When Amelia finished, Mrs. Ramos showed her picture to the whole class. Then she pasted a bright red star on the top.

By the end of the day, everybody in class had learned Amelia's name. Finally, here was a place where she wanted to stay.

Response Corner

1. How does the harvest affect the lives of the Martinez family?
2. Do you think that it is difficult for children of migrant farm workers, such as Amelia, to attend school? Explain.

Lesson 1

Time

1905 — 1945 — 1985

- **1947** California votes to create a statewide freeway system
- **1950** California's population reaches more than 10 million
- **1959** The silicon chip is invented

WHAT TO KNOW
How did California grow and change after World War II?

✓ Identify the reasons for the growth of California's population after World War II.

✓ Explain where and why some industries developed in California after the war.

VOCABULARY
- **diverse economy** p. 394
- **technology** p. 394
- **freeway** p. 395
- **commute** p. 395
- **urban sprawl** p. 395
- **high-tech** p. 396
- **silicon chip** p. 396
- **aerospace** p. 396

PEOPLE
Sally Ride

PLACES
Fremont
Pasadena

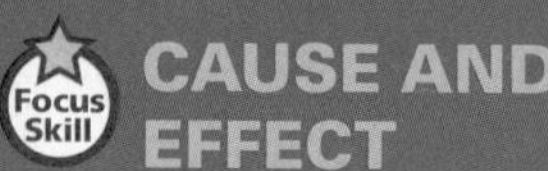

Focus Skill **CAUSE AND EFFECT**

California Standards
HSS 4.4, 4.4.4, 4.4.5, 4.4.6

Changes After World War II

YOU ARE THERE Gasoline is no longer in short supply, as it was during the war. Now it seems as if everyone is driving a new car, going everywhere. You hope that today your father will take the family in his new car to one of the new drive-in restaurants. Friends have told you that you can order food at the curb and eat inside the car! This is just one way life has changed since World War II ended.

In the 1940s and 1950s, many businesses in California took advantage of the growing popularity of automobiles.

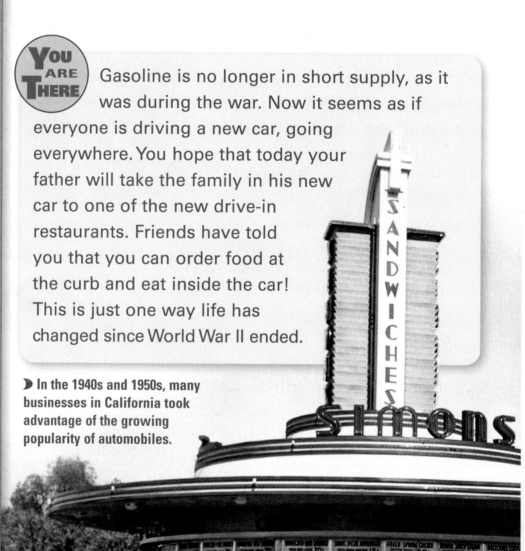

California Booms Again

In the years during and just after World War II, California's population grew quickly. In 1940, the state's population was almost 7 million. By 1950, that number had grown to more than 10 million.

Much of this growth had to do with the war. Many of the workers who had taken wartime jobs in California stayed in the state after the war ended. Among these workers were African Americans. Many people who had come from Mexico to plant, tend, and harvest crops in California also stayed. These braceros were not United States citizens when they came, but they played an important role in the strengthening of California's agricultural industry.

Analyze Graphs **Between 1940 and 1960, California's population more than doubled.**

By about how many people did California's population increase between 1940 and 1960?

In addition to drive-in restaurants, Californians could take their cars to drive-in movies.

Another increase in population occurred when about 300,000 members of the armed services came back to California from the war. Through the GI Bill of Rights, they could receive government money to go to college, to learn new job skills, and to pay for housing. Many stayed in California to start new lives.

The large population growth was a challenge for existing businesses, services, housing, and roads. At the same time, it provided the opportunity for California's economy to grow.

READING CHECK **CAUSE AND EFFECT**
What was the effect of World War II on California's population?

An Industrial Power

Before the war, California's aviation, shipbuilding, oil, and moviemaking industries were well developed. So was large-scale commercial agriculture. Using irrigation systems, farms in the Central and Imperial Valleys grew huge amounts of crops.

After World War II, the state's economy became more diverse. A **diverse economy** is one that is based on many industries. New industries made clothing, shoes, chemicals, refrigerators, and building materials, such as concrete.

The automobile industry grew quickly after World War II. New automobile factories opened in **Fremont**. By December 2002, a factory in Fremont had produced 5 million vehicles!

In Santa Clara County, the electronics industry grew. Stanford Research Park soon became home to companies that developed electronic technologies. **Technology** is the use of knowledge or tools to make or do something.

These new industries led to a boom in construction. Industries needed factories and office buildings, and the people who worked in them needed places to live and shop. Workers built new houses, schools, and office buildings. Other workers built reservoirs, dams, and power plants to make electricity and provide water.

READING CHECK **CAUSE AND EFFECT**
What led to a construction boom in California after World War II?

Workers at the Hughes Aircraft Company in Culver City completed the *Hercules* seaplane in 1947. It is still one of the largest planes ever built.

FAST FACT

The *Hercules* was nicknamed the "Spruce Goose" because it was built mostly of wood. The plane was flown only once, on November 2, 1947. The flight lasted about one minute and covered a distance of about one mile.

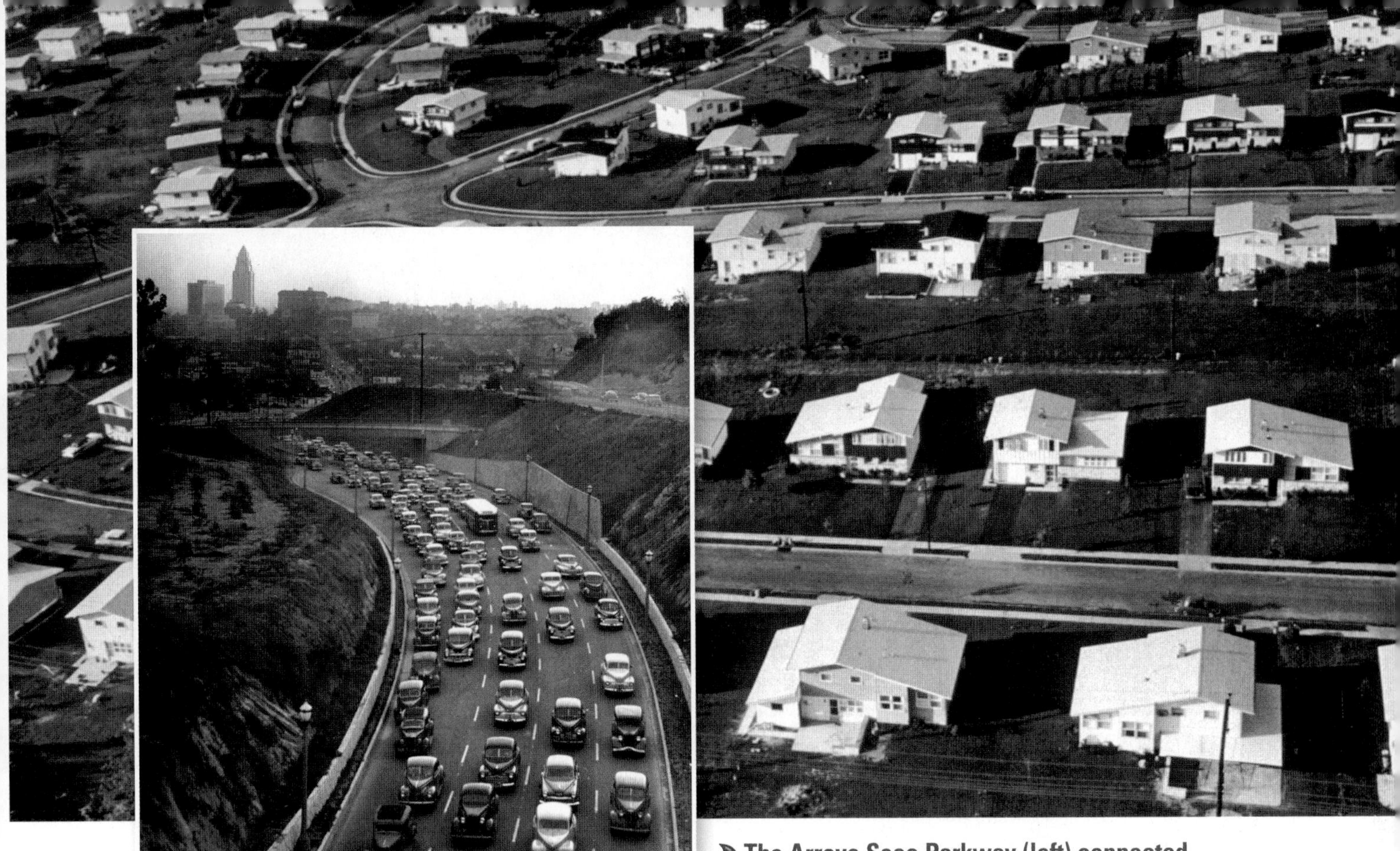

The Arroyo Seco Parkway (left) connected subdivisions like the one above to Los Angeles.

Californians on the Move

When the Arroyo Seco (uh•ROY•oh SEH•koh) Parkway opened in 1940, it began a new chapter in California history. The parkway became known as the Pasadena Freeway, the state's first **freeway**. There are no tolls, or charges, on this wide, divided highway, and traffic moves quickly.

During World War II, few major roads were built in California. Car traffic began to increase, and by the time the war ended, California had about 3 million cars on its highways. In 1947, state lawmakers voted to create a 12,500-mile freeway system. The system would connect the state's largest cities and metropolitan areas. The new freeways allowed workers to easily **commute**, or travel between work and home. As a result, workers could live farther from their jobs.

Near cities, California builders constructed whole communities at once. Some of these communities, also called subdivisions, had hundreds of houses that looked almost alike. Communities began to spread out and away from urban centers, and huge suburbs grew up near cities such as Los Angeles. The result was **urban sprawl**, or the outward spread of urban areas.

READING CHECK **CAUSE AND EFFECT**
What caused the rapid spread of urban areas in California in the late 1940s?

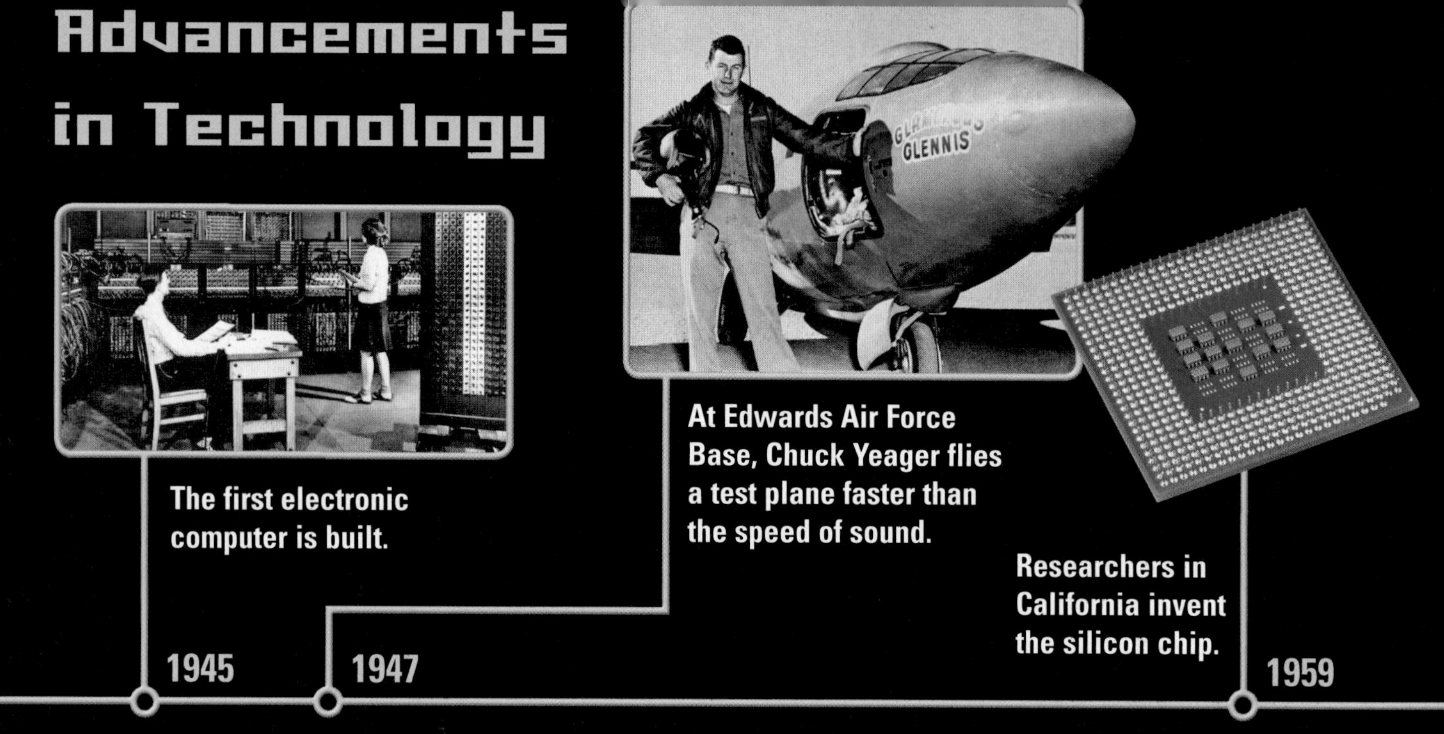

Advancements in Technology
GLAMOROUS GLENNIS
The first electronic computer is built.
1945
At Edwards Air Force Base, Chuck Yeager flies a test plane faster than the speed of sound.
1947
Researchers in California invent the silicon chip.
1959

Into the Space Age

When World War II ended, the defense industry—military bases and the factories that made supplies for them—remained important to California's economy. Many scientists stayed in California after the war to develop computers, jet planes, and other new advancements. Edwards Air Force Base, in Kern County, soon became a major testing ground for new jets.

Other scientists went to work in the many new high-tech industries in California, such as the communications industry. **High-tech** industries are those that invent, build, or use computers and other kinds of electronic equipment. More than 200 high-tech electronic companies opened in the San Francisco area alone.

In 1959, another big advance in technology occurred. Researchers in California invented the **silicon chip**. The chip is a tiny device that can store millions of bits of information. Silicon chips made computers smaller, faster, and less expensive to make and buy.

New computers and jets soon made travel in space possible. Scientists in California were leaders in starting the **aerospace** (AYR•oh•spays) industry, which builds and tests equipment for air and space travel. During the 1950s, Sacramento became home to the nation's largest rocket-engine testing and development site.

In 1966, scientists at the Jet Propulsion (pruh•PUHL•shuhn) Laboratory, in **Pasadena**, guided an uncrewed spacecraft to land on the moon. Three years later, they helped astronauts reach the moon.

The crew of *Apollo 11* lands on the moon.

1969

Steve Jobs and Steve Wozniak start one of the first successful personal computer companies.

1976

The space shuttle program begins.

1981

In 1983, **Sally Ride**, who was born in California, became the first American woman to travel in space.

READING CHECK **CAUSE AND EFFECT**
How did developments in technology create new industries in California?

Summary

During and after World War II, California's population grew. Scientists made great advances in the aerospace and computer industries.

REVIEW

1. How did California grow and change after World War II?
2. Explain how the **aerospace** industry became a **high-tech** industry.
3. Why did building freeways in California become important after World War II?

CRITICAL THINKING

4. ANALYSIS SKILL **Make It Relevant** How are the communities built in the 1940s and 1950s like many communities today?
5. How did population growth create both challenges and opportunities for California after World War II?
6. **Write a Brochure** You are the mayor of a California city in the 1950s. Write a brochure to get out-of-state workers to move to your city.
7. Focus Skill **CAUSE AND EFFECT** On a separate sheet of paper, copy and complete the graphic organizer below.

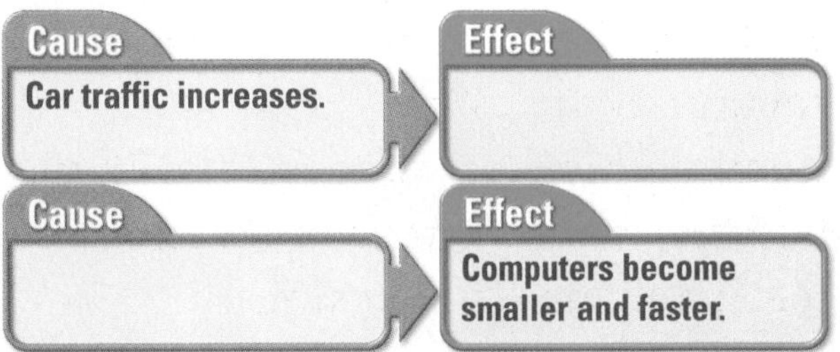

Cause	Effect
Car traffic increases.	
	Computers become smaller and faster.

Map and Globe Skills

Read a Road Map

WHY IT MATTERS

When people plan trips by car, they often use road maps. A road map shows more than just the roads that are between places. It also tells how far it is between the places. Knowing distances can help people choose the best routes to take from place to place.

WHAT YOU NEED TO KNOW

A road map usually includes an index to help you locate places. Imagine that you want to find Bakersfield on the road map on page 399. Find Bakersfield in the index. Next to Bakersfield, you'll see *E-3*. Bakersfield is located near where *E* across and *3* down meet.

On many road maps, highways are marked with small wedges called distance markers. The number between two wedges is the distance covered in miles by that section of the road. To figure out the distance from one place to another, add up the distances of all the sections of road between the two places.

PRACTICE THE SKILL

Use the road map on page 399 to answer the questions.

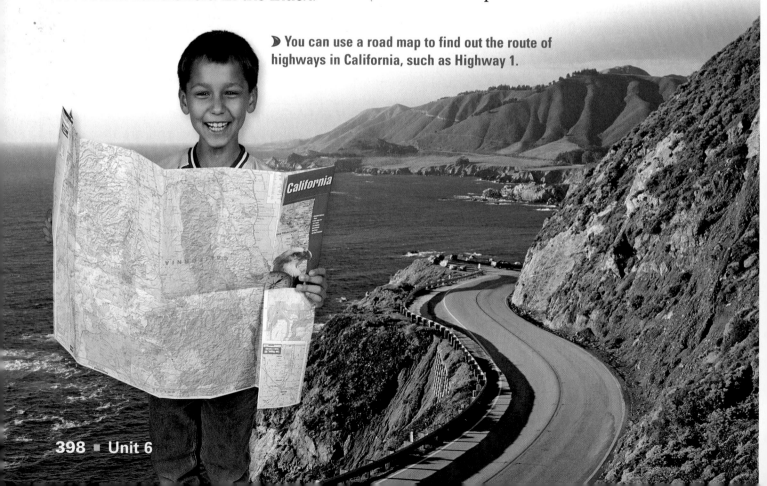

You can use a road map to find out the route of highways in California, such as Highway 1.

1. Use the index to find San Jose and Los Angeles on the map. Which interstate highway would you use to drive between these two cities?
2. Which road would you take to get from Fresno to Bakersfield? What is the distance?

APPLY WHAT YOU LEARNED

ANALYSIS SKILL Plan a road trip between two places in California. Use a road map to decide the best routes and figure out the distance in miles.

Practice your map and globe skills with the **GeoSkills CD-ROM**.

Road Map of California

Interstate highway
United States highway
State highway
★ State capital
Metropolitan area
23 Distance (in miles)

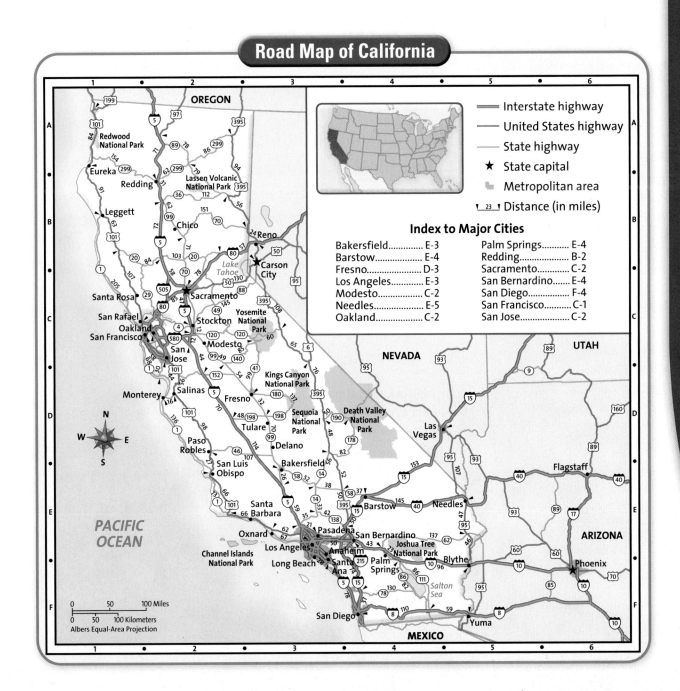

Index to Major Cities

City	Grid	City	Grid
Bakersfield	E-3	Palm Springs	E-4
Barstow	E-4	Redding	B-2
Fresno	D-3	Sacramento	C-2
Los Angeles	E-3	San Bernardino	E-4
Modesto	C-2	San Diego	F-4
Needles	E-5	San Francisco	C-1
Oakland	C-2	San Jose	C-2

OREGON
NEVADA
UTAH
ARIZONA
MEXICO
PACIFIC OCEAN

0 50 100 Miles
0 50 100 Kilometers
Albers Equal-Area Projection

Lesson 2

1905 1945 1985

1965 Cesar Chavez leads a nationwide boycott of grapes

1969 American Indians take over Alcatraz Island in San Francisco Bay

WHAT TO KNOW
How did California change as groups worked to secure equal rights?

- Describe the struggle for equal rights.
- Analyze the effects of the Civil Rights movement in California.

VOCABULARY
segregation p. 401
civil rights p. 401
labor union p. 402
strike p. 403
boycott p. 403

PEOPLE
Martin Luther King, Jr.
Sylvia Mendez
Jackie Robinson
Cesar Chavez
Dolores Huerta
Yvonne Brathwaite Burke
Dalip Singh Saund

PLACES
Delano
Alcatraz Island

CAUSE AND EFFECT

California Standards
HSS 4.4, 4.4.6, 4.4.8

Rights for All Californians

YOU ARE THERE You're a student at the University of California, Berkeley. It's 1957. **Dr. Martin Luther King, Jr.**, a minister from Georgia, is giving a speech. He tells the audience that he believes all people should have equal rights under the law. "We have a great opportunity in America to build here a great nation, a nation where all men live together as brothers. . . . We must keep moving toward that goal."*

*Martin Luther King, Jr. From a speech given at the University of California at Berkeley, June 4, 1957.

Dr. Martin Luther King, Jr., came to California several times to speak about equal rights for all people.

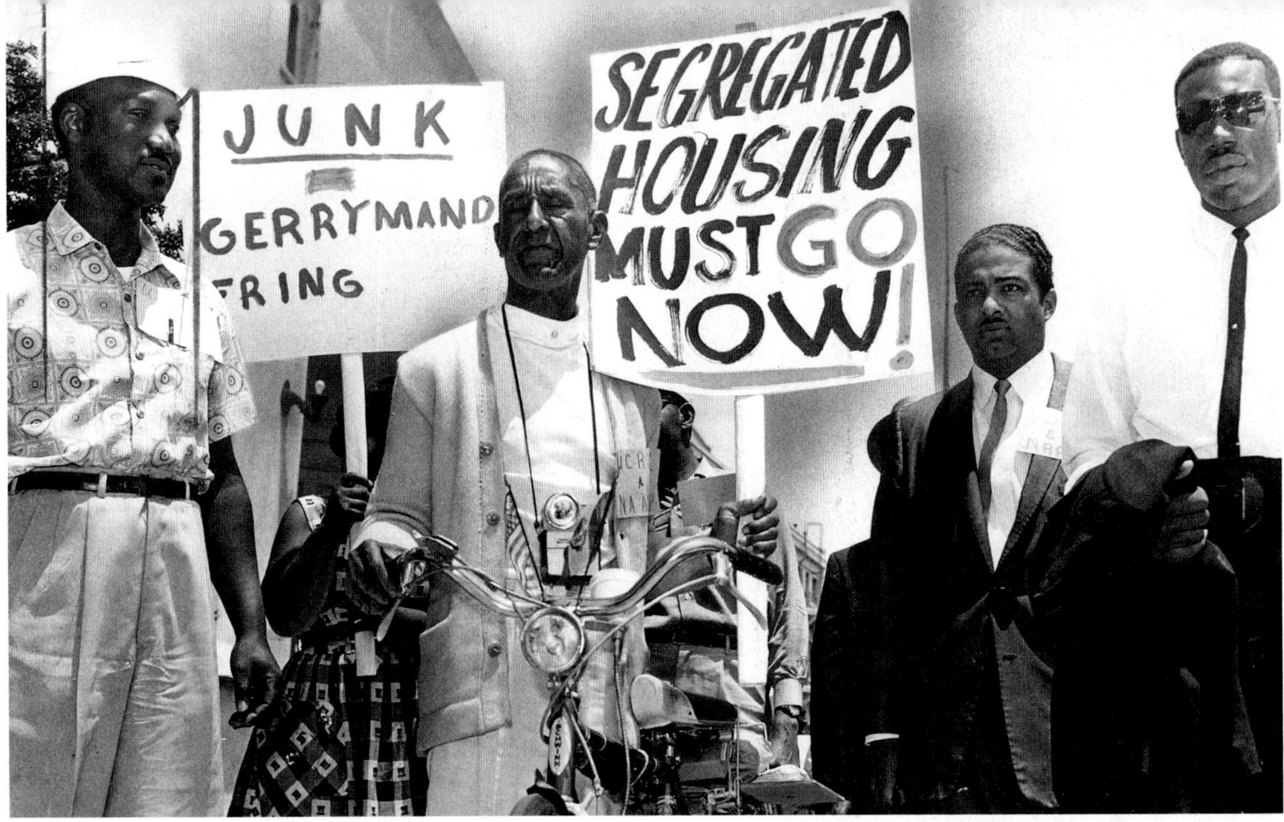

Californians fought for fair housing laws.

Confronting Discrimination

California's economy boomed after World War II, but not all people enjoyed the same opportunities. Throughout the United States, some groups, such as Latinos, African Americans, and Asian Americans, continued to face discrimination. They were often kept out of higher-paying jobs, and they were not allowed to live in certain neighborhoods. Because of this **segregation**, their children often went to poor schools.

In 1944, the parents of **Sylvia Mendez** wanted to send her to a public school in Westminster, California, but only white children attended this school. When Sylvia's parents were told she could not attend because she was Mexican American, they sued the school district and won. Segregation in California schools ended the next year.

In 1947, **Jackie Robinson**, who had grown up in Pasadena, became the first African American to play major-league baseball. This helped end segregation in professional sports.

During the 1950s and 1960s, more people joined the Civil Rights movement. **Civil rights** are the rights of citizens to equal treatment. One of the movement's leaders was Dr. Martin Luther King, Jr. He led peaceful protests to bring attention to the lack of civil rights. In time, leaders who supported civil rights were elected, and more civil rights laws were passed.

READING CHECK **CAUSE AND EFFECT**
How did California's school system change in the 1940s?

A UFW Poster

Analyze Posters (ANALYSIS SKILL)

This 1978 poster calls for people to boycott lettuce and grapes.

1. **On the sun is the UFW symbol.**
2. **Farmworkers work in a lettuce field.**

◆ **What do you think the sun with the UFW symbol represents?**

Migrant Farmworkers

In the Central Valley and elsewhere, farmworkers also faced discrimination. In general, these workers and their families—many of them Latinos—had been treated unfairly for many years. Laws in the early 1960s set wages at a minimum of $1.25 per hour. Most farmworkers were paid about 90 cents per hour.

Then, in 1962, **Cesar Chavez** (SAY•zar CHAH•vez), **Dolores Huerta** (doh•LOH•res HWAIR•tah), and others formed a labor union. A **labor union** is an organization of workers.

▶ **Cesar Chavez led a march in support of the grape pickers strike in 1965.**

Dolores Huerta

Yvonne Brathwaite Burke

Dalip Singh Saund

The goal of the labor union was to improve farmworkers' lives. The National Farm Workers Association, which later became the United Farm Workers (UFW), organized workers to push for higher pay, improved housing, and better working conditions.

In 1965, Chavez led a strike of grape pickers in the Central Valley town of **Delano**. A **strike** is when workers stop working to get employers to listen to their needs.

Chavez also called for a boycott of grapes. A **boycott** is a decision by a group of people not to buy something until a certain problem is fixed. It is a form of protest. As more people across the country joined the boycott, the grape growers began to lose money. Finally, in 1970, the growers agreed to give the workers more pay and better working conditions. The workers' strike and the grape boycott were a success.

READING CHECK **CAUSE AND EFFECT**
What effect did the boycott have on grape growers in California?

Civil Rights for Other Groups

By the 1960s, women, like other groups, had joined the fight for equal rights. In 1972, **Yvonne Brathwaite Burke** became the first African American woman from California elected to the United States House of Representatives. Soon Asian American and Latino women from California were elected to positions in government. In 1993, California became the first state to have only women—Barbara Boxer and Dianne Feinstein—represent it in the United States Senate.

Asian groups faced discrimination, too. Until 1952, people from Asian countries were not allowed to become United States citizens. During the 1940s, **Dalip Singh Saund,** a Sikh immigrant from India, worked to change that law. In 1956, Saund became the first Sikh and first Asian American member of Congress.

▶ **The Indians who took over Alcatraz Island in 1969 called their group "Indians of All Tribes."**

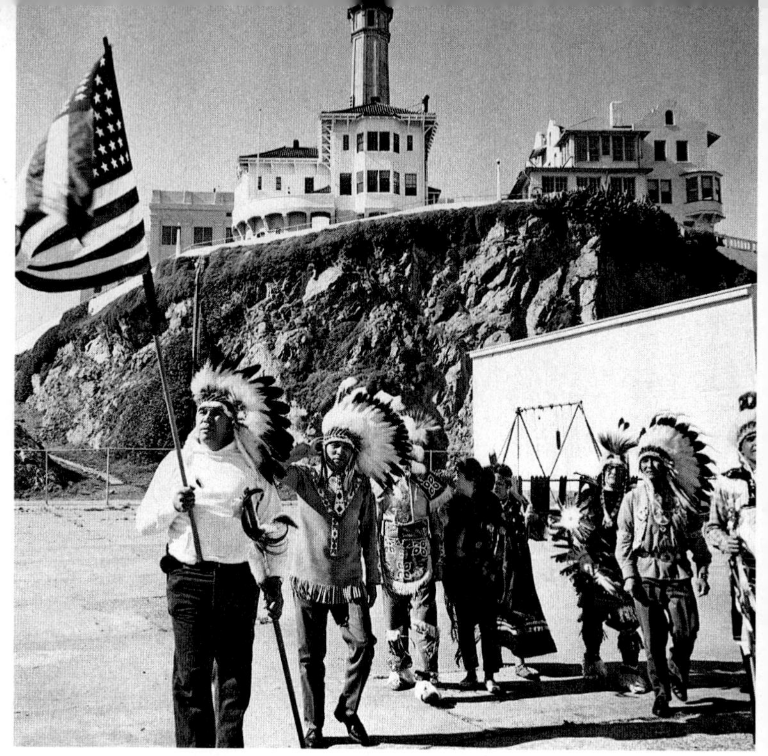

American Indians were another group working for equal rights in the 1960s. Some tribes came together to push for improved education for Indian children. Others worked to protect their rights to tribal lands.

In 1969, a group of American Indians took over **Alcatraz** (AL•kuh•traz) **Island** in San Francisco Bay. The island, which had once been Indian land, was the site of a former United States prison. To them, the island was a symbol of all the land once held by the American Indians. The protestors stayed on the island for nearly two years, calling attention to the American Indian Civil Rights movement.

READING CHECK **GENERALIZE**
What were many groups in the 1940s, 1950s, and 1960s fighting for?

Summary

In the 1940s, 1950s, and 1960s, many groups worked for equal rights. African Americans, Latinos, Asian Americans, and American Indians worked for civil rights. Women worked to gain equal rights.

REVIEW

1. How did California change as groups worked to secure equal rights?
2. Use the terms **strike** and **boycott** to describe how farmworkers in California won better treatment.
3. Why was the UFW formed? What happened as a result?

CRITICAL THINKING

4. ANALYSIS SKILL Why do you think it was important to civil rights leaders that protests be peaceful?
5. **Make a Poster** Choose one of the groups fighting for equal rights. Make a poster calling attention to one of the issues important to that group.
6. Focus Skill **CAUSE AND EFFECT** On a separate sheet of paper, copy and complete the graphic organizer below.

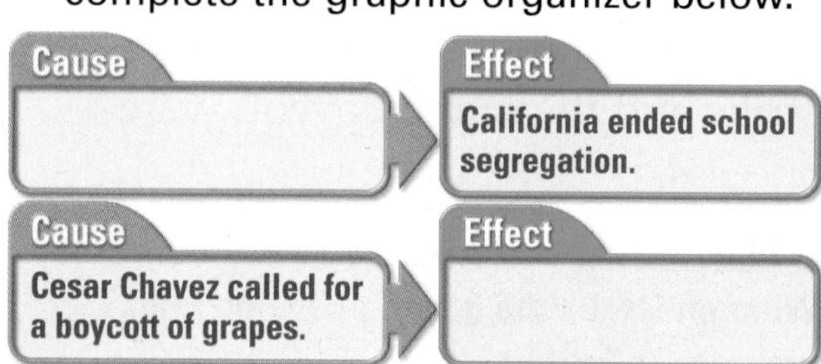
Cause
Effect
California ended school segregation.
Cause
Cesar Chavez called for a boycott of grapes.
Effect

Cesar Chavez

Biography

Trustworthiness
Respect
Responsibility
Fairness
Caring
Patriotism

*"Together, all things are possible."**

Cesar Chavez was born in 1927, on a farm near Yuma, Arizona. When he was ten years old, his family had to close down the farm. The family moved to California, where they became migrant farmworkers.

Chavez's early life was hard. He was expected to work long hours, but he received little pay. He went to more than 30 schools because his family moved often to find work. After he finished the eighth grade, Chavez quit school to work full-time in the fields. In this way, he helped his family earn a living.

As leader of the UFW, Cesar Chavez organized a grape pickers' strike in 1965.

In 1962, Chavez helped start the National Farm Workers Association–later known as the United Farm Workers. The union's purpose was to organize migrant farmworkers to work for better working conditions and higher pay. The year after his death, Chavez was awarded the Presidential Medal of Freedom, one of the nation's highest awards.

*Cesar Chavez. From a speech given during his Fast for Life in 1988. www.ufw.org/cecstory.htm

Why Character Counts

In what ways did Cesar Chavez show his deep concern for the lives of migrant farmworkers?

Bio Brief

1927 Born

1962 Chavez and others organize the United Farm Workers

1965 Leads a strike and a boycott to help grape pickers

1993 Died

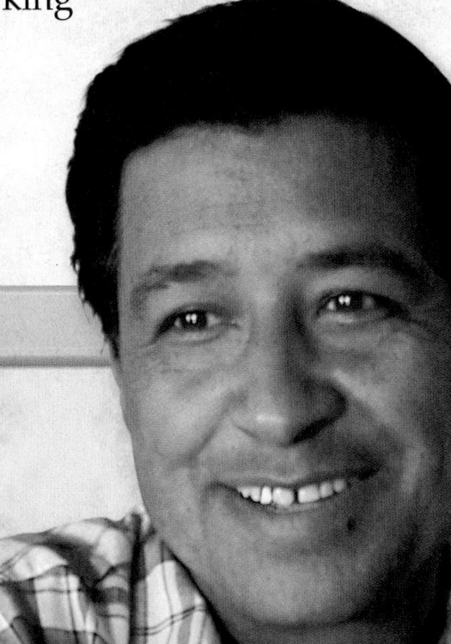

GO ONLINE **Interactive Multimedia Biographies**
Visit MULTIMEDIA BIOGRAPHIES at www.harcourtschool.com/hss

Lesson 3

Time

1905 | 1945 | 1985

1952
Citizenship Day becomes a national holiday

1964
For the first time, California has more people than any other state

WHAT TO KNOW
How have immigration and migration changed California?

- Describe how immigration has affected the population of California.
- Explain how people throughout the state honor and celebrate culture.

VOCABULARY
multicultural p. 407
ethnic group p. 408
heritage p. 408

CAUSE AND EFFECT

California Standards
HSS 4.4, 4.4.4

A Diverse State

YOU ARE THERE You are staring out the airplane window as the plane lands in San Francisco. You are from Bangladesh, a country in Asia, but San Francisco is going to be your new home. You are excited! You wonder what your new home will be like. The weather in Bangladesh is always warm. Elephants and tigers live in the forest near your family's rice farm. Will San Francisco be at all like Bangladesh?

California's diverse population has made the state a more interesting place to live.

A Booming Population

Today, more than 35 million people live in California—more than in any other state. Part of California's population boom is the result of people migrating to the state from other places in the United States. It is also due to increases in the birth rate and to immigration.

Many immigrants have come from Mexico, Central America, and South America. Others have come from Laos, Cambodia, and Vietnam. These three countries are in southeastern Asia, a region damaged by war. Other Asian immigrants have come from India, Bangladesh, the Philippines, China, and South Korea. Immigrants have also come from countries in Europe, and from African nations such as Kenya and Nigeria.

Each immigrant group has brought its culture to California. The languages immigrants speak, the foods they eat, and their religious beliefs all reflect their cultures. The diverse cultures of immigrants have made California a **multicultural** state.

California's Foreign-Born Population, 2000

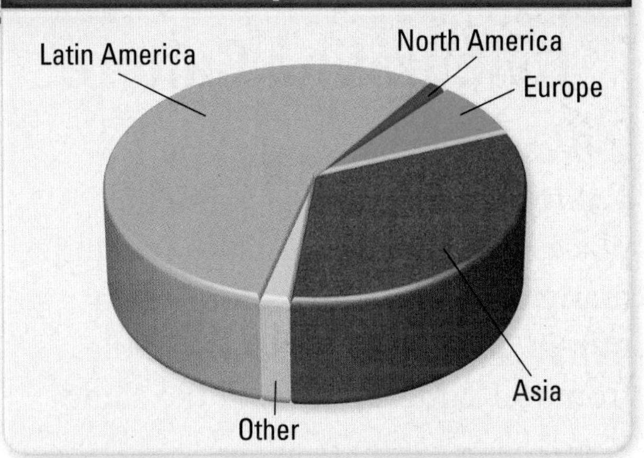

Analyze Graphs **People from many different regions and of many different backgrounds live in California.**

- **From which region did most of California's foreign-born population come in 2000?**

Many immigrants in California are legal immigrants. This means that they have permission from the government to live in the United States. Some people, however, find ways to enter the country illegally. The government has passed laws to make it harder for these illegal immigrants to stay in the United States.

READING CHECK **CAUSE AND EFFECT**
How has immigration affected the culture of California?

Children play traditional Japanese drums at a festival.

Celebrating Culture

Because so many people in California have come from other places, the state's population includes many different ethnic groups. An **ethnic group** is a group of people from the same country, of the same race, or with a shared culture. Each ethnic group has brought some of its own culture to California.

The people of California work to keep their cultures alive and to share their history and heritage with others. **Heritage** includes the traditions, beliefs, and ways of life that have been handed down from the past. Many California cities have cultural festivals, or celebrations, each year.

In Los Angeles and San Diego, Cinco de Mayo celebrates Mexican heritage. In Sonora, people from Ireland, Scotland, and Wales hold a Celtic Celebration. In Yuba City, the Punjabi American Festival celebrates the heritage and contributions

CITIZENSHIP

Democratic Institutions

All people born in the United States are citizens. Immigrants to the United States may follow certain steps to become citizens.

In 1940 the United States Congress decided that a day should be set aside to honor the country's new citizens. At first it was called I Am an American Day. Then in 1952, the name was changed to Citizenship Day. September 17 was chosen as Citizenship Day because the United States Constitution was signed on that date in 1787. Citizenship Day honors all United States citizens.

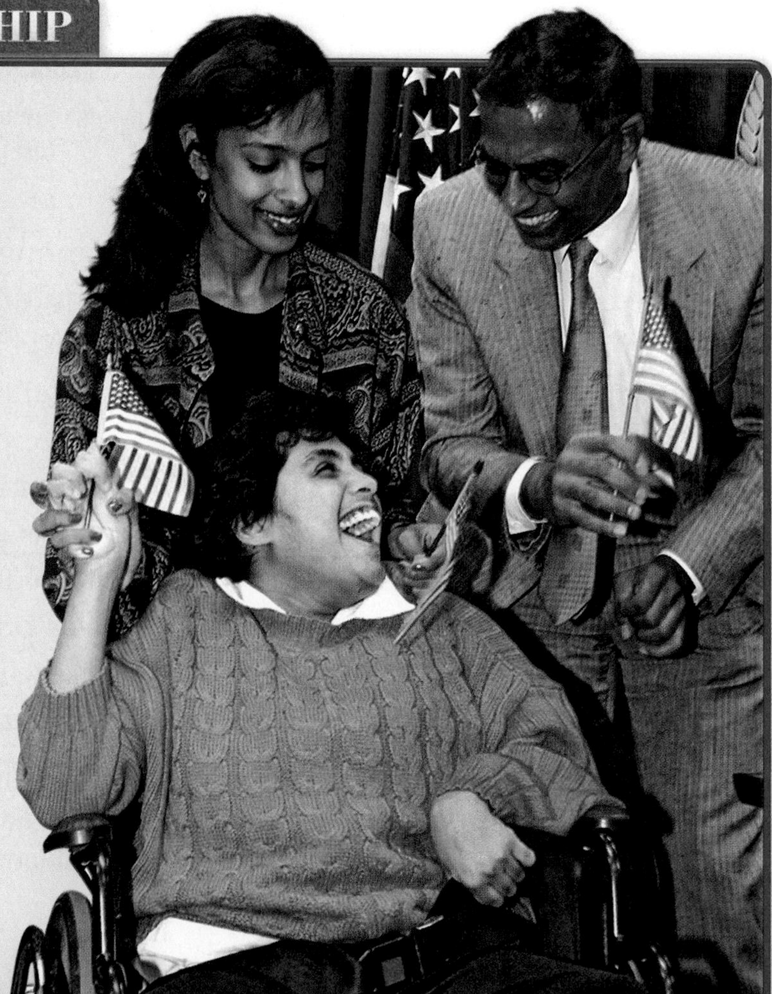

of people from the Punjab region of India. Many Punjabis are members of the Sikh religion. In 2004, about 13,000 people went to the festival to learn about Sikh culture.

Almost all cultural festivals include traditional food, music, singing, and dancing. In Los Angeles, the Watts Towers Day of the Drum focuses on one musical instrument. People from different cultures listen to and learn about drum music.

READING CHECK **SUMMARIZE**
How do Californians share the heritage and history of different groups of people?

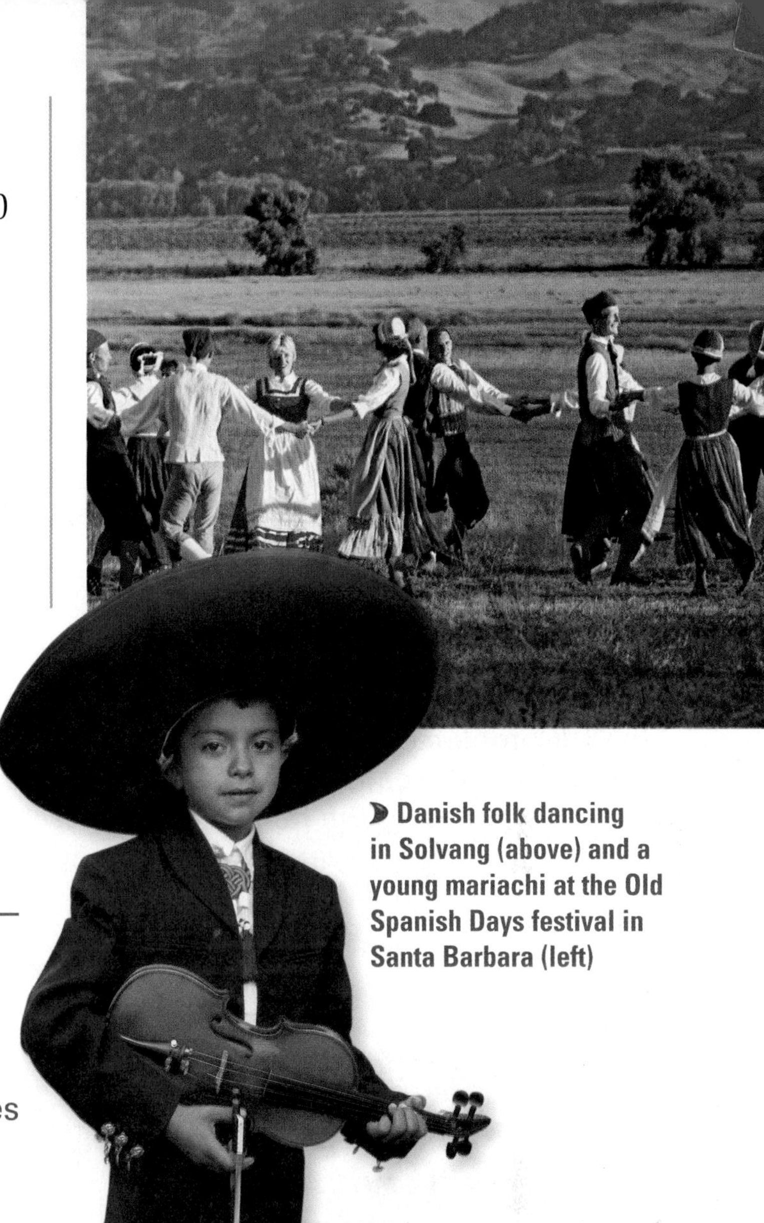

Danish folk dancing in Solvang (above) and a young mariachi at the Old Spanish Days festival in Santa Barbara (left)

Summary

California continues to attract immigrants from many parts of the world. The diverse groups of people living in California today celebrate their cultures and share them during festivals.

REVIEW

1. How have immigration and migration changed California?
2. Use the term **heritage** to explain why it is important for people to hold cultural festivals.
3. What can people learn at the Punjabi American Festival?

CRITICAL THINKING

4. ANALYSIS SKILL How has California become a multicultural state? How has this affected life in California?
5. ANALYSIS SKILL What hopes do you think immigrants today share with immigrants of the past?
6. **Write a Paragraph** Think about things in your community that show it is a multicultural place. Write a paragraph describing those things.
7. Focus Skill **CAUSE AND EFFECT**
On a separate sheet of paper, copy and complete the graphic organizer below.

Cause	Effect
Immigration to California continues.	
	California is a multicultural state.

Chapter 10 Review

Time

1945

1955

1945
World War II ends as Japan surrenders

1959
The silicon chip is invented

Reading Social Studies

A **cause** is an action or event that makes something happen. An **effect** is what happens as a result of an action or event.

Focus Skill Cause and Effect

Complete the graphic organizer below to show that you understand the causes and effects of key events that helped shape California in the half century after World War II. A copy of this graphic organizer appears on page 114 of the Homework and Practice Book.

Into Modern Times

Cause	Effect
Workers who come to California during the war decide to stay.	
Some groups in California face discrimination.	

California Writing Prompts

Write a Report Write a report explaining some ways in which the people of California work to keep their cultures alive. Include examples mentioned in Chapter 10 as well as others you know from your own experience.

Write a Summary Imagine you are a historian writing an encyclopedia article about California and its role in space travel. Write a brief summary of how Californians helped develop the United States' space program.

1965 1975 1985

1965
Cesar Chavez leads a nationwide boycott of grapes

1969
American Indians take over Alcatraz Island in San Francisco Bay

Use Vocabulary

Identify the term that correctly matches each definition.

technology, p. 394
commute, p. 395
civil rights, p. 401
strike, p. 403

1. to travel between work and home
2. citizens' rights to equal treatment under the law
3. when workers refuse to work unless they get better treatment
4. the use of knowledge or tools to make or do something

Use the Time Line

 **Use the summary time line above to answer these questions.**

5. In what decade did Cesar Chavez lead a grape boycott and Native Americans take over Alcatraz Island?
6. How many years after the end of World War II was the silicon chip invented?

Apply Skills

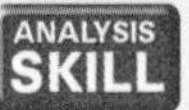 **Read a Road Map**

7. Look at the road map on page 399. Which highways would you take to travel from Sacramento to Monterey?

Recall Facts

Answer these questions.

8. How did building new freeways after World War II change where people lived?
9. How did Cesar Chavez help improve the lives of farmworkers in California?
10. What are some ways in which immigrants have contributed to California's culture?

Write the letter of the best choice.

11. What was one effect of population growth in California after World War II?
    A a depression
    B a shortage of workers
    C a natural disaster
    D a construction boom
12. What was one result of the Civil Rights movement?
    A Leaders who supported civil rights were elected to office.
    B Segregation was allowed in schools.
    C More freeways were built.
    D Women got the right to vote.

Think Critically

13. ANALYSIS SKILL Would you have boycotted California-grown grapes in the 1960s? Why?
14. ANALYSIS SKILL How did cars and freeways contribute to urban sprawl?

Petersen Automotive Museum

GET READY

By the 1950s, automobiles had become an important part of everyday life in the United States, especially in southern California. At the Petersen Automotive Museum in Los Angeles, you can see how automobiles have developed over the years and how they have affected culture in southern California and around the world.

Visitors can walk through "streetscapes," which show how cars have changed over time. The museum also houses exhibits featuring motorcycles, race cars, and movie and celebrity cars. The May Family Discovery Center is filled with hands-on exhibits and a driving simulator.

WHAT TO SEE

These 1950s cars parked outside of this diner complete the streetscape and highlight its time period.

LOCATE IT

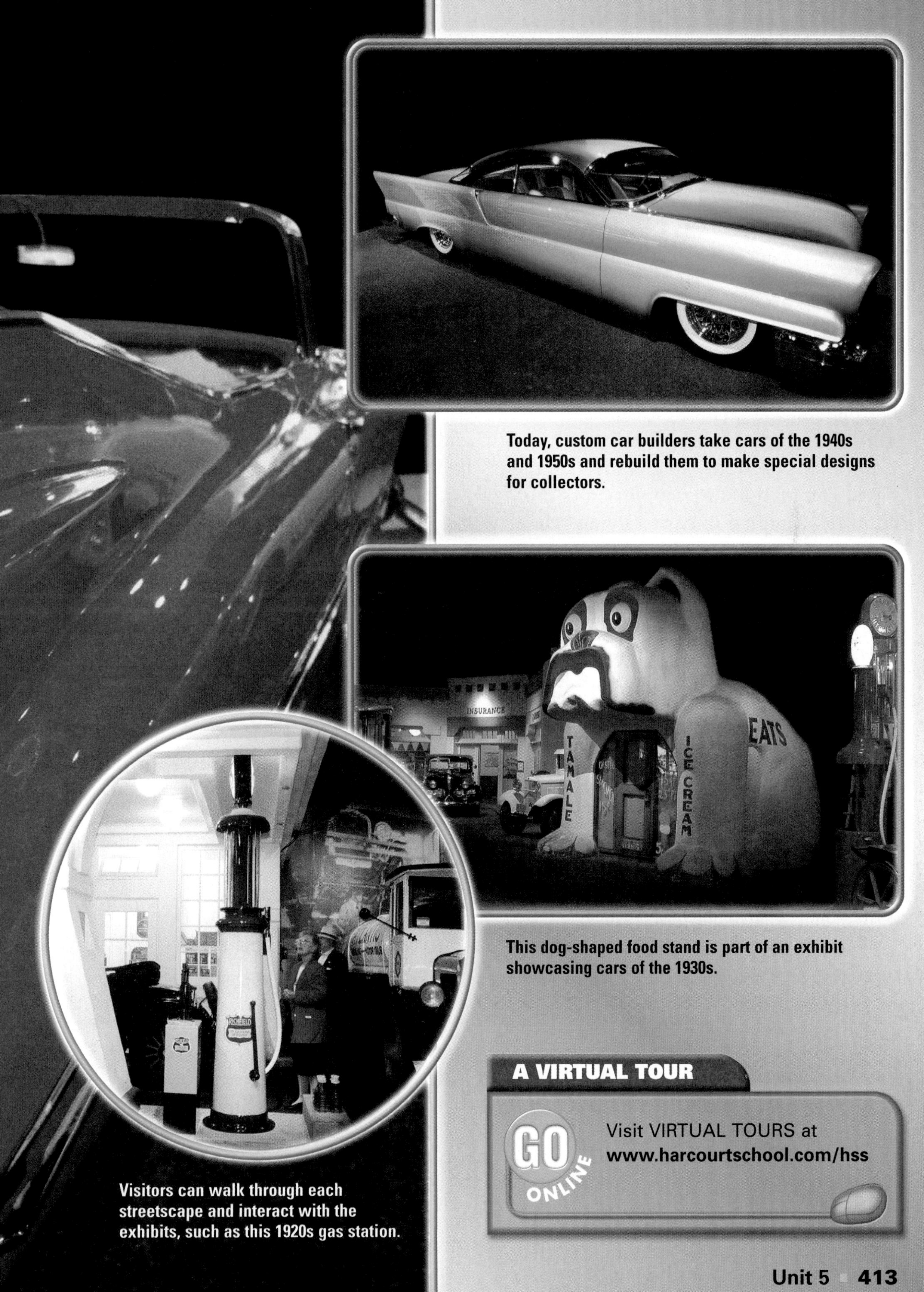

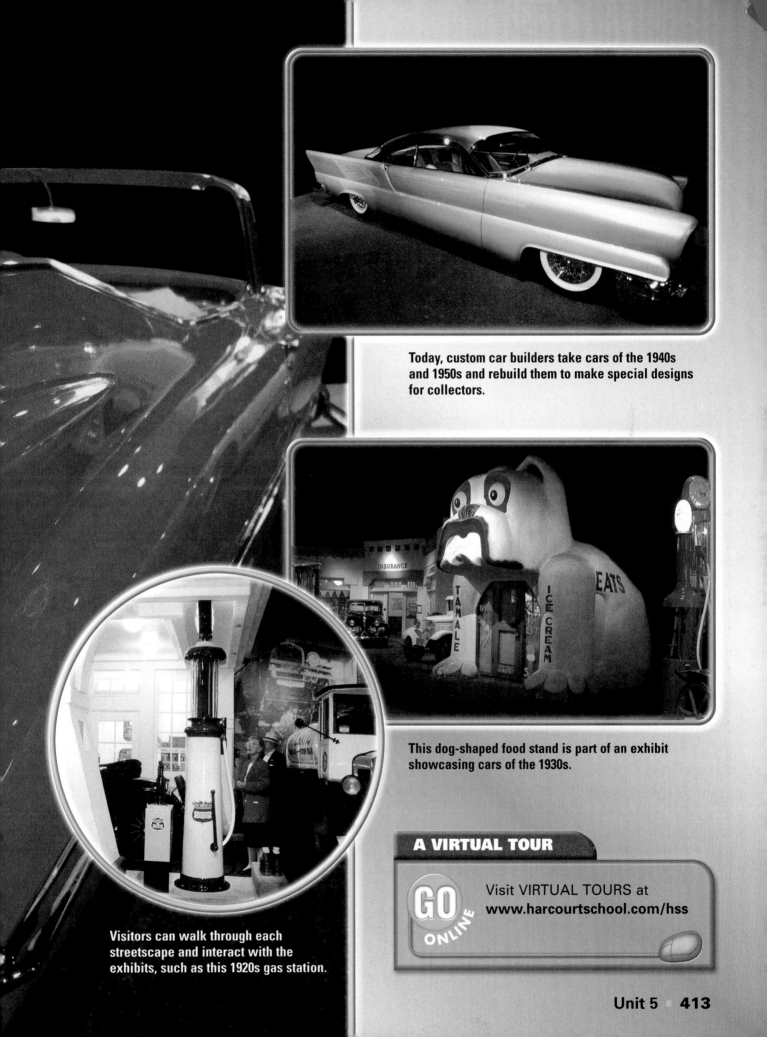

Today, custom car builders take cars of the 1940s and 1950s and rebuild them to make special designs for collectors.

This dog-shaped food stand is part of an exhibit showcasing cars of the 1930s.

Visitors can walk through each streetscape and interact with the exhibits, such as this 1920s gas station.

A VIRTUAL TOUR

GO ONLINE Visit VIRTUAL TOURS at **www.harcourtschool.com/hss**

Review

THE BIG IDEA

Growth and Change Human and natural events changed California, the United States, and the world during the twentieth century.

Summary

Solving Problems

In the early 1900s, the opening of the Panama Canal and the demand for goods during World War I caused California's economy to grow. When the Great Depression hit, people across the country struggled to earn a living. Many came to California hoping to find work, but jobs were scarce. To deal with high unemployment, the government hired people to work on public projects.

The country's entry into World War II put people to work and brought more newcomers to the state. By the war's end, California's population was larger and more diverse. The state's industries had grown larger and stronger as well.

Starting in the 1940s, Californians fought for equality and civil rights. Some ran for public office to make changes. Others formed labor unions and organized boycotts and strikes. Today, California still attracts newcomers from around the world, who add to the state's cultural diversity.

Main Ideas and Vocabulary

Read the summary above. Then answer the questions that follow.

1. What is unemployment?
- **A** military supplies and weapons
- **B** changing something for the better
- **C** a time when many businesses fail
- **D** the number of people without jobs

2. How did the government respond to the Great Depression?
- **A** It built the Panama Canal.
- **B** It hired people to work on public projects.
- **C** It gave women equal pay for equal work.
- **D** It started labor unions.

3. What are civil rights?
- **A** rules of polite behavior
- **B** strikes and boycotts
- **C** public offices
- **D** equal treatment under the law

4. How did California's population change during World War II?
- **A** It became segregated.
- **B** It became smaller and less diverse.
- **C** It became larger and more diverse.
- **D** It did not change.

Recall Facts

Answer these questions.

5. What reforms did Hiram Johnson help make as governor of California?
6. What caused the movie industry to develop and grow in southern California?
7. What was life like for migrant workers in California during the Depression?
8. What happened to the Japanese Americans who lived in California during World War II?
9. How did California's economy become more diverse after World War II?

Write the letter of the best choice.

10. After which of these events did the United States enter World War II?
    - **A** the opening of the Panama Canal
    - **B** the stock market crash of 1929
    - **C** the attack on Pearl Harbor
    - **D** the grape pickers' strike of 1965
11. Automobiles helped create urban sprawl by
    - **A** keeping metropolitan areas from growing.
    - **B** polluting the air.
    - **C** using gasoline.
    - **D** allowing people to live in one place and work in another.
12. What was the name of California's first freeway?
    - **A** Arroyo Seco Parkway
    - **B** El Camino Real
    - **C** Highway 1
    - **D** Golden Gate Freeway
13. How did migrant farm workers improve their working conditions?
    - **A** They told people to buy more grapes.
    - **B** They formed a labor union and went on strike.
    - **C** They kept a union from forming.
    - **D** They decided not to protest.

Think Critically

14. ANALYSIS SKILL How do you think the automobile changed where people lived?
15. ANALYSIS SKILL During the 1960s, many Californians fought for civil rights, equality in the workplace, and the fair treatment of farm workers. Do you think it is still important to fight for equal rights today? Explain.

Apply Skills

Read a Road Map

Look at the road map below to answer these questions.

16. How many miles is it from Bakersfield to Needles? Which highways would you take to get from one place to the other?
17. What route would you take to go from San Luis Obispo to Joshua Tree National Park? What is another route you could take?

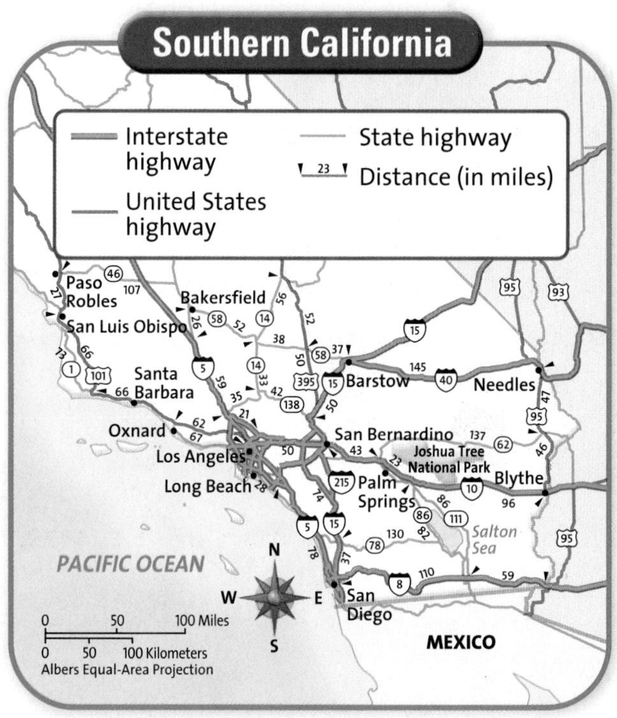

Unit 5

Activities

Read More

- *Cesar Chavez: Yes We Can!* by Josh Daniel.

- *Golden Gate Bridge* by Belinda Hulin.

- *On the Home Front* by Madeline Boskey.

Show What You Know

Unit Writing Activity

Write a Summary Choose a person or group from the unit and imagine that you have been chosen to write a speech about them. Your speech should summarize the contribution of the person or group and give details about their effect on others. Make sure to include significant details and to express main ideas in your speech.

Unit Project

Design a Scrapbook Design a scrapbook that honors a notable person, event, or achievement in California during the twentieth century. Write a short paragraph that summarizes that person, event, or achievement. Include illustrations in your scrapbook.

GO ONLINE Visit ACTIVITIES at **www.harcourtschool.com/hss**

California Today and Tomorrow

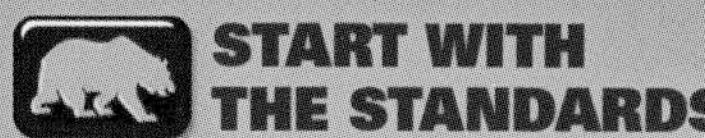

START WITH THE STANDARDS

California History-Social Science Standards

4.1 **Students demonstrate an understanding of the physical and human geographic features that define places and regions in California.**

4.4 **Students explain how California became an agricultural and industrial power, tracing the transformation of the California economy and its political and cultural development since the 1850s.**

4.5 **Students understand the structures, functions, and powers of the local, state, and federal governments as described in the U.S. Constitution.**

The Big Idea

GOVERNMENT AND LEADERSHIP

Californians are proud of their history, government, and heritage.

What to Know

- What industries are important to the California economy today?
- How are arts and California's public education system important?
- What are the functions of each level of government?

Show What You Know

★ **Unit 6 Test**

Writing: An Information Report

Unit Project: A Bulletin Board

SAN DIEGO
CA

Time

California Today and Tomorrow

1994 A strong earthquake shakes southern California

2001 California faces energy shortages and blackouts, p. 451

1985 1990 1995

At the Same Time

1986 The space shuttle *Challenger* explodes

1989 The Berlin Wall comes down, marking the end of the Cold War

1993 European Union begins

California Today and Tomorrow

2003 Californians vote to recall Governor Gray Davis, p. 475

2003 Brush fires burn more than 750,000 acres in southern California

Present More than 6 million students attend public school in California, p. 447

2000

PRESENT

2000 George W. Bush is elected President in the closest presidential election in United States history

2001 Terrorists attack the World Trade Center and the Pentagon

Unit 6

Earl Warren

1891–1974

- Governor of California from 1943 to 1953
- Chief Justice of the United States Supreme Court from 1953 to 1969

Paul R. Williams

1894–1980

- Architect from California
- Helped design the Theme Building at Los Angeles International Airport, the Hollywood YMCA, Saks Fifth Avenue in Beverly Hills, and the Los Angeles County Courthouse

People

1890 | 1910 | 1930

- 1891 • Earl Warren
- 1894 • Paul R. Williams
- 1907 • John Wayne
- 1911 • Ronald Reagan
- 1933 • Dianne Feinstein

Dianne Feinstein

1933–

- First woman to be elected mayor of San Francisco, serving from 1978 to 1988
- First female senator from California—first elected in 1992
- Reelected to the Senate in 1994 and again in 2000

Judith Baca

1946–

- Artist who created the *Great Wall of Los Angeles*, a mural that stretches for a half mile
- Received a 2001 Education Award from the National Hispanic Heritage Awards

John Wayne

1907–1979

- Movie star known for playing tough heroes in movies such as *The Green Berets* and *True Grit*
- Tried to enlist in the Army during the Vietnam War but was rejected due to an old injury and his age

Ronald Reagan

1911–2004

- Served two terms as governor of California, from 1966 to 1974
- Served two terms as President of the United States, from 1980 to 1988
- Before his political career, he had a career as an actor

1950 | 1970 | 1990 | PRESENT

1974

1980

1979

2004

1946 • Judith Baca

1947 • Arnold Schwarzenegger

1952 • Amy Tan

Arnold Schwarzenegger

1947–

- Former bodybuilder, born in Austria, who has won many bodybuilding titles, including Mr. Olympia and Mr. Universe
- Star of many action films
- Elected governor of California in 2003

Amy Tan

1952–

- Chinese American author who writes about growing up in Chinese and American cultures
- Her first book, *The Joy Luck Club*, was made into a film

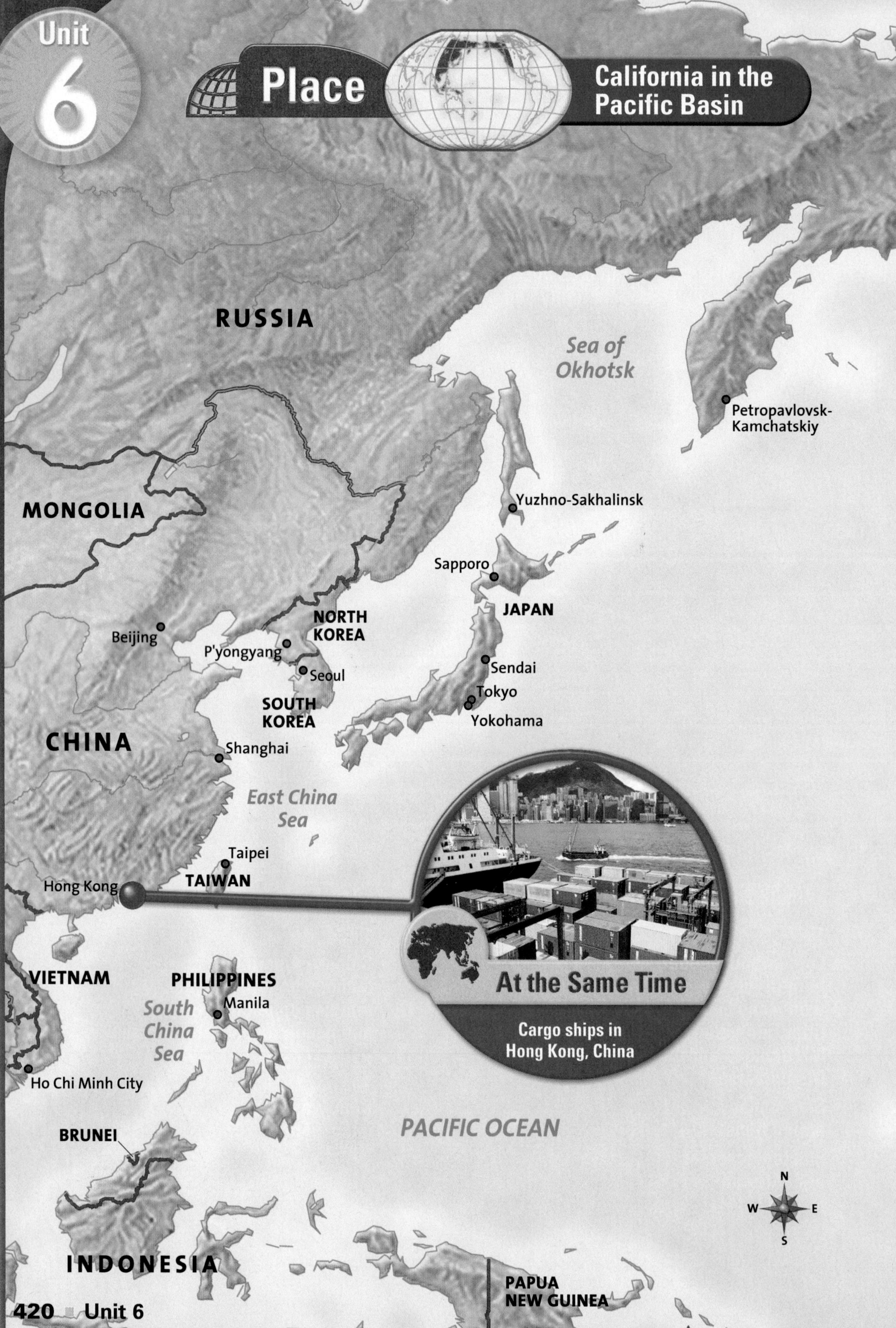

Cargo ships in Hong Kong, China

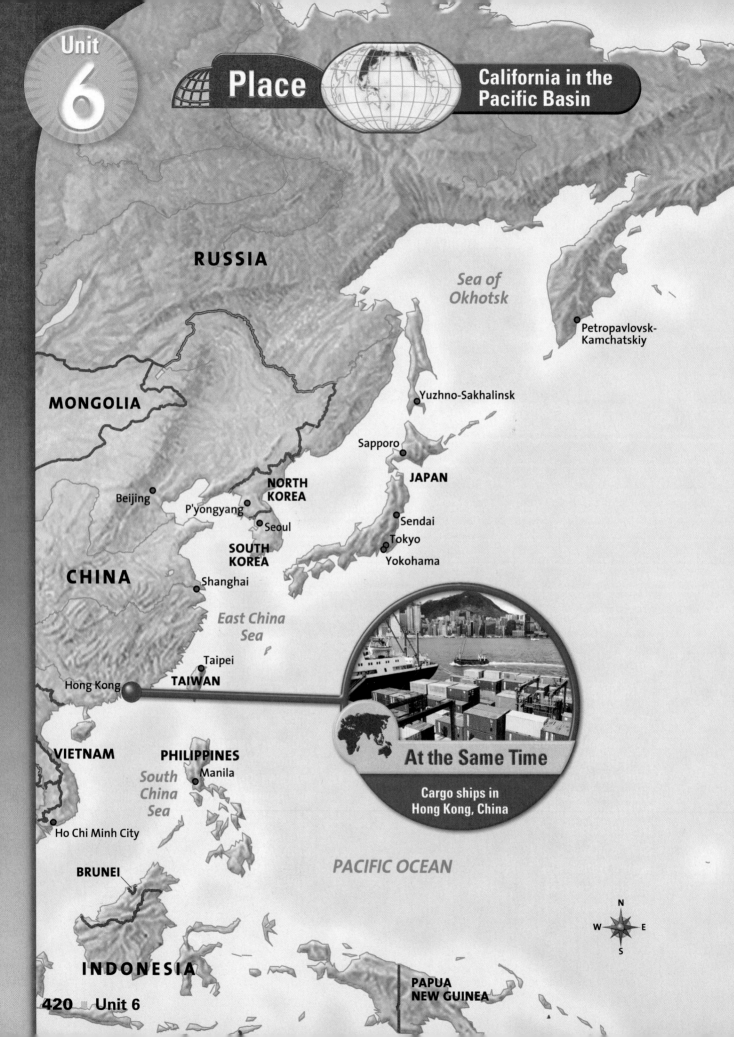

A sawmill in northern California

High-tech workers in Silicon Valley

Farmers in the Imperial Valley

Unit 6 Reading Social Studies

Focus Skill Summarize

When you summarize, you state in your own words a shortened version of what you read.

Why It Matters

Summarizing a passage can help you understand and remember the most important information.

Key Fact	Summary
Important idea from the reading	Important information you read, shortened and written in your own words
Key Fact: Important idea from the reading	

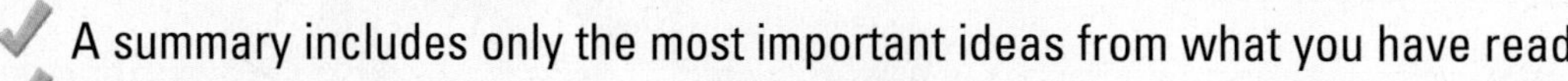

✓ A summary includes only the most important ideas from what you have read.
✓ Always use your own words when you summarize.

Practice the Skill

Read the paragraphs that follow. Write a summary for the second paragraph.

Facts

In 1969, a group of American Indians took over Alcatraz Island in San Francisco Bay, the site of a former United States prison. The island had once been Indian land. The protesters stayed on the island for nearly two years. The protest made many people aware of the American Indian Civil Rights movement. (A group of American Indians took over Alcatraz Island to bring attention to their cause.)

Summary

Today, Alcatraz Island is a national park. The prison there was closed in 1963, but the prison buildings still stand. Park rangers give tours of the prison, and many visitors come each year to hear about the criminals who were jailed there.

Apply What You Learned

 **Summarize** **Read the paragraphs, and answer the questions.**

Protecting California's Environment

During the gold rush, people damaged streams and rivers. Since that time, Californians have worked to solve problems in the environment caused by humans. In fact, Californians have become leaders in protecting the air, water, and soil.

People began working to protect the state's natural resources as early as the 1800s. In 1890, a naturalist named John Muir convinced Congress to protect natural areas in California. That year, Yosemite, Sequoia, and General Grant (now Kings Canyon) became California's first national parks.

During the early 1900s, the environment in California changed again. Many factories were opening up. People traveled on a system of freeways. By the 1940s, gases from cars and factories led to air-pollution problems. The dirty air in southern California became dangerous to people, animals, and plants.

In 1959, the state government passed a law that set standards for air quality in California. People had to test and control the gases coming out of factories, cars, and trucks. The law was the first of its kind in the nation. Four years later, the federal government passed the Clean Air Act to set national standards for air quality.

Then, in 1970, the federal government created the Environmental Protection Agency, or EPA. This agency helps protect the environment and people's health.

Summarize

1. **How would you describe the environmental problems that Californians have faced?**
2. **What activities have contributed to air pollution in California?**
3. **How has government responded to problems in the environment?**

Designing special cars that use less gas is one way people can protect the environment.

Study Skills

SKIM AND SCAN

Skimming and scanning are two ways to learn from what you read.

- **To skim, quickly read the lesson title and the section titles. Look at the pictures and read the captions. Use this information to identify the main topics.**
- **To scan, look quickly through the text for specific details, such as key words or facts.**

SKIM	SCAN
Lesson: A Modern Economy **Main Idea:** California has a strong, diverse economy. **Titles/Headings:** A Strong Economy, Technology and Trade **Visuals:** ______	**Key Words and Facts** • international trade • California's history shaped its economy. • Silicon Valley • ______ • ______ • ______

Apply As You Read

Before you read, skim the text to find the main idea of each section. Then look for key words. If you have questions, scan the text to find the answers.

California History-Social Science Standards, Grade 4

4.1 Students demonstrate an understanding of the physical and human geographic features that define places and regions in California.
4.4 Students explain how California became an agricultural and industrial power, tracing the transformation of the California economy and its political and cultural development since the 1850s.

CHAPTER

The Golden State

Independence Day fireworks burst over the Golden Gate Bridge, one of California's most beloved symbols.

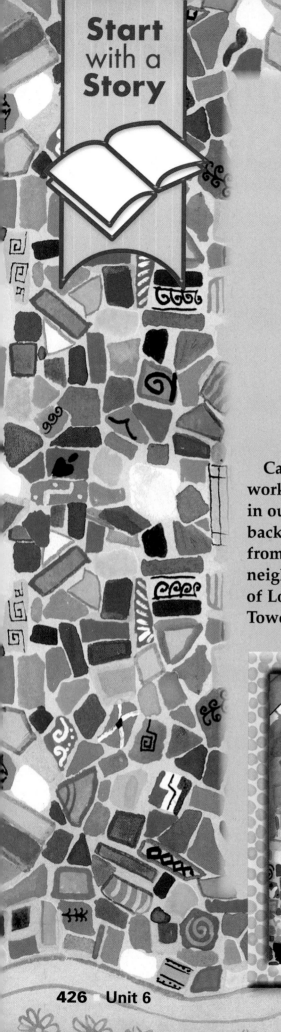

Start with a Story

The Wonderful Towers of Watts

by Patricia Zelver
illustrated by Frané Lessac

California has many fine museums filled with beautiful works of art. However, one of the most unusual art forms in our state rises from what was once Simon Rodia's backyard in Watts. Rodia spent more than 30 years, from 1921 to 1954, building three colorful towers in his neighborhood, which is now in the South Central part of Los Angeles. Read to learn how Rodia built his Watts Towers.

Old Sam's real name was Simon Rodia. He was a small man who dressed in ragged overalls, a shirt with sleeves cut off, and a greasy hat. His arms and face were always covered with dust.

Simon Rodia had come from Italy as a young man and spoke with a thick accent. He bought a little bungalow in Watts, a poor neighborhood that was half town, half country, outside the city limits of Los Angeles. He baked his bread in an outdoor oven he had made, just like the oven his mother had used in the old country. Sometimes he was friendly and smiled at people with a gap-toothed smile; other times his thoughts seemed far away and he would speak to no one.

Old Sam worked as a laborer at Taylor's Tilery. Every evening he got off the streetcar carrying a large burlap sack of broken colored tiles.

"What's Old Sam going to do with those?" people said.

On weekends Old Sam walked down to the vacant lot by the railroad tracks and collected things that people thought were better thrown away. He brought home blue Milk of Magnesia bottles, broken bits of colored pottery, even pieces of broken mirrors.

Sometimes he paid the neighborhood kids pennies or cookies to bring him empty green soda pop bottles and sacks of seashells.

"What does Old Sam want with all that junk?" people wondered.

Old Sam spent most of his money on sacks of cement, sand, and steel. People could hear him working in his backyard, behind a high fence.

"Old Sam, what's he up to?" they said.

One day, to the neighbors' amazement, something strange and beautiful rose over the fence in Sam's backyard. It was a lacy web of steel, covered with a skin of concrete in which Old Sam had stuck glittering bits of tile, glass, mirrors, pottery, and seashells. Was Old Sam building a fairy castle? A church spire? A tower on which he could climb to the sky?

Everyone stared in wonder at Old Sam's creation.

Sam went on working. He worked all by himself for thirty-three years in all kinds of weather, high off the ground with only a window washer's belt to keep him from falling. While he worked he listened to opera music on an old gramophone. His favorite singer was Enrico Caruso. Old Sam could be heard singing along with him.

The children of the neighborhood grew up and had their own children, who watched Old Sam's towers soaring into the sky. Old Sam was getting older, too, but he went on working, just as before.

Sometimes Old Sam invited the neighborhood children into his yard, which was now surrounded by a decorated wall. Inside, the children found a magical city with little streets, squares, and fountains. The walks and walls were covered with starfish patterns, heart shapes, seashells, colorful tiles decorated with peacocks, and a golden bumblebee. Stuck into the cement were all sorts of curious objects which Old Sam had collected over the years. A teapot spout. A cowboy boot. Faucet handles. Horseshoes. Even willowware plates.

Newspaper reporters heard about the towers and came to see them and to talk to Old Sam.

"What do they mean?" they asked him.

Old Sam just smiled.

"Where are your plans?" they said.

Old Sam pointed to his head.

"Why did you do it?" they said.

"I just felt like it." Old Sam said.

Rodia's work has been preserved, and people from all over the world still come to visit his wonderful towers.

Response Corner

1. What do you think the Watts Towers meant to Old Sam?
2. Make a list of objects from your community that you might use to build a work of art. Draw a plan for your creation.

Lesson 1

A Modern Economy

WHAT TO KNOW
What are the most important parts of California's economy?

- ✓ Explain the reasons for the size and strength of California's economy.
- ✓ Describe the industries that play an important role in the economy of California.

VOCABULARY

international trade p. 431
import p. 433
interdependence p. 433
food processing p. 434
service industry p. 435
tourism p. 435

PLACES

Silicon Valley
Pacific Basin

Focus Skill **SUMMARIZE**

California Standards
HSS 4.4, 4.4.6

YOU ARE THERE

You look carefully at the microchip you have just made. It will now be tested by different machines to make sure it works. If the chip passes all the tests, it will be used in a powerful new computer. The company you work for is just one of the many high-tech companies in California. Companies like yours make up an important part of California's economy—one of the largest economies in the world.

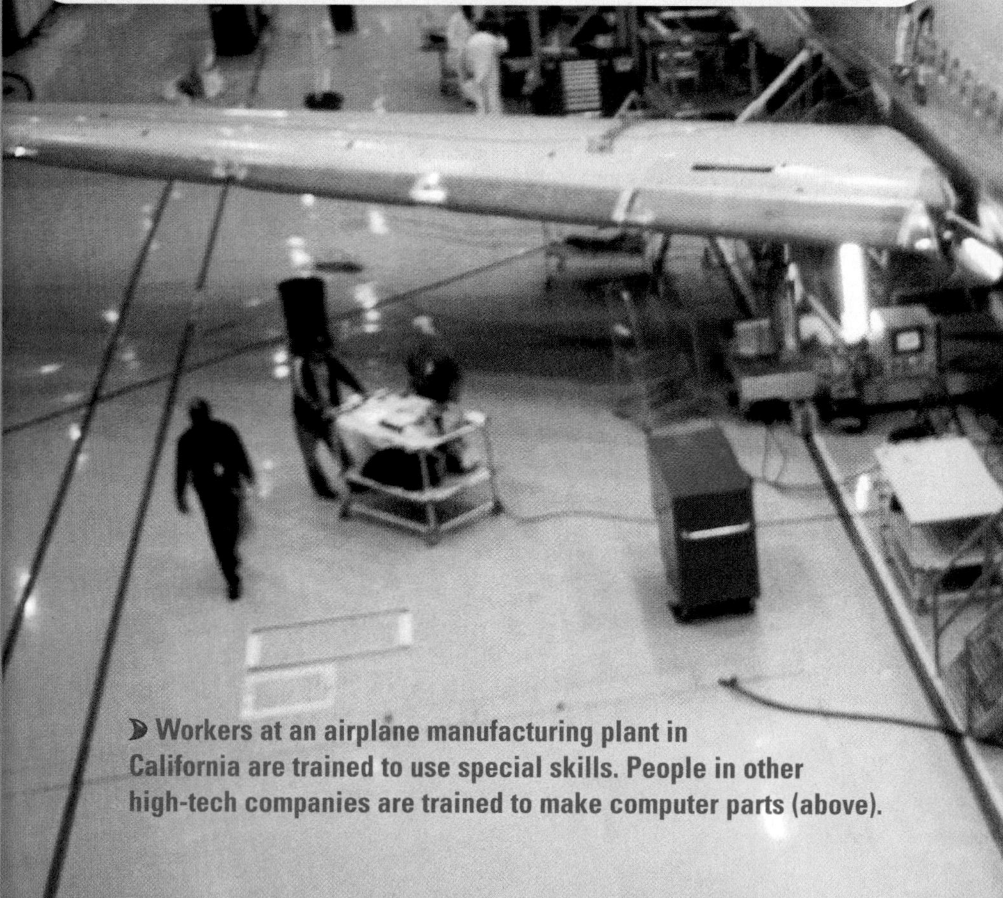

➤ Workers at an airplane manufacturing plant in California are trained to use special skills. People in other high-tech companies are trained to make computer parts (above).

A Strong Economy

Each year, California produces about $1.4 trillion in products and services. In fact, California leads all states in manufacturing, and its economy is larger than the economies of most countries.

One reason that California's economy is strong is geography. Large areas of rich farmland make California a leading producer of vegetables, fruits, and dairy products. Its beaches and mountains draw millions of visitors. Also, the state's location on the Pacific Ocean is good for **international trade**, or trade with other countries. Today, California leads all states in international trade.

California's history has also shaped its economy. The gold rush, the building of the railroads, two world wars, and other events have led to the growth of new industries.

California's economy depends on the skills of its people. Actors in Los Angeles, engineers in Santa Clara, farmers near Fresno, and dockworkers in San Diego add to the state's economy.

READING CHECK **SUMMARIZE**
What makes California's economy strong?

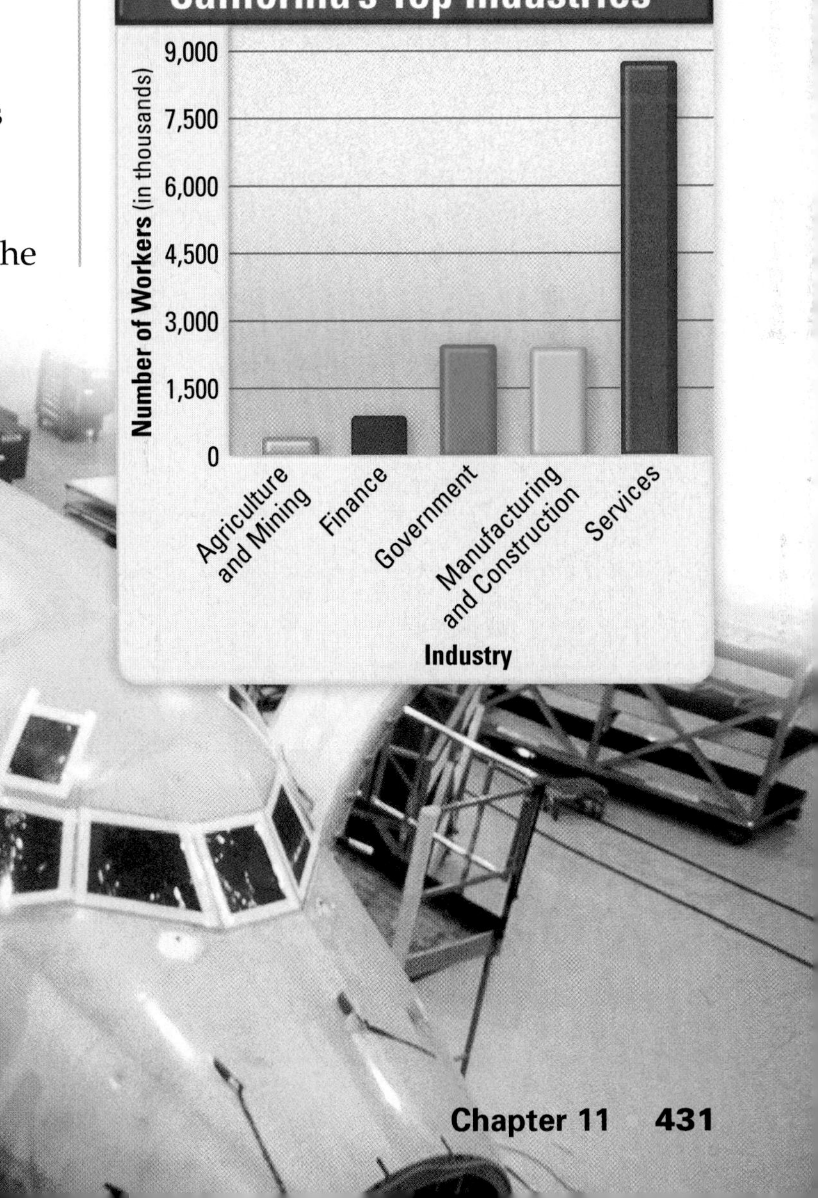

Analyze Graphs **California's economy is made up of several strong industries.**

Which industry employs the most workers in California?

High-Tech Manufacturing

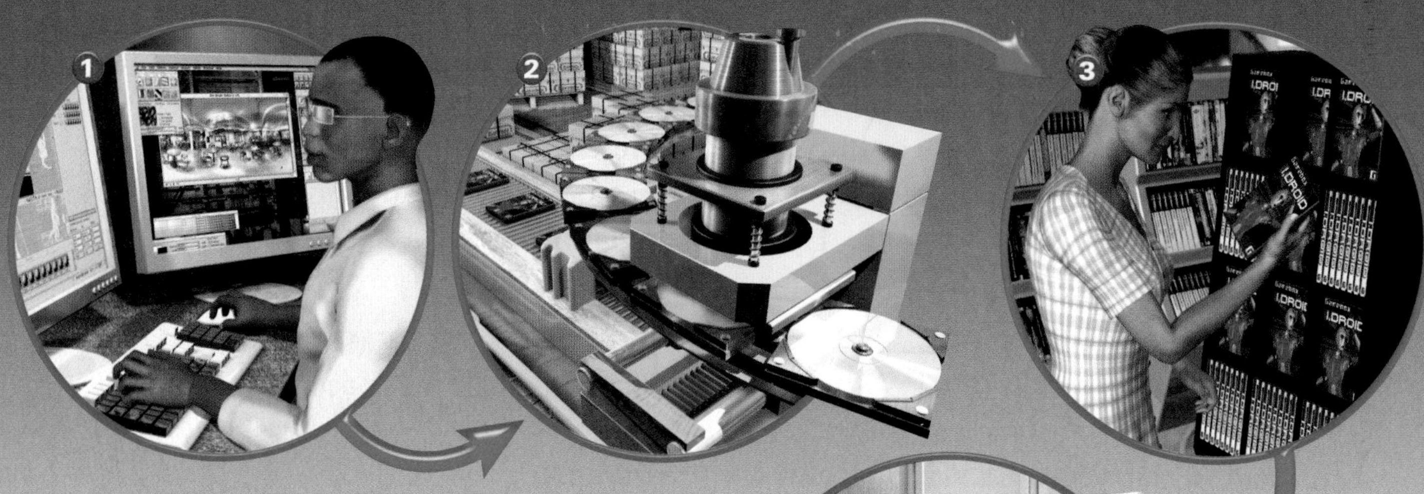

Analyze Illustrations **Video games are one product that is made in Silicon Valley. ❶ Designers use computers to form pictures and sound. ❷ Workers assemble materials. ❸ The games are shipped to stores and sold. ❹ Users enjoy the games at home.**

❖ What steps must happen before the games are shipped to stores?

GEOGRAPHY

Silicon Valley

California became a center for high-tech industries in part because some graduates from Stanford University near Palo Alto did not want to move to eastern states for jobs. A few graduates started their own computer companies near Palo Alto. As more computer companies were started there, the area became a high-tech center. In the 1970s, the area from Palo Alto to San Jose began to be called "Silicon Valley."

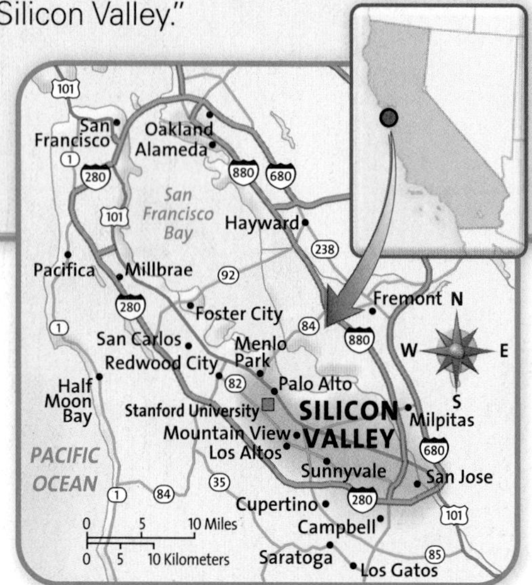

Technology and Trade

High technology plays a key part in California's economy. As early as 1951, high-tech companies were started near Palo Alto and San Jose. Today, the area has so many computer companies it is known as **Silicon** (SIH•lih•kuhn) **Valley**, after the silicon chips in computers.

High-tech companies are also located in other parts of California. Many are in Orange, San Bernardino, Los Angeles, San Diego, San Mateo, and Marin Counties. About 400,000 Californians work for companies that make high-tech products.

High technology has changed the way many people live. Silicon chips are used in everyday things, such as toys. In addition, about half of the homes in the United States today have computers.

Many of California's high-tech products are exported to other countries. In fact, about half of all California exports are high-tech products. Other top exports are machinery and food products.

Exports from California and other states are shipped from California to other ports along the **Pacific Basin**. In fact, the state exports goods worth almost $50 billion to Asia each year. California also sends many goods to Mexico and Canada.

In addition to shipping exports, California receives **imports**, or goods from other countries. Top imports to the United States include automobiles, electronics, and food. Many imports to the United States are shipped to California ports such as Los Angeles, Long Beach, San Diego, Oakland, and San Francisco.

Trade helps create **interdependence** between Californians and people in other places. Interdependence means that people in each place depend on the others for goods and products.

READING CHECK GENERALIZE
How are imports related to interdependence?

California's Top Trading Partners, 2003

RANK	IMPORTS	EXPORTS
1	China	Japan
2	Japan	Mexico
3	Mexico	China
4	Korea	Korea
5	Taiwan	Taiwan
6	Malaysia	Singapore
7	Germany	Hong Kong
8	Thailand	Australia

Analyze Tables This table shows California's top trading partners.

From which country does California import the most goods?

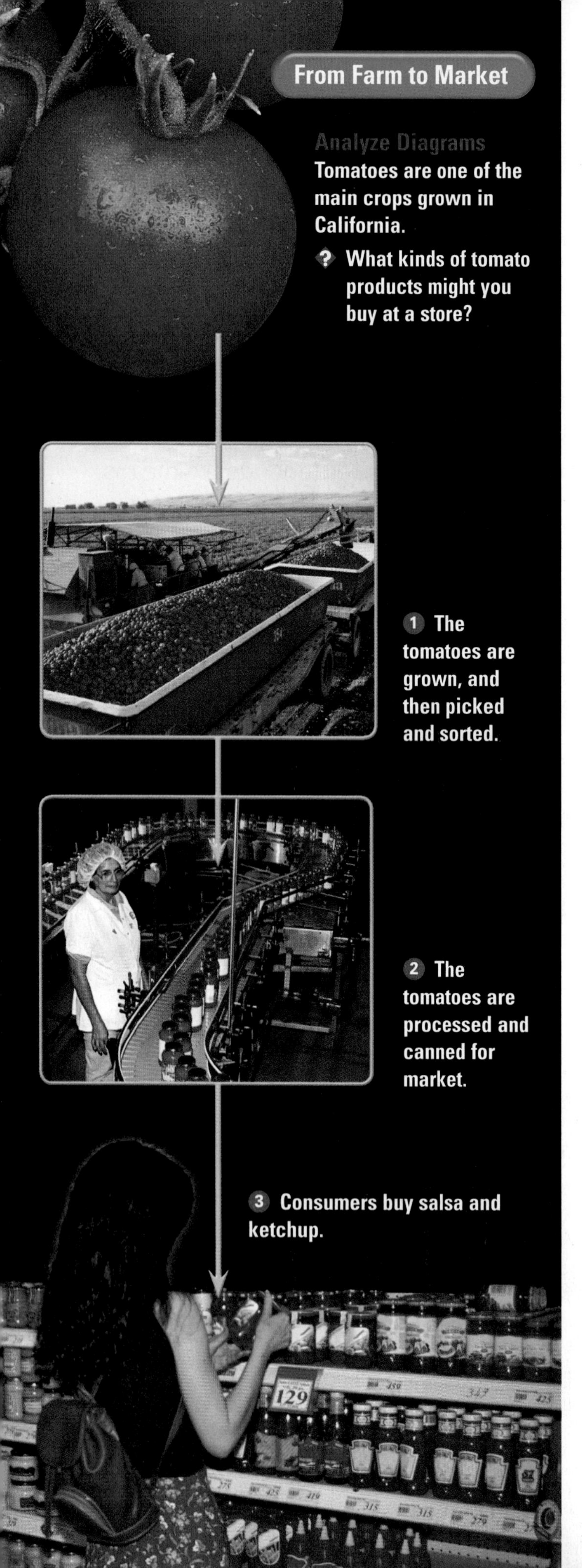

Analyze Diagrams
Tomatoes are one of the main crops grown in California.

? What kinds of tomato products might you buy at a store?

1 The tomatoes are grown, and then picked and sorted.

2 The tomatoes are processed and canned for market.

3 Consumers buy salsa and ketchup.

An Agricultural Giant

For more than 50 years, California has produced more agricultural goods than any other state. In fact, about half of all vegetables, fruits, and nuts grown in the United States are grown in California. Agriculture provides jobs for more than 1 million Californians. Many work as farmers, scientists, or field workers. Workers in the state also have jobs in **food processing**—the cooking, canning, drying, freezing, and preparing of foods for market.

California's geography is well suited to agriculture. The climate and soil support many kinds of plants. In fact, California grows almost all of the almonds, apricots, olives, avocados, and grapes for sale in the United States.

The land of California is also good for raising farm animals. Ranching is very important to the economy of the state. Today, California is a leader in production of beef and dairy products in the United States.

Most of the food produced in California is eaten in the United States. However, Californians also earn about $6 billion each year from food exports. People in Japan, countries in Europe, Canada, Mexico, and China all eat foods that are produced in California.

READING CHECK **MAIN IDEA AND DETAILS**
How is agriculture important to California's economy?

The Service Industry

Businesses that provide services for people instead of making things belong to the **service industry**. Cashiers, waiters, and taxi drivers are all workers in the service industry.

Tourism, the business of serving visitors, brings a lot of money into California. Each year, more than 50 million tourists come to the state. Tourists help the economy by staying in hotels, eating at restaurants, and buying souvenirs.

READING CHECK **CAUSE AND EFFECT**
How do visitors to California affect service industries in the state?

Summary

California has a strong economy because of the state's history, its geography, and its people. Manufacturing, service industries, agriculture, and international trade are all important parts of California's economy.

REVIEW

1. What are the most important parts of California's economy?
2. Describe how **imports** are a part of **international trade**.
3. How has geography affected California's economy?

CRITICAL THINKING

4. ANALYSIS SKILL How is California's history connected to its modern economy?
5. **Make a Brochure** Imagine that you plan to open a business. Select a business, and research different places in California for your location. Make a brochure that describes the business and the location.
6. Focus Skill **SUMMARIZE**
On a separate sheet of paper, copy and complete the graphic organizer below.

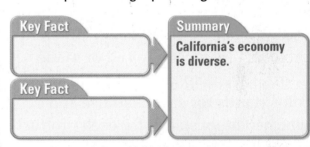

Key Fact	Summary
	California's economy is diverse.
Key Fact	

➤ Tourists from all over the world visit California's famous theme parks.

Read a Land Use and Products Map

WHY IT MATTERS

Where are most goods in California manufactured? In what parts of the state do you find farms? To find answers to these questions, you need a map that shows **land use**, or how most of the land in a place is used.

WHAT YOU NEED TO KNOW

The map on page 437 is a land use and products map of California. It uses colors to show how most of the land in a place is used. The map also uses symbols to show where different products are mostly raised or made. Look at the map key to see which color stands for each land use and which symbol stands for each product.

PRACTICE THE SKILL

Use the land use and products map to answer these questions.

1. Which color shows areas where land is used for manufacturing?
2. Where are California's grape-producing regions?
3. What parts of California are used very little for economic purposes?

APPLY WHAT YOU LEARNED

ANALYSIS SKILL **Make It Relevant** Draw a land use map of the area near your community. Use the map on page 437 and reference books to find out how people use the land in that area. Include a map key.

Practice your map and globe skills with the **GeoSkills CD-ROM**.

People use the land and coastal waters of California to cut lumber, catch fish, and grow crops.

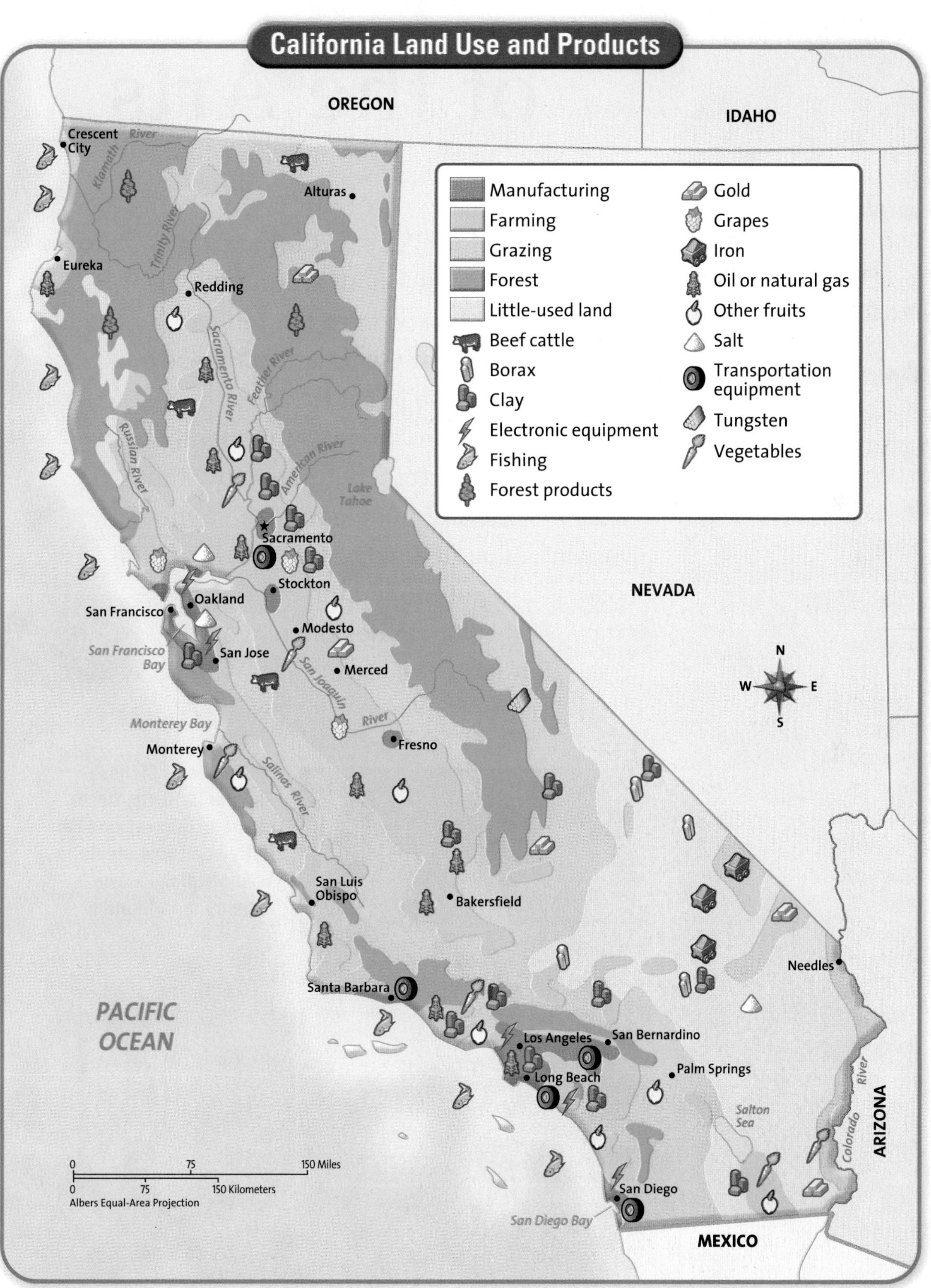
California Land Use and Products
OREGON
IDAHO
NEVADA
ARIZONA
MEXICO
PACIFIC OCEAN
Manufacturing
Farming
Grazing
Forest
Little-used land
Beef cattle
Borax
Clay
Electronic equipment
Fishing
Forest products
Gold
Grapes
Iron
Oil or natural gas
Other fruits
Salt
Transportation equipment
Tungsten
Vegetables
Crescent City
Eureka
Redding
Alturas
Sacramento
Stockton
Oakland
San Francisco
San Jose
Modesto
Merced
Fresno
Monterey
Monterey Bay
San Francisco Bay
San Luis Obispo
Bakersfield
Santa Barbara
Los Angeles
San Bernardino
Long Beach
Palm Springs
San Diego
San Diego Bay
Needles
Salton Sea
Lake Tahoe
Klamath River
Trinity River
Sacramento River
Feather River
American River
Russian River
San Joaquin River
Salinas River
Colorado River
N
S
E
W
0 75 150 Miles
0 75 150 Kilometers
Albers Equal-Area Projection

Map and Globe Skills

Lesson 2

A State of the Arts

WHAT TO KNOW
In what ways is California an important center of culture?

- Describe the development of the entertainment industry in California.
- Analyze the impact of twentieth-century Californians on the nation's artistic and cultural development.

VOCABULARY
special effects p. 439

PEOPLE
John Wayne
Ansel Adams
Judith Baca
Isamu Noguchi
Jack London
William Saroyan
Amy Tan
Dave Brubeck
Isadora Duncan
Julia Morgan
Paul R. Williams
Frank O. Gehry

SUMMARIZE

California Standards
HSS 4.4, 4.4.9

YOU ARE THERE Click! click! click! Camera flashes go off all around you as the movie star steps onto the red carpet. You're here at Grauman's Chinese Theater to see the latest Hollywood movie. Many have come to the theater just to see the actors, but you know that it takes many other people to make a movie. Directors, sound and lighting workers, film editors, computer operators, makeup artists, and costume designers work in the film industry, too.

Grauman's Chinese Theater (left), the Oscar statuette (above), and the Hollywood sign are three symbols of the movie industry in California.

Lights, Camera, Action!

The film industry has been important in California since the early 1900s. During the 1930s and 1940s, a time known as the Golden Age of Hollywood, about 400 films a year were made by movie companies. These companies were also called studios.

Over time, studios became known for the kinds of movies they made. For example, the Walt Disney studio made animated films. The Warner Brothers studio was known for action films, and Metro-Goldwyn-Mayer was known for its movie stars. Other studios made musicals, comedies, or westerns.

Many actors also became known for playing certain kinds of roles in movies. One of these was **John Wayne**. He was born in Iowa, but moved to California when he was six. Wayne made more than 170 movies, many of them westerns.

Workers in the film industry often use computers to make special effects for movies.

Today, California's film companies continue to make many movies and television shows. Some of these shows have amazing special effects. **Special effects** are ways of making things that are not real look real on film. With technology, filmmakers can make an imaginary space voyage look as real as a car ride through a neighborhood.

READING CHECK **SUMMARIZE**
What was the Golden Age of Hollywood?

The landscape of southern California has inspired artist David Hockney. He painted *Pacific Coast Highway and Santa Monica* in 1993.

The Arts in California

California is home to a large number of talented artists. To show their work, the state has many theaters, music centers, and museums. At the J. Paul Getty Center in Los Angeles, visitors view great works of art from around the world. The Oakland Museum of California has California art from the 1800s through today, including paintings from the time of the gold rush.

California also has museums that focus on the history and culture of certain groups. The California African American Museum is in Los Angeles. Sacramento is home to the California State Indian Museum. The Asian Art Museum in San Francisco shows works by Asians. Many Chicano artists, or artists of Mexican heritage, show their works at the Centro Cultural de la Raza in San Diego.

California has long been home to fine artists of all kinds. The photographs of **Ansel Adams** capture the rugged beauty of California's land. Painter **Judith Baca** makes huge wall designs called murals. She then works with hundreds of people who paint the murals. Many of the painters who help Baca are teenagers. One of her murals, *The Great Wall of Los Angeles*, shows the history of ethnic groups in California. **Isamu Noguchi**

A sculpture by Isamu Noguchi

Judith Baca

Amy Tan

Dave Brubeck

(EE•sah•moo noh•GOO•chee) was a sculptor born in Los Angeles. He is known for making large sculptures, stone gardens, and even playgrounds.

Many writers have also come from California. Author **Jack London**, who grew up in the San Francisco Bay area, wrote many exciting adventure tales. **William Saroyan** (suh•ROY•uhn), an Armenian American, wrote about the joys and troubles of immigrants. **Amy Tan** continues to write about the experiences of Chinese Americans.

California has also given the world talented musicians and dancers. **Dave Brubeck**, from Concord, formed a popular jazz group in the 1950s. **Isadora Duncan** was born in San Francisco in 1878. She created new dance styles based on ancient Greek dramas. Duncan's style greatly influenced later dancers.

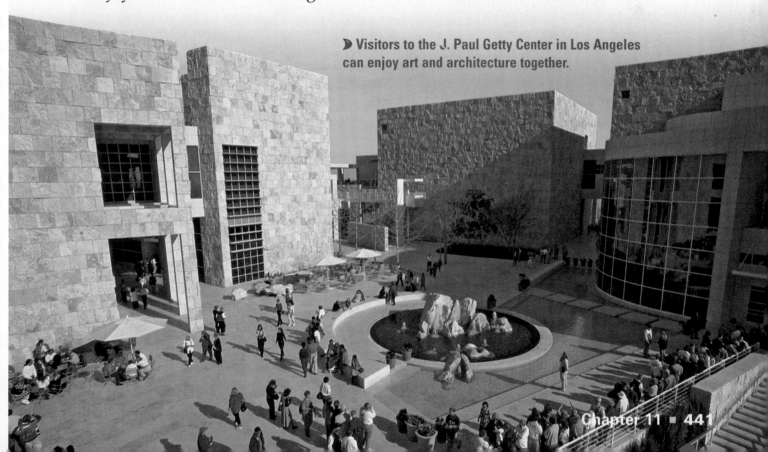

➤ Visitors to the J. Paul Getty Center in Los Angeles can enjoy art and architecture together.

The Walt Disney Concert Hall in Los Angeles

California has also been home to notable architects. **Julia Morgan** designed the Hearst Castle in San Simeon. The LAX Theme Building at the Los Angeles International Airport was designed with the help of **Paul R. Williams. Frank O. Gehry** designed the Walt Disney Concert Hall.

READING CHECK SUMMARIZE
How have Californians influenced the arts?

Summary

Californians have been influential in the arts, including in film, the visual arts, music, writing, dance, and architecture. World-famous museums provide many opportunities to enjoy art and culture in California. The work of Califonia artists often shows the natural beauty of the state.

REVIEW

1. In what ways is California an important center of culture?
2. Use the term **special effects** to describe how movies are made in Hollywood.
3. Name four California artists and the types of work they are known for.

CRITICAL THINKING

4. **Make It Relevant** What kind of art is most important to you? Why?
5. ANALYSIS SKILL Do you think it is important for California to support the arts? Why or why not?
6. **Make a Table** In a table, categorize the Californians you read about in this lesson as artists, writers, musicians, dancers, or architects.
7. Focus Skill **SUMMARIZE**
On a separate sheet of paper, copy and complete the graphic organizer below.

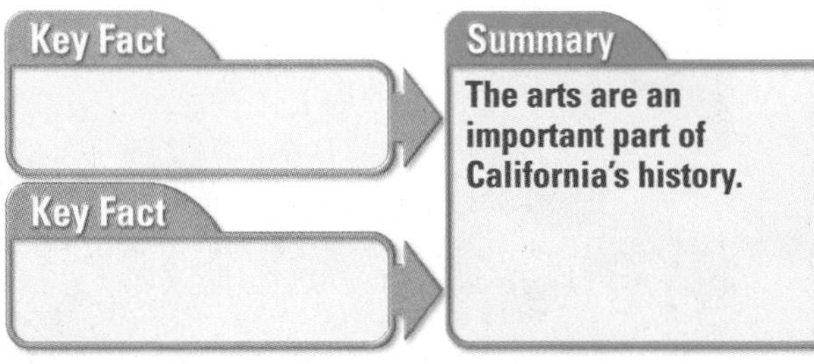
Key Fact
Key Fact
Summary
The arts are an important part of California's history.

Walt Disney

Biography

Trustworthiness

Respect

Responsibility

Fairness

Caring

Patriotism

As a young boy, Walt Disney became interested in drawing. While in grade school, he took drawing classes. As Disney grew older, he knew he wanted to become a film-maker or a cartoonist.

Walt Disney explains his idea for a new form of transportation at his theme park.

After World War I, Disney began working as a commercial artist. In 1923, he moved to Los Angeles, where he set up a movie studio. In 1928, he introduced the world to Mickey Mouse with the film *Steamboat Willie*—the first cartoon with sound. In 1937, he released the first full-length cartoon film, *Snow White and the Seven Dwarfs*. After that, he went on to create many other films.

With the money made from his films, Walt Disney built Disneyland, a theme park that opened in 1955. He said, "Disneyland will never be completed. It will continue to grow as long as there is imagination left in the world."*

*Walt Disney. From a speech given at the opening of Disneyland. July 17, 1955.

Why Character Counts

How do you know Walt Disney respected imagination and creativity?

Bio Brief

1901 Born — **1966** Died

1923 Moves to Los Angeles to work in the film industry

1928 Introduces Mickey Mouse, his most famous animated character

1937 Disney's film *Snow White and the Seven Dwarfs* is a huge success

1955 Disneyland opens in Anaheim, California

GO ONLINE

Interactive Multimedia Biographies
Visit MULTIMEDIA BIOGRAPHIES at www.harcourtschool.com/hss

PRIMARY SOURCES

Ansel Adams's Photographs

As a child, Ansel Adams lived in San Francisco. He was an only child who had problems fitting in at school. Adams spent much time as a boy alone and outdoors. Later in his life, he joined a group called the Sierra Club, which is concerned about saving the natural environment.

In 1922, Adams first published his photographs in the Sierra Club *Bulletin*. From then on, Adams became very well known for his black-and-white images of nature.

This is the kind of camera Ansel Adams used to take some of his photographs.

The photographer uses this switch to open the shutter to allow light to filter through the lens.

The lens filters light and projects the image onto the photographic plate.

A photographic plate records the image the photographer is shooting.

Flowers on a dogwood tree in Yosemite National Park

ANALYSIS SKILL Analyze Artifacts

1. What do many of Ansel Adams's photographs have in common?
2. How would you describe Adams's style of photography?
3. Do you think that Adams's work might inspire other photographers? Explain.

GO ONLINE Visit PRIMARY SOURCES at www.harcourtschool.com/hss

A snow-covered tree in Yosemite National Park

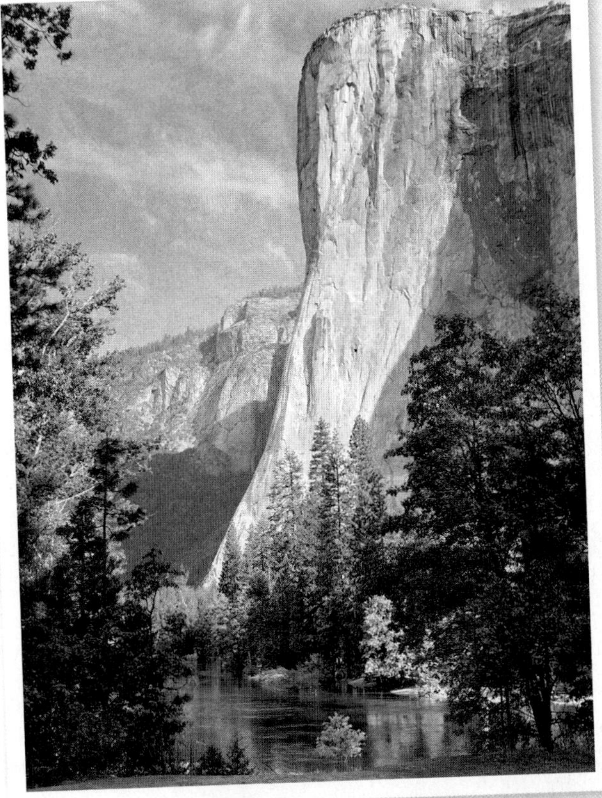

El Capitan in Yosemite National Park

Lesson 3 Education in California

WHAT TO KNOW
What are some of the ways that education will help ensure a bright future for California?

- ✓ Describe how and why California's public education system was developed.
- ✓ Explain how public education is funded and operates in California today.

VOCABULARY
public school p. 447
private school p. 447
generation p. 449

PEOPLE
Robert Semple

SUMMARIZE

California Standards
HSS 4.4, 4.4.8

YOU ARE THERE You and your classmates are watching red worms wriggle through a bin filled with shredded paper and vegetable waste from the school cafeteria. The worms are composting the garbage, or breaking it down into dark, earthy material called compost.

This is just one way students in your school learn about the world around them. Like students everywhere, they read, and listen to the teachers and each other. Schools provide you with an opportunity for a bright future.

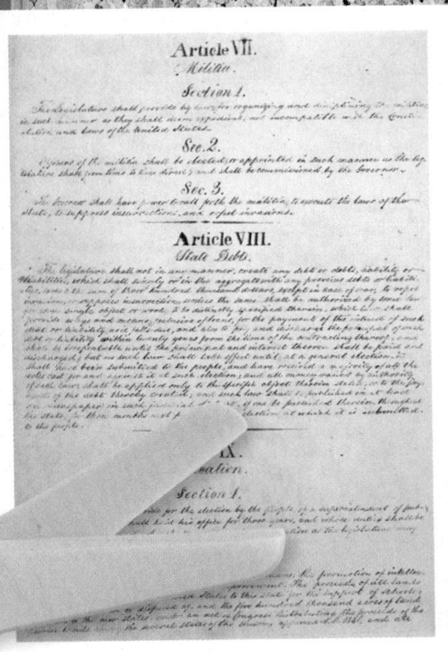
Article VII.
Militia.
Section 1.
Sec. 2.
Sec. 3.
Article VIII.
State Debts.
Section 1.

1849: The state constitution calls for public schools.

1850: The first public school in California funded by tax money is opened in San Francisco.

1852: Mills College, a women's college, is founded in Oakland.

Schools in California

In 1849, at California's first constitutional convention, delegate **Robert Semple** said,

> **"If the people are to govern themselves . . . they must be educated; they must educate their children."***

When California became a state, the new state constitution set up **public schools**. The first public school paid for by city taxes opened in San Francisco in 1850. San Francisco's first public high school opened six years later, in 1856.

*Will C. Wood, State Superintendent of Public Instruction. From *The Bulletin.* Diamond Jubilee Edition, 1925.

Today, more than 6 million students attend public schools in California, more than in any other state. There are about 9,000 public schools in the state. These schools are funded mostly by city, county, and state taxes.

More than 600,000 students in California attend **private schools**. Private schools generally do not get money from taxes. Instead, these schools are funded mostly by private groups and individuals. Students usually pay tuition, or money, to attend private schools. There have been private schools in California since the time the Spanish ruled Alta California.

READING CHECK **SUMMARIZE**
How did public schools in California begin?

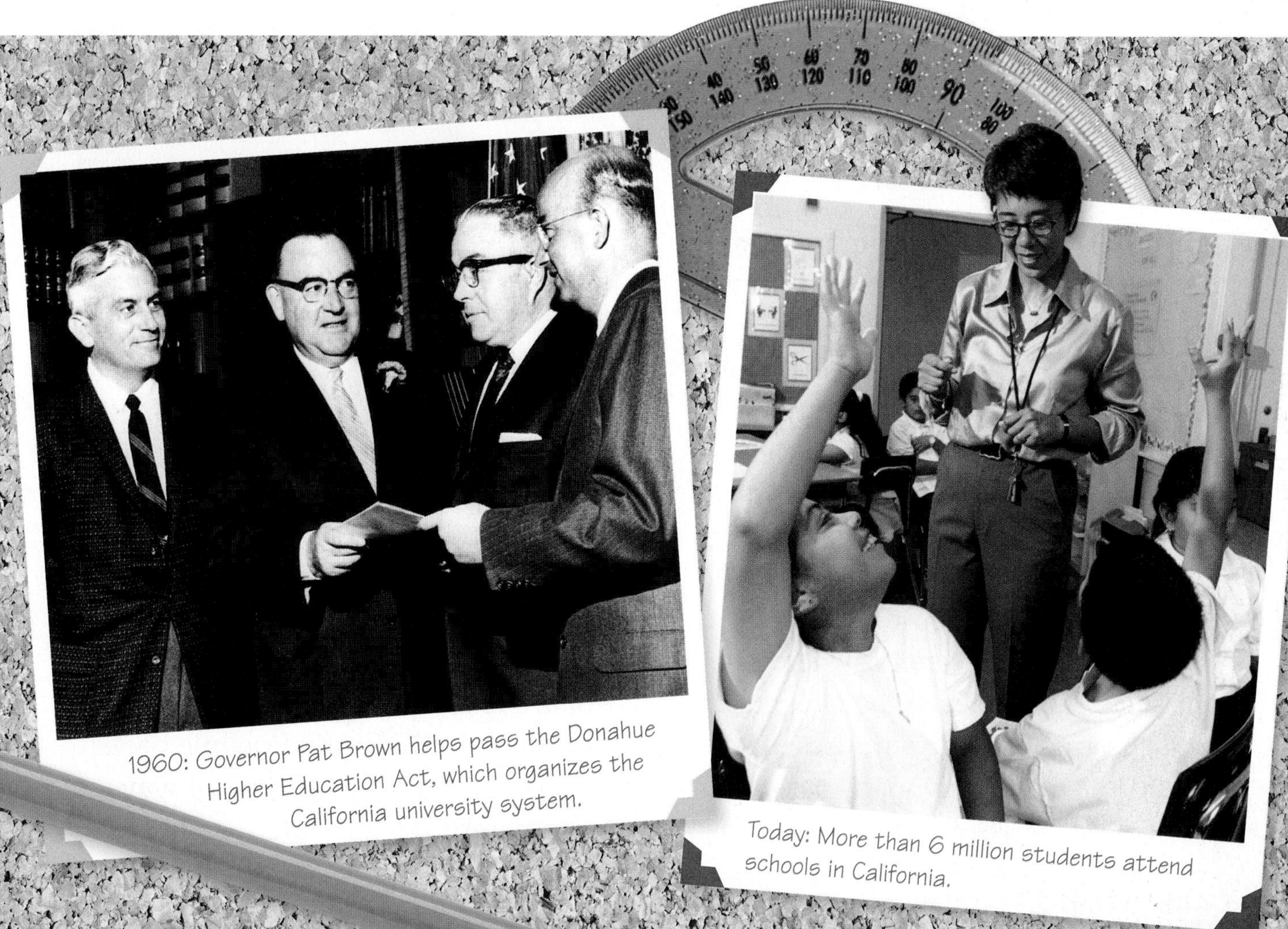

1960: Governor Pat Brown helps pass the Donahue Higher Education Act, which organizes the California university system.

Today: More than 6 million students attend schools in California.

➤ Thousands of students graduate (right) from California colleges and universities each year. As part of their studies, many students conduct scientific research (above).

Educating for the Future

California's first constitution also set up a state university system. Today, California has the largest system of colleges and universities in the United States. Public colleges and universities receive some money from the state government. However, students must also pay to attend. Several state and national programs help students who cannot pay the full cost.

California's university system includes 9 branches of the University of California and 22 campuses of California State University. Besides large universities, California also has many community colleges, which offer two-year programs. Some students choose to attend private colleges. One of the first private colleges in the state, Mills College, was begun in 1852 as a college for women.

The purpose of California's educational system is to prepare students for the future. Educated people have the training needed to think of ways to help improve the state. They help businesses grow. They think of new ways to protect the environment for future generations. A **generation** is a group of people born and living at about the same time. Educated people can also communicate with others to get things done, helping them be more active citizens.

READING CHECK **MAIN IDEA AND DETAILS**
Who pays for public colleges and universities?

Summary

Ever since the state's first constitutional convention, public and private schools have been important to Californians. A good education helps prepare students for the future.

Pasadena hosts the Rose Bowl, a football game between top college teams.

REVIEW

1. What are some of the ways that education will help ensure a bright future for California?
2. Explain the difference between a **public school** and a **private school**.
3. Why are educated Californians more active citizens?

CRITICAL THINKING

4. ANALYSIS SKILL Do you think that California's education system will need to continue to grow and develop? Explain.
5. **Plan for the Future** Think of some jobs that you might want to have in the future. Choose one, and write a paragraph describing the education you think you will need in order to work at this job.
6. Focus Skill **SUMMARIZE**
On a separate sheet of paper, copy and complete the graphic organizer below.

Key Fact	Summary
California has a public education system.	
Key Fact	

Lesson 4

Overcoming Challenges

WHAT TO KNOW

What are some of the challenges facing Californians in the twenty-first century?

- ✓ Describe how Californians use natural resources to provide energy.
- ✓ Explain how Californians plan for the future of the state.

VOCABULARY

energy crisis p. 451
long-term planning p. 451
conservation p. 451
renewable p. 451
nonrenewable p. 451
pollution p. 451
deficit p. 452

SUMMARIZE

California Standards

HSS 4.1, 4.4

YOU ARE THERE

You're reading a good book when suddenly the lights go out. Looking out the window, you see that all of the other homes on the block are dark, too. Has a power line been knocked down? Has your local power station had an accident? You turn on a battery-powered radio, but there are no reports of downed power lines or accidents. Puzzled, you wonder what else could have caused the power outage.

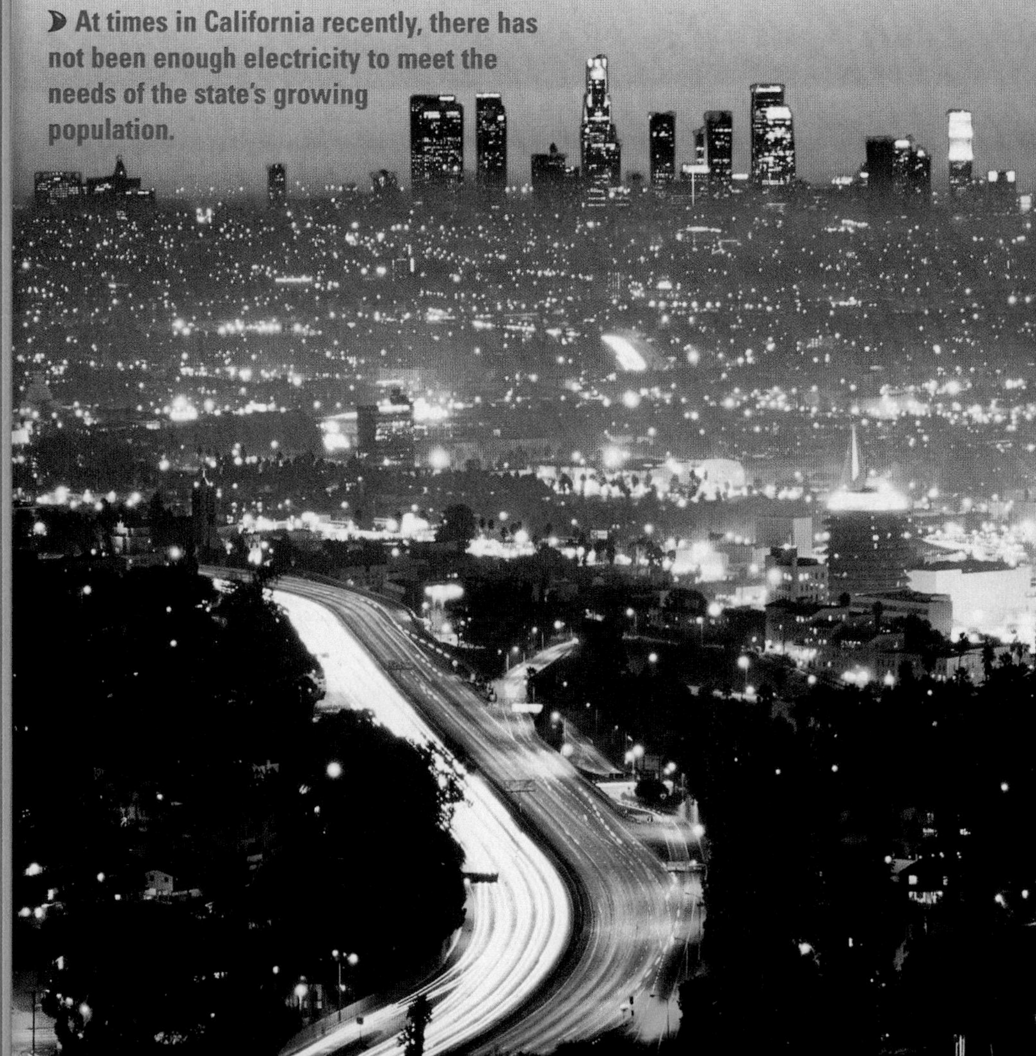

At times in California recently, there has not been enough electricity to meet the needs of the state's growing population.

Planning for the Future

As California has grown, water projects and power plants have been built. In the 1990s and early 2000s, however, California had to deal with an energy crisis. An **energy crisis** happens when there is not enough power to meet demand.

Californians try to prevent such shortages and other problems through **long-term planning**, or making choices based on how they will affect life in the future. **Conservation**—the protection and wise use of natural resources—is one kind of long-term planning.

People use natural resources for almost everything they need. Some resources, such as trees, are **renewable**. They can be made again by nature or people. Others, such as oil and minerals, are **nonrenewable**. They cannot be made again.

Sometimes people's activities cause pollution. **Pollution** is anything that makes a natural resource dirty or unsafe to use. Californians are working to meet their growing needs and at the same time reduce pollution. Researchers have also found ways to make products, such as cars, that cause less pollution. They are also looking for new ways to use energy from renewable resources.

READING CHECK **SUMMARIZE**
What are the two types of natural resources?

These volunteers clean up after an oil spill at Newport Beach. Oil spills in the ocean can harm wildlife and spoil beaches.

California's Economic Future

Californians also use long-term planning when making economic choices. The state government provides services to help citizens, businesses, farms, schools, and the environment. To pay for these services, the state collects tax money. If the state cannot collect enough money through taxes, it may also borrow money.

In recent years, California and many other state governments have faced budget deficits. A **deficit** (DEH•fuh•suht) means that the state has spent more money than it has. As a result, the state has to borrow money to continue providing services. State leaders now must try to find ways to pay off the budget deficit. They also must look for ways to keep the state government running without creating a larger deficit.

Because of the large number of people who live in the state—and

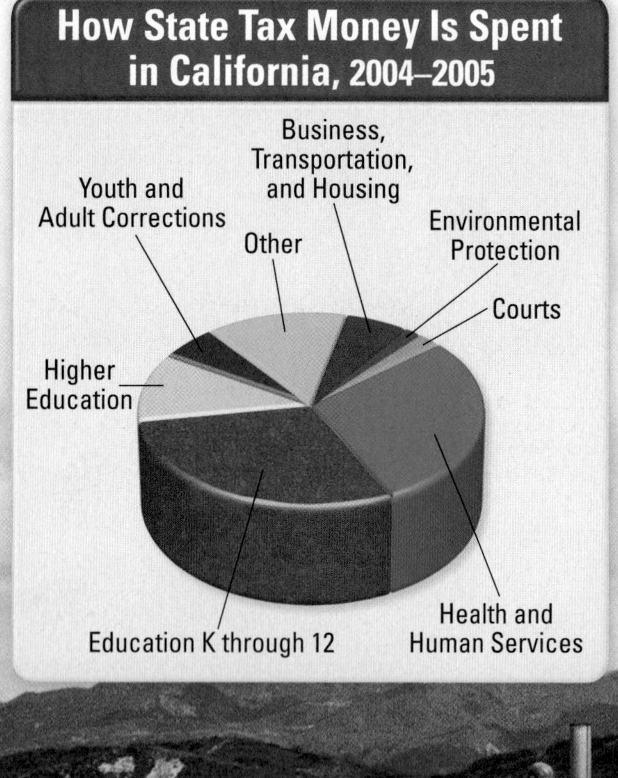

Analyze Graphs **Money collected from state taxes is used to pay for many state services, such as highway construction (below).**

For which services does California spend the most tax dollars?

because the state continues to grow—California will face many challenges in the future. But through education, research, and long-term planning, Californians have opportunities to make sure that the state's future stays bright.

READING CHECK DRAW CONCLUSIONS
How do you think Californians will overcome the budget deficit?

Summary

As California grows, it faces certain challenges. Research and education will help Californians find ways to conserve natural resources and reduce pollution. With planning, they can ensure that there is enough energy for the state and enough money to continue to provide services.

REVIEW

1. What are some of the challenges facing Californians in the twenty-first century?
2. How might energy produced from a **renewable resource** help prevent energy shortages?
3. What have Californians done to help protect the state's environment?

CRITICAL THINKING

4. ANALYSIS SKILL What are some reasons that conservation of resources will continue to be necessary in the future?
5. **Design a Button** Design a button or a bumper sticker showing a way to conserve a natural resource. Explain how your idea will help conserve that natural resource.
6. Focus Skill **SUMMARIZE**
On a separate sheet of paper, copy and complete the graphic organizer below.

Key Fact	Summary
Californians work to protect natural resources.	
Key Fact	

Solve a Problem

WHY IT MATTERS

Think about some problems you have had to solve in the past few weeks. Perhaps you had trouble learning how to do something new. Maybe you did not do as well as you would have liked to on a test and you want to do better next time. Or perhaps you did not have enough money to buy something you really wanted.

People everywhere have problems at some time. Learning how to solve problems is an important skill that you can use now and in the future.

These windmills in Tracy, California, use energy from the wind to turn machines that make electricity.

WHAT YOU NEED TO KNOW

Here are some steps you can use to help you solve a problem.

Step 1 **Identify the problem.**

Step 2 **Find out more information about the problem. Identify the cause or causes of the problem.**

Step 3 **Think of possible solutions to the problem.**

Step 4 **Evaluate the solutions by weighing the advantages and disadvantages of each.**

Step 5 **Choose the best solution, and plan how to carry out that solution.**

Step 6 **Follow your plan. Then think about how well your solution worked. Did it solve the problem? If not, try other solutions until the problem is solved.**

PRACTICE THE SKILL

In the lesson, you read about California's difficulty with providing reliable sources of energy. Think about what might be done to keep energy shortages from happening. Then answer the following questions.

1. How could Californians decrease demand for electric power?
2. How could Californians increase the supply of electric power?

Solar panels collect energy from the sun.

3. What do you think is a wise solution to prevent future energy shortages?

APPLY WHAT YOU LEARNED

Make It Relevant Look around your community. Identify a problem that is important to you. Then use the steps listed in What You Need to Know to solve this problem. Share your ideas with your classmates.

Critical Thinking Skills

Reading Social Studies

When you **summarize**, you restate the key points, or most important ideas, in your own words.

Summarize

Complete the graphic organizer to show what you have learned about the industries, activities, and institutions in California.
A copy of this graphic organizer appears on page 126 of the Homework and Practice Book.

The Golden State

Key Fact

California has a powerful economy supported by international trade and the agriculture, high tech, and service industries.

Key Fact

California's educational system prepares students for the future.

Summary

California Writing Prompts

Write a Summary Imagine you are working to protect and preserve California's environment. Write an article that summarizes the natural resources found in California and calls for their protection.

Write a Report Write a report about the public school system in California. Include information about the history of California's schools as well as how they are organized and funded.

Use Vocabulary

Use each vocabulary word in a sentence that helps explain its meaning.

1. **international trade,** p. 431
2. **import,** p. 433
3. **service industry,** p. 435
4. **special effects,** p. 439
5. **conservation,** p. 451
6. **nonrenewable,** p. 451
7. **pollution,** p. 451
8. **deficit,** p. 452

Apply Skills

ANALYSIS SKILL **Read a Land Use and Products Map** Use the map on page 437 to answer the questions.

9. How is most of the land near Bakersfield used?
10. How is most of the land around Fresno used?
11. Around what city would you find most of the state's salt?
12. What types of products would you find in Los Angeles?

Solve a Problem

13. Imagine you are the governor of California at the time of the energy crisis in the 1990s. What are some questions you might ask to help you find a solution to the problem?

Recall Facts

Answer these questions.

14. How does California's location on the Pacific Ocean benefit its economy?
15. In what ways is California an agricultural giant?
16. How has technology affected the kinds of movies that can be made?

Write the letter of the best choice.

17. What is the name of the area in northern California that is home to many computer companies?
    A High-Tech Valley
    B San Joaquin Valley
    C Silicon Valley
    D Death Valley
18. Which California writer celebrates the culture of Chinese Americans in his or her work?
    A Jack London
    B William Saroyan
    C Robert Frost
    D Amy Tan

Think Critically

19. Which part of California's economy do you think would be most difficult for the state to be without? Why?
20. ANALYSIS SKILL How might California be different if filmmakers had not come to Hollywood in the early 1900s? Explain your answer.

Study Skills

POSE QUESTIONS

Asking questions as you read can help you understand what you are learning.

- **Form questions as you read. Think about why and how events happened and how events and ideas are related.**
- **Use the questions to guide your reading. Look for the answers as you read.**

Californians and Government	
Questions	Answers
What makes the United States Constitution important?	It continues to shape the United States government and can be changed to fit the changing needs or wishes of the people.

Apply As You Read

As you read, write down any questions you have about events, ideas, primary sources, people, or places discussed in the chapter. Then read on to look for the answers.

California History-Social Science Standards, Grade 4

4.5 Students understand the structures, functions, and powers of the local, state, and federal governments as described in the U.S. Constitution.

CHAPTER

Californians and Government

▶ Visiting the California State Capitol in Sacramento

I Love You, California

by F. B. Silverwood

The California state legislature designated "I Love You, California" as the state song in 1951. It was not until 1988, however, that the song became the state song by law.

I love you, California, you're the greatest state of all.
I love you in the winter, summer, spring and in the fall.
I love your fertile valleys; your dear mountains I adore.
I love your grand old ocean and I love her rugged shore.

Chorus:
Where the snow crowned Golden Sierras
Keep their watch o'er the valleys bloom,
It is there I would be in our land by the sea,
Ev'ry breeze bearing rich perfume.
It is here nature gives of her rarest. It is Home Sweet Home to me.
And I know when I die I shall breathe my last sigh
For my sunny California.

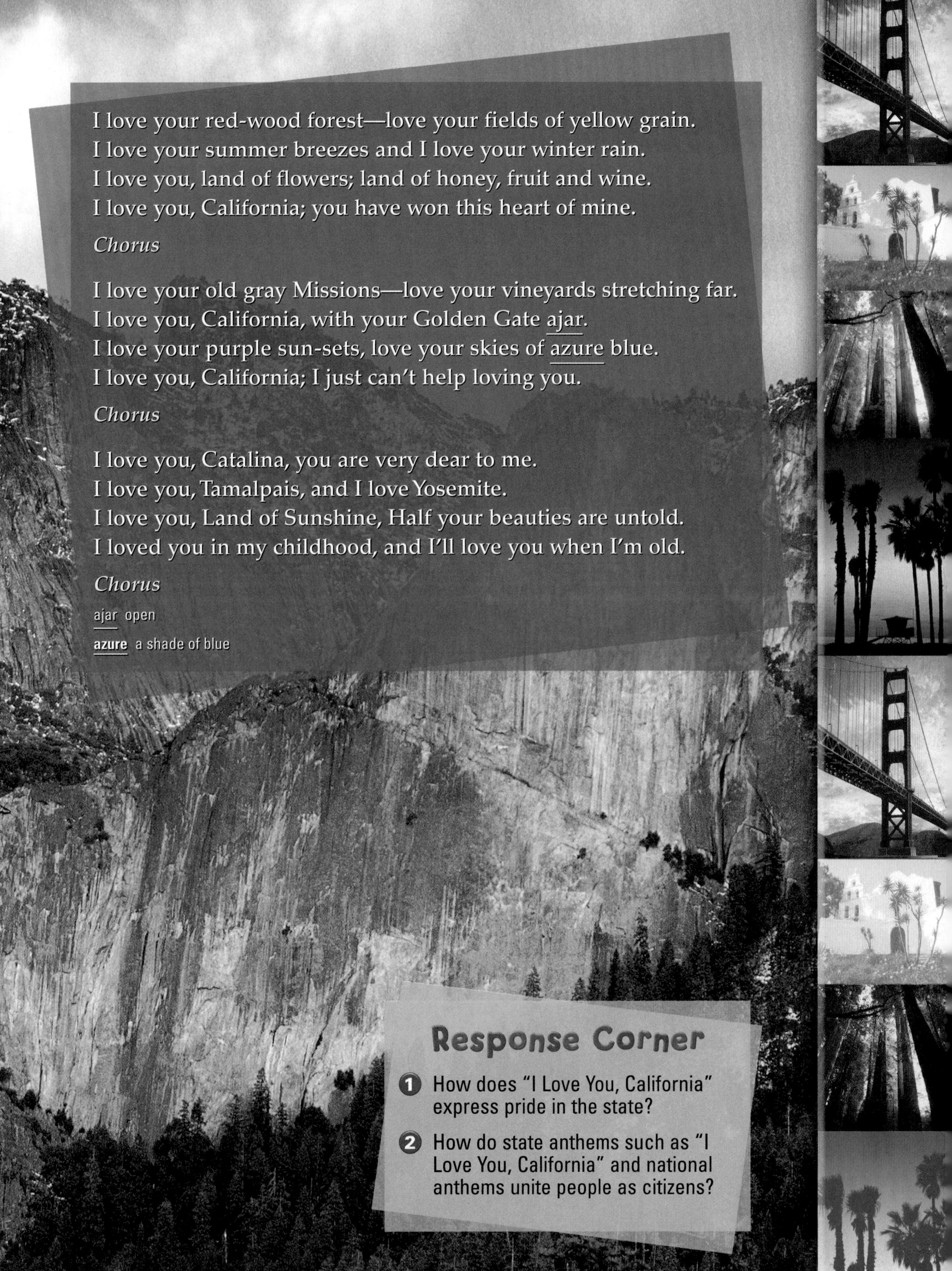

I love your red-wood forest—love your fields of yellow grain.
I love your summer breezes and I love your winter rain.
I love you, land of flowers; land of honey, fruit and wine.
I love you, California; you have won this heart of mine.

Chorus

I love your old gray Missions—love your vineyards stretching far.
I love you, California, with your Golden Gate ajar.
I love your purple sun-sets, love your skies of azure blue.
I love you, California; I just can't help loving you.

Chorus

I love you, Catalina, you are very dear to me.
I love you, Tamalpais, and I love Yosemite.
I love you, Land of Sunshine, Half your beauties are untold.
I loved you in my childhood, and I'll love you when I'm old.

Chorus

ajar open

azure a shade of blue

Response Corner

1. How does "I Love You, California" express pride in the state?
2. How do state anthems such as "I Love You, California" and national anthems unite people as citizens?

Lesson 1

A Plan for Government

WHAT TO KNOW
Why is the United States Constitution important?

- ✓ Explain the structure and purpose of the United States government.
- ✓ Describe the shared powers of federal, state, and local governments, and tell how the levels are similar and different.

VOCABULARY
democracy p. 463
federal p. 463
Cabinet p. 465
tax p. 466

PEOPLE
Dianne Feinstein
Barbara Boxer
Herbert Hoover
Richard Nixon
Ronald Reagan
Stephen J. Field
Earl Warren
Anthony Kennedy

SUMMARIZE

California Standards
HSS 4.5, 4.5.1, 4.5.3

YOU ARE THERE You're gazing at downtown Los Angeles from the backyard of your hillside home. The sky is clear today, but on some days, you can barely see the city. You know that the United States has clean-air laws. You know that California has similar laws. Perhaps your community does, too. But which level of government is responsible for making sure that the air in your community is clean? Chances are that each level of government plays a role.

This painting by Howard Chandler Christy shows the signing of the United States Constitution in 1787.

The Constitution

The United States is a democracy. A **democracy** is a form of government in which the people rule by making decisions themselves or by electing people to make decisions for them. In a democracy, people make decisions by voting.

The United States Constitution was written in 1787. It is the plan for our national, or **federal**, government. It explains how the federal government is organized and what its purpose is. The Constitution says that the government will work toward fairness and peace, defend the nation, and secure its well-being.

The Constitution also gives states the right to form their own governments. In turn, states allow areas within their borders to form local governments. As a result, the United States has three levels of government—national, state, local.

The power to govern is shared among all three levels. However, the Constitution is the supreme, or highest, law of the land. The Constitution is kept up to date through amendments. The first ten amendments, known as the Bill of Rights, list the freedoms promised to all United States citizens.

READING CHECK **SUMMARIZE**
What is the United States Constitution?

The Federal Government

The federal government is located in Washington, D.C. The United States Constitution divides the federal government into three branches, or parts—the legislative, executive (ig•ZEH•kyuh•tiv), and judicial (ju•DIH•shuhl) branches. The United States Constitution makes the branches equal so that no one branch can rule over the other two branches.

Congress is the legislative, or lawmaking, branch. This branch makes laws for the entire nation. Congress has two houses—the Senate and the House of Representatives. The Senate has 100 members. Each state elects two senators. California made history by becoming the first state to elect women—**Dianne Feinstein** and **Barbara Boxer**—to fill both of its Senate seats.

The House of Representatives has 435 members. The number of representatives a state elects depends on how many citizens it has. States with larger populations, such as California, Texas, and New York, have more representatives. California has the most, 53.

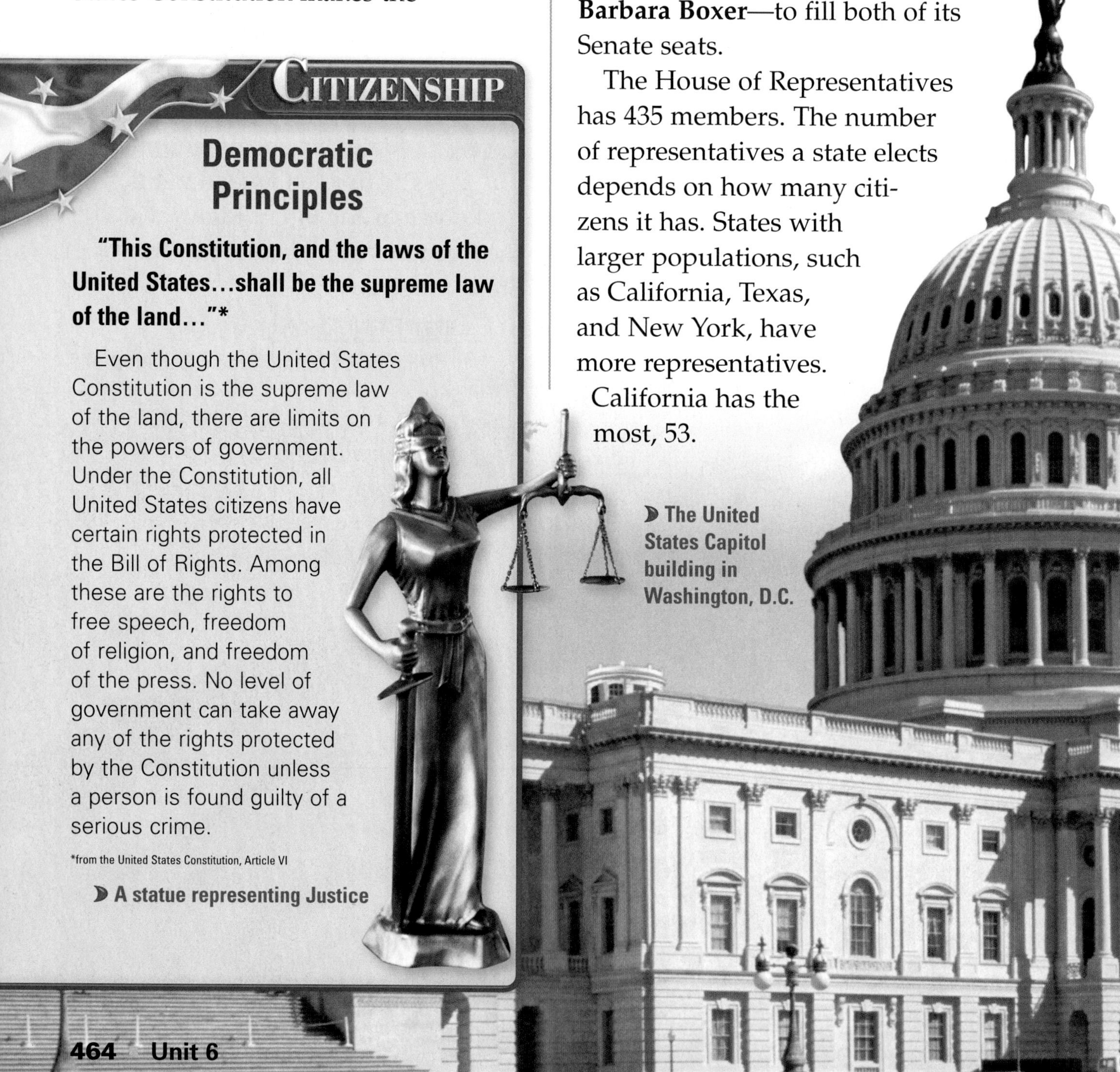

CITIZENSHIP

Democratic Principles

"This Constitution, and the laws of the United States...shall be the supreme law of the land..."*

Even though the United States Constitution is the supreme law of the land, there are limits on the powers of government. Under the Constitution, all United States citizens have certain rights protected in the Bill of Rights. Among these are the rights to free speech, freedom of religion, and freedom of the press. No level of government can take away any of the rights protected by the Constitution unless a person is found guilty of a serious crime.

*from the United States Constitution, Article VI

A statue representing Justice

The United States Capitol building in Washington, D.C.

The executive branch makes sure that the laws made by Congress are carried out. The President is the head of the executive branch. Three people from California—**Herbert Hoover, Richard Nixon,** and **Ronald Reagan**—have been elected President. Other members of the executive branch include the Vice President and the President's Cabinet. The **Cabinet** is a group of the President's most important advisers.

The judicial branch is made up of the United States Supreme Court and all the other federal courts. Justices, or judges, on the Supreme Court are appointed by the President and approved by the Senate. Once appointed, justices serve for life.

Three Californians have served on the Supreme Court. President Abraham Lincoln appointed **Stephen J. Field** in 1863. **Earl Warren** was the chief justice, or head judge, of the Supreme Court from 1953 to 1969, and **Anthony Kennedy** is a justice now.

The Supreme Court decides if laws passed by Congress or actions taken by the President agree with the Constitution. It also decides whether the laws and courts of California and the other states follow the Constitution. Decisions made by the Supreme Court apply to everyone in the United States.

READING CHECK **SUMMARIZE**
What is the function of each of the three branches of the federal government?

Analyze Tables **No branch of the federal government is more powerful than the others.**

Why do you think the federal government has three branches?

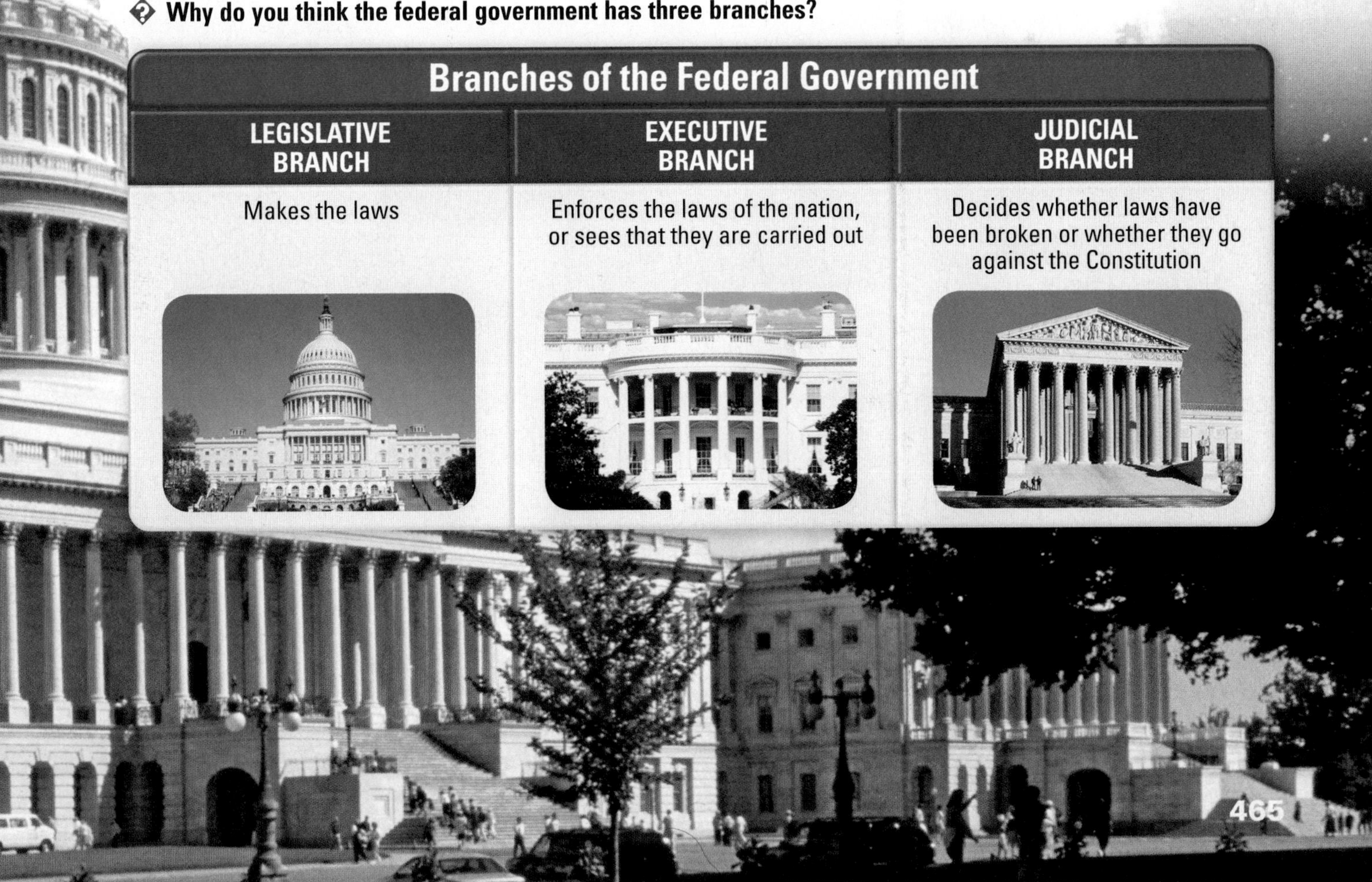

Branches of the Federal Government

LEGISLATIVE BRANCH	EXECUTIVE BRANCH	JUDICIAL BRANCH
Makes the laws	Enforces the laws of the nation, or sees that they are carried out	Decides whether laws have been broken or whether they go against the Constitution

Different Levels of Government

The levels of government—federal, state, and local—are alike in many ways. For example, governments at the federal and state levels follow written constitutions, and duties at each level are divided among three branches.

All levels of government operate only by the consent, or approval, of the citizens. Each level must obey the Constitution and the laws passed by the United States Congress. And each level must follow the rule of law. This means that government and elected officials must obey the same laws that all other citizens obey.

The levels of government share some duties. Each makes laws and ensures that laws are followed. All levels of government also collect taxes. A **tax** is money that a government collects from its citizens, often to pay for services. Tax money is also used to pay government workers and to pay for government equipment.

While they are alike in many ways, the levels of government also have important differences. For example, only the federal government has the power to declare war on another nation. The federal government also controls the nation's military forces.

Scope of Jurisdiction

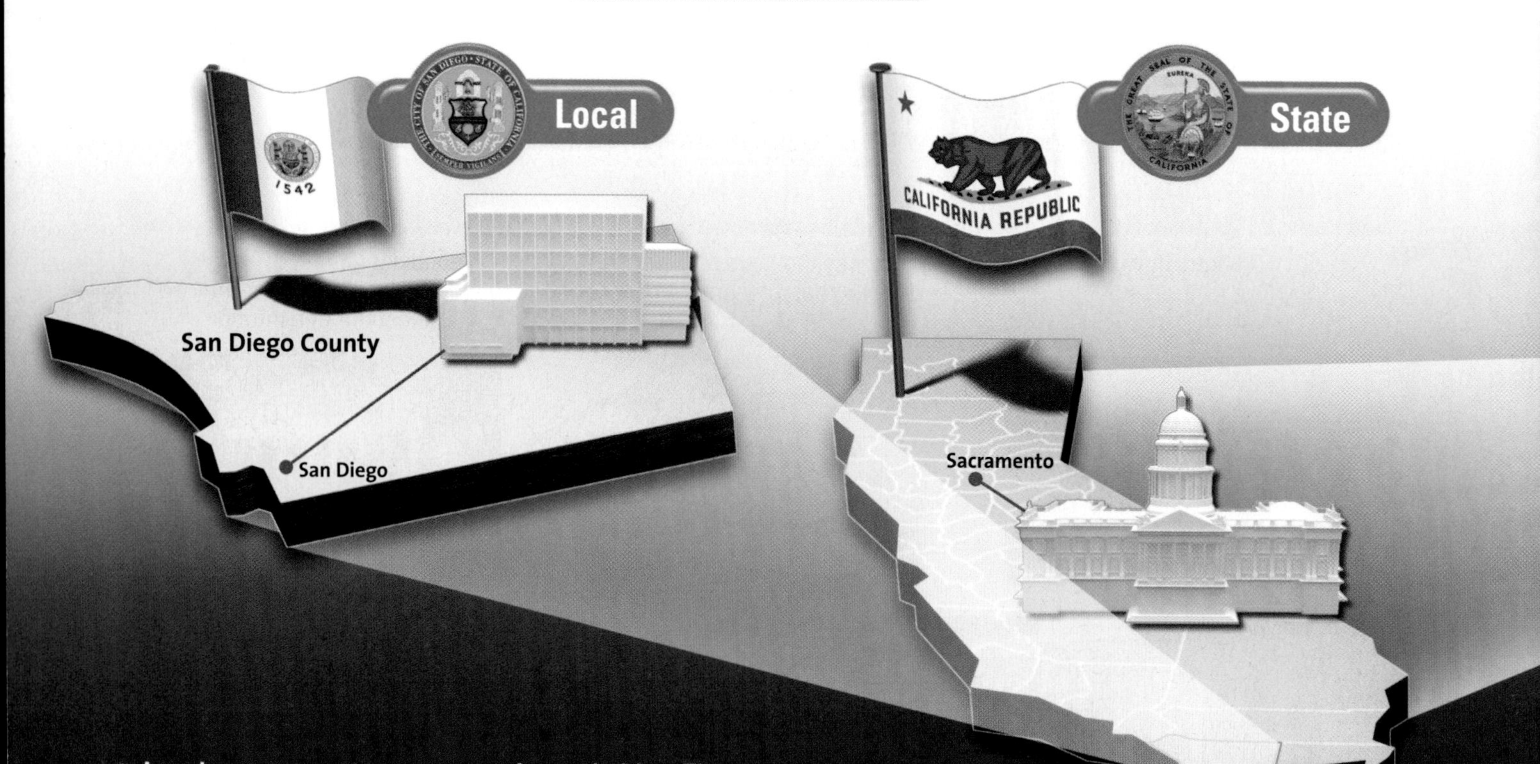

Local governments govern counties and cities. The state government in Sacramento governs all of California. The federal government in Washington D.C., oversees the whole country.

Only the federal government can print money and set up post offices. The federal government also manages trade between states and between the United States and other countries. The federal government has other duties, too, including caring for national parks and historic sites.

Laws created by the three levels of government differ, and they affect different groups of people. Laws passed by the United States Congress apply to all people in the United States. Laws passed by the California state legislature affect only the people within California. Local governments pass laws that apply to the people in particular counties, cities, or towns.

All levels of government have their own courts. However, the United States Supreme Court—the nation's highest court—has the final decision in resolving disputes. State courts deal with cases related to state laws, and local courts deal with cases related to local laws.

State and local governments also have special responsibilities. For example, state governments issue driver's licenses. State and local governments hold elections and provide for the health and safety of citizens.

READING CHECK COMPARE AND CONTRAST
How are the federal, state, and local governments alike?

Analyze Diagrams

Which level of government usually governs a larger area, state government or county government?

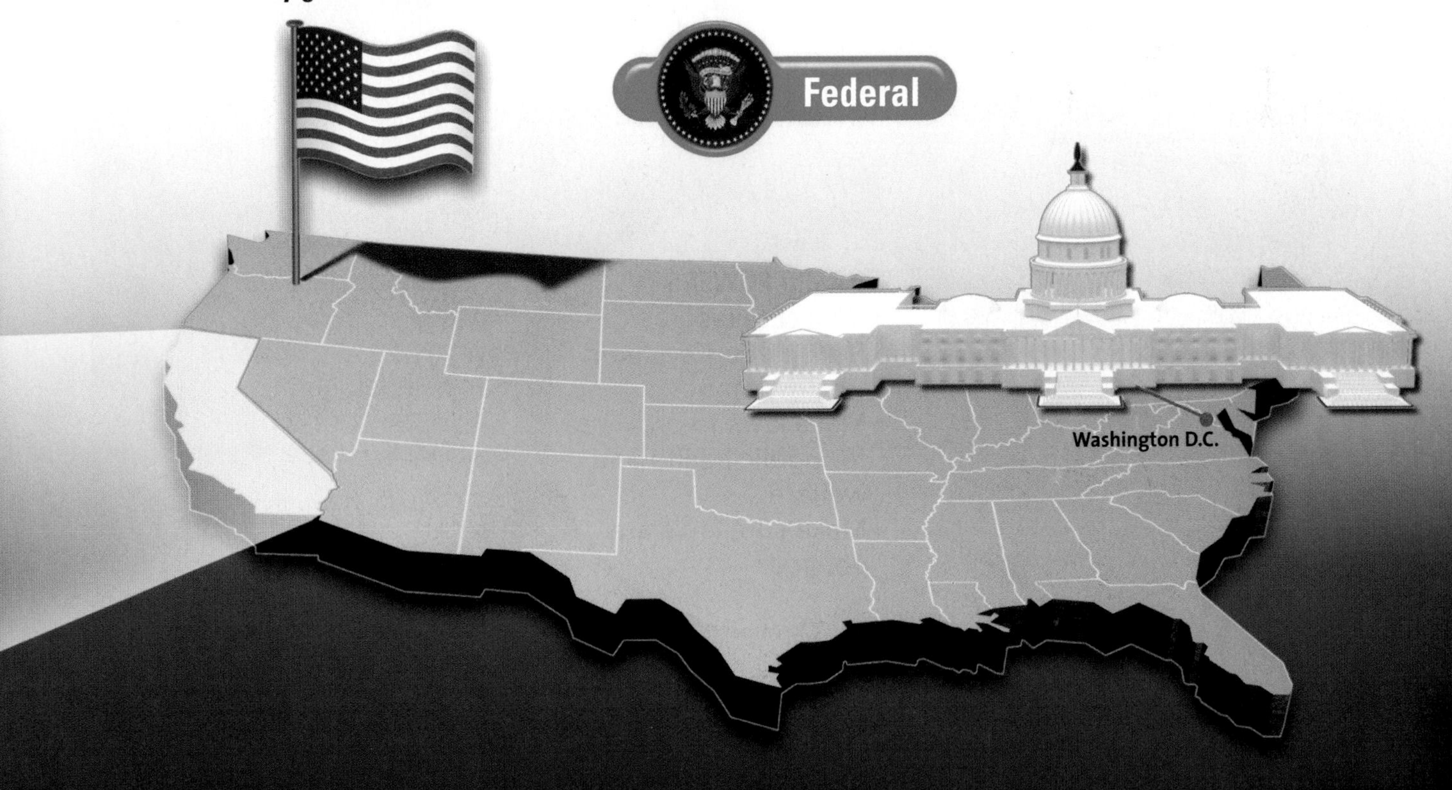

Sharing Responsibilities

Although federal, state, and local governments have different jobs to do, they share responsibilities and powers to reach their goals. For example, each level collects and borrows money to spend on public programs.

Most local governments collect property taxes on homes, businesses, and farms. The federal government and some state governments also collect income taxes, or taxes on the amount of money a person earns. States also collect money through sales taxes—taxes on goods that people buy.

The three levels of government often work together to serve people. For example, the local government takes care of the water pipes in its area. The state government takes care of the reservoirs and canals that collect and carry water to different parts of the state. For major water projects, the federal government provides money to the states.

The three levels of government also work together to provide for public health and safety. For example, local governments keep track of the sources of air pollution in their regions. Some states test cars and trucks to make sure that they are not polluting too much. The federal government sets national

Analyze Tables **Local, state, and federal governments share powers that allow them to work together to help people.**

Why do you think each level of government has the power to collect taxes?

Federal System of Government

SOME POWERS OF FEDERAL GOVERNMENT

- Control trade between states and with foreign countries
- Create and maintain an army and a navy
- Print and coin money
- Admit new states
- Make laws for immigration and citizenship
- Declare wars and make peace

SOME POWERS OF STATE GOVERNMENT

- Set up public schools
- Set up local governments
- Conduct elections
- Control trade within the state
- Make laws for marriage and divorce
- Set qualifications for voting

SHARED POWERS

- Collect taxes
- Set up court systems
- Borrow money
- Make laws to provide for public health and welfare
- Make sure laws are obeyed

SOME POWERS OF LOCAL GOVERNMENT

- Set up local services such as fire protection and waterworks
- Set up local libraries and parks

SKILL Analyze Maps The federal government operates eight national parks, 18 national forests, and one national seashore in California. The state government operates almost 100 state parks.

Place Which national park is nearest to Palm Springs?

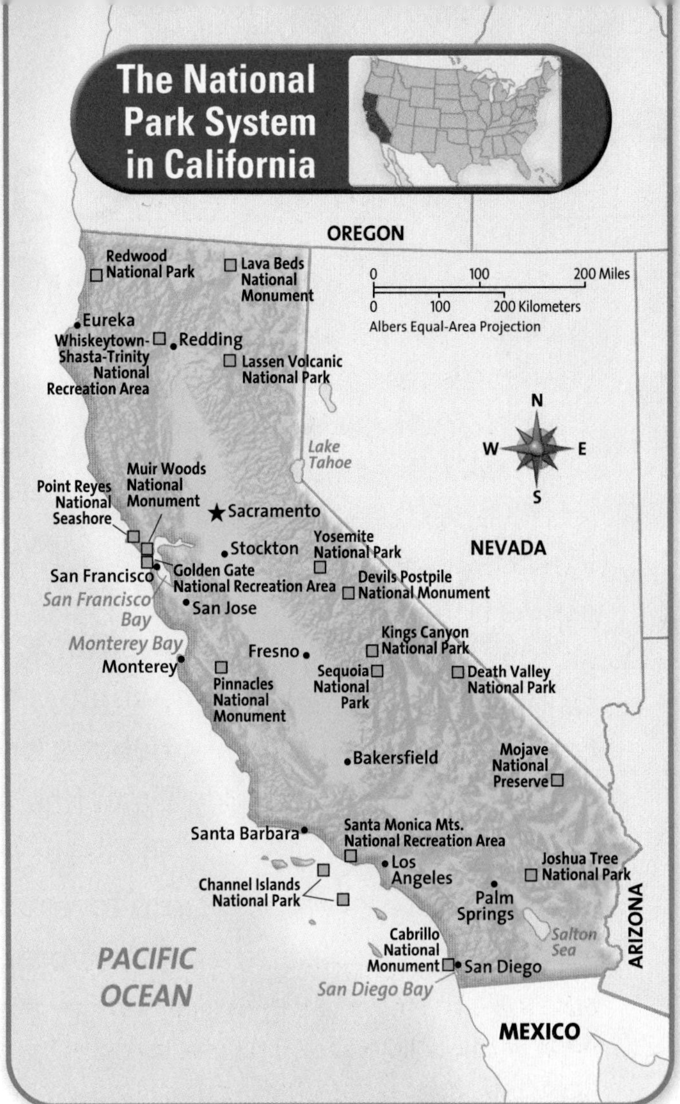

standards to make sure air quality is good. In this way, the levels of government work together for the good of all citizens.

READING CHECK SUMMARIZE

What are some things that the levels of government provide by working together?

Summary

Government in the United States is divided into three levels—federal, state, and local. Federal and state governments have three branches. All three levels of government work together and share responsibilities.

REVIEW

1. Why is the United States Constitution important?
2. Use the term **Cabinet** to explain the work of the executive branch of the federal government.
3. In what ways is the federal government more powerful than state or local governments?

CRITICAL THINKING

4. SKILL Why do you think the authors of the United States Constitution set up three branches of government?
5. How does the federal government help unite people in California and the rest of the states?
6. **Write a Pamphlet** Think about what someone who is new to the United States should know about the Constitution. Write a pamphlet in which you describe the Constitution.
7. **SUMMARIZE**
   On a separate sheet of paper, copy and complete the graphic organizer below.

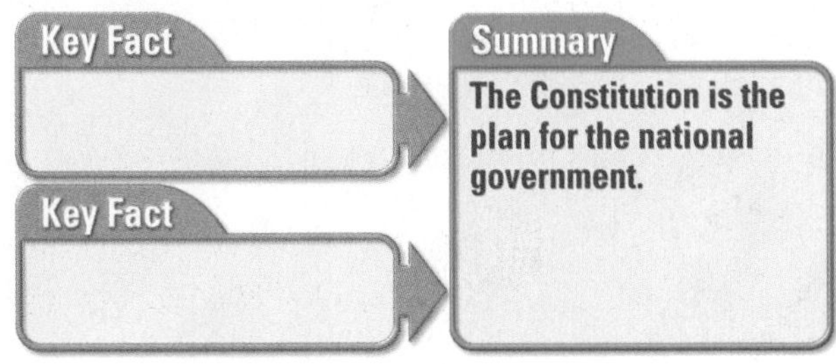

Lesson 2

California State Government

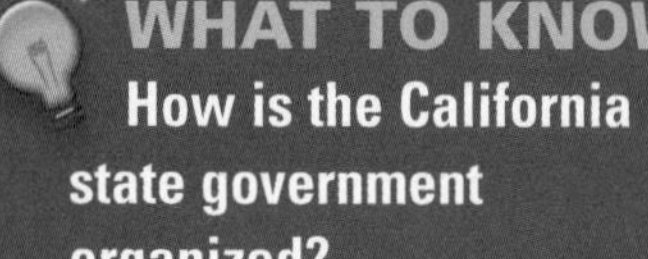

WHAT TO KNOW
How is the California state government organized?

- Analyze the purpose of and the key principles in the California Constitution.
- Describe the work of each branch of state government, and describe the roles of officials in each branch.

VOCABULARY
bill p. 472
budget p. 473
veto p. 473
recall p. 475
initiative p. 475
petition p. 475
referendum p. 476

PEOPLE
Ronald M. George
Gray Davis
Arnold Schwarzenegger

PLACES
Sacramento

SUMMARIZE

California Standards
HSS 4.5, 4.5.2, 4.5.3, 4.5.4

YOU ARE THERE It's election day, and you're at the voting booth. Finally, you're 18 years old—old enough to vote for the first time. You have listened to the people who are running for office debate, or discuss, the issues. Each has a different plan to make the state a better place. Now it's up to you to decide who will get your vote.

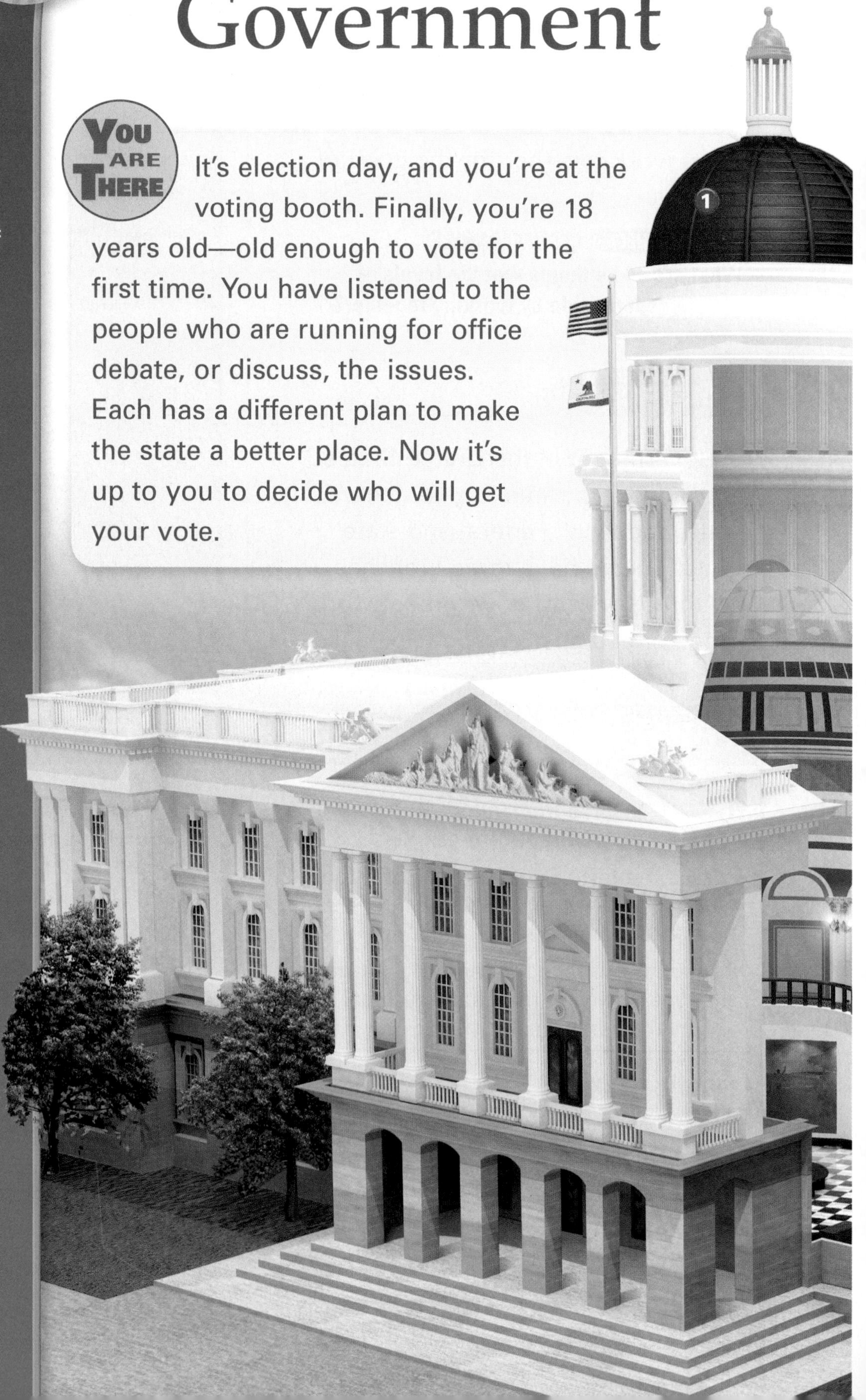

1

The California Constitution

Before newly elected California officials and employees take office, they make a public promise that begins with these words:

> "I will support and defend the Constitution of the United States and the Constitution of the State of California . . ."*

In doing so, they promise to follow the laws laid out in both documents.

The California Constitution is the written plan for the state government. It is similar in many ways to the United States Constitution.

Like the United States Constitution, the California Constitution sets up a government with three branches. These branches are modeled after the executive, legislative, and judicial branches of the federal government.

Another part of the California Constitution—the Declaration of Rights—lists the rights and freedoms of citizens. Many of these rights and freedoms are also listed in the United States Constitution.

READING CHECK **SUMMARIZE**
What is the purpose of the California Constitution?

*From the California Oath of Office. California Constitution, Article 20 miscellaneous subjects. www.leginfo.ca.gov.

The State Capitol

The California state capitol building in Sacramento was completed in 1874.

1. **capitol dome**
2. **The Historic Offices**
3. **The State Senate Chamber**

Which branch of the state government is located in the capitol building?

The Great Seal of the State of California

Analyze Artifacts **The California state seal is used on all official state papers.**

1. **The seal features California's motto, *Eureka*, which means "I have found it."**
2. **Minerva, the Roman goddess of wisdom, holds a shield on which there are 31 stars. The stars stand for the number of states in the Union at the time that California joined the United States.**
3. **The grape vine and wheat at Minerva's feet stand for California's many agricultural products.**

Why do you think a grizzly bear, a gold miner, and ships are also shown on the seal?

California's Legislature

In California, the legislative branch is called the California State Legislature. It is similar to the United States Congress in many ways. The state legislature has two parts, known as houses—the senate and the assembly. Members represent the different districts, or parts, of the state.

The California Senate has 40 members, called senators. Voters in each district elect state senators to four-year terms. Each senator may serve no more than two terms. The California Assembly has 80 members. They are elected to two-year terms and may serve no more than three terms.

The two houses meet in the state capitol in **Sacramento**. Members of each house can present **bills**, or plans for new laws. Each house first works

The state legislature meets inside the capitol building to discuss, debate, and vote on laws.

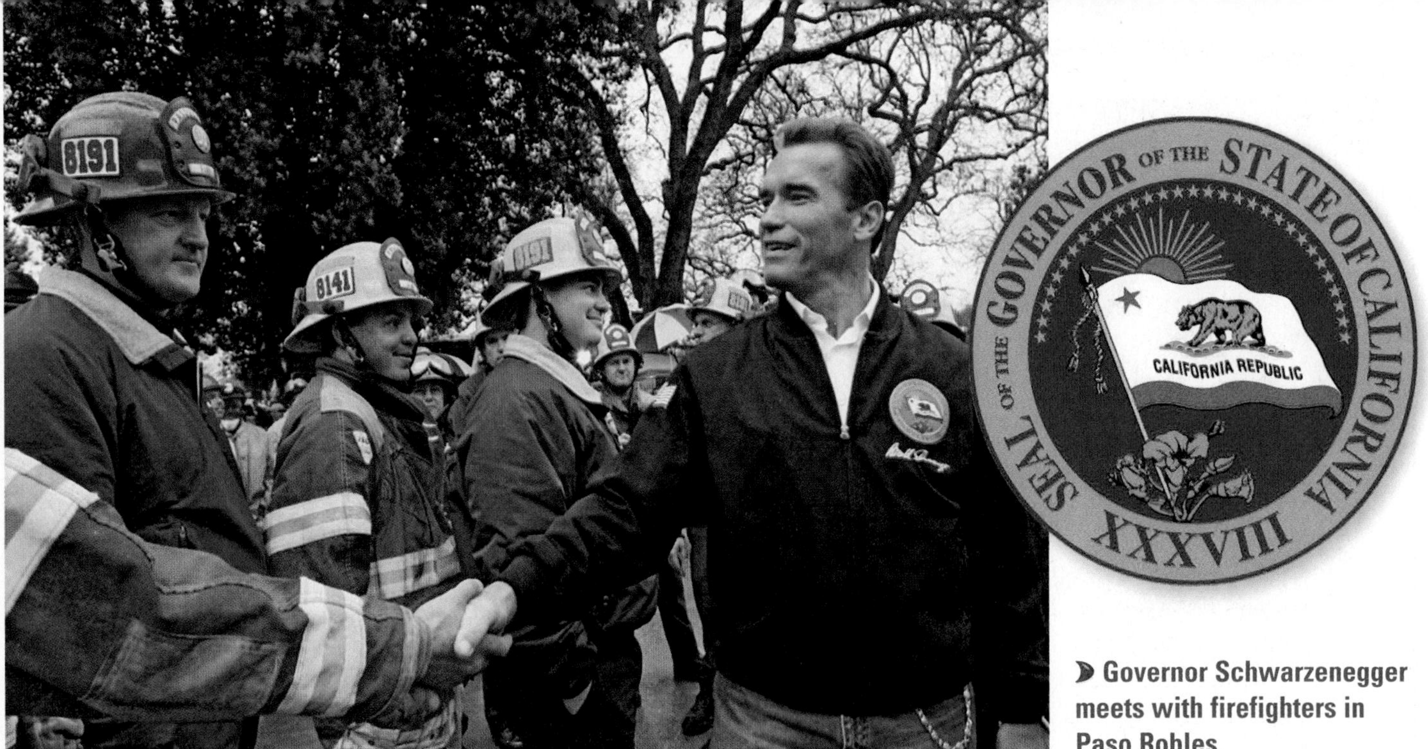

Governor Schwarzenegger meets with firefighters in Paso Robles.

on bills by itself. Bills that are passed, or agreed to, by one house are sent to the other house for its approval.

The state legislature also decides how state taxes will be spent. State taxes are used to operate the state government. Taxes also pay for roads, buildings, schools, parks, and programs to help citizens.

READING CHECK **SUMMARIZE**
What are the two houses of the California State Legislature?

California's Executive Branch

The governor is the leader of the state's executive branch. State voters elect the governor to serve a four-year term. In addition to enforcing laws, the governor's office creates a **budget**, or written plan for how to spend state money. The governor then gives the budget to the legislature for its approval. The governor can also suggest bills to the legislature.

All bills are approved by both houses of the legislature. If they are approved, they are then given to the governor. If the governor signs a bill, it becomes law. If the governor takes no action on a bill, it becomes a law after 12 days.

If the governor does not agree with a bill, he or she can **veto** (VEE•toh), or reject, it. The legislature can still pass a vetoed bill but only if two-thirds of the members of both houses vote for it. The governor also chooses leaders to run government agencies and departments, such as the Department of Motor Vehicles.

READING CHECK **DRAW CONCLUSIONS**
How can the governor of California stop a bill from becoming law?

Chief Justice Ronald George (left) swears in Justices Marvin Baxter, Kathryn Werdegar, and Carlos Moreno (left to right) to the California Supreme Court.

California's Judicial Branch

The judicial branch is made up of all state courts. State judges make sure that California laws are used fairly. They also decide if the laws agree with the state constitution.

The California Supreme Court is the state's highest court. It is made up of seven judges called justices. One of these is chosen as the chief justice. The current chief justice is **Ronald M. George**. The supreme court hears cases about the rights and freedoms of California citizens. The justices also deal with questions having to do with the California Constitution.

Under the California Supreme Court are six state courts of appeal. In law, to appeal is to ask for another trial. The courts of appeal hear cases that challenge a decision made earlier in a lower court. Judges study the arguments on both sides. They then decide whether to support or reject the lower court's decision.

Justices of the supreme court and courts of appeal are appointed by the governor. Voters are then asked to approve the governor's choices. If approved, a justice serves for 12 years. Judges in lower courts are elected directly by voters.

READING CHECK **GENERALIZE**

Why is the California Supreme Court important?

California Voters

The California Constitution gives the state's voters some special powers. Voters in many other states do not have these powers.

Voters in every state elect their governor and the members of their state legislature. But in California and just a few other states, voters can also **recall** their officials, or remove them from office. In the fall of 2003, for the first time in California's history, citizens voted to recall the elected governor. Governor **Gray Davis** was recalled, and **Arnold Schwarzenegger** (SHWAW•tzuh•neh•ger) was elected to take his place.

Voters in California also have the power to pass initiatives (ih•NIH•shuh•tivz). An **initiative** is a law made directly by voters instead of by a legislature.

For an initiative to be passed, it must go through a certain process. First, voters sign a petition (puh•TIH•shuhn) saying that they want a new law. A **petition** is a signed request for action. If enough voters sign the petition, the initiative is presented to all California voters at the next election. If more than half the voters vote to support the initiative, it becomes law. California citizens can also make changes to their state constitution in this way.

CITIZENSHIP

Democratic Principles

"All political power is inherent in the people…they have the right to alter or reform [the government] when the public good may require."*

In 1911, leaders changed the California Constitution to allow for recall, initiative, and referendum. Recently, California citizens used their right to petition for the recall of any elected official. During a special election in 2003, Californians voted on whether Governor Gray Davis should be removed from office. They also voted on who should replace him if he were removed.

Almost 9 million Californians voted in the recall election. Nearly 5 million votes were in favor of recalling Governor Davis. To replace him as governor, more than 4 million voters chose Arnold Schwarzenegger.

*from the California State Constitution, Article II, Section 1

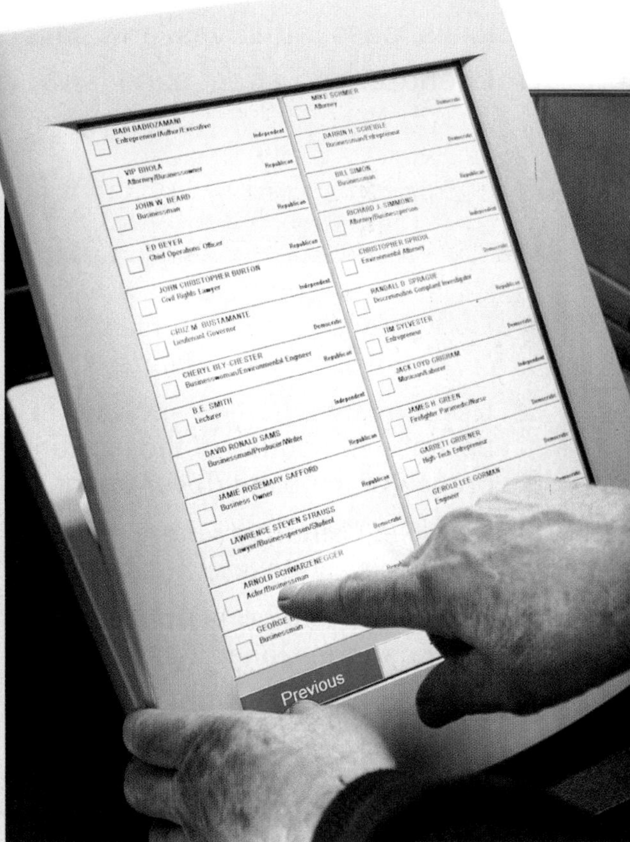

In 2003, Californians voted on who should replace Governor Gray Davis.

If voters do not like a law passed by the state government, they can take action against it. They can sign a petition asking that a referendum (reh•fuh•REN•duhm) be held. A **referendum** is an election in which voters can decide whether to keep or do away with an existing law.

READING CHECK SUMMARIZE
How do the recall, initiative, and referendum processes give power to voters?

Summary

The California Constitution sets up a government with three branches. California voters elect the governor, members of the legislature, and judges. They can also recall elected officials, pass initiatives, and pass referendums to affect state laws.

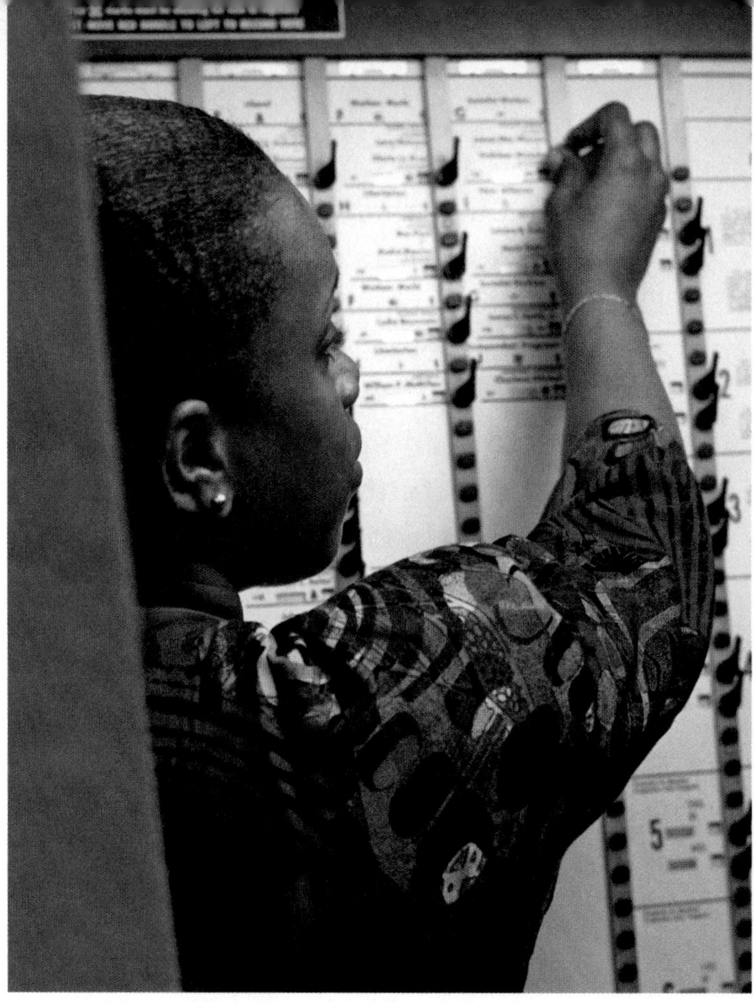
In each election, California voters have an opportunity to have a voice in their government.

REVIEW

1. How is the California state government organized?
2. Use the terms **budget** and **veto** to describe the duties of the executive branch of the state government.
3. How can California voters make changes to state laws?
4. How is the California Constitution similar to the United States Constitution?

CRITICAL THINKING

5. ANALYSIS SKILL Why is it important for California voters to be able to make changes to the laws of their state?
6. **Deliver a Speech** Imagine that you are one of the leaders in the state government, such as governor or chief justice. In a speech to the class, describe the work you do and why your work is important.
7. Focus Skill **SUMMARIZE**
On a separate sheet of paper, copy and complete the graphic organizer below.

Key Fact	Summary
The governor enforces laws.	
Key Fact	
The governor can veto a bill.	

Ronald Reagan

Biography

Trustworthiness
Respect
Responsibility
Fairness
Caring
Patriotism

*"My fellow citizens, our nation is poised for greatness. We must do what we know is right and do it with all our might."**

Ronald Wilson Reagan was born in 1911 in Illinois. He spent his childhood in the town of Dixon. As a teenager, he rescued 77 people while working as a lifeguard. After finishing college, Reagan worked as a radio sports announcer. In 1937, he went to Hollywood to act in films. Reagan starred in many movies and served as president of the actors' union for several years.

Ronald Reagan gives a speech as governor of California in 1966.

Reagan also became active in politics. In 1966, he was elected to the first of two terms as governor of California. In 1980 and again in 1984, he was elected President of the United States.

As President, Reagan worked to make the federal government smaller and to keep the United States strong against the enemies of democracy.

*From Ronald Reagan's second Presidential Inauguration speech, January 21, 1985.

Why Character Counts

How do Ronald Reagan's words and actions show his patriotism toward the United States?

Bio Brief

1911 Born — 2004 Died

1966 Elected to the first of two terms as governor of California

1980 Elected to the first of two terms as President of the United States

1994 Announces that he has Alzheimer's disease, an illness that attacks the brain

Interactive Multimedia Biographies
Visit MULTIMEDIA BIOGRAPHIES at www.harcourtschool.com/hss

Read a Flowchart

WHY IT MATTERS

Some information is easier to understand when it is presented in a drawing. The drawing on these pages is a flowchart. A **flowchart** is a drawing that shows the steps in a process. The arrows in a flowchart help you see the order of the steps.

WHAT YOU NEED TO KNOW

The flowchart shows how the California state government makes new laws. The first box of the flowchart shows the first step in passing a law. In this step, a member of the California Senate or California Assembly writes a bill. A bill may begin in either of the two houses.

In the second step, the bill is sent to a special committee. A committee is a small group of lawmakers from either legislative house. Committee members study the bill and then tell the other members of their house whether they

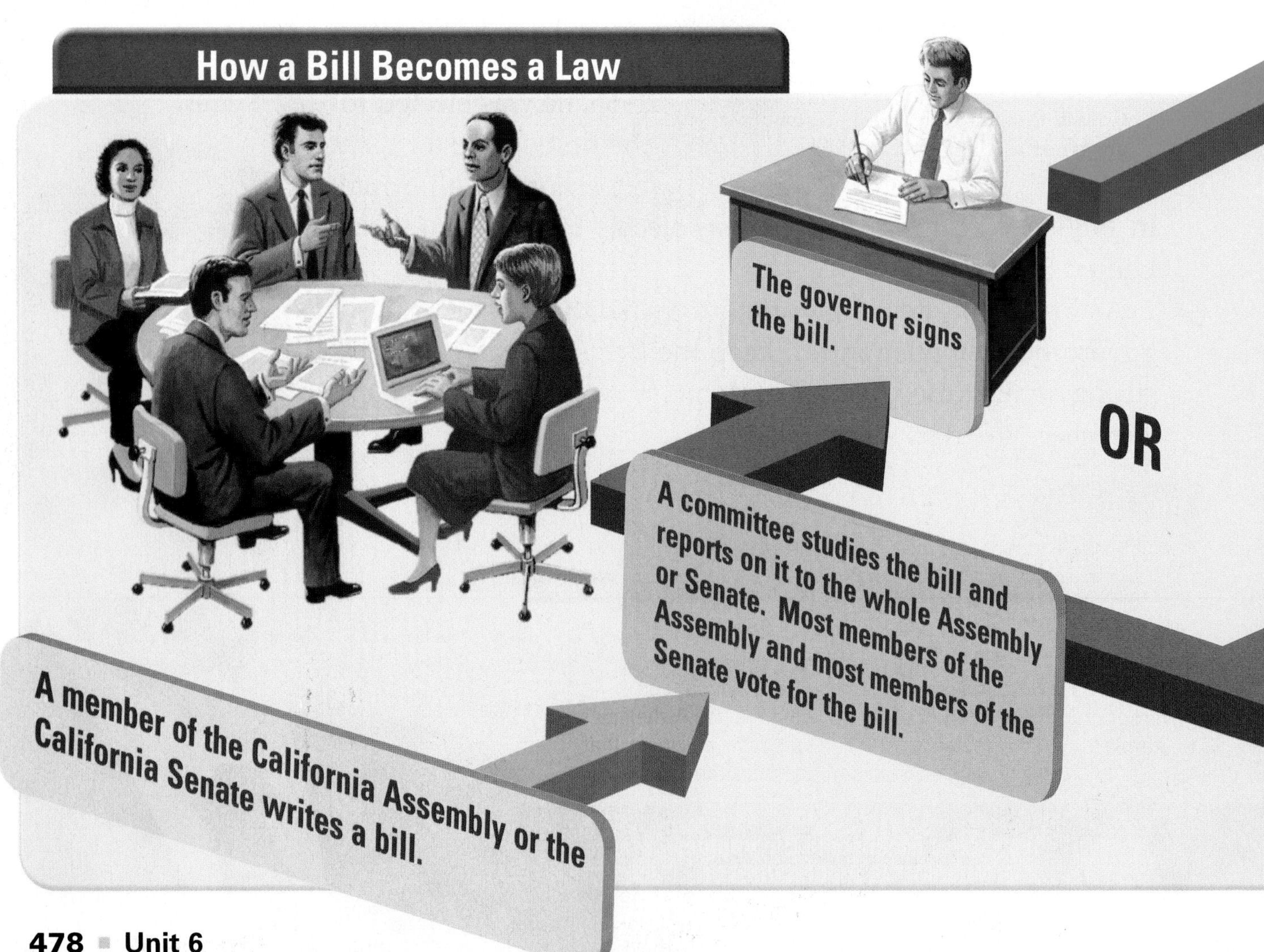
How a Bill Becomes a Law
A member of the California Assembly or the California Senate writes a bill.
A committee studies the bill and reports on it to the whole Assembly or Senate. Most members of the Assembly and most members of the Senate vote for the bill.
The governor signs the bill.
OR

think the proposed bill would make a good law.

Read the rest of the steps in the flowchart to find out what else must happen for a bill to become a law.

PRACTICE THE SKILL

Use the flowchart to answer these questions.

1. What happens after both the California Assembly and the California Senate approve a bill?
2. What actions can the governor take when he or she receives a bill?
3. How can a bill become a law if the governor vetoes it?

APPLY WHAT YOU LEARNED

Make It Relevant Work with a partner to create a process for making decisions in your class. Make a flowchart to show the steps in the process and how they connect. Write each step on a strip of paper. Then paste the strips, in order, onto posterboard, and connect the steps with arrows. Share your flowchart with your classmates.

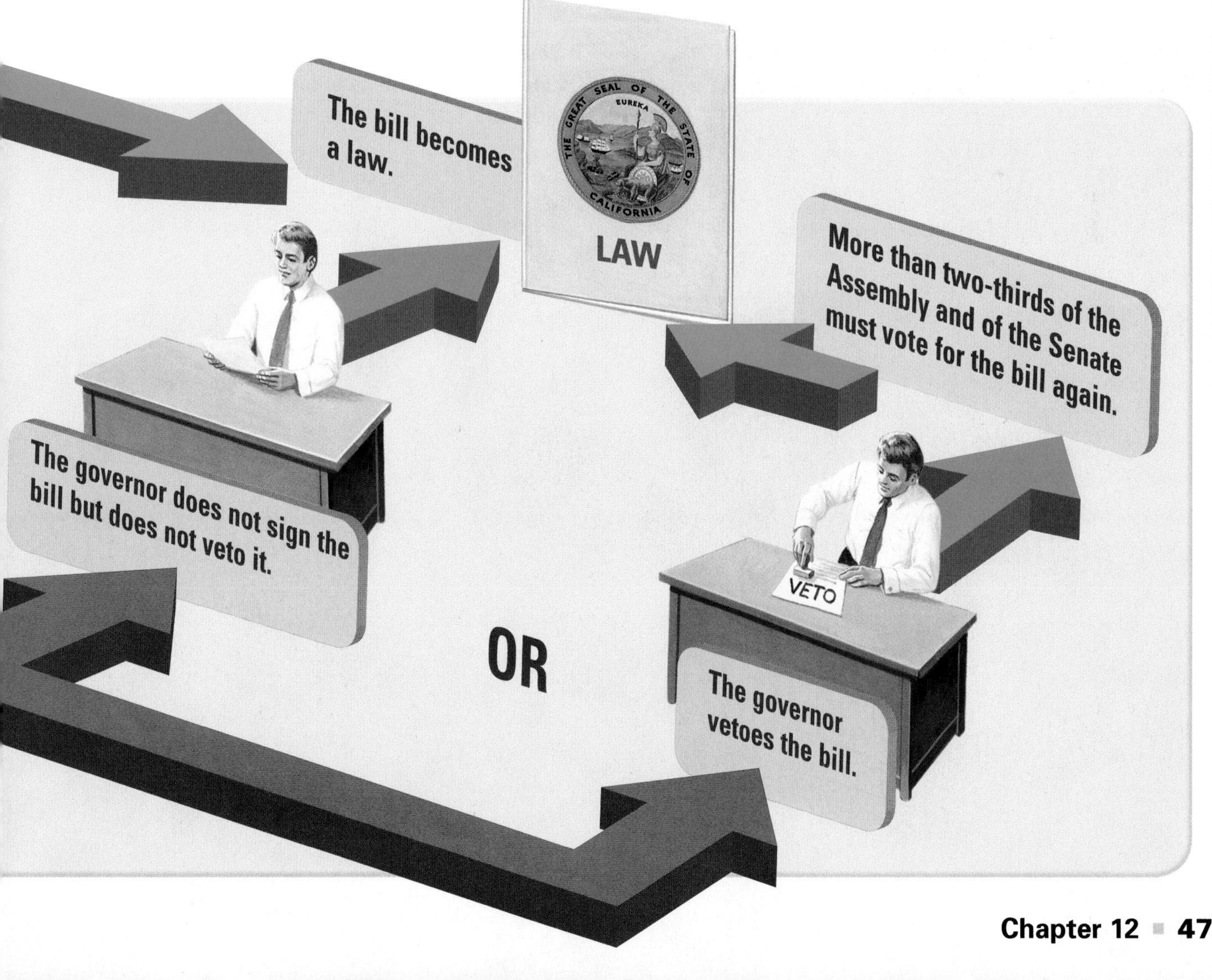

The bill becomes a law.
THE GREAT SEAL OF THE STATE OF CALIFORNIA
EUREKA
LAW
More than two-thirds of the Assembly and of the Senate must vote for the bill again.
The governor does not sign the bill but does not veto it.
OR
VETO
The governor vetoes the bill.

Chart and Graph Skills

Lesson 3

Local Governments

WHAT TO KNOW

How are California's local governments organized, and what do they do?

- ✓ Summarize how California's local governments are organized.
- ✓ Describe the function of each part of California's local governments.
- ✓ Explain the functions of California's special forms of local government.

VOCABULARY

county p. 481
county seat p. 481
board of supervisors p. 481
jury trial p. 482
municipal p. 483
city manager p. 484
special district p. 485
regional body p. 485
rancheria p. 486
sovereign p. 486

SUMMARIZE

California Standards
HSS 4.5, 4.5.3, 4.5.5

YOU ARE THERE It's been several months since the city closed its park for repairs. Now you walk past the new playground and beds of freshly planted flowers to join a large group of people gathered in front of a stage. Soon the mayor arrives and gives a speech, thanking the many people who worked on the park. Then she cuts a ribbon, and the park is reopened.

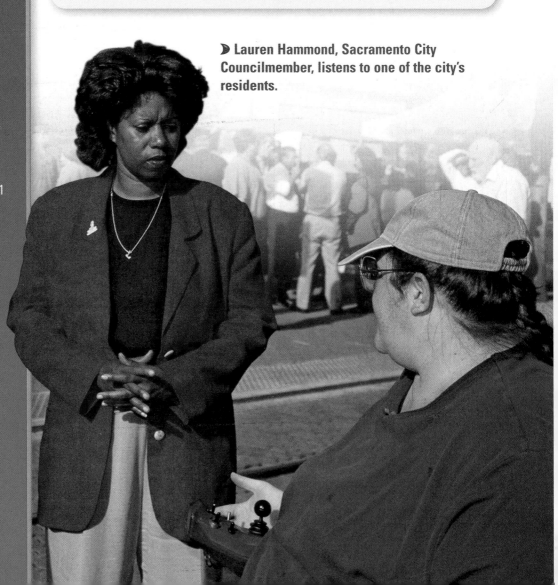

Lauren Hammond, Sacramento City Councilmember, listens to one of the city's residents.

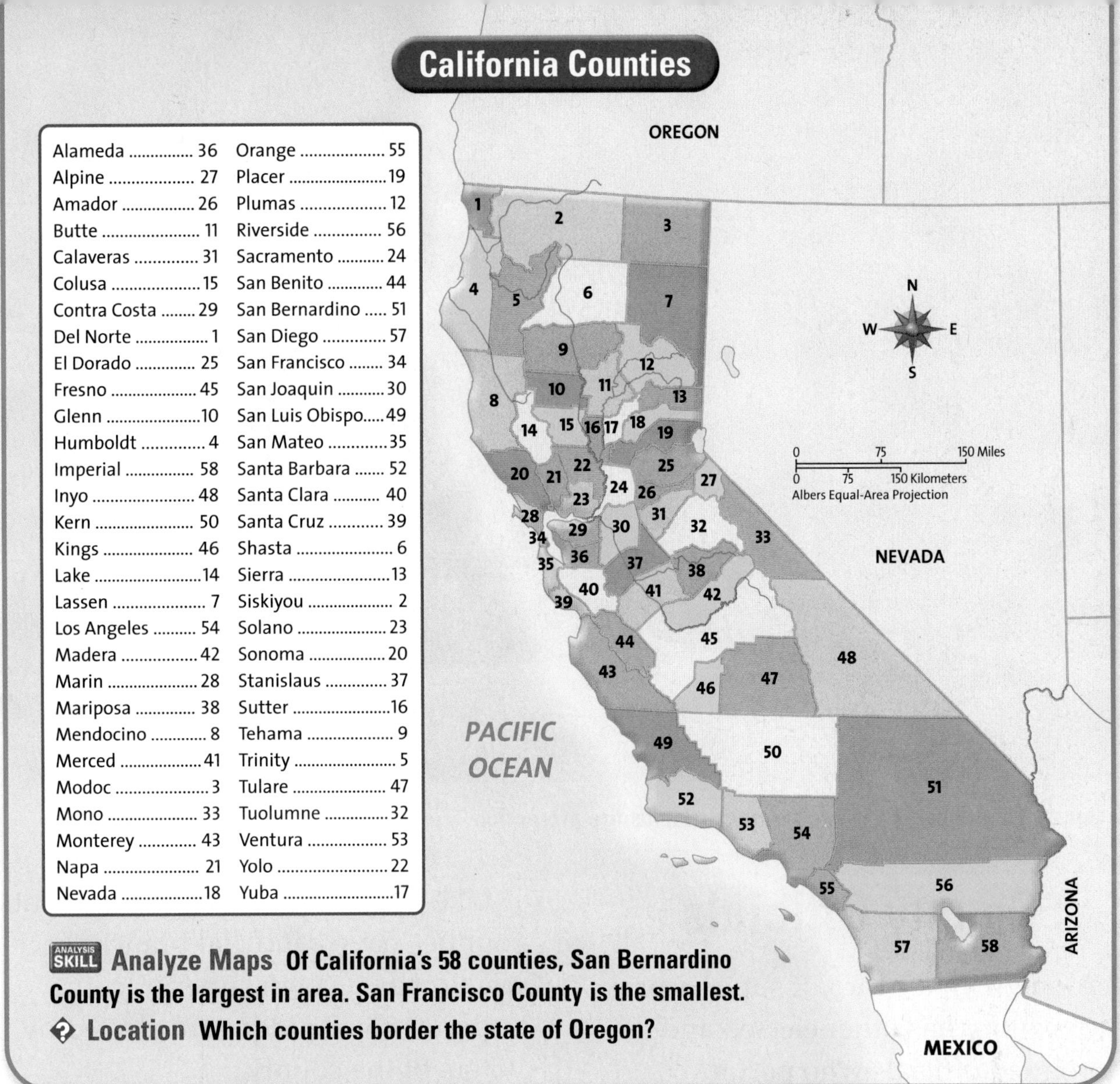

ANALYSIS SKILL Analyze Maps **Of California's 58 counties, San Bernardino County is the largest in area. San Francisco County is the smallest.**

Location **Which counties border the state of Oregon?**

County Governments

In addition to a state government, California also has county and city governments. These local governments make laws that apply only to the counties and cities. The highest level of local government is county government. A **county** is a section of a state.

The center of each county's government is called the county seat. A **county seat** is the city where the main government offices of the county are located.

The voters in each county elect a group of people to lead the government. This group is called the **board of supervisors**. In most counties, board members do the work of both the legislative and the executive branches. They make laws for the county and also decide how to spend tax money. County governments do a wide range of jobs, from running airports to picking up garbage.

READING CHECK **SUMMARIZE**

What does the board of supervisors in most county governments do?

County governments provide services such as fire protection.

County Officials

Along with a board of supervisors, each county has other elected and appointed officials who perform a variety of jobs. These include enforcing laws, making sure elections are fair, and providing health care.

Each county has a sheriff chosen by voters to head the sheriff's department. The sheriff's job is to protect people and to make sure laws are obeyed in the county. The sheriff also runs the county jails.

Other county officials are the treasurer and the district attorney. The treasurer keeps track of the county's tax money and pays the county's bills. The district attorney represents the county in court cases.

Like state and federal governments, counties have a judicial branch. Each county has its own superior court. Superior court judges are elected by voters of the county.

Jury trials are often held in superior courts. In a **jury trial**, a group of citizens called a jury attends a trial and then decides whether the person on trial is guilty or not guilty.

Each county has an office of education headed by an elected superintendent of schools. The office of education works with both the state board of education and local school districts to provide quality education to all students in the county.

READING CHECK MAIN IDEA AND DETAILS
What are some of the jobs of people who work for county governments?

Municipal Governments

California has 478 communities that are set up as cities. More than three-fourths of all Californians live in cities. As a result, **municipal** (myu•NIH•suh•puhl), or city, governments often have the most direct effect on citizens' lives.

Municipal governments pass local laws and see that those laws are obeyed. They provide fire and police protection as well as many other services. They develop and maintain schools, libraries, parks, city jails, and other facilities. In addition, they run city recycling programs, keep local streets in good condition, and do many other important jobs.

Two kinds of cities described in the California Constitution are general law cities and charter cities. General law cities are organized by the state legislature and follow rules made by the state legislature. About three-fourths of California cities are general law cities.

Charter cities may form in communities of 3,500 people or more. The charter is an official document that tells how a city's government is set up. Unlike general law cities, charter cities set up their own rules for city government. General law cities usually follow the rules outlined in the state constitution.

READING CHECK **MAIN IDEA AND DETAILS**
What are the two kinds of cities described by the California Constitution?

This officer (right) works for the San Francisco Police Department in an area of San Francisco known as Japantown. Garbage pickup (below) is another service that city governments provide.

Forms of Municipal Governments

Different cities have different forms of municipal government. One common form is the mayor-council form. In cities with this type of government, voters elect a mayor and a city council. The mayor leads the executive branch. He or she makes sure that city laws are carried out. The mayor also hires people to run city departments.

In the mayor-council form of municipal government, the city council serves as the legislative branch. It makes laws for the city and collects taxes. Many large California cities use this form of government.

Another form of municipal government is the council-manager form. About three-fourths of the cities in California have this form of municipal government.

In the council-manager form, voters elect a city council to make the laws. They often do not elect the mayor. Instead, the city council names one of its members as mayor. The mayor represents the city at special events. The city council also hires a **city manager**. The city manager runs the city under the direction of the city council. The city manager, in turn, hires workers for city departments.

READING CHECK **MAIN IDEA AND DETAILS**
What are the two common forms of municipal government in California?

Municipal government meetings are usually open to the public.

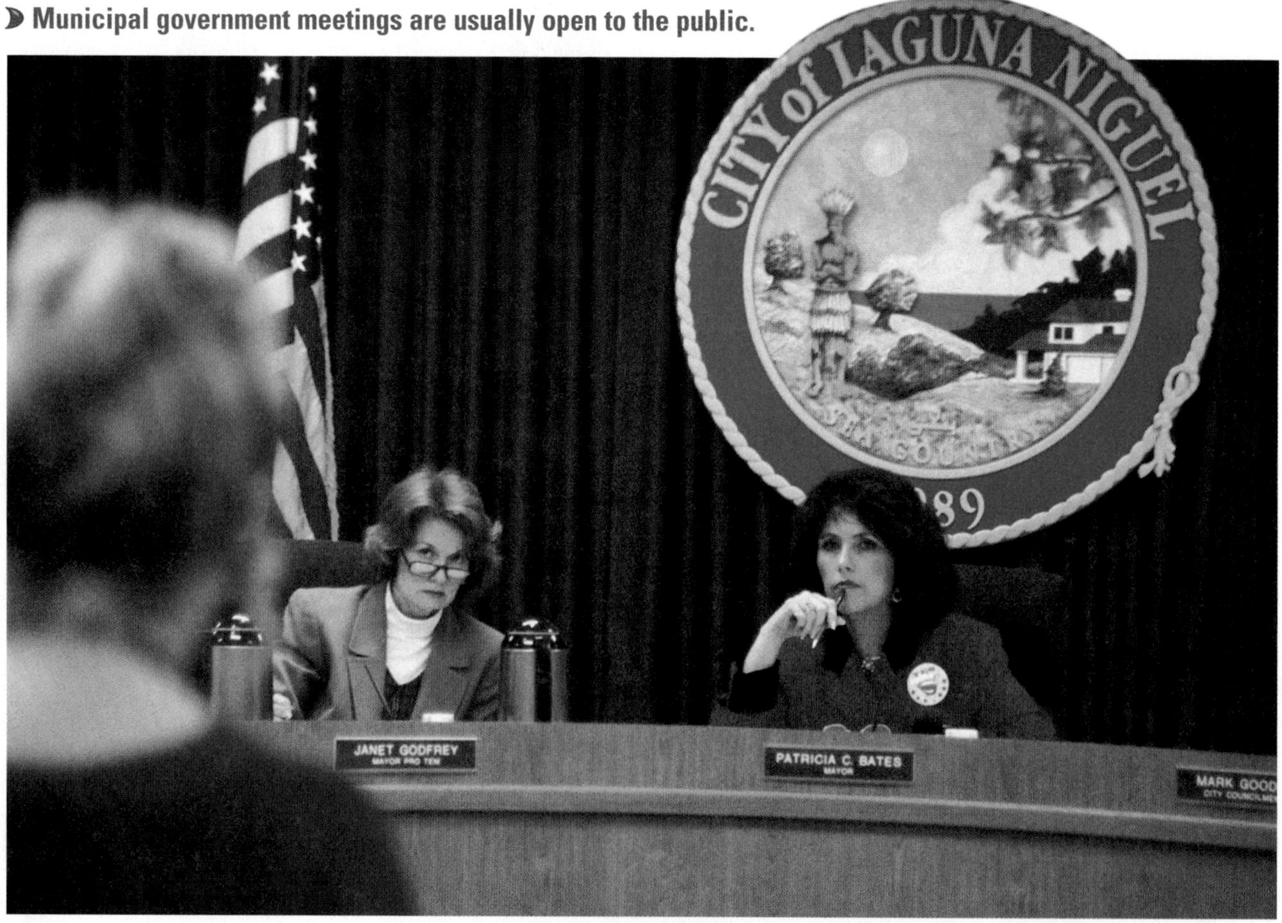

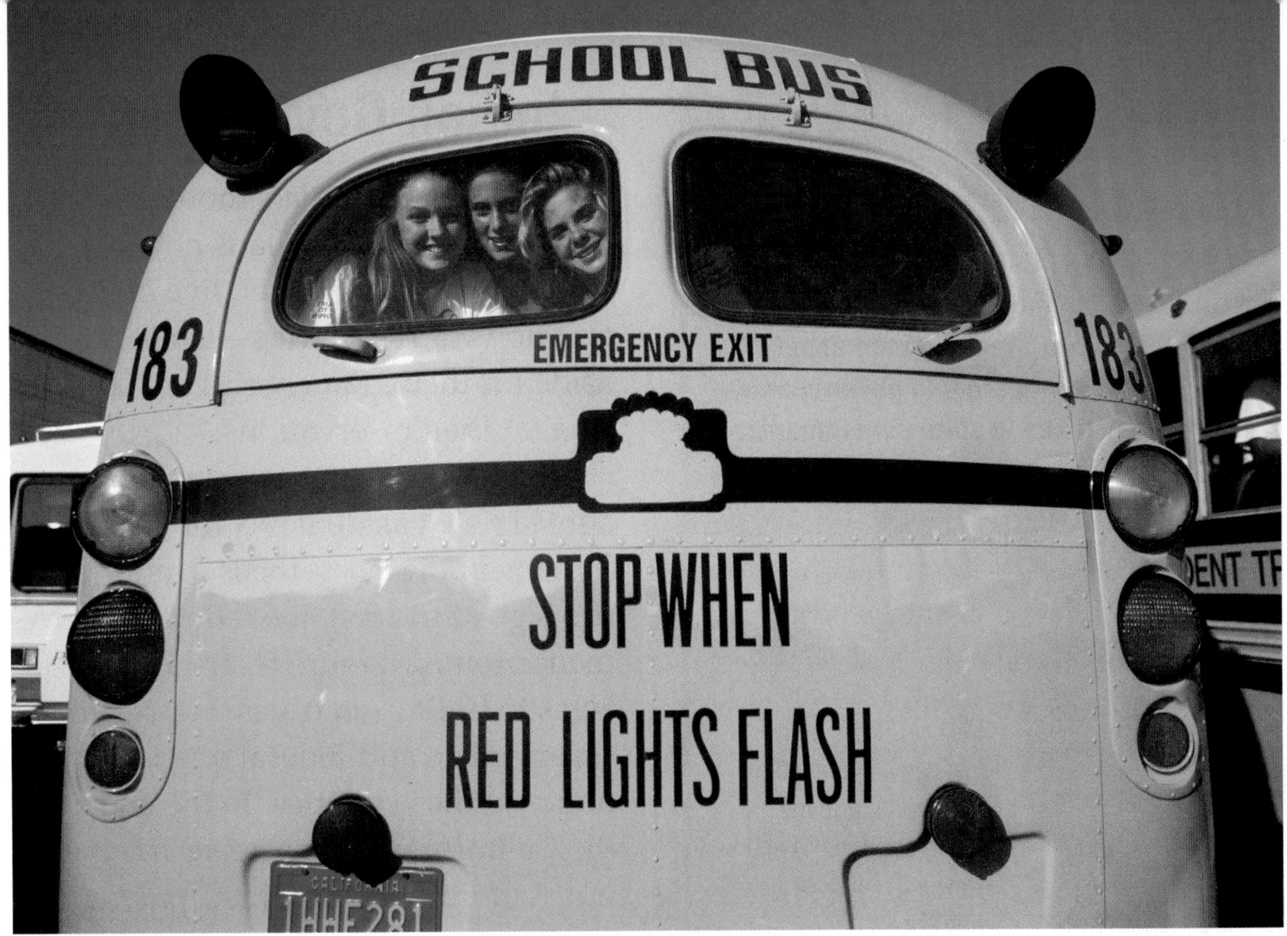

There are more than 1,050 school districts in California. They help manage the more than 9,050 public schools in the state.

Special Districts and Regional Bodies

Another kind of local government in California is a special district. **Special districts** are groups set up to deal with certain services or problems. Sometimes they provide services that are not provided by county or city governments. They have power to raise and spend money to try to improve services or to fix problems.

Several governments often work together to run a special district. School districts, water districts, irrigation districts, and flood-control districts are examples of special districts.

For problems that affect large areas, Californians may form special government groups called regional bodies. A **regional body** is a group made up of people, usually from several cities or counties, who work together to create a plan for a large area.

The Metropolitan Transportation Commission (MTC) is one of the regional bodies in the San Francisco Bay area. Among other things, the MTC decides how to spend federal money on transportation projects for the area.

READING CHECK **DRAW CONCLUSIONS**
How might it be helpful for a number of counties to work together to create plans for transportation projects?

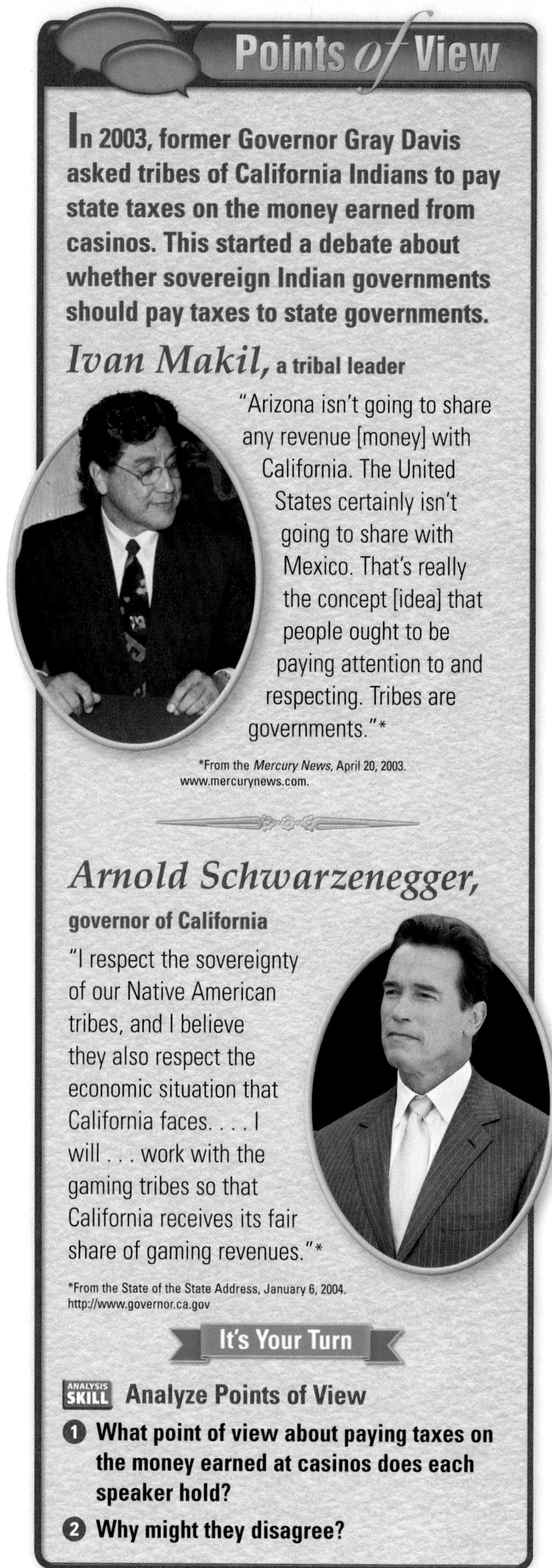

Points of View

In 2003, former Governor Gray Davis asked tribes of California Indians to pay state taxes on the money earned from casinos. This started a debate about whether sovereign Indian governments should pay taxes to state governments.

Ivan Makil, **a tribal leader**

"Arizona isn't going to share any revenue [money] with California. The United States certainly isn't going to share with Mexico. That's really the concept [idea] that people ought to be paying attention to and respecting. Tribes are governments."*

*From the *Mercury News*, April 20, 2003. www.mercurynews.com.

Arnold Schwarzenegger,
governor of California

"I respect the sovereignty of our Native American tribes, and I believe they also respect the economic situation that California faces. . . . I will . . . work with the gaming tribes so that California receives its fair share of gaming revenues."*

*From the State of the State Address, January 6, 2004. http://www.governor.ca.gov

It's Your Turn

ANALYSIS SKILL **Analyze Points of View**

1. **What point of view about paying taxes on the money earned at casinos does each speaker hold?**
2. **Why might they disagree?**

Indian Governments

Many of California's more than 330,000 American Indians now live in cities. Some, however, live on reservations or **rancherias**—lands set aside for them. Rancherias are usually smaller than reservations.

The United States government first agreed to set aside lands for California Indians in the early 1850s. Under treaties signed in 1852, the federal government promised more than 7 million acres to California tribes. However, several state and federal officials opposed these treaties. In the end, the California Indians never received much of this land. By 1900, only about 6,000 of the 16,000 California Indians had received lands on reservations.

Today, the federal government recognizes 109 Indian tribes in California. These tribes have the right to form **sovereign** (SAH•vuh•ruhn), or free and independent, governments on their lands. A tribe with this type of government is considered its own nation in many ways. It governs itself apart from federal, state, or local governments.

Many tribes have constitutions that tell how their governments are to be set up. Most are governed by a tribal council, a group of leaders elected by tribe members. Many also have their own tribal laws as well as tribal courts to settle disagreements.

In 1976, the state government formed the California Native American Heritage Commission.

California Indians who serve on this commission work with federal, state, and tribal governments to protect Indian culture. The commission also works to protect and preserve lands that are important to the history and religion of California Indians.

READING CHECK COMPARE AND CONTRAST
How are reservations different from rancherias?

Summary

County and city governments in California handle many important jobs not done by the state government. Special districts and regional bodies deal with problems that are not handled by state, county, or city governments. California Indians on reservations and rancherias have the right to form their own governments, elect leaders, and make and enforce laws.

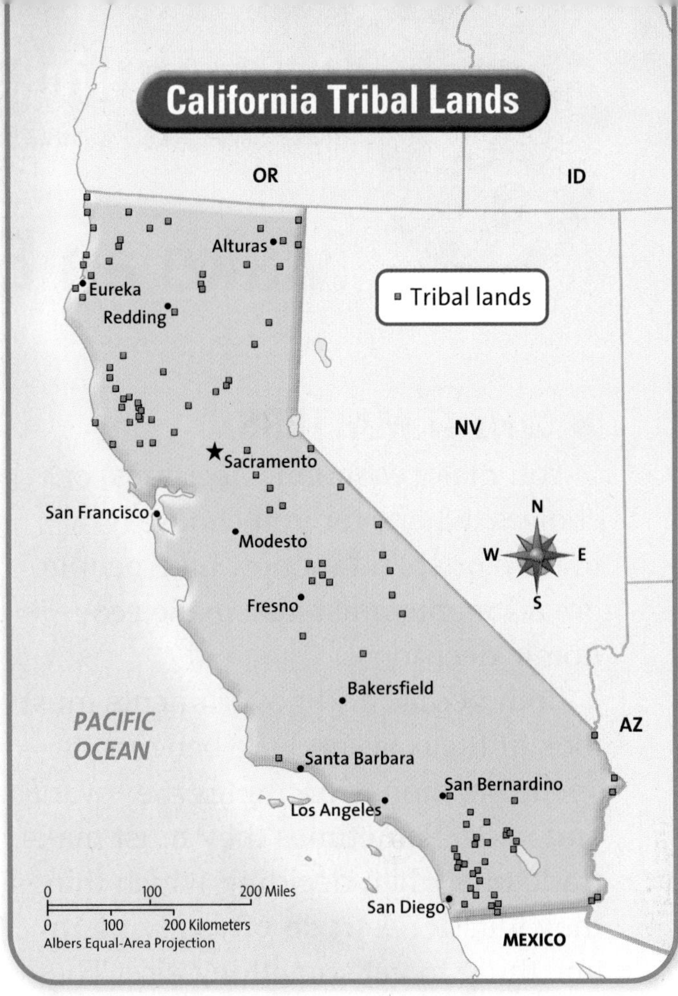

ANALYSIS SKILL Analyze Maps This map shows existing tribal lands of Indians in California.

Regions In what parts of California are most of the tribal lands located?

REVIEW

1. How are California's local governments organized, and what do they do?
2. Why are **regional bodies** formed?
3. What kind of local government is a school district?

CRITICAL THINKING

4. ANALYSIS SKILL What costs and benefits might a mayor or city council think about when deciding whether to fix up a local park?
5. ANALYSIS SKILL Why do you think the number of California counties has grown from 27 in 1850 to 58 today, even though the state has not grown in land area?
6. **Create a City Government Brochure** Make an illustrated brochure about your city government. Show how your city is governed and the services that are provided.
7. Focus Skill **SUMMARIZE**
On a separate sheet of paper, copy and complete the graphic organizer below.

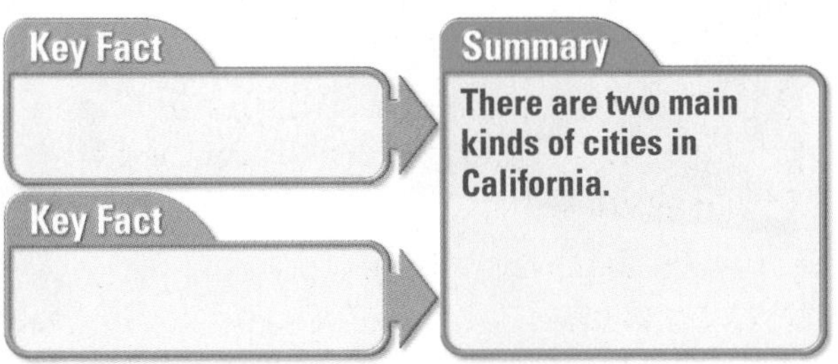

Critical Thinking Skills

Make an Economic Decision

WHY IT MATTERS

You make economic decisions, or choices, whenever you choose how to save or spend money. Like people, governments must also make economic decisions.

Both people and governments must look at the costs and the benefits of spending money on things they want and need. Sometimes they must make trade-offs when deciding which things they will do. A **trade-off** is giving up one thing to get something else. The thing that is given up is called the **opportunity cost**.

WHAT YOU NEED TO KNOW

Following the steps below can help you make a thoughtful economic decision.

Step 1 **Identify your goal and the resources you have to meet that goal.**

Step 2 **Identify the alternatives.**

Step 3 **Think about the advantages and disadvantages of each alternative.**

Step 4 **Choose and identify the opportunity cost of each choice.**

People make economic decisions when they use banks (left) or purchase goods or services (below).

PRACTICE THE SKILL

Imagine you are the mayor of a city in California. The municipal government has money available for a public project. There is enough money to build a bike path or a basketball court, but not both. Which project would you approve? Why?

Think about the steps and about the information and questions below. Then make your decision.

1. A bike path in your community would make riding safer for people who ride bikes to work or for fun.
2. A basketball court would give people a place to play and could be used for after-school programs.
3. What are the trade-offs of each choice? What are the opportunity costs?

APPLY WHAT YOU LEARNED

ANALYSIS SKILL **Make It Relevant** Imagine that you have $5 to spend. You want to buy a book and rent a movie, but you do not have enough money for both. Explain to a partner the trade-offs and the opportunity costs of your choice.

Some communities have used part of their budgets to build public bike trails.

Citizenship

Be an Active Citizen

VOTE

I Voted

"To vote is like the payment of a debt— a duty never to be neglected, if its performance is possible."*

—President Rutherford B. Hayes

The writers of the United States Constitution were not sure their government would last. No other nation had ever had a government like the one described by the Constitution. No other people had ever had the rights that American citizens enjoyed. It would be up to the people to keep their government going and to protect their freedoms. The country would need responsible, active citizens.

Active citizens vote. They stay informed about the issues by reading newspapers and books and by watching or listening to

*From the *Diary and Letters of Rutherford Birchard Hayes: Nineteenth President of the United States*, 1879.

Reading the newspaper is one way for citizens to stay informed.

Proud to be a REPUBLICAN

When they vote, people may choose to support certain political parties (above).

news. They may also volunteer to register others to vote, work for political candidates, volunteer at voting stations, and attend political rallies.

In addition to the rights protected by the United States Constitution, Californians have special rights under the state constitution. In California, citizens can recall state officials, pass initiatives, and ask for referendums.

By using their rights, active citizens in California can work to improve their government and their communities. Many California leaders, such as William Byron Rumford, Odis Jackson, Cesar Chavez, and Dolores Huerta, were all active citizens who used their constitutional rights to fight for fair treatment.

Think About It!

Make It Relevant
Why is it important to be an active citizen?

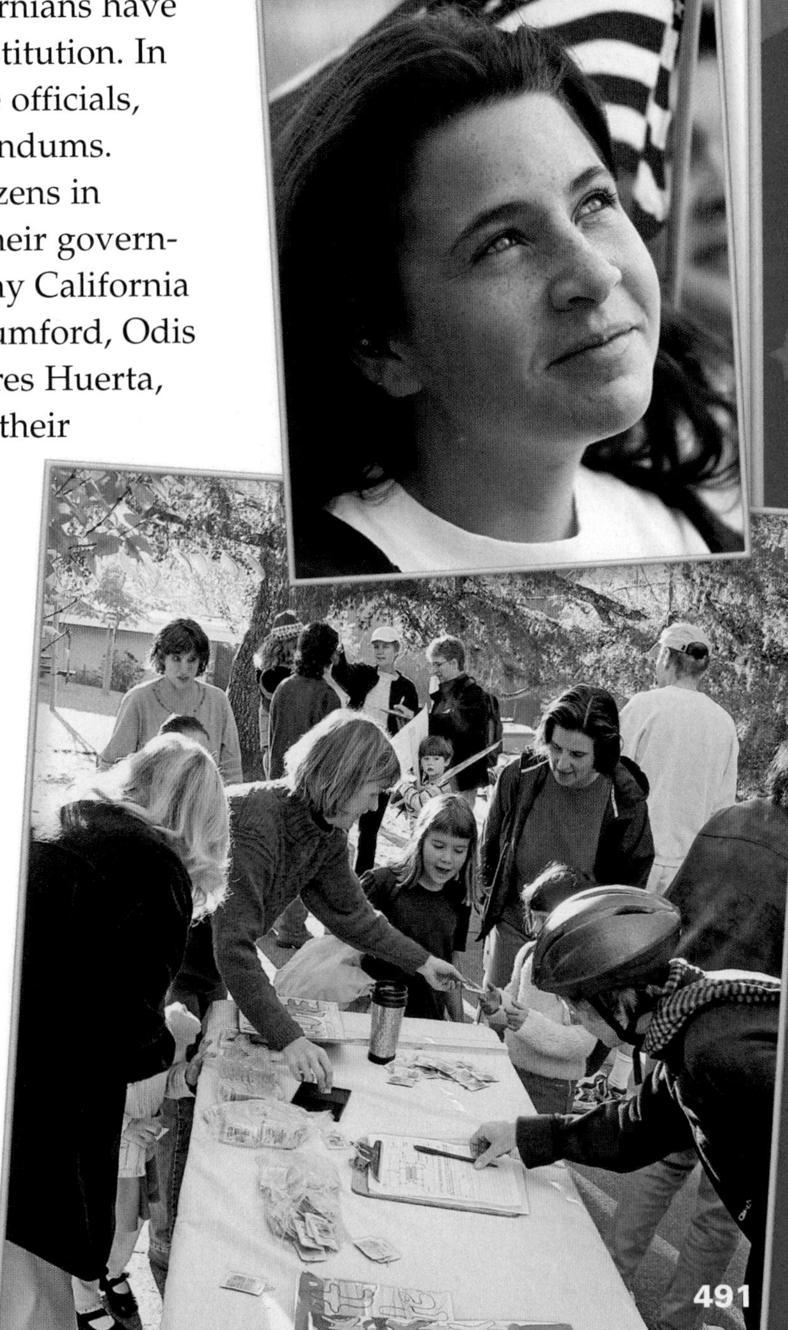

In order for a democracy to work, the government needs active, involved citizens. These people are signing a petition to get their local government to build a crosswalk at a dangerous intersection.

Reading Social Studies

When you **summarize**, you restate the key points, or most important ideas, in your own words.

Summarize

Complete this graphic organizer to summarize how federal, state, and local governments work together for the good of all citizens. A copy of this graphic organizer appears on page 138 of the Homework and Practice Book.

Californians and Government

Key Fact

All levels of government operate only with citizens' approval.

Key Fact

Each level of government can only exist with written laws that are accepted by the people.

Summary

California Writing Prompts

Write a Summary Imagine you are going to teach a group of second graders about government in California at the state and local levels. Write a speech that summarizes how each level is organized.

Write a Report Write a report about an elected government official you read about in this chapter. Explain the duties of a person in that position, and tell why the job is important in the running of the government.

Use Vocabulary

Use a term from the list to complete each sentence.

democracy, p. 463
federal, p. 463
budget, p. 473
veto, p. 473
recall, p. 475
county, p. 481

1. Voters in California can _____ the governor.
2. The governor decided to _____ the bill.
3. The United States Supreme Court is part of the _____ government.
4. San Bernardino is the largest _____ in California.
5. The new state _____ calls for spending more money on after-school programs.
6. In a _____, people make decisions by voting.

Apply Skills

Read a Flowchart

7. Examine the flowchart on pages 478 and 479 to answer the question. What happens before a bill is voted on by members of the California Assembly and Senate?

Make an Economic Decision

8. ANALYSIS SKILL Think about an economic decision you or someone you know has made recently. What were some of the trade-offs involved? What were some of the opportunity costs?

Recall Facts

Answer these questions.

9. How are the jobs of United States Senator, state assembly member, and county supervisor alike?
10. Which branch of the California state government prepares the state budget?
11. What special powers does the California Constitution give the state's voters that voters in many other states do not have?
12. What special rights do Indian tribes in California have?

Write the letter of the best choice.

13. What is the highest level of local government in California?
    A municipal government
    B county government
    C school district
    D state supreme court
14. Who is head of the state's executive branch of government?
    A governor
    B county sheriff
    C President of the United States
    D chief justice of the Supreme Court

Think Critically

15. ANALYSIS SKILL Do you think it is a good idea to give voters the power to recall officials? Explain.
16. Why might it be necessary to create a special district or regional body to fix a problem?

Balboa Park

GET READY

In 1868, city leaders in San Diego set aside 1,400 acres of land for a public park. Today, it is known as Balboa Park, the largest urban cultural park in the United States. The park is home to 15 museums, 85 cultural and recreational organizations, and many performing arts groups. At a large sports complex, you can play tennis, golf, swim, or bike. You can also visit the Japanese Friendship Garden, the House of Pacific Relations, WorldBeat Center, and the Centro Cultural de la Raza. Also in Balboa Park is the San Diego Zoo, which has thousands of animals. With the many attractions at Balboa Park, visitors can explore the worlds of art, culture, and nature.

LOCATE IT

WHAT TO SEE

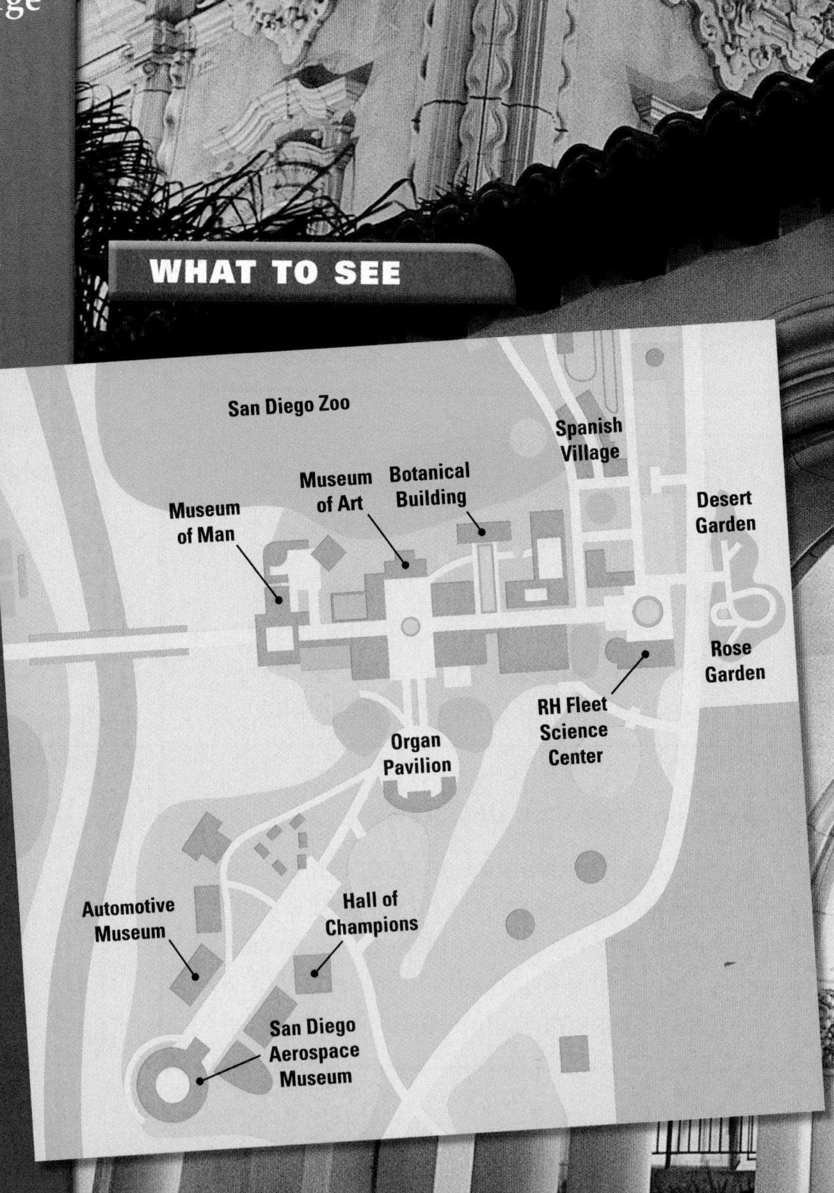

With more than 4,000 animals at the San Diego Zoo, you can see everything from a small caterpillar to a giant polar bear!

At the Aerospace Museum in Balboa Park, you can see historic airplanes like this one.

The Botanical Building in Balboa Park is filled with more than 2,000 different plants.

Review

THE BIG IDEA

Government and Leadership Californians are proud of their history, government, and heritage.

Summary

Building a Prosperous State

California's growth and success is based on many factors, including its people, location, history, and government. The state's economy depends on the skills of its people in different industries, such as agriculture, electronics, film, and tourism. In addition, California's location on the Pacific Ocean gives its economy a boost by making it a center for trade with other countries on the Pacific Basin.

For the state to run well, Californians depend on leaders and officials in local, state, and federal governments to work together on important issues and public projects. State officials must follow the United States Constitution and the California Constitution as well as laws passed by local, state, and federal legislators. Among the duties of state government are making laws and using tax money to ensure the health, safety, and well-being of all Californians.

Main Ideas and Vocabulary

Read the summary above. Then answer the questions that follow.

1. What does the term tourism refer to?
   A movies filmed in color
   B countries along the Pacific Basin
   C agricultural products
   D the business of serving visitors

2. What is one major benefit of California's location on the Pacific Ocean?
   A trade with other Pacific Basin countries
   B public projects along the coast
   C fertile lands for agriculture
   D rugged coastline for action films

3. What does federal mean?
   A powerful
   B local
   C national
   D international

4. Which laws do California's state officials pledge to obey?
   A federal, local, and state laws
   B federal laws only
   C state laws only
   D local laws only

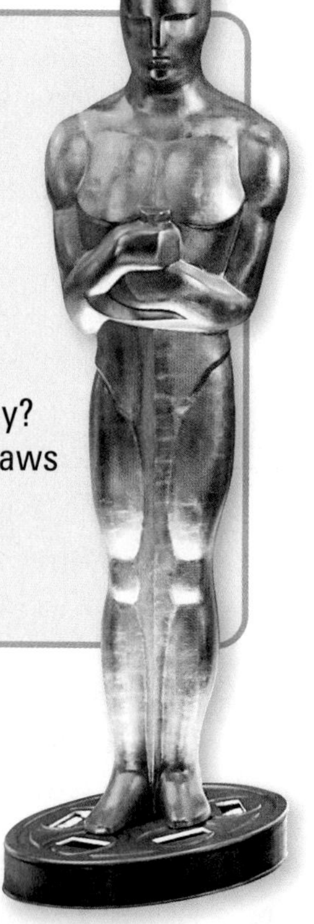

Recall Facts

Answer these questions.

5. How does California benefit from international trade?
6. To what places does California export agricultural products?
7. What are some powers the federal government has that state governments do not have?
8. What are the three branches of California's state government? What is each branch responsible for?
9. How can California voters bypass the state's legislature to make new laws or get rid of laws that already exist?
10. How does the state get money to pay for services to help its residents and businesses?

Write the letter of the best choice.

11. Which of these people was a well-known architect in California?
    - **A** Julia Morgan
    - **B** Amy Tan
    - **C** Judith Baca
    - **D** Ansel Adams
12. Why does California have the most people in the United States House of Representatives?
    - **A** California is the state with the largest population.
    - **B** California has the best leaders.
    - **C** California holds more elections than any other state.
    - **D** California is the largest state in land area.
13. How did California voters remove Governor Gray Davis from office?
    - **A** by debate
    - **B** by veto
    - **C** by recall
    - **D** by trial

Think Critically

14. ANALYSIS SKILL How might a diverse economy be important to a state and its workers?
15. Which level of government do you think has the greatest impact on your life? Explain why.

Apply Skills

Read a Land Use and Products Map

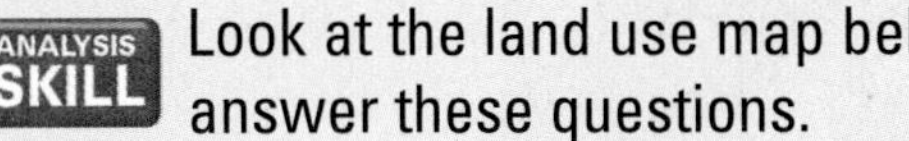
ANALYSIS SKILL Look at the land use map below to answer these questions.

16. How is most land in the Los Angeles area used?
17. What is the most common land use in the northwestern part of the state? in the Central Valley?

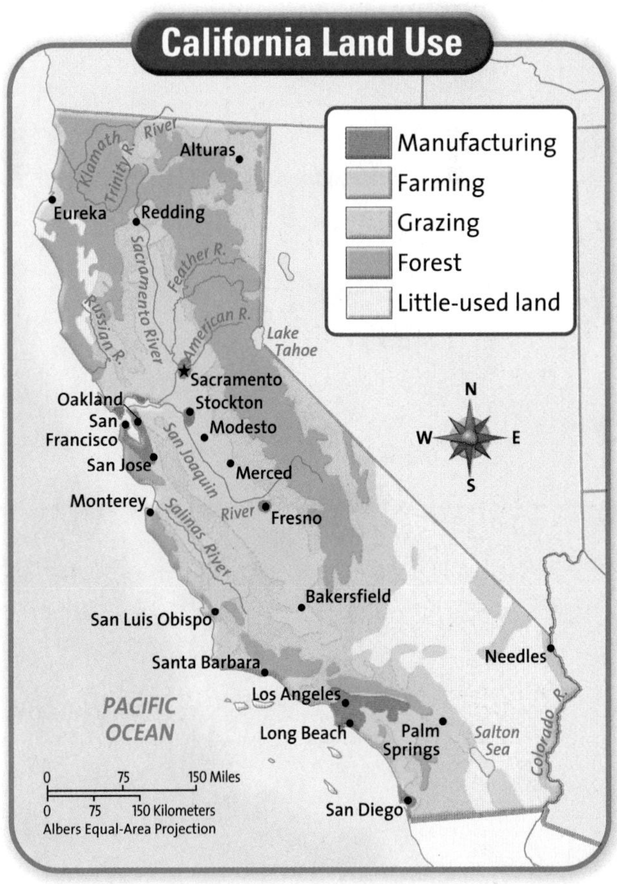

Unit 6

Activities

Read More

- *Twentieth-Century Californians* by Lisa Jo Rudy.

- *Creating Yosemite National Park* by Lisa Jo Rudy.

- *Sacramento: A Capital City* by Sheila Sweeny.

Show What You Know

Unit Writing Activity

Write an Information Report Write a brief report about a part of life in California today, such as education, government, the arts, or the economy. Your report should pose a question about the topic you have chosen. Use facts and details in your report to answer the question you pose about the topic. Gather information from more than one source if possible.

Unit Project

Make a California Bulletin Board Make a bulletin board display about present-day California. Include pictures and drawings of people, places, and events that are important to the state and to your community. Write short passages about the people, places, and events displayed on your bulletin board.

GO ONLINE Visit ACTIVITIES at **www.harcourtschool.com/hss**

For Your Reference

ATLAS

R2 The World: Political
R4 The World: Physical
R6 Western Hemisphere: Political
R7 Western Hemisphere: Physical
R8 United States: Overview
R10 United States: Political
R12 United States: Physical
R14 California: Political
R15 California: Physical
R16 California: Climate
R17 California: Vegetation
R18 Canada
R19 Mexico

ALMANAC

R20 Facts About California
R22 Facts About California Counties
R26 Facts About California Governors

RESEARCH HANDBOOK

R28

BIOGRAPHICAL DICTIONARY

R38

GAZETTEER

R44

GLOSSARY

R50

INDEX

R58

The World: Political

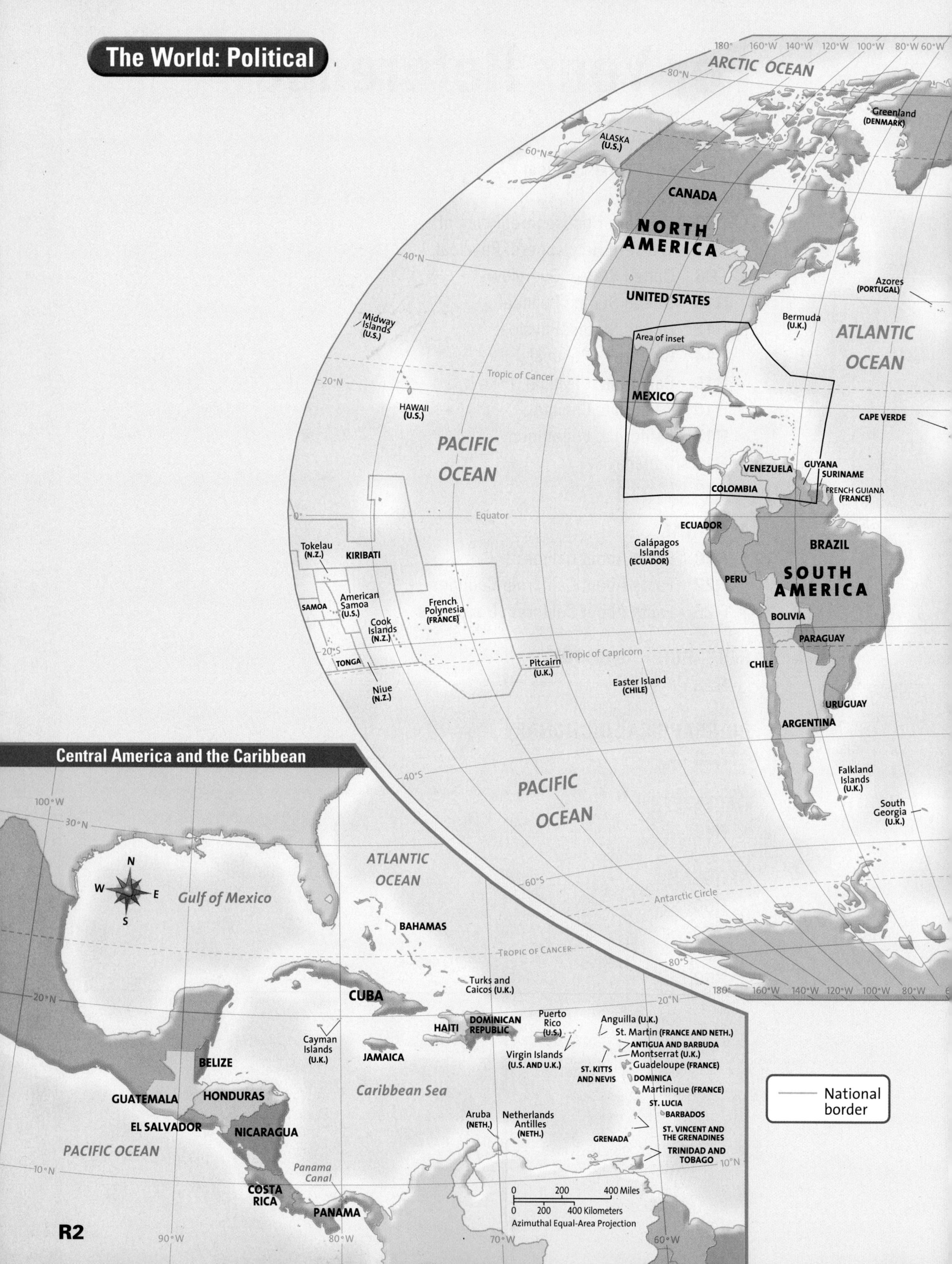

ARCTIC OCEAN
Greenland (DENMARK)
ALASKA (U.S.)
CANADA
NORTH AMERICA
UNITED STATES
Azores (PORTUGAL)
Bermuda (U.K.)
ATLANTIC OCEAN
Midway Islands (U.S.)
Area of inset
Tropic of Cancer
MEXICO
HAWAII (U.S.)
CAPE VERDE
PACIFIC OCEAN
VENEZUELA
GUYANA
SURINAME
COLOMBIA
FRENCH GUIANA (FRANCE)
Equator
ECUADOR
Galápagos Islands (ECUADOR)
BRAZIL
Tokelau (N.Z.)
KIRIBATI
SOUTH AMERICA
PERU
American Samoa (U.S.)
SAMOA
French Polynesia (FRANCE)
Cook Islands (N.Z.)
BOLIVIA
PARAGUAY
Tropic of Capricorn
TONGA
Pitcairn (U.K.)
CHILE
Niue (N.Z.)
Easter Island (CHILE)
URUGUAY
ARGENTINA
Falkland Islands (U.K.)
PACIFIC OCEAN
South Georgia (U.K.)
Antarctic Circle
Central America and the Caribbean
ATLANTIC OCEAN
Gulf of Mexico
BAHAMAS
TROPIC OF CANCER
Turks and Caicos (U.K.)
CUBA
Puerto Rico (U.S.)
Anguilla (U.K.)
HAITI
DOMINICAN REPUBLIC
St. Martin (FRANCE AND NETH.)
Cayman Islands (U.K.)
ANTIGUA AND BARBUDA
Montserrat (U.K.)
Virgin Islands (U.S. AND U.K.)
JAMAICA
ST. KITTS AND NEVIS
Guadeloupe (FRANCE)
BELIZE
DOMINICA
Martinique (FRANCE)
Caribbean Sea
ST. LUCIA
GUATEMALA
HONDURAS
BARBADOS
Aruba (NETH.)
Netherlands Antilles (NETH.)
EL SALVADOR
NICARAGUA
ST. VINCENT AND THE GRENADINES
GRENADA
TRINIDAD AND TOBAGO
PACIFIC OCEAN
Panama Canal
COSTA RICA
PANAMA
0 200 400 Miles
0 200 400 Kilometers
Azimuthal Equal-Area Projection
National border

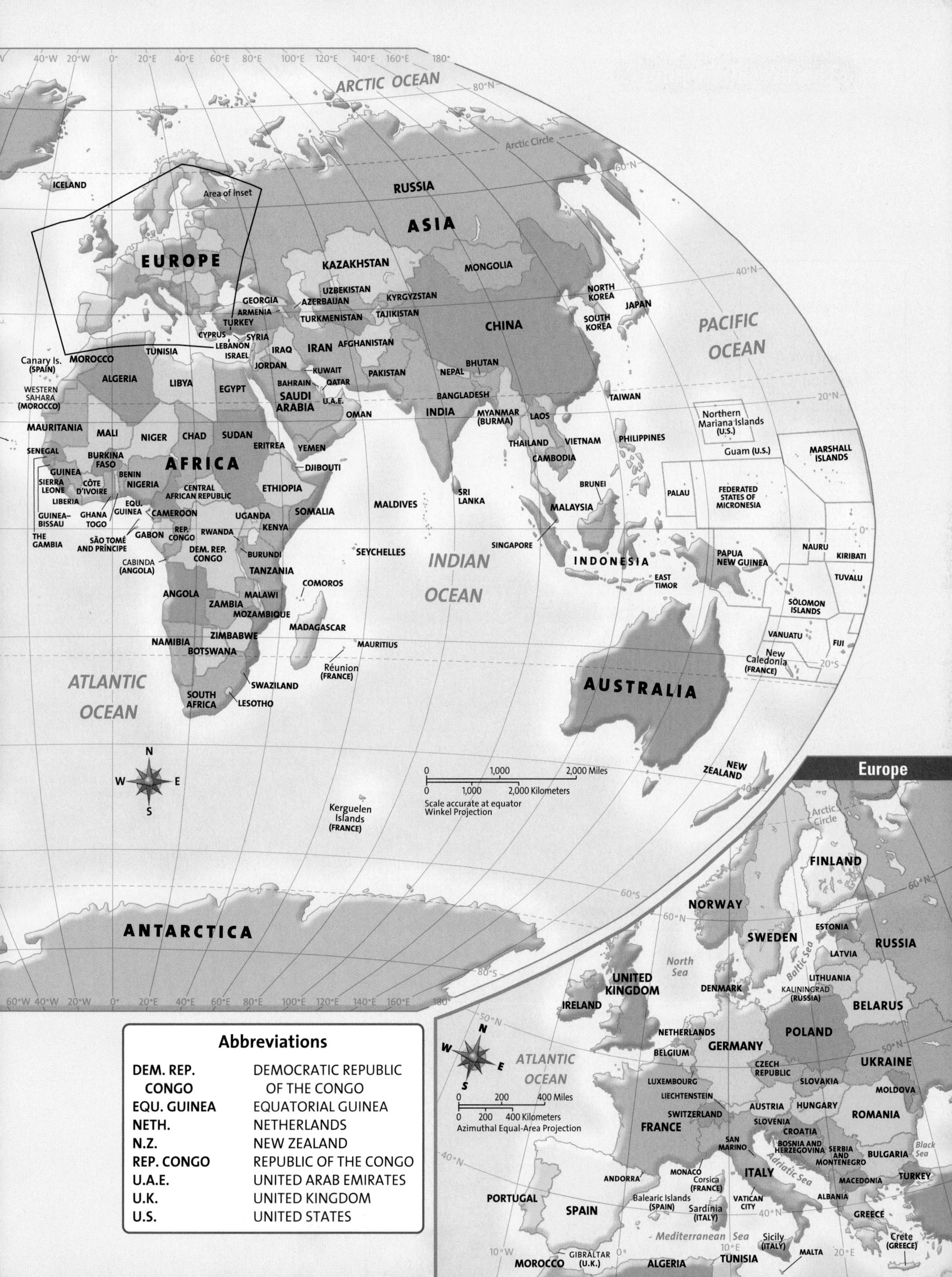
ARCTIC OCEAN
Arctic Circle
ICELAND
Area of inset
RUSSIA
ASIA
EUROPE
KAZAKHSTAN
MONGOLIA
UZBEKISTAN
KYRGYZSTAN
GEORGIA
AZERBAIJAN
ARMENIA
TURKMENISTAN
TAJIKISTAN
TURKEY
NORTH KOREA
SOUTH KOREA
JAPAN
CHINA
PACIFIC OCEAN
CYPRUS
SYRIA
LEBANON
ISRAEL
TUNISIA
IRAQ
IRAN
AFGHANISTAN
JORDAN
KUWAIT
BAHRAIN
QATAR
PAKISTAN
NEPAL
BHUTAN
Canary Is. (SPAIN)
MOROCCO
ALGERIA
LIBYA
EGYPT
SAUDI ARABIA
U.A.E.
OMAN
BANGLADESH
INDIA
MYANMAR (BURMA)
LAOS
TAIWAN
WESTERN SAHARA (MOROCCO)
Northern Mariana Islands (U.S.)
MAURITANIA
MALI
NIGER
CHAD
SUDAN
ERITREA
YEMEN
THAILAND
VIETNAM
PHILIPPINES
Guam (U.S.)
MARSHALL ISLANDS
SENEGAL
BURKINA FASO
AFRICA
DJIBOUTI
CAMBODIA
GUINEA
BENIN
SIERRA LEONE
CÔTE D'IVOIRE
NIGERIA
CENTRAL AFRICAN REPUBLIC
ETHIOPIA
SRI LANKA
BRUNEI
PALAU
FEDERATED STATES OF MICRONESIA
LIBERIA
EQU. GUINEA
GHANA
TOGO
CAMEROON
UGANDA
SOMALIA
MALDIVES
MALAYSIA
GUINEA-BISSAU
THE GAMBIA
SÃO TOMÉ AND PRÍNCIPE
GABON
REP. CONGO
RWANDA
KENYA
SINGAPORE
CABINDA (ANGOLA)
DEM. REP. CONGO
BURUNDI
SEYCHELLES
INDIAN OCEAN
INDONESIA
PAPUA NEW GUINEA
NAURU
KIRIBATI
TANZANIA
EAST TIMOR
TUVALU
COMOROS
ANGOLA
MALAWI
ZAMBIA
MOZAMBIQUE
SOLOMON ISLANDS
MADAGASCAR
ZIMBABWE
NAMIBIA
BOTSWANA
MAURITIUS
VANUATU
FIJI
New Caledonia (FRANCE)
Réunion (FRANCE)
ATLANTIC OCEAN
SWAZILAND
AUSTRALIA
SOUTH AFRICA
LESOTHO
NEW ZEALAND
0 1,000 2,000 Miles
0 1,000 2,000 Kilometers
Scale accurate at equator
Winkel Projection
Kerguelen Islands (FRANCE)
ANTARCTICA
N S E W
Abbreviations
DEM. REP. CONGO DEMOCRATIC REPUBLIC OF THE CONGO
EQU. GUINEA EQUATORIAL GUINEA
NETH. NETHERLANDS
N.Z. NEW ZEALAND
REP. CONGO REPUBLIC OF THE CONGO
U.A.E. UNITED ARAB EMIRATES
U.K. UNITED KINGDOM
U.S. UNITED STATES
Europe
Arctic Circle
FINLAND
NORWAY
ESTONIA
SWEDEN
RUSSIA
LATVIA
North Sea
Baltic Sea
LITHUANIA
UNITED KINGDOM
DENMARK
KALININGRAD (RUSSIA)
IRELAND
BELARUS
NETHERLANDS
POLAND
GERMANY
BELGIUM
ATLANTIC OCEAN
CZECH REPUBLIC
UKRAINE
LUXEMBOURG
SLOVAKIA
0 200 400 Miles
0 200 400 Kilometers
Azimuthal Equal-Area Projection
LIECHTENSTEIN
MOLDOVA
AUSTRIA
HUNGARY
SWITZERLAND
ROMANIA
FRANCE
SLOVENIA
CROATIA
SAN MARINO
BOSNIA AND HERZEGOVINA
SERBIA AND MONTENEGRO
Black Sea
BULGARIA
Adriatic Sea
MONACO
ANDORRA
Corsica (FRANCE)
ITALY
MACEDONIA
TURKEY
PORTUGAL
Balearic Islands (SPAIN)
Sardinia (ITALY)
VATICAN CITY
ALBANIA
SPAIN
GREECE
Mediterranean Sea
Sicily (ITALY)
Crete (GREECE)
GIBRALTAR (U.K.)
MOROCCO
ALGERIA
TUNISIA
MALTA

The World: Physical

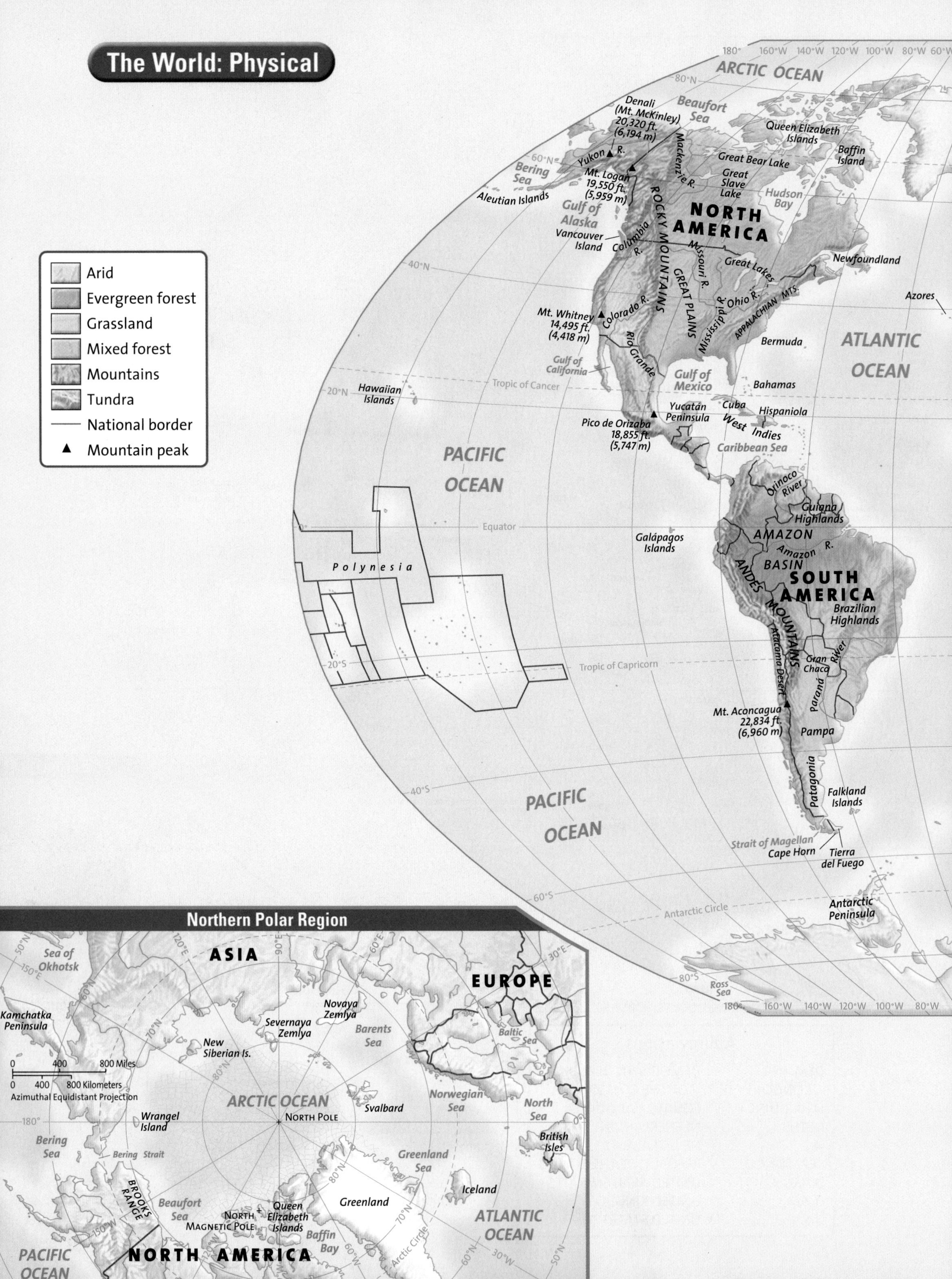

Arid
Evergreen forest
Grassland
Mixed forest
Mountains
Tundra
National border
Mountain peak
ARCTIC OCEAN
Beaufort Sea
Denali (Mt. McKinley) 20,320 ft. (6,194 m)
Queen Elizabeth Islands
Baffin Island
Yukon R.
Mt. Logan 19,550 ft. (5,959 m)
Mackenzie R.
Great Bear Lake
Great Slave Lake
Bering Sea
Aleutian Islands
Gulf of Alaska
Hudson Bay
ROCKY MOUNTAINS
NORTH AMERICA
Vancouver Island
Columbia R.
Missouri R.
Great Lakes
Newfoundland
GREAT PLAINS
Ohio R.
Mississippi R.
APPALACHIAN MTS.
Azores
Mt. Whitney 14,495 ft. (4,418 m)
Colorado R.
Rio Grande
Bermuda
ATLANTIC OCEAN
Gulf of California
Gulf of Mexico
Tropic of Cancer
Bahamas
Hawaiian Islands
Yucatán Peninsula
Cuba
Hispaniola
West Indies
Pico de Orizaba 18,855 ft. (5,747 m)
Caribbean Sea
PACIFIC OCEAN
Orinoco River
Guiana Highlands
Equator
Galápagos Islands
AMAZON BASIN
Amazon R.
Polynesia
SOUTH AMERICA
ANDES MOUNTAINS
Brazilian Highlands
Atacama Desert
Gran Chaco
Paraná River
Tropic of Capricorn
Mt. Aconcagua 22,834 ft. (6,960 m)
Pampa
Patagonia
Falkland Islands
PACIFIC OCEAN
Strait of Magellan
Cape Horn
Tierra del Fuego
Antarctic Peninsula
Antarctic Circle
Ross Sea
180° 160°W 140°W 120°W 100°W 80°W 60°W
80°N 60°N 40°N 20°N 20°S 40°S 60°S 80°S
Northern Polar Region
Sea of Okhotsk
ASIA
EUROPE
Kamchatka Peninsula
Novaya Zemlya
Severnaya Zemlya
Barents Sea
New Siberian Is.
Baltic Sea
0 400 800 Miles
0 400 800 Kilometers
Azimuthal Equidistant Projection
ARCTIC OCEAN
NORTH POLE
Norwegian Sea
North Sea
Svalbard
Wrangel Island
British Isles
Bering Sea
Bering Strait
Greenland Sea
BROOKS RANGE
Iceland
Beaufort Sea
NORTH MAGNETIC POLE
Queen Elizabeth Islands
Greenland
ATLANTIC OCEAN
Baffin Bay
Arctic Circle
PACIFIC OCEAN
NORTH AMERICA

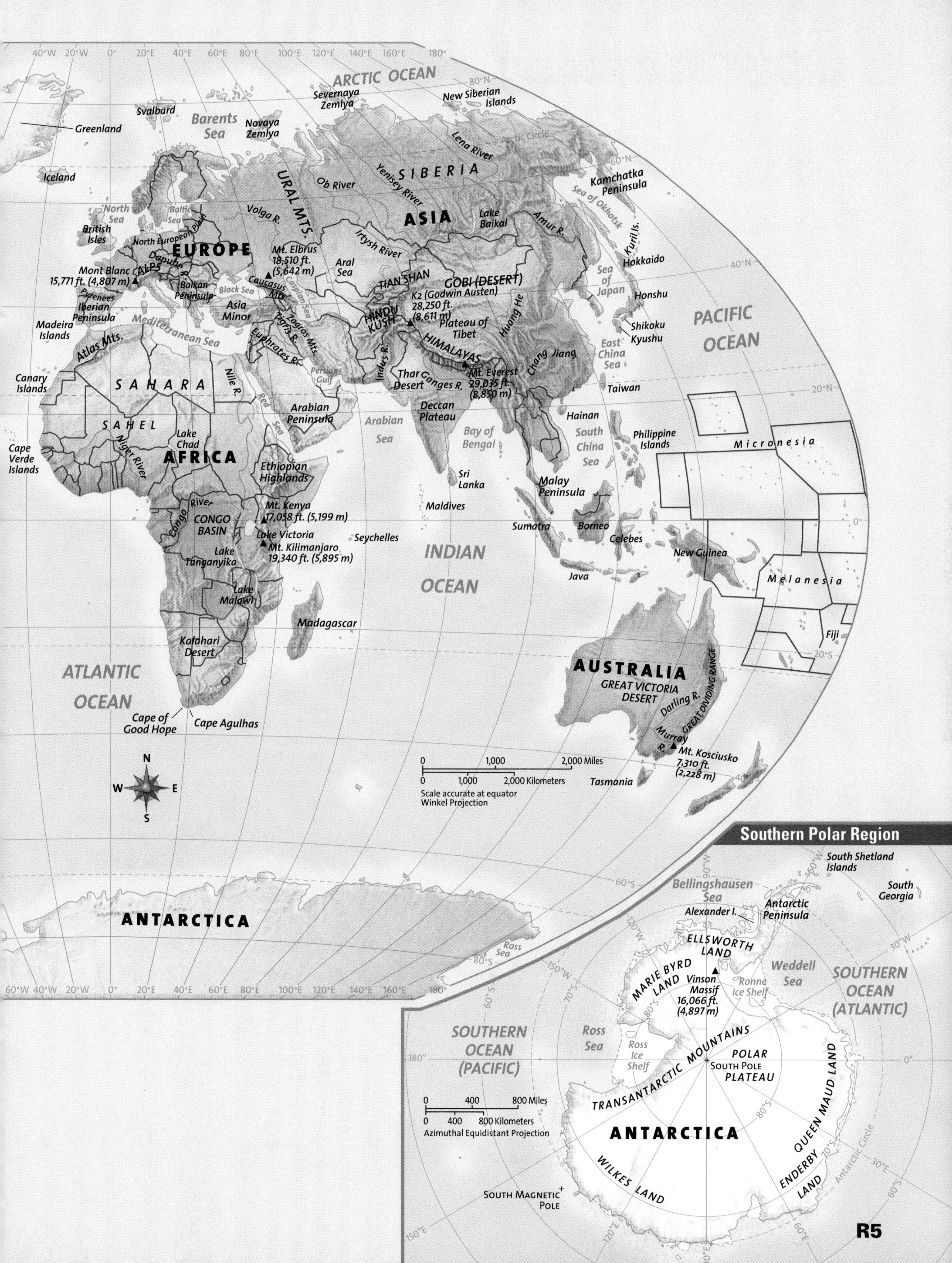

ARCTIC OCEAN
Severnaya Zemlya
New Siberian Islands
Svalbard
Barents Sea
Novaya Zemlya
Greenland
Arctic Circle
Lena River
Iceland
URAL MTS.
Ob River
Yenisey River
SIBERIA
Kamchatka Peninsula
Sea of Okhotsk
North Sea
Baltic Sea
Volga R.
ASIA
Lake Baikal
Amur R.
British Isles
North European Plain
EUROPE
Mt. Elbrus 18,510 ft. (5,642 m)
Irtysh River
Aral Sea
Kuril Is.
Hokkaido
Mont Blanc 15,771 ft. (4,807 m)
ALPS
Danube R.
Caucasus Mts.
Caspian Sea
TIAN SHAN
GOBI (DESERT)
Sea of Japan
Pyrenees
Balkan Peninsula
Black Sea
K2 (Godwin Austen) 28,250 ft. (8,611 m)
Honshu
Iberian Peninsula
Asia Minor
HINDU KUSH
Plateau of Tibet
Huang He
Shikoku
Kyushu
PACIFIC OCEAN
Madeira Islands
Mediterranean Sea
Tigris R.
Zagros Mts.
Euphrates R.
HIMALAYAS
Atlas Mts.
Indus R.
Chang Jiang
East China Sea
Nile R.
Persian Gulf
Thar Desert
Ganges R.
Mt. Everest 29,035 ft. (8,850 m)
Canary Islands
SAHARA
Taiwan
Red Sea
Arabian Peninsula
Deccan Plateau
Hainan
SAHEL
Arabian Sea
Bay of Bengal
South China Sea
Philippine Islands
Micronesia
Lake Chad
Cape Verde Islands
Niger River
AFRICA
Ethiopian Highlands
Sri Lanka
Malay Peninsula
Congo River
Mt. Kenya 17,058 ft. (5,199 m)
Maldives
CONGO BASIN
Lake Victoria
Seychelles
Sumatra
Borneo
Celebes
Mt. Kilimanjaro 19,340 ft. (5,895 m)
Lake Tanganyika
INDIAN OCEAN
New Guinea
Java
Melanesia
Lake Malawi
Madagascar
Fiji
Kalahari Desert
ATLANTIC OCEAN
AUSTRALIA
GREAT VICTORIA DESERT
GREAT DIVIDING RANGE
Darling R.
Murray R.
Cape of Good Hope
Cape Agulhas
Mt. Kosciusko 7,310 ft. (2,228 m)
Tasmania
0 1,000 2,000 Miles
0 1,000 2,000 Kilometers
Scale accurate at equator
Winkel Projection
N
W
E
S
ANTARCTICA
Ross Sea
Southern Polar Region
South Shetland Islands
South Georgia
Bellingshausen Sea
Alexander I.
Antarctic Peninsula
ELLSWORTH LAND
MARIE BYRD LAND
Vinson Massif 16,066 ft. (4,897 m)
Ronne Ice Shelf
Weddell Sea
SOUTHERN OCEAN (ATLANTIC)
SOUTHERN OCEAN (PACIFIC)
Ross Sea
Ross Ice Shelf
TRANSANTARCTIC MOUNTAINS
POLAR PLATEAU
SOUTH POLE
QUEEN MAUD LAND
0 400 800 Miles
0 400 800 Kilometers
Azimuthal Equidistant Projection
ANTARCTICA
WILKES LAND
ENDERBY LAND
SOUTH MAGNETIC POLE
Antarctic Circle

Western Hemisphere: Political

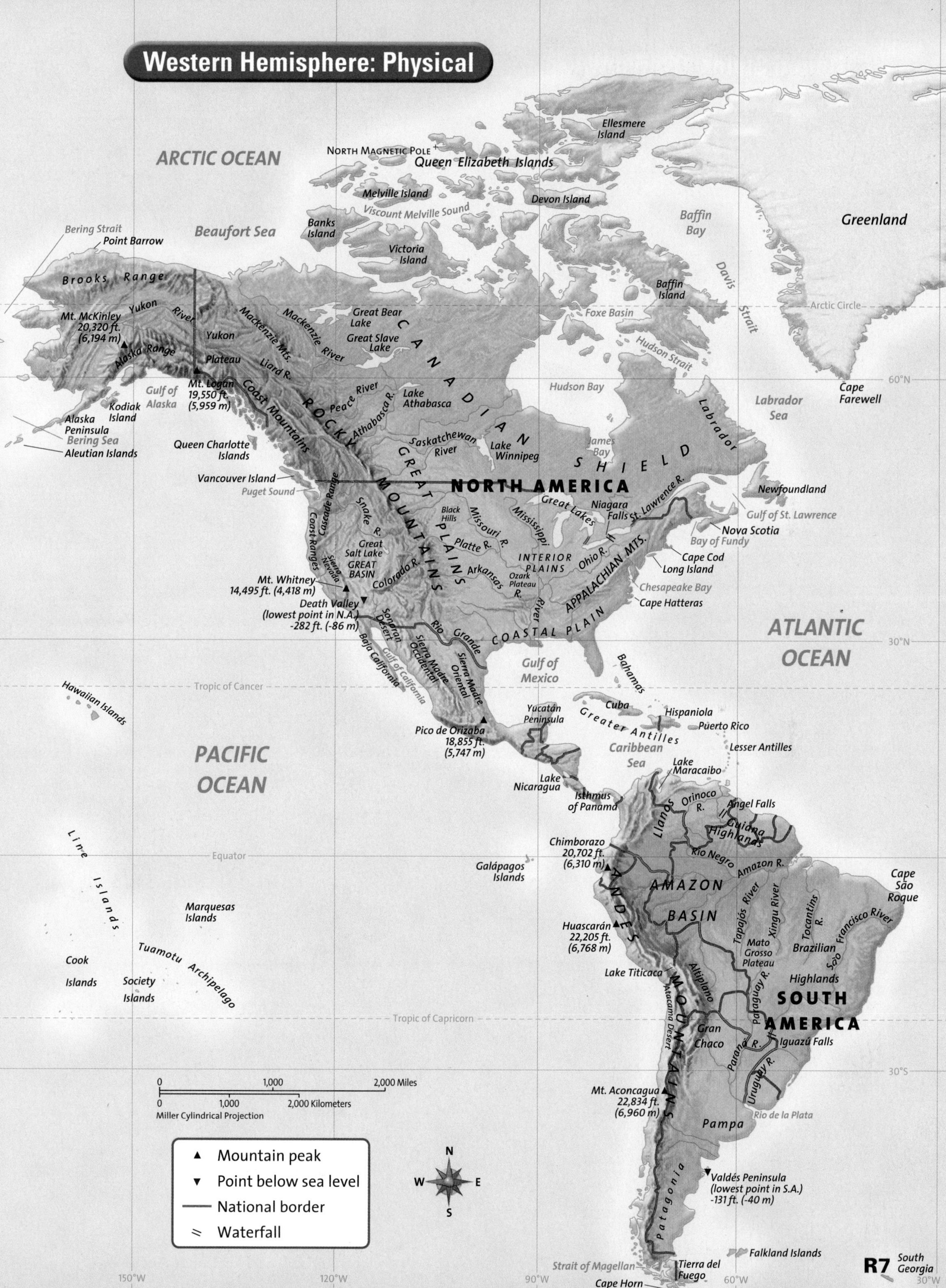
Western Hemisphere: Physical
ARCTIC OCEAN
North Magnetic Pole
Queen Elizabeth Islands
Ellesmere Island
Melville Island
Devon Island
Viscount Melville Sound
Banks Island
Beaufort Sea
Baffin Bay
Greenland
Bering Strait
Point Barrow
Victoria Island
Baffin Island
Brooks Range
Davis Strait
Arctic Circle
Foxe Basin
Mt. McKinley 20,320 ft. (6,194 m)
Yukon River
Mackenzie Mts.
Mackenzie River
Great Bear Lake
Great Slave Lake
CANADIAN SHIELD
Yukon Plateau
Alaska Range
Liard R.
Hudson Strait
Mt. Logan 19,550 ft. (5,959 m)
Gulf of Alaska
Peace River
Lake Athabasca
Hudson Bay
Labrador
60°N
Cape Farewell
Labrador Sea
Kodiak Island
Alaska Peninsula
Bering Sea
Aleutian Islands
Coast Mountains
ROCKY MOUNTAINS
Athabasca R.
Saskatchewan River
Lake Winnipeg
James Bay
Queen Charlotte Islands
GREAT PLAINS
Vancouver Island
Puget Sound
NORTH AMERICA
Newfoundland
Cascade Range
Snake R.
Black Hills
Missouri R.
Mississippi River
Great Lakes
Niagara Falls
St. Lawrence R.
Gulf of St. Lawrence
Coast Ranges
Great Salt Lake
Platte R.
Nova Scotia
Bay of Fundy
Sierra Nevada
GREAT BASIN
INTERIOR PLAINS
Ohio R.
Cape Cod
Long Island
Colorado R.
Arkansas R.
Ozark Plateau
APPALACHIAN MTS.
Mt. Whitney 14,495 ft. (4,418 m)
Chesapeake Bay
Death Valley (lowest point in N.A.) -282 ft. (-86 m)
Cape Hatteras
Sonoran Desert
Rio Grande
COASTAL PLAIN
ATLANTIC OCEAN
30°N
Baja California
Gulf of California
Sierra Madre Occidental
Sierra Madre Oriental
Gulf of Mexico
Bahamas
Tropic of Cancer
Hawaiian Islands
Cuba
Yucatán Peninsula
Greater Antilles
Hispaniola
Puerto Rico
Pico de Orizaba 18,855 ft. (5,747 m)
Caribbean Sea
Lesser Antilles
PACIFIC OCEAN
Lake Maracaibo
Lake Nicaragua
Isthmus of Panama
Orinoco R.
Angel Falls
Llanos
Guiana Highlands
Line Islands
Chimborazo 20,702 ft. (6,310 m)
Rio Negro
Equator
Amazon R.
Galápagos Islands
Cape São Roque
ANDES MOUNTAINS
AMAZON BASIN
Marquesas Islands
Tapajós River
Xingu River
Tocantins R.
São Francisco River
Huascarán 22,205 ft. (6,768 m)
Mato Grosso Plateau
Brazilian Highlands
Tuamotu Archipelago
Cook Islands
Society Islands
Lake Titicaca
Altiplano
Paraguay R.
SOUTH AMERICA
Atacama Desert
Tropic of Capricorn
Gran Chaco
Paraná R.
Iguazú Falls
0 1,000 2,000 Miles
0 1,000 2,000 Kilometers
Miller Cylindrical Projection
30°S
Uruguay R.
Mt. Aconcagua 22,834 ft. (6,960 m)
Rio de la Plata
Pampa
Mountain peak
Point below sea level
National border
Waterfall
N
W
E
S
Patagonia
Valdés Peninsula (lowest point in S.A.) -131 ft. (-40 m)
Falkland Islands
Strait of Magellan
Tierra del Fuego
Cape Horn
South Georgia
150°W
120°W
90°W
60°W
30°W

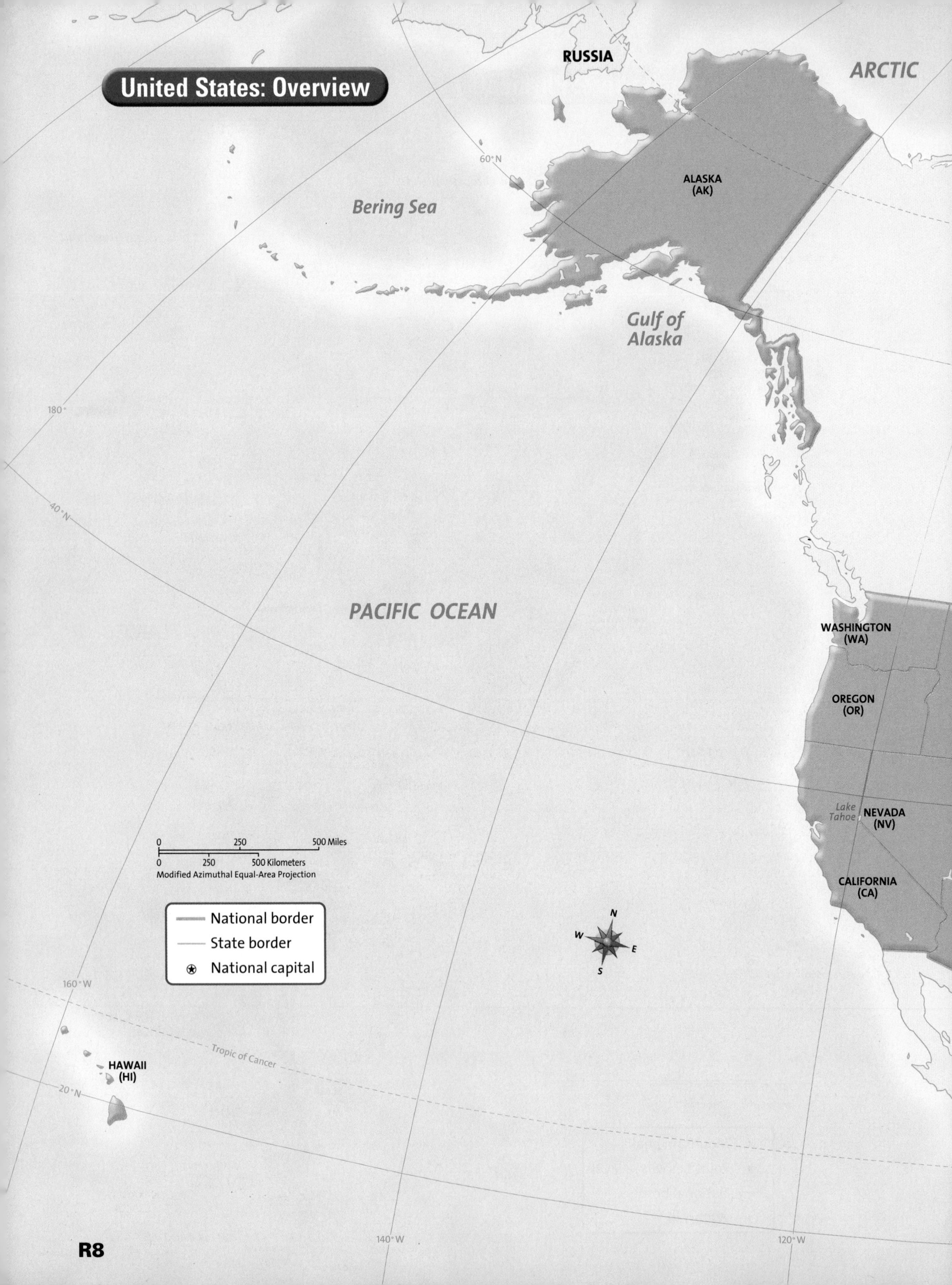
United States: Overview
RUSSIA
ARCTIC
ALASKA
(AK)
Bering Sea
60° N
Gulf of
Alaska
180°
40° N
PACIFIC OCEAN
WASHINGTON
(WA)
OREGON
(OR)
Lake
Tahoe
NEVADA
(NV)
CALIFORNIA
(CA)
0
250
500 Miles
0
250
500 Kilometers
Modified Azimuthal Equal-Area Projection
National border
State border
National capital
N
W
E
S
160° W
Tropic of Cancer
HAWAII
(HI)
20° N
140° W
120° W

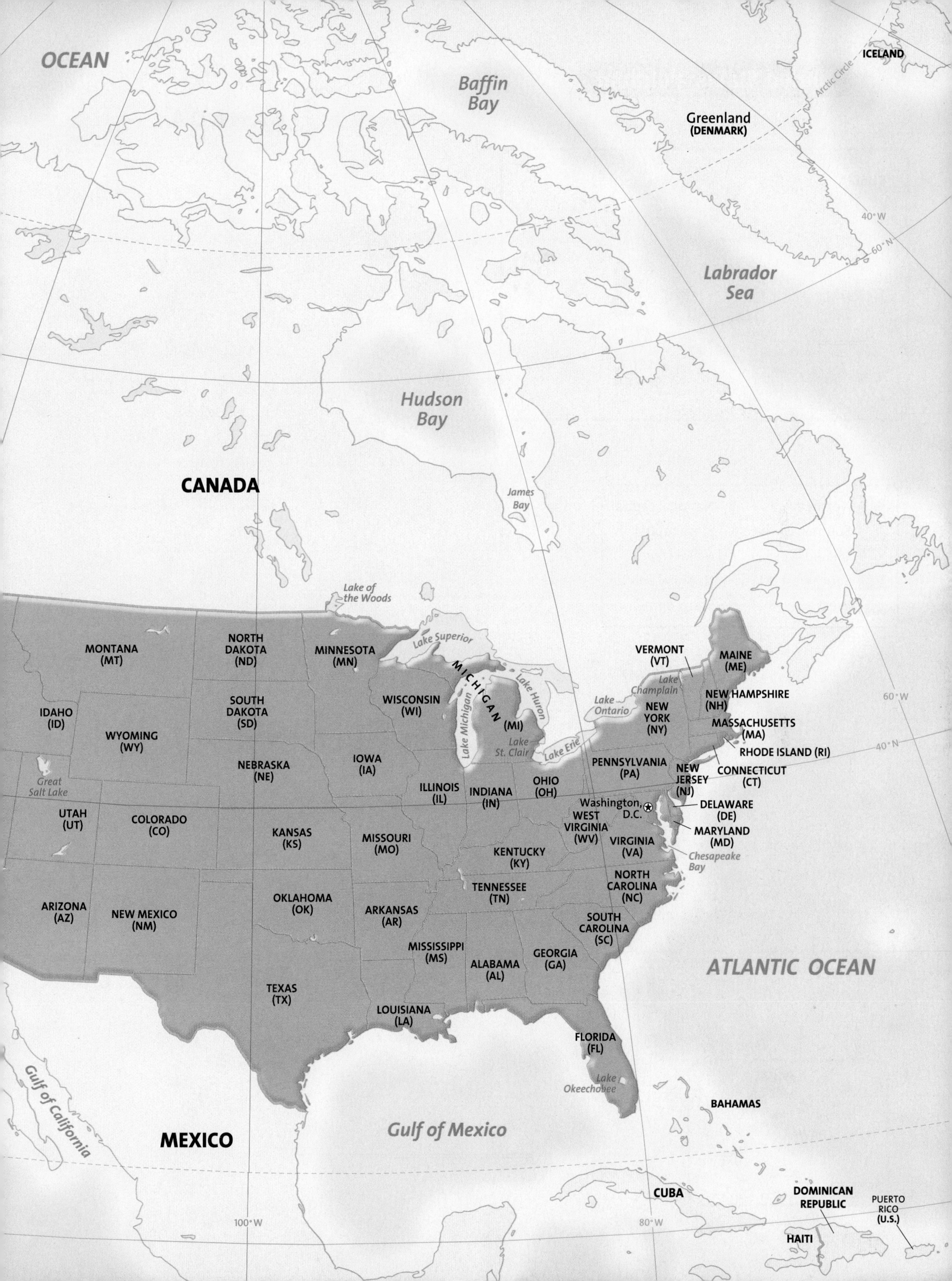

OCEAN
Baffin Bay
ICELAND
Arctic Circle
Greenland (DENMARK)
40° W
60° N
Labrador Sea
Hudson Bay
CANADA
James Bay
Lake of the Woods
Lake Superior
MICHIGAN
Lake Huron
Lake Michigan
MONTANA (MT)
NORTH DAKOTA (ND)
MINNESOTA (MN)
VERMONT (VT)
MAINE (ME)
Lake Champlain
NEW HAMPSHIRE (NH)
60° W
WISCONSIN (WI)
Lake Ontario
IDAHO (ID)
SOUTH DAKOTA (SD)
NEW YORK (NY)
(MI)
MASSACHUSETTS (MA)
WYOMING (WY)
Lake St. Clair
Lake Erie
RHODE ISLAND (RI)
40° N
IOWA (IA)
PENNSYLVANIA (PA)
NEBRASKA (NE)
NEW JERSEY (NJ)
CONNECTICUT (CT)
Great Salt Lake
ILLINOIS (IL)
INDIANA (IN)
OHIO (OH)
Washington, D.C.
DELAWARE (DE)
UTAH (UT)
COLORADO (CO)
WEST VIRGINIA (WV)
KANSAS (KS)
MISSOURI (MO)
VIRGINIA (VA)
MARYLAND (MD)
KENTUCKY (KY)
Chesapeake Bay
NORTH CAROLINA (NC)
TENNESSEE (TN)
ARIZONA (AZ)
NEW MEXICO (NM)
OKLAHOMA (OK)
ARKANSAS (AR)
SOUTH CAROLINA (SC)
MISSISSIPPI (MS)
ALABAMA (AL)
GEORGIA (GA)
ATLANTIC OCEAN
TEXAS (TX)
LOUISIANA (LA)
FLORIDA (FL)
Lake Okeechobee
Gulf of California
BAHAMAS
MEXICO
Gulf of Mexico
CUBA
DOMINICAN REPUBLIC
PUERTO RICO (U.S.)
100° W
80° W
HAITI

United States: Political

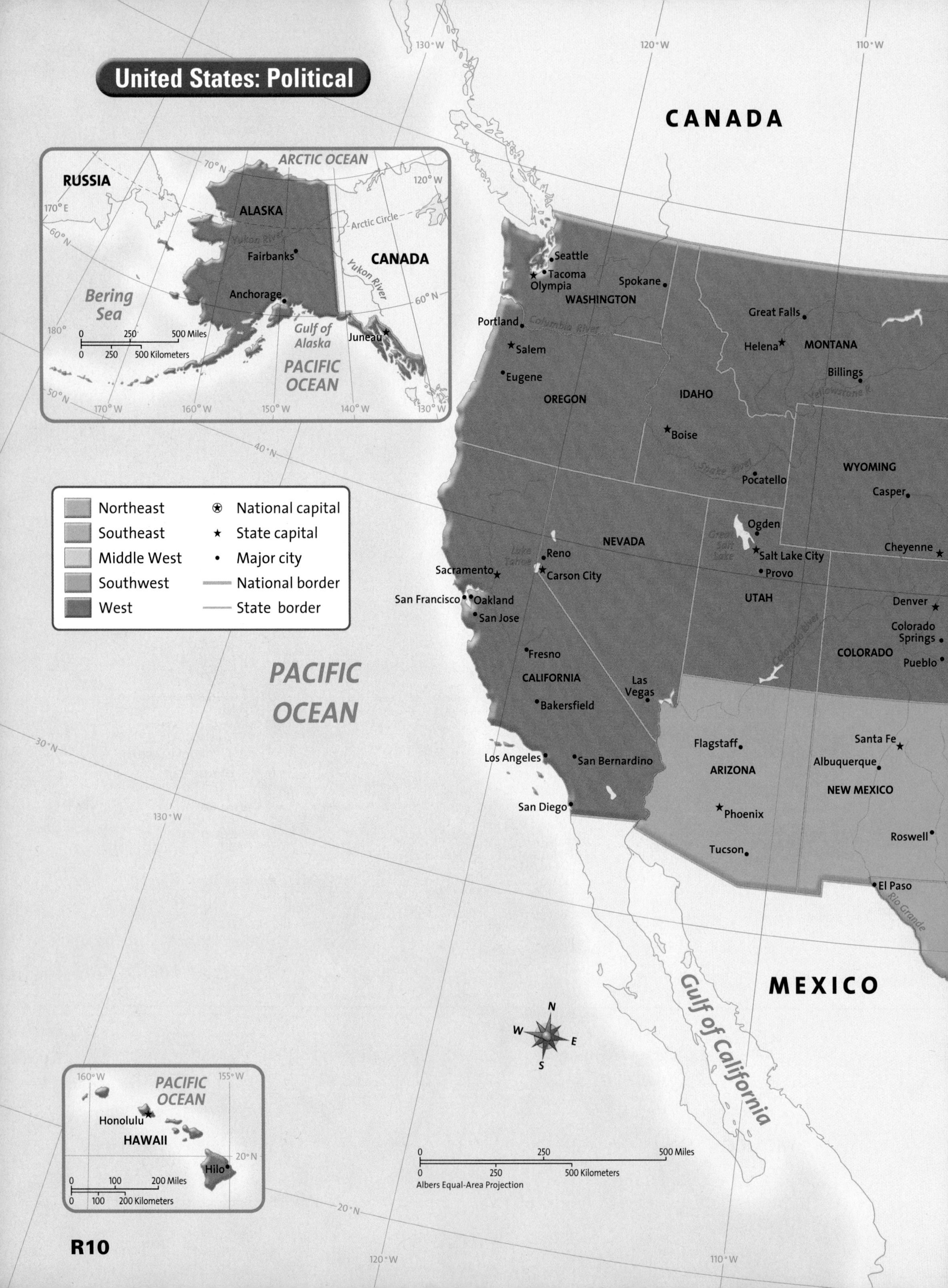

CANADA
ARCTIC OCEAN
RUSSIA
ALASKA
Arctic Circle
Yukon River
Fairbanks
CANADA
Bering Sea
Anchorage
Gulf of Alaska
Juneau
PACIFIC OCEAN
0 250 500 Miles
0 250 500 Kilometers
Seattle
Tacoma
Olympia
Spokane
WASHINGTON
Portland
Columbia River
Salem
Eugene
OREGON
Great Falls
Helena
MONTANA
Billings
Yellowstone R.
IDAHO
Boise
Snake River
Pocatello
WYOMING
Casper
Northeast
Southeast
Middle West
Southwest
West
National capital
State capital
Major city
National border
State border
NEVADA
Lake Tahoe
Reno
Sacramento
Carson City
Ogden
Great Salt Lake
Salt Lake City
Provo
Cheyenne
San Francisco
Oakland
San Jose
UTAH
Denver
Colorado Springs
COLORADO
Pueblo
Colorado River
Fresno
CALIFORNIA
Las Vegas
Bakersfield
PACIFIC OCEAN
Los Angeles
San Bernardino
Flagstaff
ARIZONA
Santa Fe
Albuquerque
NEW MEXICO
San Diego
Phoenix
Tucson
Roswell
El Paso
Rio Grande
MEXICO
Gulf of California
N
S
E
W
PACIFIC OCEAN
Honolulu
HAWAII
Hilo
0 100 200 Miles
0 100 200 Kilometers
0 250 500 Miles
0 250 500 Kilometers
Albers Equal-Area Projection

100°W
90°W
80°W
70°W
50°N
40°N
30°N
70°W
80°W
100°W
90°W
CANADA
Lake of the Woods
Lake Superior
Lake Michigan
Lake Huron
Lake Ontario
Lake Erie
Lake St. Clair
Lake Champlain
St. Lawrence River
Mississippi River
Missouri River
Platte River
Arkansas River
Ohio River
Red River
Lake Texoma
Rio Grande
Chesapeake Bay
Lake Okeechobee
ATLANTIC OCEAN
Gulf of Mexico
BAHAMAS
CUBA
NORTH DAKOTA
Grand Forks
Fargo
Bismarck
SOUTH DAKOTA
Pierre
Rapid City
Sioux Falls
MINNESOTA
Duluth
St. Paul
Minneapolis
NEBRASKA
Omaha
Lincoln
IOWA
Sioux City
Cedar Rapids
Davenport
Des Moines
KANSAS
Topeka
Wichita
Kansas City
MISSOURI
Jefferson City
Springfield
St. Louis
WISCONSIN
Green Bay
Madison
Milwaukee
MICHIGAN
Sault Sainte Marie
Grand Rapids
Lansing
Flint
Detroit
ILLINOIS
Rockford
Chicago
Peoria
Decatur
Springfield
INDIANA
Gary
South Bend
Indianapolis
Evansville
OHIO
Toledo
Cleveland
Akron
Columbus
Dayton
Cincinnati
KENTUCKY
Louisville
Frankfort
Lexington
WEST VIRGINIA
Wheeling
Charleston
PENNSYLVANIA
Pittsburgh
Harrisburg
Philadelphia
NEW YORK
Buffalo
Rochester
Syracuse
Albany
New York City
VERMONT
Burlington
Montpelier
NEW HAMPSHIRE
Concord
Manchester
MAINE
Augusta
Portland
MASSACHUSETTS
Boston
Worcester
RHODE ISLAND
Providence
CONNECTICUT
Hartford
Bridgeport
NEW JERSEY
Newark
Trenton
DELAWARE
Wilmington
Dover
MARYLAND
Baltimore
Annapolis
Washington, D.C.
VIRGINIA
Richmond
Roanoke
Newport News
Norfolk
Virginia Beach
NORTH CAROLINA
Winston-Salem
Greensboro
Raleigh
Charlotte
TENNESSEE
Nashville
Knoxville
Chattanooga
Memphis
SOUTH CAROLINA
Columbia
Charleston
GEORGIA
Atlanta
Macon
Columbus
Savannah
ALABAMA
Huntsville
Birmingham
Montgomery
Mobile
MISSISSIPPI
Meridian
Jackson
Biloxi
FLORIDA
Tallahassee
Jacksonville
Orlando
Tampa
St. Petersburg
West Palm Beach
Miami
ARKANSAS
Fort Smith
Little Rock
LOUISIANA
Shreveport
Baton Rouge
New Orleans
OKLAHOMA
Tulsa
Oklahoma City
TEXAS
Amarillo
Lubbock
Fort Worth
Dallas
Abilene
Odessa
Austin
Beaumont
Houston
San Antonio
Laredo
Corpus Christi

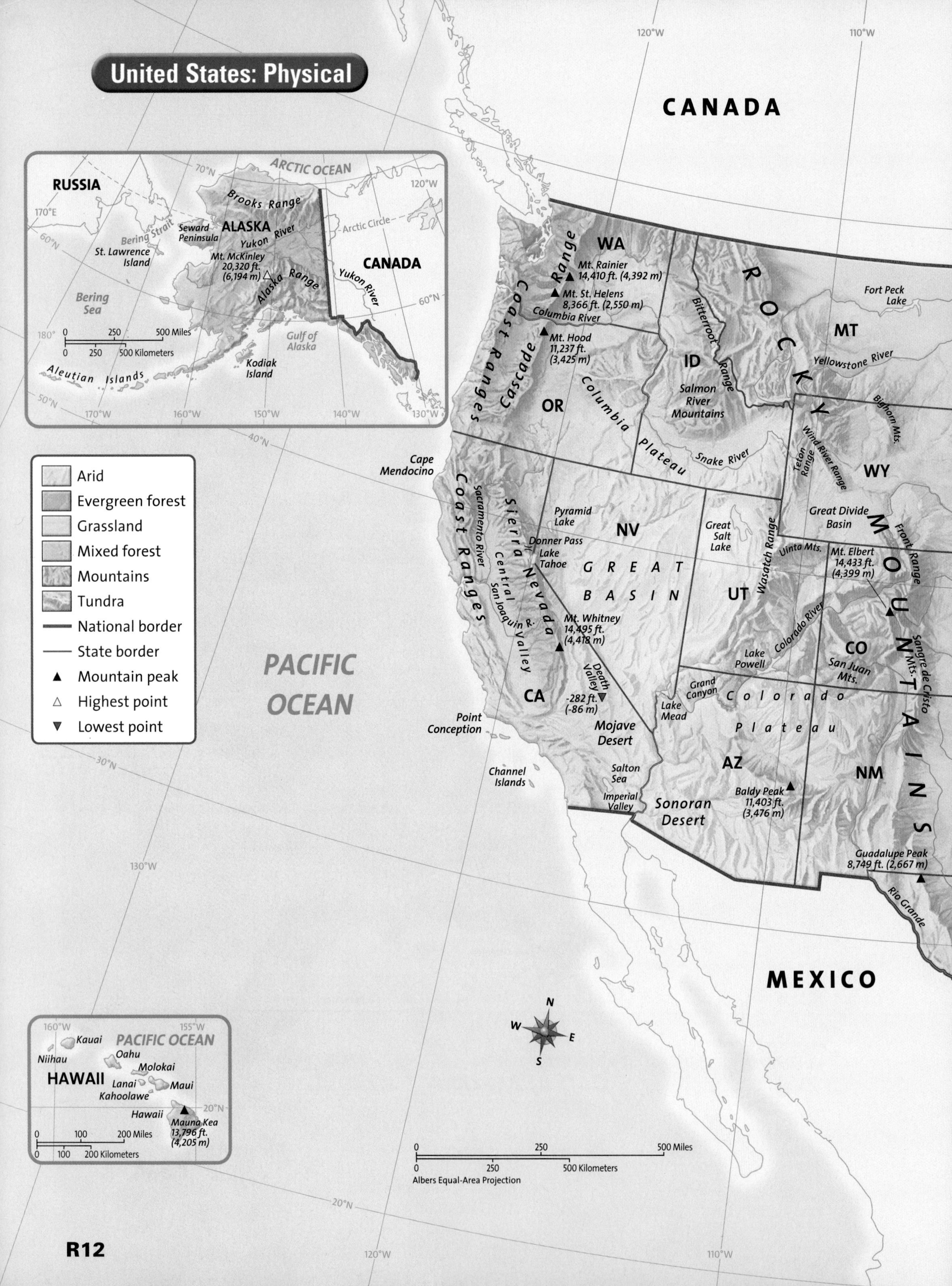
United States: Physical
CANADA
MEXICO
PACIFIC OCEAN
RUSSIA
ARCTIC OCEAN
ALASKA
Brooks Range
Bering Strait
Seward Peninsula
Yukon River
Arctic Circle
St. Lawrence Island
Mt. McKinley 20,320 ft. (6,194 m)
Alaska Range
Bering Sea
Gulf of Alaska
Kodiak Island
Aleutian Islands
0 250 500 Miles
0 250 500 Kilometers
Arid
Evergreen forest
Grassland
Mixed forest
Mountains
Tundra
National border
State border
Mountain peak
Highest point
Lowest point
WA
OR
CA
ID
NV
UT
AZ
MT
WY
CO
NM
Coast Ranges
Cascade Range
Mt. Rainier 14,410 ft. (4,392 m)
Mt. St. Helens 8,366 ft. (2,550 m)
Columbia River
Mt. Hood 11,237 ft. (3,425 m)
Columbia Plateau
Snake River
Bitterroot Range
Salmon River Mountains
ROCKY MOUNTAINS
Fort Peck Lake
Yellowstone River
Bighorn Mts.
Teton Range
Wind River Range
Great Divide Basin
Front Range
Cape Mendocino
Sacramento River
Sierra Nevada
Pyramid Lake
Donner Pass
Lake Tahoe
Central Valley
San Joaquin R.
GREAT BASIN
Great Salt Lake
Wasatch Range
Uinta Mts.
Mt. Elbert 14,433 ft. (4,399 m)
Mt. Whitney 14,495 ft. (4,418 m)
Death Valley
-282 ft. (-86 m)
Colorado River
Lake Powell
San Juan Mts.
Sangre de Cristo Mts.
Grand Canyon
Lake Mead
Colorado Plateau
Point Conception
Mojave Desert
Channel Islands
Salton Sea
Imperial Valley
Sonoran Desert
Baldy Peak 11,403 ft. (3,476 m)
Guadalupe Peak 8,749 ft. (2,667 m)
Rio Grande
HAWAII
Kauai
Niihau
Oahu
Molokai
Lanai
Maui
Kahoolawe
Hawaii
Mauna Kea 13,796 ft. (4,205 m)
0 100 200 Miles
0 100 200 Kilometers
0 250 500 Miles
0 250 500 Kilometers
Albers Equal-Area Projection
N
E
S
W
120°W
110°W
130°W
40°N
30°N
20°N

CANADA
ATLANTIC OCEAN
Gulf of Mexico
BAHAMAS
CUBA
GREAT PLAINS
INTERIOR PLAINS
CENTRAL PLAINS
APPALACHIAN MOUNTAINS
PIEDMONT
COASTAL PLAIN
Ozark Plateau
ND
SD
NE
KS
OK
TX
MN
IA
MO
AR
LA
WI
IL
MS
MI
IN
KY
TN
AL
OH
WV
VA
NC
SC
GA
FL
PA
NY
MD
DE
NJ
CT
RI
MA
VT
NH
ME
Lake of the Woods
Upper Red Lake
Lower Red Lake
Leech Lake
Mesabi Range
Mille Lacs Lake
Isle Royale
Lake Superior
Keweenaw Peninsula
Upper Peninsula
Lake Sakakawea
Lake Oahe
Black Hills
Missouri River
Sand Hills
North Platte R.
Platte River
South Platte R.
Smoky Hills
Red Hills
Llano Estacado
Edwards Plateau
Pecos River
Rio Grande
Colorado River
Brazos River
Sabine River
Red River
Canadian River
Arkansas River
Lake Texoma
Ouachita Mountains
Missouri River
Lake of the Ozarks
Harry S. Truman Reservoir
Mississippi River
Wisconsin River
Lake Winnebago
Lake Michigan
Lower Peninsula
Lake Huron
Lake St. Clair
Lake Erie
Lake Ontario
Niagara Falls
Finger Lakes
Adirondack Mountains
Lake Champlain
St. Lawrence River
Green Mts.
White Mts.
Connecticut R.
Hudson R.
Moosehead Lake
Mt. Katahdin 5,269 ft. (1,606 m)
Mt. Washington 6,288 ft. (1,917 m)
Cape Ann
Cape Cod
Long Island
Illinois River
Wabash River
Ohio River
Allegheny Mts.
Potomac R.
Delaware Bay
Cape Charles
Chesapeake Bay
James R.
Roanoke R.
Albemarle Sound
Cape Hatteras
Cape Fear River
Cape Fear
Cumberland Gap
Lake Barkley
Cumberland R.
Mt. Mitchell 6,684 ft. (2,037 m)
Tennessee R.
Savannah River
Clark Hill Lake
Stone Mountain
Oconee R.
Ocmulgee R.
Altamaha R.
Chattahoochee R.
Alabama R.
Tombigbee R.
Okefenokee Swamp
St. Johns River
Cape Canaveral
Toledo Bend Reservoir
Sam Rayburn Reservoir
Lake Maurepas
Lake Pontchartrain
Mobile Bay
Mississippi Delta
Galveston Bay
Tampa Bay
Lake Okeechobee
Everglades
Cape Sable
Florida Keys
Straits of Florida
100°W
90°W
80°W
70°W
50°N
40°N
30°N

California: Political
OREGON
IDAHO
NEVADA
ARIZONA
MEXICO
PACIFIC OCEAN
State capital
County seat
Other city
National border
State border
County border
Crescent City
DEL NORTE
Yreka
SISKIYOU
MODOC
Alturas
Goose Lake
HUMBOLDT
Eureka
Weaverville
TRINITY
SHASTA
Redding
Shasta Lake
LASSEN
Susanville
Red Bluff
TEHAMA
PLUMAS
Quincy
Pyramid Lake
MENDOCINO
GLENN
Willows
Chico
BUTTE
SIERRA
Downieville
Oroville
Nevada City
NEVADA
Truckee
COLUSA
Colusa
Ukiah
LAKE
Lakeport
YUBA
Yuba City
Marysville
SUTTER
PLACER
Auburn
Lake Tahoe
YOLO
Woodland
SONOMA
Santa Rosa
NAPA
Napa
Placerville
EL DORADO
Markleeville
ALPINE
Sacramento
SACRAMENTO
AMADOR
Jackson
Sonoma
Petaluma
MARIN
Fairfield
SOLANO
CALAVERAS
San Andreas
Bridgeport
San Rafael
Martinez
CONTRA COSTA
Berkeley
Stockton
SAN JOAQUIN
TUOLUMNE
Sonora
Mono Lake
MONO
San Francisco
SAN FRANCISCO
Oakland
ALAMEDA
San Francisco Bay
Modesto
STANISLAUS
Redwood City
SAN MATEO
MARIPOSA
Mariposa
San Jose
SANTA CLARA
Merced
MADERA
SANTA CRUZ
Santa Cruz
MERCED
Madera
FRESNO
Monterey Bay
Hollister
Salinas
SAN BENITO
Fresno
Independence
Monterey
INYO
Visalia
Tulare
TULARE
Hanford
KINGS
MONTEREY
Lake Mead
SAN LUIS OBISPO
Ridgecrest
Bakersfield
KERN
San Luis Obispo
Santa Maria
SANTA BARBARA
Barstow
Needles
SAN BERNARDINO
Lompoc
VENTURA
Santa Clarita
LOS ANGELES
Santa Barbara
Ventura
Oxnard
Burbank
Glendale
Pasadena
San Bernardino
Los Angeles
Torrance
Riverside
Long Beach
Anaheim
Huntington Beach
Santa Ana
ORANGE
Palm Springs
RIVERSIDE
Blythe
Salton Sea
Oceanside
Escondido
IMPERIAL
SAN DIEGO
San Diego
El Centro
San Diego Bay
Klamath River
Pit River
Trinity River
Eel River
Sacramento River
Feather R.
Russian River
American River
Stanislaus
San Joaquin River
Kings River
Salinas River
Kern
Cuyama R.
Santa Ynez River
Santa Clara R.
Colorado River
N
S
E
W
0 75 150 Miles
0 75 150 Kilometers
Albers Equal-Area Projection
42°N
41°N
40°N
39°N
38°N
37°N
36°N
35°N
34°N
33°N
32°N
124°W
123°W
122°W
121°W
120°W
119°W
118°W

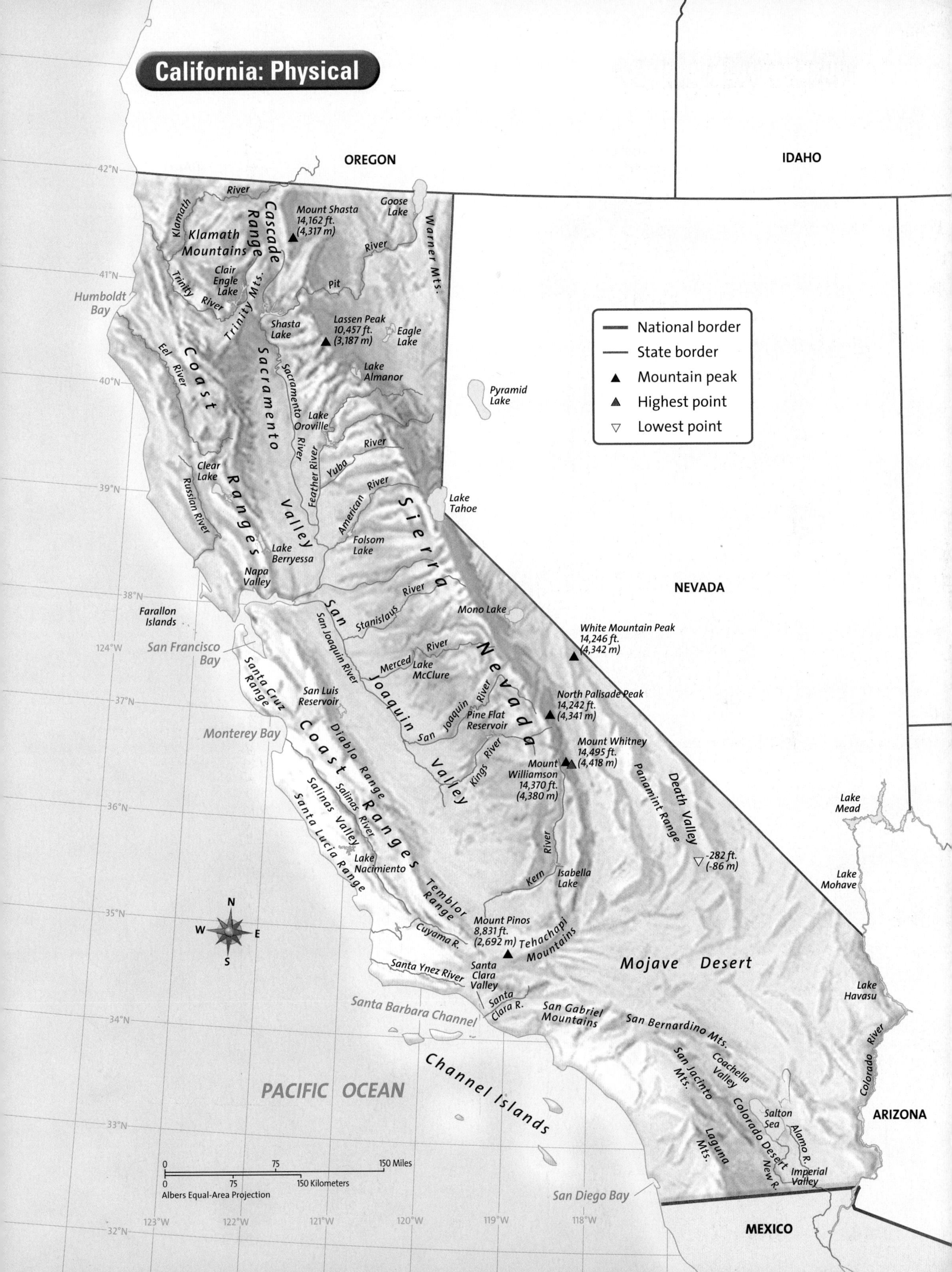
California: Physical
OREGON
IDAHO
NEVADA
ARIZONA
MEXICO
PACIFIC OCEAN
National border
State border
Mountain peak
Highest point
Lowest point
Mount Shasta 14,162 ft. (4,317 m)
Lassen Peak 10,457 ft. (3,187 m)
White Mountain Peak 14,246 ft. (4,342 m)
North Palisade Peak 14,242 ft. (4,341 m)
Mount Whitney 14,495 ft. (4,418 m)
Mount Williamson 14,370 ft. (4,380 m)
Mount Pinos 8,831 ft. (2,692 m)
-282 ft. (-86 m)
Klamath Mountains
Cascade Range
Trinity Mts.
Warner Mts.
Coast Ranges
Sacramento Valley
Sierra Nevada
San Joaquin Valley
Death Valley
Panamint Range
Santa Cruz Range
Diablo Range
Salinas Valley
Santa Lucia Range
Temblor Range
Tehachapi Mountains
Mojave Desert
San Gabriel Mountains
San Bernardino Mts.
San Jacinto Mts.
Coachella Valley
Laguna Mts.
Colorado Desert
Imperial Valley
Napa Valley
Santa Clara Valley
Channel Islands
Farallon Islands
Humboldt Bay
San Francisco Bay
Monterey Bay
Santa Barbara Channel
San Diego Bay
Klamath River
Trinity River
Pit River
Eel River
Russian River
Sacramento River
Feather River
Yuba River
American River
San Joaquin River
Stanislaus River
Merced River
Kings River
Kern River
Salinas River
Cuyama R.
Santa Ynez River
Santa Clara R.
Colorado River
New R.
Alamo R.
Goose Lake
Clair Engle Lake
Shasta Lake
Eagle Lake
Lake Almanor
Lake Oroville
Pyramid Lake
Clear Lake
Lake Tahoe
Folsom Lake
Lake Berryessa
Mono Lake
Lake McClure
San Luis Reservoir
Pine Flat Reservoir
Lake Nacimiento
Isabella Lake
Lake Mead
Lake Mohave
Lake Havasu
Salton Sea
N
S
E
W
0 75 150 Miles
0 75 150 Kilometers
Albers Equal-Area Projection
42°N
41°N
40°N
39°N
38°N
37°N
36°N
35°N
34°N
33°N
32°N
124°W
123°W
122°W
121°W
120°W
119°W
118°W

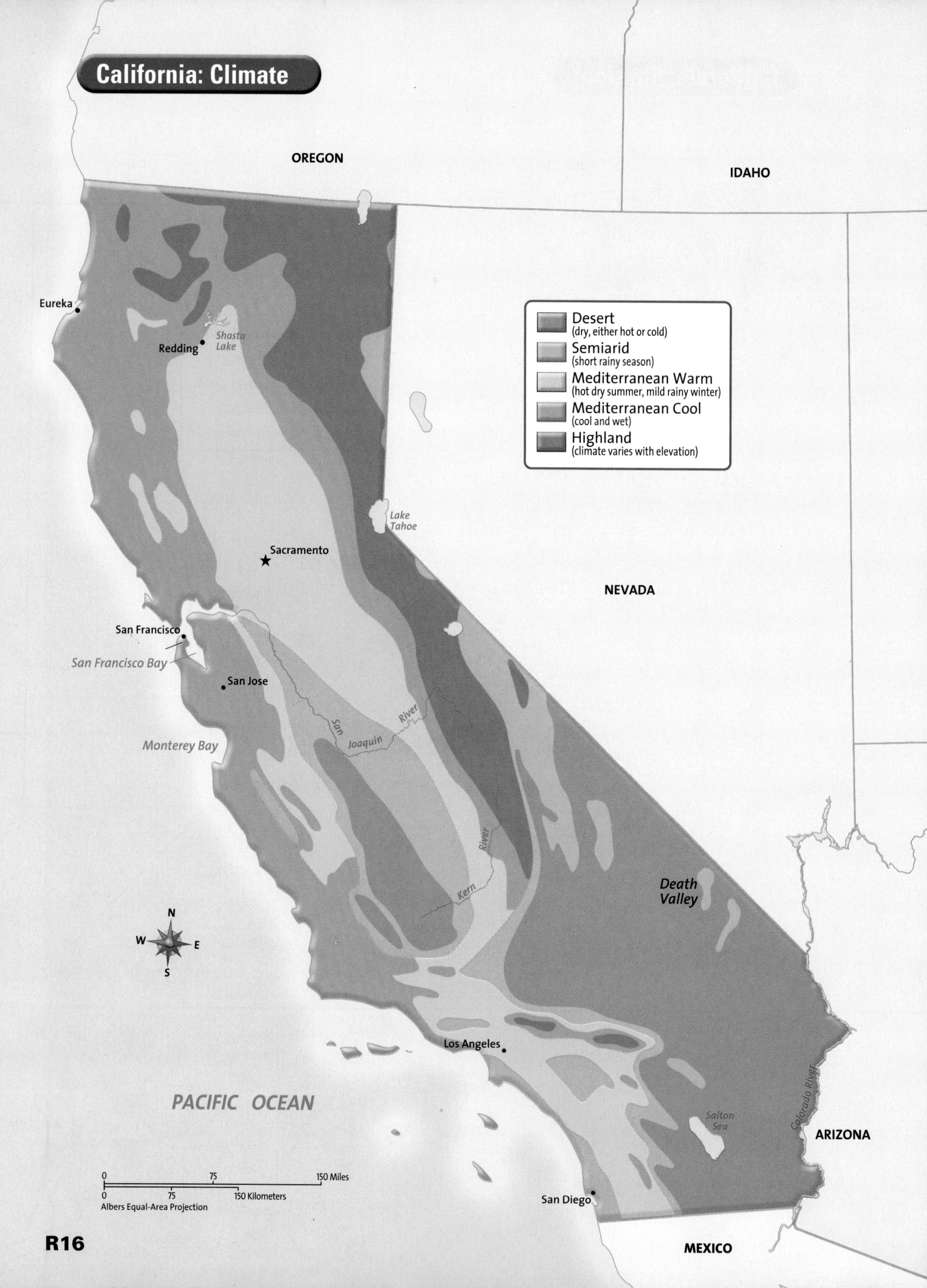

California: Climate
OREGON
IDAHO
NEVADA
ARIZONA
MEXICO
PACIFIC OCEAN
Desert
(dry, either hot or cold)
Semiarid
(short rainy season)
Mediterranean Warm
(hot dry summer, mild rainy winter)
Mediterranean Cool
(cool and wet)
Highland
(climate varies with elevation)
Eureka
Redding
Shasta Lake
Lake Tahoe
Sacramento
San Francisco
San Francisco Bay
San Jose
Monterey Bay
San Joaquin River
Kern River
Death Valley
Los Angeles
Salton Sea
Colorado River
San Diego
N
E
S
W
0
75
150 Miles
0
75
150 Kilometers
Albers Equal-Area Projection

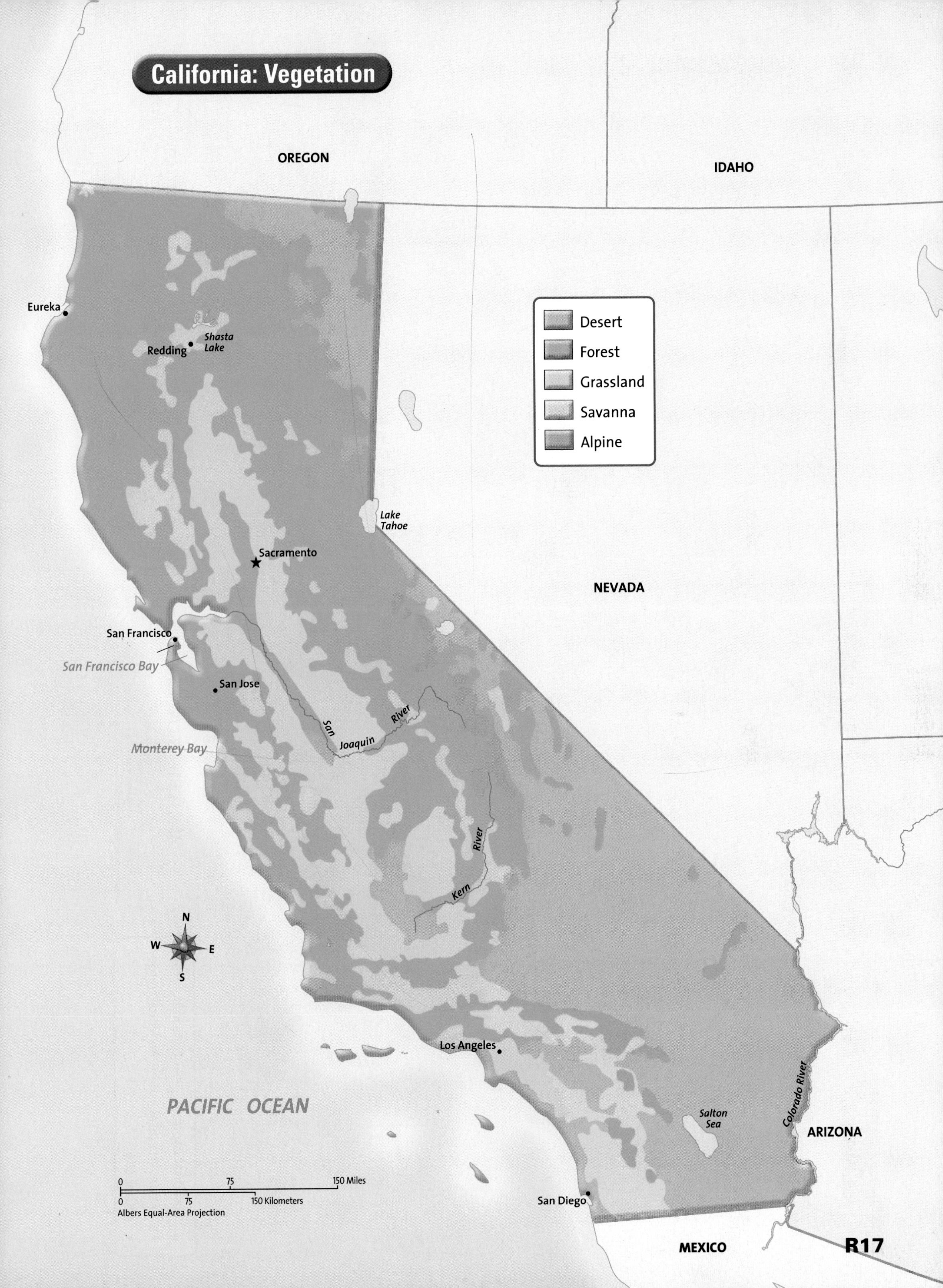
California: Vegetation
OREGON
IDAHO
NEVADA
ARIZONA
MEXICO
PACIFIC OCEAN
Desert
Forest
Grassland
Savanna
Alpine
Eureka
Redding
Shasta Lake
Lake Tahoe
Sacramento
San Francisco
San Francisco Bay
San Jose
Monterey Bay
San Joaquin River
Kern River
Los Angeles
Salton Sea
Colorado River
San Diego
N
W
E
S
0
75
150 Miles
0
75
150 Kilometers
Albers Equal-Area Projection

Canada

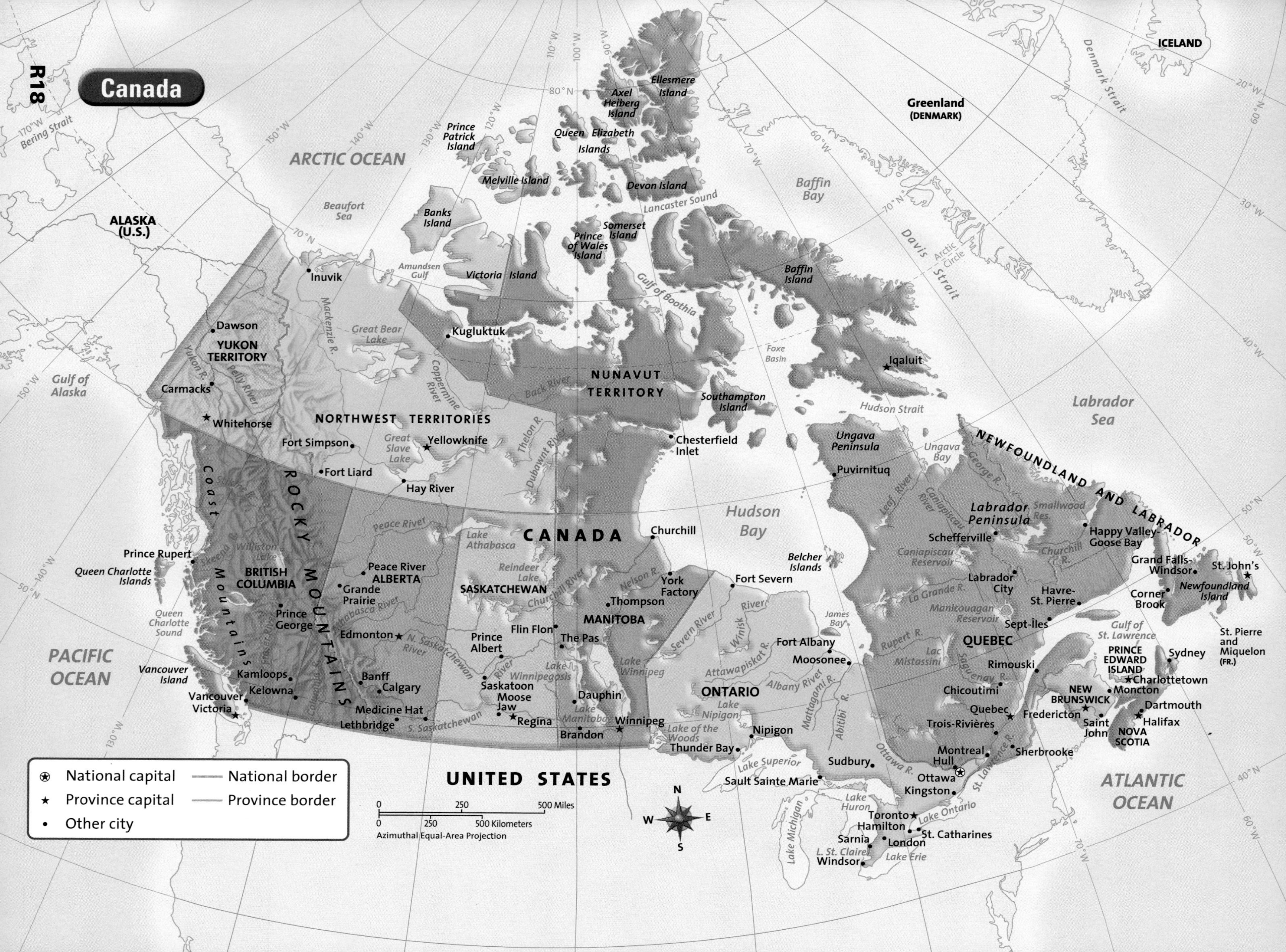
CANADA
UNITED STATES
ALASKA (U.S.)
Greenland (DENMARK)
ICELAND
ARCTIC OCEAN
PACIFIC OCEAN
ATLANTIC OCEAN
Beaufort Sea
Baffin Bay
Labrador Sea
Hudson Bay
Gulf of Alaska
Bering Strait
Denmark Strait
Davis Strait
Hudson Strait
Lancaster Sound
Gulf of Boothia
Foxe Basin
Amundsen Gulf
James Bay
Ungava Bay
Gulf of St. Lawrence
Queen Charlotte Sound
Arctic Circle
YUKON TERRITORY
NORTHWEST TERRITORIES
NUNAVUT TERRITORY
BRITISH COLUMBIA
ALBERTA
SASKATCHEWAN
MANITOBA
ONTARIO
QUEBEC
NEWFOUNDLAND AND LABRADOR
NEW BRUNSWICK
PRINCE EDWARD ISLAND
NOVA SCOTIA
ROCKY MOUNTAINS
Coast Mountains
Ellesmere Island
Axel Heiberg Island
Queen Elizabeth Islands
Devon Island
Prince Patrick Island
Melville Island
Banks Island
Victoria Island
Somerset Island
Prince of Wales Island
Baffin Island
Southampton Island
Belcher Islands
Ungava Peninsula
Labrador Peninsula
Newfoundland Island
Queen Charlotte Islands
Vancouver Island
St. Pierre and Miquelon (FR.)
Mackenzie R.
Yukon R.
Pelly River
Coppermine River
Back River
Thelon R.
Dubawnt River
Peace River
Athabasca River
N. Saskatchewan River
S. Saskatchewan
Churchill River
Nelson R.
Severn River
Winisk River
Attawapiskat R.
Albany River
Mattagami R.
Abitibi R.
Ottawa R.
St. Lawrence R.
Saguenay R.
Rupert R.
La Grande R.
Caniapiscau River
Leaf River
George R.
Churchill R.
Stikine R.
Skeena R.
Fraser River
Columbia R.
Great Bear Lake
Great Slave Lake
Lake Athabasca
Reindeer Lake
Lake Winnipegosis
Lake Manitoba
Lake Winnipeg
Lake of the Woods
Lake Nipigon
Lake Superior
Lake Michigan
Lake Huron
L. St. Claire
Lake Erie
Lake Ontario
Williston Lake
Lac Mistassini
Caniapiscau Reservoir
Manicouagan Reservoir
Smallwood Res.
Dawson
Carmacks
Whitehorse
Inuvik
Fort Simpson
Fort Liard
Yellowknife
Hay River
Kugluktuk
Iqaluit
Chesterfield Inlet
Churchill
York Factory
Thompson
Fort Severn
Prince Rupert
Prince George
Kamloops
Kelowna
Vancouver
Victoria
Peace River
Grande Prairie
Edmonton
Banff
Calgary
Medicine Hat
Lethbridge
Prince Albert
Saskatoon
Moose Jaw
Regina
Flin Flon
The Pas
Dauphin
Brandon
Winnipeg
Thunder Bay
Nipigon
Sault Sainte Marie
Sudbury
Fort Albany
Moosonee
Toronto
Hamilton
St. Catharines
London
Sarnia
Windsor
Kingston
Ottawa
Hull
Montreal
Trois-Rivières
Quebec
Sherbrooke
Chicoutimi
Rimouski
Sept-Îles
Havre-St. Pierre
Labrador City
Schefferville
Puvirnituq
Happy Valley-Goose Bay
Grand Falls-Windsor
Corner Brook
St. John's
Sydney
Charlottetown
Moncton
Fredericton
Saint John
Dartmouth
Halifax
80° N
70° N
60° N
50° N
40° N
170° W
150° W
140° W
130° W
120° W
110° W
100° W
90° W
70° W
60° W
40° W
30° W
20° W
N
E
S
W
0
250
500 Miles
0
250
500 Kilometers
Azimuthal Equal-Area Projection
National capital
Province capital
Other city
National border
Province border

Mexico

UNITED STATES
MEXICO
Gulf of Mexico
PACIFIC OCEAN
Bay of Campeche
Caribbean Sea
Yucatán Channel
Gulf of California
Gulf of Tehuantepec
BELIZE
GUATEMALA
HONDURAS
EL SALVADOR
BAJA CALIFORNIA
BAJA CALIFORNIA SUR
SONORA
CHIHUAHUA
COAHUILA
NUEVO LEÓN
TAMAULIPAS
SINALOA
DURANGO
ZACATECAS
SAN LUIS POTOSÍ
NAYARIT
AGUASCALIENTES
GUANAJUATO
QUERÉTARO
HIDALGO
JALISCO
COLIMA
MICHOACÁN
MÉXICO
DISTRITO FEDERAL
MORELOS
TLAXCALA
PUEBLA
VERACRUZ
GUERRERO
OAXACA
TABASCO
CHIAPAS
CAMPECHE
YUCATÁN
QUINTANA ROO
Tijuana
Mexicali
Ensenada
Puerto Peñasco
Sonoran Desert
Nogales
Ciudad Juárez
Nueva Casas Grandes
Villa Ahumada
Guadalupe
Cedros Island
Eugenia Point
Hermosillo
Guaymas
Ciudad Obregón
Navojoa
Yaqui R.
Chihuahua
Conchos R.
Delicias
Hidalgo del Parral
Rio Grande
Rio Bravo
Nuevo Laredo
Monclova
Reynosa
Matamoros
Saltillo
Monterrey
Loreto
Los Mochis
Torreón
Culiacán
La Paz
San Lucas
Cape San Lucas
Mazatlán
Durango
Concepción del Oro
Ciudad Victoria
SIERRA MADRE OCCIDENTAL
SIERRA MADRE ORIENTAL
Tropic of Cancer
Fresnillo
Zacatecas
Ciudad Mante
Tampico
Ciudad de Valles
San Luis Potosí
Aguascalientes
Marías Islands
San Blas
Tepic
Santiago R.
León
Irapuato
Guanajuato
Querétaro
Poza Rica
Puerto Vallarta
Cape Corrientes
Guadalajara
Lerma R.
Lake Chapala
Revillagigedo Islands
Socorro Island
Morelia
Mexico City
Pachuca
Jalapa Enríquez
Veracruz
Toluca
Tlaxcala
Puebla
Cuernavaca
Uruapán
Colima
Tecomán
Balsas River
Lázaro Cárdenas
Chilpancingo
SIERRA MADRE DEL SUR
Acapulco
Oaxaca
Puerto Escondido
Salina Cruz
Coatzacoalcos
Isthmus of Tehuantepec
Villahermosa
Usumacinta R.
Tuxtla Gutiérrez
Comitán
Tapachula
Ciudad del Carmen
Campeche
Mérida
Yucatán Peninsula
Chetumal
Cancún
Cozumel Island
N
S
E
W
30°N
20°N
110°W
100°W
90°W
National border
State border
National capital
State capital
Other city
0
150
300 Miles
0
150
300 Kilometers
Azimuthal Equal-Area Projection

Almanac

FACTS ABOUT CALIFORNIA

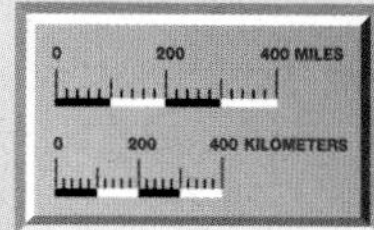

CLIMATE

POPULATION*

LEADING PRODUCTS AND RESOURCES

CALIFORNIA

LAND

Highest Point: Mt. Whitney in the Sierra Nevada 14,495 feet

Lowest Point: Death Valley 282 feet below sea level

SIZE

Area: 158,648 square miles

Greatest Distance North/South: 646 miles

Greatest Distance East/West: 560 miles

Coastline: 840 miles

CLIMATE

Average Temperature: 75°F in July, 44°F in January

Average Yearly Rainfall: 22 inches

POPULATION*

Total Population: 33,871,648*

Population Density: 217.2 people per square mile

Population Distribution: Urban 94.5 percent Rural 5.5 percent

*the most recent figure available

LEADING PRODUCTS AND RESOURCES

Crops: Grapes, nursery products, cotton, almonds, hay, lettuce, tomatoes, strawberries, oranges, broccoli, carrots

Livestock: Cattle, poultry, sheep

Fishing: Sea urchin, crab, squid, tuna

Timber/lumber: Fir, pine, redwood

Manufacturing: Computer and electronic equipment, food products, pharmaceuticals, transportation equipment

Mining: Petroleum, natural gas, sand and gravel, boron, gold, silver, asbestos, gypsum

California is the third largest state in size among all the states. Only Alaska and Texas are larger.

The lowest recorded temperature in California was –45°F at Boca on January, 20, 1937. The highest temperature ever recorded in California—or anywhere else in the United States—was 134°F in Death Valley on July 10, 1913.

California has more people than any other state. In fact, one out of every eight people in the United States lives in California.

GOVERNMENT

Elected Officials: 4-year terms: Governor, Lieutenant Governor, Secretary of State, Controller, Attorney General, Treasurer, Superintendent of Public Instruction

State Senate: 40 senators, 4-year terms

State Assembly: 80 members, 2-year terms

Counties: 58

United States Senators: 2 senators, 6-year terms

United States Representatives: 53 representatives, 2-year terms

STATE SYMBOLS

Animal: Grizzly bear

Bird: California valley quail

Colors: Blue and gold

Dance: West coast swing dancing

Fish: Golden trout

Flower: Golden poppy

Folk Dance: Square dance

Fossil: Saber-tooth cat

Gemstone: Benitoite

Insect: California dogface butterfly

Marine Fish: Golden orange fish

Marine Mammal: California gray whale

Mineral: Gold

Reptile: Desert tortoise

Rock: Serpentine

Soil: San Joaquin soil

Tree: California redwood

The world's tallest tree currently standing is located in California's Mendocino County. The 367-foot redwood is about as tall as a 37-story building, and the tree is still growing!

Even after the gold rush in 1849, mining experts claim that only 10 percent of California's gold has been discovered.

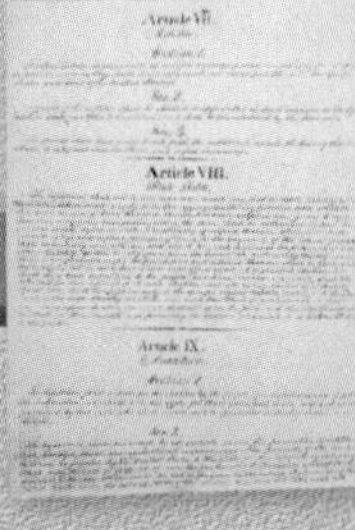

The California state constitution takes up a lot of space—it is more than 10,000 pages long. It has been changed more than 500 times since 1879.

Almanac
Facts About California Counties

County Name	County Seat	Population*	Year Organized	Named For
Alameda	Oakland	1,443,741	1853	"grove of trees" in Spanish
Alpine	Markleeville	1,208	1864	the mountainous Sierra Nevada
Amador	Jackson	35,100	1854	José María Amador, settler
Butte	Oroville	203,171	1850	Sutter Buttes or the Butte River
Calaveras	San Andreas	40,554	1850	"skulls" in Spanish
Colusa	Colusa	18,804	1850	a village of the Patwin Indians
Contra Costa	Martinez	948,816	1850	"opposite coast" in Spanish
Del Norte	Crescent City	27,507	1857	"of the north" in Spanish
El Dorado	Placerville	156,299	1850	"the gilded" or "the golden" in Spanish
Fresno	Fresno	799,407	1856	"ash tree" in Spanish
Glenn	Willows	26,453	1891	Hugh J. Glenn, physician and wheat grower
Humboldt	Eureka	126,518	1853	Friedrich Heinrich Alexander von Humboldt, German naturalist
Imperial	El Centro	142,361	1907	Imperial Land Company
Inyo	Independence	17,945	1866	Indian word for "where the great spirit dwells"
Kern	Bakersfield	661,645	1866	Edward M. Kern, topographer and artist

* The population figures are the most recent estimates.

County Name	County Seat	Population*	Year Organized	Named For
Kings	Hanford	129,461	1893	Kings River
Lake	Lakeport	58,309	1861	Clear Lake
Lassen	Susanville	33,828	1864	Peter Lassen, pioneer
Los Angeles	Los Angeles	9,519,338	1850	"the angels" in Spanish
Madera	Madera	123,109	1893	"lumber" in Spanish
Marin	San Rafael	247,289	1850	Marin, a mythical Indian leader, or "mariner" in Spanish
Mariposa	Mariposa	17,130	1850	"butterfly" in Spanish
Mendocino	Ukiah	86,265	1850	Antonio de Mendoza or Lorenzo Suarez de Mendoza, viceroys of New Spain
Merced	Merced	210,554	1855	Merced River, *merced* meaning "mercy" in Spanish
Modoc	Alturas	9,449	1874	Modoc Indian tribe
Mono	Bridgeport	12,853	1861	tribe of the Shoshone Indians
Monterey	Salinas	401,762	1850	Count of Monterey, a viceroy of New Spain, or Monterey Bay
Napa	Napa	124,279	1850	Wappo or Pomo Indian word, possibly meaning "village" or "fish"
Nevada	Nevada City	92,033	1851	Sierra Nevada, *nevada* meaning "snow-covered" in Spanish
Orange	Santa Ana	2,846,289	1889	the fruit
Placer	Auburn	248,399	1851	surface gold deposits

*The population figures are the most recent estimates.

County Name	County Seat	Population*	Year Organized	Named For
Plumas	Quincy	20,824	1854	"feathers" in Spanish, for the Feather River
Riverside	Riverside	1,545,387	1893	location near river
Sacramento	Sacramento	1,223,499	1850	Holy Sacrament
San Benito	Hollister	53,234	1874	St. Benedict
San Bernardino	San Bernardino	1,709,434	1853	St. Bernard of Siena
San Diego	San Diego	2,813,833	1850	St. Didacus
San Francisco	San Francisco	776,733	1850	St. Francis of Assisi
San Joaquin	Stockton	563,598	1850	St. Joachim
San Luis Obispo	San Luis Obispo	246,681	1850	St. Louis of Toulouse
San Mateo	Redwood City	707,161	1856	St. Matthew
Santa Barbara	Santa Barbara	399,347	1850	St. Barbara
Santa Clara	San Jose	1,682,585	1850	St. Clare of Assisi
Santa Cruz	Santa Cruz	255,602	1850	"holy cross" in Spanish
Shasta	Redding	163,256	1850	Shasta Indian tribe
Sierra	Downieville	3,555	1852	Sierra Nevada, *sierra* meaning "mountain range" in Spanish
Siskiyou	Yreka	44,301	1852	"bobtailed horse" in Cree or "six boulders" in French
Solano	Fairfield	394,542	1850	Chief Solano or St. Francis Solano

* The population figures are the most recent estimates.

County Name	County Seat	Population*	Year Organized	Named For
Sonoma	Santa Rosa	458,614	1850	Chief Tsonoma or Wintu Indian word, possibly meaning "nose"
Stanislaus	Modesto	446,997	1854	Chief Estanislao
Sutter	Yuba City	78,930	1850	John Augustus Sutter
Tehama	Red Bluff	56,039	1856	Indian word, possibly for "lowlands" or "shallow"
Trinity	Weaverville	13,022	1850	Trinity River
Tulare	Visalia	368,021	1852	"rush" or "reed" in Spanish, possibly from "cattail" in Aztec
Tuolumne	Sonora	54,501	1850	Indian word for "cluster of stone wigwams"
Ventura	Ventura	753,197	1873	St. Bonaventure
Yolo	Woodland	168,660	1850	Yolo Indian tribe, possibly meaning "place abounding in rushes"
Yuba	Marysville	60,219	1850	Maidu Indian village or tribal name

* The population figures are the most recent estimates.

Almanac
Facts About California Governors

Governor	Birth/Death	Place of Birth	Political Party	Term
Peter Burnett	(1807–1895)	Nashville, Tennessee	Independent Democratic	1849–1851
John McDougall	(c.1818–1866)	Ross County, Ohio	Independent Democratic	1851–1852
John Bigler	(1805–1871)	Carlisle, Pennsylvania	Democratic	1852–1856
Neely Johnson	(1825–1872)	Johnson Township, Indiana	American (Know-Nothing)	1856–1858
John Weller	(1812–1875)	Montgomery, Ohio	Democratic	1858–1860
Milton Latham	(1827–1882)	Columbus, Ohio	Democratic	1860
John Downey	(1827–1894)	Roscommon County, Ireland	Democratic	1860–1862
Leland Stanford	(1824–1893)	Watervliet, New York	Republican	1862–1863
Frederick Low	(1828–1894)	Frankfort, Maine	Union	1863–1867
Henry H. Haight	(1825–1878)	Rochester, New York	Democratic	1867–1871
Newton Booth	(1825–1892)	Salem, Indiana	Republican	1871–1875
Romualdo Pacheco	(1831–1899)	Santa Barbara, California	Republican	1875
William Irwin	(1827–1886)	Butler County, Ohio	Democratic	1875–1880
George Perkins	(1839–1923)	Kennebunkport, Maine	Republican	1880–1883
George Stoneman	(1822–1894)	Busti, New York	Democratic	1883–1887
Washington Bartlett	(1824–1887)	Savannah, Georgia	Democratic	1887
Robert Waterman	(1826–1891)	Fairfield, New York	Republican	1887–1891
Henry Markham	(1840–1923)	Wilmington, New York	Republican	1891–1895

Governor	Birth/Death	Place of Birth	Political Party	Term
James Budd	(1851–1908)	Janesville, Wisconsin	Democratic	1895–1899
Henry Gage	(1852–1924)	Geneva, New York	Republican	1899–1903
George Pardee	(1857–1941)	San Francisco, California	Republican	1903–1907
James Gillett	(1860–1937)	Viroqua, Wisconsin	Republican	1907–1911
Hiram Johnson	(1866–1945)	Sacramento, California	Republican	1911–1917
William Stephens	(1859–1944)	Eaton, Ohio	Republican	1917–1923
Friend William Richardson	(1865–1943)	Friends Colony County, Michigan	Republican	1923–1927
Clement Calhoun Young	(1869–1947)	Lisbon, New Hampshire	Republican	1927–1931
James Rolph	(1869–1934)	San Francisco, California	Republican	1931–1934
Frank Merriam	(1865–1955)	Hopkinton, Iowa	Republican	1934–1939
Culbert Olson	(1876–1962)	Fillmore, Utah	Democratic	1939–1943
Earl Warren	(1891–1974)	Los Angeles, California	Republican	1943–1953
Goodwin Knight	(1896–1970)	Provo, Utah	Republican	1953–1959
Edmund G. Brown	(1905–1996)	San Francisco, California	Democratic	1959–1967
Ronald Reagan	(1911–2004)	Tampico, Illinois	Republican	1967–1975
Edmund G. Brown, Jr.	(1938–)	San Francisco, California	Democratic	1975–1983
George Deukmejian	(1928–)	New York City, New York	Republican	1983–1991
Pete Wilson	(1933–)	Lake Forest, Illinois	Republican	1991–1999
Gray Davis	(1942–)	New York City, New York	Democratic	1999–2003
Arnold Schwarzenegger	(1947–)	Thal Styria, Austria	Republican	2003–

Research Handbook

Before you can write a report or complete a project, you must gather information about your topic. You can find some information in your textbook. Other sources of information are technology resources, print resources, and community resources.

Technology Resources

- Internet
- Computer disk
- Television or radio

Print Resources

- Almanac
- Atlas
- Dictionary
- Encyclopedia
- Nonfiction book
- Periodical
- Thesaurus

Community Resources

- Teacher
- Museum curator
- Community leader
- Older citizen

Technology Resources

The main technology resources you can use for researching information are the Internet and computer disks. Your school or local library may have CD-ROMs or DVDs that contain information about your topic. Other media, such as television and radio, can also be good sources of current information.

Using the Internet

The Internet contains vast amounts of information. By using a computer to go online, you can read documents, see pictures and artworks, listen to music, take a virtual tour of a museum and read about current events. Keep in mind that some websites might contain mistakes or incorrect information. To get accurate information, be sure to visit only trusted websites, such as museum and government sites. Also, try to find two or more websites that give the same facts.

Plan Your Search

- Identify the topic to be researched.
- Make a list of questions that you want to answer about your topic.

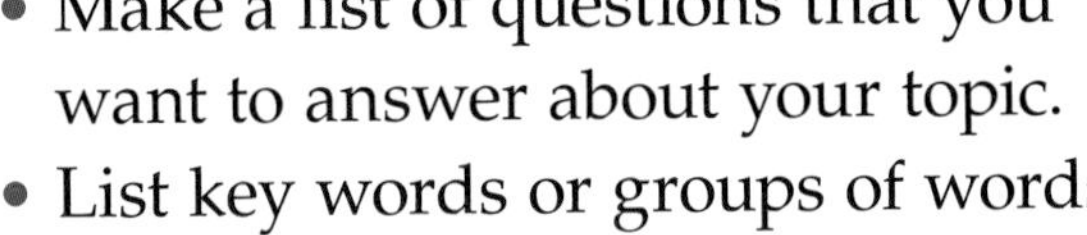

- List key words or groups of words that can be used to write or talk about your topic.
- Look for good online resources to find answers to your questions.

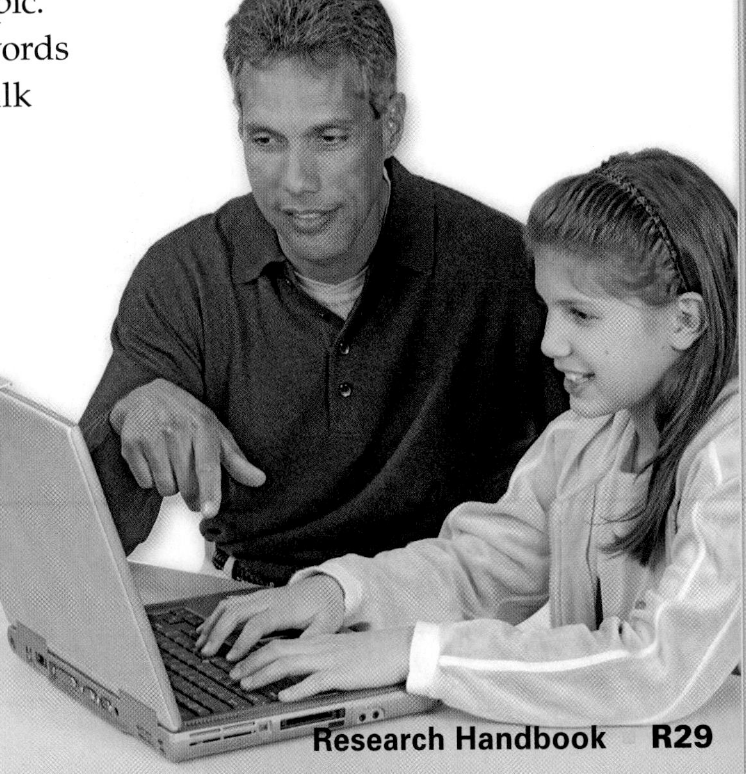

Use a Search Engine

A search engine is an online collection of websites that can be sorted by entering a key word or group of words. There are many different search engines available. You may want to ask a librarian, a teacher, or a parent for suggestions on which search engine to use.

Search by Subject To search by subject, or topic, use a search engine. Choose from the list of key words that you made while planning your search, and enter a key word or group of words in the search engine field on your screen. Then click SEARCH or GO. You will see a list of websites that have to do with your topic. Click on the site or sites you think will be most helpful. If you do not find enough websites listed, think of other key words or related words, and search again.

Search by Address Each website has its own address, called a Uniform Resource Locator, or URL for short. To get to a website using a URL, simply type the URL in the LOCATION/GO TO box on your screen and hit ENTER or click GO.

Use Bookmarks The bookmark feature is an Internet tool for keeping and organizing URLs. If you find a website that seems helpful, you can save the URL so that you can quickly return to it later. Click BOOKMARKS or FAVORITES at the top of your screen, and choose ADD. Your computer makes a copy of the URL and keeps a record of it.

Print Resources

Books in libraries are organized through a system of numbers. Every book has its own number, known as a call number. The call number tells where in the library the book can be found. Some reference books, such as encyclopedias, are usually kept in a separate section of a library. Each book there has R or RE—for *reference*—on its spine. Most reference books can only be used in the library. Most libraries also have a special section for periodicals, which include magazines and newspapers.

Almanac

An almanac is a book or electronic resource that contains facts about different subjects. The subjects are listed in alphabetical order in an index. Many facts that involve numbers and dates are shown in tables or charts. New almanacs are published each year, with the most current information.

Atlas

An atlas is a book of maps. It gives information about places. Different kinds of atlases show different places at different times. Your teacher or librarian can help you find the kind of atlas you need for your research.

Dictionary

A dictionary gives the correct spelling of words and their definitions, or meanings. It also gives the words' pronunciations, or how to say the words aloud. In addition, many dictionaries have lists of foreign words, abbreviations, well-known people, and place names.

de•mand\di-ˊmand*n* **1:** the act of demanding or asking with authority **2:** the desire or need for a procuct or service
de•pend\di-ˊpend*vi* **1:** to be undecided **2:** to rely on for help
de•pos•it\di-ˊpä-zit*vb* **1:** to put money into a bank account **2:** to place for safekeeping or as a pledge

Dictionary entry

Encyclopedia

An encyclopedia is a book or set of books that gives information about many different topics. The topics are arranged alphabetically. An encyclopedia is a good source to use when beginning your research. In addition to words, electronic encyclopedias often have sound and video clips.

Capitol, United States, houses the United States legislative branch, or Congress. The Capitol building is in Washington, D.C., on Capitol Hill. The Capitol is a government building and a symbol of the United States. Visitors from different countries visit the Capitol each year. The public can go inside and see where the House of Representatives and the Senate meet.

In 1792 the government held a special contest. Architects from around the country competed to see whose design for the Capitol would be chosen. Amateur architect and doctor William Thornton submitted the winning entry. In 1793, construction of the Capitol began. Congress held its first meeting in the new Capitol in 1800. During the War of 1812, British troops set fire to the building in the year 1814. Congress could not return to the Capitol until 1819.

The Capitol is modeled on the architecture used by Romans. The Capitol's 540 rooms include offices and reception rooms. In these rooms are keepsakes from United States history and works of art from memorable artists. The center of the Capitol, also known as the Rotunda, is beneath the dome. It is more than 95 feet in diameter and 185 feet high. The large center dome is painted white to match the rest of the marble building. On top of the dome is the Statue of Freedom. The statue is a woman with a headdress of eagle feathers, holding a shield and sword.

Many state funerals for famous United States citizens, such as Abraham Lincoln and Ronald Reagan, have been held in the Rotunda under the dome ceiling. Painted in 1865, *The Apotheosis of George Washington* by an Italian painter Constantino Brumidi, decorates the dome ceiling.

To the north of the Rotunda is the Senate wing of the Capitol. This wing has rooms open to the public where visitors can watch the Senate in session. The old Supreme court chamber is also housed in this wing. The chamber looks much like it did in 1859. This is where the court met during 1810 to 1859. The President's room is also located on the Senate side. It is one of the most decorated rooms. Portraits of George Washington and a large bronze chandelier decorate this room.

South of the Rotunda is the House of Representatives' wing. Located in this wing are the House Chamber and the Statuary Hall. The House Chamber has rooms open to the public for viewing. The Statuary Hall contains statues of notable Americans. In 1857, an extension to the House wing was completed. Thomas Ustick Walter, co-founder of the American Institute of Architects, built it. Walter is responsible for the fireproof cast-iron dome on top of the building's center completed in 1866. It replaced the small wood-constructed dome built in 1824.

In 1962, architect J. George Stewart completed the eastward expansion of the Capitol's center. Today, the Capitol covers 4 acres and has five levels. It is part of the Capitol Complex.

The Capitol Complex consists of the United States Botanical Garden Conservatory, United States Supreme Court, office buildings for the House of Representatives and Senate, and the Library of Congress.

Chapter 1 · 217

Encyclopedia article

Nonfiction Books

A nonfiction book gives facts about real people, places, and things. All nonfiction books in a library are arranged in order and by category according to their call numbers. To find a book's call number, you use a library's card file or computer catalog. You can search for a book in the catalog by subject, author, or title.

Periodicals

A periodical is published each day, each week, or each month. Periodicals are good resources for current information on topics not yet found in books. Many libraries have a guide that lists magazine articles by subject. Two such guides are the *Children's Magazine Guide* and the *Readers' Guide to Periodical Literature.* The entries in guides are usually in alphabetical order by subject, author, or title.

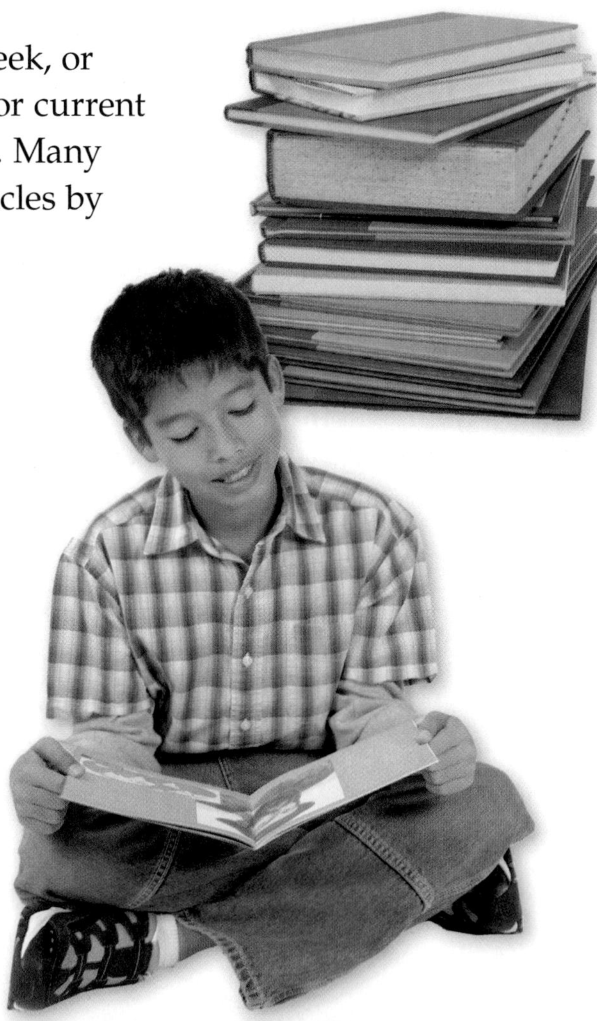

Thesaurus

A thesaurus (thih•SAWR•uhs) gives synonyms (SIH•nuh•nimz), or words that mean the same or nearly the same as another word. A thesaurus also gives antonyms (AN•tuh•nimz), or words that have the opposite meanings. Using a thesaurus can help you find words that better describe your topic and make your writing more interesting.

Community Resources

Many times, people in your community can tell you information about your research topic. You can learn facts, opinions, or points of view by asking these people thoughtful questions. Before you talk to any of them, always ask a teacher or a parent for permission.

Listening to Find Information

It is important to plan ahead whenever you talk with people as part of your research. Planning ahead will help you gather the information you need. Follow these tips as you gather information from people in your community.

Before

- Find out more about the topic you want to discuss.
- Think about the kind of information you still need.
- Consider the best way to gather the information you need.
- List the people you want to talk to.
- Make a list of useful questions you want to ask.

During

- Speak clearly and loudly enough when asking questions.
- Listen carefully. Make sure you are getting the information you need. You may think of more questions to ask based on what you hear.
- Be polite. Do not talk when the other person is speaking.
- As you listen, write down the important ideas and details in your own words. Taking notes will help you remember what you hear.
- Write down the person's exact words if you think you will want to quote them in your report. If possible, use a tape recorder. Be sure to ask the speaker for permission in advance.

After

- Thank the person you spoke with.
- Follow up by writing a thank-you note.

Writing to Get Information

You can also write to people in your community to gather information. You can send them an e-mail or a letter. Keep these ideas in mind as you write:

- Write neatly or use a computer.
- Say who you are and why you are writing.
- Check your spelling and punctuation.
- If you are writing a letter, provide a self-addressed, stamped envelope for the person to send you a response.
- Thank the person.

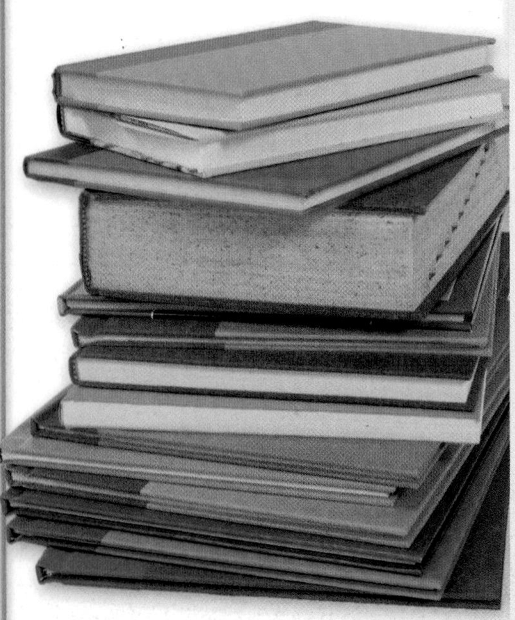

222 Central Avenue
Bakersfield, CA 93301
October 25, 20- -

Bureau of Tourism
Attn: Ms. Stephanie Nguyen
123 Main Street
Sacramento, CA 94211

Dear Ms. Nguyen:

My name is David Thomas, and I am writing this letter to see if you can send me some information about scenic attractions in the state of California. My family is planning a vacation next month, and we would like to visit some of the attractions in the northern part of the state. Please send a brochure listing the scenic attractions and a highway map. I understand this is a service you provide for those planning vacations in the area. I am excited about visiting your part of the state.

Thank you for your help.

Sincerely,

David Thomas

David Thomas
222 Central Avenue
Bakersfield, CA 93301

Bureau of Tourism
Attn: Stephanie Nguyen
123 Main Street
Sacramento, CA 94211

Reporting

Written Reports

Your teacher may ask you to write a report about the information you find. Knowing how to write a report will help you make good use of the information. The following tips will help you write your report.

Before Writing

- Choose a main idea or topic.
- Think of questions about your topic. Questions should be clear and focus on specific ideas.
- Gather information from more than one source. You may use print resources, technology resources, or community resources. Be sure to look for answers to your questions.
- Take notes on the information you find.
- Review your notes to be sure you have the information you need. Write down ideas and details about your topic to put in your report.
- Use your notes to make an outline of the information you found. Organize your ideas in a way that is easy to understand.

Citing Sources

An important part of research and writing is citing, or listing, sources. When you cite a source, you keep a written record of where you got your information. The list of sources will make up a bibliography. A bibliography is a list of the books, periodicals, and other sources that you used to find the information in your report.

Outline

The California Capitol Building

I. Where, when, and why the capitol building was constructed

A. The capitol building was built in Sacramento.

1. In 1849, the capital was in San Jose.
2. In 1852, the capital moved from San Jose to Vallejo.
3. Later, the capital was moved to Benicia and then to Sacramento.

B. The population of California increased, creating a need for a capitol building.

1. People wanted a symbol to represent the state of California.
2. In 1854, Sacramento's statehouse became the new capitol building.

C. Many important decisions are made in the capitol building.

1. Government representatives make new laws.
2. Government officials meet to talk about California issues.

D. Knowing about the state capitol is important for good citizenship.

1. The building includes information everyone should know.
2. Citizens vote for people who represent them.

Bibliography

Hernandez, Elizabeth. *Sacramento Through the Years.* San Antonio, Texas: Old Alamo Press, 2004

Wyatt, Adam. *The History of California.* Philadelphia, Pennsylvania: Scenic River Publishing, 2003

Bibliography Card

Wyatt, Adam. *The History of California.* Philadelphia, Pennsylvania: Scenic River Publishing, 2003, page 25.

San Jose was the first state capital of California. Eventually the state government moved to Sacramento in 1854.

THE CALIFORNIA CAPITOL BUILDING	
Reading Notes	**Class Notes**
• The California Legislature first met at the Capitol building in 1869 • Government representatives make laws in the Capitol building • Government representatives vote on issues there • The capital of California was San Jose in 1849 • In 1852, the capital moved to Vallejo • The Sacramento statehouse became the new Capitol building	• Visitors can tour the offices of the California attorney general, secretary of state, treasurer, and governor • Outside the building is a statue of Junipero Serra • Around the building are 40 acres of garden • The capital moved from San Jose to Vallejo to Sacramento, when the statehouse became the Capitol building • The Capitol building is a symbol for the people of California • The Capitol building was built out of the statehouse and took four more years to complete

RESEARCH HANDBOOK

Write a First Draft

- Use your notes and your outline to write a draft of your report. Keep in mind that your purpose is to share information.
- Write in paragraph form. Develop your topic with facts, details, examples, and explanations. Each paragraph should focus on one new idea.
- Get all your ideas down on paper. You can correct errors and make changes in the next step.

Revise

- Read over your draft. Does it make sense? Does it have a beginning, a middle, and an end? Have you answered all your questions?
- Rewrite sentences that are unclear or poorly worded. Move sentences that seem out of place.
- Add details when needed to support your ideas.
- If too many sentences are alike, make some sentences shorter or longer to keep your report interesting.
- Check any quotations to be sure you have shown someone's exact words and that you have noted the source correctly.

Proofread and Edit

- Proofread your report, checking for errors.
- Correct any errors in spelling, capitalization, or punctuation.

Publish

- Make a neat, clean copy of your report.
- Include illustrations, maps, or other drawings to help explain your topic.

Rough draft

Allison Cesareo
Social Studies

A History of the Capitol Building in Sacramento, California

The capitol Building in Sacramento California is a very important place. The capitol building is the place where our state government works on making new laws. It is also where our government officials meet to talk about important issues happening in California. Many people do not know about the history of the capitol building because it was build before many of today's California citizens were born. There are many interesting historical facts about the Capital building in Sacramento, California. It is important to know who made the decision to build it, where it was built, when it was built, and what happens in the capitol building today.

The capitol Building in Sacramento was not always the location of our state's government offices. A long time ago, the capitol of California was located in San Jose in the year 1849. In 1852 the capital of California moved from San jose to Vallejo, California. At that time, Vallejo was not a good place for the capitol building. The work on the building took a long time and it was very expensive. Then, in 1853, the capital moved to Benicia where it remained until the city of Sacramento offered its courthouse as the new capitol building. In 1854, Sacramento's courthouse became the new statehouse. The building that the first session held its meeting in is not the same building that serves as today's capitol building. When the capital first moved to Sacramento, members of the legislature were happy to have a place to meet that would stand as a symbol of the great State of California. But, soon after, the city began to grow. As the population increased, so did the need for a new Capitol building.

Final draft

Allison Cesareo
Social Studies

A History of the Capitol Building in Sacramento, California

The capitol building in Sacramento, California, is a very important place. The capitol building is the place where our government representatives make new laws. It is also where our government officials meet to talk about important issues happening in California. Many people do not know about the history of the capitol building because it was built before many of today's California citizens were born. There are many interesting historical facts about the capitol building, which is located in Sacramento, California. It is important to know where it was built, when it was built, and what happens in the capitol building today.

The capitol building in Sacramento was not always the location of our state's government offices. In 1849, the capital of California was located in San Jose. In 1852, California's capital moved from San Jose to Vallejo, California. At that time, Vallejo was not a good place for the capitol building because work on the building took a long time and it was very expensive. In 1853, the capital of California moved to Benicia where it remained until the city of Sacramento offered its courthouse as the new capitol building. In 1854, Sacramento's courthouse became the new statehouse. The building in Sacramento that held the first state sesssion in 1854 is not the same building that serves as today's California capitol building.

When the state capital was first moved to Sacramento, members of the legislature were happy to have a nice place to meet that would serve as a symbol of the great state of California. But, soon after, the city began to grow. As the population increased, so did the need for a new Capitol building.

Proofreading marks and their meanings	
Word	**Meaning**
^	Insert word.
^,	Insert comma.
¶	Start a new paragraph.
≡ (cap)	Use capital letter.
(delete mark)	Delete.
(lc)	Use lowercase letter.

Oral Presentations

Sometimes you may be asked to give an oral presentation. Like a written report, the purpose of an oral presentation is to share information. These tips will help you prepare an oral presentation:

- Follow the steps described in Before Writing to gather and organize information.
- Use your notes to plan and organize your presentation. Include an introduction and a conclusion in your report.
- Prepare note cards that you can refer to as you speak.
- Prepare visuals such as illustrations, diagrams, maps, or other graphics to help listeners better understand your topic.
- Practice your presentation.
- Be sure to speak clearly and loudly enough. Keep your listeners interested in your report by using facial expressions and hand movements.

Biographical Dictionary

The Biographical Dictionary provides information about many of the people introduced in this book. Also included are some other famous Californians you might like to know about. Names are listed alphabetically by last name, and pronunciation guides are provided for hard-to-pronounce names. Following each name are the birth and death dates of that person, if known. If the person is still alive, only the year of birth appears. A brief description of the person's main achievement is then given. The page number that follows tells where the main discussion of that person appears in this book. (You can check the Index for other page references.) Guide names at the top of each page help you quickly locate the name you need to find.

A

Abdul-Jabbar, Kareem *1947–* Basketball star for the University of California at Los Angeles and the Los Angeles Lakers.

Abiko, Kyutaro *1865–1936* Founder of Yamato Colony, a 3,000-acre Japanese immigrant farming community in the Central Valley. p. 315

Adams, Ansel *1902–1984* Photographer known for his photographs of the West, including the Sierra Nevada. p. 444

Allensworth, Allen *1842–1914* One of the founders of Allensworth, a town settled by African Americans. p. 321

Anza, Juan Bautista de (AHN•sah, HWAN bow•TEES• tah day) *1736–1788?* Spanish soldier who led settlers to Alta California in 1774 on a new overland route. p. 122

Asisara, Lorenzo *1819–?* California Indian born and raised at Mission Santa Cruz. p. 152

Austin, Mary *1868–1934* American author who moved to California with her family in 1888. p. 317

B

Baca, Judith (bah•kah) *1946–* Artist who created a mural titled *The Great Wall of Los Angeles* in the 1970s and 1980s. p. 440

Bartleson, John Along with John Bidwell, a leader of the Bartleson-Bidwell expedition. In 1841, this became the first group of American settlers to cross overland into California. p. 200

Beckwourth, James *1798–1866* Trailblazer and trapper; he made several overland trips to California in the 1830s and 1840s. Beckwourth Pass is named for him. p. 195

Bering, Vitus *1681–1741* Danish explorer sailing for Russia, discovered that North America and Asia are separate continents. p. 119

Bidwell, John *1819–1900* Along with John Bartleson, a leader of the Bartleson-Bidwell expedition. In 1841, this became the first group of American settlers to cross overland into California. p. 200

Bono, Sonny *1935–1998* Singer and songwriter who was elected mayor of Palm Springs and later to the United States House of Representatives.

Boxer, Barbara *1940–* United States senator from California; she was first elected in 1992. p. 464

Bradley, Thomas *1917–1998* First African American mayor of Los Angeles; he served from 1973 to 1993.

Brannan, Samuel *1819–1889* Businessperson from San Francisco who was the first to announce the discovery of gold in California, in 1848. p. 227

Brathwaite Burke, Yvonne W. *1932–* First African American woman to serve in the California State Assembly, in 1966; the first African American woman from California to serve in the United States House of Representatives, in 1972; elected Los Angeles County Supervisor, in 1992. p. 403

Briones de Miranda, Juana (bree•OH•nays day meer•AHN•dah) *1802–1889* Owner of Rancho La Purísima Concepción, near San Jose, during the period of Mexican rule. p. 169

Brubeck, Dave *1920–* Successful jazz pianist from Concord; started the Dave Brubeck Quartet. p. 441

Burbank, Luther *1849–1926* Scientist who mixed seeds from different kinds of plants to create new and better kinds of plants. The city of Burbank is named for him. p. 304

Burnett, Peter H. *1807–1895* First governor of California, from 1849 to 1851. p. 249

Butterfield, John *1801–1869* Founder of the first regular mail service between California and the East. p. 280

C

Cabrillo, Juan Rodríguez (kah•BREE•yoh, rohd•REE•ges) *1499?–1543* Spanish explorer; he reached San Diego Bay in 1542. p. 112

Carlos III *1716–1788* Spanish king who ordered the settlement of Alta California in the 1760s. p. 118

Carson, Kit *1809–1868* Trailblazer who led John C. Frémont to California. Carson Pass in the Sierra Nevada is named for him. p. 214

Castro, José *1810?–1860?* General in charge of the Mexican army in California during the Bear Flag Revolt. p. 209

Cermeño, Sebastián Rodríguez (sair•MAY•nyoh) Spanish trader who sailed to California from the Philipines in 1595. p. 114

Chaffey, George *1848–1932* Engineer of irrigation systems in southern California in the late 1800s and early 1900s. p. 305

Chavez, Cesar (CHAH•vez, SAY•zar) *1927–1993* Labor leader and organizer of the United Farm Workers. p. 405

Clappe, Louise *1819–1906* Writer who wrote a series of letters describing her life as a woman in a mining camp during the gold rush. p. 233

Cook, James *1728–1779* English explorer who sailed the world and mapped the coasts of eastern Canada, Australia, New Zealand, and western North America. p. 119

Cortés, Hernando (kawr•TEZ, er•NAHN•doh) *1485–1547* Spanish conquistador; he conquered the Aztec and claimed Baja California for Spain. p. 111

Crespí, Juan (kres•PEE) *1721–1782* Spanish missionary and explorer; he traveled to California in the late 1760s and early 1770s with Junípero Serra. p. 120

Crocker, Charles *1822–1888* Member of the "Big Four," who ran the Central Pacific and Southern Pacific Railroads in the middle to late 1800s. p. 288

D

Dana, Richard Henry *1815–1882* Author who wrote about his voyage to California in *Two Years Before the Mast.* p. 160

Davis, Gray *1942–* Elected governor of California in 1998; became first governor of California to be recalled, in 2003. p. 475

Davis, William 1822–1909 Businessperson and writer; wrote *Sixty Years in California*, published in 1889. p. 165

DiMaggio, Joe *1914–1999* Professional baseball player from Martinez; he played for the New York Yankees.

Disney, Walt *1901–1966* Creator of animated movies and popular children's characters and builder of Disneyland in Anaheim in 1955. p. 443

Doheny, Edward (duh•HEE•nee) *1856–1935* Discoverer of oil in Los Angeles in 1892. p. 324

Donner, Eliza *1843–1922* Daughter of George Donner; she traveled with the Donner party to California and later wrote about the journey. p. 205

Donner, George *1784–1847* Leader of an expedition that traveled from Missouri to California in 1846, which became known as the Donner party. p. 202

Donner, Jacob *1790–1846* Along with his brother, George Donner, leader of the Donner party. p. 202

Doolittle, James *1896–1993* General in the United States Army and Congressional Medal of Honor winner; born in Alameda. p. 383

Douglas, Donald *1892–1981* Founder of an aviation company in Los Angeles in 1920.

Drake, Francis *1543?–1596* First English explorer to reach the Pacific coast of the Americas and to reach present-day California. p. 113

Duncan, Isadora *1878–1927* American dancer from San Francisco. p. 441

E

Eastwood, Clint *1930–* Movie actor and director; he served as mayor of Carmel from 1986 to 1988.

Echeandía, José María (eh•chay•ahn•DEE•ah) *?–1855* Governor of California under Mexican rule from 1824 to 1831. p. 192

Espinosa, Fermina (ay•spee•NOH•sah) *1779?–1865?* Rancho owner in California.

Eu, March Fong *1927–* First Asian American woman elected to the California State Assembly; she was elected in 1966.

F

Feinstein, Dianne *1933–* United States senator from California; she was first elected in 1992. She also served as mayor of San Francisco from 1978 to 1988. p. 464

Field, Stephen J. *1816–1899* California Supreme Court justice. p. 465

Figueroa, José (fee•gay•ROH•ah) *1792?–1843?* Governor of California under Mexican rule from 1833 to 1835. p. 152

Frémont, Jessie Ann Benton *1824–1902* Wife of explorer John C. Frémont; she helped him write a popular book about the western United States. p. 201

Frémont, John C. *1813–1890* Explorer of the western United States in the 1840s. Later, he was a leader of the Bear Flag Revolt, one of the first two United States senators from California, and a presidential candidate in 1856. p. 201

Fry, Johnny *1840–1863* First rider of the Pony Express to travel east to west. p. 281

G

Gálvez, José de (ga h l •ves) *1729–1787* Government official of New Spain who sent expeditions to San Diego and Monterey Bays in 1769. p. 120

BIOGRAPHICAL DICTIONARY

Gehry, Frank O. *1929–* Architect in Santa Monica who designed many prominent buildings, including the Walt Disney Concert Hall in Los Angeles. p. 442

George, Ronald M. *1940–* Chief Justice of the California Supreme Court, appointed in 1996. p. 474

Giannini, Amadeo Pietro (jee•ah•NEE•nee, ah•mah•DAY•oh PYEH•troh) *1870–1949* Banker; his bank grew into what is now one of the largest banks in the world. p. 332

Gibbs, Mifflin *1823–1915* Founder of the *Mirror of the Times,* the first newspaper owned by African Americans in California. p. 240

Gillespie, Archibald A United States Marine, who, along with John C. Frémont, became a leader of the Bear Flaggers. p. 214

Gonzales, David M. (guhn•ZAH•luhs) *1923–1945* Congressional Medal of Honor winner from Pacoima. p. 383

Gwin, William M. *1805–1885* One of the first two United States senators from California; he served from 1850 to 1855 and from 1857 to 1861. p. 250

Hallidie, Andrew Smith (hal•uh•dee) *1836–1900* Inventor of the cable car. p. 340

Hamilton, Billy First Pony Express rider to travel west to east over the Sierra Nevada. p. 281

Hearst, Phoebe Apperson *1842–1919* One of the founders of the National PTA; mother of William Randolph Hearst.

Hearst, William Randolph *1863–1951* Politician and publisher of a San Francisco newspaper, the *Examiner.*

Hidalgo y Costilla, Miguel (ee•DAHL•goh ee kohs•TEE•yah, mee•GAYL) *1753–1811* Mexican priest whose 1810 speech, known as *el Grito de Dolores,* marked the beginning of the Mexican War for Independence. p. 149

Hoover, Herbert *1874–1964* Thirty-first President of the United States; a resident of California p. 465

Hopkins, Mark *1813–1878* Member of the "Big Four," who ran the Central Pacific and Southern Pacific Railroads in the middle to late 1800s. p. 288

Hoya, Oscar de la *1973–* Boxer from East Los Angeles who won a gold medal in the 1992 Olympics.

Huerta, Dolores (HWAIR•tah, doh•LOH•res) *1930–* Labor leader and an organizer of the United Farm Workers. p. 402

Hughes, Howard *1905–1976* Pilot and business leader active in California aviation.

Huntington, Collis P. *1821–1900* Member of the "Big Four," who ran the Central Pacific and Southern Pacific Railroads in the middle to late 1800s. p. 288

Ishi *1861?–1916* Considered by many to be the last survivor of the Yahi, a California Indian tribe. p. 93

Jackson, Helen Hunt *1830–1885* Writer who in the 1880s brought attention to the poor treatment of American Indians by the United States government.

Jackson, Odis African American lawyer who protested when a builder refused to sell him a house in a new Los Angeles suburb in 1963. p. 491

Jobs, Steven *1955–* Computer designer who started a successful personal computer company with Steven Wozniak in the Silicon Valley in 1976. p. 397

Johnson, Hiram *1866–1945* Governor of California from 1911 to 1917 and a United States senator from 1917 to 1945. p. 358

José, Nicolas A California Indian who led a rebellion at Mission San Gabriel in 1785. p. 136

Joyner-Kersee, Jackie *1962–* University of California at Los Angeles graduate and gold medalist in the pentathlon and long jump in the 1988 Olympics and in the heptathlon in the 1992 Olympics.

Judah, Theodore D. *1826–1863* Engineer who founded the Central Pacific Railroad and planned the route of the first transcontinental railroad. p. 287

Kaiser, Henry *1882–1967* Business leader whose shipyards in California built many of the vessels used by the United States armed forces during World War II. p. 380

Kearny, Stephen Watts (KAR•nee) *1794–1848* General in the United States Army during the Mexican-American War. p. 214

Keith, William *1839–1911* Scottish-born artist famous for his paintings of Yosemite Valley. p. 317

Kennedy, Anthony *1936–* United States Supreme Court justice from Sacramento. p. 465

Kientepoos, Chief *1837?–1873* Modoc Indian chief; also known as Captain Jack. p. 320

King, Martin Luther, Jr. *1929–1968* African American civil rights leader who worked to end segregation in nonviolent ways. p. 400

Kwan, Michelle *1980–* American figure skater from Torrance.

Lange, Dorothea *1895–1965* Photographer known for her pictures of migrant workers and families, taken during the 1930s. p. 375

Leidesdorff, William *1810–1848* African American who built the first hotel and helped found the first school in San Francisco in the 1840s.

Lockheed, Allan *1889–1969* Along with his brother, Malcolm, and John K. Northrop, he founded an aviation company in California in the early 1900s.

Lockheed, Malcolm *1887–1958* Along with his brother, Allan, and John K. Northrop, he founded an aviation company in California in the early 1900s.

London, Jack *1876–1916* Author from San Francisco; he wrote adventure stories, including *The Call of the Wild*. p. 441

Lopez, Nancy *1957–* Professional golfer from Torrance.

Lu Ng (LOO ING) Chinese immigrant who traveled to California during the gold rush. p. 229

M

Marsh, John *1799–1856* Early American pioneer who settled in Los Angeles in 1836. p. 200

Marshall, James *1810–1885* Carpenter at Sutter's Mill; he claimed to be the first to discover gold there in 1848, which led to the California gold rush. p. 227

Martin, Glenn *1886–1955* Builder of California's first airplane factory, in Santa Ana in 1909. p. 363

Mason, Biddy *1818–1891* Former slave who became one of the wealthiest African Americans in Los Angeles during the late 1800s. She donated much of her time and money to helping others. p. 253

Mayer, Louis B. *1885–1957* Owner of a film company in Los Angeles that later became Metro-Goldwyn-Mayer (MGM). p. 365

Maynard, Robert *1937–1993* Owner of the *Oakland Tribune* in the 1980s; he was the first African American to own a major metropolitan newspaper in the United States.

Megquier, Mary Jane (meh•GWEER) Forty-niner who went to California with her husband, Thomas, in search of gold. p. 240

Mendez, Sylvia *1936–* Her court case ended school segregation in California. p. 401

Molina, Gloria *1948–* First Hispanic woman elected to the California State Assembly, in 1982, and the Los Angeles City Council, in 1987.

Morgan, Julia *1872–1957* San Francisco architect who designed Hearst Castle in San Simeon. p. 442

Morrow, Irving *1884–1952* One of the designers of the Golden Gate Bridge.

Morse, Samuel F. B. *1791–1872* One of the inventors of the telegraph and the creator of Morse code. p. 284

Muir, John (MYUR) *1838–1914* Naturalist and conservation leader. p. 25

Mulholland, William (muhl•HAH•luhnd) *1855–1935* Engineer of the Los Angeles Aqueduct. p. 325

Nahl, Charles Christian *1818–1878* German-born painter, famous for depicting life in California gold-mining camps. Also designed the bear on the California state flag. p. 317

Neve, Felipe de *1728–1784* Governor of Alta California from 1777 to 1782. p. 130

Ng Poon Chew (N POON CHEE•oh) *1866–1931* Chinese immigrant who established the first Chinese language daily newspaper in California.

Nixon, Richard *1913–1994* Thirty-seventh President of the United States; born in Yorba Linda. p. 465

Noguchi, Isamu *1904–1988* Sculptor from Los Angeles. p. 440

Nolan, Mae Ella *1886–1973* First woman from California elected to the United States House of Representatives; she was elected in 1922.

Northrop, John K. *1895–1981* Along with the Lockheed brothers, he founded an aviation company in California in the early 1900s.

Ochoa, Ellen (oh•CHOH•ah) *1958–* Astronaut from Los Angeles; she flew on the space shuttle *Discovery* in 1993.

Pattie, James Ohio *1804–1850?* Trailblazer who traveled to California with his father, Sylvester Pattie. p. 193

Pattie, Sylvester Trailblazer who traveled to California with his son, James Ohio Pattie. p. 193

Patton, George *1885–1945* General in the United States Army; born in San Gabriel.

Pelosi, Nancy *1940–* Member of the United States House of Representatives from California; she is the first woman to lead a major political party in Congress.

Pico, Andrés *1810–1876* Californio general during the Mexican-American War. p. 216

Pico, Pío *1801–1894* Last Mexican governor of Alta California; he served from 1845 to 1846. Brother of Andrés Pico. p. 158

Polk, James K. *1795–1849* Eleventh President of the United States. p. 207

Portolá, Gaspar de (pawr•toh•LAH) *1723?–1784?* Spanish army captain and government official who led a land expedition to Alta California in 1769 to establish settlements. p. 120

R

Reagan, Ronald *1911–2004* Fortieth President of the United States. A resident of California, he also served as governor of California from 1967 to 1975. p. 477

Reed, Virginia *1833–1921* Daughter of James Reed, a leader of the Donner party. p. 203

Ride, Sally *1951–* Astronaut from Encino; she became the first woman from the United States to fly in space when she flew on the space shuttle *Challenger* in 1983. p. 397

Riley, Bennett *1787–1853* Military general and governor of California after it gained independence from Mexico; helped California become a state by calling for a convention to decide California's future. p. 247

Rivera, Diego (ree•VAY•rah) *1886–1957* Mexican artist known for his murals, including those he painted for San Francisco's Art Institute and City College.

Rivera y Moncada, Fernando (ree•VAY•rah ee mohn•KAH•dah) *1711?–1782?* Spanish army captain who led a land expedition to Alta California in 1769 to establish settlements. p. 120

Robinson, John (Jackie) *1919–1972* University of California at Los Angeles athlete who in 1947 became the first African American to play major-league baseball. p. 401

Rodia, Simon (Sam) (roh•DEE•uh) *1879–1965* Artist who in the 1920s built the sculpture *Watts Towers,* which is located in the Watts neighborhood of Los Angeles. p. 426

Roosevelt, Franklin D. *1882–1945* Thirty-second President of the United States. p. 373

Roosevelt, Theodore *1858–1919* Twenty-sixth President of the United States. p. 329

Roybal-Allard, Lucille *1941–* First Hispanic woman from California elected to the United States House of Representatives; she was elected in 1992.

Ruíz, Bernarda (roo•EES, bair•NAR•dah) *1802–1880* Californio woman who convinced John C. Frémont not to punish the Californios for fighting the Americans in the Mexican-American War. p. 216

Russell, William H. Founder of the Pony Express.

Ryan, T. Claude *1898–1982* Builder of the plane, named *Spirit of St. Louis,* that Charles Lindbergh flew across the Atlantic Ocean in 1927.

Sánchez, José Bernardo *1778–1831* Head of the San Gabriel Mission who welcomed trailblazer Jedediah Strong Smith in the late 1820s. p. 192

Saroyan, William (suh•ROY•uhn) *1908–1981* Armenian American writer from Fresno. p. 441

Saund, Dalip Singh (SAND) *1899–1973* First Asian American elected to Congress; he served from 1957 to 1963. p. 403

Schwarzenegger, Arnold (SHWAW•tzuh•neh•ger) *1947–* Elected governor of California in 2003 to replace recalled Governor Gray Davis; Hollywood actor and former professional body builder. p. 475

Seidner, Cheryl A. *1950–* American Indian leader; elected tribal chairperson of the Wiyot tribe in 1996. p. 89

Semple, Robert Delegate to California's first constitutional convention in 1849. p. 447

Serra, Junípero (SAIR•rah, hoo•NEE•pay•roh) *1713–1784* Spanish priest; he founded many of the California missions from 1769 to 1784. p. 123

Severance, Caroline (SEH•vuh•ruhns) *1820–1914* A leader of the movement for women's rights in California. p. 359

Shima, George *1865?–1926* Japanese immigrant who became known as the "Potato King" for growing most of California's potato crop in the early 1900s. p. 307

Sloat, John D. *1781–1867* Officer in the United States Navy during the Mexican-American War, took control of Monterey. p. 213

Smith, Jedediah Strong *1799–1831* Trailblazer and trapper; he traveled overland to California in the late 1820s. p. 192

Solá, Pablo Vicente de *1761?–1826?* Last Spanish governor of Alta California before the Mexican War for Independence. p. 151

Stanford, Leland *1824–1893* Member of the "Big Four," who ran the Central Pacific and Southern Pacific Railroads in the middle to late 1800s. Governor of California from 1862 to 1863. p. 288

Stearns, Abel *1789–1871* Early settler of California. p. 199

Steinbeck, John *1902–1968* Author from Salinas; he described the experiences of migrants to California in his novel *The Grapes of Wrath.* p. 371

Stockton, Robert F. *1795–1866* Officer in the United States Army during the Mexican-American War. p. 214

Strauss, Joseph B. *1870–1938* American engineer who designed and oversaw construction of the Golden Gate Bridge. p. 373

Strauss, Levi *1830–1902* German immigrant to California during the gold rush who made his fortune selling to miners "jeans" made of canvas and, later, denim. p. 238

Strong, Harriet Russell *1844–1929* Californian who worked to improve crops in California. p. 304

Sutter, John Augustus *1803–1880* Swiss immigrant who founded Sutter's Fort in the Central Valley. Gold was discovered near his mill in 1848. p. 199

Tac, Pablo *1822–1841* A Luiseño Indian who wrote a diary about his life at Mission San Luis Rey. p. 138

Tan, Amy *1952–* Chinese American author from Oakland. p. 441

Tibbets, Eliza *1825–1898* Orange grower whose seedless oranges sparked California's citrus industry in the late 1800s. Wife of Luther Calvin Tibbets. p. 303

Tibbets, Luther Calvin Orange grower whose seedless oranges sparked California's citrus industry in the late 1800s. Husband of Eliza Tibbets. p. 303

Toypurina (toy•poo•REE•nuh) *1761–1799* Gabrielino Indian woman who led Indians in a revolt at the San Gabriel Mission. p. 136

Uchida, Yoshiko (oo•CHEE•dah, yoh•shee•koh) *1921–1992* Japanese American author from Berkeley; she wrote about her experiences in a relocation camp during World War II in *The Invisible Thread.*

Valdez, Luis *1940–* A film director and playwright; he founded the El Teatro Campesino and is considered the father of Mexican-American theater.

Vallejo, Mariano (vuh•LAY•hoh, mah•ree•AHN•oh) *1808–1890* Californio rancho owner and Mexican general who surrendered to the Bear Flaggers in 1846. p. 159

Vischer, Edward A rancho worker who lived in California during the time of Mexican rule. p. 166

Vizcaíno, Sebastián (vees•kah•EE•noh) *1550?–1616* Spanish explorer; he sailed to Monterey Bay in the early 1600s and recommended establishing Spanish settlements there. p. 114

Vuich, Rose Ann First woman in the California State Senate; she was elected in 1976.

Walker, Joseph Reddeford *1798–1876* Trailblazer who found a route through a mountain pass, later named for him, in the Sierra Nevada in 1834. p. 194

Warren, Earl *1891–1974* Governor of California from 1943 to 1953 and chief justice of the United States Supreme Court from 1953 to 1969. p. 465

Watson, Diane E. *1933–* First African American woman elected to the California State Senate; she was elected in 1978.

Wayne, John *1907–1979* Actor known for his performances in westerns. p. 439

Wiggin, Kate Douglas *1856–1923* Educator and writer; started the first kindergarten free of cost in San Francisco in 1878. p. 317

Williams, Paul R. *1894–1980* Architect from southern California who designed the LAX Theme Building at the Los Angeles International Airport. p. 442

Williams, Serena *1981–* Professional American tennis player raised in Compton, California.

Williams, Venus *1980–* Professional American tennis player raised in Compton, California.

Wozniak, Steven *1950–* Computer designer who started a successful personal computer company with Steven Jobs in the Silicon Valley in 1976. p. 397

Yamaguchi, Kristi *1971–* Ice skater from Fremont who won a gold medal in the 1992 Olympics.

Yeager, Chuck (YAY•ger) *1923–* United States Air Force test pilot; in 1947, he became the first pilot to fly at supersonic speeds, at Edwards Air Force Base in California. p. 396

Yee Fung Cheung (YEE FUHNG JEH•uhng) *1825?–1907* Chinese immigrant who became a well-respected herbalist in California in the middle to late 1800s. p. 293

Young, Ewing *1792?–1841* Trapper and trailblazer who helped develop the Old Spanish Trail in the early 1830s. p. 194

Gazetteer

The Gazetteer is a geographical dictionary that can help you locate some of the places discussed in this book. Place names are listed alphabetically, and hard-to-pronounce names are followed by pronunciation guides. A description of the place is then given. The absolute location, or latitude and longitude, of each city is provided. The page number that follows tells where each place is shown on a map. Guide words at the top of each page help you locate the place name you need to find.

A

Alameda A city built on an island; an important port in the San Francisco Bay area. (38°N, 122°W) p. 432

Alcatraz Island (AL•kuh•traz) An island in San Francisco Bay; the site of a former prison; the site of an Indian civil rights protest. p. 315

Alta California Upper California; the name used by the Spanish to describe the stretch of land they controlled along the Pacific Ocean and above Baja California. p. 113

Alturas A city in northeastern California; county seat of Modoc County. (41°N, 121°W) p. 39

American River A tributary of the Sacramento River. p. 27

Anaheim A large city in southwestern California. (34°N, 118°W) p. 17

Angel Island An island in San Francisco Bay; a former detention center for immigrants; a state park since 1963. p. 315

Auburn A city in eastern California, northeast of Sacramento; county seat of Placer County. (39°N, 121°W) p. R14

B

Baja California (BAH•hah) Lower California; a peninsula in northwestern Mexico that borders southern California. p. 113

Bakersfield A city in the San Joaquin Valley; county seat of Kern County. (35°N, 119°W) p. 17

Barstow A city in southern California. (35°N, 117°W) p. 39

Bear River A tributary of the Feather River. p. 232

Beckwourth Pass A mountain pass through the Sierra Nevada; named for trailblazer James Beckwourth. p. 202

Berkeley A city in the San Francisco Bay area; site of the University of California at Berkeley. (38°N, 122°W) p. 335

Big Pine A town in the Owens Valley. (37°N, 118°W) p. 326

Bishop A city in eastern California in the Owens Valley. (37°N, 118°W) p. 326

Blythe A city in southeastern California, near the Colorado River. (34°N, 115°W) p. 399

Bodega Bay A small natural harbor along the California coast, north of San Francisco. p. 160

Brawley A city in the Imperial Valley. (33°N, 116°W) p. 305

Bridgeport A village in eastern California; county seat of Mono County. (38°N, 119°W) p. R14

Burbank A city north of Los Angeles. (34°N, 118°W) p. R14

C

Cabrillo National Monument A national monument in southwestern California, where Juan Rodríguez Cabrillo first sighted land in 1542. p. 469

Calexico A city in southern California, on the Mexican border. (33°N, 115°W) p. 305

California Trail An overland route that settlers took from Missouri to California in the mid-1800s. p. 202

Cape Mendocino (men•duh•SEE•nō) A point of land that extends into the Pacific Ocean in present-day Humboldt County. p. 113

Cascade Range A range of mountains that lies north of the Sierra Nevada. p. 20

Central Valley One of the four natural regions in California. p. 20

Channel Islands A group of eight islands off the southern coast of California. p. 20

Channel Islands National Park A national park off the southern coast of California; it has examples of volcanic activity. p. 469

Chico A city in northern California, north of Sacramento; home of California State University at Chico. (40°N, 122°W) p. 17

Chocolate Mountains A mountain range in southern California, in the Imperial Valley. p. 305

Clair Engle Lake A lake in northwestern California. (41°N, 123°W) p. R15

Clear Lake A lake in northern California. (39°N, 123°W) p. R15

Coachella A city in southeastern California. (34°N, 116°W) p. 305

Coachella Valley A valley within the Desert Region of California. p. R15

Coast Ranges Several small mountain ranges that lie along the California coast and reach north into Oregon and Washington. p. 20

Coloma A town on the American River. (39°N, 121°W) p. 232

Colonel Allensworth State Historic Park A state historical park on the site of Allensworth, a town founded by Colonel Allen Allensworth in 1908; the only town in California founded and run by African Americans. p. 319

Colorado Desert A desert south of the Mojave Desert. p. 20

Colorado River A river that flows from Colorado to the Gulf of California; part of it forms the border between California and Arizona. p. 20

Colusa A city in north-central California on the Sacramento River; county seat of Colusa County. (39°N, 122°W) p. R14

Cosumnes River (kuh•SUHM•nuhs) A tributary of the Mokelumne River. p. 232

Crescent City A city on the northwestern coast of California; county seat of Del Norte County. (42°N, 124°W) p. 17

Cuyama River A river in southern California. p. R15

D

Death Valley The lowest point in California and in the Western Hemisphere; at one point, it lies 282 feet below sea level. p. 27

Death Valley National Park A national park located in eastern California. p. 469

Delano A town in the Central Valley. (36°N, 119°W) p. 399

Devils Postpile National Monument A national monument in Madera County, in central California; it features unusual rock formations that look like piles of fence posts. p. 469

Diablo Range (dee•AH•bloh) One of the mountain ranges that make up the Coast Ranges. p. R15

Domínguez Rancho A rancho in southern California; the site of a battle between Californios and U.S. soldiers during the Mexican-American War. p. 215

Downieville A village in northeastern California, northeast of Sacramento; county seat of Sierra County; began as a mining town. (40°N, 121°W) p. 232

Dust Bowl Parts of Oklahoma, Texas, Kansas, Colorado, and New Mexico that suffered from drought and severe dust storms in the 1930s. p. 370

E

Eagle Lake A lake in northern California. p. R15

Eastern Hemisphere The half of Earth made up of Europe, Asia, Africa, Australia, and the waters and islands around them. p. 16

Eel River A river in northwestern California. p. 63

El Camino Real A road that connected the missions and presidios of Alta California. p. 127

El Centro A city in the southeastern corner of California; county seat of Imperial County. (33°N, 116°W) p. 305

Escondido A city in the southwestern corner of California, north of San Diego. (33°N, 117°W) p. 95

Eureka A city on the northwestern coast of California; county seat of Humboldt County. (41°N, 124°W) p. 17

F

Fairfield A city in central California, southwest of Sacramento; county seat of Solano County. (38°N, 122°W) p. R14

Farallon Islands (FAIR•uh•lahn) A group of small, rocky islands off the central coast of California. p. R15

Feather River A tributary of the Sacramento River. p. 20

Florin A city in central California, south of Sacramento, was founded by Japanese immigrants. (38°N, 121°W) p. 22

Folsom Lake A lake in north-central California. p. R15

Fort Ross State Historic Park A state historic park at the site of a Russian settlement in northern California, built in 1812. p. 160

Fremont A city in western California, southeast of Oakland. (38°N, 122°W) p. 432

Fresno A city in the San Joaquin Valley; county seat of Fresno County. (37°N, 120°W) p. 17

G

Golden Gate A narrow body of water that connects San Francisco Bay to the Pacific Ocean. (38°N, 122°W) p. 315

Goose Lake A lake in northeastern California, on the California-Oregon border. p. R15

Gulf of California A part of the Pacific Ocean, located off the northwestern coast of Mexico. p. 113

H

Hanford A city in southwest-central California; county seat of Kings County. (36°N, 120°W) p. R14

Healdsburg A city in western California, northwest of Santa Rosa. (39°N, 123°W) p. 160

Hetch Hetchy Aqueduct A water project completed in 1931 that supplies water from the Hetch Hetchy Valley to San Francisco. p. 335

Hetch Hetchy Reservoir A lake in central California, formed by the O'Shaughnessy Dam. p. 335

Hetch Hetchy Valley A valley in the Sierra Nevada, located in Yosemite National Park. p. 335

Hollister A city in western California, east of Monterey Bay; county seat of San Benito County. (37°N, 121°W) p. R14

Hollywood A district in Los Angeles; center of the movie industry. (34°N, 118°W) p. 415

Holtville A city in the Imperial Valley. (33°N, 115°W) p. 305

Humboldt Bay A natural harbor on the northern coast of California. (41°N, 124°W) p. 27

Huntington Beach A city on the coast of southern California. (34°N, 118°W) p. R14

Imperial A city in the southeastern corner of California, in the Imperial Valley, north of El Centro. (33°N, 116°W) p. 305

Imperial Valley A valley within the Desert Region of California, near the Mexican border. p. 305

Independence A town in eastern California, east of Fresno; county seat of Inyo County. (37°N, 118°W) p. 39

Indio A city in southeastern California, southeast of San Bernardino. (34°N, 116°W) p. 305

Isabella Lake A lake in southern California. p. R15

Isthmus of Panama A narrow stretch of land in Central America, connecting North America and South America. p. 229

Jackson A city in central California; county seat of Amador County. (38°N, 121°W) p. R14

Joshua Tree National Park A national park located in southern California, known for its unusual desert plants. p. 469

Kern River A river in south-central California. p. R15

Kings Canyon National Park A national park located along the Kings River in south-central California, in the Sierra Nevada; known for its unusual canyons. p. 469

Klamath Mountains (KLA•muhth) One of the mountain ranges that make up the Coast Ranges. p. 20

Klamath River A river in northwestern California. p. 27

Lake Almanor A lake in northeastern California. p. R15

Lake Berryessa A lake in northern California. p. R15

Lake Oroville A reservoir in northern California formed by Oroville Dam. p. R15

Lake Tahoe (TAH•hoh) One of California's two largest lakes; located in the Sierra Nevada, on the California-Nevada border. p. 17

Lakeport A city in western California; county seat of Lake County. (39°N, 123°W) p. R14

Lassen Peak A mountain peak with an elevation of 10,457 feet; located in the Cascade Range; part of Lassen Volcanic National Park; last erupted in 1921. p. 27

Lassen Volcanic National Park A national park in northeastern California, in the Cascade Range. p. 469

Lava Beds National Monument A national monument located in northern California; known for its volcanic landscape features. p. 469

Lompoc A city in southwestern California, near the Pacific Ocean. (35°N, 120°W) p. 95

Lone Pine A town in the Owens Valley. (36°N, 118°W) p. 326

Long Beach A city in California's Coastal Region; about 20 miles south of Los Angeles. (34°N, 118°W) p. 29

Los Altos A city in the Santa Clara Valley near San Jose. (37°N, 122°W) p. 432

Los Angeles A city in southwestern California; more than 15 million people live in the Los Angeles metropolitan area; county seat of Los Angeles County. (34°N, 118°W) p. 17

Los Angeles Aqueduct An aqueduct that carries water from the Owens River to Los Angeles. p. 326

Los Angeles River A river in Los Angeles; before construction of the Los Angeles Aqueduct, it gave Los Angeles most of its water. p. 326

Madera A city in central California, located 20 miles northwest of Fresno; county seat of Madera County. (37°N, 120°W) p. 17

Mariposa An unincorporated settlement in central California; county seat of Mariposa County. (37°N, 120°W) p. R14

Markleeville A town in eastern California; county seat of Alpine County. (39°N, 120°W) p. R14

Martinez A city in western California; county seat of Contra Costa County. (38°N, 122°W) p. R14

Marysville A city in north-central California; county seat of Yuba County. (39°N, 122°W) p. R14

Merced (mer•SED) A city in central California; county seat of Merced County. (37°N, 120°W) p. 296

Merced River (mer•SED) A tributary of the San Joaquin River. p. 232

Mission San Diego de Alcalá The first Spanish mission established in Alta California, founded in 1769 by Father Serra in San Diego. p. 127

Modesto A city on the Tuolumne River in central California; county seat of Stanislaus County. (38°N, 121°W) p. 17

Mojave Desert (moh•HAH•vee) A large desert area between the southern Sierra Nevada and the Colorado River. p. 20

Mokelumne River (moh•KEH•luh•mee) A tributary of the San Joaquin River. p. 232

Mono Lake A lake in eastern California, near Nevada. p. 326

Monterey A historic town located on the coast of California; original state capital of California. (37°N, 122°W) p. 17

Monterey Bay A natural harbor near Monterey. p. 20

Mount Pinos (PEE•nohs) The tallest peak in the Coast Ranges, with an elevation of 8,831 feet. p. 27

Mount Shasta A mountain peak with an elevation of 14,162 feet; located in the Cascade Range. p. 27

Mount Whitney The tallest peak in California, with an elevation of 14,495 feet; located in the Sierra Nevada. p. 27

Muir Woods National Monument (MYUR) A national monument located 12 miles northwest of San Francisco. p. 469

N

Napa A city in west-central California; county seat of Napa County. (38°N, 122°W) p. R14

Napa Valley A valley in the Coast Ranges, located north of San Francisco. p. R15

Needles A city in southeastern California, on the Colorado River. (35°N, 115°W) p. 17

Nevada City A city in eastern California; county seat of Nevada County. (39°N, 121°W) p. R14

New River A river in southern California. p. 305

North Pole The northernmost location on Earth. (90°N) p. 16

Northern Hemisphere The half of Earth located north of the equator. p. 16

Oakland A large city and port in northern California, on San Francisco Bay opposite San Francisco; county seat of Alameda County. (38°N, 122°W) p. 17

Oceanside A city in the southwestern corner of California. (33°N, 117°W) p. 95

Old Spanish Trail A route from Santa Fe, New Mexico, to southern California. p. 202

Oroville A city in north-central California on the Feather River; county seat of Butte County. (40°N, 122°W) p. R14

Owens Lake A lake that gets its water from the Owens River; now nearly dry. p. 326

Owens River A river that flows through the Sierra Nevada; water from the river is diverted to the Los Angeles Aqueduct that supplies water to the city of Los Angeles. p. 326

Oxnard A city in southwestern California. (34°N, 119°W) p. 399

Pacific Basin Lands surrounded by the Pacific Ocean as well as lands that border the Pacific Ocean. p. 420

Palm Springs A city in southern California. (34°N, 117°W) p. 17

Palo Alto A city in the Santa Clara Valley; site of Stanford University. (37°N, 122°W) p. 432

Panamint Mountains A mountain range in eastern California, west of Death Valley; its highest peak is Telescope Peak at 11,049 feet. p. R15

Pasadena A city northeast of Los Angeles. (34°N, 118°W) p. 399

Paso Robles (pa•SOH ROH•buhlz) A city in southwest California, on the Salinas River. (35°N, 120°W) p. 399

Petaluma A city in western California, on the Petaluma River, south of Santa Rosa; site of a former rancho owned by Mariano Vallejo. (38°N, 123°W) p. 158

Pinnacles National Monument A national monument in west-central California; it features spirelike rock formations. p. 469

Pit River A tributary of the Sacramento River. p. R15

Placerville A city in the Central Valley; county seat of El Dorado County; began as a mining town. (39°N, 121°W) p. 232

Point Conception A piece of land that extends into the Pacific Ocean south of Santa Barbara County. p. 113

Point Reyes National Seashore A national seashore along the California coast north of San Francisco Bay. p. 469

Q

Quincy An unincorporated village in northeastern California; county seat of Plumas County. (40°N, 121°W) p. R14

R

Red Bluff A city in northern California; county seat of Tehama County. (40°N, 122°W) p. R14

Redding A city in northern California, on the Sacramento River; county seat of Shasta County. (41°N, 122°W) p. 17

Redwood City A city in western California, west of San Francisco Bay; county seat of San Mateo County. (37°N, 122°W) p. R14

Redwood National Park A national park located along the northwestern coast of California; its groves of ancient trees include some of the world's tallest. p. 469

Ridgecrest A city in southern California, northeast of Bakersfield. (36°N, 118°W) p. 326

Riverside A city in southern California, located east of Los Angeles; county seat of Riverside County. (34°N, 117°W) p. 95

Russian River A river in northwestern California. p. 160

S

Sacramento A city in the Central Valley; California's state capital; county seat of Sacramento County. (39°N, 121°W) p. 22

Sacramento River A river that flows through the Sacramento Valley. p. 20

Sacramento Valley A valley that forms the northern part of the Central Valley. p. 20

Salinas A city in western California; county seat of Monterey County. (37°N, 122°W) p. 399

Salinas River A river in western California. p. 326

Salton Sea One of California's two largest lakes; located in the Imperial Valley. p. 305

San Andreas (an•DRAY•uhs) A village in central California; county seat of Calaveras County. (38°N, 121°W) p. R14

San Andreas Fault A fault more than 600 miles long that begins off the coast of northern California and runs to the southeast. p. 42

San Bernardino A city located about 55 miles east of Los Angeles; county seat of San Bernardino County. (34°N, 117°W) p. 17

San Bernardino Mountains A mountain range in southern California. p. 27

San Diego A city located 12 miles north of California's border with Mexico; county seat of San Diego County. (33°N, 117°W) p. 17

San Diego Bay A natural harbor near San Diego. (33°N, 117°W) p. 20

San Francisco A city in northern California; county seat of San Francisco County. (38°N, 122°W) p. 17

San Francisco Bay A natural harbor near San Francisco. (38°N, 122°W) p. 27

San Gabriel A city about 10 miles east of Los Angeles. (34°N, 118°W) p. 193

San Jacinto Mountains (hah•SEEN•toh) A range of mountains southeast of Los Angeles, near the San Bernardino Mountains. p. 120

San Joaquin River (wah•KEEN) A river that flows through the San Joaquin Valley. p. 20

San Joaquin Valley (wah•KEEN) A valley that forms the southern part of the Central Valley. p. 20

San Jose (hoh•ZAY) A city in west-central California; county seat of Santa Clara County. (37°N, 122°W) p. 17

San Juan Capistrano (ka•puh•STRAW•no) A city in Orange County; the site of a mission founded by Father Serra in 1776. p. 152

San Luis Obispo (LOO•is uh•BIS•poh) A city near the California coast, about halfway between Los Angeles and San Francisco; county seat of San Luis Obispo County. (35°N, 121°W) p. 39

San Luis Reservoir A lake in central California, formed by the San Luis Dam. (37°N, 121°W) p. R15

San Pasqual A town in southern California, where the soldiers of General Kearny and Andrés Pico fought in 1846 during the Mexican-American War. (33°N, 117°W) p. 215

San Pedro Bay A body of water off the coast of southern California that includes the human-made Los Angeles harbor. p. 326

San Rafael (rah•fah•EL) A city in western California; county seat of Marin County. (38°N, 123°W) p. 399

Santa Ana A city in southwestern California; county seat of Orange County. (34°N, 118°W) p. 399

Santa Barbara A city located along the central coast of California; county seat of Santa Barbara County. (34°N, 120°W) p. 17

Santa Barbara Channel A body of water that separates mainland California from the Channel Islands. p. 71

Santa Clara River A river in southern California. p. 326

Santa Cruz A city at the north end of Monterey Bay; county seat of Santa Cruz County. (37°N, 122°W) p. 17

Santa Cruz Mountains One of the mountain ranges that make up the Coast Ranges. p. R15

Santa Lucia Mountains (loo•SEE•uh) One of the mountain ranges that make up the Coast Ranges. p. R15

Santa Monica A city on the southern coast of California; west of Los Angeles. (34°N, 118°W) p. 95

Santa Rosa A city 50 miles northwest of San Francisco, in the Sonoma Valley; county seat of Sonoma County. (38°N, 123°W) p. 399

Santa Ynez River A river in southern California. p. R15

Sausalito A city in western California, on San Francisco Bay; northwest of San Francisco. (38°N, 122°W) p. 315

Sebastopol A city in western California, southwest of Santa Rosa. (38°N, 123°W) p. 160

Sequoia National Park (sih•KWOY•uh) A national park in south central California, in the Sierra Nevada; established in 1890; contains Mount Whitney. p. 469

Shasta Lake A reservoir in northern California; formed by Shasta Dam. p. R15

Sierra Nevada (see•AIR•ah neh•VAH•dah) California's largest mountain range; it stretches north and south across much of the eastern part of the state. p. 20

Silicon Valley An area in western California, between San Jose and Palo Alto; the name refers to the area's computer industry, which makes and uses silicon chips. p. 432

Sonoma A city north of San Francisco. (38°N, 122°W) p. 157

Sonora A city in central California; county seat of Tuolumne County. (38°N, 120°W) p. R14

South Pole The southernmost location on Earth. (90°S) p. 16

Southern Hemisphere The half of Earth located south of the equator. p. 16

Stanislaus River A tributary of the San Joaquin River. p. 232

Stockton A city in the San Joaquin Valley; county seat of San Joaquin County. (38°N, 121°W) p. 17

Susanville A city in northeastern California; county seat of Lassen County. (40°N, 121°W) p. R14

Sutter's Fort A settlement also known as New Helvetia, or New Switzerland, built by John Sutter near the Sacramento and American Rivers. (39°N, 121°W) p. 198

Sutter's Mill The site at Coloma where gold was found in California in 1848. (39°N, 121°W) p. 227

Trinity River A river in northern California. p. 63

Tulare A city in south-central California. (36°N, 119°W) p. 296

Tuolumne River (tu•AH•luh•mee) A tributary of the San Joaquin River; site of a dam that provides water for San Francisco. p. 232

Ukiah (yoo•KY•uh) A city in western California, on the Russian River; county seat of Mendocino County. (39°N, 123°W) p. R14

Ventura A city in southwestern California; county seat of Ventura County. (34°N, 119°W) p. 95

Visalia A city in central California; county seat of Tulare County. (36°N, 119°W) p. R14

Walker Pass A mountain pass through the Sierra Nevada; named for trailblazer Joseph Reddeford Walker. p. 193

Weaverville An unincorporated settlement in northwestern California; county seat of Trinity County. (41°N, 123°W) p. R14

Western Hemisphere The half of Earth made up of North America and South America and the waters and islands around them. California is in the United States, in North America, in the Western Hemisphere. p. 16

Willows A city in northern California; county seat of Glenn County. (40°N, 122°W) p. R14

Woodland A city in north-central California; county seat of Yolo County. (39°N, 122°W) p. R14

Yosemite National Park (yoh•SEH•muh•tee) A national park located in the central Sierra Nevada; established in 1890. p. 469

Yreka (wy•REE•kuh) A city in northern California; county seat of Siskiyou County. (42°N, 123°W) p. R14

Yuba City A city in north-central California, on the Feather River; county seat of Sutter County. (39°N, 122°W) p. R14

Yuba River A tributary of the Feather River. p. 232

Glossary

The Glossary contains important history and social science words and their definitions, listed in alphabetical order. Each word is respelled as it would be in a dictionary. When you see the mark ´ after a syllable, pronounce that syllable with more force. The page number at the end of the definition tells where the word is first used in this book. Guide words at the top of each page help you quickly locate the word you need to find.

add, **ā**ce, **câ**re, p**ä**lm; **e**nd, **ē**qual; **i**t, **ī**ce; **o**dd, **ō**pen, **ô**rder; t**o͝o**k, p**o͞o**l; **u**p, b**û**rn; y**o͞o** as *u* in *fuse*; **oi**l; p**ou**t; **ə** as *a* in *above*, *e* in *sicken*, *i* in *possible*, *o* in *melon*, *u* in *circus*; **ch**eck; ri**ng**; **th**in; **th**is; **zh** as in *vision*

A

absolute location (ab´sə•lo͞ot lō•kā´shən) The exact position of a place on Earth, using lines of latitude and longitude. p. 16

adapt (ə•dapt´) To change one's way of life to adjust to the environment. p. 41

aerospace (ar´ō•spās) Having to do with building and testing equipment for air and space travel. p. 396

agriculture (a´gri•kəl•chər) Farming. p. 87

alcalde (äl•käl´dā) A mayor of a town in Spanish California. p. 131

amendment (ə•mend´mənt) An addition or change to a constitution. p. 359

ancestor (an´ses•tər) An early family member. p. 57

aqueduct (a´kwə•dəkt) A large pipe or canal that carries water from one place to another. p. 325

arid (ar´əd) Dry, or having little rainfall. p. 87

artifact (är´ti•fakt) Any object made by people in the past. p. 60

aviation (ā•vē•ā´shən) The making and flying of airplanes. p. 363

B

barter (bär´tər) To trade one kind of item for another, usually without exchanging money. p. 160

benefit (be´nə•fit) Something that is helpful or gained. p. 111

bill (bil) A plan for a new law. p. 472

board of supervisors (bōrd əv sü´pər•vī•zərz) An elected group of people who govern a county. p. 481

boom (bo͞om) A time of fast economic growth. p. 324

boycott (boi´kät) A decision by a group of people not to buy something until a certain problem is fixed. p. 403

bracero (brä•ser´ō) A skilled Mexican worker who came to California to work during World War II. p. 381

bribe (brīb) To promise money or a gift to a person to get him or her to do something. p. 359

budget (bə´jət) A written plan for how to spend money. p. 473

C

Cabinet (kab´nit *or* ka´bə•nit) A group of the President's most important advisers. p. 465

Californio (ka•lə•fôr´nē•ō) The name that the Spanish-speaking people of Alta California called themselves. p. 151

canal (kə•nal´) A waterway dug across land. p. 305

cardinal direction (kär´də•nəl də•rek´shən) North, south, east, or west. p. I21

cause (kôz) Something that makes something else happen. p. 154

century (sen´shə•rē) A period of 100 years. p. 132

GLOSSARY

ceremony (ser´ə•mō•nē) A celebration to honor a cultural or religious event. p. 64
character traits (kar´ik•tər trāts) Traits displayed by people, such as trustworthiness, respect, responsibility, compassion, and patriotism. p. I5
chronology (krə•nä´lə•jē) Time order. p. I13
city manager (si´tē ma´ni•jər) A person hired by a city council to run the city under the direction of the city council. p. 484
civil rights (si´vəl rīts) The rights of citizens to equal treatment. p. 401
claim (klām) The area a miner said belonged to him or her. p. 230
classify (kla´sə•fī) To group information. p. 74
climate (klī´mət) The kind of weather a place has most often, year after year. p. 29
coastal plain (kōs´təl plān) An area of low land that lies along the shoreline. p. 20
colony (kä´lə•nē) A settlement that is ruled by a faraway government. p. 119
commercial farm (kə•mûr´shəl färm) A farm that grows crops only to sell. p. 301
communication (kə•myo͞o•nə•kā´shən) The sending and receiving of information. p. 279
commute (kə•myo͞ot´) To travel back and forth between work and home. p. 395
compass rose (kəm´pəs rōz) The direction marker on a map. p. I21
competition (käm•pə•ti´shən) The contest among companies to get the most customers or sell the most products. p. 296
compromise (käm´prə•mīz) An agreement in which each side in a conflict gives up some of what it wants. p. 250
Congress (kän´•grəs) The part of the United States government that makes laws. p. 250
conquistador (kän•kēs´tə•dôr) Any of the Spanish conquerors in the Americas. p. 111
consequence (kän´sə•kwens) What happens because of an action. p. 376
conservation (kän•sər•vā´shən) The protection and wise use of natural resources. p. 451
constitution (kän•stə•to͞o´shən) A plan of government. p. 249
consumer (kən•so͞o´mər) A person who buys a product or a service. p. 238
consumer good (kən•so͞o´mər go͝od) A product made for people to use. p. 362
continent (kän´tən•ənt) One of the seven largest land areas on Earth. p. I16
convention (kən•ven´shən) An important meeting. p. 247
cooperate (kō•ä´pə•rāt) To work together. p. 71
coordinate grid system (kō•ôrd´nət grid´ sis´təm) The grid system formed by lines of latitude and longitude, which cross to make a pattern of squares on a map. p. 17
cost (kôst) The value of something given up in order to gain something. p. 111
county (koun´tē) A section of a state. p. 481
county seat (koun´tē sēt) A city where the main government offices of the county are located. p. 481
criollo (krē•ōl´yō) A person born of Spanish parents in Mexico. p. 149
culture (kəl´chər) A way of life. p. 59
custom (kəs´təm) A usual way of doing things. p. 138

D

decade (de´kād) A period of ten years. p. 132
deficit (de´fə•sət) The result of spending more money than is available. p. 452
delegate (de´li•gət) A person who is chosen to speak and act for the people who elected him or her. p. 247
delta (del´tə) Land built up from soil carried by rivers. p. 22
demand (di•mand´) A need or a desire for a good or service by people willing to pay for it. p. 191
democracy (di•mä´krə•sē) A form of government in which the people rule by making decisions themselves or by electing people to make decisions for them. p. 463
depression (di•pre´shən) A time when there are few jobs and people have little money. p. 369
derrick (der´ik) A tower built over an oil well to hold the machines used for drilling. p. 324

discrimination (dis•kri•mə•nā´shən) The unfair treatment of people because of such things as their religion, their race, or their birthplace. p. 242

diseño (di•sān´yō) A hand-drawn map that shows the boundaries of a land grant. p. 157

diverse economy (dī•vûrs´ i•kä´nə•mē) An economy that is based on many industries. p. 394

division of labor (də•vi´zhən əv lā´bər) Having different workers do different jobs. p. 79

documentary source (dä•kyə•men´tə•rē sōrs) A source of information that is often produced at the time an event takes place, often by a person who actually experienced the event. p. 204

double-bar graph (də´bəl•bär graf) A kind of bar graph that compares two sets of numbers. p. 336

drought (drout) A long time with little or no rain. p. 32

E

economy (i•kä´nə•mē) The way people in a place or region use resources to meet their needs. p. 135

effect (i•fekt´ *or* ē•fekt´) What happens as a result of something else happening. p. 154

elevation (e•lə•vā´shən) The height of the land. p. 26

energy crisis (e´nər•jē krī´səs) A problem that happens when there is not enough power to meet demand. p. 451

entrepreneur (än•trə•prə•nər´) A person who sets up a new business. p. 238

equator (i•kwā´tər) The imaginary line that divides Earth into the Northern Hemisphere and the Southern Hemisphere. pp. I16, 13

ethnic group (eth´nik grōōp) A group of people from the same country, of the same race, or with a shared culture. p. 408

evidence (e´və•dəns) Proof. p. I3

expedition (ek•spə•di´shən) A journey into an area to learn more about it. p. 120

export (ek´spōrt) A product shipped from one country to be sold in another; to sell goods to people in another country. p. 301

F

fact (fakt) A statement that can be checked and proved to be true. p. 196

fault (fôlt) A crack in Earth's surface. p. 42

federal (fe´də•rəl) National. p. 463

fertile (fûr´təl) Good for growing crops. p. 22

fiction (fik´shən) Made-up writing. p. 204

fiesta (fē•es´tə) A party. p. 167

flowchart (flō´chärt) A drawing that shows the steps in a process. p. 478

food processing (fōōd prä´se•sing) The cooking, canning, drying, freezing, and preparing of foods for market. p. 434

forty-niner (fôr•tē•nī´nər) A person who went to California in 1849 to search for gold. p. 228

freeway (frē´wā) A wide, divided highway with no cross streets or stoplights. p. 395

frontier (frən•tir´) Land beyond the settled part of a country. p. 191

G

galleon (ga´lē•ən *or* gal´yən) A large Spanish trading ship. p. 114

generation (je•nə•rā´shən) A group of people born and living at about the same time. p. 449

glacier (glā´shər) A huge, slow-moving mass of ice. p. 57

gold rush (gōld rəsh) A huge movement of people going to a place to look for gold. p. 227

government (gə´vərn•mənt) A system for deciding what is best for a group of people. p. 70

granary (grā´nə•rē *or* gra´nə•rē) A place for storing acorns and grains. p. 78

grid system (grid sis´tem) An arrangement of lines that divide something, such as a map, into squares. p. I22

growing season (grō´ing sē´zən) The period of time when the weather is warm enough for crops to grow. p. 43

H

hacienda (ä•sē•en´də) The main house on a rancho. p. 159

harbor (här´bər) A protected area of water where ships can dock safely. p. 20

hatch lines (hach līnz) A pattern of diagonal lines often used on historic maps to indicate land that was claimed by two or more countries. p. 219

hemisphere (he´mə•sfir) A half of Earth. pp. I17, 13

heritage (her´ə•tij) Traditions, beliefs, and ways of life that have been handed down from the past. p. 408

high-tech (hī´tek) Shortened form of the words *high technology;* having to do with inventing, building, or using computers and other kinds of electronic equipment. p. 396

human feature (hyōō´mən fē´chər) A feature, such as a building or bridge, that has been made by people. p. I14

humid (hyōō´məd) Damp or moist. p. 32

hydroelectric power (hī•drō•i•lek´trik pow´ər) Electricity produced by using waterpower. p. 325

I

immigrant (i´mi•grənt) A person who comes from another place to live in a country. p. 199

immigration (i•mə•grā´shən) The process of people leaving one country to live in another. p. 315

import (im´pôrt) A good, or product, that is brought into one country from another to be sold; to bring in goods from another country to sell. p. 433

independence (in•də•pen´dəns) Freedom. p. 149

industry (in´dəs•trē) All the businesses that make one kind of product or provide one kind of service. p. 41

inflation (in•flā´shən) A sharp increase in prices. p. 239

initiative (i•ni´shə•tiv) A law made directly by voters instead of by a legislature. p. 475

inset map (in´set map) A small map within a larger map. p. I20

interdependence (in•tər•di•pen´dəns) The depending on one another for resources and products. p. 433

intermediate direction (in•tər•mē´dē•ət də•rek´shən) A direction between the cardinal directions—northeast, southeast, southwest, and northwest. p. I21

international trade (in•tər•nash´nəl trād) Trade with other countries. p. 431

interpret (in•tûr´prət) To explain. p. I3

invest (in•vest´) To buy something, such as a share in a company, in the hope that it will be worth more in the future. p. 288

irrigation (ir•ə•gā´shən) The use of canals, ditches, or pipes to carry water to dry places. p. 23

isthmus (is´məs) A narrow piece of land that connects two larger land areas. p. 228

J

jury trial (jŏŏr´ē trīl) A trial in which a group of citizens decides whether a person accused of a crime or other wrongdoing should be found guilty or not guilty. p. 482

L

labor (lā´bər) Work. p. 166

labor union (lā´bər yōōn´yən) An organization of workers whose goal is to improve working conditions. p. 402

land grant (land grant) A gift of land given by the government. p. 157

land use (land yo͞os) How most of the land in a place is used. p. 436

legend (le´jənd) A story handed down over time. p. 60

legislature (le´jəs•lā•chər) A group of officials elected to make laws. p. 249

levee (le´vē) A high wall made of earth to help control flooding. p. 305

line graph (līn graf) A graph that uses a line to show changes over time. p. 244

lines of latitude (līnz əv la´tə•to͞od) A set of lines that run east and west drawn on maps and globes. They are measured in degrees north and south from the equator. p. 16

lines of longitude (līnz əv län´jə•to͞od) A set of lines that run north and south, from the North Pole to the South Pole, drawn on maps and globes. They are measured in degrees east and west from the prime meridian. p. 16

location (lō•kā´shən) Where something can be found. p. I14

locator (lō´kā•tər) A small map or globe that shows where the place on the main map is located within a state, a country, a continent, or in the world. p. I21

long-term planning (long´tərm plan´ing) Making choices that are based on how they will affect life in the future. p. 451

M

manifest destiny (ma´nə•fest des´tə•nē) The idea that the United States should expand to reach from the Atlantic Ocean to the Pacific Ocean. p. 207

map legend (map´ le´jənd) The part of a map that explains what the symbols on the map stand for; also known as a map key. p. I20

map scale (map skāl) The part of a map that compares a distance on the map to a distance in the real world. p. I21

map title (map tī´təl) The words that tell you the subject of a map. p. I20

mestizo (me•stē´zō) A person of both European and Indian heritage who lived in Mexico or another part of New Spain. p. 149

metropolitan area (me•trə•pä´lə•tən ar´ē•ə) A large city together with nearby cities and suburbs. p. 36

migrant worker (mī´grənt wûr´kər) A worker who moves from place to place, harvesting crops. p. 371

migration (mī•grā´shən) The movement of people from one place to another within a country. p. 315

mission (mi´shən) A religious settlement. p. 119

missionary (mi´shə•ner•ē) A person who teaches a religion to others. p. 119

modify (mo´də•fī) To change. p. 37

multicultural (məl•tē•kəlch´rəl) Having many different cultures. p. 407

municipal (myo͝o•ni´sə•pəl) Having to do with a city. p. 483

munitions (myo͝o•ni´shənz) Military supplies and weapons. p. 380

N

natural region (na´chə•rəl rē´jən) A region made up of places that share the same kinds of physical, or natural, features, such as plains, mountains, valleys, or deserts. p. 19

natural resource (na´chə•rəl rē´sōrs) Something found in nature, such as water, soil, or minerals, that people can use to meet their needs. p. 35

naturalist (na´chə•rə•list) A person who studies nature and works to protect it. p. 335

neophyte (nē´ə•fīt) A person who is new to the Catholic faith. p. 135

nonrenewable (nän´ri•no͞o´ə•bəl) Something that cannot be made again by nature or by people. p. 451

O

ocean current (ō´shən kər´ənt) A stream of water that moves through the ocean. p. 114

GLOSSARY

opinion (ə•pin′yən) A statement that tells what the person who makes it thinks or believes. p. 196

opportunity cost (ä•pər•to͞o′nə•tē kôst) The thing that is given up to get something else. p. 488

P

pass (pas) An opening between high mountains. p. 194

peninsula (pə•nin′sə•lə) Land that has water almost all around it. p. 112

petition (pə•ti′shən) A signed request for action. p. 475

petroleum (pə•trō′lē•əm) Another name for oil. p. 324

physical environment (fi′zi•kəl in•vī′rən•mənt) Surroundings consisting of a place's physical features, landforms, and climate. p. 35

physical feature (fi′zi•kəl fē′chər) A feature, such as a mountain or river, that has been formed by nature. p. I14

pioneer (pī•ə•nir′) One of the first settlers in a place. p. 200

plaza (pla′zə) An open square where people can gather. p. 130

point of view (point əv vyo͞o) A person's set of beliefs that have been shaped by factors such as whether that person is old or young, male or female, rich or poor. p. I4

political boundary (pə•li′ti•kəl boun′drē) The imaginary line marking the limits of a nation. p. 218

pollution (pə•lo͞o′shən) Anything that makes a natural resource dirty or unsafe to use. p. 451

population density (pä•pyə•lā′shən den′sə•tē) The number of people who live in an area of a certain size. p. 38

precipitation (pri•si•pə•tā′shən) Water that falls to Earth's surface as rain, sleet, hail, or snow. p. 29

prejudice (pre′jə•dəs) The unfair feeling of hate or dislike for members of a certain group because of their background, race, or religion. p. 318

presidio (pri•sē′dē•ō) A Spanish fort. p. 128

primary source (prī′mer•ē sōrs) A record made by people who were present when an event took place. p. 124

prime meridian (prīm mə•ri′dē•ən) The imaginary line that divides Earth into the Western Hemisphere and the Eastern Hemisphere. pp. I17, 13

private school (prī′vət sko͞ol) A school that is funded and run by individuals or groups instead of by a government agency. p. 447

public school (pə′blik sko͞ol) A school that is free to students, supported by tax dollars, and run by a government agency. p. 447

pueblo (pwe′blō) A farming community in Spanish California. p. 130

R

rain shadow (rān sha′dō) The drier side of a mountain. p. 32

rancheria (ran′chə•rē′ə) Land in California set aside for American Indians. p. 486

rancho (ran′chō) A cattle ranch. p. 158

ratify (ra′tə•fī) To approve. p. 249

rebel (re′bəl) A person who fights against the government. p. 210

recall (ri•kôl′) To remove an official from his or her job. p. 475

recycle (rē•sī′kəl) To use again. p. 381

referendum (re•fə•ren′dəm) An election in which voters can decide whether to keep or do away with an existing law. p. 476

reform (ri•fôrm′) To change for the better. p. 359

region (rē′jən) A place with at least one physical or human feature that makes it different from other places. p. I15

regional body (rē′jə•nəl bä′dē) A group made up of people, usually from several cities or counties, who work together to create a plan for a large area. p. 485

relative location (re′lə•tiv lō•kā′shən) Where a place is in relation to one or more other places on Earth. p. 14

relief (ri•lēf′) The differences in the heights of land shown in maps. p. 26

relocation camp (rē•lō•kā´shən kamp) A prison-like camp where Japanese Americans were sent after the bombing of Pearl Harbor. p. 382

renewable (ri•nōō´ə•bəl) Something that can be made again by nature or people. p. 451

republic (ri•pub´lik) A form of government in which people elect their leaders. p. 210

research (rē•sərch) To study carefully. p. I2

reservation (re•zər•vā´shən) Land set aside by the government for use by American Indians. p. 319

reservoir (re´zər•vwär) A lake made by people to collect and store water. p. 325

resolve (ri•zälv´) To settle. p. 254

revolt (ri•vōlt´) To fight against. p. 136

right (rīt) A freedom that belongs to a person. p. 213

rural (rŏŏr´əl) Like, in, or of the country. p. 36

S

scarce (skers) Limited. p. 44

sea level (sē le´vəl) Land that is level with the surface of the ocean. p. 24

secondary source (se´kən•der•ē sōrs) A record of an event that was made by people who were not present when an event took place. p. 124

secularization (se•kyə•lə•rə•zā´shən) The end of church rule of the missions. p. 152

segregation (se•gri•gā´shən) Keeping people of one race or culture separate from other people. p. 401

service (sûr´vəs) An activity that someone does for others for pay. p. 41

service industry (sûr´vəs in´dəs•trē) Businesses that do things for people instead of making things. p. 435

shaman (shä´mən) A religious leader. p. 64

shortage (shôr´tij) A lack of something. p. 380

silicon chip (si´li•kən chip) A tiny device that can store millions of bits of information. p. 396

silt (silt) Fine grains of soil and rock. p. 87

sovereign (sä´və•rən) Free and independent. p. 486

special district (spe´shəl dis´trikt) A group set up to deal with a certain service or problem. p. 485

special effect (spe´shəl i•fekt´) A way of making things that are not real look real on film. p. 439

specialize (spe´shə•līz) To work at one kind of job and learn to do it well. p. 79

spring (spring) A flow of water from an opening in the ground. p. 85

squatter (skwä´tər) Someone who lives in a place without permission. p. 209

stagecoach (stāj´kōch) An enclosed wagon pulled by a team of horses. p. 280

stock (stäk) A share of ownership in a company. p. 369

strike (strīk) A time when workers stop working to get employers to listen to their needs. p. 403

suburb (su´bərb) A town or small city near a large city. p. 36

suffrage (su´frij) The right to vote. p. 359

supply (sə•plī´) An amount of a good or a service that is offered for sale. p. 191

surplus (sur´•pləs) An extra amount. p. 58

T

tallow (ta´lō) Animal fat used to make soap and candles. p. 160

tax (taks) Money that a government collects from its citizens, often to pay for services. p. 466

technology (tek•nä´lə•jē) The use of knowledge or tools to make or do something. p. 394

telegraph (te´lə•graf) A machine that uses electricity to send messages over wires. p. 282

tenant farmer (te´nənt fär´mər) A farmer who pays rent to use a piece of land. p. 302

time zone (tīm zōn) A region in which people use the same time. p. 298

tourism (tŏŏr´i•zəm) The business of serving visitors. p. 435

trade (trād) The exchanging, or buying and selling, of goods. p. 67

trade-off (trād´ôf) Giving up one thing to get something else. p. 488

trailblazer (trāl´blā•zər) A person who makes a new trail for others to follow. p. 192

transcontinental railroad (trans•kän•tən•en´təl rāl´rōd) A railroad that crosses the North American continent, linking the Atlantic and Pacific coasts. p. 287

treaty (trē´tē) A written agreement between groups or countries. p. 216

tribe (trīb) An American Indian group with its own leaders and lands. p. 59

tributary (tri´byə•ter•ē) A river that flows into a larger river. p. 22

tropics (trä´piks) Earth's warmest regions, between the Tropic of Cancer and the Tropic of Capricorn. p. 16

U

unemployment (ən•im•ploi´mənt) The number of workers without jobs. p. 369

urban (ûr´bən) Like, in, or of a city. p. 36

urban sprawl (ûr´bən sprôl) The outward spread of urban areas. p. 395

V

vaquero (vä•ker´ō) A cowhand. p. 165

vegetation (ve•jə•tā´shən) Plant life. p. 30

veto (vē´tō) To reject. p. 473

vigilante (vi•jə•lan´tē) A person who takes the law into his or her own hands. p. 242

W

wagon train (wa´gən trān) A group of wagons, each pulled by horses or oxen. p. 200

weir (wir) A fence-like structure built across a river in order to trap fish. p. 64

wind pattern (wind pa´tərn) The general direction of the wind. p. 114

GLOSSARY

Index

The Index lets you know where information about important people, places and events appears in the book. All entries are listed in alphabetical order. For each entry, the page reference indicates where information about that entry can be found in the text. Page references for illustrations are set in italic type. An italic *m* indicates a map. Page references set in boldface type indicate the pages on which vocabulary terms are defined. Guide words at the top of each page help you identify which words appear on each page.

Abdul-Jabbar, Kareem, R38
Abiko, Kyutaro, 315, R38
Absolute location, **16**
  See also Map and Globe Skills
Achumawi tribe, *m59,* 77, *m77*
Acorns, 3, 64, 65, 70, 72, 78–79, 80, *81,* 84, 85, 92, *187*
Actors, 431
Adams, Ansel, 440, *444,* R38
Adams, Ernest H., 331
Adapt, **41**, 58, R50
Advertisements and advertising, *229, 303,* 323, *342*
Aerospace, **396**
Aerospace industry, 351, *380,* 396
Aerospace Museum (Balboa Park), *495*
Africa, 111
African American(s), 393, 418
  Allensworth, Allen, 266
  California statehood and, 250
  in civil rights movement, 400, 401
  contributions of, 178, 347
  discrimination and prejudice against, 224–225, 242, 318–319, 401
  end of segregation of, 401
  and gold rush, 228, 240
  in government, 347
  leaders, 178, 253, 319, 321, 400, 401, 403
  in Los Angeles, 178
  settlers, 130, 315
  women, 224–225, 253, 347, 403
  in World War II, 380–381
Aftercastle, *114*
Agricultural industry, 393, *436*
Agriculture (farming), 87
  in Alta California, 130–131
  in Central Valley, 43, 301
  changes in, 393
  in deserts, 87
  drought and, 370–371
  farmworkers in, *370, 402,* 403, 405
  fertile soil and, 43, 271
  during the Great Depression, 370–371
  growing season, 303
  hydraulic mining and, 241
  immigrants and, 333, 381
  irrigation and, 326–327, 374
  as major industry, 311, 431, 434
  in Mexican California, 158–159
  of Native Californians, 87
  railroads and, 304
  tenant farmers in, 302
  water control and, 305, 374
  See also Crops; Ranchos
Air pollution, 423, 468–469
Airplanes, *378*
  See also Aerospace industry
Alameda, R44
Alameda, California, *m432*
Alaska, 19
Alcalde, **130**
Alcatraz Island, 400, *404,* 422, R44
Allensworth, 266, *319,* 321
Allensworth, Allen, *266,* 319, 321, *321,* R38
Allensworth State Historical Park, 319
Allies, in World War II, 379
Almanac, I13, R20–R27, R28, R31
Almonds, 43, 434
Alta California, 128–129, 130, 151, 178, 192–193
  agriculture in, 130–131
  borders of, *m180–181*
  Californios in, 151
  everyday life in, 134–136
  exploration of, 112–115
  geographical barriers to, 120–121
  isolation of, 191
  Mexican refusal to sell, 208
  in Mexican War for Independence, 148–151
  missions in, 97, 98, 127
  population of, *130*
  presidios in, 128–129
  ranchos in, 158–159
  routes to, *m120*
  settlers in, 119
  travel from Mexico to, 99, 120–121
Altman, Linda Jacobs, 390–391
Alturas, 39, R44
Alzheimer's disease, 477
***Amelia's Road* (Altman),** 390–391
Amendment, **359**
American Indian Civil Rights movement, 404
American Indians, 57, 86, 400, 404, *404*
  See also California Indians
American Red Cross, 46, *47*
American Revolution, 149, 150, 154
American River, 22, 78, 179, 226, 227, R44
Anaheim, *m17, 36,* 317, 323, 443
Analyze
  artifacts, *64, 82–83, 162–163, 234–235, 284–285, 366–367, 444–445, 472*
  diagrams, *20–21, 32, 434*
  drawings, *292*
  graphs, *39, 130, 139, 237, 301, 316, 393, 407, 431, 452*
  illustrations, *13, 23, 432*
  maps, *m20, m29, m30, m49, m57, m59, m63, m69, m77, m157, m215, m229, m232, m255, m279, m280–281, m296, m335, m370, m481, m487*
  points of view, 141, 209, 250, 329, 486
  posters, 402
  tables, *36, 283, 465*
Ancestors, **57**, 73, 86, R50
Angel Island, 314, *314, m315,* R44
Anián, Strait of, 111, 112
Animals
  beavers, 190
  bighorn sheep, *23*
  coyote, *23*
  earliest, 56, 57, 58
  extinct, 58
  Gambel's quail, *23*
  habitats of, 7
  jackrabbit, *23*
  mountain lion, *23*
  as natural resources, 434
  oil spills and, 451
  otters, 190
  rattlesnake, *23*
  Scott's oriole, *23*
  as state symbols, 257
  tortoise, *23*
  See also Hunting; *individual animals*
Animation, 439
Ansel Adams's photographs, 444–445
Anza, Juan Bautista de, 118, *122, m175*
Anza's Expedition, 1775–1776, *m175*
Apollo 11, *397*
Appalachian Mountains, *m5*
Appelbaum, Ellen, 176
Appointed officials, 482
Apricots, 43, 434
Aqueduct, **325**, 334, R50
Architecture, *41, 44, 442*
Arden, *m22*
Argentina, 150
Arid, ***87***, R50
Arizona, 14, *m14, m17,* 207, 216, 405
Armenian immigrants, 317
Armies, 320, 379
Arroyo Seco Parkway, *395*
Art, *71,* 440–442
  See also Museums
Art activities, 429
  build a museum display, 176
  create a travel poster, 45
  create an advertisement, 383
  design a button, 453
  design a scrapbook, 416
  draw a cartoon, 297
  draw a mural, 88, 161
  make a brochure, 435
  make a city government brochure, 487
  make a poster, 404
  make illustrations, 67

Artifacts, 2, 3, *51,* 60, *61,* 72, *82, 82–83, 92–93, 124, 174,* R50
Arts, 440–442
Ashley–Henry trapping expedition, 195
Asia, 57, 111, 229, 315, 317, 406, 433
Asian Americans, 346, 401, 403, 404, 419
Asian Art Museum (San Francisco), 440
Asian immigrants, 407
Asisara, Lorenzo, 99, 141, *141,* 152
Assembly chamber, *470*
Astaire, Fred, *366*
Astrolabe, *116*
Astronaut, 347, 396, *397*
Atlantic Ocean, *m5, m13,* 113, 360
Atlas, *mR2–R19,* R28, R31
Atlatl, 58
Auburn, R44
Austin, Mary, 317, R38
Australia, 229
Australia, trade with, 433
Autograph cards, *226*
Automobile industry, 394
Automobiles, 324, 362, 392, 412, 413, 423
Aviation, 363
Aviation industry, 351, 363, *380,* 381, 394, 396, *430–431*
Avocados, 434
Awards, 383, *438, 496*
Axis Powers, in World War II, 379
Aztec civilization, 111, 182

Baca, Judith, 418, *418,* 440, *441,* R38
Badger, 52, *53, 55*
Badwater Basin, 7
Baja California, 99, 110, 112, 130, R44
Bakersfield, *m17,* 296, 324, 398, R44
Bangladesh, 406
Banks, *238,* 369, *488*
Baptisms, 167
Barges, 188
Barley, 159
Barstow, R44
Barter, 160, R50
Bartleson, John, 200, R38
Bartleson-Bidwell expedition, 198, 200–201, *m202*
Baseball, 401
Baskets and basket weaving, 58, 59, 60, *62,* 65, 66, *67, 76,* 77, 79, 82, *83,* 86, 89, *92,* 93
Battle of Olompali, 210
Battle of Rio San Gabriel, *215*
Battle of San Pasqual, 215
Baxter, Marvin, *474*
Beaches, *451*
Beads, 66
 See also Shells
Beakhead, *115*
Beans, 85, 159
Bear Flag Republic, 210
Bear Flag Revolt, 99, 206, 210, *211*
Bear River, *m232,* R44
Bears, 44, *52,* 52–55, *55*
Beavers, 190, 191
Beckwourth, James, 178, *178,* 194, 195, *195,* R38
Beckwourth Pass, 194, 195, *m202,* R44
Beckwourth Trading Post, *195*
Beef products, 434
Beliefs. *See* California Indians; Religion
Bells, *136*
Benefit, 111, R50
Benicia, 250
Bering, Vitus, 119, R38
Berkeley, R44
Berries, 58, 63, 64, 66, 77
Bibliography, R35
Bidwell, John, 179, *179,* 200, *300,* 300–301, R38
Bidwell-Bartleson expedition, *m202*
Big Four, *288,* 296–297
Big idea, I8
Big Pine, R44
Bighorn sheep, *23*
Bike trails, *489*
Bill, 472, R50
Bill of Rights, 463
Bio Brief Timeline. *See* Biographies
Biographical Dictionary, R38–R43
Biographies, I12
 Allensworth, Allen, 321
 Beckwourth, James, 195
 Briones, Juana, 169
 Chavez, Cesar, 405
 Disney, Walt, 443
 Lange, Dorothea, 375
 Mason, Biddy, 253
 Mayer, Louis B., 365
 Muir, John, 25
 Reagan, Ronald, 477
 Seidner, Cheryl A., 89
 Serra, Junípero, 123
 Shima, George, 307
 Yee Fung Cheung, 293
Birds, 23, 58, *60,* 65
Bishop, R44
Blacksmiths, 159, *261*
Blazing Trails to California **(Skelton),** 264
Blythe, R44
Board of supervisors, 481, R50
Boating, 43
Boats and ships, *41, 237*
 barges, 188
 California (ship), 183
 California Indian Boats by Tribe, *75*
 canoes, 2, 62
 cargo ships, *420*
 clipper ships, 183, *228, m229*
 container ships, *433*
 ferries, 237, 372
 Flying Cloud (ship), 183
 kayak, *41*
 riverboat, *43,* 228
 San Carlos, 108
 U.S.S. Ohio (ship), 360
 White Swallow (ship), *183*
Bodega, R44
Bodega Bay, 160
Bono, Sonny, R38
Bookmarking, R30
Boom, 324, R50
Bootman, Colin, 224–225
Boots, 160
Boston, 161
Botanical Building (Balboa Park), *495*
Boundaries, 248
Bows and arrows, *93*
 See also Tools
Boxer, Barbara, 403, 464, R38
Boycott, *402,* 403, R50
Braceros, 381, 393, R50
Branches of the Federal Government, *465*
Branches of government, 464–465, 471
Brands, 165
Brannan, Samuel, 227, 242, R38
Brathwaite Burke, Yvonne, 347, *403*
Brawley, R44
Brazil, 303
Bribe, 359, R50
Bridgeport, R44
Bridges, 372–373
Briones de Miranda, Juana, 98, *98,* 166, 169, *169,* R38
Britian, 151, 379
British colonies, 149
Brown, Edmund G. (Pat), *447*
Brubeck, Dave, 441, *441,* R38
Brush fires, 32, 46, 417
Budget, 452, 473, R50
Building styles, 45
Bullfights, 167
Bumper stickers, *491*
Bunting, Eve, 354–357
Burbank, 380, R44
Burbank, Luther, 304, R38
Burnett, Peter H., 249, R38
Buses, *43*
Bush, George, 385
Bush, George W., 417
Butterfield, John, 280, R38

Cabinet, 465, R50
Cable cars, 268, 340–341, *340–341*
Cabrillo, Juan Rodríguez, 110, 112, *112, 113,* R38
Cabrillo National Monument (San Diego), 469, R44
Cactus, 7, 85, 87
Cahuenga Pass, 216
Cahuilla tribe, 3, *m59, m85,* 85–86, 87
Calexico, R44
Calhoun, John C., *250*
California: Climate, *mR16*

California: Physical, *mR15*
California: Political, *mR14*
California: Vegetation, *mR17*
California African American Museum (Los Angeles), 440
California Assembly, 472
California capitol, *22, 251, 271, 470–471*
California Constitution, 246, 248–250, *446,* 471, 483
California Counties, *m481,* R22–R25
California Cowhand (Chevat), 176
California Equal Suffrage Association, *359*
California flag, *256*
California geography, *m27,* 248
California government, 359, 470–479
California governors, R26–R27
California history
  Bear Flag Republic, 210–211
  Dust Bowl and, 370–371
  European settlement, 315
  Great Depression, 369
  Mexican–Americans, 401, 402, 403
  statehood, 177, *223, 246,* 246–250
  war milestones, 381
  women, 157, 240
  in World War I, 361
  in World War II, 379–381
California Indian artifacts, 64, 82–83
California Indian Seal, *257*
California Indians, *56, 58,* 107, *107,* 123, 127, 129, 130, 139, 188, 230
  cultivation of land, 85, 87, 135
  discrimination against, 242, 319–320
  economic activities, 486
  geographic distribution, *59, m63*
  languages, 59, 77, 89
  legends, 60–61
  and mission secularization, 152–153
  and physical environment, 59, 63, 64
  ranchos, 166
  religious beliefs, 59, 64, 72, 80, *86*
  use of sea resources, 70
  villages, 1, 59, *m59*
  See also Artifacts; *specific tribes*
California Land Use, *m497*
California Land Use and Products, *m437*
California Latitude and Longitude, *m17*
California Native American Heritage Commission, 486–487
California poppy (state symbol), *257*
California Senate, 472
California Southern Railroad, 296
California state animal, *257*
California state bird, 256
California state constitution, 447
California state dance, 256
California state fife-and-drum band, 256
California state flag, *210, 262*
California state flower, *257*
California state government, 470–476
California State Indian Museum (Sacramento), 440
California State Legislature, *472,* 472–473
California state seal, *257*
California state song, 257, 460–461
California state symbols, *257*
California state tree, 257
California state university system, 448
California statehood, *254*
California Supreme Court, *474*
California Trail, *m202,* R44
California Tribal Lands, *m487*
California in the United States, 1886, *m268–269*
California Wheat Production 1850–1890, *301*
California in the World, *m13*
California's Foreign-Born Population, 2000, *407*
California's Largest Cities, *36*
California's Population, 1769–1848, *130*
California's Population, 1850–1890, *245*
California's Population, 1940–1960, *393*
California's public education system, 447, 448–449
California's Top Industries, *431*
California's Top Trading Partners, 2003, *433*
Californios, 151, 153, 160, 179, 208, 214, 215, 242, R50
Camera, *444*
Camping, *44*
Camps. *See* Migrant camps; Tent camps
Canada, *m13,* 25, *mR18*
  trade with, 434
Canal, 305, 360, R50
Candle making, 160
Canoes, 62, 63, 64, *64,* 70, *74, 75*
Canyons, 85
Capitol building, *251,* 464–465, *470–471*
Captain Jack, 266
  See also Kientepoos, Chief
Cardinal directions, R50
Caring, 169, 253, 375
Carlos III, *118,* 119, R38
Carmel Mission, 121, *172,* 172–173, *173*
Carmichael, *m22*
Cars, 451
Carson, Kit, R38
Carving, 72
Cascade Range, 21, R44
Cashiers, 435
Casinos, 486
Castro, José, 209, 210, R38
Catholic religion, 108
Cattle, 43, 122, 127, 135, *156–157,* 158, *165,* 166, 199
Cattle ranches. *See* Ranchos
Cause, 154, R50
Cause and effect, 350
CD–ROMs, R29
Celebrations, 167, 408, 409
  See also specific celebrations
Celtic Celebration, 408
Central America, 315, 407
Central Japanese Association, 384
Central Pacific Railroad, 271, 288, *288, 296*
Central Valley Project (CVP), 374
Central Valley Region, *m4,* 19, 22, *m27,* 30, 35, 43, 77, 301, *301,* 317, 394, R44
Centro Cultural de la Raza (San Diego), 440, 494
Century, 132, R50
Ceremonies, 64, 71, 73, 80, 86, 89, R51
Cermeño, Sebastián Rodríguez, *m113, 113,* 114, 182, R39
Cesar, Julio, 140
Cesar Chavez: Yes We Can (Daniel), 416
Chaffey, George, 305, R39
Channel Islands, 2, 20, 69, R44
Channel Islands National Park, 469, R44
Channel Islands National Park (Skelton), 96
Character traits, R51
Chart and graph activities, 15, 442
Chart and Graph Skills, I11
  bar graph, 39
  compare tables, 74–75, 91
  create a chart, 15
  create a weather chart, 33
  K-W-L chart, 184
  read a double-bar graph, 336–337
  read a flowchart, 478–479
  read a line graph, 244–245
  read a time line, 132–133
Charter cities, 483
Chavez, Cesar, 345, 400, *402,* 402–403, 405, *405,* 491, R39
Chemehuevi tribe, *m59*
Chemical industry, 394
Chevat, Richie, 176
Chickens, 135
Chico, R44
Children in History
  Games for Miwok children, 80
  Mamie Tape, 318
  Pablo Tac, 138
  Virginia Reed, *203*
  Weedpatch Camp, *371*
Children's Magazine Guide, R32
Chile, 150
China, 229, 407
  trade with, 434
Chinatowns, *38,* 316, *316*
Chinese, discrimination against, 242, *243,* 289, *314,* 318
Chinese Americans, *240, 317*
Chinese Exclusion Act, 318
Chinese immigrants, 289

Chinese New Year, *317*
Chinese workers, 289, *290–291,* 291, 306, 316–317
Chocolate Mountains, R44
Christianity, 111, 127
See also Religion
Chronology, R51
Chumash Indians, 112
Chumash Painted Cave State Historic Park, *71, m71*
Chumash tribe, 2, *m59,* 68, 69, *70,* 70–71, *86*
Cinco de Mayo, 408
Cities, 483
Citing sources, R35
Citizens, 382
Citizenship, I12
Be an Active Citizen, 490–491
Democratic Institutions, 408
Democratic Principles, 150, 464, 475
Democratic Values, 248, 359
Helping in Times of Need, 46–47
Symbols of Pride, 256
Citizenship Day, 406, 408
Citrus fruits, 303, *311*
City commission, 485
City council, 484
City manager, 484, R51
City services, *483*
Civil Practice Act of 1850, 224
Civil rights, 401, R51
Civil Rights movement, 401
Civil War, 289, 321
Claim, 230, R51
Clair Engle Lake, R44
Clams, 63, 70
Clappe, Louise, 179, *179,* 233, *233*
Clapper board, *367*
Clark, William, 97
Classify, 74, R51
Clay, Henry, *250*
Clay pots. *See* Pottery
Clean air laws, 462
Clear Lake, 66
Climate, 29, 29–33, 43, 45, 57, 69, 77, 323, 434, R51
Clipper ships, 183, 228
A Closer Look
Building the Railroad, *290*
The Golden Gate Bridge, 373
Hydraulic Mining, *241*
Making Acorn Flour, *78–79*
A Presidio, *128–129*
A Rancho, 167
A Spanish Galleon, 114
A Spanish Mission, *137*
The State Capitol, 471
A Wagon Train, *200*
Clothing, 60, 65, 160, 191, 234, 238–239
Clothing industry, 394
Clyman, James, *192*
Coachella, R44
Coachella Valley, 23
Coast Ranges, 20, 21, R44
Coast redwoods. *see* Redwoods
Coastal plain, 20, R51
Coastal region, *m4,* 19, 20, 41, 42, 65, 68, *m69*
Cohan, George M., 361
Colleges and universities, 448
Coloma, 227, R44
Coloma schoolhouse, *261*
Colombia, 150
Colonel Allensworth State Historic Park, R45
Colony, 119, R51
Colorado, 216, 370
Colorado Desert, *m20,* 23, 305, R45
Colorado River, *m4,* 6, 14, 23, 87, 192, R45
Colton Hall (Monterey), *223,* 248
Colusa, R45
Coming to California **(Kim),** 344
Commercial farms, 301, 394, R51
Committee of Vigilance, 236, *242*
Communication, 279, R51
Community colleges, 448
Community leaders, R28
Community resources, R28, R33
Commute, 395, R51
Compare and contrast, 182
Compass rose, 162, R51
Competition, 296, 323, R51
Composting, 446
Compromise, 250, R51
Compromise of 1850, 250, *254*
Computer disk, R28
Computer industry. *See* High-tech industry
Computer operators, 438
Computers, *396,* R30
Conduct an interview, 283
Conflicts, 254
Congress, U.S., 250, 408, 464, 467
Congressional Medal of Honor
Doolittle, James, 346, 383
Gonzales, David M., 346, 383
Conquistador, 111, R51
Consequence, 376, R51
Conservation, 451, R51
Constitution, 249, R51
Constitution of the United States, 359, *462–463,* 486
Construction industry, 394, *431*
Consumer, 238, *434,* R51
Consumer goods, 362, *434*
Continents, R51
Convention, 247, R51
Cook, James, 98, 99, 119
Cooperate, 71, R51
Coordinate grid system, 17, R51
Corn, 85, 87, 159
Cortés, Hernando, 110, 111, 112, *113,* 182, R39
Cost, 111, R51
Costanoan tribe, *m59*
Costume designers, 438
Cosumnes River, *m232,* R45
Council Bluffs, Iowa, 286
Council-manager form of municipal government, 484
County, 481, R51
County governments, 481–482
County jails, 482
County seat, 481, R51
Courts, 486
Cowhands (vaqueros), *164, 165*
Cowhides, 160, *161,* 188
Coyotes, *23*
Crabs, 70
Cradles (bed), 65
Cradles (mining tool), 231
Create a display, 498
Create an advertisement, 383
Creating Yosemite National Park **(Rudy),** 498
Crescent City, *m17,* R45
Crespí, Juan, 98, 120, R39
Crime-prevention groups, 47
Criollos, 149, 154, R51
Critical Thinking Skills, I11
analyze, 24, 81
compare primary and secondary sources, 124
distinguish fact from fiction, 204
distinguish fact from opinion, 196–197
identify multiple causes and effects, 154–155
make an economic decision, 488–489
make it relevant, 24
make a thoughtful decision, 376–377
solve a problem, 454–455
Crocker, Charles, 288, R39
Crops, 43, 159, 305
barley, 159
beans, 85, 87, 159
corn, 85, 87, 159
melons, 87
peas, 159
pumpkins, 87
squash, 85
wheat, 159
See also specific crops
Crosby, Helen, 251
Crow Indians, 195
Cry of Dolores *(el Grito de Dolores),* 149
Cultural heritage
Bear Flag, *210*
California Indians Today, 86
Chinese New Year, *317*
Culture, 59, 408, 409
Custom, 138, R51
Cuyama River, R45
Cuyama Valley, 2, 69

D

D-Day invasion, 381, *381*
Dairy products, 431, 434
Damashek, Sandy, 264
Dams, 394
Dana, Richard Henry, 160, R39
Dance, 86, *409*
Davis, Gray, 417, 475, 486, R39
Davis, William, 165, R39
The Dawn of the World: Myths and Tales of the Miwok Indians of California (Merriam), 60
De la Guerra, Pablo, *252*
De Solá, Pablo Vicente, 151
Death Valley, *m4,* 7, 19, 24, *24,* R45
Death Valley National Park, *m469,* R45
Decade, 132, R51
Declaration of Rights, 471
Deed, *253*
Deer, *11,* 44, *55,* 58, *58,* 63, 72
Defense industry, 396
Deficit, 452, R51
Delano, 403, R45
Delegate, *247,* 248, R51
Delta, 22, R51
Demand, 191, R51
Democracy, 150, 463, R51
Denmark, 315
Department of Motor Vehicles (DMV), 473
Depression, 369, R51
Derricks, *324,* 324, *362,* R51
Desert areas, 3
Desert collared lizard, *7*
Desert plants, 44
Desert region, 19, 23–24, 44, 45, *84*
Deserts, *m4,* 7, 14
Devil's Postpile National Monument, *m469,* R45
Diablo Range, R45
Diaries, 138
  Eliza P. Donner Houghton, 205
Diary writing activities, 233
Dictionary, R28, R31
DiMaggio, Joe, R39
Directors, 438
Disaster relief, 46–47
Disaster teams. *See* Neighborhood Watch
Discrimination, 242, 289, 318, 371, 401, R52
Diseases, 138
Diseños, 157, *162–163,* R52
Disney, Walt, *443,* R39
Distance markers, 398
Distances, comparing on maps, 398
District attorney, 482
Diverse economy, 394, R52
Diversity, 406–409
Division of labor, 79, R52
Dockworkers, 431
Documentary sources, 204, R52
Dogwood tree, *445*
Doheny, Edward, 324, R39
Dolores, Mexico, 148
Domínguez Rancho, 214, R45
Donahue Higher Education Act, *447*
Donner, Eliza, *205,* R39
Donner, George, 202, R39
Donner, Jacob, 202, R39
Donner Lake, 202
Donner party, 198, 202–203, *m202*
Doolittle, James, 346, 383, R39
Double-bar graph, 336, R52
Doves, 7
Downieville, R45
Drake, Francis, 113, *113,* R39
Draw conclusions, 270
Drive-in movies, *393*
Drive-in restaurants, *392*
Drought, 32, 87, 370, R52
Dugout canoes. *See* Canoes
Duncan, Isadora, 441, R39
Dust, in Owens Valley, 327
Dust Bowl, 370–371, *m370, 375,* R45
Dust storm, *376*
DVDs, R29

E

Eagle Lake, R45
Early European Explorers to Alta California, *m113*
Early Mail Routes in California, *m280–281*
Earth geography, 16
Earthquakes, 42, 46, 47, *47,* 72, 330–331, *330–331*
Eastern Hemisphere, 13, 16, R45
Eastwood, Clint, R39
Echeandía, José María, 192, R39
Economic decisions, *488*
Economy, 135, 238–239, R52
  of California, 151, 238–239, 351, 359, 361, 430–431, 452–453
Editing, R36
Education, 168, 393, 446–449
Edwards Air Force Base, 345, *396,* 397
Eel River, R45
Effect, 154, R52
  See also Cause; Cause and effect
El Camino Real, 126, 127, R45
El Capitan, 52, *445*
El Centro, R45
El Grito de Dolores (the Cry of Dolores), 149
"El Ranchito," 178
Elected officials, 464
Elections. *See* Referendums
Electric power, 394, *450*
Electricity, 282, 325
Electronics industry, 394, 396
Elephants, 406
Elevation, 26, *m27, m95,* R52
Elevations of Southern California, *m95*
Elk, 58, *58,* 62, 63, 64
The Emigrants' Guide to Oregon and California (Hastings), 202
Encyclopedia, R32
Energy crisis, 451, R52
Engineers, 431
England, 113
English colonies, 97
Entertainment Industry, 363–364
Entrepreneurs, 238, 238–239, *239,* R52
Environment, 59, 240–241, 423
Equal rights, 400
Equator, 13, 16, 29, R52
Esselen tribe, *m59*
Ethnic groups, 408, R52
Eu, March Fong, R39
Eureka, *m17,* R45
Eureka (state motto), 472
Europe, 229, 315, 379, 434
European settlements in California, 289, 315
Europeans, 118
Evidence, R52
Executive branch, 464, 473, 484
Expedition, R52
Expedition of the Donner Party and Its Tragic Fate, The (Donner), 205
Expeditions, 99, 106–109
Exploration, 111–117
Explorers, 111, *113,* 201
Exploring California's Coast (Friedman), 176
Explosives, 291
Export markets, 433
Exports, 301, 434, R52
Eyewitness accounts, 203, 205

F

Fact, 196, R52
Factories, 380, 394
Facts About California, R20–R21
Facts About California Counties, R22–R25
Facts About California Governors, R26–R27
Fairfield, R45
Fairness, 321, 405
Families, on ranchos, 167–168
Farallon Islands, 20, R45
Farmers, *302,* 421, 431, 434
Farming, 85, 135, 268, 301, 370
  in the Central Valley, *268*
Farmland, 44
Farms, 43, 301
Farmworkers, *370, 402,* 403
  See also Migrant farmworkers
Fast Fact
  abandoned ships, 237
  Cabrillo, Juan Rodríguez, 112
  California statehood, 251
  California's population, 35
  climbing California's fourteeners, 21
  Death Valley, 24

gold seekers, 231
Great Depression, 369
Monterey Convention, 247
presidios, 129
Queen Calafia, 111
Rendezvous, 191
sailors, 115
San Francisco, 316
transcontinental railroad workers, 290
Faults, *42, 45,* R52
Favorites, R30
Feather River, 78, R45
Feather River Valley, 32
Feathers, 66
Federal, 463, R52
Federal government, 464–465
Federal Radio Commission, 363
Feinstein, Dianne, 403, 418, *418,* 464, R39
Ferndale, *38*
Ferries, 237
Fertile, 22, R52
Fertile soil, 43, 198, 271, 431, 434
Fiction, 204, R52
Fiddletown, *266*
Field, Stephen J., 283, 465, R39
Field Trips, I12
Balboa Park, 494, *494*
Carmel Mission, 172–173
Marshall Gold Discovery State Historic Park, 260–261
Petersen Automotive Museum, 412–413
San Francisco Cable Car Museum, 340–341
State Indian Museum, 92–93
Field workers, 434
Fiestas, 167, R52
Figs, 317
Figueroa, José, 151, 152, R39
Film and television production, 363–364, *364, 366–367,* 394, 439, *439*
Film editors, 438
Film industry. *See* Film and television production
Finance, *431*
Fire department, *482,* 483
Fire in the Valley **(West),** 312–313
Firefighters, *46, 473*
Fires, 33, 72
Fireworks, *425*
First African Methodist Episcopal Church, 178
First Salmon ceremony, 64
Fishing, 43, 44, 58, 64, 66, 77, 80
Fishing industry, *40, 436*
Flags, 210
Flood control districts, 485
Floods, 32, 46, 305
Florida, 119
Florin, *m22,* 333
Flour, 78
Flowcharts, 478–479, *479,* R52
Flower, state, 19
Folsom Lake, R45
Font, Pedro, 141, *141*
Food exports, 434
Food gathering, 58
Food processing, 434, R52
Food products, 433
Foothill Farm, *m22*
Foothills, 3
Forecastle, *115*
Forest fires, 32, *33,* 46
Forest products, 14, 41, 44
Forests, 14
Fort Ord, 379
Fort Ross, *160,* R45
Fort Ross State Historic Park, *m160*
Forts, 199
Forty-niners, 226, 228, 228–229, R52
442 Regimental Combat Team, 382
Fourteeners, 21
Foxes, 7, 52, 54, *55*
France, 301, 360, 379
Free and Slave States in 1850, *m255*
Free state, 224, 249
Freedoms, 463
Freeways, *389,* 395, 395
Fremont, California, 394, *432,* R45
Frémont, Jessie Ann Benton, *201,* R39
Frémont, John C., 178, *178, 201, 208,* 209, 214, R39
Fresno, *m17, 36,* 296, R45
Friant–Kern Canal, *374*
Friedman, Nan, 176
Frontier, 191, R52
Fruits, 64, 431, 434
apricots, 43, 434
citrus, 266
figs, 317
grapefruits, 303
grapes, 107, 305, 317, 403, 434
kiwifruits, 43
lemons, 303
melons, 43, 87, 305, 317
oranges, 266, *300,* 303, *303*
peaches, 43, 391
strawberries, 317, 333, *333*
Fry, Johnny, 281, R39
Fuerte de los Rusos, 160
Fugitive Slave Act, 250
Fur traders, 160
Fur trappers, *191*
Furs, 188

Gable, Clark, *365*
Gabrielino tribe, 2, *m59,* 69, *m69,* 72–73, *73,* 86, 98
Galleon, 114, *114–115,* R52
Galley, *114*
Gálvez, José de, 120, R39
Gambel's quail, *23*
Games, 80
Gardens, 440
Garland, Sherry, 186–189
Gas masks, *361*
Gasoline, 324
Gatherers, 58, 66, 70, 78, 80
Gavel, *474*
Gazetteer, R44–R49
Gehry, Frank O., 442
General law cities, 483
Generation, 449, R52
Genthe, Arnold, 375
Geography
Angel Island, 315, *m315*
Chumash Painted Cave State Historic Park, 71, *m71*
Fort Ross, 160, *m160*
Imperial Valley, 305, *m305*
A Northern Passage, 119, *m119*
Sacramento, 22, *m22*
San Andreas Fault, 42, *m42*
Silicon Valley, 432, *m432*
A Western State, 14, *m14*
Geography terms, I18–I19
Geologist, *45*
George, Ronald M., *474,* R40
GeoSkills CD-ROM, 17, 26, 39, 117, 219, 299, 436
German immigrants, 317
German soldiers, *381*
Germany, 379
trade with, 433
GI Bill of Rights, 393
Giannini, Amadeo Pietro, 332–333, R40
Giant sequoias, 31, *31*
Gibbs, Mifflin, 236, *240,* R40
Gillespie, Archibald, 214, R40
"Giver of Life," 72
Glaciers, 57, R52
Glossary, R50–57
GO Online
activities, 96, 176, 344
multimedia biographies, 123, 169, 195, 253, 293, 307, 321, 365, 375, 405, 443, 477
primary sources, 83, 163
virtual tours, 93, 173, 261, 341, 413, 495
Goats, 135
Going for the Gold **(Widener),** 264
Gold, 113, 177, 227
Gold mining, 179, 229, 230–231, 472
Gold rush, 22, 227, 301, R52
Golden Age of Hollywood, 439
Golden Gate, 373, R45
Golden Gate Bridge, 368, *372–373, 425*
Golden Gate Bridge **(Hulin),** *416*
Golden poppy (state flower), 19
The Golden Spike **(Skelton),** 344
Golf courses, 44, *45*
Gonzales, David M., 346, 383, R40
Goose Lake, R45
Government, 70, 71, 466–467, R52

levels of, 466–467, *466–467*
powers of, 464
programs of, 374
Governors, 358, 417, 419, R26–R27
Granary, 78, 87, R52
Grapefruits, 303
Grapes, 107, 305, 317, 403, *405*, 434, 472
Grapes of Wrath, The (Steinbeck), 347, 371
Grass, 44
Gray fox, 52, *55*
Great Basin, 200
Great Depression, 369
Great Pathfinder (John C. Frémont), 178
Great Plains, *m5*, 189
Great Salt Lake, Utah, 192, 202
Great Seal of the State of California, *496*
The Great Wall of Los Angeles, 440
Gregory, Kristiana, 274–277
Grid system, R53
Grizzly bear (state animal), 52–55, 257, 472
Groups, working together in, 58
Growing seasons, 43, R53
Growth, 333, 393
Guidebook writing activity, 203
Gulf of Mexico, *m5*
Gum Sam ("Gold Mountain"), 229
Gwin, William M., *250*, R40

Hacienda, 159, R53
Hahn, William, *295*
Hallidie, Andrew Smith, 340, R40
Hamilton, Billy, 281, R40
Hammond, Lavren, *480*
Hanford, R45
Harbors, 20, 323
Hardware, 160
Harvest Dance, *73*
Hastings, Lansford W., 202
Hatch lines, 219, R53
Hats, 65
Hawaiian Islands, 99
Hayes, Benjamin, 224–225
Hayes, Rutherford B., 490
Healdsburg, 160, R45
Hearst, Phoebe Apperson, R40
Hearst, William Randolph, R40
Hearst Castle, 442
Hemisphere, 13, R53
Hercules ("Spruce Goose"), *394*
Heritage, 408, R53
Hetch Hetchy Aqueduct, 330, 335, *m335*, R46
Hetch Hetchy Valley, 334, *334*
Hidalgo y Costilla, Miguel, 149, *151*, *154*, *155*, R40
Hides. *See* Cowhides
High school, 249
High-tech, 396, R53
High-tech industry, 396, 430, 432–433
Highway 1, *398*
Highway construction, *452*
Highway system, 333, 362, 392
Hiking, 44
Himler, Ron, 146–147
Hispanic Americans. *See* Latinos
Historic sites, 467
Historical maps, 116–117, 175
Hockney, David, 440
Hollister, R46
Hollywood, 364, R46
Hollywood sign, *367*, *438–439*
Hollywood YMCA, 418
Holtville, R46
Hong Kong, 420, 433
Hoover, Herbert, 465, R40
Hopkins, Mark, 288, R40
Horse races, 167
Horses, *103*, 122, 135, 159, 164
Hotels, 44, 240
Houghton, Eliza P. Donner, 205
House of Pacific Relations, 494
House of Representatives, 403, 464
Houses, *44*, 65, *66*, *72*, 76, 78, 80, *85*, 86, 87, 112, 136, *337*, 394
How a Bill Becomes a Law, 478–479
How the Robin Got His Red Breast, 60
How State Tax Money Is Spent in California, 2004–2005, 452, *452*
Hoya, Oscar de la, R40
Huerta, Dolores, 345, 346, 402, *403*, 491, R40
Hughes, Howard, R40
Hughes Aircraft Company, *394*
Human features, R53
Humboldt Bay, R46
Humid, 32, R53
Hunting, 58, *58*, 66, *70*, 78, *80*, *93*
Huntington, Collis, P., 288, R40, R44
Hupa tribe, *m59*, 63, *m63*, *64*, 65
Hydraulic mining, 241
Hydroelectric power, 325, R53

I Am an American Day. *See* Citizenship Day
I Love You, California (Silverwood)(state song), 460–461
Ice, 304
Ice Age, 57
Idaho, *m17*
Immigrants, 199, 242, 267, *314*, 317, 333, 407, *407*, R53
Immigrants in California, 1900, *316*
Immigration, 315, 407, R53
Imperial, R46
Imperial Valley, 6, 23, 305, *m305*, 394, 421, R46
Import, 433, R53
Independence, 149, R53
India, 407
India Association of America, 346
Indian culture, 487
Indian governments, 486
Indian Island, 89
Indiana, 25
Indio, R46
Industry, 41, R53
Inflation, 239, R53
Influenza, 138
Information storage, 396
Initiative, 470, 475, 491
Inset map, R53
Interdependence, 433, R53
Interior Plains, *m5*
Intermediate direction, R53
International trade, 431, 433, 434, R53
Internet, R28
Interpret, R53
Interviews, R33
Invest, 288, R53
Ipai tribe. *See* Kumeyaay tribe
Ireland, 407
Irish immigrants, 289
Irish potato famine, 177
Irish workers, 289, 291
Irrigation, 23, 44, R53
Irrigation districts, 305, 485
Irrigation projects, 312–313
Irrigation systems, 394
Irving, Washington, 197
Isabella Lake, R46
Ishi, *93*, R40
Ishi (Sweeny), 96
Isthmus, 228, R53
Isthmus of Panama, 228, R46
Italian immigrants, 317
Italy, 301
Iwasaki, Laura, 354
Iwasaki, Shiro, 357

J. Paul Getty Center (Los Angeles), 440, *441*
Jackrabbit, *23*
Jackson, R46
Jackson, Helen Hunt, R40
Jackson, Odis, R40
Jails, 483
January Temperatures in California, *m29*
Japan, 15, 379, *381*
trade with, 433
Japanese Americans, 307, 333, 375, 382, *382*, *385*
Japanese Association of America, 307
Japanese farm workers, *333*
Japanese Friendship Garden, 494
Japanese immigrants, 307, 317

Japantown, *483*
Jeans, 234, 238–239
Jet Propulsion Laboratory, 396
Jets, *351*
Jewelry, 67
Jimmy Spoon and the Pony Express (Gregory), 274–277
Jobs, 373
Jobs, Steven, *397,* R40
Johnson, Hiram, *358,* 358–359, R40
José, Nicolas, 136, R40
Joshua Tree National Park, 469, R46
Joyner-Kersee, Jackie, R40
Judah, Theodore, *267,* 287, R40
Judges, 482
Judicial branch, 464, 465, *465,* 474, 482
July Temperatures in California, *m29*
Jury trial, 482, R53
Justice, *464*
Justices, of state Supreme Court, *474*

Kaiser, Henry J., 380, R40
Kansas, 370
Kansas City, Missouri, 323
Karuk tribe, *m59,* 63, *m63*
Kearny, Stephen Watts, 214, R40
Keel, *114*
Keith, William, 317, R40
Kelsey, Nancy, *248*
Kennedy, Anthony, 465, R40
Kennedy, John F., 345
Kentucky, 321
Kenya, 407
Kern County, 396
Kern River, *m4,* R46
Kientepoos, Chief, *267,* 320, *320,* R41
Kilimanjaro, *21*
Kindergartens, 317
King, Martin Luther, Jr., *400,* 401, R41
Kings Canyon National Park, 423, 469, R46
Kiwifruits, 43
Klamath Indians, 266
Klamath Mountains, R46
Klamath River, 2, 64
Korea, trade with, 433
Kumeyaay tribe, *m59,* 69, *69,* **69,** *m69,* *72,* 72–73
Kwan, Michelle, R41

La Brea Tar Pits, 99
La Purísima Mission, 146–147
Labels, *303*
Labor, 166, R53
Labor union, 402, R53
Laguna Beach, 69
Lake Almanor, R46
Lake Berryessa, R46
Lake Oroville, R46
Lake Tahoe, *m4,* 6, *m17,* 21, *26,* R46
Lakeport, R46
Land, 67
Land Act of 1851, 251
Land bridge, 57
Land grants, 156, **157,** 199, 251–252, 291, R53
  See also Diseños
Land management, 72
Land routes to California, 191, 193
Land use, 72, 434, 436, *m437,* R54
Landforms, *m4,* 45, 52
Landforms in California, *m4–5*
Landmarks, 162
Landscape, 44, *45*
Landslides, 46
Lange, Dorothea, 374, 375, *375,* R41
Language, 59
Laos, 407
Lassen Peak, 21, R46
Lassen Volcanic National Park, 469, R46
"Last Spike," *288*
Lasuén, Fermín Francisco de, 141, *141*
Latinos, 401, 402, 403
Latitude and Longitude Grid, *16*
Laurgaard, Rachel K., 204
Lava Beds National Monument, 469, R46
Lawmakers, 249
Laws, 466
Legends, 60, R54
  Chumash, 71
  Gabrielino, 72
  Miwok, 52–55, 60–61
  See also specific legends
Legislative branch, 464, 484
Legislature, **249,** 483, R54
Leidesdorff, William, R41
Lemons, 303
Lessac, Frané, 426–429
Letter writing activities, 122
Lettuce, 305
Levee, **305,** 306, *306,* 317, R54
Lewis, Meriwether, 97
Libraries, 483
The Life of a Forty-Niner, 234
Lifeguards, *40*
Lindbergh, Charles, *362*
Line graph, **244,** R54
Lines of latitude, **16,** R54
Lines of longitude, **16,** R54
Literature
  Amelia's Road (Altman), 390–391
  With Corporal Tapia: from a Personal Tour of La Purisima (Young), 146–147
  Fire in the Valley (West), 312–313
  The Grapes of Wrath (Steinbeck), 371
  How the Robin Got His Red Breast, 60
  Jimmy Spoon and the Pony Express (Gregory), 274–277
  Open Hands, Open Heart: The Story of Biddy Mason (Robinson), 224–225
  Sierra (Siebert), 10–11
  So Far from the Sea (Bunting), 354–357
  Two Bear Cubs: A Miwok Legend from California's Yosemite Valley (San Souci), 52–55
  Valley of the Moon: the Diary of Maria Rosalia de Milagros (Garland), 186–189
  Voyage of Faith: Father Serra in California (McGovern), 106–109
  The Wonderful Towers of Watts (Zelver), 426–429
Livestock, 43
Lizards, 7
Local governments, 467, 480
  See also County governments; Indian governments; Municipal governments; Special districts; Regional body
Location, *12,* R54
  California, 13–15
Locator, R54
Lockheed, Allan, R41
Lockheed, Malcolm, R41
Lompoc, R46
London, Jack, 441, R41
Long Beach, *36,* 323, 380, R46
Long-term planning, **451,** 452, 453, R54
Lopez, Nancy, R41
Los Altos, R46
Los Altos, California, *m432*
Los Angeles, *m17,* 36, *36,* 42, 69, 99, 159, 178, 199, 214, 296, 322, 323, 360, *383,* 395, 408, 409, 442, R46
Los Angeles Aqueduct, 267, 322, 325, *326, m326, 328*
Los Angeles County, 2, 433
Los Angeles County Courthouse, 418
Los Angeles International Airport, 418, 442
Los Angeles Plaza Church, *369*
Los Angeles pueblo, 130
Los Angeles River, 325, R46
Lu Ng, 229
Lugo family, *168*
Luiseño tribe, *m59,* 69, 72–73, 138
Lumber, 44, *436*

M

Machinery, 433
Madera, *m17,* R46
Magellan, Ferdinand, 182
Maidu tribe, 3, *m59,* 76, *77,* **77,** *m77,* 78–79
Mail delivery, 271, 274
Main idea and details, 6
Major Gold Mining Towns, 1849–1859, *m232*
Major Mountains of the World, *m20–21*
Makeup artists, 438

Makil, Ivan, *486*
Making Movies in California, 366
Malaysia, trade with, 433
Malibu, 69
Mammoths. *See* Woolly mammoths
Manifest destiny, *207,* **207,** 216, R54
Manly, William Lewis, 7
Manufacturing industry, 394, *431*
Manzanar War Relocation Camp, 354–357, *355, 356, 357, 358,* 382
Manzanita, *187*
Map activities, 24, 26, 81
Map and Globe Skills, I11
California Atlas, 96
Follow Routes on a Historical Map, 116–117, 175
Read a Land Use and Products Map, 436–437, 497
Read a Population Map, 38–39
Read a Road Map, 398–399
Read a Time Zone Map, 298–299, 343
Read and Compare Historical Maps, 218–219, 263
Use an Elevation Map, 26, 95
Use Latitude and Longitude, 16–17
Map legend, R54
Map scale, R54
Map title, R54
Mapmakers, 201
Maps
Angel Island, *m315*
Anza's Expedition, 1775–1776, *m175*
California: Climate, *mR16*
California: Physical, *mR15*
California: Political, *mR14*
California: Vegetation, *mR17*
California Counties, *m481*
California in the United States, 1886, *m268–269*
California Land Use, *m497*
California Land Use and Products, 436, *m437*
California Latitude and Longitude, *m17*
California Tribal Lands, *m487*
Canada, *mR18*
Dust Bowl, *m370*
Early European Explorers to Alta California, *m113*
Early Mail Routes in California, *m280–281*
Elevations in California, *m27*
Elevations of Southern California, *m95*
Fort Ross State Historic Park, *m160*
Free and Slave States in 1850, *m255*
Hetch Hetchy Aqueduct, *m335*
Imperial Valley, *m305*
January Temperatures in California, *m29*
July Temperatures in California, *m29*
Los Angeles Aqueduct, *m326*
Major Gold Mining Towns, 1849–1859, *m232*
Mexican California, 1840, *m180–181*
Mexican-American War in California, *m215*
Mexico, *mR19*
National Park System in California, *m469*
Natural Regions of California, *m20*
A Northern Passage, *m119*
Overland to California, *m202*
Pacific and Mountain Time Zones, *m343*
Pacific Basin, *m420–421*
Pacific Routes of the Spanish Galleons, *m117*
Population Density in California, *m39*
Precipitation in California, *m30*
Railroad Companies, Late 1880s, *m296*
Routes to Alta California, 1769–1776, *m120*
Routes of Early People, *m57*
Routes of the Forty-Niners, *m229*
Sacramento, *m22*
San Andreas Fault, *m42*
Sending Messages Across the Country, *m278–279*
Silicon Valley, *m 432*
Some California Tribes, *m59*
Some Tribes of the Desert, *m85*
Some Tribes of the Northern Coast, *m63*
Some Tribes of the Southern Coast, *m69*
Southern California, *m415*
Spanish Missions, 1769–1823, *m127*
Trailblazers from the United States, *m193*
Transcontinental Railroad, *m289*
Transportation in California, *m348–349*
The United States, 1845, *m218*
The United States, 1848, *m219*
United States: Overview, *mR8–R9*
United States: Physical, *mR12–R13*
United States: Political, *mR10–R11*
United States Time Zones, *m299*
Western Hemisphere: Physical, *mR7*
Western Hemisphere: Political, *mR6*
Western United States, 1845, *m263*
Western United States, 1848, *m263*
World: Physical, *mR4–R5*
World: Political, *mR2–R3*
Mare Island, *361*
Mariachi, *409*
Marin County, 372, 433
Mariposa, R46
Markleeville, R47
Marsh, John, 198, 200, R41
Marshall, James, *226,* 227, R41
Marshall Gold Discovery State Historic Park, 260–261
Martin, Glenn, 363, R41
Martin, John, 106–109
Martinez, R47
Marysville, 237, *244,* R47
Mason, Biddy, 178, *178,* 224–225, 253, *253,* R41
Massachusetts, 199
Mastodons, 57
Mayer, Louis B., 364, 365, *365,* R41
Maynard, Robert, R41
Mayor-council form of municipal government, 484
Mazellan, Ron, 274–277
McGovern, Jim, 106–109
Measles, 138
Measuring Worm, 52–55, *54*
Medals, 346, 383, 405
Medicine, 266, 293
Megaphone, *365–366*
Megquier, Mary Jane, 240, R41
Melons, 43, 305, 317
Mendez, Sylvia, 401, R41
Merced, 296, R47
Merced River, 52, *m232,* R47
Mesquite, 85
Mestizo, 149, 154, R54
Metcalf, Victor H., 332
Metro-Goldwyn-Mayer (MGM), 364, 439
Metropolitan area, 36, R54
Metropolitan Transportation Commission (MTC), 485
Mexican American. *See* Latinos
Mexican Americans, 401
Mexican California, 208–209
Mexican California, 1840, *m180–181*
Mexican citizenship, 157
Mexican immigrants, 393
Mexican rancho period, 156–159
Mexican rule in California, 150–153
Mexican Settlements in California, *m157*
Mexican War for Independence, 148–151, 154
Mexican workers, 381
Mexican-American War, 212–217, *213*
Mexican-American War in California, *m215*
Mexicans, 242
Mexico, *m5, 13,* 23, 42, 59, 111, 150, *151,* 199, 213, 229, 381, 407, *mR19*
conquest of, 103, 111
trade with, 433, 434
Mexico City, 111, 161, 208
Mexico independence, 97, 151
Mickey Mouse, 443
Microchips, *430*
Middle West, *m14*
Migrant camps, *370, 377,* 390–391
See also Tent Camps

Migrant farmworkers, 405
Migrant Mother **(Lange),** *375*
Migrant workers, 370–371, **371,** 390–391, 402–403, 405, R54
Migration, **315,** *370, 376,* R54
Mill Valley, R47
Mills College, *446,* 448
Minerals, 14, 44, 451
Miners, 229–231, *230,* 237, 317
Minerva (Roman goddess), 472
Mineta, Norman, *385*
Mining, 22
Mining camps, *232,* 232–233
Mining industry, 44
Minor, Wendall, 10–11
Miranda, Juana Briones de, 166, 169
Mirror of the Times **(newspaper),** 236, 240
Mission bells, *121*
Mission life, *135*
Mission San Antonio, 126
Mission San Carlos, *153*
Mission San Carlos Borroméo del Carmel. *See* Carmel Mission
Mission San Diego, *121,* 136
Mission San Diego de Alcalá, 127, R47
Mission San Francisco Solano, 126, *136*
Mission San Gabriel, 98, 136, 192
Mission San Juan Capistrano, *152*
Mission San Luis Obispo, 126, 136
Mission San Luis Rey, 138, *140*
Mission Santa Barbara, *134*
Mission Santa Barbara **(Appelbaum),** 176
Mission Santa Clara, 138
Mission Santa Cruz, 99, 152
Missionary, 98, 119, R54
Missions, 98, 118, **119,** 127, *127, 137*
Mississippi River, *m5*
Missouri, 189, 200, 202
Missouri River, *m5*
Miwok artifacts, *82, 83*
Miwok tribe, 52–55, *m59, m77,* 80
Modesto, *m17,* 296, R47, R54
Modify, 37
Modoc tribe, *m59,* 266, 319–320
Modoc War, 267
Mojave Desert, 23, *m85,* 192, *196,* 325, 351, R47
Mojave pottery, *83*
Mojave tribe, *m59, 87,* **87,** 87–88, *88*
Mokelumne River, *m232,* R47
Molasses, 160
Molina, Gloria, R41
Money, 467
Mono Lake, R47
Monorail, *443*
Mont Blanc, *20*
Monterey, 122, 150, 151, *208,* 213, *213,* 246, 250, 379, R47
Monterey Bay, 99, 110, 114–115, 118, 120, 121, 182, R41, R47
Monterey Convention, *223,* 247
Moon, 396, *397*
Moreno, Carlos, *474*
Morgan, Julia, 442, R41
Mormon Island Emporium, 235
Morrow, Irving, R41
Morse, Samuel F.B., *282, 284,* R41
Morse code, 282
Mortar and pestle, *92*
Mount Diablo, 80
Mount Everest, *21*
Mount McKinley, *21*
Mount Pinos, R47
Mount Shasta, 21, R47
Mount Whitney, *m4,* 19, *20,* 21, R47
Mountain lion, *23,* 52, *53, 55*
Mountain men (fur trappers), 191–194
Mountain ranges, 14
Mountain region, *m4,* 19, 21, 31, 44, 45, 77
Mountain sheep, 44
Mountains, major, *20–21*
Mouse, *55*
Movie camera, *367*
Movies. *See* Film and television production
Muir, John, 25, *25,* 31, 267, 334–335, R41
Muir Woods National Monument, *m469,* R47
Mules, 122, 228
Mulford, Prentice, 231
Mulholland, William, *267,* 325, *325,* R41
Multicultural, 407, **407,** R54
Municipal, 483, R54
Municipal governments, 483–484, *484*
Munitions, 380, R54
Murals, 45, 440
Museum curators, R28
Museums
Aerospace Museum (Balboa Park), *495*
Petersen Automotive Museum, 412–413
San Francisco Cable Car Museum, 340–341
Watts Towers, 426–429
Music, ***I Love You, California*** **(Silverwood),** 460–461
Mussel Slough, *300,* 302

Nahl, Charlesz Christian, 317, R41
Napa, R47
Napa Valley, 20, 317, R47
NASA, 351
National Baseball Hall of Fame, 347
National Farm Workers Association. *See* United Farm Workers of America (UFW)
National Hispanic Heritage Awards, 418
National Park System in California, *m469*
National parks, 25, 467, *469*
National Women's Hall of Fame
Huerta, Dolores, 346
Ride, Sally, 347
Native Americans. *See* California Indians
Native Californians. *See* California Indians
Native Sons Monument, *256*
Natural disasters, 46–47
Natural regions, 19, R54
Natural Regions of California, 19, *m20*
Natural resources, 14, 35, 44, 59, 63, 69, 77, 82, 423, 451, R54
Naturalist, 335, R54
Navel oranges, *300,* 303
Needles, *m17,* R47
Neighborhood Watch, 47, *47*
Neighborhoods, 47
Neophyte, 135, R54
Nepewo, 64
Nevada, 14, *m14, m17,* 24, 216
Nevada City, R47
Neve, Felipe de, 130, R41
New Deal, 373–374, *374*
New Helvetia, 188, 199
New Mexico, 119, 194, 207, 215, 216, 370
New River, R47
New Spain, 111, 127, 146–147
Newport Beach, *451*
News writing activities, 344
Ng Poon Chew, R41
Nigeria, 407
Nisenan tribe, *m59,* **77,** *m77*
Nixon, Richard, 465, R41
Nobel Prize for Literature, 347
Noguchi, Isamu, 440, *440,* R41
Nolan, Mae Ella, R41
Nomads, *56–57,* 57
Nonfiction books, R28, R32
Nonrenewable, 451, R54
North Africa, 379
North America, 7, *13,* 14, 57, 228
North Pole, 13, 16, 29, R47
Northeast, *m14*
Northern California, 2
Northern Hemisphere, 13, 16, R47
Northridge, 47
Northrop, John K., R41
Nuts, 58, 64, 77, 434
acorns, 85
almonds, 43, 434
pine nuts, 66
piñions, 85
pistachio nuts, 317
walnuts, 43

INDEX

Oahu, Hawaii, 378
Oak trees, 84
Oakland, *m17, 36,* 333, *359,* R47
Oakland Museum of California, 440
Ocean currents, 114, 120, R54
Oceans, 57
Oceanside, R47
Ochoa, Ellen, R41
"The Octopus," 296
Office of education, 482
Officials, 482
O'Gorman, Juan, 154
Ohio River, *m5*
Oil, 451
Oil derricks in Southern California, *268*
Oil industry, 324, 359, *362,* 380, 394
Oil rigs. *see* Derricks
Oil spills, *451*
Okies, 371
Oklahoma, 370, 371
Old Spanish Days festival, 409
Old Spanish Trail, 194, *m202,* R47
Older citizens, R28
Olive press, *131*
Olives, 43, 131, 317, 434
Olsen, Barbara, 186–189
On the Home Front **(Boskey)**, *416*
Open Hands, Open Hearts: The Story of Biddy Mason **(Robinson)**, 224–225
Opinion, 196, R55
Opinion writing activities, 196–197
Opportunity cost, 488, R55
Oral presentations, R37
Orange County, 2, 433
Orange groves, 303
Oranges, 266, *300,* 303, *303,* 304, *342*
Orcas, *435*
Order of the Rising Sun, 307
Oregon, 14, *m17,* 21, 201, 319
Oregon Trail, 200, 201, *m202*
The Original Morse code, *283*
Oroville, R47
Oscar statuette, *438, 496*
Otters, 190
"Over There," 361
Overland Mail Act, *278*
Overland Mail Service, 280
Overland to California, *m202*
Owens Lake, 326–327, R47
Owens River, 267, 312–313, 325, 328, 329, R47
Owens Valley, 312–313, 317, 326–327, 328–329, 382
Oxnard, R47

Pacific Basin, 14–15, **15**, *m420–421,* 433, R47
Pacific Coast, 14, 207
Pacific Coast Highway and Santa Monica, *440*
Pacific and Mountain Time Zones, *m343*
Pacific Ocean, 2, *m4, 13,* 14, *m17,* 30, 70, 114, 360
Pacific Railroad Act, 286, 288, *294*
Pacific Routes of the Spanish Galleons, *m117*
Pacoima, 346
Palm Springs, *m17,* R47
Palo Alto, 432, R47
Panama, 360
Panama, Isthmus of, 360, *360*
Panama Canal, 360, *360*
Panamint Mountains, R47
Paper, 44
Paraguay, 150
Parks, 483
Balboa Park, 494–495
See also Theme parks; National parks
Participation Skills, I11
Resolve Conflict, 254
Parties, 167
Pasadena, 401, *449,* R47
Pasadena Freeway, 394, 395
Paso Robles, *473,* R47
Pass, 194, R55
Patriotism, *477*
Pattie, James Ohio, 193–194, R41
Pattie, Sylvester, 193, R41
Patty Reed's Doll: The Story of the Donner Party **(Laurgaard)**, 204
Peaches, 43, 391
Pearl Harbor, 378, *378,* 379
Pearson, Erik, 42
Peas, 159
Pelosi, Nancy, R42
Peninsula, 112, R55
Pentagon, *417*
People, I8
Periodicals, R28, R32
Pesticides, 346
Petaluma, 159, 160, R47
Peters, Charles, 237
Petersen Automotive Museum, 412–413
Petitions, 475, *491,* R55
Petroleum, 324, *362,* R55
Philippine Islands, 114, 182, 407
Photography, 374, 375, 440, 444
Physical environment, 35, R55
Physical features, R55
Pico, Andrés, *159,* 216, *216, 252,* R42
Pico, Pío, 158–159, 178, *178, 209,* R42
Pictographs, *71*
Pigeons, 80
Pine nuts, 66
Pine trees, *187*
Piñion nuts, 85
Pinnacles National Monument, 469, R47
Pioneers, 200, R55
Pirates, 115, 150
Pistachio nuts, 317
Pit River, R47
Place, I8
Place (geography), I14
Pacific Basin, *420–421*
Placerville, R47
Plank canoes. *See* Canoes
Plants
cactus, 85
creosote bush, *23*
in the desert region, *23*
Joshua Tree, *23*
mesquite, 85, 87
piñion nuts, 85
prickley pear cactus, *23*
screwbeans, 85
tule, 70
yucca, *23*
See also Nuts; Vegetables
Plants and animals of the Desert Region, 23
Plateau, R55
Platte River, *m5*
Playgrounds, 441
Plaza, 130, R55
Plaza Hidalgo, *155*
Poetry, "Sierra" (Siebert), 10–11
Point of View, R55
Point Reyes National Seashore, 469, R48
Points of View
Californios and the United States, 209
The Mission System, 140–141
Relocation of Japanese Americans, 384
Statehood for California, 250
Taxes on Indian Gaming, *486*
Whose Water Is It?, 328–329
Polar bears, *495*
Police department, 483, *483*
Political boundary, 218, R55
Political parties, *491*
Politics, 491
Polk, James K., 206, 207, 228
Pollution, 451, 462, R55
Pomo tribe, *m59, m63,* 66, 93
Pony Express, 274–277, *278,* 281, *281, 282*

***The Pony Express* (Skelton),** *344*
Poppy, golden (state flower), 19
Population, 207, *235,* 237, *237,* 242–243, 333, 371, 380–381, 393, 406, 407
Population density, 36, **38,** 44, 130, 336–337, 393, R55
Population Density in California, *m39*
Population of Native Californians, *139*
Population of San Francisco, *237*
Portolá, Gaspar de, 98, 99, 106, 120, 121, 123, R42
Post office, 467
"Potato King," 267, 307
Potatoes, 267, 306
Pottery, 3, 58, 59, 60, *83,* 86, 87, *88*
Potts, Marie, 76
Poway, *m17*
Power, 450
Power outage, 450
Power plants, 394
Precipitation, **29,** *30,* 31, R55
Precipitation in California, *m30*
Prejudice, **318,** R55
Presidential Medal of Freedom, 405
Presidios, 126, **128,** 128–129, R55
Primary source, **124**
Primary Sources
Ansel Adam's Photographs, *444–445*
California Indian Artifacts, 82–83
A Diseño, 162–163
Great Seal of the State of California, *472*
The Life of a Forty-Niner, 234
Making Movies in California, 366
The Telegraph, 284
The Transcontinental Railroad, 292
A UFW Poster, 402
Yurok Coin Purse, *64*
Prime meridian, **13,** R55
Print resources, R28
Private schools, **447,** R55
Products, 431, *434, 437*
Promontory, Utah, 286, 291
Proofreading, R36
Property ownership, 248
Property taxes. *See* Taxes
Protest, *401, 404*
Public health, 468
Public schools, *249,* 318, 417, *446,* **447,** 448, R55
Public transportation, 41
Publishing a report, R36
Pueblos, 126, **130,** 130–131, 152, 159, R55
Pulitzer prize, 347
Punjabi American Festival, 408

Q

Quails, 7
***Qua-o-ar* ("Giver of Life"),** 2, 72
Queues, *243*
Quincy, R47

R

Rabbits, 7, 58, *58,* 72, 87
Raccoons, 87
Radios, 352, *363*
Railroad companies, *297*
Railroad Companies, Late 1880s, *m296*
Railroads, 267, 271, *287, m289,* 302, *304,* 323
Rain, 30
Rain shadow, **32,** R55
Raisins, 160
Rancherias, 166, **486,** R55
Rancheros, 251–252
Ranching, 103, 434
A Rancho in Mexican California, *180*
Rancho La Brea Tar Pits, 99
Rancho La Purísima Concepción, *169*
Rancho Petaluma, *159*
Ranchos, 158, 158–159, 164–168, 187, 251–252, R55
Rankin, John, *385*
Ratify, **249,** R55
Rattles, *70,* 86
Rattlesnakes, *23,* 87
Readers' Guide to Periodical Literature, R32
Reading Skills
cause and effect, 32, 42, 58, 115, 121, 171, 203, 209, 217, 251, 280, 289, 320, 327, 359, 361, 369, 371, 379, 381, 393, 394, 395, 397, 401, 403, 407, 435
compare and contrast, 20, 21, 66, 73, 86, 182–183, 191, 193, 199, 207, 213, 227, 229, 233, 237, 239, 247, 249, 304, 467, 487
draw conclusions, 61, 136, 139, 168, 194, 243, 270–271, 279, 283, 287, 292, 295, 297, 301, 302, 306, 315, 319, 323, 325, 331, 364, 373, 383, 453, 473, 485
generalize, 37, 102–103, 111, 119, 127, 131, 135, 149, 151, 157, 159, 161, 165, 240, 252, 317, 360, 363, 382, 404, 433, 474
main idea and details, 6–8, 13, 15, 19, 22, 24, 29, 30, 33, 35, 37, 41, 43, 45, 48, 57, 59, 61, 63, 67, 69, 71, 77, 81, 85, 122, 136, 153, 241, 434, 449, 482, 483, 484
summarize, 31, 32, 65, 79, 88, 113, 129, 166, 201, 211, 231, 281, 303, 324, 333, 335, 374, 409, 431, 439, 442, 447, 451, 463, 465, 469, 471, 476, 481
Reading Social Studies, I9
cause and effect, 350–351, 386, 410
compare and contrast, 182, 220, 258
draw conclusions, 308, 338
generalize, 142, 170
main idea and details, 6, 48, 90
summarize, 422–423, 456, 492
Reagan, Ronald, *419,* 465, 477, *477,* R42
Reata, 165
Rebel, **210,** R55
Recall, **475,** R55
Reclamation Service project, 312–313
***Recollections of My Youth at San Luis Rey Mission* (Cesar),** 140
Recreation, *41,* 43, *44,* 232–234
Recycle, **381,** 483, R55
Red Bluff, R48
Redding, *m17,* R47
Red-Tailed Hawk, 52, *55*
Redwood National Park, 469, R48
Redwoods, 30, 66
Reed, Virginia, 204, R42
Referendums, 475, **476,** 491, R55
Reform, **359,** R55
Refrigerated railroad cars, 271, 304, *304*
Refrigerators, 394
Regional body, **485,** R55
Regions, *370,* R55
Regions of California, 18–24, 62–67, 68–73
Relationship to the Constitution of the United States, 471
Relative location, **14,** R55
Relief, **26,** R55
Religion, 1, 3, 64, 65, 136
Religious services, 233
Relocation of California Indians, 319–320
Relocation camps, 375, 378, *382,* **382,** 385, R55
See also individual camps
Relocation of Japanese Americans, *384,* 384–385
Renewable, **451,** R55
Reporting, R35
Reports, R35
Republic, **210,** R56
Research, R56
Research Handbook
community resources, R28
print resources, R28
technology resources, R28
Reservations, **319,** 319–320, 486, R56
Reservoirs, **325,** 394, R56
Resolve Conflict, **254,** R56

Resources, 66, 70
Respect, 25, 195, 443
Responsibilities of citizens, 490–491
Responsibility, 89, 123, 365
Revising a report, R36
Revolt, 136, R56
Rhode Island, 12
Ribbon Falls, 21
Rice, 317
Richmond, 380
Ride, Sally, 347, 396, R42
Ridgecrest, R48
Right, 213
Rights of citizens, 463
Riley, Bennett, 247, R42
Rio Grande, *m5*
River rafting, 44
Rivera, Diego, R42
Rivera y Moncada, Fernando, 120, R42
Riverboats, 228
Rivers, 63
Riverside, 303, R48
Road Map of California, *m399*
Road maps, 398–399
Robinson, Deidre, 224–225
Robinson, John (Jackie), 347, 401, R42
Rock art, *71*
Rock climbing, 21, 44
Rockets, 396
Rocks, 44
Rocky Mountains, *m5*, 87, 190, 191
Rodia, Simon, 426, R42
Rogers, Ginger, *366*
Rogers, Will, *329*
Role-playing activity, 73, 131, 243
Roman Empire, 1
Roosevelt, Franklin D., 368, 373, R42
Roosevelt, Theodore, 14, *25*, *329*, R42
Rose Bowl (Pasadena), *449*
Round houses, 80
Routes, *57*, 191
Routes to Alta California, 1769–1776, *m120*
Routes to California, 228, *229*
Routes of Early People, *m57*
Routes of the Forty-Niners, *m229*
Roybal-Allard, Lucille, R42
Ruiz, Bernarda, 179, *179*, 216, R42
Rural, 36, R56
Rural areas, 44
Russell, Majors, and Waddell company, 274
Russell, William H., R42
Russia, 151, 160
Russian River, 66, 160, R48
Russians, 118, 119
Ryan, T. Claude, R42

S

Sacramento, *m17*, *36*, 80, 188, 250, *266*, 271, 274, 281, 286, 296, 396, 472, R48
Sacramento: A Capital City (Sweeny), 498
Sacramento County, 333
Sacramento Delta, 267, 316–317
Sacramento River, *m4*, 22, 78, 230, 237, 305, 374, R48
Sacramento Valley, 3, 22, 178, 199, 271, 317
Saddlemakers, 159
Saks Fifth Avenue, 418
Salinan tribe, *m59*, *m69*
Salinas, R48
Salinas River, R48
Salinas Valley, 20
Salmon, 64
Salton Sea, 6, *m17*, 23, *37*, R48
San Andreas, R48
San Andreas Fault, *42*, *m42*, R48
San Bernardino, *m17*, 323, R48
San Bernardino County, 32, 433
San Bernardino Mountains, 3, 85, 192
San Diego, 30, *36*, 69, 97, 106–109, 123, 127, 151, 323, *361*, 380, R48
San Diego Bay, 35, 99, 108, 112, 120, 121, 128, R48
San Diego County, 32, 433
San Diego de Alcalá, 121, *124*
San Diego Zoo, 494, *495*
San Franciscans, *332*
San Francisco, *m17*, 22, 30, *34*, *35*, *36*, *38*, *41*, 42, 151, 206, 214, 236, 295, *316*, 330, 372, 440, 444, 447, *483*, R48
San Francisco Bay, 20, 35, 66, 121, 188, 372, R48
San Francisco earthquake (1906), 330–333
San Francisco News, 385
San Francisco Police Department, *483*
San Francisco presidio, 129
San Gabriel, R48
San Gabriel pueblo, 130
San Jacinto Mountains, 3, 85, 120, 122, R48
San Joaquin River, *m4*, 22, 230, 237, *244*
San Joaquin River delta, 306
San Joaquin Valley, 2, 22, 80, 193, 302, 317, 319, 321, 371, 374, R48
San Jose, *m17*, *36*, 166, 250, 432, R48
San José de Guadalupe pueblo, 130
San Luis Obispo, 136, R48
San Luis Reservoir, R48
San Mateo County, 433
San Pasqual, R48
San Pasqual, Battle of, 215
San Pedro, 214
San Pedro Bay, 323, R48
San Rafael, R48
San Souci, Daniel, 52–55
San Souci, Robert D., 52–55
Sanchez, Enrique O., 390–391
Sánchez, José Bernardo, R42
Sanson, Nicholas, 124
Santa Ana, *36*, 363, R48
Santa Ana Valley, 317
Santa Barbara, *m17*, *41*, *51*, *71*, *323*, *409* R48
Santa Clara County, 394
Santa Clara River, R49
Santa Clara Valley, 20
Santa Cruz, *m17*, R49
Santa Cruz Mountains, R49
Santa Cruz pueblo, 130
Santa Fe, 194
Santa Fe Railroad, 323
Santa Fe Trail, *m202*
Santa Lucia Mountains, R49
Santa Monica, 380, R49
Santa Rosa, R49
Santa Rosa Mountains, 84–85
Santa Ynez River, R49
Saroyan, William, 441, R42
Saund, Dalip Singh, 346, *403*, R42
Sausalito, R49
Saving the Redwoods (Sweeny), 96
Sawmills, 421
Scarce, 44, 239, R56
School bus, *485*
School districts, 482
Schools, *249*, 317, 394, 401, 447, 483
Schwarzenegger, Arnold, *419*, *473*, 475, *486*, R42
Scientists, 396, 434
Scope of Jurisdiction, 466–467
Scott's oriole, *23*
Sculptures, 440
Sea level, 24, R56
Sea lions, 63
Search engines, R30
Sebastopol, 160, R49
Secondary source, 124, R56
Secularization, 152, R56
Seed beater, 78–79, *79*
Segregation, 401, R56
Segregation in schools, 447
Seidner, Cheryl A., 89, R42
Semple, Robert, 447, R42
Senate, 464
Senators, 178, 472
Sending Messages Across the Country, *m278–279*
Sequoia National Park, 31, 423, 469, R49
Sequoias. *See* Giant Sequoias; Trees
Serra, Junípero, 97, 98, 106–109, *109*, 118, 120, *121*, 123, *123*, *173*, R42
Serrano tribe, *m59*, *m85*, 86
Service, 41, R56
Service industry, 431, 435, 452, R56
Settlements, 160, 237
Settlers, 131, 207
Severance, Caroline, 359, R42
Shamans, 64, 81, 98, R56
Shang Dynasty (China), 1
Shared powers of government, 468
Shasta, Mount, R47
Shasta Dam, 380
Sheep, 127, 135, 159

Shellfish, 63
Shells, 2, 64, 65, *66*, 67, *67*, *70*, 72, *83*, 86
Sheriff, 482
Shima, George, *267*, 306, 307, *307*, R42
Shipbuilding industry, 380–381, 394
Shipping industry, 41
Ships, 472
Shortage, 380, 451, R56
Siebert, Diane, 10–11
"Sierra" (Siebert), 10–11
Sierra Club, 266, 444
Sierra Club *Bulletin*, 444
Sierra Nevada, 3, 6, 10–11, 21, 22, 23, 31, 77, 78, 80, 178, 193, 201, 202, 230, 287, 325, R49
Sikh religion, 409
Silicon chips, 392, *396*, **396**, 432, 433, R56
Silicon Valley, *m421*, 432–433, *m432*, R49
Silk, 111
Silt, 87, **R56**
Silverwood, F.B., 460–461
Singapore, trade with, 433
Skelton, Renee, 264
Skiing, 44
Skills lessons. *See* Chart and Graph Skills; Critical Thinking Skills; Map and Globe Skills; Participation Skills; Reading Skills
Slave, 224, 228
Slave state, 224, 248–249, 250
Slavery, 224, 248–249, 250, 321
Sloat, John D., 213, R42
Smallpox, 138
Smith, Jedediah Strong, 190, 192, *192*, *196*, R42
Smith, Robert, 224–225, 253
Snakes, 7
Snow, 44, 201, 202–203
Snow White and the Seven Dwarfs, 443
Snowboarding, 44
***So Far from the Sea* (Bunting)**, 354–357
Soapmaking, 136, 160
Soapstone, 2, 72
Soentpiet, Chris K., 354–357
Soil, 43, 370, 434
Solá, Pablo Vicente de, 151, R42
Solar power, *455*
Soldiers, 289, *379*, *383*, 393
Solvang, 315, *409*
Some California Tribes, *m59*
Some Tribes of the Central Valley and Mountains, *m77*
Some Tribes of the Desert, *m85*
Some Tribes of the Northern Coast, *m63*
Some Tribes of the Southern Coast, *m69*
Songs, 86, 460
Sonoma, 126, 127, 157, 214, R49
Sonoma Valley, 20, 317
Sonora, 408, R49
Sonoran Desert, 122
Sound and lighting workers, 438
Sound movies. *See* Film and television production
Soup kitchen, *368*, *369*
South, *m14*
South America, *13*, 57, 97, 111, 150, 188, 228, 229, 315, 407
South Pacific, 379
South Pole, 13, 16, R49
Southern California, 2, *m415*
Southern Hemisphere, 13, 16, R49
Southern Pacific Railroad Company, *294*, 296, *296*, 302, 323
Sovereign, 486, R56
Soviet Union, 379
Space program, 396
Space shuttles, 345, *397*
Spain
exploration by, 110–115, 116–117
Mexican independence from, 148–153, 154–155
settlements by, 118–122, 126–131, 134–139, 140–141
Spanish California
everyday life in, **126–131**, 134–139
missions in, 121, 123, 126, 127, *m127*, 134–139, 140–141
Spanish-Mexican Seal, *257*
Spanish missions, 121, 123, 126, 127, 134–139, 140–141
Spanish Missions, 1769–1823, *m127*
Spanish rule, inequality under, 154
Speaking activities
debate, 327
deliver a speech, 476
Spearing, Craig, 312–313
Special districts, 485, R56
Special effects, *439*, **439**, R56
Specialize, 79, R56
Speech writing activities, 194
Spices, 111, 160
Springs, 85, R56
"Spruce Goose," 394
Squash, 85
Squatter, 209, R56
Squirrels, *58*
St. Francis Dam, 267, 327, *327*
St. Joseph, Missouri, 274, 281
Stagecoach, *273*, **280**, *281*, R56
Stanford, Leland, 288, R42
Stanford Research Park, 394
Stanford University, 432
Stanislaus River, *m232*, R49
Starr, Kevin, I1
Start with a Biography, ***Open Hands, Open Heart: The Story of Biddy Mason* (Robinson)**, 224–225
Start with a Poem, ***Sierra* (Siebert)**, 10–11
Start with a Song, ***I Love You, California***, 460–461
Start with a Story
Amelia's Road (Altman), 390–391
Fire in the Valley (West), 312–313
Jimmy Spoon and the Pony Express (Gregory), 274–277
So Far from the Sea (Bunting), 354–357
Two Bear Cubs: A Miwok Legend from California's Yosemite Valley (San Souci), 52–55
Valley of the Moon: The Diary of Maria Rosalia de Milagros (Garland), 186
Voyage of Faith: Father Serra in California (McGovern), 123
With Corporal Tapia: from A Personal Tour of La Purísima (Young), 146–147
The Wonderful Towers of Watts (Zelver), 426–429
State board of education, 482
State capitol, 22, 471
State government, 467
State highway system, 330
State Indian Museum, 92–93
State legislature, 483
Statehood, 254
Statue of Liberty, *269*
Steamboat Willie, 443
Steamships, 183
Stearns, Abel, 199, R43
Steinbeck, John, 347, 371, R43
Stiers, George, 281
Stock, 369, R56
Stock market, 368
Stock market crash of 1929, 369
Stockton, *m17*, 80, 237, 296, R49
Stockton, Robert F., 214, R43
***The Story of Levi Strauss* (Damashek)**, 264
Strait of Anián, 111, 112
Strait of Magellan, 113
Strauss, Joseph B., 373, R43
Strauss, Levi, 234, 238, *238*, R43
Strawberries, 317, 333
Strike, *402*, 403, R56
Strong, Harriet Russell, 304, R43
Students, *448*
Study skills
connect ideas, 272
make an outline, 8
organize information, 222
pose questions, 458
preview and question, 352
skim and scan, 424
take notes, 144
understand vocabulary, 50
use a K-W-L chart, 184
use an anticipation guide, 310
use visuals, 104
write to learn, 388
Subdivisions, *395*
Suburb, 36, R56
Suez Canal, 295
Suffrage, 359, R56
Sugar, 160
Summarize, 422
Superintendent of schools, 482
Superior courts, 482
Supervisors, board of
Supply, 191, R56

Supreme Court, 418, *465,* 467
Surplus, 58, R56
Sutter, Johann, 160, 179, *179,* 188, 199, *199,* 227, 230, R43
See also Sutter's Fort
Sutter's Fort, 179, 186, 188, 199, 203, 210, *m232,* R49
Sutter's Mill, 226, *227, 261,* R49
See also Coloma
Sweat lodge, 65, 71, 80
Swimming, 43
Swing Time, 366
Symbols, 3, 256, 425, *438–439*

Tables
California Indian Boats by Tribe, *75*
California Indian Tribes by Kind of Boat, *75*
California's Largest Cities, *36*
California's Top Trading Partners, 2003, *433*
Tac, Pablo, 138, *138*
Tahoe, Lake, 6, 21, *26*
Taiwan, trade with, 433
"Talkies," 363, 364
See also Film and television production
Tallow, 160, *161,* 188, R56
Tan, Amy, *419,* 441, *441,* R43
Tape, Mamie, *318*
Tar, 2, 70, 72
See also La Brea Tar Pits
Tax, 466, 468, 486, R56
Taxi drivers, 435
Tea, 160
Teachers, 168, R28
Technology, 394, *396,* 432–433, R56
Technology resources, R28
Telegraph, *m278, 282,* **282,** 282–283, *284, 285,* R56
Telephones, *362*
Television and radio, 439, R28
Temperatures, *m29*
See also Climate
Tenant farmer, 302, R56
Tenochtitlán, Mexico, 111
Tent camps, 371
Texas, 19, 119, 212, 213, 370
Thailand, trade with, 433
Theme parks, *435,* 443
Thesaurus, R32
Tibbets, Eliza, *266, 303,* R43
Tibbets, Luther Calvin, 303, R43
Tiburon, R49
Tigers, 406
Timber, 14
Timber industry, 41, 44
Time, I8
Time lines, I10, I12
advances in technology, 396–397
Allensworth, Allen, 321
Beckwourth, James, 195
Briones, Juana, 169
chapter review, 90–91, 142–143, 220, 258, 308–309, 338–339, 386–387, 410–411
Chavez, Cesar, 405
Disney, Walt, 443
Early California History, 132
Lange, Dorothea, 375
Mason, Biddy, 253
Mayer, Louis B., 365
Mexican-American War, 212, 214
Mexico and California, 151
A Modern Way of Life, 362–363
Muir, John, 25
people, 2, 98–99, 178–179, 266, 346–347, 418–419
Reagan, Ronald, 477
Seidner, Cheryl A., 89
Serra, Junípero, 123
Shima, George, 307
The Transcontinental Railroad, 288
unit preview, 1, 97, 177, 265, 417
World War II, 381
Yee Fung Cheung, 293
See also Chart and Graph Skills
Time zones, 298, *m299,* R56
Tinsmiths, *238*
Tipai tribe. *See* Kumeyaay tribe
Tipton, Missouri, 280
Tolowa tribe, *m59*
Tomatoes, 305, 434, *434*
Tomols. *See* Canoes
Tongva tribe. *See* Gabrielino tribe
Tools, 57, 58, 60, 62, 64, 70, 79, 230, *234–235*
Topanga, 69
Tortoise, *23*
Tourism, 435, R56
Toypurina, 98, 136, R43
Tracy, 454
Trade, 67, 68, 86, 107, 111, 151, 156, 160–161, *161,* 207, 287, 360, 433, 467, R56
Trade links with the Pacific Basin, 431
Trade-off, 488, R57
Trailblazers, 192, 193, R57
Trailblazers from the United States, *m193*
Trails, 200–201
See also specific trails
Train station, *295*
Transcontinental railroad, 267, *286–287,* **287,** 288–292, *m289, 294,* R57
Transit system, *43*
Transportation, 35, 41, *273, 348–349,* 362, *443, 485*
Transportation in California, *m348–349*
Transportation equipment, *41*
Trappers, 190, 191–194, 195
Travel, 362
Treasurer, 482
Treaty, 216, 486, R57
Treaty of Cahuenga, 214, 216
Treaty of Guadalupe Hidalgo, 212, 214, 216, 248
Trees, 44, 451
buckeye, 60
dogwood, *445*
fruit, 266
giant cedar, 63
giant Sequoias, 31
navel oranges, 300
oak, 63, 80, 84
pine, 66
redwood, 30, 62, 63
willow, 80
Tribal constitutions, 486
Tribal council, 486
Tribal courts, 486
Tribal lands, *487*
Tribal laws, 486
Tribal leaders, 486
Tribes, 59, 486, R57
See also California Indians
Tributary, 22, R57
Trinity River, 65, R49
Tropics, 16, R57
Trustworthiness, 293, 307
Tulare, R49
Tulare River, R49
Tule, 70, 80–81
Tule balsas. *See* Canoes
Tule Lake war relocation camp, 382
Tuolumne Dam, *m335*
Tuolumne River, *m232,* 334, *m335,* R49
Turtles, 70, 72, 73
Twain, Mark, 26
Twentieth-Century Californians **(Rudy),** *498*
Two Bear Cubs **(San Souci),** 52–55
Two Years Before the Mast **(Dana),** 160–161

Uchida, Yoshiko, R43
A UFW Poster, 402
Ukiah, R49
Unemployment, *369,* **369,** R57
Union Pacific Railroad, 288, 289, *296*
United Farm Workers of America (UFW), 345, 346, 402, 403
United States, *12–13,* 151, 188, 463
The United States, 1845, *m218*
The United States, 1848, *m219*
United States: Overview, *mR8–R9*
United States: Physical, *mR12–R13*
United States Army, 320
United States Capitol, *464, 465*
United States Congress, *254*
United States Constitution, *462–463, 463*
United States Time Zones, *m299*

Universities and colleges, *400, 446,* 448
University of California Berkeley, *400*
University of California branches, 448
Urban, **36,** R57
Urban Populations in California, *336–337*
Urban sprawl, **395,** R57
URL, R30
Utah, *m17,* 192, 216

Vacuum machines, 362
Valdez, Luis, R43
Valencia oranges, 303
Vallejo, 250
Vallejo, Mariano Guadalupe, 99, *158,* 159, *209,* 248, 249, R43
Vallejo, Salvador, *252*
Valley of the Moon: The Diary of Maria Rosalia de Milagros **(Garland),** 186–189
Vancouver, George, 129
Vancouver Island, 99, 119
Vaqueros, *164, 165,* **165,** R57
Vegetables, 431, 434
avocados, 434
beans, 85, 87, 159
corn, 85, 87, 159
lettuce, 305
peas, 159
potatoes, 267
pumpkins, 87
squash, 85
tomatoes, 305, 434
Vegetation, **30,** R57
Venezuela, 150
Ventura, 324, R49
Veto, **470,** **473,** R57
Video games, *432*
Vietnam, 407
Vietnam War, 345
Vigilantes, **242,** 242–243, R57
Village crier, 81
Villages, 1, 3, 59, *63,* 65, 66, *68,* 70, 71, 78, 80
See also Rancherias
Vineyards. *See* Grapes
Virginia City, *266*
Visalia, R49
Vischer, Edward, 166, R43
Vizcaíno, Sebastián, 110, *113,* 114–115, 182, R43
Volcanoes, 21
Volunteers, 46–47, *47*
Voting, *475, 476,* 490–491, *491*
Voting age, 359
Voting rights, 358
Voting Rights Act of 1965, 359
Vuich, Rose Ann, R43

W

Wagon train, *185,* **200,** 200–201, R57
Wah Hing, 266. *See* Yee Fung Cheung
Waiters, 435
Walker, James, 164
Walker, Joseph Reddeford, 190, 194, *197,* R43
Walker Pass, 190, *194, m202,* R49
Walnuts, 43
Walt Disney Concert Hall, *442*
Walt Disney studio, 439
Wappo tribe, *m59*
Warner Brothers studio, 439
Warren, Earl, 418, *418,* 465, R43
Wars
Mexican War for Independence, 148–151
Mexican-American War, 212–217
Vietnam War, 345
World War I, 361
World War II, 345, 354–357, 378–383
Washing machines, 362
Washington, 21
Washington, D.C, 464
Washington navels. *See* Oranges
Washo tribe, *m59*
Water, 44
See also Glaciers
Water districts, 485
Water projects, 305, 313, 334–335, 374, 394, 468
Water rights, 328–329
Water sports, 43
Watson, Diane E., R43
Watterson, Mark, 329
Watterson, Wilfred, 329
Watts Towers Day of the Drum, 409
Wayne, John, *419,* 439, R43
Wealth, 2, 67
Weather, 43, 44, *44*
Weaverville, R49
Weaving, 136
Website, R30
Webster-Ashburton Treaty, 177
Weddings, 167
Weedpatch Camp, *371*
Weir, **64,** *65,* R57
Werdegar, Kathryn, *474*
West, *m14*
West, Tracey, 312–313
Western Hemisphere, 13, 16, 19, 24, R49
Western Hemisphere: Political, *mR6*
Western State, *m14*
Western Union, 282–283
Western United States, 1845, *m263*
Westerns (movies), 439
Westminster, 401
Wheat, 159, 199, 300–301, 472
White House, *465*
Why Character Counts, 169, 195, 253, 293, 307, 321, 443, 477
Widener, Sandra, 264
Wiggin, Kate Douglas, 317, R43
Wildcats, 44
Wildfires, 46
See also Fires
Williams, Paul R., 418, *418,* 442, R43
Williams, Serena, R43
Williams, Venus, R43
Willows, R49
Wind, 30
Wind patterns, 114, 120, R57
Windmills, *454*
Wine, 317
With Corporal Tapia: from A Personal Tour of La Purísima **(Young),** 146–147
Wiyot tribe, *m59,* **63,** *m63,* 89
Women, 157, 166, 396
and the gold rush, 240
in government, 347, 403
and property ownership, 248
senators, 418
voting rights, 358
Women workers, 166, 381
Women's rights movement, 403
The Wonderful Towers of Watts **(Zelver),** 426
Woodland, R49
Woodpeckers, 65
Woolly mammoths, 56, *57*
World: Physical, *mR4–R5*
World: Political, *mR2–R3*
World Trade Center, *417*
World War I, 358, 361
World War II, 345, 346, 354–357, 378–383, *381*
WorldBeat Center, 494
Worms, 446
Wozniak, Steven, *397,* R43
Wright Act, 305
Writing a first draft, R36
Writing activities, 374, I11
advertisement, 383
article, 320
billboard, 306
brochure, 397
diary entry, 233
fact book, 264
headlines, 153
information reports, 48, 264
journal entry, 115, 217
legends, 61
letter, 139, 168
narrative, 176, 344
news reports, 252
newspaper advertisement, 306
newspaper editorial, 335
pamphlet, 469
paragraph, 409, 449
publish a newspaper, 344
report, 37, 498
script, 211, 364
speech, 292
summary, 48, 96, 416
Writing to get information, R34
Wyoming, 216

Yahi Indian tribe, 93
Yamaguchi, Kristi, R43
Yamato Colony, 315
Yeager, Chuck, 351, *396,* R43
Yee Fung Cheung, *266,* 293, *293,* R43
Yerba Buena, 169
Yokuts tribe, 3, *m59,* 77, *m77,* 80–81
Yosemite National Park, 21, 267, 334, 423, *445,* R49
Yosemite Valley, 25, 52–55, *61,* 267
Young, Ewing, 194, R43
Young, Robert, 146–147
Yreka, R49
Yuba City, *m17,* 408, R49
Yuba River, 78, *m232,* R49
Yuma tribe, *m59*
Yurok coin purse, *64*
Yurok tribe, 2, *m59,* 62, 63, *m63,* 65

Zelver, Patricia, 426–429

For permission to reprint copyrighted material, grateful acknowledgment is made to the following sources:

Boyds Mills Press, Inc.: From *The Wonderful Towers of Watts* by Patricia Zelver, illustrated by Frané Lessac. Text copyright by Patricia Zelver; illustrations copyright by Frané Lessac.

Caxton Printers of Caldwell, Idaho: From *Patty Reed's Doll: The Story of the Donner Party* by Rachel K. Laurgaard. Text copyright 1956 by Caxton Printers, Ltd., renewed 1984 by Rachel Kelley Laurgaard.

Clarion Books/Houghton Mifflin Company: From *So Far from the Sea* by Eve Bunting, illustrated by Chris K. Soentpiet. Text copyright © 1998 by Eve Bunting; illustrations copyright © 1998 by Chris K. Soentpiet.

Facts On File, Inc.: Untitled Maidu Indian poem from *The First Americans: California Indians* by C. L. Keyworth.

HarperCollins Publishers: From *Sierra* by Diane Siebert, illustrated by Wendell Minor. Text copyright © 1991 by Diane Siebert; illustrations copyright © 1991 by Wendell Minor.

Kessinger Publishing, LLC: From "How *Wit'-tab-bah* the Robin got his Red Breast" in *The Dawn of the World: Myths and Tales of the Miwok Indians of California,* collected and edited by C. Hart Merriam.

Lee & Low Books Inc., New York, NY 10016: From *Amelia's Road* by Linda Jacobs Altman, illustrated by Enrique O. Sanchez. Text copyright © 1993 by Linda Jacobs Altman; illustrations copyright © 1993 by Enrique O. Sanchez.

Lerner Publications Company, a division of Lerner Publishing Group: From "With Corporal Tapia" in *A Personal Tour of La Purísima* by Robert Young. Text copyright 1999 by Robert Young.

Deidre Robinson Powell: From *Open Hands, Open Heart: The Story of Biddy Mason* by Deidre Robinson. Text copyright © 1998 by Deidre Robinson.

Scholastic Inc.: From *Valley of the Moon: The Diary of María Rosalia de Milagros* by Sherry Garland. Text copyright © 2001 by Sherry Garland. From *Jimmy Spoon and the Pony Express* by Kristiana Gregory. Text copyright © 1994 by Kristiana Gregory.

Silver Moon Press: From *Fire in the Valley* by Tracey West. Published by Silver Moon Press, 1993.

Smithsonian Institution University Press: From "My Words are Tied in One," translated by A. L. Kroeber in *Bureau of American Ethnology Bulletin 78*. Text copyright 1925 by The Smithsonian Institution.

Yosemite Association: From *Two Bear Cubs: A Miwok Legend from California's Yosemite Valley,* retold by Robert D. San Souci, illustrated by Daniel San Souci. Text copyright © 1997 by Robert D. San Souci; illustrations copyright © 1997 by Daniel San Souci.

PHOTO CREDITS

PLACEMENT KEY: (t) top; (b) bottom; (l) left; (r) right; (c) center; (bg) background; (fg) foreground; (i) inset.

COVER

Cover: Gibson Stock Photography (Juan Cabrillo statue); Bill Lies/California Stock Photo (Golden Gate Bridge); Allen Birnbach/Masterfile (Death Valley); Jim Schwabel/Index Stock(Blooming Plants on Coast).

Endsheet imagery: Jim Schwabel/Index Stock(Blooming Plants on Coast); Gibson Stock Photography (Juan Cabrillo statue); Allen Birnbach/Masterfile (Death Valley).

TITLE PAGE AND TABLE OF CONTENTS

iv The Field Museum #CSA1926; iv Cosmo Condina/Mira.com; iv Craig Aurness/Corbis; iv Galen Rowell/Corbis; iv Justin Pumfrey/Taxi/Getty Images; iv Courtesy of State Museum Resource Center/California State Parks; iv Marilyn "Angel" Wynn/Nativestock.com; iv Marilyn "Angel" Wynn/Nativestock.com; iv Mark Segal/Panoramic Images; iv Tony Freeman/PhotoEdit; iv StockImage/ImageState; vi The Granger Collection, New York; vi Courtesy of the Oakland Museum of California; vi Laurence Parent Photography; vi California Historical Society, Gift of Mr. and Mrs. Reginald Walker; FN-30659; vi Robert Fried Photography; vi Gary Conner/Index Stock Imagery; vi Seaver Center for Western History Research/Los Angeles County Museum of Natural History; vi Call number 1971.008-FR, Courtesy of The Bancroft Library University of California, Berkeley; vi Call number 1963.002:1389-B, Courtesy of The Bancroft Library University of California, Berkeley; vi Gunter Marx Photography/Corbis; viii Hulton Archive/Getty Images; viii The Society of California Pioneers, #20066; viii Smithsonian American Art Museum, Washington, DC/Art Resource, NY; viii Call number 1905.16242:042--CASE, Courtesy of The Bancroft Library University of California, Berkeley; viii Stock Montage; viii California Historical Society, FN-13679; viii Levi Strauss & Co.; x Brown Brothers; x California Historical Society, FN-10528; x Zefa/Index Stock Imagery; x Everett Collection; x Huntington Library/SuperStock; x Riverside Municipal Museum; x Bank of Stockton Photo Collection; x Union Pacific Railroad Museum; x Courtesy of State Museum Resource Center, California State Parks; xii Eric Saund, Ph.D.; xii Lambert/Archive Photos/Hulton Archive/Getty Images; xii Huntington Library/SuperStock; xii Arthur Schatz/Time Life Pictures/Getty Images; xii Library of Congress, Prints & Photographs Division, [reproduction number, LC-USZC4-2420]; xii Library of Congress, Prints & Photographs Division, [reproduction number, LC-USW361-128]; xii Harold Lloyd Trust/Getty Images; xii California Historical Society, FN-19319; xiv Kevin Winter/Getty Images Editorial; xiv Da Silva Peter/Corbis/Sygma; xiv Zefa/Index Stock Imagery; xiv Mark Jenkinson/Corbis; xiv Bettmann/Corbis; xiv Frank Capri/Hulton Archive/Getty Images; xiv Judy Baca and detail of the World Wall, Triumph of the Hearts, 1990/www.sparcmurals.org/Courtesy of Social and Public Art Resource Center/SPARC; xiv Bettmann/Corbis; xiv ML Sinibaldi/Corbis; xiv Sonja Jimenez/Tom Myers Photography; xiv Neil Lukas/Dorling Kindersley Ltd. Picture Library.

INTRODUCTION

I14 Joseph Sohm; ChromoSohm Inc./Corbis; I14 Tony Craddock/Stone/Getty Images; I15 Randy Wells/Stone/Getty Images; I15 Morton Beebe/Corbis; I15 Royalty-Free/Corbis; I4 Edward S. Curtis/National Geographic Image Collection; I4 Courtesy of State Museum Resource Center/California State Parks; I4 Richard Cummins/Corbis; I4 Spencer Grant/PhotoEdit; I6 Mark Leibowitz/Masterfile; I6 The Granger Collection, New York; I6 Huntington Library/SuperStock; I6 Comstock Images/Alamy Images; I6 Ted Streshinsky/Corbis; I6 Royalty-Free/Corbis.

UNIT 1

1 Haggin Collection, The Haggin Museum, Stockton, California; 4 (b) Richard Price/Taxi/Getty Images; 4 (c) Mark E. Gibson/Ambient Images; 4 (t) Jon Arnold/Danita Delimont Stock Photography; 5 Tony Craddock/Stone/Getty Images; 7 Gerald L. French/ThePhotoFile; 7 David A. Northcott/Corbis; 8 Craig Aurness/Corbis; 15 Craig Aurness/Corbis; 18 Warren Marr/Panoramic Images; 18 Greg Probst/Stone/Getty Images; 18 Robert Harding World Imagery/Alamy Images; 19 J. David Andrews/Masterfile; 19 Galen Rowell/Mountain Light Photography; 21 Galen Rowell/Corbis; 21 Mark E. Gibson/Ambient Images; 22 Tom Myers Photography; 24 Mitchell Funk/Image Bank/Getty Images; 25 (b) Corbis; 25 (t) The Granger Collection, New York; 28 Justin Pumfrey/Taxi/Getty Images; 30 Bruce Burkhardt/Corbis; 31 Mark E. Gibson/Ambient Images; 31 StockImage/ImageState; 33 Gary Crabbe/Ambient Images; 34 Bonhams, London, UK/Bridgeman Art Library; 34 Mark Segal/Panoramic Images; 36 Philip Condit II/Stone/Getty Images; 37 Galen Rowell/Mountain Light Photography; 38 Mark Richards/PhotoEdit; 38 Thomas Hallstein/Ambient Images; 40 Gibson Stock Photography; 40 Tony Freeman/PhotoEdit; 41 Cindy Charles/PhotoEdit; 41 Ian Vorster/Earthscape Imagery; 41 Cosmo Condina/Mira.com; 42 Joseph Sohm; ChromoSohm Inc./Corbis; 42 Lloyd Cluff/Corbis; 43 Sally Myers/Tom Myers Photography; 43 Tom Myers Photography; 43 Greig Cranna/Index Stock Imagery; 44 Robert Holmes/Corbis; 44 C. Moore/Corbis; 44 Gibson Stock Photography; 45 Gibson Stock Photography; 45 Gibson Stock Photography; 45 Roger Ressmeyer/Corbis; 46 (l) AP/Wide World Photos; 46 (r) Mark Richards/PhotoEdit; 47 (bl) Mark Downey/Ambient Images; 47 (br) Lou Dematteis/The Image Works, Inc.; 47 (t) Mark E. Gibson/Gibson Stock Photography; 50 David Muench/Corbis; 61 John Senser; 64 (b) Library of Congress, Prints & Photographs Division, Edward S. Curtis Collection,

[reproduction number, LC-USZ62-118588]; 64 (inset) Victor R. Boswell, Jr./National Geographic Image Collection; 65 Library of Congress, Prints & Photographs Division, Edward S. Curtis Collection, [reproduction number, LC-USZ62-83962]; 66 (l) Library of Congress, Prints & Photographs Division, Edward S. Curtis Collection, [reproduction number, LC-USZ62-98673]; 66 (r) Library of Congress, Prints & Photographs Division, Edward S. Curtis Collection, [reproduction number, LC-USZ62-102994]; 67 Marilyn "Angel" Wynn/Nativestock.com; 70 (l) Call number 1989.061, Courtesy of The Bancroft Library University of California, Berkeley; 70 (r) Marilyn "Angel" Wynn/Nativestock.com; 71 Marilyn "Angel" Wynn/Nativestock.com; 72 (b) Library of Congress, Prints & Photographs Division, Edward S. Curtis Collection, [reproduction number, LC-USZ62-98666]; 73 Kayte Deioma Photography; 74 (b) Roberts Photograph Collection/Humbolt State University Library; 74 (inset) Courtesy of the Phoebe Apperson Hearst Museum of Anthropology and the Regents of the University of California, 15-18588 Pomo; 75 Santa Barbara Museum of Natural History; 79 (t) The Field Museum #CSA1926; 81 Call number 1978.008 W/22c/P3 no.9, Courtesy of The Bancroft Library University of California, Berkeley; 82 (b) Marilyn "Angel" Wynn/Nativestock.com; 82 (t) Call number 1978.008 W/22t/P1:4--PIC, Courtesy of The Bancroft Library University of California, Berkeley; 83 (bl) Marilyn "Angel" Wynn/Nativestock.com; 83 (br) Courtesy of the Phoebe Apperson Hearst Museum of Anthropology and the Regents of the University of California, call numbers 1-13771 & 1-1730; 83 (tl) Bruce Farnsworth/PlaceStockPhoto.com; 83 (tr) Stephen Trimble Photography; 86 AP/Wide World Photos; 87 (b) Western History Collectiont, X32566/Denver Public Library; 88 Courtesy of the Phoebe Apperson Hearst Museum of Anthropology and the Regents of the University of California, mohave woman with olla; 92 Sally Myers/Tom Myers Photography; 92 (b) California State Department of Parks and Recreation, California State Indian Museum/Betty Sederquist; 92 (c) California State Department of Parks and Recreation, California State Indian Museum/Betty Sederquist; 92 (t) Sally Myers/Tom Myers Photography; 93 Sally Myers/Tom Myers Photography; 93 (bl) Tom Myers Photography; 93 (br) California State Department of Parks and Recreation, California State Indian Museum/Betty Sederquist; 93 (cr) California State Department of Parks and Recreation, California State Indian Museum/Betty Sederquist; 93 (tc) California State Department of Parks and Recreation, California State Indian Museum/Betty Sederquist; 93 (tr) California State Department of Parks and Recreation, California State Indian Museum/Betty Sederquist; 94 (t) J. David Andrews/Masterfile; 96 Harcourt; 97 David David Gallery/SuperStock; 103 Remington, Frederic (1861-1909) / Private Collection,/ Bridgeman Art Library; 103 Rich Reid/National Geographic Image Collection.

UNIT 2

Opener 104-105 Kirkendall / Spring Photographers; 110 The Granger Collection, New York; 110 Archivo Iconografico, S.A./Corbis; 111 The New York Public Library/Art Resource, NY; 111 The Granger Collection, New York; 112 Artist Richard Schlecht/National Park Service, Cabrillo National Monument; 113 The San Diego Historical Society Photograph Collection, www.sandiegohistory.org; 113 The San Diego Historical Society Photograph Collection, www.sandiegohistory.org; 113 The Granger Collection, New York; 113 Stock Montage; 116 The Granger Collection, New York; 118 Archivo Iconografico, S.A./Corbis; 119 Stapleton Collection/Corbis; 120 The Granger Collection, New York; 120 Laurence Parent Photography; 122 New Mexico State Museum, Santa Fe/Juan Bautista de Anza National Historic Trail; 123 (b) Santa Barbara Mission Archive Library; 123 (t) The Granger Collection, New York; 124 Hulton Archive/Getty Images; 124 Lowell Georgia/Corbis; 125 Gibson Stock Photography; 125 Harcourt; 125 National Park Service, Juan Bautista de Anza National Historic Trail; 126 Call number 1963.002:1389-B, Courtesy of The Bancroft Library University of California, Berkeley; 130 Call number 1953.004--FR, Courtesy of The Bancroft Library University of California, Berkeley; 131 Courtesy of the Oakland Museum of California; 132 National Palace Mexico City / Dagli Orti/Art Archive; 132 Seaver Center for Western History Research/Los Angeles County Museum of Natural History; 132 PlaceStockPhoto.com; 133 Richard Cummins/Corbis; 133 New Mexico State Museum, Santa Fe/Juan Bautista de Anza National Historic Trail; 134 Gary Conner/Index Stock Imagery; 135 North Wind Picture Archives; 136 Courtesy of the Oakland Museum of California; 136 Michael Freeman/Corbis; 140 ART on FILE/Corbis; 141 (b) Richard Cummins/Corbis; 143 (tc) Artist Richard Schlecht/National Park Service, Cabrillo National Monument; 143 (tc) The Granger Collection, New York; 144 Bill Manns/Art Archive; 150 National History Museum Mexico City/Dagli Orti/Art Archive; 151 The Granger Collection, New York; 151 Corbis; 151 VintagePostcards.com; 152 California Historical Society, FN-08260; 153 Courtesy of the Mission Inn Foundation & Museum, From the Collection of the Historic Mission Inn Corporation; 154 The Granger Collection, New York; 155 Robert Fried Photography; 157 California Historical Society, Gift of Mr. and Mrs. Reginald Walker; FN-30659; 158 Bonnie Kamin/PhotoEdit; 159 Call number 19xx.039:33--FR, Courtesy of The Bancroft Library University of California, Berkeley; 161 Seaver Center for Western History Research/Los Angeles County Museum of Natural History; 161 Call number Vallejo, Mariano G.--POR 64, Courtesy of The Bancroft Library University of California, Berkeley; 162 Call number Land Case Map D-972, Courtesy of The Bancroft Library University of California, Berkeley; 164 Call number 1971.008-FR, Courtesy of The Bancroft Library University of California, Berkeley; 165 Call number 1963.002:1350--FR, Courtesy of The Bancroft Library University of California, Berkeley; 168 Seaver Center for Western History Research/Los Angeles County Museum of Natural History; 169 (t) Palo Alto Historical Association; 171 (tc) Call number Land Case Map D-972, Courtesy of The Bancroft Library University of California, Berkeley; 172 (b) Foster Travel Publishing; 172 (t) Call number 1978.023-4, Courtesy of The Bancroft Library University of California, Berkeley; 173 Robert Holmes/Corbis; 173 (tc) Lowell Georgia/Corbis; 173 (tl) Robert Harding World Imagery/Alamy Images; 173 (tr) Dave Bartruff/Corbis; 174 (b) Museum of the American West; 174 (t) Courtesy of the Oakland Museum of California; 176 Harcourt; 177 Call number 1963.002:1522--FR, Courtesy of The Bancroft Library University of California, Berkeley; 178 National Portrait Gallery/Smithsonian Institution; 183 So Hing-Keung/Corbis; 183 New-York Historical Society, New York, USA/Bridgeman Art Library; 184 SuperStock.

UNIT 3

Opener 190-191 Walters Art Museum/Bridgeman Art Library; 192 Courtesy Don Prechtel @ prechtelfineart.com/Holt-Atherton Special Collections/University of the Pacific Libraries; 194 Joslyn Art Museum, Omaha, Nebraska; 195 (b) Nevada Historical Society; 195 (t) Gibson Stock Photography; 196 Private Collection/Bridgeman Art Library; 197 Joslyn Art Museum, Omaha, Nebraska; 198 The Huntington Library, Art Collections, and Botanical Gardens, San Marino, California/SuperStock; 199 Oakland Museum of California, Oakland Museum Kahn Collection; 201 David J. & Janice L. Frent Collection/Corbis; 203 James L. Amos/Corbis; 205 Call number Donner, Eliza--POR 1, Courtesy of The Bancroft Library, University of California, Berkeley; 206 The New York Public Library/Art Resource, NY; 207 Corbis; 209 Anaheim Public Library; 209 Hulton Archive/Getty Images; 209 Call number Vallejo, Mariano G.--POR 5, Courtesy of The Bancroft Library University of California, Berkeley; 210 The Society of California Pioneers, #20066; 210 Joseph Sohm; ChromoSohm Inc/Corbis; 210 Stock Montage; 216 Call number Pico, Pio--POR 3, Courtesy of The Bancroft Library University of California, Berkeley; 221 (tc) Stock Montage; 222 Betty Sederquist/Ambient Images; 226 Call number Marshall, James--POR 4, Courtesy of The Bancroft Library University of California, Berkeley; 226 Courtesy of the Oakland Museum of California; 226 Smithsonian Institution, National Museum of American History; 227 Call number 1963.002:0197--A, Courtesy of The Bancroft Library University of California, Berkeley; 228 The Granger Collection, New York; 228 The Granger Collection, New York; 230 California Historical Society, FN-13679; 230 Hulton Archive/Getty Images; 231 Smithsonian American Art Museum, Washington, DC/Art Resource, NY; 232 Call number 1963.002.1501--FR, Courtesy of The Bancroft Library University of California, Berkeley; 234 (bl) Levi Strauss & Co.; 234 (c) Jules Frazier/PhotoDisc; 234 (tr) The Society of California Pioneers, #C002881 trans.20025; 235 (b) Courtesy of the Oakland Museum of California;

235 (t) Courtesy of the Oakland Museum of California, Collection of Norm Wilson; 236 Call number 1963.002:1356--FR, Courtesy of The Bancroft Library University of California, Berkeley; 237 Fine Arts Museums of San Francisco, Museum Purchase, the M.H. de Young Endowment Fund, 39.3; 238 (bl) Call number 1905.16242:042--CASE, Courtesy of The Bancroft Library University of California, Berkeley; 238 (br) The Society of California Pioneers, #C002926 trans.20022; 239 Advertising Archive; 239 British Columbia Archives, Call Number B-01601/British Columbia Archives; 240 (t) Levi Strauss & Co.; 242 Collection of The New-York Historical Society, negative #77212d; 242 Mary Evans Picture Library; 243 Call number 1905.17500 v.29:32--ALB, Courtesy of The Bancroft Library University of California, Berkeley; 243 Courtesy of the Oakland Museum of California, Gift of anonymous donor; 247 Dave G. Houser/Corbis; 249 San Francisco History Center, San Francisco Public Library; 249 Call number 1905.16242:037--CASE Courtesy of The Bancroft Library University of California, Berkeley; 250 The Granger Collection, New York; 250 The Granger Collection, New York; 250 Call number Gwin, William--POR 3, Courtesy of The Bancroft Library University of California, Berkeley; 251 California Historical Society, FN-24053; 251 Call number 1963.002:1462--C Courtesy of The Bancroft Library University of California, Berkeley; 252 Call number Pico, Pio--POR 1, Courtesy of The Bancroft Library University of California, Berkeley; 253 (l) Ruth Wallach/ University of Southern California Library; 254 North Wind Picture Archives; 256 (br) Harcourt; 256 (l) Heidi Zeiger Photography; 257 (b) Paul A. Souders/Corbis; 257 (bl) Betty Sederquist/Ambient Images; 257 (c) Ian Vorster/Earthscape Imagery; 257 (tc) ART on FILE/Corbis; 257 (tl) California State Library/California State Capitol Museum; 257 (tr) California State Library/California State Capitol Museum; 259 (tl) Hulton Archive/Getty Images; 259 (tr) Call number 1963.002:1462--C Courtesy of The Bancroft Library University of California, Berkeley; 260 Betty Sederquist/Ambient Images; 260 (bl) David Sanger Photography; 260 (br) Tom Myers Photography; 261 California Department of Parks and Recreation Photographic Archives/California State Parks; 261 Gary Moon; 261 Betty Sederquist; 261 (bl) Tom Myers Photography; 261 (tc) Nik Wheeler; 262 (b) Joseph Sohm; ChromoSohm Inc/Corbis; 264 Harcourt; 265 Call number 1963.002:1363--FR, Courtesy of The Bancroft Library University of California, Berkeley; 267 Courtesy of the Oakland Museum of California, Oakland Museum Kahn Collection; 268 (b) The Granger Collection, New York; 268 (c) Anaheim Public Library; 268 (t) Bettmann/Corbis; 269 Museum of the City of New York/Corbis; 271 Bob Rowan; Progressive Image/Corbis; 271 Darryl Torckler/Taxi/Getty Images.

UNIT 4

Opener 272-273 David Stoecklein/Corbis; 280 Western History Collection, Z8926/Denver Public Library; 281 Bettmann/Corbis; 282 Bettmann/Corbis; 282 The Granger Collection, New York; 284 Information Technology and Society Division, National Museum of American History/Smithsonian Institution; 284 Stock Montage; 285 Library of Congress, The Papers of Samuel Finley Breese Morse Manuscript Division; 286 Bettmann/ Corbis; 288 (cl) California Historical Society, FN-10528; 288 (cr) Corbis; 288 (l) Southern Pacific Bulletin/California State Railroad Museum; 288 (r) The Granger Collection, New York; 292 The Granger Collection, New York; 293 D'Agostini Photography; 294 (b) Union Pacific Railroad Museum; 294 (t) California State Railroad Museum; 296 Call number 1963.002:0211--C, Courtesy of The Bancroft Library University of California, Berkeley; 296 Fine Arts Museums of San Francisco, Museum Purchase, Gift of the M. H. de Young Endowment Fund, 54936; 297 Call number xfF850 W18 v.9:520-521, Courtesy of The Bancroft Library University of California, Berkeley; 298 California State Railroad Museum; 298 MODIS/NASA Media Resource Center; 299 (t) California Historical Society, FS-26852; 300 PhotoDisc; 300 Frank S Balthis Photography; 300 Meriam Library, Special Collections, CSU, Chico, Bidwell Mansion State Historic Park, catalog #sc16940; 302 Library of Congress, Prints & Photographs Division, Panoramic Photographs Collection, [reproduction number, LC-USZ62-127860]; 302 (b) Riverside Municipal Museum; 302 (inset) Huntington Library/SuperStock; 303 David Fraizer/The Image Works, Inc.; 307 (b) Bank of Stockton Photo Collection; 307 (c) Call number 1905.02724--PIC, Courtesy of The Bancroft Library University of California, Berkeley; 309 (tl) The Granger Collection, New York; 310 California Historical Society, FS-26852; 314 Courtesy of State Museum Resource Center, California State Parks; 316 Brown Brothers; 317 Mark Downey/Ambient Images; 318 Permission granted by Jack Kim/Berkeley Architectural Heritage Association; 319 Ted Streshinsky/Corbis; 320 Courtesy of the Autry National Center/ Southwest Museum, Los Angeles. Photo #N.24776; 321 (l) Courtesy of California State Parks/California State Parks; 321 (r) California Historical Society, FN-32157; 322 Call number 1964.056:15--PIC, Courtesy of The Bancroft Library University of California, Berkeley; 322 (l) Anaheim Public Library; 324 Brown Brothers; 325 (inset) Everett Collection; 325 (t) Corbis; 326 Brown Brothers; 327 Bettmann/Corbis; 328 [LIPP Box 78, no.304], Joseph Barlow Lippincott Papers, Water Resources Center Archives, University of California, Berkeley; 329 (b) Stock Montage; 329 (c) Laws Railroad Museum & Historical Site; 329 (t) Bettmann/Corbis; 330 Library of Congress, Prints & Photographs Division, Panoramic Photographs Collection, [reproduction number, LC-USZ62-123116]; 331 (inset) Underwood & Underwood/Corbis; 332 Call number 1958.021 v.4:22--fALB, Courtesy of The Bancroft Library University of California, Berkeley; 332 (b) San Francisco History Center, San Francisco Public Library; 333 Japanese American Archival Collection. Department of Special Collections and University Archives. The Library. California State University, Sacramento; 334 San Francisco Public Utilities Commission Photographic Archive; 337 J. A. Kraulis/ Masterfile; 339 (tc) Library of Congress, Prints & Photographs Division, Panoramic Photographs Collection, [reproduction number, LC-USZ62-123116]; 339 (tr) Corbis; 340 (b) Gibson Stock Photography; 340 (inset) Heidi Zeiger Photography; 340 (inset) Heidi Zeiger Photography; 340 (t) Cable Car Museum; 341 San Francisco Department of Public Transportation; 341 Hulton Archive/Getty Images; 341 (br) Heidi Zeiger Photography; 341 (cl) Heidi Zeiger Photography; 341 (tl) Hulton Archive/Getty Images; 342 (b) The Granger Collection, New York; 342 (t) Huntington Library/SuperStock; 344 (b) Harcourt.

UNIT 5

Opener 345-345 Mark Gibson/Ambient Images; 348 (b) Arthur Schatz/Time Life Pictures/Getty Images; 348 (t) Lawrence Migdale Photography; 349 (b) Roger Ressmeyer/Corbis; 349 (t) Royalty-Free/ Corbis; 351 Bettmann/Corbis; 351 Bettmann/ Corbis; 358 Call number Johnson, Hiram-- POR 28, Courtesy of The Bancroft Library University of California, Berkeley; 359 (t) California Historical Society, FN-19319; 360 Corbis; 360 Underwood & Underwood/Corbis; 360 Corbis; 361 (c) Corbis; 361 (l) Burns Archive; 361 (r) Burns Archive; 362 (c) Dagli Orti (A)/Art Archive; 362 (l) Topical Press Agency/Hulton Archive/Getty Images; 362 (r) Photofest; 363 Science Museum, London / Topham-HIP/The Image Works, Inc.; 363 (c) Harold Lloyd Trust/Getty Images; 363 (l) Photofest; 364 Underwood Photo Archives/ SuperStock; 365 (b) Bettmann/Corbis; 365 (t) ZUMA Movie Stills Library/Zuma Press; 366 (bl) Everett Collection; 366 (tr) Bettmann/ Corbis; 367 Burke/Triolo Productions/ Brand X Pictures/Robertstock.com; 367 (bl) Bettmann/Corbis; 367 (br) Hot Ideas/Index Stock Imagery; 367 (cl) Hot Ideas/Index Stock Imagery; 368 American Stock/Archive Photos/Hulton Archive/Getty Images; 370 (b) Retrofile.com; 370 (t) Corbis; 371 Leo Hart Collection/Jerry Stanley; 374 Loomis Dean/ Time Life Pictures/Getty Images; 375 (b) The Granger Collection, New York; 375 (t) Corbis; 376 Corbis; 376 Dorothea Lange/Resettlement Administration/Time Life Pictures/Getty Images; 376 (inset) Corbis; 378 Mort Künstler; 378 (r) Bettmann/Corbis; 379 (b) Shades of L.A. Archives/Los Angeles Public Library; 379 (t) San Francisco History Center, San Francisco Public Library; 380 Library of Congress, Prints & Photographs Division, [reproduction number, LC-USW361-128]; 380 (inset) Corbis; 381 Bettmann/Corbis; 381 (c) Mary Evans Picture Library; 381 (l) Corbis; 381 (r) Bettmann/Corbis; 382 Call number 1967.014 v.19 CB-8--PIC, Courtesy of The Bancroft Library University of California, Berkeley; 382 Call number 1967.014 v19 8 CA-926--PIC Courtesy of The Bancroft Library University of California, Berkeley; 383 Bettmann/Corbis; 384 Corbis; 385 Joe Raedle/ Getty Images; 385 (br) Corbis; 385 (l) Getty Images Editorial; 385 (tr) Time Life Pictures/ Getty Images Editorial; 387 (tc) California Historical Society, FN-19319; 387 (tc) Burns Archive; 388 Nik Wheeler; 392 Huntington Library/SuperStock; 393 Allan Grant/Time Life Pictures/Getty Images; 394 Bettmann/ Corbis; 395 (inset) Time Life Pictures/Getty Images; 395 (t) Lambert/Archive Photos/ Hulton Archive/Getty Images; 396 (c) Bettmann/Corbis; 396 (l) Everett Collection; 396 (r) Intel Corporation; 397 (c) AP/Wide World Photos; 397 (l) Photo by Charles M. Duke Jr./NASA/Zuma Press; 397 (r) Corbis; 398 (b) Greg Probst Photography; 398 (inset) Harcourt; 400 SuperStock; 401 (t) Herald

Examiner Collection/Los Angeles Public Library; 402 (b) 1976 George Ballis/Take Stock; 402 (inset) Library of Congress, Prints & Photographs Division, [reproduction number, LC-USZC4-2420]; 403 Eric Saund, Ph.D.; 403 (c) Yvonne Braithwaite Burke; 403 (l) 1976 George Ballis/Take Stock; 404 Bettmann/ Corbis; 405 (b) Arthur Schatz/Time Life Pictures/Getty Images; 405 (t) Arthur Schatz/ Time Life Pictures/Getty Images; 406 Kayte M. Deioma/PhotoEdit; 407 Donna Day/ ImageState; 408 (b) AP/Wide World Photos; 408 (t) Tony Freeman/PhotoEdit; 409 (c) Isaac Hernandez/Mercury Press International; 409 (t) Ted Streshinsky/Corbis; 411 (tl) Arthur Schatz/Time Life Pictures/Getty Images; 411 (tr) Intel Corporation; 412 David Peevers/ Lonely Planet Images; 412 (inset) Petersen Automotive Museum; 413 (bl) Gibson Stock Photography; 413 (br) Petersen Automotive Museum; 413 (tr) David Peevers/Lonely Planet Images; 414 (b) Intel Corporation; 414 (t) California Historical Society, FN-19319; 416 Harcourt.

UNIT 6

Opener 417-418 Chris Daniels/Corbis; 419 White House Historical Association (White House Collection) (48); 420 (t) James Marshall/Corbis; 421 (b) Grant Heilman Photography; 421 (c) Mark Richards/ PhotoEdit; 421 (t) Phil Schermeister/Corbis; 423 Ulf Wallin/Image Bank/Getty Images; 430 (inset) Tomi/PhotoLink/PhotoDisc; 431 Spencer Grant/PhotoEdit; 431 Lee Foster/ Bruce Coleman Inc.; 434 (b) V.O. Press/ PhotoEdit; 434 (bc) Spencer Grant/PhotoEdit; 434 (t) Rosalind Creasy/Peter Arnold, Inc.; 434 (tc) Grant Heilman Photography; 435 Mark Richards/PhotoEdit; 436 (c) Catherine Karnow/Corbis; 436 (l) Ed Kashi/ IPN/Kashi Photo Archive; 436 (r) Renee Lynn/Photo Researchers, Inc.; 438 (b) Thomas Del Brase/Photographer's Choice; 438 (inset) Joseph D. Kulisics; 438 (t) Kevin Winter/ Getty Images Editorial; 439 (t) Da Silva Peter/Corbis/Sygma; 440 David Hockney "Pacific Coast Highway and Santa Monica" 1990. Oil on canvas 91 1/4" x 137 1/4" © David Hockney; 440 Reproduced with the permission of The Noguchi Museum, New York, Smithsonian American Art Museum, Washington, DC, Art Resource, NY; 441 (b) Richard R. Hansen/Photo Researchers, Inc.; 441 (c) James Salzano; 441 (tc) Allan Grant/ Time Life Pictures/Getty Images; 441 (tl) Frank Capri/Hulton Archive/Getty Images; 441 (tr) Judy Baca and detail of the World Wall, Triumph of the Hearts, 1990/www.sparcmurals.org/Courtesy of Social and Public Art Resource Center/SPARC; 442 (t) Sonja Jimenez/Tom Myers Photography; 443 (b) Bettmann/Corbis; 443 (t) Bettmann/ Corbis; 444 Ansel Adams Publishing Rights Trust/Corbis; 444 National Museum of Photography, Film & Television/Science & Society Picture Library; 444 (bl) Ansel Adams Publishing Rights Trust/Corbis; 444 (tl) Call number Adams, Ansel--POR 4, Courtesy of The Bancroft Library University of California, Berkeley; 445 (bl) Ansel Adams Publishing Rights Trust/Corbis; 445 (r) Ansel Adams Publishing Rights Trust/Corbis; 445 (tl) Ansel Adams Publishing Rights Trust/Corbis; 446 (b) Eadweard Muybridge, Special Collections, F.W. Olin Library, Mills College; 446 (l) The Granger Collection, New York; 446 (r) California State Archives; 447 (bl) John Elk III Photography; 447 (br) Zefa/ Index Stock Imagery; 447 (cl) Call number UARC PIC 15:270, Courtesy of The Bancroft Library University of California, Berkeley; 447 (cr) Frank S Balthis Photography; 448 Joseph Sohm/ ChromoSohm Inc/Corbis; 448 (t) Bilderberg/Voltz/Peter Arnold, Inc.; 449 AP/Wide World Photos; 450 Mark Jenkinson/ Corbis; 451 Joseph Sohm; ChromoSohm Inc./Corbis; 452 Mick Roessler/Index Stock Imagery; 454 ML Sinibaldi/Corbis; 455 (b) Dynamic Graphics Group/Creatas/Alamy Images; 455 (t) L Lefkowitz/Taxi/Getty Images; 458 Shubroto Chattopadhyay/Index Stock Imagery; 462 Robert Weinreb/Bruce Coleman Inc.; 462 The Granger Collection, New York; 463 (c) Burke/Triolo Productions/ Brand X Pictures; 463 (t) Tony Freeman/ PhotoEdit; 464 Warner J. Bertsch/Bruce Coleman Inc.; 464 Wendell Metzen/Index Stock Imagery; 465 Tony Freeman/PhotoEdit; 465 Craig Aurness/Corbis; 469 Phil Lauro/ Index Stock Imagery; 472 (b) AP/Wide World Photos; 472 (c) Neil Lukas/Dorling Kindersley Ltd. Picture Library; 473 (l) Nick Ut/Pool/Corbis; 473 (r) California Office of the Governor; 474 (b) Siede Preis/PhotoDisc; 474 (t) AP/Wide World Photos; 475 Neema Frederic/Gamma Press, Inc.; 476 SuperStock; 477 (b) Bettmann/Corbis; 477 (t) Tom Myers Photography; 480 Tom Myers Photography; 482 Jonathan Nourok/PhotoEdit; 483 Robert Fried Photography; 483 Omni Photo Communications Inc./Index Stock Imagery; 484 Spencer Grant/PhotoEdit; 484 Joseph Sohm; ChromoSohm Inc./Corbis; 485 Joseph Sohm; ChromoSohm Inc./Corbis; 486 AP/ Wide World Photos; 486 (t) AP/Wide World Photos; 488 (l) Bill Aron/PhotoEdit; 488 (r) Jonathan Nourok/PhotoEdit; 489 David Young-Wolff/PhotoEdit; 490 (b) David Young-Wolff/PhotoEdit; 490 (t) William Whitehurst/ Corbis; 490 (tl) Steve Solum/Bruce Coleman Inc.; 491 (br) Mark Richards/PhotoEdit; 491 (c) Annie Griffiths Belt/Corbis; 491 (t) VictoryStore.com; 491 (tr) VictoryStore.com; 494 Royalty-Free/Corbis; 495 Jim Sugar/ Corbis; 495 Gibson Stock Photography; 495 (bl) John Warden/Stone/Getty Images; 495 (cr) MaryAnn and Bryan Hemphill/Index Stock Imagery; 496 (b) Kevin Winter/Getty Images Editorial; 496 (t) Neil Lukas/Dorling Kindersley Ltd. Picture Library.

All other photos from Harcourt School Photo Library and Photographers: Ken Kinzie, April Riehm and Doug Dukane.

All maps created by MapQuest.com

California History–Social Science Standards and Analysis Skills

CALIFORNIA STANDARDS

Source for California Standards: California Department of Education

History–Social Science Content Standards
California: A Changing State

Students learn the story of their home state, unique in American history in terms of its vast and varied geography, its many waves of immigration beginning with pre-Columbian societies, its continuous diversity, economic energy, and rapid growth. In addition to the specific treatment of milestones in California history, students examine the state in the context of the rest of the nation, with an emphasis on the U.S. Constitution and the relationship between state and federal government.

4.1 Students demonstrate an understanding of the physical and human geographic features that define places and regions in California.

4.1.1 Explain and use the coordinate grid system of latitude and longitude to determine the absolute locations of places in California and on Earth.

4.1.2 Distinguish between the North and South Poles; the equator and the prime meridian; the tropics; and the hemispheres, using coordinates to plot locations.

4.1.3 Identify the state capital and describe the various regions of California, including how their characteristics and physical environments (e.g., water, landforms, vegetation, climate) affect human activity.

4.1.4 Identify the locations of the Pacific Ocean, rivers, valleys, and mountain passes and explain their effects on the growth of towns.

4.1.5 Use maps, charts, and pictures to describe how communities in California vary in land use, vegetation, wildlife, climate, population density, architecture, services, and transportation.

(continued)

4.2 Students describe the social, political, cultural, and economic life and interactions among people of California from the pre-Columbian societies to the Spanish mission and Mexican rancho periods.

4.2.1 Discuss the major nations of California Indians, including their geographic distribution, economic activities, legends, and religious beliefs; and describe how they depended on, adapted to, and modified the physical environment by cultivation of land and use of sea resources.

4.2.2 Identify the early land and sea routes to, and European settlements in, California with a focus on the exploration of the North Pacific (e.g., by Captain James Cook, Vitus Bering, Juan Cabrillo), noting especially the importance of mountains, deserts, ocean currents, and wind patterns.

4.2.3 Describe the Spanish exploration and colonization of California, including the relationships among soldiers, missionaries, and Indians (e.g., Juan Crespi, Junipero Serra, Gaspar de Portola).

4.2.4 Describe the mapping of, geographic basis of, and economic factors in the placement and function of the Spanish missions; and understand how the mission system expanded the influence of Spain and Catholicism throughout New Spain and Latin America.

4.2.5 Describe the daily lives of the people, native and nonnative, who occupied the presidios, missions, ranchos, and pueblos.

4.2.6 Discuss the role of the Franciscans in changing the economy of California from a hunter-gatherer economy to an agricultural economy.

4.2.7 Describe the effects of the Mexican War for Independence on Alta California, including its effects on the territorial boundaries of North America.

4.2.8 Discuss the period of Mexican rule in California and its attributes, including land grants, secularization of the missions, and the rise of the rancho economy.

(continued)

4.3 Students explain the economic, social, and political life in California from the establishment of the Bear Flag Republic through the Mexican-American War, the Gold Rush, and the granting of statehood.

4.3.1 Identify the locations of Mexican settlements in California and those of other settlements, including Fort Ross and Sutter's Fort.

4.3.2 Compare how and why people traveled to California and the routes they traveled (e.g., James Beckwourth, John Bidwell, John C. Fremont, Pio Pico).

4.3.3 Analyze the effects of the Gold Rush on settlements, daily life, politics, and the physical environment (e.g., using biographies of John Sutter, Mariano Guadalupe Vallejo, Louise Clappe).

4.3.4 Study the lives of women who helped build early California (e.g., Biddy Mason).

4.3.5 Discuss how California became a state and how its new government differed from those during the Spanish and Mexican periods.

(continued)

4.4 Students explain how California became an agricultural and industrial power, tracing the transformation of the California economy and its political and cultural development since the 1850s.

4.4.1 Understand the story and lasting influence of the Pony Express, Overland Mail Service, Western Union, and the building of the transcontinental railroad, including the contributions of Chinese workers to its construction.

4.4.2 Explain how the Gold Rush transformed the economy of California, including the types of products produced and consumed, changes in towns (e.g., Sacramento, San Francisco), and economic conflicts between diverse groups of people.

4.4.3 Discuss immigration and migration to California between 1850 and 1900, including the diverse composition of those who came; the countries of origin and their relative locations; and conflicts and accords among the diverse groups (e.g., the 1882 Chinese Exclusion Act).

4.4.4 Describe rapid American immigration, internal migration, settlement, and the growth of towns and cities (e.g., Los Angeles).

4.4.5 Discuss the effects of the Great Depression, the Dust Bowl, and World War II on California.

4.4.6 Describe the development and locations of new industries since the turn of the century, such as the aerospace industry, electronics industry, large-scale commercial agriculture and irrigation projects, the oil and automobile industries, communications and defense industries, and important trade links with the Pacific Basin.

4.4.7 Trace the evolution of California's water system into a network of dams, aqueducts, and reservoirs.

4.4.8 Describe the history and development of California's public education system, including universities and community colleges.

4.4.9 Analyze the impact of twentieth-century Californians on the nation's artistic and cultural development, including the rise of the entertainment industry (e.g., Louis B. Meyer, Walt Disney, John Steinbeck, Ansel Adams, Dorothea Lange, John Wayne).

(continued)

4.5 Students understand the structures, functions, and powers of the local, state, and federal governments as described in the U.S. Constitution.

4.5.1 Discuss what the U.S. Constitution is and why it is important (i.e., a written document that defines the structure and purpose of the U.S. government and describes the shared powers of federal, state, and local governments).

4.5.2 Understand the purpose of the California Constitution, its key principles, and its relationship to the U.S. Constitution.

4.5.3 Describe the similarities (e.g., written documents, rule of law, consent of the governed, three separate branches) and differences (e.g., scope of jurisdiction, limits on government powers, use of the military) among federal, state, and local governments.

4.5.4 Explain the structures and functions of state governments, including the roles and responsibilities of their elected officials.

4.5.5 Describe the components of California's governance structure (e.g., cities and towns, Indian rancherias and reservations, counties, school districts).

Kindergarten Through Grade Five

History–Social Science Content Standards

Historical and Social Sciences Analysis Skills

The intellectual skills noted below are to be learned through, and applied to, the content standards for kindergarten through grade five. They are to be assessed *only in conjunction with* the content standards in kindergarten through grade five.

In addition to the standards for kindergarten through grade five, students demonstrate the following intellectual, reasoning, reflection, and research skills:

Chronological and Spatial Thinking

1. Students place key events and people of the historical era they are studying in a chronological sequence and within a spatial context; they interpret time lines.
2. Students correctly apply terms related to time, including *past, present, future, decade, century,* and *generation.*
3. Students explain how the present is connected to the past, identifying both similarities and differences between the two, and how some things change over time and some things stay the same.
4. Students use map and globe skills to determine the absolute locations of places and interpret information available through a map's or globe's legend, scale, and symbolic representations.
5. Students judge the significance of the relative location of a place (e.g., proximity to a harbor, on trade routes) and analyze how relative advantages or disadvantages can change over time.

(continued)

Research, Evidence, and Point of View

1. Students differentiate between primary and secondary sources.
2. Students pose relevant questions about events they encounter in historical documents, eyewitness accounts, oral histories, letters, diaries, artifacts, photographs, maps, artworks, and architecture.
3. Students distinguish fact from fiction by comparing documentary sources on historical figures and events with fictionalized characters and events.

Historical Interpretation

1. Students summarize the key events of the era they are studying and explain the historical contexts of those events.
2. Students identify the human and physical characteristics of the places they are studying and explain how those features form the unique character of those places.
3. Students identify and interpret the multiple causes and effects of historical events.
4. Students conduct cost-benefit analyses of historical and current events.

Death Valley National Park, in California